HELLENIC STUDIES 15

THE CULTURE OF *KITHARÔIDIA*

Recent Titles in the Hellenic Studies Series

http://chs.harvard.edu/chs/publications

The Culture of *Kitharôidia* by Timothy Power
Copyright © 2010 Center for Hellenic Studies, Trustees for Harvard University
All Rights Reserved.
Published by Center for Hellenic Studies, Trustees for Harvard University,
  Washington, DC.
Distributed by Harvard University Press, Cambridge, Massachusetts, and
  London, England
Printed in Ann Arbor, MI by Edwards Brothers, Inc.

LIBRARY OF CONGRESS CATALOGING-IN-PUBLICATION DATA:
  Power, Timothy Conrad.
  The culture of kitharôidia / by Timothy Power.
    p. cm. -- (Hellenic studies ; 15)
  Includes bibliographical references and index.
  ISBN 978-0-674-02138-9 (alk. paper)
  1. Music, Greek and Roman--History and criticism. 2. Songs with cithara--
History and criticism. 3. Nero, Emperor of Rome, 37-68. 4. Terpander. 5.
Music--Social aspects--Greece--History--To 146 B.C. 6. Music--Social aspects--
Greece--History--146 B.C.-323 A.D. 7. Musicians--Greece. I. Title. II. Series.

ML169.P69 2010
780.938--dc22

                                                        2010026469

THE CULTURE OF *KITHARÔIDIA*

Timothy Power

CENTER FOR HELLENIC STUDIES
Trustees for Harvard University
Washington, D.C.
Distributed by Harvard University Press
Cambridge, Massachusetts, and London, England
2010

Acknowledgments

THIS BOOK was a long time in the making. I could neither have begun nor completed it without the understanding and support of my wonderful mother and father, Michele and Conrad, and my dear sisters, Suzanne and Stephanie. I am indebted for intellectual and moral support to all my colleagues and friends at Harvard University, University of Washington, Seattle, the Center for Hellenic Studies, and Rutgers University. Noel Spencer's editorial acumen was invaluable. I am enormously grateful to Valerie Woelfel for the graceful and thoughtfully rendered line drawings that she produced. Very special thanks to my very patient Jessica; a series of vigorous pats to Frances, our gray cat.

Contents

Contents

Preface

THIS BOOK EXAMINES the origins, development, and elaboration of *kithar-ôidia* in its social and political contexts and in its relation to other poetic, musical, and discursive forms and practices. It is thus, in part, an archaeology of a performative practice (singing to the *kithara*) and a song genre, the citharodic *nomos*; a social history of the production and consumption of professional agonistic music in ancient Greece and Rome; and a consideration of the cultural politics of *kitharôidia*: how different regions, cities, and individuals competed to "possess" this prestigious musical medium, and what role it was seen to play in the life of the communities in which it was cultivated. What I think will emerge is an appropriately nuanced picture of the aesthetic and socio-political complexity and dynamism of *kitharôidia*. And by retraining a spotlight on the citharode, I hope to reconfigure the traditional scholarly staging of Archaic and Classical Greek song culture (and its Hellenistic and Imperial legacies), showing that *kitharôidia* acts alongside better-studied genres, epic, lyric, and dramatic, in one mutually antagonistic and promiscuous performance ensemble. Far from being a minor player, it deserves to take a place at center stage.

If, as one student of Greek song has memorably put it, dithyramb is the "ugly sister of the Dionysian family"—tragedy and comedy are the belles of the ball—then *kitharôidia* has been treated like an often forgotten, rarely spoken of, and indeed rather mysterious uncle in the family of lyric, or, to be more widely inclusive, melic poetry.[1] The favorite sons of this family are sympotic monody (e.g. most of Alcaeus, Sappho, Anacreon) and the narrative, cultic, and epinician choral melic performed on festive and ceremonial public occasions (most of Alcman, Simonides, Stesichorus, Ibycus, Pindar, and Bacchylides). These deprecating familial metaphors are of course meaningful only in terms of the interests and prejudices of modern scholarship, for both the choral, aulodic dithyramb and the solo song of the competitive

---

[1] Wilson 2003a: "Ugly sister" (164).

kithara-singer had a prominence in Greek and Greco-Roman antiquity that is completely disproportionate to the scant attention they have received from historians of the poetry of these eras. Indeed, both forms enjoyed a vigorous longevity that attests to their persistent relevance. Dithyramb was performed at least as early as the seventh century BCE and was still going strong throughout the Hellenistic and Roman Imperial periods. The case is even more striking with *kitharôidia*: citharodic performance was formally instituted in Sparta in the first half of the seventh century BCE and continued to be featured, in the same basic form, as the main attraction at Panhellenic and local festival musical contests, not to mention in non-competitive concerts, well into the late Empire. Part I of the present book examines the career of the most famous Imperial citharode, the Emperor Nero; his was a bizarrely singular career to be sure, a product of its time, yet one that consciously and creatively drew upon persistent musical, mythical, and political themes and models running through the entire history of the medium, going back to the Archaic period. *Kitharôidia* was arguably the musico-poetic performance genre that was enjoyed by the greatest number of people in the greatest number of places over the greatest length of time in the ancient Mediterranean world. If nowadays it is treated like a minor form, an antiquarian curiosity, relegated to cursory discussions in the handbooks of ancient literary and musical history, the reality in Greek and Roman antiquity was radically different.

In terms of genre and occasion, *kitharôidia* was intermediately positioned, and so has tended to get lost in the interstices between the specialized areas of scholarship on Greek song culture.[2] It falls in between two melic macrogenres, private lyric monody and public choral song. Like the former, it was solo song accompanied by stringed instrument; like the latter, it was generally performed out of doors, before the scrutiny of a large festival audience, and often in a competitive setting. Unlike both, it was mostly performed by individual professionals, a fact that brings it closer to *rhapsôidia*, which also shared with *kitharôidia* the musical contest as its primary occasion, not to mention, at least at an early stage, a good deal of common form and content. Plato in fact groups *kitharôidia* and *rhapsôidia* together under the rubric of solo song, *monôidia*, in his discussion of competitive festival music performance in *Laws* 764d–e. Of course, poets such as Sappho and Alcaeus could and did compose choral songs, Pindar and Bacchylides

---

[2]   Herington 1985 represents a significant exception to this tendency.

composed solo *skolia*, and the choral songs of a Simonides, for instance, could be reperformed solo by individual symposiasts (e.g. Aristophanes *Clouds* 1354–1357).[3] But it is crucial to note: not one of the nine canonical melic poets was a practicing citharode, nor is there any testimony that indicates any one of them composed citharodic *nomoi* or indeed any solo pieces intended for public performance on the concert *kithara*. *Kitharôidia* cleaved more closely to the generally inclusive civic ideology of choral song, and, as we will see again and again in accounts of citharodic performance, it carried much the same charge of maintaining *kosmos*, musical and political order, in the community. Yet *kitharôidia* differed greatly from choral melic in its overall disposition. It was more secular than religious, more thoroughly professional than amateur, more a demonstration of personal skill, charisma, and the individual performer's body than of corporate solidarity and the "body politic," more Panhellenic than epichoric, less an expression *of* the community than entertainment and edification *for* it.

But the general scholarly neglect suffered by *kitharôidia* is due foremost to the paucity of preserved citharodic texts. The same is true to some extent for dithyramb, though there the state of textual preservation is far better. We have only a small number of fragments, under twenty, and several of those of disputed generic status, from works that were originally composed and performed by citharodes. Fortunately, one undisputed fragment among these is a substantial excerpt from a citharodic *nomos* by Timotheus of Miletus entitled *Persians*, discovered in 1902 on a fourth-century BCE papyrus unearthed at Abusir in Egypt.[4] Although no musical notation was included on the papyrus, the text is a precious example of the stylistically innovative citharodic poetry of the later fifth and early fourth centuries BCE. In the final section of the preserved text, which is examined in detail in Part IV, we hear Timotheus speak *in propria persona* about his own *kitharôidia* and its contemporary reception, a unique and profoundly revealing instance of an individual citharode's self-presentational interaction with his audience.

---

[3] On the performative and occasional mutability of Archaic monody and choral melic, see Davies 1988; Cingano 2003.

[4] Wilamowitz produced the first edition in 1903, with an exegesis of the text and a discussion of *kitharôidia*, which remains still the most engaging treatment of the subject. The last decade has seen the publication of a new edition of *Persians* and the other, shorter citharodic (and dithyrambic) fragments of Timotheus (Hordern 2002), which includes a helpful philological commentary. An earlier commentary by Janssen (1984) delves more deeply into the sociohistorical context of *Persians*.

Much less survives of Archaic and early Classical citharodic song. We have only a handful of fragments of poetry, none more than two lines, attributed to Terpander, whom the ancient sources generally concur in regarding as the founder of the "classical" citharodic practice that predated Timotheus. Antonietta Gostoli (1990) has assembled these fragments with commentary, along with the ancient testimonia relevant to the life and work of Terpander. As we will see in Part III, it is in fact the latter that are more valuable for understanding the history of *kitharôidia* than the former. Indeed, as if to balance out our lack of citharodic texts, we have a relative abundance of literary and visual testimonia. Citharodes—unsurprisingly, given their cultural centrality—are everywhere: in drama, history, philosophy, oratory, and above all in a rich tradition of popular anecdote recorded by the antiquarians; they are painted on Attic pots of all sizes and shapes; their victories are commemorated on numerous inscribed dedications. From these sources we may extract some sense of what the citharodes were singing; this is a main focus of Part II. But, more broadly, they reflect how the culture of *kitharôidia* was imagined by both the citharodes and the various strata of their Greek and Roman audiences, from high to low, across time and space. Indeed, we have as much ancient testimony about *kitharôidia* as we have about drama or rhapsodic epic poetry, though much of it has not yet been organized, analyzed, and contextualized in the manner it deserves. This study aims to do just that. It is, however, necessarily selective in nature. I see it as a first step toward understanding *kitharôidia* within its broader social and cultural contexts. My hope is that future work on the subject by myself and others will fill in the outlines I am sketching out here.

A brief note on the structure and organization of the book. It is divided into four main parts (designated by upper-case Roman numerals), each of which is divided into sections (designated by Arabic numerals); some of the longer sections are further divided into subsections (designated by lower-case Roman numerals). Because I treat a number of the same figures, texts, and themes from different perspectives in different parts of the book, a fair amount of internal cross-referencing has been unavoidable. A reference such as III.3, for instance, indicates Part III, Section 3; II.9.i indicates Part II, Section 9, subsection i. The running heads, with part number on the left-hand page and section number on the right-hand page will, I hope, assist the reader in quickly navigating these internal references.

Part I

Princeps Citharoedus

1 Setting the Scene: A Citharode in Naples

He made his performance debut at Naples, and, even though the theater was rocked with a sudden earthquake, he did not cease singing until he had finished the *nomos* that he had begun. In the same city he sang frequently over the course of several days. Even when he took a short time to refresh his voice, he could not bear to remain out of sight, but went from the baths to the theater and, while dining in the middle of the orchestra surrounded by the people, he promised in Greek that after he had had a little something to drink he would ring out something packed full of sound. He was taken moreover with the rhythmic laudations of the Alexandrians in the audience, who had thronged into Naples from a recently arrived fleet, and summoned more men from Alexandria. Not stopping at that, he selected young men of the order of knights and more than five thousand strapping youths drawn from the plebeian class, to be divided into groups and learn by heart the Alexandrian styles of applause (they called them "buzzings," "rooftiles," and "bricks"), and to practice them vigorously while he sang.

Suetonius Life of Nero 20.2–3

Hitherto he had sung in the privacy of home or in the gardens during the games of the Juvenalia, but he now thought little of those games, as they were too sparsely attended and too restricted in size for so great a voice. Nevertheless, since he did not dare to make a beginning at Rome, he chose Naples, because it was a Greek city. Starting out from there he might cross into Achaea, and, winning the prestigious and sacred garlands of antiquity, evoke, with still greater fame, the enthusiasm of the citizens. Thus a crowd of townspeople was brought together, with those whom the report of such an event had attracted from the neighboring towns and colonies, and those who followed Caesar to pay him honor or to provide various other services, as well as some companies of soldiers—these all filled the theater of the Neapolitans. There an event occurred, which many thought ill-omened, but which he [the performer] took to be a sign of providence and divine favor: after the people who had been in attendance exited, the theater collapsed, empty and without harming anyone. And so he composed a song of thanks to the gods, celebrating the good fortune that attended the recent downfall.

Tacitus Annals 15.33.2–34.1

I N 64 CE the citizens of Naples and nearby settlements, along with some visiting Romans and an enthusiastic contingent of Alexandrian sailors who happen to be in town on shore leave, gather in the city's theater to witness a musical spectacle. The spectacle is conceptually and visually direct: one man performing alone on the stage. It is of a type that has a long, continuous tradition behind it, going back well over six hundred years to early Hellenic antiquity. The audience is in store for a show that audiences in Archaic Sparta, Periclean Athens, and Ptolemaic Alexandria before it have experienced in much the same form. Yet ancient and basic as it is, the spectacle, even without the peculiar twist that this one has, could still generate excitement in an Imperial culture jaded by novel spectacles of a far more elaborate nature.

A man walks onto the stage. He is Roman, but he is costumed in the distinctly Greek fashion that is traditional for performers such as he. Neither Tacitus nor Suetonius supply details about his outward appearance that day, but we can make some reasonable suppositions based on visual and literary representations of other men like this man, on other occasions like this one. (Performers of this sort are typically men, although, as we will soon see, the occasional woman is attested in the Hellenistic period and after.) He is dressed in a long, sumptuous robe, a chiton probably dyed a deep purple, that falls straight down over his feet, which are shod in buskins; on top of this chiton a lighter mantle, adorned with gold-embroidered patterns, covers his upper torso.[1] In all likelihood he wears a gold wreath in his hair. In his left arm he cradles

---

[1] The straight-hanging chiton worn by the citharode is called by Dio Cassius 63.17.5 and 63.22.4 the ὀρθοστάδιον (on which see scholia *ad* Aristophanes *Lysistrata* 45). In the same passages Dio has the performer wearing *kothornoi* 'buskins', which are more commonly associated with post-Classical tragic actors. Citharodes in Greek vase

upright a broad, magnificent stringed instrument, perhaps made of gleaming ivory into which precious metals and gems have been inlaid. It has a flat bottom, a voluminous resonating sound-box, and at least seven, perhaps as many as eleven or twelve animal-gut *khordai* 'strings' stretching from the bridge at the base to the rotating tuning bar, the *zugon*, held in place across the tall arms at the top, where they are fastened around the leather bands (*kollopes*) that hold them tight. The sound box narrows at each top corner into two convex horns that flare out, then taper and turn in, meeting the delicate ornamental volutes at the base of the blocky, straight arms that extend well above the player's head. Flowing down from its rear side is a broad cloth, decorated with geometric or floral motifs, extending almost to the ground. When the citharode begins to move in time with his music, this banner-like cloth will wave hypnotically, "echoing and reinforcing the movements of the performer."[2]

This splendid object is the *kithara* (κιθάρα; *cithara* in Latin), what Aristotle calls a *tekhnikon organon*, an instrument designed for use by the *tekhnitês*, a master technician of instrumental performance, typically a professional virtuoso.[3] This 'concert lyre' is to the smaller, bowl-shaped tortoise-shell lyre (*khelus*) played by amateur musicians and schoolboys what a concert grand piano is to an upright spinet or a technologically sophisticated electric guitar is to the simple acoustic folk

---

paintings are normally barefoot (e.g. Plate 9), although some wear low-cut footwear (e.g. Plate 1).

[2]   Herington 1985:17, from his description of a depiction of a citharode by the Berlin Painter on an early fifth-century BCE amphora (New York, Metropolitan Museum of Art, Fletcher Fund, 1956 [56.171.38]).

[3]   Aristotle *Politics* 8.1341a18–19. The sketch of costume and *kithara* given here is a loose composite of late Archaic and Classical Attic vase paintings and descriptions in Roman-era literary sources (e.g. *Rhetorica ad Herennium* 4.60; Ovid *Metamorphoses* 11.165–169; Lucian *The Uncultured Book Collector* 8–11, Dio Cassius 63.22.4). While the late literary sources offer a rather gaudier, more luxurious image of the *kithara* player than the vase paintings, the similarities strongly suggest continuity in the performers' self-presentation from early Greek to later Roman times. See the detailed discussion of instrument and costume, with illustrations, in Bélis 1995, Paquette 1984:90–102, and Maas and Snyder 1989:58–68 and 171–175. The *kithara* underwent morphological changes during the Hellenistic period that were probably reflected in Nero's instrument. By the Imperial period some *kitharai* seem to have acquired a slimmer, more elongated profile than their more robust Classical ancestors. A good example is to be seen in one of the Spada reliefs from second-century CE Rome that shows Amphion and his brother Zethus (or perhaps Hermes; see Newby 2002:134–137, with fig. 4.9), or in a fresco fragment with a seated Apollo from the Palatine Antiquarium (inv. 379982). But it is impossible to say whether these thinner instruments were regularly played by professional citharodes of the Empire. Cf. n163 below.

guitar.[4] It is a heavy, unwieldy instrument, whose weight is supported against the chest of the singer by a decorated sling looped over his right shoulder and braced around his left wrist.[5] With the fingers of his right hand the man clutches by its handle a long, spoon-shaped device, the *plêktron*, which is attached to the body of the *kithara* by a cord. The man stands ready to strike the strings with this plectrum; his left hand is poised on the reverse side of the sound box, just above its upper edge, his fingertips pressed against those strings whose sound he will want to damp when he strikes the first notes.

The performer's elaborate costume, his instrument, and its accoutrements are unmistakably those of a *kitharôidos* (κιθαρῳδός), a citharode, a singer (ᾠδός, a contracted form of ἀοιδός) to the *kithara*. His art, *tekhnê*, a unified combination of vocal and instrumental music, is called *kitharôidia* (κιθαρῳδία). It had long enjoyed the greatest prestige of any solo musical performance genre throughout the Greek-speaking Mediterranean and would continue to command the highest respect well into the late Empire, thanks in large part to this very performer.

2. The Emperor-Citharode and Other Pretenders

The performer's identity, however, is what makes this occasion, which in other respects conforms to type, highly anomalous. The man with the *kithara* happens to be the most powerful man in the world. He is the Emperor Nero. But let us try for now not to focus too much on this fact, as difficult as that may be, and pretend that the audience in Naples is doing the same—a still more difficult proposition. Let us instead consider, as we have already done, what would have been typically citharodic about Nero's otherwise extraordinary performance.

---

[4]   On this important distinction, with its attendant occasional, gender, class, ethical, even moral dimensions, see Maas and Snyder 1989: "[The *kithara*] was *not* a lyre played by an amateur for idle amusement at a dinner party or by young school boys or by Athenian wives entertaining one another in the women's quarters of their houses" (58).

[5]   The sling or strap is designated the *telamôn* or *aortêr* (from *aierein* 'to raise up'), as in a scholion to *Iliad* 15.256, which claims that Apollo's epithet χρυσάωρ means 'of the golden *aortêr*' (rather than 'of the golden sword [*aôr*]'). The etymology is fanciful, but it reflects assumptions about the "glitz" of the citharode's outfit. The sling is called *balteus* or *balteum* in Latin: Apuleius *Florida* 15.9. The excess end of the tied-off strap is sometimes shown hanging down from the side of instrument in the vase paintings. In some images this excess resembles a spare set of strings, but this is likely because it has been tasseled or fringed to add decorative fancy to the costume. See Maas and Snyder 1989:67–68.

This approach would please the emperor himself. Ever caught up in fictions and fantasies, he preferred to maintain the modest pretense that he was a citharode like any other, although, as he knew as well as anyone, modesty was a virtue as disingenuous in a citharode as in an emperor.[6] That Nero was genuinely committed to the *tekhnê* of *kithara* singing there can be no doubt, however; that he was widely thought to be at least a mediocre musician, at best a fairly decent one, is something that emerges from even the most hostile traditions, in which the main aesthetic charge brought against him—greatly muted next to the morally, politically, and sexually charged abuse his musical ambitions provoked—is that he played and sang for too great a length of time, though not necessarily badly.[7] The "Lucianic" dialogue *Nero* offers what seems the most objective assessment of his abilities. One character in the dialogue, Menecrates, observes that some are amazed at Nero's *phônê* 'voice', while others laugh at it. His interlocutor, Musonius, explains that the emperor's savvy choice of musical material and his carefully practiced performance technique distract from his natural deficiencies; he can put on a perfectly good show, or a reasonable simulacrum thereof, as long as he remains within his limits:

> In fact, Menecrates, his voice (*phthegma*) is neither admirable nor ridiculous, for nature (*phusis*) has made him tolerably and moderately musical. His voice is naturally hollow and low, as his throat is constricted, and because it is his songs have a sort of buzzing sound to them. But the tones of his voice are smoothed over when he trusts not in his natural ability, but in crowd-pleasing harmonic colorings, attractively composed melodies, well-controlled singing to the *kithara* (χρωμάτων δὲ φιλανθρωπίᾳ καὶ μελοποιίᾳ εὐαγώγῳ μὲν δὴ καὶ κιθαρῳδίᾳ εὐσταλεῖ), and in choosing the right moment to walk, stand, and change position, and in swaying his head in time to the music; then the only disgrace is that a king should seem to strive for perfection in these matters. But if he should imitate

---

6 See e.g. Tacitus *Annals* 16.4; cf. Suetonius *Nero* 23.2 on Nero's studied attempts to pass himself off as just another citharodic agonist.

7 See e.g. Suetonius *Nero* 23.2, 39.3; Champlin 2003:57. Overplaying: Suetonius *Nero* 23.2, an account of Nero's literally captive audiences in Greece. The claim by Vindex that Nero was a *malus citharoedus* 'bad citharode' (Suetonius *Nero* 41.1) was a taunt meant to hurt the emperor's feelings (which it did); it was not an honest assessment based on personal experience. Texts relating to Nero's citharodic career are collected in Wille 1967:338–357.

his betters, how great is the laughter that falls over the spectators!

"Lucian" *Nero* 6–7[8]

Even if some audiences could not resist laughing at his apparent over-reaching, Nero was deadly, obliviously serious about winning the same acclaim his musical "betters" enjoyed; his quest for perfection in *kitharôidia* was no lark. Although he began his training much later in life than a professional citharode, who, typically brought up in a family of professional musicians, would have begun his vocational studies as a young boy, he likely devoted more energy to the music of the *kithara* than he did to anything else in his entire life. According to Suetonius *Nero* 20.1, at least five years before his appearance in Naples Nero had begun to study under the personal tutelage of the most highly esteemed citharode of the day (*citharoedum vigentem tunc praeter alios*), a Greek named Terpnus, whose very name advertises the awesome musical pleasure, *terpsis*, his talent produces in his listeners, and also hearkens back to the legendary founder of the medium, Terpander of Lesbos. He had honed his relatively weak singing voice through the same grueling regimen of exercises and deprivations that the professionals followed, although the routine seems more appropriate for Olympic athletes than musicians. Lying on his back, he balanced a heavy lead plate on his chest, a procedure intended to increase lung capacity and stamina of breath, and he habitually purged and maintained a strict diet—no fruit!—in the interest of vocal strength and clarity.

Shortly before his death, Nero fantasized about murdering the Senate, burning down Rome, and sailing off to Alexandria, a hotbed of citharodic culture at the time, to enjoy his life's second act as a private citizen and a professional *citharoedus*. There, he reckoned in a famously pathetic line, τὸ τέχνιον ἡμᾶς διαθρέψει 'My art, such as it is, will get me by'.[9] Although he tried his hand, intently, at all sorts of musical, dramatic, and athletic activities in the final decade of his life, *kitharôidia* was the vocation that first and last defined Nero's artistic and

---

[8] Translation based on Macleod 1967:515. Nero's voice seems to have been his primary drawback. Dio Cassius 61.20.2 says that his voice is *brakhu kai melan* 'small and indistinct'; in Suetonius *Nero* 20.1 it is "weak and husky" (*exiguae vocis et fuscae*). Warmington 1977:78 notes, however, that a *vox fusca* might not have been a total liability. He compares Quintilian 11.3.171, which says that such a voice was "suitable for conveying emotional, pitiful and dramatic situations."

[9] Dio Cassius 63.27.2; cf. Suetonius *Nero* 40.2.

performative aspirations.[10] This fact is better reflected in the ancient sources than in the modern scholarship on Neronian "theatricality," which has tended to focus on the emperor qua actor or simply "performer," reductively eliding his dramatic and citharodic endeavors, and thereby overlooking the culturally specific semiotics of the latter.[11] Indeed, Nero may not even have begun in earnest his acting career, or, more accurately, his career as a *tragoedus*, a histrionic singer of tragic songs (*tragoedia cantata*), until the lead-up to his tour of Greece, in 66 CE.[12] It is true that many in Rome, both critics and admirers, initially, at least, lacked the proper cultural frame of reference to decode those semiotics, which were informed by distinctly Hellenic concepts of music's role in social and political life. But Nero appreciated them very well, and this nuanced appreciation had much to do with his choice to pursue *kitharôidia* as intently as he did. And so, even if he did eventually become more profligate with his talents, it is more appropriate to speak of Nero, as Juvenal *Satire* 8.198 does, as a *princeps citharoedus*, than it is to take Pliny the Younger's famous tag too literally and so confine him to the status of *imperator scaenicus* 'actor-emperor' (*Panegyricus* 46.4). In the widest, most culturally unspecific sense, Nero was essentially an actor; but the primary role he brought before the public on the stages of Rome and Greece, his true star turn, was the role of the citharode.

Indeed, the emperor had become so deeply identified as a *citharoedus* in the popular imagination that in the years following his death two of the three pretenders who emerged in the Greek East claiming to be Nero were in fact citharodes, or at least men with sufficient musical skills to pretend to be citharodes. From the elitist, anti-Neronian perspective, these revenant impostors were fittingly debased specters of the hypertheatricalized regime of simulacra and simulations that Nero had brought to pass in Rome and across the Empire—if an emperor could play the citharode, then it is no surprise if a citharode should attempt to play the emperor.[13] But from a more objective viewpoint,

---

[10] Cf. Griffin 1984:201.

[11] See e.g. the otherwise excellent studies of Dupont 1985, Bartsch 1994, Edwards 1994. These authors do not, to be fair, completely neglect Nero's fundamentally musical persona, but Beacham 1999 and Champlin 2003 are far more attentive to Nero's citharodic efforts. See too the less sophisticated but still useful Gyles 1947 and 1962.

[12] See Lesky 1949:397–398 = 1966:343–344, who notes that in Tacitus' *Annals*, which as we have it covers events through 66 CE, Nero is referred to always as a *citharoedus*, with the sole exception of 15.67.2, in which one of the members of the Pisonian conspiracy of 65 CE calls him *histrio* 'actor'. But even here we may be wary of taking this as a literal reference to acting, as is the case with *scaenicus* 'stage player' at *Annals* 15.59.2 (cf. n193 below).

[13] See Edwards 1994 on Nero's subversive confounding of reality and appearance.

the seemingly bizarre phenomenon of these citharodic False Neros is a straightforward attestation of the actual popular favor accorded to Nero's own distinctive fusion of political and citharodic charisma. This particular combination must have aroused sufficiently positive enthusiasm among the general population, especially in Greece (see e.g. Dio Cassius 63.10.1), for the pretenders to emulate it in their own bids for power. Yet it is unlikely to have aroused such genuine enthusiasm had Nero been a bad citharode. Tacitus, a staunch critic of Nero's musical activities, indirectly acknowledges this when he describes the initial success of the first False Nero as due to his "skill at the *cithara* and singing, which, in addition to his likeness in facial appearance to Nero, lent a greater plausibility to the deception."[14]

Within his lifetime, Nero inspired a more prosaic group of imitators, small-time buskers who roamed through the *urbs* performing the emperor's repertoire for audiences willing and unwilling. In *Life of Apollonius of Tyana* 4.39 Philostratus describes the tactics of one such street musician, a drunken hustler really, but not a musically untalented one, who approaches Apollonius and his friends while they are staying at an inn near the gates of the city. The man, equipped with a *kithara* and "all the fittings (*skeuê*) proper for a citharode," demands payment (*misthos*) for his performance of Nero's songs (*melê*), and he threatens to have those who refuse to listen or to pay arrested for impiety. This cut-rate "citharode" also shows off a used *kithara* string, claiming that he acquired it from Nero's very own *kithara* at the cost of two *minae*, and swearing, disingenuously to be sure, that he will sell the string only to "one of the very best (*aristoi*) citharodes, those who compete at Delphi." It is more than likely that many other Neronian strings were bought and sold in Rome and throughout the Empire at large. But the *princeps* was not the only citharode whose discarded paraphernalia, authentic or not, were highly valued. As we will see in Section 7, the circulation of these sorts of souvenir and keepsake objects, small relics of the citharode's celebrity aura, was but one index of the popular fascination with *kitharôidia*.

---

[14] Tacitus *Histories* 2.8: *citharae et cantus peritus, unde illi super similitudinem oris propior ad fallendum fides.* Tacitus reports two versions of the citharodic pretender's background: he was either a slave from Pontus or a freedman from Italy.

3. Showing Off: Citharodic Glamour and the Economics of Visual Display

i. How *skeuê* makes the citharode

The theatergoers in Naples take in the presence of the citharode and grow quiet. A powerful visual impact is made even before the music begins. The *kithara* alone inspires wonder and curiosity. The majority of spectators would rarely lay eyes on such an instrument outside of the occasional frame of citharodic performance. Few non-professionals would own or even come into personal contact with one, and then only the very rich.[15] The musician himself is to be looked at as much as heard; he projects the image of creative and technical mastery even before he proves it in execution. The most remarkable aspect of his spectacular self-presentation is his performance outfit, the *skeuê*, which recurs as the focal point in many an ancient literary account or visual depiction of *kitharôidia*. The *skeuê* is really a costume ensemble, consisting not only of the garment or garments worn by the citharode, but of various decorative and practical apparatus as well, the support strap, the plectrum and its cord, a crown, the embroidered cloth that hangs from the base of the *kithara*, and even the *kithara* itself.

The powerful effect rendered by the *skeuê* is vividly illustrated, and interestingly problematized, by a story related in Lucian *The Uncultured Book Collector* 8–11. A wealthy man from Tarentum, Evangelus, sets out to win the Pythian citharodic *agôn* 'contest' at Delphi—no small feat. Such *mousikoi agônes* 'musical contests' were the primary arena for the high-level display of *kitharôidia* and other solo musical forms, and the Panhellenic Pythian contest of citharodes was long among the most prestigious and competitive, from its establishment in the Archaic period well into the late Empire. Evangelus pins his slim hopes of victory at this major event not on his skill or musicality—he is in fact horribly untalented—but on the finery of his gold-plated, bejeweled *kithara*, a visual *thauma* 'marvel', his purple, gold-embroidered raiment (*esthês*), and a gold, emerald-studded laurel wreath.[16] He takes the stage, resplendent

---

[15] Strictly speaking, the proverb *non omnes qui habent citharam sunt citharoedi* 'Not all who hold a *cithara* are citharodes' (Varro *De re rustica* 2.1.3) is thus true, but not entirely felicitous: most people who possessed *kitharai* were indeed citharodes. The luxurious ornamentation of *kitharai* in the Imperial era would only have put them further out of common reach.

[16] Evangelus inevitably recalls another *arriviste* citharode from Italy, Nero, whose tour of the Greek contest circuit included the Pythian games, although Nero is not the

in his *skeuê*, "dazzling the theater in advance (of the music) and filling the spectators with the hope of experiencing something marvelous" (προεκπλήξας τὸ θέατρον καὶ θαυμαστῆς ἐλπίδος ἐμπλήσας τοὺς θεατάς, 9). This "shock and awe" is much the desired effect, but the ocular spell is broken rather than intensified by the musical performance itself, which is intolerably flawed. The audience breaks out into laughter, always a sure sign of the failure of the performance ritual, the rude signal that the musician's temporary license to manipulate mass emotion has been irredeemably revoked.[17] The judges have a crying, humiliated Evangelus whipped for his hubristic presumption in appearing at the games. In keeping with the reductive moral logic of the story, victory goes instead to the more humbly attired, but far more talented Eumelus, an Elean, whose name indicates genuine musical skill ('Melody Man'), not just the "promise" or "boast" of it, as is intimated by the name Evangelus.[18] Eumelus plays a plain, old wooden *kithara* and wears no *skeuê* to speak of, merely an outfit "worth barely ten drachmas," but his impressive exhibition of *tekhnê* justly trumps the empty flashiness of the rich man, which a gloating Eumelus calls ἄτεχνος τρυφή 'luxuriousness devoid of *tekhnê*'.

This anecdote had life long before Lucian. It appears in less fleshed-out form in the first-century BCE treatise called the *Rhetorica ad Herennium* (4.60), and there it seems already to have acquired folktale status. Where or when it was first told we cannot be sure, although we may be tempted to conjecture a connection to some burlesque treatment of the star citharode Nicocles (third century BCE), a Tarentine, who won a whopping six times at the Pythian *agôn*, as well as at practically every other citharodic *agôn* attached to a major Hellenistic festival, including the Great Panathenaia, the Isthmia, the Argive Hekatomboia, the Basileia at Macedonia and at Alexandria, and others. The ostentatious style of the monument celebrating these victories (IG II² 3779), which was displayed conspicuously along the Sacred Way in Athens (Pausanias 1.37.2), strongly suggests that Nicocles was a man

---

primary object of Lucian's satire.

[17] Such a breakdown of consensus between audience and (rhapsodic) performer, the moment when the latter realizes he has lost not only audience favor but, still worse, his prize money, is dramatically evoked in Plato *Ion* 535e.

[18] Eumelus' Elean provenance also has symbolic force. Elis was the home of the Olympic festival, which, until the time of Nero's tour of Greece in 66/7 CE, when the program was altered to accommodate the emperor's citharodic endeavors (Suetonius *Nero* 23.1), hosted no *mousikoi agônes*, only athletic games, at which the athletes famously competed in the nude. Eumelus embodies the "stripped-down," spiritually aristocratic ethos/aesthetic of the Olympics.

who would not be shy about embracing the kind of splendor Lucian ascribes to Evangelus. In any case, the story is almost surely apocryphal, for the simple reason that, the glaring exception of Nero aside, an unproven musician, much less a completely untalented one such as Evangelus, could not have passed muster with the organizing officials of the contests, the *agônothetai*. At world-famous *mousikoi agônes* such as those of the Pythia, only the very best, the acknowledged stars such as Nicocles, would have been granted the coveted opportunity to compete, as the number of open slots was necessarily limited by the temporal constraints of a festival.[19] From the perspective of one less-than-stellar citharode in Neronian Rome, the street busker we encountered above, the citharode who is ranked among the best (*aristoi*) is also one who is fit to compete at Delphi (κιθαρῳδός ... τῶν ἀρίστων τε καὶ ἀγωνιουμένων Πυθοῖ, Philostratus *Life of Apollonius of Tyana* 4.39).

By the same token, it is highly unlikely that a citharode sufficiently accomplished to win at Delphi would ever perform there, or at any contest or concert of any size, in any locale, wearing a paltry ten-drachma robe. The costly finery of an Evangelus was surely the rule for citharodic performance, not the exception. To put it more strongly, such finery was a requisite for an agonistic and concert career of any distinction. Successful citharodes, and large-scale, public musical performers in general, proleptically dressed for success; theirs was a winner's game. Xenophon's Socrates thus advises those who want to be perceived as talented auletes to emulate "the externals of the art" (τὰ ἔξω τῆς τέχνης), above all by flaunting "fine *skeuê*" (*Memorabilia* 1.7.2).[20] This strategy was especially apparent in the practice of wearing

---

[19] Three to five contestants seems to have been the rule at major citharodic *agônes*: five at the Panathenaia in the first half of the fourth century BCE (IG II² 2311.4–11, in the restored text of Shear 2003); three at the fourth-century festival of Artemis in Eretria (IG XII ix 189) and perhaps at Delphi as well (according to Lucian *The Uncultured Book Collector* 9, a third citharode, Thespis of Thebes, competed against Eumelus and Evangelus). See Bélis 1995:1052; 1999:133–134. The vetting of potential competitors could have taken place at the assembly before the *agôn*, the *proagôn*. Such an event is attested for Eretrian *mousikoi agônes*: IG XII ix 189.22.

[20] See Vos 1986:128, Wilson 2002:51–52, and Miller 1997:162–175 on the costume of auletes, players of the reed-blown pipes called *auloi*. At the Pythian contests it was traditional for auletes to wear specific raiment called the *Puthikê stolê*. The famous aulete Chrysogonus, decked out in these distinctive garments, played the *auloi* aboard the trireme carrying Alcibiades back from exile (Athenaeus 12.535d; Plutarch *Alcibiades* 32.2). The virtuoso's costume was no doubt as much a feature of the political theater as his music. Athenian dramatic, dithyrambic, and theoric choruses were often lavishly costumed. See Plutarch *Nicias* 3.4–6 for a particularly grandiose case. Funding for choral *skeuê* (and that of the accompanying aulete) was provided by the wealthy citizen *khorêgos*, and as such the costume was a reflection of his own desire

ornamental *stephanoi*, crowns or wreaths, during performance. These *stephanoi* simultaneously advertised their wearers' previous agonistic victories and created the impression that they were again worthy of distinction in the present performative context, be it contest or concert. Gold and silver crowns were in fact conferred as prizes in the *mousikoi agônes* at some festivals, including the Great Panathenaia in Athens. These could be and surely were melted down by victors to redeem their cash value, but presumably they were in some cases worn at subsequent performances as testament to recent triumph.[21]

As the most conspicuous advertisement of the combined cultural and economic capital that the serious citharode was expected to possess—a "poor" or "humble" citharode such as Eumelus is in reality as much an oxymoron as a totally unskilled one—the vigilant maintenance of the status symbol that is the *skeuê* represented a necessary reinvestment of earned income. Citharodes were self-promoting impresarios, entrepreneurs who had to spend money to make money; the best became quite rich while doing so. Depictions of elaborately garbed citharodes on Archaic and Classical Attic vases attest to the antiquity of this truth. After all, who else was paying for these *skeuai* but the musicians themselves? The first prize at the fourth-century BCE Panathenaic citharodic *agôn* was a golden olive branch crown worth 1,000 drachmas plus a flat cash award of 500 silver drachmas—an enormous payday. Runners-up took home more than respectable sums as well: second prize was 1,200 drachmas cash, the third 600, the fourth 400, and the fifth 300.[22] In the relative terms of the ancient Athenian economy, the fourth-place finisher earned from his one semi-successful agonistic appearance at the Panathenaic festival an amount equal to more than one year's wages earned by a skilled craftsman.[23]

---

for social distinction. The *khorêgos* himself wore an eye-catching outfit to match that of his chorus: Demosthenes 21.16, 22. Cf. Wilson 2000:86–88.

[21] Cf. Boyd 1994:112n8, who argues that the golden wreath that Socrates imagines the rhapsode Ion wearing to the Panathenaia (*Ion* 541b-c) is the same one he received as prize at the Asclepieia in Epidaurus.

[22] As recorded in the Panathenaic prize inscription IG II² 2311. The section recording the second through fourth prizes in *kitharôidia* is damaged (lines 8–11), but Kotsidu 1991:101, 212n240 makes convincing arguments for these amounts. On the inscription, see now Shear 2003, who proposes slightly different reconstructions of the prize amounts for citharists and aulodes (95).

[23] Miller 2004:134, who estimates that the first prize amount for citharodes would be roughly equivalent to 150,000 dollars US, while a fifth-place contestant still earned the equivalent of several thousand dollars. Athens was a remarkably lucrative market for citharodes, but other cities offered them relatively high payouts as well. See the discussion of the Eretrian Artemisia below.

Citharodes far out-earned fellow musicians as well; winning citharists won a crown worth only 300 drachmas and a 200-drachma cash prize, while first-place winners in *aulos* singing, *aulôidia*, went home with a crown worth 300 drachmas, the same as the last-place citharode.[24] There is no good reason to believe that these prize amounts did not have scaled equivalents in the fifth and sixth centuries.[25]

This last point has been overlooked in recent histories of ancient Greek music, which tend to view the commodification of musical performance as a symptom of the hyperprofessionalization of popular music culture in late Classical Athens, the era of the so-called New Music. This view does have grounding in the ancient sources. One fourth-century BCE critic, probably Aristoxenus of Tarentum, says that the music of his time was composed in a "money-making style" ("Plutarch" *On Music* 12.1135c), an assessment seemingly confirmed in the anecdotal traditions surrounding financially successful star virtuosos such as the fourth-century Athenian citharist Stratonicus, who in story after story openly boasts of the riches his music has brought him. But the sources must be treated with care. We should be wary of characterizing agonistic musicians of the Archaic and earlier Classical periods as Eumeluses, noble servants of the Muse, eager only for prestige, and later fifth- and fourth-century musicians as a new generation of mercantile fortune hunters. This would be to accept uncritically the reductive claims of fourth-century elites such as Aristoxenus, who tend to mystify the whole of old-fashioned *mousikê* as aristocratic and economically disinterested, while framing the "crowd-pleasing" contemporary music they object to on social and aesthetic grounds as purely commercial in intent.[26]

---

[24] The prize amounts for the citharist are those proposed by Shear 2003:95; Kotsidu 1991:101 proposes a prize of 500 drachmas and a crown worth 300 drachmas.

[25] Aristotle *Constitution of Athens* 60.3: "The prizes for winners in the *mousikoi agônes* are of silver and gold." Kotsidu 1991:100 argues that cash prizes were instituted only after restoration of the democracy in 403–402 BCE, but it seems unlikely that itinerant musicians would ever have been awarded the cumbersome oil-filled amphorae awarded to athletic victors. See Herington 1985:246n28; Davison 1958:38. See further Part IV.7n158.

[26] Such reductionism colors the following assessment from Bélis 1995: "Alors qu'à l'epoque classique, les musiciens accomplissent leur métier en recherchant moins la fortune que les couronnes conquises dans les concours sacrés, à partir du quatrième siècle, leurs ambitions sont de connaître aussi vite que possible la gloire ... et, simultanément, d'amasser des richesses" (1057). This is not to say that glory and renown were not important to Archaic and Classical citharodes, only that the accrual of wealth was equally important, and increasingly feasible with the expansion of contests and patronage opportunities in the sixth and early fifth century BCE.

Similarly, Stratonicus' boldly mercantile persona must be taken in proper context. While it may represent a novel mode of self-presentation among music professionals, the economic mentalities and practicalities it so frankly acknowledges—Stratonicus unapologetically claims, for instance, that "from the Muses I have received all the Greeks as my *telos* [that is, a source of tax revenue], from whom I exact a wage (*misthos*) for their *amousia* 'lack of musicality'" (Athenaeus 8.350e)—go back well before the fourth century.[27] A logic of exchange of musical pleasure for material goods is already constituent of the model of the Homeric *aoidos* 'bard', who is a *dêmioergos* 'worker for the community' on the level of a builder, doctor, or seer (*Odyssey* 18.383–385).[28] Archaic *kitharôidia*, practiced in a world of increased commercial sophistication, festal organization, and tyrannical patronage, represents a metastasis of that older logic; the *dêmioergos* has become a long-distance, large-scale merchant of his *tekhnê*.[29] Such transformation is neatly reflected in the Herodotean account of the Lesbian citharode Arion's return journey to Corinth, where he enjoys the long-term patronage of the tyrant Periander, from Sicily and Italy, where he has earned an enormous sum of money (*khrêmata megala*, 1.24.1). Herodotus does not say, but the money was presumably earned from either giving public concerts, winning (and perhaps organizing) *mousikoi agônes*, entering the service of wealthy patrons, or some combination of these ventures, all of which

---

[27] The rhetoric involved in fashioning this persona is complex. In part it is an attempt to compensate for the lower socioeconomic status of the citharist relative to the citharode; IG II² 2311.15–17 (in the restored text of Shear 2003) shows that citharists earned about half what citharodes did at the Panathenaia. It is also a response to the conservative critics of his music. Cf. Wilson 2004:291, who observes that Stratonicus "appears to have been unconcerned to conceal the economics at the base of his career." Not only is Stratonicus unapologetic about the commodified status of his music, he is eager to advertise it (cf. n70 below). His self-presentation as a Panhellenic touring musician amounts to a recuperation of the stigmatization of musical performance for pay, *misthos*, that we see framed by elites such as Aristoxenus. At the same time, Stratonicus appropriates the prejudices of that elite ideology, effecting a *détournement* of its snobbery to ennoble his own commercial activity. For it is the Muses themselves who authorize him to exploit, for monetary gain, the *amousia* of the mass audiences he entertains. For extra measure, Stratonicus adds a hint of royal entitlement to his self-fashioning with the metaphor latent in *telos*. As Gulick 1996:88 notes, "Stratonicus alludes to the custom of assigning certain towns and villages for the support of favorites at court." Cf. Athenaeus 1.29f, where this custom is connected to the Persian court.

[28] Compare the image of the itinerant singer as hungry *gastêr* 'stomach' in Hesiod *Theogony* 26–28, which "serves as the symbol for the dependence of the poet ... on the patronage of a localized audience" (Nagy 1990b:190).

[29] Cf. Murray 1993:240 on the "complex international market economy" in place by the mid sixth century BCE.

would have been open to the enterprising Archaic citharode. It is no coincidence that the Herodotean narrative repeatedly (four times) focuses on Arion's impressive *skeuê* after the mention of the riches he has earned on his Western tour: *skeuê* and monetary earnings are cognate, mutually reinforcing.[30] It is telling that the only other figure in Herodotus besides Arion of whom the phrase "all his *skeuê*" is used—a pleonastic phrase echoing the rich excess of the ceremonial outfit—is the Persian king, Xerxes (7.15.3), the ultimate exemplar of conspicuous wealth and luxury.[31] We will return to Arion's costume below.

In the Greco-Roman era, when, thanks to an expanded agonistic and concert market for music, moneymaking opportunities became more frequent and more rewarding, the circular logic of the economics of visual display became ever more overheated. In his version of the Arion tale in *Dialogues of the Sea Gods*, Lucian has the citharode returning to his hometown of Methymna from his lucrative stint in Corinth, not to perform music, but to "make a display of his riches" (ἐπιδείξασθαι τὸν πλοῦτον, 8.2). The musical performative connotations of ἐπιδείξασθαι are unmistakable; Lucian repeats the word when Arion "shows off" his gold and silver to the sailors on board the ship to Lesbos. By having Arion make performative displays (*epideixeis*) of his material wealth rather than his *tekhnê*, which we should expect, Lucian alludes wittily, and with some exaggeration, to the thoroughgoing conflation of money, luxury, and music in the citharodic performance culture of his own time, perhaps with implicit reference to the sumptuous *skeuê*, which, following Herodotus, he twice mentions in his description of Arion. By the time of Lucian and Nero it was nothing less than *mos* 'custom' for an *eximius citharoedus* 'star citharode' such as the one mentioned by Juvenal, Seleucus—the name, probably the satirist's invention, evokes the luxurious splendor of the Seleucid East—to "gleam in a golden mantle."[32] The

---

[30] We may note how Herodotus emphatically inscribes Arion in a world of monetary exchange. After he makes his *khrêmata megala*, he "hires" (*misthôsasthai*) a Corinthian ship to take him home. Herodotus' account no doubt reflects the commercialized musical culture of the time in which he composed (c. 430s BCE), but that does not mean it tells us nothing about the economic realities of Archaic *kitharôidia*, of which Arion is an idealized exemplar. Wilson 2004:285 perhaps overstates the case when he argues that Arion's tour is purely a retrojection of "contemporary [i.e. later fifth-century] musical practices and mentalities" onto the Archaic past. Of course, the emphasis on money and commerce in the Herodotean account reflects the context of Arion's tenure in Periandrean Corinth, known for its trade and its wealth—a logical base from which *kitharôidia* could be commodified on an international scale.

[31] Cf. Herington 1985:16.

[32] *Satire* 10.210–212: *nam quae cantante uoluptas | sit licet eximius, citharoedo siue Seleuco | et quibus aurata mos est fulgere lacerna* ("For what pleasure is there in a singer, even if he

17

heightened "glam factor" informed the manufacture of the *kithara* as well, which was now engineered, as Lucian puts it, to be a "grand marvel for the eyes" (θαῦμα μέγα τοῖς ὁρῶσιν), replete with rare gems, woods, and metals, and even decorated with reliefs. The *kithara* of Evangelus, surely not a complete fabrication of Lucian's ecphrastic imagination, features a relief of Apollo, Orpheus, and the Muses. Apuleius, writing around the time of Lucian, imagines Apollo, "radiant in purple," playing a lyre intricately decorated with gold, ivory, and precious jewels in his contest against the *aulos*-playing satyr, Marsyas (*Florida* 3.11). It seems appropriate that Nero would gravitate to the musical medium that not only had traditionally enjoyed the most cultural prestige and celebrity, but that was also the most conspicuously lucrative.

While Eumelus' charge of ἄτεχνος τρυφή neatly characterizes the garish excesses surrounding the uninformed cultural aspirations of ignorant *nouveaux riches*—the uncultured *citharoedus* Evangelus is explicitly portrayed as a counterpart to the wealthy yet uncultured book collector attacked by Lucian throughout his treatise—for citharodes and the majority of people in their audiences a flamboyant *skeuê* was hardly at odds with the "eumelic" *tekhnê* possessed by its wearer. Rather, the *skeuê* was viewed as the appropriately grand, material manifestation of that immaterial, invisible, yet nonetheless rich and powerful possession. The moralizing dichotomy drawn in Lucian's anecdote between seeming and being is hardly applicable to *kitharôidia*, a "show business" in which visual and audial *terpsis* 'pleasure' are mutually reinforcing and less is never more. The more mainstream appreciation of citharodic splendor informs Apuleius' brief account of the contest between Apollo and Marsyas in *Florida* 3. Apuleius inverts the assumptions about the fundamental incompatibility between style and substance that we see in Lucian. Here, it is the barbaric Marsyas

---

is outstanding, even Seleucus the citharode and those whose custom it is to gleam in a golden mantle"). The lines belong to a list of geriatric miseries. The inability to enjoy the definitive musical pleasure, *kitharôidia*, is prominent among them, thanks not only to the loss of hearing but, significantly, of *sight* as well. Courtney 1980 *ad loc.* thinks that *quibus* implicitly refers to *tibicines*, or auletes, since these musicians are associated with the *lacerna* 'mantle', while the more conspicuous item of the citharode's *habitus* is the chiton. But Roman descriptions of citharodic *skeuê* do take both garments into account. Nero wears a purple chiton and a gold-adorned *khlamus*, a mantle analogous to the *lacerna* (Hallet 2005:334–335), on his triumphant return to Rome (Suetonius *Nero* 25.1); cf. Apuleius *Florida* 15.8; *Rhetorica ad Herennium* 4.60. Philostratus the Elder *Imagines* 1.10 ascribes a magical, prismatic charm to the multi-colored *khlamus* of Amphion. At least in the fourth century BCE, the *khlamus*-mantle is called the *epiporpama*, after the *porpê* 'brooch' that fastens the garments together at the shoulder (Plato fr. 10 K-A, with Pollux *Onomasticon* 10.190).

who boasts that his physical ugliness, the humbleness of his art, *aulos* playing, and his poverty belie an "inner beauty," whereas Apollo's beautiful appearance, fine garments, and deluxe lyre are *blandimenta nequaquam virtuti decora, sed luxuriae accommodata* 'empty delights in no way ornamenting virtue, but fit only for luxury'. The judges, the Muses and Minerva, will have none of this, and they award victory to the musically superior and, accordingly, better-dressed Apollo. In this contest, as was generally true in real life, it is the poor, unadorned musician who is defeated and humiliated.[33]

Lucian's moralizing above all recalls Socratic/Platonic attempts to discredit the value of "sensational" demotic musical forms by way of valorizing the supposedly honest and accordingly unspectacular pursuit of philosophy. (Perhaps the Evengelus fable could be traced to some post-Platonic critic of popular music.) Indeed, the *skeuê* of the rhapsode, which by the later fifth century BCE closely imitated that worn by the citharode, emerges in the Platonic dialogue *Ion* as the (ironized) focus of Socrates' attentions. This is unsurprising, as the *Ion* represents Plato's most sustained critique of large-scale musico-poetic spectacle and the charisma of its producers, which are both iconicized by the *skeuê*. At the very beginning of the dialogue, Socrates tendentiously foregrounds the close association between the *tekhnê* and *skeuê* of the star rhapsode Ion: "[I envy you rhapsodes] for the fact that it is always appropriate to your *tekhnê* that you should adorn your body with beautiful garments and look as attractive as possible" (τὸ σῶμα κεκοσμῆσθαι ἀεὶ πρέπον ὑμῶν εἶναι τῇ τέχνῃ καὶ ὡς καλλίστοις φαίνεσθαι, 530b). Later, at 535b, Socrates evokes the image of Ion reciting an especially pathetic episode from Homer while "adorned in intricately embroidered clothing and a golden wreath" (κεκοσμημένος ἐσθῆτι ποικίλῃ καὶ χρυσοῖσι στεφάνοις; cf. 541b–c). The philosopher wants to demystify the *skeuê* and, by extension, the musical *tekhnê* it signifies by teasing out what he sees as the vanity, spiritual emptiness, and cynical demagoguery projected by both.[34] Socrates' mistrust of musicians and their

---

[33] As a high-profile sophistic performer himself (see e.g. *Florida* 9), Apuleius must have well appreciated the celebrity citharode's twin cultivation of talent and image. His telling of the Marsyas and Apollo story in some sense begs to be read as quasi-autobiographical: Apuleius, like Apollo *kitharôidos*, embodies both substance and style, gracefully reconciling the contrasting personae of philosophical heavyweight and dashing, charismatic sophist. The accusers who brought Apuleius to court on a charge of witchcraft had tried to impugn his intellectual pursuits by calling him a "handsome philosopher" (*Apology* 4.1). For the "philosophical" bias against the visually attractive, see Zanker 1995:235.

[34] Cf. Murray 1996:102.

finery is surely "countercultural," but not unique. Other critics of populist musical spectacle will seize upon the effeminate and Eastern connotations of citharodic dress. Lucian's τρυφή insinuates both.

ii. Citharodes on parade

Far from restricting the extravagance of the *skeuê*, the authorities that
sponsored citharodic performance at civic festivals officially promoted
its display. An inscribed decree from the minor Euboean *polis* of Eretria
details the institution of an ἀγῶν μουσικῆς 'contest of music' at the
city's Artemisia festival (IG XII ix 189, c. 341/0 BCE). The roster of musicians who are to compete is fairly typical for the fourth century BCE:
rhapsodes, boy aulodes (singers to the *aulos*), citharists, parody-singers,
and citharodes. (The omission of auletes and adult aulodes from the
lineup is somewhat unexpected, however.) Notably, the inscription
records that competitors are expected to perform music not only at
the *agôn* proper, but also at the festival's cultic centerpiece, the sacrifice, while decked out in all their stage costume. It is decreed that the
city requires that

> τοὺς δὲ τὴν μουσικὴν ἀγωνιζομένους πάντα[ς] | ἀγωνίζεσθαι
> προσόδιον τεῖ θυσίει ἐν τεῖ αὐλεῖ ἔ- | [χο]ντας τὴν σκευὴν
> ἥμπερ ἐν τοῖ ἀγῶνι ἔχουρ[ι]

all those competing in music compete in the *prosodion* 'processional song' for the sacrifice in the *aulê* [an open courtyard
area], wearing the very *skeuê* they wear in the *agôn* proper.

IG XII ix 189.13–15

The musicians' playing of the sacrificial *prosodion* is surely connected to
the sacrificial procession, or *pompê*, in which it is later stipulated they
must also participate, and in which, it is entirely reasonable to assume,
they are also to wear their *skeuai*:

> συμπο- | μπευόντων δὲ καὶ οἱ τῆς μουσικῆς ἀγωνισταὶ πάντ- |
> ες, ὅπως ἂν ὡς καλίσστη ἡ πομπὴ καὶ ἡ θυσίη γίνηται.

Let all of the competitors in *mousikê* also take part in the
pompê so that the *pompê* and the sacrifice may be as splendid
as possible.

IG XII ix 189.38–40

Cities financed *mousikoi agônes*, even modest ones such as those in Eretria, whose operating budget was capped at the lowly sum of 1,000 drachmas (IG XII ix 189.4), for a set of interrelated reasons.[35] Obviously, there is the motivation to delight the citizenry, but also to raise the profile of the important civic cult to which the *agônes* are attached, to advertise the city's cultural prestige, to compete for glory and distinction with other cities hosting contests, and to foster and to demonstrate to all, both citizen and stranger, their political soundness and communal harmony, ideals that resonate especially well in the organization of an orderly musical competition. Eretria instituted the musical *agôn* at the Artemisia as a way of symbolically marking a new political dawn following its liberation at the hands of Athens from the Macedonian-backed strongman Cleitarchus; the final lines (44–45) of the inscription optimistically assert that the *agôn* will be held in the prescribed fashion "for as long as the Eretrians are free, prospering, and ruling themselves." But *mousikoi agônes* served to stimulate the local economy as well, by attracting large, exuberant crowds eager to listen to and look at the visiting star musicians, even the presumably "B-list" stars who would perform at the small-time Artemisia. The festival context of most *agônes* was a site of intensive mercantile activity—at the Artemisia a tax-free market was conveniently in effect (lines 32–34)—and a well-attended *agôn* could mean a good deal of commercial revenue for the citizens of the host *polis*.[36] As Hermes puts it in Aristophanes *Wealth* 1162–1163, "It is most appropriate for Wealth to hold musical and gymnastic *agônes*." As god of commerce (*empolaios*) and contests (*enagônios*), Hermes knows whereof he speaks.

The Eretrian decree implicitly invokes self-promotional and economic motives: the musical *agôn* is intended to add splendor to the preexisting festival (ὡς κάλλιστα ἄγωμεν), thereby enticing "as many people as possible to participate in the sacrifice" (θύω[ριν ὡς πλεῖ]στοι, 2). The pious desire to propitiate Artemis with a grand sacrifice aside, a capacity crowd at the sacrifice means higher attendance at the festival as a whole, and accordingly more money and recognition generated by it. To this end, by requiring the musical *agônistai* to

---

[35] To put the smallness of this amount in perspective: at the fourth-century BCE Great Panathenaia a second-place winner in the citharodic *agôn* would alone take home 1,2000 drachmas cash (IG II² 2311.8).

[36] Cf. Csapo and Slater 1994:204; Hasebroek 1965:167; de Ligt and de Neeve 1988. For the commercial ambience surrounding the early Panathenaic *mousikoi agônes* (probably) held in the Agora, see Kotsidu 1994:169.

21

appear "in character," as it were, outside the *agôn* proper, the Eretrian magistrates contrive to infuse the sacrificial *pompê* with the splendor and excitement of the musical contest, thus maximally capitalizing on their thousand-drachma investment.[37] Procession and sacrifice themselves become theatricalized, staged as the scene of an informal *agôn*, in which the musicians compete both in displaying their prowess in playing the *prosodion* and, as the inscription emphatically stipulates, in displaying their best *skeuê*.[38] The lavish costumes of musicians, and the distinctively agonistic "roles" they signify, are temporarily repurposed by the city to serve more comprehensively its festal self-marketing.

A late parallel to the Artemisia regulations comes by way of the official rules for third-century CE *mousikoi agônes* held in another small community, the Egyptian town of Karanis. The rules stipulate that the κιθαριστὴς κύκλιος, the 'cyclic citharist' who accompanies competing choruses, must wear his *skeuê* "during exits (ἐξόδους)" as well, presumably, as entrances (P.Mich. 4682 ii.25–26). The papyrus text is partly illegible in this spot, but the sense seems to be that the citharist is required to wear his costume—the same one he wears for his own solo performances, perhaps—for some duration longer than the actual performance event.[39]

---

[37] The *pompê* probably already featured an impressive military display: Strabo 10.1.10. On the performative nature of *pompai,* see Kavoulaki 1999. Another section of the Eretrian inscription records that musicians are to be paid a stipend of one drachma per day leading up to the *agôn* (lines 21–23). Such stipends were likely not uncommon. Itinerant *agônistai* could be treated by "patron" cities as temporary retainers during festival times, not merely as performers who passed through to win prizes on *agôn* day and then moved on. More generally, in the time immediately before and after the contest proper the citharode would very much have been on display in the city, engaging in all sorts of informal contests, interventions, and displays, musical and verbal, doing the "off-stage" cultural work of *kitharôidia,* at *proagônes,* civic events, public discourses, semi-public exchanges of "shop talk" between *agônistai* at parties, private entertainments, etc. The anecdotal tradition surrounding the "witty" citharist Stratonicus offers an invaluable window onto the politics of the para-agonistic scene (see evidence collected in Gilula 2000). Plato's *Ion* is a stylized dramatization of a conversation about contests and *mousikê* held in the run-up to the Panathenaic *agônes.* See Nagy 2002 on refractions of para-Panathenaic discourse in Plato.

[38] It is unclear in what sense exactly the musicians are to "compete" in the sacrificial *prosodion;* cf. von Prott and Ziehen 1906:255. The verb in the inscription, *agônizesthai,* does mean 'to compete', and rather than take it to mean merely 'participate' or 'perform', as it might in some Hellenistic festival inscriptions (cf. Slater 2007:34–35), we should here, I think, respect its original semantics, attenuated as they might be— thus my "informal *agôn*" above—and see in the use of the word a statement of the city's agenda of "agonization." It is remarkable that in Attic iconography, at least, string players are never shown accompanying sacrifice at the altar itself, only auletes (Nordquist 1992:155). As auletes are not explicitly mentioned in the Eretrian inscription, we may assume the case was different at the Artemisia.

[39] See Pearl 1978.

At the Artemisia, as at the Panathenaia and most other local festivals with thematic or chrematitic *mousikoi agônes*, i.e. games that award victors with prizes of cash and valuables, *khrêmata*, rather than wreaths, *stephanoi*, the notionally sole prizes at the stephanitic contests, which claimed international, "sacred" status, the winning citharodes receive *athla* 'prizes' of the highest value.[40] The first-place citharode takes home 200 drachmas, the second-place, 150, and the third-place, 100 (lines 15–20). The total expenditure on these prizes, 450 drachmas, thus represents close to half the total prize budget, and with this significant investment in citharodic culture, modest as it is in comparison with the exorbitant outlay in Athens, Eretrian authorities were clearly counting on a high yield of prestige, visibility, and profit for the city.[41] Accordingly, we should expect that the citharodes took pride of place in the extra-agonistic displays, and that their *skeuai* were especially grand. We may compare representations of *kithara* players participating in the sacrifical *pompê* in Athens. A richly illustrated early example is to be found on a black-figured Attic amphora by the Painter of Berlin 1686 from around 540 BCE.[42] The reverse shows four musicians, two auletes and two *kithara* players, providing music for the processional ceremony shown on the obverse, the leading of a sacrificial ox to the altar of Athena. All four musicians are attired in sleeveless, full-length chitons decorated with intricate patterns and designs, although the garb of the two string players—we cannot tell whether these are citharodes, citharists, or both—is arguably more luxurious than that of the auletes. It is possible that the *pompê* depicted on the Berlin amphora is meant to be a stylized representation of the Panathenaic procession itself, and that the musicians are not merely

---

[40] In reality, even self-advertised stephanitic contests, such as the "sacred games" of the Pythia and their derivatives in Naples and elsewhere, likely offered cash or valuables to musical victors as supplements to the crown awards. Cf. Slater 2007:38–40; Pleket 2004. The symbolic capital of prestige earned at the stephanitic *agônes* was necessary to build a reputation, but financial capital was necessary to sustain a citharodic career.

[41] By comparison, the three top prizes for citharists amount to 235 drachmas, those for rhapsodes, 170 drachmas; the boy aulodes are allotted prizes totaling 100 drachmas, and the parodists receive only 60. The strong emphasis on string music at the Artemisia, to the detriment of *aulos*-based forms, is noteworthy. Perhaps a deliberate "niche" marketing/branding strategy lies behind it, a plan to make the most of limited resources in order to put the Artemisia on the geomusical map as a small but attention-worthy center of one field of musical *tekhnê*. The inclusion of auletic and adult aulodic events would have stretched the budget too thin, making it difficult to attract high-caliber citharodes (and citharists).

[42] Staatliche Museen zu Berlin F 1686. See Shapiro 1992:54–55, with fig. 34, a, b: "The Berlin amphora ... gives us our first glimpse of the colorful and elaborate costumes characteristic of professional musicians at Athens."

hired ceremonial hands or amateurs, but competitors in the festival's musical *agôn*, which at this time the Peisistratid tyrants were intent on making into a Panhellenically prestigious cultural event. Similarly, the four *kithara* players and four auletes sculpted on the north and (probably) the south sides of the Parthenon frieze (c. 440 BCE), which most scholars believe represents an idealized Panathenaic *pompê*, could be *agônistai* at the festival, although it has also been suggested that they are non-competitive Athenian citizens.[43] In any case, the costume worn by the musicians, thick himations draped over ankle-length, sleeved chitons, distinguishes them as the most conspicuously attired participants in the sacrifical procession.[44]

iii. Technicolor dreamcoat

But the *skeuê* does more than distinguish its wearer as a high-value star showman. It works a more sublime sort of theatrical magic as well. We should avoid equating agonistic and concert *kitharôidia* in any strong sense with drama, either theatrical or cultic-ritual. To borrow a useful analytical category from modern-day performance theory, citharodic performance was a "nonmatrixed" event; that is, it was not "subtended by matrices of fictional time, place, and character."[45] Although a citharode could histrionically occupy any number of fictional roles in the course of bringing to musical life the partly mimetic, partly diegetic poetic texts he typically sang, the citharode's identity qua citharode was at no point entirely submerged in such role-playing, as an actor's identity (ideally) would have been; audience members never forgot they were being entertained by a virtuoso *kitharôidos* in the here-and-now.[46] But *kitharôidos* was itself a part to be played; the citharode

---

[43] So Bundrick 2005: "Although many of the musicians employed for Athenian rituals were likely hired professionals, in the case of the Parthenon frieze with its apparent emphasis on the Athenian *demos*, these particular musicians are probably citizens too" (152). If they are citizens, the *kithara* players, at least, might belong to the aristocratic clan of the Euneidai, whose members, we learn from Harpocration s.v. Εὐνεῖδαι, "were citharodes who provided service for religious rituals."

[44] On the ornamented sleeved chiton (*khitôn kheiridotos*), see Miller 1997:156–165, who suggests that fifth-century musicians were drawn to the garment for its connotations of Eastern sumptuousness; cf. Bundrick 2005:166.

[45] Kirby 1965:14–16, as condensed in Auslander 2006:102.

[46] On "mixed mode" poetry, mimetic and diegetic, of which Homeric epic is the primary example, see Plato *Republic* 392e–394c. The "new *nomos*" of the later fifth century BCE did, however, involve a greater emphasis on theatrical mimesis, which compromised, yet still did not entirely obscure, the integrity of the citharode's traditional persona; see Section 17 below; Part IV.11.iv.

not only performed music and poetry, he performed the traditional, generic musical persona of the *kitharôidos*, a role ideally graced with the aura of the supernatural, the sacred, even the (Apollonian) divine.[47] The *skeuê* vividly marks the ritualized assumption of this larger-than-life persona in the moment of performance, symbolically mediating the transformation of the performer's identity from ordinary musician to extraordinary *kitharôidos*. Like the modern-day superhero who must change into costume in order to assume his powers, when the citharode put on his *skeuê* he became "another man," the musical magician capable of wonders. Or, to invoke what is perhaps a closer parallel, we may compare the ritual garments of the Siberian shaman, whose donning, as Mircea Eliade argues, marks the mystical moment of transition when the shaman "transcends profane space and prepares to enter into contact with the spiritual world."[48]

The transfiguring force of the citharode's costume should be traced back to the colorfully decorated "sacral dress" worn by his distant ancestors, the lyre players of Late Minoan and Mycenaean palatial culture, whose musico-hieratic role in cultic ritual is strongly suggested by the extant iconography, although it is by no means exactly comprehensible. In some cases, notably the outsized bard depicted on a wall painting from the Throne Room at Pylos (c. 1300 BCE), who wears a full-length, horizontally striped robe and holds a swan-necked lyre, elaborately accoutered musicians may represent semi-divine musical heroes or even the epiphanic forms of gods, perhaps of Apollo himself.[49] During the Dark Age, the elaborate *skeuê*, along with the

---

[47] On the concept of musical personae, derived from Goffman's "presentation of self," see Auslander 2006: "Musical performance may be defined ... as *a person's representation of self within a discursive domain of music*. I posit that in musical performance, this representation of self is the direct object of the verb *to perform*. What musicians perform first and foremost is not music, but their own identities as musicians, their musical personae" (102). See too Nagy 1996 on the mimetic reenactment of ritual personae in Archaic and Classical Greek performance culture.

[48] Eliade 1964:147. On parallels between the shaman and Orpheus, see Graf 1987; Freiert 1991; McGahey 1994:3–26.

[49] On Minoan-Mycenaean musicians, see Anderson 1994:6–14; "sacral dress": Nilsson 1971:155–164. The bird depicted rising up next to the Pylos bard may indicate that this is an epiphany of Apollo (so Anderson). Otherwise, the summoned bird, as well as the rocky outcropping on which the bard sits, which suggests a wild terrain "outside a constructed human environment" (Younger 1998:48), could identify him as Orpheus. Compare the lyre player in a striped robe standing beneath two flying birds on a Late Minoan IIIB pyxis in Chania, Crete (Maas and Snyder 1989:16, fig. 2b). Cf. Langdon 1992:76–78. For Near Eastern parallels, see Franklin 2006a:53–54. The processional lyre players depicted on paintings from Hagia Triada, Crete, who wear ankle-length, vertically banded robes, very closely resemble Archaic/Classical citharodes; these

heptatonic instruments that the Minoan-Mycenaean musicians seem to have cultivated, may have fallen out of use. In Geometric art musicians are generally depicted without clothing. This could merely be representational convention, but it is notable that in Homeric epic no mention at all is made of the mode of dress of *phorminx*-playing bards.

In what is likely the earliest image of an agonistic citharode, on a late-eighth- or early-seventh-century BCE stamnos from the northern Aegean island of Lemnos (Athens, National Museum 19272), the citharode wears a thigh-length garment that is exquisitely decorated and clearly a forerunner to later Archaic full-length costumes.[50] The wearing of *skeuê* was perhaps "rediscovered" only in the late eighth and early seventh century BCE, with the emergence of the solo citharodic tradition, above all on the eastern Aegean island of Lesbos and surrounding territories, and later throughout Ionian Greece. This emergence coincides with the so-called Orientalizing period, and it is possible that the Lesbian citharodes were inspired by Near Eastern musical technology they encountered in Lydia to develop the heptachord *kithara*, which was itself a sort of rediscovery of the "lost" Bronze Age seven-stringed instrument.[51] Similarly, the early citharodes of Eastern Greece could have adapted the sumptuous ceremonial dress of Oriental musicians in the designs of their *skeuê*. The "sacral dress" of the Minoan-Mycenaean musicians is likely to have been already derived from Near Eastern apparel.[52] The associations of the citharodic *skeuê* with the exotic glamour of the East no doubt contributed to its powers of charm and fascination. As we will see in Part IV.10, the designation of the concert *kithara* as "Asiatic" that begins to appear in literature of the fifth century BCE reflects a wider tendency of citharodes

---

are presumably mortal ritual officiants. See discussion and illustrations in Anderson 1994:7–9 and Maas and Snyder 1989:2–3, 16.

[50] Cf. discussion of this image in Part III.11.

[51] For a plausible reconstruction of the Archaic rediscovery of lost Minoan-Mycenaean musical technology via the culture of Mermnad Lydia, see Franklin 2002 and 2008; cf. Boardman 1980:97–98. It is telling that the earliest surviving image of Apollo playing a seven-stringed *kithara*, painted on a later seventh-century amphora from the island of Melos (Athens, National Museum 911, Maas and Snyder 1989:42, fig. 2), appears in a markedly Orientalizing context. Apollo stands in a chariot drawn by four winged horses, exotic creatures derived from the Near Eastern bestiary.

[52] Evans 1928:721; cf. Anderson 1994:8. On Greek adoption and adaptation of Eastern fashions in general, see Miller 1997:153–187, especially 161–162 on musicians' dress. West 1992:55 considers the patterned cloth that citharodes drape from their instruments to be "inspired by oriental pomp" (see e.g. Plates 1, 9). Similar textile adornments are shown suspended from the vertical harps of musicians on seventh-century BCE Assyrian reliefs.

to fashion their performative self-presentation with romanticized touches of the Orient.

The supernatural aura of the *skeuê* probably dissipated over time, even as citharodic costume became ever more luxuriously elaborate, but in the Archaic and earlier Classical periods the *skeuê* was no doubt thought to possess real talismanic powers. In his account of Arion's performance on board a ship traveling from Italy to Corinth, Herodotus places repeated emphasis on the role of the *skeuê* in the wondrous proceedings.[53] We are told that Arion makes sure to appear before the sailors, who plan to rob and murder him, with his *kithara* and ἐν τῇ σκευῇ πάσῃ "in all his *skeuê*" (1.24.4; cf. 1.24.5; Lucian *Dialogues of the Sea Gods* 8.2). Plutarch, who also relates this detail in his version of the tale, calls the *skeuê* an *enagônios kosmos* 'adornment for the contests' (*Banquet of the Seven Sages* 18.161c). Even under the dire circumstances of this impromptu concert, the citharode, ever the competitive showman, dons his iconic costume, the symbol of his success and wealth; it is as if the performance would be illegitimate without it. But implicit here too is the sense that the *skeuê* is worn for supernatural protection, that it induces an altered state in which the wondrous is possible.[54] Arion leaps into the sea "with all his *skeuê*" (σὺν τῇ σκευῇ πάσῃ, 1.24.5), where he is rescued by dolphins and miraculously brought safely to Corinth, still wearing his *skeuê*, of course (1.24.6). When the sailors later show up in Corinth, Arion appears before them once again in costume, looking just as he did on the ship, shocking them into confessing their crime. Herodotus figures this second "performance" as a kind of divine epiphany (*epiphanênai*, 1.24.7); specifically, Arion in the fullness of his citharodic persona resembles none other than Apollo *kitharôidos*. Although Herodotus does not make it explicit, one assumes that Arion will subsequently recover the money stolen from him by the sailors. At the denouement of Arion's amazing life-and-death adventure, then, the mystical and mercantile dimensions of his citharodic persona converge upon the image of his *skeuê*.

---

[53] Cf. Gray 2001:14n1; Herington 1985:16.

[54] Aelian *Historical Miscellanies* 3.43 records an anecdote that also attests to the sacred aura of citharodic *skeuê*, although in this case it fails to save the life of its wearer. The Sybarites slaughter a citharode, despite the fact that he had fled to the altar of Hera and was still wearing his stage costume (*sun autêi stolêi*). The hubristic disrespect for the altar is significantly parallel to that for the *stolê* as the Sybarites kill this 'therapôn (servant) of the Muses'. Perhaps their own excess luxury in dress (Athenaeus 15.518e–519b) has caused them to lose sight of the special status accorded to citharodic costume.

4. Apollonian Assimilations and Orphic Icons

Indeed, every citharode may be perceived as a spectacular representation, *mimêsis*, of the god Apollo, although that popular perception must have become considerably "secularized" by the time of Nero and Lucian. That is, audiences recognized still a notional assimilation between god and mortal, but not the epiphanic implications of the citharode's appearance.[55] The second-century CE literary historian Proclus, putting forth the theory that the genre of citharodic song called the *nomos* was derived from the choral song called the paean, records a bit of lore from Delphi that stands as a local *aition* of the performance of *kitharôidia* there:

> Χρυσόθεμις ὁ Κρὴς πρῶτος στολῇ χρησάμενος ἐκπρεπεῖ
> καὶ κιθάραν ἀναλαβὼν εἰς μίμησιν τοῦ Ἀπόλλωνος μόνος
> ᾗσε νόμον, εὐδοκιμήσαντος δὲ αὐτοῦ διαμένει ὁ τρόπος τοῦ
> ἀγωνίσματος·

> Chrysothemis the Cretan, wearing conspicuous raiment and taking up the *kithara* in reenactment (*mimêsis*) of Apollo, was the first man to sing by himself a *nomos*; and since he won acclaim, this style of competitive performance persists to this day.

> Proclus Chrestomathia ap.
Photius Bibliotheca 320b1–4

Crucial to the performative *mimêsis* of Apollo enacted prototypically by the legendary citharode Chrysothemis, reputedly the first winner at the Pythian citharodic *agôn* (Pausanias 10.7.2), is the στολὴ ἐκπρεπής 'conspicuous raiment', which historical competitors in the contest long continued to wear.[56] The logic of myth and ritual in the matter of the *skeuê* is uroboric: mortal citharodes dress up as their patron god Apollo, who in turn is costumed as a mortal citharode. The Pythian section of the *Homeric Hymn to Apollo* thus opens with an iconic image of Apollo making his way to Delphi accoutered as a concert citharode,

---

[55] Yet Nero felt a real kinship with Apollo *kitharôidos*; he was deeply invested in the ideal of the divine citharode. See Suetonius *Nero* 53, Pliny *Natural History* 30.14, Dio Cassius 63.20.5 on Nero's Apollonian fixation. Further sources collected in Miller 2000:410n5. The official designation for Neronian citharodic performance came to be "divine voice" after 65 BCE: Suetonius *Nero* 21.1, Dio Cassius 63.20.5. Cf. Kauppi 2006:60–61.

[56] Cf. n20 above on the distinctive *stolê* of auletic competitors at the Pythian contests, which was likely emulative of citharodic costume.

"playing on the hollow *phorminx*, wearing divine, perfumed garments" (182–184). Archaic and early Classical Attic vase paintings of citharodic scenes seem deliberately to invite confusion between divine model and mortal reenactor. We will examine this visual "feedback loop" between the two at greater length in Part IV.

Apollo *kithârôidos*, sometimes alone, sometimes leading the chorus of the Muses or in the company of other Olympian gods, would be familiar to all who had seen the many images of the god in that aspect on Greek pottery, votive objects, and in statuary. This iconic image had become well known in Rome as well. Some of the spectators in Naples may have been holding Roman coins, issued under Nero himself, with images of Apollo in full citharodic *habitus* on the reverse.[57] A magnificent statue of Apollo in full citharodic costume supposedly created by the fourth-century BCE sculptor Scopas of Paros stood in the cella of the Augustan temple of Apollo on the Palatine for all to see.[58] Wealthy Romans had since the Republican period been appropriating Greek statues of Apollo *citharoedus* for display in their private villas, as the bronze Apollo found at the so-called Casa del Citarista in Pompeii indicates.[59] Tacitus in fact has Nero making rhetorical appeal to the familiarity of such model images by way of justifying his own musical vocation: citharodic songs were "sacred to Apollo," argues the *princeps*, and "this outstanding and prescient divinity was represented in the *ornatus* 'fine attire' of a *citharoedus* not only in Greek cities but in Roman temples" (*Annals* 14.14.1).

The sight of the citharode may also have evoked the mythic charge of Orpheus or Amphion, proto-citharodic culture heroes, one imposing order and control on the chaos of the natural world, nearly

[57] These coins were minted between 62 and 65 CE. Suetonius thought they were struck to commemorate Nero's tour of Greece in 66–67 and that the citharode portrayed on them was the emperor (*Nero* 25.2). But see Champlin 2003:117, with illustration in Griffin 1984, fig. 31. *Kitharai* (but not citharodes) had been featured on Roman coins going back to the second century BCE (Wille 1967:214). Various Greek municipalities, especially ones with strong Apollonian and/or citharodic connections such as Delos, Mytilene, and Methymna (Richter 1965:68, figs. 269–270; Schefold 1997:156–157, Abb. 70) had been striking coins with Apollo *kithârôidos* or the *kithara* alone since the fifth century BCE.

[58] Pliny *Natural History* 36.25; Propertius *Elegies* 2.31.16 (*Pythius in longa carmina ueste sonat* 'The Pythian god wearing his long garment performs his songs'); Ovid *Metamorphoses* 11.165–169 may also be an ecphrasis of the statue. Roccos 1989, however, argues that the Palatine Apollo was a Roman work modeled on the Athenian cult statue of Apollo Patroos by Euphranor.

[59] See Roccos 2002 for a fascinating reconstruction of the "narrative" contextualization of statues of long-robed Apollo *citharoedus* on the private grounds of Imperial villas.

transcending the irrevocable power of death itself, the other sounding into harmonic motion the inert stones that would form the walls of the Theban *polis*. These divine and mythical models and paradigms remained very much "in play" in the living culture of Imperial *kithar-ôidia*. An elaborately garbed, youthful citharode performing before an appreciative audience is depicted on a second- or third-century CE applique medallion from the Rhone valley. Above him an inscription reads *NICA APOLLO* 'Be victorious, Apollo'. The figure depicted is most likely a mortal citharode who is being accorded the most fulsome praise by the spectators at the performance; that is, they identify him with the patron god of his art.[60] A roughly contemporary epigram from the *Latin Anthology* (103 Kay = 114R) compares the awesome talent of a performing citharode, "skilled in making songs with his Apolline plectrum" (1), to the preternatural musical feats of Amphion and Orpheus. The epigram is one of a series in the *Anthology* dedicated to populist spectacles—other poems treat pantomime and tight-rope walking—and this context suggests that, despite the poet's high literary tone, the vision of the citharode as a latter-day Orpheus or Amphion was not simply a socially detached ecphrastic topos, but an actual reflection of popular mentality.[61] At least one real-life citharode of the Empire was named Amphion (CIL 6, 10124b).

Such encomiastic assimilation of real to mythical citharode had a long pre-Roman history. A striking example has been preserved on an artifact of citharodic culture that predates the medallion by well over 600 years. A black-figured oinochoe from Athens shows a figure in full citharodic garb mounting a *bêma*, the platform reserved for competitors at musical games. An inscription framing the image reads *khaire Orpheus* 'Hail, Orpheus'.[62] Perhaps the inscription straightforwardly indicates that the musician is meant to be *the* Orpheus, imagined here, uniquely in Greek art and poetry, in an explicitly agonistic context.[63] Alternatively, it has been suggested that the musician is a real-life citharode, whose greeting to the legendary singer is recorded in the inscription.[64] Another interpretation of the image would be to integrate these

---

[60] Thus Péché and Vendries 2001:74, with illustration.

[61] Cf. Kay 2006:136–155.

[62] Villa Giulia M 354; Seebass 1991:19, with fig. 6; Shapiro 1992:69.

[63] Thus Seebass 1991:19.

[64] Amyx 1976:28; cf. Bundrick 2005:118. I note that the phrase *khaire Orpheus* corresponds to a type of hymnic closing formula whereby the performer bids adieu to the divinity he has been singing, e.g. *Homeric Hymns* 12.6. Citharodes as well as rhapsodes sang hymns, so perhaps the inscription quotes the text of a citharodic hymn to Orpheus that the citharode has been performing. This interpretation is enticing,

two readings. The figure is meant to be a real citharode; the inscription, however, represents not his voice, but that of a fan in the festival audience, who lauds him as an "Orpheus" incarnate.[65] Secondarily, the inscription prompts or "scripts" the praise uttered by anyone looking at the depicted musician and, as was the ancient habit, reading aloud the inscribed greeting. The reception of the image thereby reenacts the mythicizing acclaim that met the live performance. The oinochoe represents a variant of the interactive dynamic that informs the *kalos*-inscription, whereby those who view a figure depicted on a vase and read the *kalos*-inscription naming him are made to participate in the celebration of the figure's fame and beauty. Such inscriptions do in fact accompany several depictions of *bêma*-mounted citharodes on Attic vases of the fifth century BCE.[66]

5. Commemorating Citharodes

Statues of mortal citharodes, living and dead, were commonly erected in their home cities and at important centers of *kitharôidia*. A statue of the semi-legendary citharode Eunomus, a Pythian victor, was erected by his fellow citizens in Epizephyrian Locri (Strabo 6.1.9). The sixth-century BCE tyrant Polycrates of Samos dedicated a statue of a beautiful young citharode in the Samian temple of Hera (Apuleius *Florida* 15.6–10). Two dedications dated to around 500 BCE, one from a citharode named Ophsios, the other from an Alkibios, have been found on the Akropolis. We know nothing about either, but we may assume that both were recent victors at the Panathenaia and had the considerable wealth to advertise their success—the dedications were probably

---

but problematic, since the citharode is depicted in pre- or post-performance mode, neither playing nor singing.

[65] The use of the Thracian-style *kithara* by some Classical citharodes surely invited such identifications. See n111 below.

[66] Slater 1999 discusses the function of the *kalos*-inscription within the Athenian "culture of fame." Citharodes labeled *kalos* are sometimes named, e.g. a red-figured krater by Polygnotus, with a young *kithara* player labeled "Nikomas *kalos*" standing before admirers (New York, The Metropolitan Museum of Art 21.88.73; Richter and Hall 1936, no. 126), a fact that prompts still another reading of the Orpheus oinochoe. Is this real-life citharode actually named Orpheus? No citharodic Orpheuses are attested, although we hear of an Orpheus of Croton, who was supposedly employed by the Peisistratids to edit the text of Homer (Tzetzes *On Comedy* p20 Kaibel; cf. *Suda* s.v. Ὀρφεύς, 657 Adler).

inscribed on pedestals supporting bronze statues of the citharodes.[67] A character in Athenaeus 1.19b notes that, while one cannot find a statue of Pindar in that poet's native Thebes, there is the famous statue of Cleon son of Pytheas, called an *aoidos* 'singer' in the funerary verse inscription that celebrates both the "heaven-reaching fame" of the victorious musician and his "glorification of the Theban fatherland" (= anon. FGE 113, 1532-1535). Pliny *Natural History* 34.59 clarifies that this Cleon was a citharode, and attributes the statue, which was spared by Alexander when he razed Thebes, to the reputed fifth-century sculptor Pythagoras of Rhegium.[68] Alexander honored his friend, the citharode Aristonicus, with a bronze statue at Delphi (Plutarch *On the Fortune of Alexander* 334e–f). A statue of the third-century BCE Nicocles of Tarentum, "most famous of all citharodes," was displayed in Athens, where he had made his home (Pausanias 1.37.2; the inscription is preserved: IG II² 3779).

Verres plundered a famous statue of a *citharista* from the city of Aspendus in Pamphylia (Cicero *Verrine Orations* 2.1.53), which he had installed at his own villa. Another statue of a citharist, Archelaus, was erected by the Milesians (Athenaeus 1.19b). The citharode Anaxenor, a favorite of Mark Antony, was honored by his native city, Magnesia on the Maeander, with a painted image in the agora showing him dressed in purple and with a bronze statue in the theater, to which was attached an honorific inscription from Homer, a rendering of *Odyssey* 9.3–4, in which the "godlike voice" of Demodocus is praised by Odysseus (Strabo 14.1.41, who records that the artisan accidentally omitted a letter from the grammatical termination of αὐδή 'voice' in the second line of the inscribed quotation, thus bringing charges of ignorance upon the people of Magnesia). In the second century CE, the city council of Argos decreed the erection of a statue in honor of M. Ulpius Heliodorus, originally of Thessalonike, who was, according to the inscribed statue base, the most theretofore agonistically successful

---

[67] IG I³ 666 and 754. See Raubitschek 1949, nos. 84 and 86; cf. Wilson 2004:284. Kotsidu 1991:80, however, argues that the dedicatory objects were more likely to have been tripods.

[68] Polemon fr. 25 Preller tells the tale, recorded in Athenaeus and Pliny, that a refugee from Thebes had successfully hidden a sum of gold in the sculpted fold of the citharode's mantle; the money was recovered after the city was restored twenty years later. As a result, Pliny tells us, the statue was nicknamed *Dicaeus* ('Just One'). The curious anecdote conflates two themes in the cultural imagination surrounding the citharode: his ability to make money and to protect cities (Thebes itself was founded by the citharode Amphion).

citharode.[69] Heliodorus' record was shattered by a citharode of the Severan period, the Pergamene native C. Antonius Septimius Poplius, who was honored with a victory statue in Smyrna, where he had received citizenship. The base of the monument survives, recording his exhaustive résumé of victories (IGR IV 1432, beginning, "The first and only citharode of the age to win the following *agônes*").

Monuments such as these constituted an off-stage (and in some cases post-mortem) extension of the high-stakes competition for prestige and recognition conducted by the living citharodes they represent, as well as the cities that hosted them.[70] Dio Cassius 63.8.4–5 says that Nero forced an aged citharode, Pammenes, whose celebrity had been at its peak during the reign of Nero's uncle, Gaius, to compete against him during his agonistic tour of Greece, so that "having beaten him, he could have his statues mutilated" (αὐτοῦ τοὺς ἀνδριάντας κράτησας αἰκίσηται; cf. Suetonius *Nero* 24), and presumably replaced with his own. Such *damnatio memoriae* is not otherwise attested, but the story, even if apocryphal, dramatizes the kind of strategic manipulation of cultural memory that was involved in the erection of citharodic statuary. It is worth noting, however, that Nero's entry into the agonistic musical culture of Greece was in some respects bizarrely conflated with Roman military-political theater, in which the punitive destruction or mutilation of opponents' images was exceedingly common. As Dio has it, the emperor staged his entire tour of the Achaean circuit of *agônes* as a military campaign (63.8.4), and celebrated a triumph on his return to Rome, during which he exhibited his "subjugated foe," the citharode Diodorus (63.20.3–4). Dio compares Nero's main citharodic competitors on the tour, Terpnus, Diodorus, and Pammenes, to the Macedonian potentates Philip, Perseus, and Antiochus, describing their defeat at the hands of the emperor in military metaphors (63.8.4–5) that probably echo the Neronian rhetoric.

---

[69] IG IV 591 (Stephanis 1988, no. 1066) records Heliodorus' multiple victories in *agônes* at the Nemean, Isthmian, Pythian, Actian and, curiously, Olympic festival; in the games at the "Shield of Argos" festival, the Sebasta in Naples, the *Koinon* of Asia, and the Urania; and in numerous other provincial *agônes*. On the inscription, see Wallner 2001, who argues that Heliodorus competed at the Olympics, where there was normally no citharodic *agôn*, as a *kêrux* 'herald'.

[70] We see an exaggerated example of such gamesmanship in an anecdote preserved in Athenaeus 8.351e–f: after a victory in Sicyon, the citharist Stratonicus dedicated a "trophy," perhaps a statue, in the Asclepieion, which was inscribed with the words "From the spoils of bad citharists." That is, the monument advertised its own status as a marker of its dedicator's economic success in the contests; it was funded with the winnings Stratonicus "took" from his opponents.

6. Erotic Audition

Beyond any divine and heroic resonances potentially evoked by his stage persona, the citharode, decked out in his stunning concert regalia, exudes a worldly sexual charisma—a powerful amalgam of visual glamour, the projection of technical wizardry, and the promise of overwhelming sensual mastery—which foreshadows that of the modern instrumental virtuoso, concert tenor, or pop star. Standing on the *bêma*, with the eyes of thousands of festival-goers fixed on him, he is an object of wonder and desire, the larger-than-life embodiment of popular acclaim, of wealth and success, of awesome artistic accomplishment.[71] It seems safe to say that no other type of musical or verbal performer in Greek or Roman antiquity, neither virtuoso auletes nor actors nor the theater-filling itinerant rhetors of the First or Second Sophistic, had exerted such consistently powerful sway over the mass libidinal imagination. And it is easy to imagine why, on this level alone, a monumental narcissist such as Nero would be drawn above all other performance media to the practice of *kitharôidia*.

The audition of citharodic music was from its very beginnings acknowledged as a fundamentally erotic experience. Thus during Hermes' primal display of lyre playing in the *Homeric Hymn to Hermes*, which is imagined at once as a foundational *lyric* performance, looking forward to the restricted use of the *khelus*-lyre in the aristocratic symposium and the schoolroom, and a public, proto-professional citharodic event, the heart, *thumos*, of the audience of one, Apollo, is overcome by γλυκὺς ἵμερος 'sweet desire' (422) and ἔρος ἀμήχανος 'irresistible longing' (434). For his part, the performer is determined to make both lyre and voice utterly seductive. The *Hymn to Hermes* describes Hermes' music making as *eratos* 'lovely' three times within six lines (421, 423, 426). The very invention of the lyre is precipitated in the *Hymn* by a mock-erotic encounter marked by the playful tone that distinguishes the poem as a whole. As the newborn Hermes first exits his mother's cave, his gaze is drawn (ἀθρήσας, 29) to the (female) tortoise "prancing along on her feet" (σαῦλα ποσὶν βαίνουσα, 28). He flirtatiously calls the dainty animal 'lovely in form', φυὴν ἐρόεσσα, and a 'companion of the feast', a δαιτὸς ἑταίρη (31; cf. 478). The latter epithet proleptically envisions the tortoise as the convivial instrument it will eventually become; at the same time, however, it figures the

---

[71] For a vivid description of a festival performer (in this case a rhapsode) transfixed by the collective gaze of an audience more than 20,000 strong, see Plato *Ion* 535d–e.

tortoise, and the lyre, as that sexually seductive (and often musically skilled) habitué of the symposium, the *hetaira* 'courtesan'.

i. Seductions of the lyre

More commonly, however, the Archaic and Classical *khelus*-lyre is associated with attractive *boys*. The *bella figura* cut by the well-bred, lyre-playing youth looms large in the early Greek pederastic imagination.[72] But, in Athens at least, this distinctly lyric sex appeal was appreciated primarily by a small, refined group of sympotic elites, who were aroused above all by the demure bearing, modesty, and self-restraint displayed by the privileged students of the *kitharistês* 'lyre teacher'. The lyre functioned almost as an incidental signifier, or a convenient focalizer, of these and related aesthetic, ethical, and even political dispositions, which were ultimately the real turn-ons.[73] The mid-fifth-century sophist Damon, an early exponent of systematized theory linking music and *êthos* 'character', says that a boy should "display not only his masculinity (*andreia*) and self-restraint (*sophrosunê*) while singing and playing the lyre, but also his sense of justice (*dikaiosunê*)" (D-K B 4)—a moral/ethical prescription with hard-to-miss erotic undertones. These are more audible in a passage from Aristophanes' *Clouds*, in which Better Argument, a caricature of an unreconstructed lyric pederast, relates a sexually charged memory of the "good old days," when naked boys walked in orderly fashion (εὐτάκτως, 964) to the *kitharistês* to learn by heart simple, traditional songs sung "in the *harmonia* 'mode' which their fathers had handed down," all the while ingenuously "keeping their thighs spread open" (966–968). Lyre playing put virtue on seductive display.

The visual culture of the symposium makes the case more explicitly. On Attic vases young lyre players attract attention, but they almost always play hard to get, assiduously resisting the advances of their would-be lovers. In some cases boys even use their lyres to fend off aggressive predators, whether divinities (Eros and Eos) or older, bearded gentlemen, idealized reflections of the desiring symposiasts who gaze at the image. This fetchingly defensive gesture nicely iconicizes how the lyre of the "good boy" both piques desire and notionally

---

[72] The eroticized tableau of beautiful young Achilles singing and playing his precious, silver-bridged *phorminx* (the Homeric "lyre") for a rapt Patroclus in *Iliad* 9.182–194 is a paradigmatic case.

[73] For the ethical and somatic comportment instilled by the *kitharistês*, see Plato *Protagoras* 326a–b.

35

guarantees its frustration, a dialectic theoretically at the heart of homoerotic courtship in Classical Athens. Another scene type involves a would-be *erastês* 'lover' offering the gift of a lyre to a properly demure young man. The gesture represents at once a generous act of pedagogy— the lyre perfectly emblematizes the cultural capital that is elite educa- tion, *paideia*—as well as a blatant ploy to outfit the boy with just the prop that will most sexually excite the older man.[74]

The erotic investment in the lyre made by Athenian sympotic elites exhibits a marked fetish character in an Attic *skolion*, or drinking song (PMG 900): "Would that I might become a beautiful ivory lyre and beautiful boys might carry me to the Dionysian chorus" (εἴθε λύρα καλὴ γενοίμην ἐλεφαντίνη | καί με καλοὶ παῖδες φέροιεν Διονύσιον ἐς χορόν). In light of the fact that Dionysian choruses, above all the dramatic and dithyrambic choruses featured at Athenian festivals dedicated to the god, were typically accompanied by the *aulos* rather than the lyre (or the *kithara*), the closing tag Διονύσιον ἐς χορόν must be slyly intended. Perhaps it is meant as a lightly polemical swipe at the demotic culture of the *polis*.[75] The unexpected image of the lyre, that fixture of the exclusive domain of elite society, "invading" the popular ranks of civic *mousikê* and there challenging the supremacy of the *aulos*, the instrument that had, by the later fifth century BCE, come to be fundamentally associated with the democratic musico- cultural apparatus, could well have brought a smile to the lips of politi- cally and culturally separatist aristocrats. However, given that the *skolion* may date to the late Archaic or early Classical period, before the *aulos* and the lyre had become ideologically polarized in the way they would become in the later fifth century, a less political interpretation is safer.[76] The "Dionysian chorus" is likely the very sympotic group to

---

[74] On the adolescent lyre player in schoolroom and courtship scenes, see discussions in Dover 1989:75, Maas and Snyder 1989:87–89, and Bundrick 2005:60–66. In at least one scene Eros has intercrural intercourse with a lyre-holding youth (fragmentary kylix by Douris, Boston, Museum of Fine Arts 13.94; see Shapiro 1981:142, with pl. 28, fig. 14). Cf. Koch-Harnack 1983:166–172 on the lyre as courting gift. Koch-Harnack points out that in some images of the symposium, (nude) young men are shown playing the lyre, and open to the sexual advances of older symposiasts (e.g. the party scene on a kylix of the Hegesiboulos Painter, New York, Metropolitan Museum of Art 07.286.47; cf. Dover 1989:96). But these may be professional, hired musicians, such as the Syracusan boy lyre player in Xenophon *Symposium* 2.1, rather than the "real thing."

[75] Thus Wilson 2004:296–297. Fabbro 1995:166–168 thinks that the chorus is a dithy- rambic chorus at the Panathenaia, but, *pace* Koller 1962, there is no firm evidence for lyric or citharodic dithyrambic performance in Athens.

[76] On this polarization, see Wilson 1999.

which the singer of the *skolion* belongs.[77] Similarly, Anacreon sings of seeing a handsome youth, Simalus, "holding a beautiful *pêktis* in the chorus" (ἐν χορῷ πηκτίδ' ἔχοντα καλήν, PMG 386). The *pêktis*, a type of harp, had no place in choral performance, but it was, according to Pindar fr. 125 S-M, a feature of the Lydian banquet; Anacreon's chorus is the Lydianizing sympotic group, which was the original audience for his songs.[78] The symposiast's wish is thus not only to be transformed into a beautiful boy's precious lyre, but also to be carried to the place where such fine things, beautiful lyres and beautiful boys, are most appreciated, the symposium. This reading of the *skolion* as a self-referential in-joke is supported by its "capping" couplet, PMG 901, which offers a heterosexual reply to the declaration of homoerotic desire that is PMG 900. The singer wishes that he were a golden ornament and that "a beautiful woman would wear me—one who had made pure her mind (καθαρὸν θεμένη νόον)." The woman evoked here is the *hetaira*, who will wear her gold jewelry to the symposium. The ironical closing tag καθαρὸν θεμένη νόον is timed to correspond to the metrically equivalent Διονύσιον ἐς χορόν of PMG 900, which, like PMG 901, is mildly salacious in tone, even suggesting a slight intimation of "corruption."[79] The denizens of the liberated Dionysian symposium dream of fulfilling their sexual fantasies by having a youthful lyre player join their "chorus."[80]

But the *skolion* expresses the truth of a larger process of musical socialization: the elite boys who today are training on the lyre in the schoolroom of the *kitharistês* will tomorrow take their place in the ranks of the symposium. The two zones are, after all, socioculturally contiguous, the former a prelude of sorts to the latter. In a well-known schoolroom scene on a red-figured cup by Douris (Antikensammlung, Staatliche Museen zu Berlin, Preussischer Kulturbesitz F 2285), we thus see two students' lyres hanging on the wall alongside two drinking

---

[77] Cf. Collins 2004:125–126.

[78] For the conceptualization of the sympotic group as a Dionysian chorus, compare Plato *Laws* 664d, 665b, 666b-d. (Collins 2004:125n41 thinks that the *khoroi* of Ion's elegiac fr. 26.11 West refer to symposia, but these might be, at least at the primary level of reference, dithyrambic festival choruses.) The *skolion* in question was probably sung to the lyre, but aulodic performance of *skolia* was also practiced (cf. Aristophanes *Wasps* 1219–1222). If PMG 900 were sung to the "Dionysian" *aulos*, then the self-referentiality of Διονύσιον ἐς χορόν would obviously be more apparent. In the sixth and early fifth centuries BCE the easy coexistence in the symposium of *auloi* and lyres, as well as the vaguely exotic baritone lyre, the *barbitos*, was common.

[79] Cf. Kurke 1997:117–118, who is less inclined to see humor in these *skolia*.

[80] Some Attic sympotic vessels imagine the realization of such fantasies; see n74 above.

cups, which are clearly intended as "symbols of the symposion at which such musical apprenticeship is directed."[81]

ii. "Amazing passion": Misgolas and company

The seductive young lyre player remained a recognizable erotic icon after the fifth century. Demosthenes, for instance, was able to insinuate that his opponent Aeschines had been aroused by the sight of a youthful Alexander singing to the lyre at a Macedonian symposium (Aeschines *Against Timarchus* 168–169).[82] In the same speech we find strong evidence too that the aristocratic romance of the lyre could extend to the world of professional *kitharôidia* as well. Aeschines speaks of one wealthy and cultivated (καλὸς κάγαθός), middle-aged Athenian named Misgolas, beyond reproach in every respect except for his "amazing passion" (δαιμονίως ἐσπουδακώς) for good-looking younger men, which translated into a particular predilection for "certain citharodes or citharists," with whom "he was accustomed always to surround himself" (ἀεί τινας ἔχειν εἰωθὼς περὶ αὐτὸν κιθαρῳδοὺς ἢ κιθαριστάς).[83] Aeschines predictably colors Misgolas' associations as scandalous or ridiculous, reserving "citharodes or citharists" for the end of the sentence, as if to maximize either the shock value or the absurdity of the company kept by the man. But his rhetoric is predictably disingenuous. Although many of the fourth-century BCE Athenian elite kept their distance from popular musicians as a point of moral principle or, more commonly, as a way of maintaining social distinction, Misgolas was surely not alone in his attraction to citharodes. Indeed, the ἤ 'or' in that closing phrase may carry its full disjunctive force, signifying a slight hedge on Aeschines' part: "citharodes, *or rather* citharists." That is, it may be one thing for a man of his stature to surround himself with citharodes, but Misgolas' enthusiasms are really déclassé—he pursues *kithara* players, whose status and prestige are considerably lower than those of the celebrated citharodes. Yet Misgolas did somehow distinguish himself among the Athenian *dêmos* as a discriminating lover of citharodes, and he is ridiculed as such in Middle Comedy plays by Alexis (fr. 3 K-A) and Antiphanes (fr. 27 K-A). In the former, a young man assures his mother that the predatory Misgolas has no sexual interest in him, since he is

---

[81]   Lissarrague 1990:138–139. For the image, see Bundrick 2005:2, fig. 1.
[82]   Discussion in Fisher 2001:314.
[83]   *Against Timarchus* 41. The speech was delivered in 346 BCE. On Misgolas, see discussion in Fisher 2001:170–172 and Dover 1989:73–74.

not a κιθαρῳδός.[84] In the latter, *The Fisherwoman*, the titular character imagines that a fish called the κίθαρος, a turbot, would be irresistible to Misgolas, since its name evokes the κιθαρῳδοί he so fervently desires:

> ἀλλὰ κίθαρος οὑτοσί,
> ὃν ἂν ἴδῃ τὰς χεῖρας οὐκ ἀφέξεται.
> καὶ μὴν ἀληθῶς τοῖς κιθαρῳδοῖς ὡς σφόδρα
> ἅπασιν οὗτος ἐπιπεφυκὼς λανθάνει.

> But this turbot (*kitharos*) here, if Misgolas sees him, he won't be able to keep his hands off. I tell you, it's really amazing, how with all the *kitharôidoi*, he sneaks his way in really close to them!

> Antiphanes *The Fisherwoman* fr. 27 K-A[85]

Both Aeschines and Antiphanes leave us to wonder how exactly Misgolas "got in" with *kitharôidoi*, and what form their association assumed. The charge implied by both authors is that Misgolas was a kind of stage-door Johnny, forming relationships with professional string musicians, presumably younger, good-looking ones—he does not seem to have cared for auletes—and discreetly angling to sleep with them, perhaps by lavishing gifts, money, lodging, and flattery.[86] (The attempts at discretion obviously failed, given the seemingly compulsive nature of his attraction; he makes a play for *all* the citharodes according to Antiphanes.) Did he sleep with them? Probably in some instances, but, although Misgolas was a notorious client of prostitutes, we need not think that as a rule the musicians in question pursued a part-time prostitution racket loosely connected to their daytime musical activity, as if they were sympotic *hetairai*, who mingled musical and sexual services. The citharode's income and the prestige of his *tekhnê* would by and large have kept him out of the straits of male prostitution. Perhaps Misgolas was content to experience close-up the eroticized glamour

---

[84] Cf. Arnott 1996:62–63.

[85] Translation adapted from Fisher 2001:172, who renders κιθαρῳδοῖς as 'lyre players', which misses the mark, as does Davidson's '*cithara*-boys' (2001:30). Misgolas does not pursue amateur lyre players or hired party boys, like the youthful lyre player in Xenophon *Symposium* 2.1, 4.53–54, but real concert musicians.

[86] An example of one such good-looking citharode from the later fifth century BCE is Arignotus, whose *kharis*, his musical and physical grace, made him "beloved to all men" (Aristophanes *Wasps* 1277–1278). Aristophanes insinuates that Arignotus was a promiscuous *erômenos* (see Totaro 1991), but that need not have been the case. Cf. Part IV.10.

of popular citharodes rather than to pursue full-fledged sexual affairs with them, as the comic poets insinuated.

According to an anecdote originally told by Antigonus of Carystus (writing c. 240 BCE), the Macedonian king Antigonus II Gonatas took a more direct approach with the citharode he fancied than did the subtle Misgolas:

> Ἀντιγόνου τοῦ βασιλέως ἐρώμενος ἦν Ἀριστοκλῆς ὁ κιθαρῳδός, περὶ οὗ Ἀντίγονος ὁ Καρύστιος ἐν τῷ Ζήνωνος βίῳ γράφει οὕτως· Ἀντίγονος ὁ βασιλεὺς ἐπεκώμαζε τῷ Ζήνωνι. καί ποτε καὶ μεθ' ἡμέραν ἐλθὼν ἔκ τινος πότου καὶ ἀναπηδήσας πρὸς τὸν Ζήνωνα ἔπεισεν αὐτὸν συγκωμάσαι αὐτῷ πρὸς Ἀριστοκλέα τὸν κιθαρῳδόν, οὗ σφόδρα ἦρα ὁ βασιλεύς.

> Aristocles the citharode was the *erômenos* 'beloved' of King Antigonus, about whom Antigonus of Carystus writes in his *Life of Zeno* the following: "King Antigonus used to go out on *kômoi* 'drunken revels' with Zeno. Coming once at dawn from some drinking, he hurried to Zeno's and convinced him to go along on a *kômos* to Aristocles the citharode, whom the king passionately desired."

Antigonus of Carystus ap. Athenaeus 8.603e[87]

The full story behind this comastic *paraclausithyron* must remain uncertain. Athenaeus calls Aristocles, a star performer of the earlier third century, the king's *erômenos*, which would indicate that the two were involved in a reciprocal romantic/sexual relationship, and presumably a high-profile one, as both *erastês* and *erômenos* were celebrities.[88] The anecdote could be read to imply that both men, along with the Stoic philosopher Zeno, were fellow travelers in an elite artistic-intellectual social circuit, which might support this view.[89] But even if they did

---

[87] Cf. Diogenes Laertius 7.13–14 for a similar account.

[88] Aristocles appears again at *Mirabilia* 169, a work (probably) by Antigonus of Carystus, in which his student Timon speaks of a special acanthus-wood *plêktron* that Aristocles handed down to him. It is likely, I think, that this Aristocles was the father of the star citharode Nicocles, a Tarentine who made his primary residence in Athens (Stephanis 1988, no. 1839).

[89] Zeno himself appears in the anecdotal tradition as an admirer of the star citharode Amoebus, but for him virtuoso cithardic performance was (apparently) less an erotic experience than an opportunity for philosophical speculation on the sublime tension between sensible musical harmony and the brute materials of the instrument that produces it: "They say that Zeno, when he was about to go to the theater to hear Amoebus sing to the *kithara*, said to his students, 'Let's go and learn what sort

move through the same social circles in Athens, Antigonus of Carystus, the original source, in fact says only that the king passionately desired the citharode, which could mean merely than that the king was a smitten fan of Aristocles. His early-morning *kômos* could thus have been nothing more than an overly enthusiastic and spontaneous expression of one-way desire. But in either case the anecdote confirms that the desires of Misgolas were hardly obscure. Antigonus' attraction to Aristocles indeed finds a telling echo in anecdotal accounts about another Hellenistic king, Ptolemy Philadelphus of Alexandria, a political rival of Antigonus, whose storied interest in the female citharode Glauce will be discussed below. In both cases the romantic pursuit of citharode by king represents an eroticized expression of a traditional theme: the attraction of royal or tyrannical power to citharodic celebrity.

In an epigram in the *Palatine Anthology* (5.99) we hear a Hellenistic music fan expressing what we may suppose were the sort of "obscene" passions nourished by a Misgolas or Antigonus, and archly euphemized by Aeschines and Antiphanes: "I wanted, citharode, to stand by you as you played, and bang your bottom [string] and loosen your middle [string]" (ἤθελον, ὦ κιθαρῳδέ, παραστάς, ὡς κιθαρίζεις, | τὴν ὑπάτην κροῦσαι, τήν τε μέσην χαλάσαι). The musico-sexual punning in the epigram's second verse goes back to Old Comedy (cf. e.g. Pherecrates *Cheiron* fr. 155 K-A), and here, as there, it is rather difficult to appreciate the joke. Simon Goldhill summarizes the problems: "[The joke] obviously gives musical terms a sexual double entendre, but what exactly is to be made of *hupatên* and *mesên*? *Krouein* is common enough for 'bang' ('strike the strings of an instrument'/'have sex'), and *chalazein*, according to Henderson, means 'to loosen by inserting the penis' as well as 'to loosen the strings of an instrument.'"[90] The lusting spectator who wants to get his hands on the citharode is certainly a man, as the masculine participle παραστάς indicates. The citharode could be a woman. Some support for this reading may come from the Pherecrates fragment, in which *Mousikê*, personified as a woman, complains of her strings/genitals being violated, "loosened." But as Goldhill points out,

---

of orderly harmony and voice (τάξεως ἐμμέλειαν καὶ φωνήν) is emitted from animal guts and sinews [the strings] and pieces of wood and bone [the frame of the *kithara*] when they are imbued with human reason (*logos*) and rhythm" (Plutarch *Moralia* 443a = SVF I, p67 fr. 299 von Arnim). Stoics believed in the power of music to transform human behavior, and Terpander's pacification of violence in Sparta seems to have been for them an item of belief (Philodemus *On Music* 1 fr. 30.31–35, p18 Kemke = Diogenes of Babylon SVF III, p232 fr. 84 von Arnim).

90 Goldhill 2005:278; Henderson 1975:177.

"'penetration' and 'banging' are gender-free in object choice." So if the citharode is a woman, we could imagine that she is one of the alluring "pop stars" who are sent mash notes from male fans elsewhere in the *Palatine Anthology* (5.222; 16.277, 278). But it is just as likely that the citharode is a younger man objectified by an older, would-be lover such as Misgolas.

The verb παρίστημι 'to stand by, near', from which the intransitive second aorist παραστάς is formed, comes freighted with male homosexual overtones by way of the ritualized pederastic culture of ancient Crete, in which the younger *erômenos* was referred to as a παρασταθείς 'the one posted beside' an older partner (Strabo 10.4.21). One scholar has suggested that a boy shown walking alongside a lyre-holding bard in a Geometric bronze sculpture from eighth-century BCE Crete, now at the Getty Museum, may be not only a helper or apprentice, but just such a *parastatheis* to the older musician.[91] The homoerotic relationship between between master citharode and student seems to have been a theme in the representation of citharodic culture, although one surely not always reflective of real practice. One tradition makes Cepion, a *mathêtês* 'student' of the Lesbian citharode Terpander, into the master's *erômenos* as well (Pollux *Onomasticon* 4.65). Another reflex of the theme is to be found, perhaps not coincidentally, in the musical history of Crete: a Cretan citharode, Ametor of Eleutherna, the progenitor of a line of *kitharôidoi* called the Ametoridai, was apparently, according to a local Eleuthernan tradition, the first to compose "erotic songs" for the *kithara* (Athenaeus 14.638b; Hesychius s.v. Ἀμητορίδας; the name, however, does sound suspiciously like a play on the Latin word for 'lover', *amator*). Of course, the sexually aggressive fan in the Hellenistic epigram makes for an antitypical *parastatheis*, but such unexpected inversion could be part of the poem's salacious wit.

iii. The promiscuous appeal of the citharode

Cithardic charisma was far more promiscuous than the exclusive allure of the schoolboy or adolescent with his tortoise-shell lyre, and, as a publicly available commodity, it had a range of appreciators well beyond aristocratic connoisseurs. The citharode was a truly egalitarian sex symbol, transcending barriers of class, age, and gender. The demographics of citharodic audiences in pre-Roman Greece could have varied greatly depending on the era or the context of the

---

91 Padgett 1995:400.

performance (Panhellenic or local festival, or a civic concert), but the testimonia suggest a consistently wide social composite of spectators. Significant inference is to be drawn from a curious passage in Plato's *Laws* (658a–d). The Athenian Stranger proposes a hypothetical *agôn* at which performers of all kinds would be invited to compete in "giving pleasure (*terpsis*) to the spectators." The Stranger expects that a rhapsode, citharode, tragedian, comedian, and puppeteer would enter the contest; he then predicts to what segments of the audience each would most appeal. The rhapsode, reciting the *Iliad* and *Odyssey* and Hesiod, would appeal to conservative older men such as the Stranger and his interlocutors; small children would enjoy the puppet show most; comedy would hold the older boys; tragedy would attract "educated women, young men, and perhaps the majority of all people" (αἵ τε πεπαιδευμέναι τῶν γυναικῶν καὶ τὰ νέα μειράκια καὶ σχεδὸν ἴσως τὸ πλῆθος πάντων). But Plato assigns *kitharôidia* no predominant type of consumer.[92] Though tragedy is posited as the ultimately inclusive medium, which was no doubt the case in fifth- and fourth-century Athens, the aporia concerning *kitharôidia* is remarkable: Plato seems unwilling or unable to define absolutely its "niche" market constituency and so passes over it entirely.

Anecdotal accounts suggest that citharodic performance could mobilize the entire population of a city like few other events. A recital given by the fourth-century BCE Aristonicus of Olynthus drew together the combined populations of the cities of the Bosporus region, all eager to hear the great virtuoso (Polyaenus *Strategems* 5.44.1). This recital played a critical role in the strategy of the Rhodian general Memnon, an early patron of the citharode—Aristonicus would later go on to serve Philip and Alexander—to capture the region. Wanting to gauge the size of the forces he would encounter when he invaded, Memnon reckoned that the most accurate way to take a census of the populace was to put on a citharodic show, an occasion so irresistible that everyone in the region would be sure to come. Polyaenus records another strategic ruse involving *kitharôidia*, in which the Macedonian dynast Antigonus I ("The One-Eyed") seized control of the citadel of Acrocorinth while the Corinthians were assembled to hear a star citharode, Amoebus, who was hired to perform at the wedding of Antigonus' son to Nicaea.[93]

---

[92] At *Laws* 718b–c tragedy is said to "offer demagoguery" for the masses (*okhlos*). At *Gorgias* 502a Socrates says that *kitharôidia* appeals to the "mass of spectators" (*okhlos theatôn*).

[93] *Strategems* 4.6.1. Polyaenus' emphatic mention of the performance of Amoebus suggests that it was as significant a draw for the "great crowd" as the wedding itself;

This power to seduce mass populations, which in both of these cases involves momentous political implications, seems proper to citharodic celebrity. Such power is presumed by the fourth-century BCE mythographer Palaephatus in his interpretation of the myth of Amphion's foundation of Thebes:

περὶ Ζήθου καὶ Ἀμφίονος ἱστοροῦσιν ἄλλοι τε καὶ Ἡσίοδος ὅτι κιθάρᾳ τὸ τεῖχος τῆς Θήβης ἐτείχισαν. δοκοῦσι δὲ ἔνιοι κιθαρίζειν <μὲν> αὐτούς, τοὺς δὲ λίθους αὐτομάτως ἀναβαίνειν ἐπὶ τὸ τεῖχος. τὸ δὲ ἀληθὲς ἔχει ὧδε· κιθαρῳδοὶ οὗτοι ἄριστοι ἐγένοντο καὶ ἐπεδείκνυντο μισθῷ. ἀργύριον δὲ οὐκ εἶχον οἱ τότε ἄνθρωποι. ἐκέλευον οὖν οἱ περὶ τὸν Ἀμφίονα, εἴ τις βούλοιτο ἀκούειν αὐτῶν, ἐρχόμενος ἐργάζεσθαι ἐπὶ τὸ τεῖχος· οὐ μέντοι οἱ λίθοι εἵποντο ἀκρώμενοι. εὐλόγως οὖν ἔλεγον οἱ ἄνθρωποι ὅτι λύρᾳ τὸ τεῖχος ἐτειχίσθη.

Hesiod (= fr. 182 M-W) and others say of Zethus and Amphion that they built the walls of Thebes with the *kithara*. Some people take this to mean that they played the *kithara* and that the stones spontaneously rose up into the walls. But the truth is as follows: these two were outstanding citharodes and they used to put on concerts in return for money. But people back then did not use money. So those in Amphion's circle told anyone who wanted to hear them to come and work on the walls. It was not that the stones listened and followed along, but people say with some reason that the walls were built with the lyre.

Palaephatus *On Unbelievable Tales* 41

The rationalizing approach to mythical exegesis taken by Palaephatus typically results in silliness, and it does here as well.[94] Nevertheless, his claim to uncovering the "truth" beneath the myth has a certain merit, at least in terms of the socioeconomic reality of contemporary *kithar-ôidia*. Palaephatus imagines Amphion and Zethus to have been like the celebrated star citharodes of his own day (κιθαρῳδοὶ οὗτοι ἄριστοι), who gave lucrative and well-attended concerts (*epideixeis*).[95] So popular

---

in retaining Amoebus, Antigonus presumably wanted to ensure that *all* potential resistors would be fully distracted by the celebration.

[94] For a judicious discussion of Palaephatus' methods, see Stern 1999.

[95] A musical Zethus is attested only here; in other accounts (e.g. Pausanius 9.5.4), Amphion alone is musical. Cf. Part II.12n305. On Amphion's foundation of Thebes, see Rocchi 1989:47–56.

were these stars that Palaephatus can posit as a rational alternative to the mystical scenario of the myth what might appear to us to be an equally "unbelievable" scenario: eager fans would commit to hard labor in exchange for the pleasure of hearing the citharodes perform. But as a metaphor, this explanation is not so far from the historical situation: star citharodes could move mass populations of cities to part with their time and money in exchange for the pleasure of their music. And, in a sense, both the myth and Palaephatus' attempted demystification of it suggest, through their respective metaphors, the rationally inexplicable influence exerted by the citharode over the body politic.

Dio Chrysostom *Oration* 19.2–4 is a vivid first-person account of the orator's own attraction to the star power of the citharode. He recounts how, while he was visiting Cyzicus, the entire civic population, 3,000 plus strong, turned out *en masse* for a performance by an unnamed star, "the best of the citharodes of the day" (ὁ ἄριστος τῶν νῦν κιθαρῳδῶν), who was reputedly even better than Arion. Dio says that a σπουδὴ ἀμήχανος 'irresistible urge' gripped the people of Cyzicus to hear this sensation. He himself was happily carried along with the crowd, which he figures as the mesmerized herd of fawns and calves that followed Orpheus' music.[96] What Dio calls the σπουδή, the enthusiastic tenor, surrounding citharodic performance, appears to be socially unmarked.[97] The pleasure produced by the citharode is all consuming.

As such, it is quite likely that even in Classical Greece women as well as men enjoyed citharodic spectacles. The literary sources are vague on this point, as they are on the notoriously vexed question of whether women attended dramatic performances, but nothing in them speaks against it, and the presence of women, or at least some women,

---

[96] We may compare the libidinal compulsion, the ἔρος ἀμήχανος, that stirs Apollo to listen to Hermes' lyre singing in *Homeric Hymn to Hermes* 434, or the "music-mad compulsion" (μουσομανὴς ἀνάγκα) experienced by one enthusiast of *kitharôidia* in Sophocles' *Thamyras* (fr. 245.1–2), lending his (or her) fascination with this predominantly Apollonian art an impetuous, Dionysiac tone. Dio also makes the telling revelation that the pleasure afforded to the masses by citharodic performance is much greater than the pleasure produced by popular rhetors and sophists such as he (19.4).

[97] The word σπουδή seems to be a *vox propria* for the passionate enthusiasm attending *kitharôidia*. Cf. scholia *ad* Aristophanes *Clouds* 964c: ἐσπούδαζον δὲ οἱ Ἀθηναῖοι περὶ κιθαρῳδίαν ("The [fifth-century] Athenians were fanatical about *kitharôidia*"); Dio Chrysostom 32.61 criticizes Nero's σπουδή for *kitharôidia*, as well as his practice (ἐμπειρία) of it; Plutarch *Dialogue on Love* 749c speaks of the σπουδαί that erupt surrounding a citharodic *agôn* in Thespiae. Plutarch *Life of Themistocles* 5.3 says that a citharist popular in Athens was σπουδαζόμενον. Aeschines *Against Timarchus* 168 mentions the "amazing σπουδή" (δαιμονίως ἐσπουδακώς) of Misgolas for the citharodes he desired.

seems to be implied in most descriptions of citharodic performances. We are fortunate, however, to have two vase paintings that would seem to indicate that women attended *mousikoi agônes* in fifth-century Athens.[98] On an Attic calyx krater from c. 430 BCE, a bearded citharode, wearing a wreath, mounts the *bêma* with his *kithara.*[99] Two winged Victories, Nikai, are on hand to mark symbolically his victory in the contest; one of them brings two metal libation bowls, *phialai,* representing the musician's cash prize. Flanking the *bêma* on one side is a bearded man, probably a judge, and on the other a seated woman, who stares intently (and perhaps longingly) at the successful competitor. A roughly contemporary oinochoe in Rome shows two female spectators gazing at a victorious musician who ascends the *bêma* with *kithara* in hand. One of the two carries *phialai,* the other sits on a hydria.[100]

The inclusion of the women in these victory scenes—both are probably set against the backdrop of the Panathenaia festival, which featured the most prestigious citharodic *agôn* of the Classical period— serves a symbolic and affective function, focalizing the desirability projected by the successful citharode and marking the field of erotic energy crackling around him.[101] Pindar aims for a similar effect in *Pythian* 9.97–99, imagining a recent victor as an object of the admiring looks of women and girls, who fantasize about having this talented athlete as son-in-law or husband: "As you were much victorious in the seasonal rites of Pallas, the maidens, each and every one, watched you in silence, praying that you, Telesicrates, might be their dearest husband, and their mothers prayed that you might be their son."[102] But

---

[98] Aristotle *Politics* 8.1341b–1342a characterizes the audience of musical *agônes* as entirely low class, tendentiously passing over the numerous aristocrats who surely watched the contests. There is no reason to believe that women (of various classes) were not caught up in the mix as well.

[99] London E 460; Bundrick 2005:169, fig. 99. The man could of course be a citharist, but this does not affect the argument.

[100] Villa Giulia 5250; Lezzi-Hafter 1976, plate 146. See Shapiro 1992:58. The hydria on which one of the women sits in the Villa Giulia scene may itself represent a prize of victory. For the motif compare a late-fifth-century *khous* (Basel, Collection of Herbert A. Cahn 649) that shows a young *kithara* player standing on the *bêma* before a Nike seated on a hydria that is probably made of metal. Here the *agôn* is presumably set at the Anthesteria festival. See discussion in Smith 2007:163–164, with fig. 8.8.

[101] Goldhill 1994:356–357 is right to remind us that we cannot be absolutely certain that, although women took part in the Panathenaic procession, they also attended the musical contests. But he is too quick to dismiss the evidence of this vase painting, nor does he acknowledge the woman spectator on the calyx krater discussed above.

[102] These "rites of Pallas" could well refer to the athletic games at the Panathenaia (cf. Scanlon 2002:223). If so, this passage could serve as indirect evidence for the presence of women at the musical games as well.

the rhetorical dimension of the painted images need not keep us from taking them as evidence for the social reality that women in Classical Athens did have the opportunity to witness citharodic performance first hand.

Subtle reflections of the citharode's potent sex appeal are detectable in literary treatments of mythical proto-citharodes as well. At Euripides *Ion* 897–906 Creusa berates Apollo, the absentee father of her son, Ion, angrily accusing the god of "making a racket on the *kithara* (κιθάρᾳ κλάζεις), singing paeans," while she and Ion suffer. This dark evocation of Apollo *kitharôidos* contrasts significantly with the earlier description of the god as an impossibly dashing citharode, "singing to the tune of the seven-stringed *kithara* ... gleaming with gold in his hair," with which Creusa prefaces the account of her rape by him (881–888). Euripides is drawing in part on the idealized Archaic and Classical representations of Apollo *kitharôidos* in painting and statuary, but this glamorously aloof Apollo evokes too the desirability and sexual confidence of the flesh-and-blood star citharode.[103]

So might the two famous Thracian lyre singers of myth, Orpheus and Thamyris. The murderous hostility of the Thracian women toward Orpheus was in some accounts explained as frustrated sexual desire. After he had lost Eurydice in Hades, Orpheus committed himself to homosexuality (e.g. Phanocles fr. 1 Powell), but, as Ovid *Metamorphoses* 10.81–82 has it, "Nevertheless, the desire possessed many women to join with the singer, and many who were rejected felt aggrieved" (*multas tamen ardor habebat | iungere se vati, multae doluere repulsae*; cf. 11.1–9 for the murder scene). The other side of the scorned women's *furor* is the consuming fascination of the Thracian men with the lyric music of Orpheus (which in another version of the myth is what angered the women in the first place; cf. Pausanias 9.30.3). Scenes of their spellbound audition are portrayed in Attic vase painting from

---

[103] It is probably relevant that the charisma and itinerant lifestyle of the professional musician could have led, even if only anecdotally, to the sort of sexual opportunism with which Creusa indicts Apollo. Some variation on this theme seems to lie behind the plot of Menander's comedy *Kitharistês*, in which the titular character, an Athenian, has an illegitimate daughter in Ephesus. The short biography by the Augustan-era historian Nicolaus of Damascus of the seventh-century BCE Magnes of Smyrna tells of a "good-looking man, known for both his poetry and *mousikê*," who traveled from city to city performing in splendid attire, sleeping along the way with smitten women—whose jealous menfolk eventually killed him, in a kind of inversion of the Orpheus myth—and becoming the boyfriend of the Lydian tyrant Gyges (FGrH 90 F 62). The Ionian Magnes is probably meant to have been an aulode or rhapsode, but the profile of the charismatic itinerant belongs to the citharode as well.

around 460 to 420 BCE.[104] Perhaps these scenes were inspired by a now-lost drama or dithyramb; perhaps too by citharodic accounts of Orpheus' life and death, which might further have provided the narrative coordinates for the dramatic and dithyrambic treatments. One dramatic influence on the iconography was surely Aeschylus' *Bassarids* (or *Bassarai*), produced around 466–459 BCE, which treated the life and death of Orpheus.[105] The paintings and their poetic source or sources could have allegorized, or been seen to allegorize, the intense enthusiasm for contemporary *kitharôidia* felt by contemporary Athenians. Taken together with the abundant scenes of Orpheus' murder, the allegory would be gendered along predictable ideological lines. Men submit peacefully and sociably to citharodic pleasures, while women, characteristically overmastered by their emotions, give way to sexual excess and impulsive violence, directed perversely at the citharode who is the object of their desire. (That is, if the account of their ambivalence we find in Ovid goes back this far.)[106] Alternately, the scenes of a youthful, distinctly Greek-looking Orpheus singing to the tortoise-shell lyre before the rapt Thracians, which appear exclusively on wine-mixing vessels, could have been intended to idealize mythically not civic *kitharôidia*, but the social and aesthetic harmony produced by lyric music within the private confines of the symposium.[107]

The myth of Thamyris related in Homer *Iliad* 2.594–600, in which the itinerant Thracian lyre singer challenges the Muses to a song contest, foregrounds his hubristic confidence in his musical abilities. Although it goes unmentioned in the Homeric account, later tellings emphasize Thamyris' physical beauty and sexual assertiveness as well. Zenobius

---

[104] See Bundrick 2005:116–126; Seebass 1991.

[105] Bundrick 2005:120 must be correct, however, to dissociate *Bassarids* from the scenes of Orpheus' murder on Attic vessels, which both predate its production and do not specifically have maenads killing Orpheus, as is seemingly the case in the play ("Eratosthenes" *Katasterismoi* 24.140). Cf. West 1990b:36–38. Could Aeschylus' play have had a citharodic source? See Part III.8.

[106] Certainly, the images of the murder are blatantly eroticized; some, such as that on an amphora by the Phiale Painter (Munich, Staatliche Antikensammlung und Glyptothek 2330; Bundrick 2005:121, fig. 73), parallel images of young lyre players pursued by excited admirers (e.g. Eos pursuing Tithonus, amphora attributed to the Group of Naples 3169, Naples 81541/H 3169; Bundrick 2005:65, fig. 37).

[107] Cf. Bundrick 2005:121–122 and 126, who thinks that the scenes recall "contemporary interest in musical *ethos*, as for example in the work of Damon." On this "elitist" reading of the Orpheus images, the maddened Thracian women intent on killing the hero might, at least in the later fifth century, have come to symbolize the forces of an anti-aristocratic demotic Athenian culture bent on diminishing the embattled prestige of elite lyric *paideia*. Orpheus is never portrayed as a citharode in fifth-century Athenian art, as he is at least once in the sixth century (see discussion above).

4.27 knows Thamyris as a practicing *kitharôidos* (ἀσκήσας κιθαρῳδίαν) who "surpassed all in beauty." (Good looks ran in the family: his grandmother was the exceedingly beautiful Philonis and his grandfather was Apollo [Hesiod fr. 64.15–16].) This handsome Thamyris stipulates that if he should defeat the Muses in the *agôn*, he is to be permitted to have intercourse with each of them. This version of the contest seems to go back at least to the fifth century BCE, when several dramatic and dithyrambic treatments of the myth, including Sophocles' *Thamyras*, were produced. Asclepiades of Tragilus (fourth century BCE), probably in his compilation of tragic myths, *Tragôidoumena*, provides an account, presumably drawn from one or more of the earlier treatments of Thamyris, that is largely similar in its details to that in Zenobius (FGrH 12 F 10).[108] It seems reasonable to assume that the heady combination of musical arrogance and sexual prowess (or vice versa) that characterized the Classical Thamyris was meant to evoke the disposition of the day's star agonistic citharodes, or at least their popular perception.[109] We may note that in some later-fifth-century vase paintings from Athens Thamyris is portrayed in the attire of a contemporary citharode or citharist, holding a *kithara*.[110] The iconography of this period also shows that real-life agonistic string players in turn visually emulated the strangely glamorous Thamyris (or perhaps Orpheus). On several vases from the second half of the fifth century, citharodic or citharistic competitors, generally younger ones, are depicted holding the so-called Thracian or Thamyris *kithara*, an instrument otherwise handled in art by the mythical Thracian lyre singers, that combines features of the concert *kithara*, the Eastern Greek *barbitos* and the old-fashioned *phorminx* to create a vaguely exotic and archaized visual profile.[111] Its curved arms are sometimes ribbed with small protuberances, giving them the appearance (at least) of horns; the effect is a very stylized naturalism or primitivism—Thracian chic.[112]

---

[108] Cf. Hall 1989:135–136.

[109] Cf. Wilson 2004:286.

[110] E.g. a volute krater by Polion (Ferrara, Museo Archeologico Nazionale T 127; c. 420 BCE), showing Thamyris *kitharôidos* (or *kitharistês*) with the Muses. Froning 1971:67–86 connects the scene to a dithyramb performed at the Hephaisteia festival.

[111] See Maas-Snyder 1989:145–147 and Bundrick 2005:26–29 for discussion and illustrations; cf. Cillo 1993. This *kithara* probably bore some relation to the *phoinix*, a lyre-like instrument whose arms were made from the horns of Libyan antelopes (Herodotus 4.192.1); Nicomedes *On Orpheus ap.* Athenaeus 14.637a–b says that the *phoinix* was employed by "Thracian kings at their feasts." See Cillo 1993:231–232.

[112] See e.g. the pelike by the Painter of Athens 1183 (Bundrick 2005:29, fig. 16). Note too the ribbing on the arms of the *kithara* held by the young citharode on the pelike of the Epimedes Painter (Plate 13). This effect is articulated in one of the fragments

The hybrid semiotics of the instrument well suit the dramatic liminality of Thamyris *kitharôidos*, a charismatic figure intriguingly poised between Thrace and Greece, mythic past and the contemporary culture of agonistic music. The fashionableness of the Thracian *kithara* may have been owed to its use on the tragic stage. Sophocles is said to have played the part of Thamyris himself, singing and playing the *kithara* (*Life of Sophocles* 24). Such borrowing from stage costume would constitute a significant development in the increased theatralization of *kitharôidia* in fifth-century Athens.

7. Juvenal on Citharodic Fandom in Rome

In post-Neronian Imperial Rome women had become open and avid consumers of *kitharôidia*. The satirist Juvenal, writing in the generation after Nero's death, suggests the extent to which the star citharodes of the Empire could inspire sexual fantasy, even obsession in their fans, including women of the most elite social rank:

> si gaudet cantu, nullius fibula durat
> vocem vendentis praetoribus. organa semper
> in manibus, densi radiant testudine tota
> sardonyches, crispo numerantur pectine chordae
> quo tener Hedymeles operas dedit: hunc tenet, hoc se
> solatur gratoque indulget basia plectro.
> quaedam de numero Lamiarum ac nominis Appi
> et farre et vino Ianum Vestamque rogabat,
> an Capitolinam deberet Pollio quercum
> sperare et fidibus promittere. quid faceret plus
> aegrotante viro, medicis quid tristibus erga
> filiolum? stetit ante aram nec turpe putavit
> pro cithara velare caput dictataque verba
> pertulit, ut mos est, et aperta palluit agna.

If your wife enjoys music, the genital clasp (*fibula*) of no one who sells his voice to the praetors will stay fast. Musical

---

from the Sophoclean *Thamyras*: Thamyris breaks the χρυσόδετον κέρας 'gold-bound horn' (fr. 246.1) of his *kithara*. Raw nature is overlaid with luxurious refinement. Cf. the silver-bridged *phorminx* (*Iliad* 9.185–189) of Achilles, a figure who shares a certain marginal status with Thamyris. Cf. Rocchi 1980. On later-fifth-century Athenian interest in things Thracian, see Parker 1996:173–174.

instruments are always in her hands; her thick sardonyx rings sparkle all over the tortoise-shell; the strings resound at the quivering quill, with which the tender Hedymeles performed his works; this she grasps, with this she consoles herself, and she lavishes kisses upon the beloved plectrum. A certain lady of the tally of the Lamiae, with the name of Appius, kept asking of Janus and Vesta, with offerings of grain and wine, whether Pollio could hope to win the crown of oak leaves at the Capitoline contests and promise victory to his lyre. What more could she have done if her husband had been sick, or if the doctors had been pessimistic about her dear little son? She stood there before the altar, thinking it no disgrace to veil her head for the sake of a *cithara*. She recited the prescribed words in the proper form, and blanched when the lamb was opened up.

Juvenal *Satire* 6.379–392[113]

There can be no doubt that these two *matronae* are figments of Juvenal's misogynistic imagination, but, satirical distortions aside, the intense emotional attachments of fan to citharodic star that are limned in this passage must have had some basis in reality. The cult of *kitharôidia* transcended class lines, but Juvenal, ever on the hunt for outrage, predictably fixates on the scandalous interpenetration of the worlds of high society and popular music. This is surely not only a satirical theme, although it is that; Juvenal draws in some measure from real-life examples. There is no reason to doubt, for instance, the gossip that the wife of Emperor Pertinax (ruled 192–193 CE), Flavia Titiana, conducted an open affair—the emperor himself approved—with a citharode (*Historia Augusta*, *Life of Pertinax* 13.8), or to think that she was the first high-status Roman wife to do so. As both reality and cultural cliché, such affairs speak to the charisma of the celebrity citharode in post-Neronian Rome.

Juvenal depicts the seduction as a two-way street: citharodes capture the erotic imagination of noblewomen, who in turn work their predatory wiles on citharodes, who are viewed as passive-aggressive sex symbols. On the one hand, there is the commodified voice of the professional citharode—he "sells his voice" (*vocem vendentis*) to the praetors, the magistrates in charge of organizing festival contests—which assimilates him to the prostitute who makes public sale of his or

---

[113] Translation is based on that of Braund 2004.

her body. Juvenal similarly paints Nero as a musical prostitute in *Satire* 8.25–26: while performing in the Greek contests, the *princeps* "enjoyed putting himself on public display (*prostitui*) with his wretched voice for foreign audiences." (Juvenal has in mind here Nero's performances as a tragic actor-singer, *tragoedus*, as much as his citharodic endeavors; Nero competed in both singing to the *kithara* and acting on his Grecian tour, and it was the latter pursuit that was more commonly associated by the Romans with prostitution.) On the other hand, the metal *fibula* that binds the citharode's genitals to prevent erections and thereby protect his celibacy marks him as one chastely devoted to his art. Infibulation, or genital binding, typically associated with athletes, was also practiced by agonistic citharodes as part of their training regimen.[114] Such athletic endurance—note the verb *durare* in line 379, with the *fibula* as the personified subject—makes the musician all the more attractive to his admirers, who themselves are ready to forsake all duty and honor to indulge their adulterous, socially transgressive passions.[115] Thus the second of Juvenal's *matronae* perverts ancient rites and the sanctity of hearth and home to assure the victory of her favorite, Pollio. The cult of *kitharôidia* has become this woman's religion; Pollio's *cithara* effectively becomes the object of worship and devotion (391), a touch that perhaps alludes to the cult of Nero's "divine voice," to which Roman nobles of a previous era were expected to make sacrifices (Tacitus *Annals* 16.22.1; Dio Cassius 62.26.3).[116]

The first woman pines for her own heartthrob, the enticingly named Hedymeles, whose limbs (*melê*), we should presume, may look or taste as sweet (*hêdu*) as his melodies (also *melê*) sound. Juvenal underlines this sexually suggestive Greek punning, which goes back as far as Old Comedy, with his Latin epithet for Hedymeles, *tener*.[117] The name

---

[114] Sexual activity was thought to degrade the singing voice. See discussion in Hall 2002:23–24.

[115] Haunting this entire passage is the specter of illegitimacy, as Braund 1992:75–76 shows. Cf. *Satire* 6.76–77, where a *citharoedus* with the imposing name of Echion (one of the hubristic Giants) threatens Rome's noble bloodlines. The vision of high society crawling with the progeny of citharodes is pure hysteria, but it reflects an actual sociocultural development: the increased participation in the Hellenic musical arts on the part of Roman elites and the increased penetration of star musicians into the ranks of the social elite. See Wille 1967:336–338.

[116] Courtney 1980:312–313 notes how Pollio's *cithara* is treated "as if it were animate." Pollio himself is imagined as speaking confidentially to it (*fidibus promittere*, 388). Juvenal perhaps has in mind the citharode's *prooimion* or *sphragis*, both sections of his song in which he might address his instrument and/or speak of his hopes of victory (cf. Terpander fr. 4 Gostoli; Timotheus *Persians* 202–236).

[117] Limbs/melodies of effeminate musicians: Cratinus fr. 276 K-A.

is clearly the satirist's invention, a vulgar variation on the speaking stage names that were assumed by or given to some real-life musicians by way of advertising their talent, e.g. Terpnus, 'Pleasurer', who was Nero's *kithara* teacher. Juvenal may even have in mind the speaking name Hedea ('Sweetie'), which belonged to a girl who won first prize in a children's citharodic contest at the Athenian Sebasteia in the first half of the first century CE.[118]

Perhaps we are to imagine Hedymeles specifically as a boy citharode; *tener* could in fact suggest that he is as young as he is lissome. Contests for boy citharists, although *not* for boy citharodes, are epigraphically attested in Athens as early as the fourth century BCE.[119] The apparent lack of formal competitions for pre-adult citharodes at this early period is worth noting. While boys were thought capable of displaying their instrumental skill on the *kithara* at major festival occasions, the virtuosic and physically demanding combination of singing and playing that is competitive *kitharôidia* was reserved for adult men. There were probably ideological considerations at work in this distinction as well. That is, *kitharôidia* was not deemed child's play. It topped the hierarchy of the solo musical performance genres, and more than any other it was traditionally thought to have the greatest sociopolitical import.[120] Mature citharodes were therefore the rule. But by the early first century CE this had changed. Boys and, at least in the remarkable case of Hedea, girls, were winning acclaim as competitive citharodes on the ever-expanding cosmopolitan Greco-Roman festival

---

[118] Hedea's victory, presumably over other boys her age, is extraordinary; no other female victors of any age in *mousikoi agônes* of any sort are attested. Hedea's father, Hermesianax of Tralles, commemorated it, along with equally unique athletic victories at the Nemean and Isthmian Games, on an inscribed statue dedicated at Delphi (SIG³ 802). See further Goldhill 2005:280–282; Bélis 1999:56–57.

[119] IG II² 2311, line 22d in the restored text of Shear 2003: παῖδες κιθαρισταί compete at the Panathenaia. These contests probably had a history going back to the Archaic period. On the obverse of a Panathenaic-type amphora from around 530 BCE (Reggio 4224; Kotsidu 1991, Tafel 8) a young musician stands atop a *bêma* playing a small-scale *kithara* before two seated spectators or judges; on the reverse Athena is depicted, suggesting the Panathenaic setting of the contest scene. There is a possibility that the youth is singing to the *kithara*, but given the fact that only boys' *kitharistikê* is later attested for the Panathenaia, this competitor is probably a citharist.

[120] At the fourth-century BCE Panathenaia there was also a boys' contest in solo singing to the accompaniment of the *aulos*, *aulôidia* (IG II² 2311, line 22a in the restored text of Shear 2003). As *kitharistikê*, solo *kithara* playing, involves only playing, so *aulôidia* too involves the display of only one musical skill, singing. Solo *aulos* playing, *aulêtikê*, and *rhapsôidia*, while single-skill media, nevertheless were practiced only by adult males at the Classical Panathenaia, presumably due to the technical and narrative virtuosity respectively demanded by each.

circuit, where the old proprieties had been largely abandoned and novelty, hybridization, and specialization were common.[121] An inscription from Iasos records the victories of a native son of that city, Phanias, in children's *kitharôidia* at the Ephesian Great Artemisia, the Claudeia on Cos, the Herakleia in Iasos, the Sebasta in Miletus, and other *hieroi agônes* 'sacred contests' (I.Iasos 1.110). A boy citharode's victory in 127 CE at the Isthmian Kaisareia is also commemorated by an inscribed dedication.[122] The evidence indicates that professionalized adolescent citharodes and contests for them were quite familiar by Juvenal's time.

It is more likely, however, that the satirist has in mind a young man, probably a *meirakion* in his late teens or a *neos* in his early twenties, who has not yet grown in (or has shaved off) his beard, and has grown his hair long, in imitation of eternally ephebic Apollo *kitharôidos*.[123] The generic name Hedymeles serves to malign this type of musician as an effeminate yet sexually compelling 'Greekling', a *cinaedus* whose attractions nevertheless threaten the virtue of Roman womanhood.[124] Juvenal is in fact activating, with the added zeal of the Roman moralizer who sees sexual deviance and debilitating, usually Greek luxuriousness in every sensual pleasure, a critical topos that Greek comic poets and cultural conservatives themselves had deployed as early as the later fifth century BCE: the negative characterization of popular music and

---

[121] On the expansive menu of festival contests and agonistic categories in the post-Classical era, see Robert 1984; Pallone 1984; Csapo and Slater 1994:186–206; Bélis 1999:113–132.

[122] Biers and Geagan 1970:80 (lines 44–46). Cf. IGSK 17 2.3813: boy citharode victorious at the Great Artemisia in Ephesus, third century CE.

[123] The majority of citharodes (and citharists) depicted on Archaic and early Classical Attic vases are bearded. Those that are unbearded, such as the Brygos Painter's citharode, represent the Apollonian *neos*-type. (Although the Brygos citharode is tagged *ho pais kalos*, this is no indication that he is an adolescent *pais*, but rather a salute to his youthful good looks; his robust neck and chest in fact signal a postadolescent age. Cf. Shapiro 2004:2 on the tag *kalos*; Davidson 2006 on age grades and age-indicative physical traits.) In the High Classical style youthful idealizing becomes the norm; citharodes and citharists are now mostly depicted as unbearded, regardless of age, although hairstyles are consistently short (see Shapiro 1992:58). It is possible, however, that this is not merely representational convention; professional citharodes may have increasingly adopted a clean-shaven look during the later fifth century BCE, which played into criticisms that they were effeminate. Phrynis the citharode was called a *gunnis* 'sissy' (scholia *ad* Aristophanes *Clouds* 971a); he is represented as beardless on a southern Italian krater of the fourth century BCE (Salerno Pc 1812), in a scene likely based on Eupolis' *Demes*. Cf. Part IV.10n283. For long hair as an affectation of Imperial citharodes, see Dio Cassius 63.9.1.

[124] Cf. Braund 1992:76 on Juvenal's articulation of this type: "[A]n adulterer may lurk under the guise of a *cinaedus*. Paradoxically, the softer he looks, the more athletic he will be in bed."

musicians, not least star citharodes, as prettified and unmanly, "soft" (*malthakos*, Plato *Symposium* 179d), if still highly sexed (Thamyris' sexual challenge to the Muses recalls this latter stereotype).[125] In Rome, a society far more anxious about the threat posed to traditional norms of masculinity by musical performance than was Classical Greece, Nero was wholly vulnerable to the charge of effeminacy because of his full-fledged musical pursuits. By extension, he exposed all Romans to an ideological embarrassment on this score, at least in the view of his traditionally minded critics.

This theme emerges consistently in the biographical traditions hostile to Nero, finding its most emphatic expression in Dio Cassius 62.6.4–5. Dio has Boudicca, the Icenian queen who galvanizes revolt against Nero's forces in Britain, channel the sentiment of the sort of old-line, traditionalist Roman elite she so conveniently resembles, when she says of him, "He has the name of a man, but in reality he is a woman; a sign of this is that he sings and plays the *kithara* and prettily adorns himself" (ὄνομα μὲν <γὰρ> ἀνδρὸς ἔχει, ἔργῳ δὲ γυνή ἐστι· σημεῖον δέ, ᾄδει καὶ κιθαρίζει καὶ καλλωπίζεται). The citharodic emperor is thus shamefully "othered" by one who is twice over an "other" herself. The self-adornment (*kallôpizetai*) must refer to the grand citharodic *skeuê* that Dio takes pains to highlight—with barely concealed disgust—in his descriptions of Nero *citharoedus* (61.20.1, 62.18.1).[126] But a wider program of cosmetic prettification associated with the self-presentation of certain citharodes is also evoked here; Boudicca is casting Nero as a kind of Hedymeles. Dio notes with contempt that during his musical tour of Greece Nero wore his hair long, yet kept his face smoothly shaven, a mannered "look" no doubt intended to emulate Apollo's beauty, but one that came off as intolerably inappropriate on "an emperor, an Augustus" (63.9.1).[127]

---

[125] Another reflex of the sexually troped music criticism of the Classical period is to be found in a contemporary of Juvenal, Dio Chrysostom 32.61–62: present-day citharodes are characterized both as violent sexual transgressors against old-time music (*arkhaia mousikê*)—this is a theme from Old Comedy, above all Pherecrates *Cheiron* fr. 155 K-A—and as singers of *aismata gunaikôn*. This latter phrase could be understood to mean 'women's songs' or 'songs sung for the enjoyment of women'. Again, the conceit of the musician as effeminate seducer is operative.

[126] Compare Philostratus *Life of Apollonius of Tyana* 5.7, in which Apollonius complains of Nero's having "cast off the *skeuê* of Augustus and Julius in exchange for that of [the citharodes] Amoebus and Terpnus."

[127] Nero's bloated face and neck, evident in the realistic portraiture on his coins of this period, must have considerably dampened the "Apollonian" effect as well. See Suetonius *Nero* 51; Griffin 1984:121.

Juvenal, however, gives no sense that Pollio—the good Roman name belongs to a real musician—is such a one. This top competitor at Domitian's prestigious Capitoline Games is clearly a more seasoned citharode than the younger Hedymeles. For Martial, Pollio is a marquee name of *kitharôidia* in late-first-century CE Rome (4.61.9). His music made him wealthy enough to acquire an impressive country estate (3.20.18). Pollio appears again in Juvenal *Satire* 7.176–177, this time commanding enormous fees as music teacher to the "sons of the swells" (*lautorum pueros*). These references all suggest an older, experienced man, at the peak of his technical mastery and fairly well integrated into respectable Roman society. Appropriately, Juvenal's Appian woman expresses her devotion to Pollio—was he her son's lyre teacher?—in a desperately serious, "adult" (and, notably, a very Roman) manner. The desire gripping the fan of Hedymeles has by contrast a more immature and blatantly sexualized cast.[128]

This well-appointed woman entertains at home on her own instrument, a testudo, the amateur tortoise-shell lyre, playing it with the "beloved plectrum" that belongs to Hedymeles.[129] This borrowed device functions as a kind of fetish object taking the place of the absent citharode; she holds it as she would her favorite, covering it with kisses and pathetically seeking emotional fulfillment in it (*hoc se solatur*). At *Satire* 6.68–70 aristocratic ladies similarly caress the props and costumes of their favorite actors, who are sorely missed during the long interval between the theatrical performances of the Plebeian and Megalensian Games. It is difficult too to resist a comparison to a modern-day rock-and-roll cliché: the guitar hero's tossing out to the adoring crowd his used guitar picks, which are eagerly claimed by fans as talismanic souvenirs of his musico-sexual aura. In our passage, however, what is left implicit but must be understood as the subtext to the woman's fixation on the plectrum is its phallic shape—apparent in much of the Greek iconography—and its typical material of manufacture, bone or

---

[128] We could compare the gushing proclamation of love (and nascent lust) by an upper-class girl for a citharodic *neos* that is imagined in *Greek Epistles* 2.5 of Aristaenetus (fifth or sixth century CE, but probably following earlier Imperial literary sources).

[129] The simple, virtuous character of the *testudo* stands in stark contrast to the sumptuous rings of Juvenal's player. There is perhaps a suggestion of a feminizing corruption of lyric music's traditional purity, as well as an allusion to the bejeweled *kitharai* of professional citharodes. Preciously adorned amateur stringed instruments have a distinguished pedigree, however: Achilles plays a *phorminx* with a silver bridge (*Iliad* 9.186).

horn.[130] The crude pun on *organa*—the woman fondles 'musical instruments' and 'male genitals'—obviously strengthens the implication.

8. Women in *kitharôidia*?

i. Maria from Pharia

The first couplet of an epigram from the *Palatine Anthology*, attributed to an early Byzantine poet, Paul the Silentiary, presents a case of *plêktron* fetishism similar to that we see in Juvenal, but with the genders turned round:

> πλῆκτρον ἔχει φόρμιγγος, ἔχει καὶ πλῆκτρον ἔρωτος·
> κρούει δ' ἀμφοτέροις καὶ φρένα καὶ κιθάρην.
> τλήμονες, οἷς ἄγναμπτον ἔχει νόον· ᾧ δ' ἐπινεύσει,
> ἄλλος ὅδ' Ἀγχίσης, ἄλλος Ἄδωνις ὅδε.
> εἰ δ' ἐθέλεις, ὦ ξεῖνε, καὶ ἀμφιβόητον ἀκοῦσαι
> οὔνομα καὶ πάτρην, ἐκ Φαρίης Μαρίη.

She holds the *plêktron* of the *phorminx* and she holds the *plêktron* of desire: she strikes with both [plectra] the heart and the

---

[130] Wood and ivory are also attested. See West 1992:65, 1990a:1–2, who notes the phallic suggestiveness of the plectrum's shape. See the plectrum held by a Roman Apollo *citharoedus* in Plate 4. Suda s.v. Σαπφώ (107 Adler) records the odd claim that Sappho invented the plectrum. Given that the apocryphal biographical information in this entry includes a marked amount of blatant sexual invective—the image is of the poet as an oversexed courtesan—her supposed invention of this phallus-shaped device may have originated in a joke about her excessive sexual appetites. The symposium, where the songs of Sappho were reperformed (Aelian via Stobaeus 3.29.58), was likely its original context; discussion of inventions, *heurêmata*, both serious and playful, was typically sympotic (see e.g. Critias D-K 88 B 2 and 6). This is noteworthy: Sappho fr. 99.5 L-P (=Alcaeus fr. 303A.5 Voigt) describes the *khordai* 'strings' of the lyre as *olisbodokoi* 'receiving the *olisbos*'. In Attic comedy, *olisbos* means 'dildo'. West believes that Sappho uses *olisbos* to denote the plectrum, with no sexual undertones; only later did the semantic development from 'plectrum' to 'dildo' take place. It is possible, however, that the epithet forms part of Sappho's originally obscene invective against her supposed rivals, the Polyanaktidai, who are mentioned in the same poem (cf. Parker [H.] 2005:7–9). Sappho would thus be insulting her aristocratic enemies' musical and moral character. But it could also be that this very song, as it circulated through Athenian symposia, inspired jokes about Sappho's invention of the *plêktron* qua sex toy. Cf. Nagy 2007a on how Sappho's own "character" could be profaned as her songs were reperformed at symposia. The plectrum could suggest violence as well as sex: in one version of the myth, a frustrated Heracles stabs his lyre teacher Linus with his plectrum (Aelian *Historical Miscellanies* 3.32).

kithara. Unhappy are those to whom her heart is unyielding. But the man to whom she shows her favor, that man is another Anchises, that man is another Adonis. And if you wish, friend, to hear her acclaimed name and her homeland: she is Maria from Pharia.

Palatine Anthology 16.278

In the final line of the poem we learn that the player of the *phorminx/ kithara,* who is represented in a painting viewed by the poet, is a woman by the name of Maria, a native of Alexandria, which is identified by the substantive epithet Pharia (by way of metonymy with its well-known cult of Isis Pharia).[131] The speaker's obsessive gaze is fixed on Maria's *plêktron,* which inspires a typically epigrammatic *jeu des mots:* the real *plêktron* with which she strikes (*krouein*) the strings, the notional *plêktron* 'goad, sting' that strikes the heart and incites desire. But there is likely a bawdier subtext to this mildly salacious wordplay: the speaker is aroused by the phallic shape of the device, the "erotic plectrum," expertly wielded by the hand of this titillating musician. In an epigram devoted to Ariadne, a *kithara* player, by Paul's contemporary Agathias, the plectrum is similarly foregrounded in the first verse, here again the focus of the erotic gaze (*Palatine Anthology* 5.222).[132]

'Maria from Pharia' (ἐκ Φαρίης Μαρίη) has the catchy ring of a stage name, one that is, as Paul puts it, ἀμφιβόητον 'acclaimed far and wide'. As early as the Hellenistic period, and certainly after, organological terminology becomes frustratingly imprecise, so we cannot know whether Paul has her playing the square-bottomed concert *kithara* of the professional citharode or the round-bottomed, smaller type of *kithara* called the *phorminx,* which is generally an instrument used by women, both free and those working in the sex and entertainment trade.[133] Perhaps this player is a *hetaira,* as the erotic dynamic in which

---

[131] Cf. Tibullus 1.3.32, with Cairns 1979:64–65.

[132] Lines 3–4 of Paul's epigram allude to the poetry of Sappho, the supposed inventor of the plectrum, specifically to the famous erotic triangulation described in the first stanze of her fr. 31: "The man to whom she nods in favor, that man is another Anchises, he is another Adonis." Paul implicitly likens Maria to Aphrodite, the lover of these mythical heroes. As such, this scenario also offers an allusive variation on the seduction scene in the *Homeric Hymn to Aphrodite.* There it is god-like Anchises who plays the lyre for a smitten Aphrodite (κιθαρίζων, 80), who in turn seduces Anchises. Scenes such as this one reflect at the level of myth the sexual charisma of the real-life lyre player (and *a fortiori* the citharode).

[133] On the *phorminx,* also called, by modern scholars, the cradle or round-based *kithara,* as a women's instrument, see Bundrick 2005:26.

Paul implicates her would immediately suggest, rather than a publicly performing citharode, although the lemma, for what it is worth, does indicate that Maria from Pharia is a *kitharôidos*.[134]

Another epigram by Paul the Silentiary finds the poem's speaker smitten with a female musician portrayed in a painting (16.277). The lemma calls this woman, probably Maria, although she goes unnamed here, a *kitharistris*, which is an unmarked designation. It could mean either 'female player of the *kithara*' or 'female player of the lyre or *phorminx*'. In the poem itself she sings to the *lura*, which is itself a generic designation for the *khelus*-lyre, *phorminx*, and *kithara*. (Similarly, the verb *kitharizein* can potentially denote the playing of any of these instruments.) Again, it is impossible to make precise sense of the various terms that are used, but it could well be that this Maria, or at least the type of Hellenistic or Imperial entertainer she represents, is an unusual, yet not singular, example of a female citharodic "pop star," as renowned for her sex appeal as for her musical talent.[135] Maria's home city of Alexandria, famous for its citharodes and its wildly enthusiastic citharodic fan culture (Dio Chrysostom 32.59–67), was as good an environment as any for this rare breed to flourish.

Simon Goldhill has recently argued that, with the exception of the clearly exceptional Hedea, we should be extremely skeptical about the very existence of female citharodes at any time or place in the ancient world; when a woman is called a *kitharôidos*, the word is *stricto sensu* misused, out of carelessness, or because the semantics of the word have in some speech communities become generalized or degraded, or in some deliberate spirit of humor or hyperbole. From this point of view, female "*kitharôidoi*" are likely to be prostitutes, *hetairai*, and/ or small-time, private musical entertainers, women more properly called *kitharistriai*, who do not even necessarily play the concert

---

[134] It is worth noting that Paul evinces interest in citharodic culture in another epigram, *Palatine Anthology* 6.54, which refers to the legendary Locrian citharode Eunomus, who won the Pythian *agôn* with the help of a cicada.

[135] The lemma to another erotic epigram in the *Palatine Anthology* reads *eis kitharôidon* (5.138), but the lovely Zenophila whom the epigram praises plays the *pêktis*, which is usually a type of many-stringed harp. Again, the organological terminology may be more poetic than technically accurate. Perhaps Zenophila plays a polychord *kithara*, common enough in late antiquity, which is here "metaphorically" called a *pêktis*. There is a similar conflation in the treatise *On the Guild of Dionysus* by the third-century BCE scholar Artemon of Cassandrea, FHG IV 342 = Athenaeus 14.636e: the polychord *kithara* of Timotheus of Miletus, no harpist he, is called the *magadis*, a type of harp.

kithara employed by the bona fide citharode.[136] Now, there do seem to be examples in which *kitharôidos* falls short of its established meaning when applied to women. Goldhill may be correct in dismissing outright two so-called citharodes, although even in the cases of these women questions of status and activity remain: a freed slave named Demetria, who appears in an Athenian manumission inscription from around 330 BCE (Δημετρ[ ] κιθαρῳδο, IG II² 1557.63), and Satyra, a woman of servile status, yet seemingly literate, in mid- to late-third-century BCE Alexandria (P.Cair.Zen. I 59087.17).[137] It is impossible to know in what exact capacity and context either woman performed music. It is possible that Satyra provided music only for convivial occasions— her name could suggest that she is something of a "party girl"—but perhaps she played the *kithara* at religious festivals as well. In a letter sent to Zenon, the administrator of the estate of her benefactor (and sometime companion?) Apollonius, finance minister to Ptolemy II Philadelphus, himself the admirer of Glauce *kitharôidos* (P.Cair.Zen. I 59028), she urges the delivery of provisions, perhaps a linen chiton like the one mentioned in another letter to Zenon (P.Cair.Zen. I 59087.17), to arrive in time for a festival of Demeter.[138] It is notable that Zenon's own patronage of a freeborn young man trained in κιθαρῳδικὴ τέχνη, a student at a school in Philadelphia presided over by Zenon, is also papy-

---

[136] We do not know what instrument was played by the *kitharistriai*, who entertained alongside *aulêtrides* and *psaltriai* (female auletes and harpists) at Classical Athenian symposia, primarily accompanying men's singing, but perhaps their own as well (cf. Plato fr. 71.12–13 K-A; Philodemus of Gadara *Epigram* 1.1). Their wage, capped and monitored by the civic bureaucrats called *astunomoi*, was no more than two drachmas per night (Aristotle *Constitution of Athens* 50.2). Did these low-rent entertainers lug large and costly *kitharai* to rowdy parties? Perhaps they did; most harps were, after all, also expensive and unwieldy. Significantly, however, in the Attic iconographical record, women, citizen or "working," are hardly ever shown playing the *kithara*. A handful of late Archaic depictions of reveling maenads and *hetairai* playing the instrument indicate that women would at least be able to play it in sympotic or comastic contexts, even if they rarely did so. (See examples and discussion in Frontisi-Ducroux and Lissarrague 1990:225, 250.) But the smaller, lighter-weight bowl lyre or *phorminx* seems more suitable to the rather basic purposes of the *kitharistria*, as they are to those of the *kitharistês* 'lyre teacher', who is never depicted holding a *kithara*. One context in which *kitharistriai* could well have played the *kithara* was the public religious festival, for which they were occasionally hired to provide music, as Menander *Epitrepontes* 477–479 attests (Habrotonon, a *psaltria*, plays for girls' choruses at the Tauropolia). Dinarchus 1.23 mentions a *kitharistria* at the Eleusinia; a woman named Seddis was employed as *kitharistria* in a temple precinct in Sardis (Sardis VII 1.3). Cf. Bélis 1999:41–42.

[137] Goldhill 2005:276–277.

[138] Cf. Menander's *hetaira* character Habrotonon, who harps for male clients as well as female festival-goers (*Epitrepontes* 477–479). On Glauce, see below.

rologically attested (P.Lond. VII 2017, c. 240 BCE). The youth in question, Heracleotes, writes a memorandum to Zenon and his colleague Nestor repeatedly asking for the restitution of an ὄργανον 'instrument', presumably a *kithara*, that had been bequeathed to him by his deceased teacher Demeas, or for the money to purchase an instrument of equivalent worth (105 drachmas) and quality. Heracleotes requires the instrument so that he might practice for upcoming festival *agônes* instituted by King Ptolemy II, the Basileia, in which he hopes to make a good showing and win a top prize.[139] What would motivate Zenon to support and outfit this budding agonistic citharode? Perhaps Heracleotes represented a financial investment for Zenon that would pay dividends in the form of cash prizes won at *agônes*—Zenon would take a cut of the citharode's winnings.[140] Perhaps too some similar "business" arrangement existed between Satyra and Apollonius.

The case of Demetria is still more mysterious: why would a female slave in late Classical Athens merit the designation *kitharôidos*? Does it speak to some extraordinary musical talent or ambition she possessed, and that perhaps played a part in her emancipation—a *kitharistria* with the ability and drive to perform as a citharode? Or is it (mis)applied in a deliberately aggrandizing sense at the instigation of either the manumitter or Demetria herself?

Goldhill's skepticism is a needed corrective to the exaggerated claim, made by one otherwise judicious student of Hellenistic performance culture, that there is "no dearth of women in the music profession with the highest status of all, that of the kitharode."[141] But while there is no doubt a dearth of female citharodes relative to males, to assume a total lack seems equally erroneous. It must be the case that women rarely, if ever, played in the same leagues as big-name male

---

[139] On the memorandum, see Bell 1925; Bélis 1999:21–22. Heracleotes also mentions the need for an *epistatês* (line 27), which Bélis translates as 'manager', to put him in competitive position in the run-up to the festival. What role the *epistatês* played in managing the career of the citharode we can only guess, but the very existence of such a figure speaks to the complexity of organization and commercialization in the citharodic culture of the Hellenistic period. See the following note.

[140] Thus Rostovtzeff 1922:174, who suggests that Zenon's and Nestor's schools were training grounds for professional musicians and athletes whose winnings the benefactors would subsequently share: "But is it not more probable that the interest was not only of a sportive character but that Zenon and Nestor were interested materially in the victory of their boys? In the Hellenistic period the Greek agones were contests of professionals and the prizes consisted not only in crowns but also in comparatively large sums of money. Large sums could be also gained by betting on the best trained boys."

[141] Lightfoot 2002:212.

citharodes, competing against them at the most prestigious *mousikoi agônes*, but what evidence we do have entitles us to conjecture that at least a few female citharodes, while perhaps never rising above the level of the "novelty act," were known to appear in public concerts and perhaps even some *agônes* from the Hellenistic period on. At the very least we can be fairly confident that, as early as the third century BCE, professional female musical entertainers and, to some degree, amateur female musicians as well, were freely adopting traits of citharodic "style," if not performing in public as citharodes in the traditional sense.

ii. Glauce: An Orpheus in Alexandria?

Consider Glauce. Alexandria again provides the backdrop for this strong citharodic contender, whose musical and erotic charms remained the stuff of legend long after her death. Aelian and Plutarch, who explicitly call Glauce a *kitharôidos*, preserve an anecdotal tradition, seemingly inspired by the myths of Orpheus, that has various animals, a dog, a ram, or a goose, falling in love with her.[142] Uncertainty, however, surrounds Glauce, just as it does Maria. Is her citharodic identity a late, fictional elaboration of her status as a musical *hetaira* in the Ptolemaic court, where she gained some notice as a composer of auletic party tunes?[143] Aelian *On the Nature of Animals* 8.11 makes Ptolemy II Philadelphus a rival to a ram for the love of Glauce, which implies her status as high-class *hetaira*. And contemporary Hellenistic writers do not call her a citharode, but rather mention her in contexts that suggest she composed music for the *aulos*.[144] But why would Glauce be recast as a citharode during the Second Sophistic? Even Goldhill, who is skeptical of the historical reality of Glauce's citharodic career, admits

---

[142] Aelian *On the Nature of Animals* 1.6, 5.29, 8.11; *Historical Miscellanies* 9.39; Plutarch *Moralia* 972f; also Pliny *Natural History* 10.51. A speaker in Plutarch *Moralia* 397a argues that the Pythian priestess should not be expected to sing as well as Glauce the *kitharôidos*.

[143] Thus Goldhill 2005:279–280.

[144] In Hedylus 1883 Gow-Page (*ap.* Athenaeus 4.176d) she is a maker of drinking songs reperformed by the aulete Theon. At Theocritus *Idyll* 4.31, Corydon, a rustic singer to the reed *surinx*, the country cousin of the *aulos*, claims he can "strike up the tunes of Glauce" (τὰ Γλαύκας ἀγκρούομαι). The scholiast to the passage calls her a *kroumatopoios*, which can in fact denote any kind of instrumental composer, but probably means aulete here (so Dorion, a famous aulete, is called a *kroumatopoios* by Hellenistic authors; see West 1992:369n34).

that, at least by the time of Plutarch and Aelian, "female citharodes were a recognizable item."[145]

The best approach to the varied testimonia is an inclusive one. That is, could not all three roles assigned to Glauce, *hetaira*, aulete, and publicly acclaimed citharode, accord with different aspects of her historical career, or at the least describe the generic profile of a successful female musician of the Hellenistic and Imperial periods?[146] Certainly, performances by female musicians in large-scale public settings are attested for Ptolemaic Alexandria, above all by Theocritus *Idyll* 15, in which an Argive woman, a πολύιδρις ἀοιδός 'skilled singer' (97), performs at a festival of Adonis, a cultic occasion that is essentially a secular concert sponsored by the royal court. In general, in the popular musical culture of the Hellenistic and Greco-Roman periods attitudes toward women's performance were relaxed; women were presented with opportunities to appear in public as recitalists and even agonistic performers that were not readily available to them in the Classical period.[147]

As the case of young Hedea demonstrates, even the highly traditional, adult male realm of *kitharôidia* opened up to female musicians. Honorary inscriptions from second-century BCE Iasos—the home of the citharodic boy wonder Phanis—and first-century BCE Delphi commemorate public performances by Kleino, daughter of Evander, and by Polygnota of Thebes, daughter of Socrates, respectively.[148] These women (or girls) were not citharodes, or at least did not appear as such on these occasions; they were female harpists who made music to choral accompaniment, *khoropsaltriai*, a class of musical performer that is not attested before the Hellenistic period. The civic honors accorded to both women as well as the inclusion of their fathers' names on the monuments would indicate that, like Hedea, they were

---

[145] Goldhill 2005:280.

[146] This is essentially the position of West 1992:378–379; 373.

[147] Discussion in Bélis 1999:37–60. Loman 2004 makes a strong argument that the number of agonistic female musicians in the Hellenistic period was considerably greater than our sources indicate. For female theatrical performers in late antiquity, see Webb 2002.

[148] Inscriptional evidence presented in Robert 1938:36–38. Kleino did not compete in contests at Iasos but rather offered *epideixeis* 'recitals' in the theater. Polygnota probably did formally compete at Delphi, as did another *khoropsaltria* from Cyme (daughter of one Aristocratus), whose name has been lost from a second-century BCE inscription (SIG 689 = Stephanis 1988, no. 2815). See discussion in Bélis 1999:53–56.

members of respectable, well-established families of professional traveling entertainers.[149]

But female musicians such as Glauce and Maria could well have straddled the worlds of the splendid royal symposium, at which they entertained the rich and powerful, and the *agôn* or, more likely, the theatrical concert, at which they entertained the masses.[150] Indeed, acclaim in one context could have made them more desirable in the other, and vice versa.[151] The history of *kitharôidia* is in fact filled with prominent names, Arion of Methymna and Timotheus of Miletus, for example, who made successful careers out of moving between private service to wealthy patrons and the lucrative public arena of festival competition and mass entertainment. (These two citharodes resemble Glauce in another respect as well: both composed for the *aulos*, specifically the aulodic dithyramb, as well as the *kithara*.) Further, Aeschines, Juvenal, and the other sources discussed above imply that at least some male citharodes were courted by wealthy admirers and entered into sexual liaisons with them. It is tempting to write off the mock-Orphic storyline about different animals, a ram, dog, or goose, falling for Glauce *kitharôidos*, and even competing with her royal suitor, as one of the tall tales told of the celebrity courtesans of the Hellenistic period. But perhaps there is some more cultural depth to it. Could we read it as an allegorical reflex of the demotic favor that Glauce (or a female

[149] Polygnota's family probably belonged to one of the performers' guilds of Dionysus that arose during the Hellenistic period. See Harmon 2005:352n5.

[150] It should be noted that Ptolemaic symposia were managed on a far grander scale than Archaic and Classical private symposia. Ptolemy Philadelphus entertained in an enormous, lavishly accoutered symposium tent (Athenaeus 5.196a–197c), in which it is easy to imagine concert performances being staged for a relatively large, while still select audience. See Murray [Oswyn] 1996, who sees the tyrants' symposia as a model for those of the Hellenistic kings: "They [the tyrants] expanded the size and expense of the *symposium* until it became almost confused with the public festival" (16).

[151] We hear of several sympotic *aulêtrides* who evoked the glamour of the Panhellenic contests by adopting *noms de guerre* such as Nemeas, Isthmias, and Pythionice. The practice was common enough in fourth-century Athens for (ineffectual) legislation to be passed against it (Polemon fr. 38 Preller = Athenaeus 13.587c). See McClure 2003:62. Straton, the fourth-century king of Sidon and a legendary hedonist, fused the thrill of the music contest with the sexual adventure of the symposium in fabulously literal fashion by having his hired female entertainers compete against one another in mock *mousikoi agônes* (Theopompus FGrH 115 F 114 = Athenaeus 12.531c). Theopompus also records that a favorite of the fourth-century BCE Phocian tyrant Phayllus, an *aulêtris* named Bromias, "would have played the *aulos* at the Pythian games had she not been prevented from doing so by the populace" (Athenaeus 13.605b)—an example of the way the private musical and erotic lives of kings or tyrants could spill out into the public performative realm. The case of Maria from Pharia could be analogous.

musician such as Glauce) won in Alexandria thanks to public concertizing?

A related zoomorphic motif appears in Dio Chrysostom 32.63–66. The orator, speaking to an Alexandrian audience, relates a humorous version of the Orpheus myth, which he claims he has heard from "a Phrygian, a kinsman of Aesop," who had himself once visited Alexandria. According to the Phrygian's tale the animals that followed Orpheus, most numerous among them birds and sheep (64), were changed by the gods into the "tribe of the Macedonians," who later settled in Alexandria (65). These origins explain why the Alexandrian *dêmos* is so mad about *kitharôidia*. Further, the Phrygian contends that Alexandrian citharodes are specifically descended from the "shameless and curious breed" of dogs inspired by Orpheus to learn to play the *kithara*. As such, the citharodic music in that city retains a "canine" quality (66). The Phrygian and his folk tale are surely inventions of Dio, but the similarities, superficial as they may be, between the tale and the anecdotal tradition surrounding Glauce are remarkable. Informing both could be some literary satire and/or popular stereotype characterizing the "wild" Alexandrian music fans as animals.[152]

There are two further cases in which we perhaps catch a fleeting glimpse of women moving, like Glauce, between the activities of the courtesan or party entertainer and a more publicly recognized role as *kitharôidos*. First, in one of the epistolary fictions of the second-century CE writer Alciphron (*Letters* 3.33), a wife berates her aged husband for falling in love with a "woman *kitharôidos*" (ἐρᾷς κιθαρῳδοῦ γυναικός) and pathetically squandering his hard-earned fortune on her. Later in the letter, however, the wife calls this woman a ἱππόπορνος 'common street-walker' and then a *hetaira*. Which is it? Does the wife use *kitharôidos* carelessly, merely to indicate that the woman, either a prostitute or a higher-status *hetaira*, makes music as part of her trade? Or does she mean it sarcastically, by way of saying that this low-class prostitute, at best a common *kitharistria*, is anything *but* a citharode? Both of these options are appealing, but the possibility remains that the husband-stealer is a likely some-time *hetaira* who also performs in some recognizable capacity as a citharode. That is, the wife alone does not choose

---

[152] Cf. Anderson 2000:156. Lucian *The Uncultured Book Collector* 12 imagines dogs being irresistibly, and violently, drawn to the son of the Lesbian tyrant Pittacus as he plays the misappropriated lyre of Orpheus. Here too a musico-political allegory may be at issue, with the dogs representing the "masses" attracted to the tyrant-musician. Plato notably singles out the "sounds of dogs and sheep and birds" as objects of mimetic imitation by the sensationalistic New Music performer (*Republic* 397a–b).

the word *kitharôidos*; it is a tag already attached to the other woman—by the husband, at least. The addition of *gunê* would thus not only "indicate how unusual it is to use the term κιθαρῳδός of a woman."[153] It would also have the effect of throwing "scare quotes" around *kitharôidos*, undercutting its customary semantics of prestige (compare condescending expressions in English such as "woman doctor"). The subtle cattiness seems entirely in keeping with the stylized mimetic verisimilitude of the *Letters*.

The second woman in question more closely resembles Glauce. She is Panthea of Smyrna, mistress of the Emperor Verus in Antioch (c. 165 BCE), who is described in Lucian's encomiastic dialogue devoted to her, *Imagines*, as one who sings beautifully, μάλιστα πρὸς τὴν κιθάραν 'most of all to the *kithara*' (13). Leisured women and girls of the Imperial era, as we will see, did practice singing to the *kithara* at home. But Panthea, called an *amica vulgaris* 'common girlfriend' in the *Historia Augusta* (*Verus* 7.10), was a *hetaira* rather than a daughter of the aristocracy. Lucian does not explicitly call Panthea a *kitharôidos*, but his extensive praise of her skill on the *kithara*, a word Lucian emphatically repeats three times, marks her as such.[154] She is compared favorably to the star citharodes of myth, Orpheus and Amphion; she is an expert at maintaining perfect rhythm and harmony, "her *kithara* a full partner in the song, her *plêktron* keeping pace with her tongue" (14). The length of the encomiastic description, and its detailed assessment of her *tekhnê*— the perfect parity between voice and instrument is a motif in the praise of citharodes, as we will see in Section 15 below—suggest that for Panthea *kitharôidia* was not merely "something that an accomplished *hetaira* might do for her man," but rather something more like a profession, and one that she exhibited to audiences in Antioch beyond Verus and his circle.[155] Panthea's career might in some respects anticipate that of another upwardly mobile Eastern Greek "working girl," Theodora, who parlayed her charms as *hetaira* and popular pantomime performer into a marriage to the Byzantine Emperor Justinian I (ruled 527–565 CE).[156]

iii. Painted women, and a citharode in Boscoreale

Speculation about female citharodes is made additionally difficult by the fact that real (not mythical or divine) women playing or singing

---

[153] Goldhill 2005:288n27.
[154] Cf. West 1992:329.
[155] The quotation is from Goldhill 2005:288n22.
[156] See Webb 2002 on the life story of Theodora, fact and fiction.

to *kitharai* in either public or private are essentially absent from the iconographical record of Archaic and Classical Greece, and the case is not much different in the Hellenistic and Roman periods.[157] Several exceptions come by way of Roman wall painting, which nevertheless present their own interpretive problems. For example, in a painting from Herculaneum (first century CE, now in the British Museum), a fully clothed, wreathed woman plays a concert *kithara* while sitting nestled against the chest of a partially nude, similarly wreathed young man, who seems to guide her right arm lightly over the strings of the instrument. An older woman stands across from the couple, observing them.[158] What is going on here? As with so many wall paintings, the otherworldly scenario is strangely ambiguous. Does the erotic tenor of the image suggest that the woman with the *kithara* is meant to be a *hetaira*? Horace *Odes* 3.9.9 describes his beloved Thracian *hetaira* as *citharae sciens*. But the standing female spectator makes this reading difficult. Is the *kithara* player instead a wife or daughter participating in some kind of stylized music lesson, or making music "together" with her husband or admirer?[159] Achilles Tatius provides literary testimony that some aristocratic women were, by at least the second century CE, playing the *kithara*, even staging mini-concerts, in the privacy of their homes. In *Leucippe and Cleitophon* 2.1 the novelist describes a well-born girl, the titular Leucippe, singing to the *kithara* for Cleitophon, who is in love with her.[160] Notably, one of the pieces she performs is a musical setting of a brief passage from the *Iliad*; such Homeric settings are well-attested citharodic practice, going back to the earliest citharodes ("Plutarch" *On Music* 3.1132b–c).

Text and image conspire to suggest that something of the technical ambition and glamour of professional *kitharôidia* had seeped into the amateur realm of women's music making under the Empire, as it had into the performative style of *hetairai*.[161] The plectrum wielded by Juvenal's lyre-playing *matrona* is another sign of this seepage, and one that suggests its erotic charge. But again, although the evidence points to both well-born and "working" women's cultivation of *kitharôidia* in

---

[157] See n136 above.

[158] Silberberg-Pierce 1993, fig. 9

[159] Cf. Silberberg-Pierce 1993:32–33.

[160] The *kithara* is not mentioned in this passage; only the term *kitharismata* is used. But in 2.7 Leucippe explicitly plays a *kithara*. Ovid is aroused by a girl playing a stringed instrument, probably a lyre, in *Amores* 2.4.27–28.

[161] A fresco from the Casa di Giasone in Pompeii (Müller 1994, fig. 49) shows a woman, probably a Muse, standing upright in a citharodic pose, but she is holding a *khelus*-lyre rather than a *kithara*.

private contexts, we might want to keep an open mind to the possibility of cultural traffic occasionally flowing in the other direction, women's publicization of their citharodic pursuits. The widely attested phenomenon of stage-struck Imperial Roman elites' public dabbling in scenic entertainments is certainly relevant to this question.[162]

An intriguing funerary inscription from Imperial Rome commemorates Auxesis, a *citharoeda* (the only place this Latin word appears) and the *optima coniunx* 'best wife' of one Gaius Cornelius Neritus (CIL VI 10125). Her musical activity is tantalizingly uncertain. In what context did she perform as *citharoeda*? Was she a former slave who provided string music at private events? (A bit odd, perhaps, for the proud husband to monumentalize this episode in her life.) Or did her own domestic cultivation of the *kithara* prompt the husband to give her the title? A third possibility exists as well, that *citharoeda* has its literal force, suggesting Auxesis pursued a more formal citharodic career, as either slave or free woman, professionally entertaining public audiences.

Still more intriguing is another fresco, from Room H of the villa of Publius Fannius Synistor at Boscoreale, currently at the Metropolitan Museum of Art, that shows a seated woman holding a large, impressively gilded *kithara* of a gracile, elongated shape (Plate 5). This instrument type, which came into fashion in the late Classical and early Hellenistic periods and continued to be used in Imperial Rome, was probably played more regularly by amateur enthusiasts and women than by male professional citharodes.[163] The woman is elegantly attired in a white himation above a long, purple chiton; she wears gold earrings, a gold headband, and bracelets. A similarly attired, younger girl looks out from behind the chair. The woman is not actively playing

---

[162] See e.g. Edwards 1997.

[163] See Maas and Snyder 1989:174–175 on this *kithara* type. The woman's *kithara* resembles that represented on a fourth-century BCE jasper scaraboid (Oxford 1921.1236, Maas and Snyder 1989:192, fig. 5), or the *kithara* held by a seated, bare-chested Apollo in another Roman fresco (Palatine Antiquarium, inv. 379982). It is also similar, but certainly not identical, to the "Italiote" *kithara*, a rectangular-shaped instrument with straight, parallel arms more practically akin to the harp than to the *kithara*, that is to be seen in the hands of wealthy domestic musicians, men and women, in south Italian vase paintings of the later fourth century BCE. Cf. Maas and Snyder, 175–178; West 1992:56, who notes that this *kithara* could have been "an import from the Levant." Its exotic origin and appearance no doubt would have made it a status symbol, as harps had been for earlier generations of Greek elites (cf. Power 2007:194–197). It does appear in the hands of a seated woman—Sappho?—in a wall painting from Stabiae, who tunes the instrument as she plucks an arched harp, *sambuca*, lying at her side (Landels 1999:76–77)—the "harmony" of harp and *kithara* in this context is telling.

the instrument, but rather tuning it; she is preparing to play. Her right hand is bent over the instrument's crossbar, altering the tension of the strings by turning their pegs. This is a conventional iconographical schema going back to Archaic vase painting—the *kithara* or lyre player reaching up to the crossbar with right hand to tune, while keeping the left hand against the strings, presumably to test their pitch as tension is drawn or released.[164] The woman does not seem to hold a *plêktron*. Although right-hand plucking was not standard playing technique on the *kithara*, contemporary wall paintings, such as the one from Herculaneum just discussed, do show seated female musicians who pluck *kitharai* with two hands, in the manner of a harp player, and the Boscoreale painter may have followed this convention.[165] The woman's left hand is potentially in position to pluck the strings from above and behind the soundbox. But perhaps the painter has simply omitted or obscured her plectrum—it could be lodged in her right palm, something occasionally implicit in Greek depictions of tuning. We should note too that this *kithara* has only five strings, which is itself most likely the result of a casual approach to organological detail rather than a deliberate representational choice.[166]

The painting has been dated to the later Republican period (c. 40–30 BCE), but there is good reason to believe that it is closely based on Hellenistic portrait models. The identity of the woman and her relation to the other figures depicted on the Boscoreale murals has been contested since the excavation of the villa in 1900. Of the many and diverse interpretations that have been offered—cultic, mythical, allegorical—two appealing prospects stand out.[167] First, it has been thought that she represents one of the *hetairai* kept by the Macedonian ruler Antigonus II Gonatas, who is accordingly depicted on the opposite wall. Antigonus' keen erotic interest in a well-known *male* citharode, at least, is anecdotally attested.[168] If this reading is correct, the musician in the painting could represent a Maria or a Glauce, her instrument and garb equally suited for a royal symposium or a public appearance, and

---

[164] Representative images in Paquette 1984:124–126.

[165] I discuss plucking and plectra in detail below. The "Italiote" *kithara* was sometimes plucked *à la harpe*, as we see on an Apulian pelike, Turin 4149; Paquette 1984:115, C22. (Note that this instrument has nine strings.)

[166] *Pace* Studniczka 1924: the instrument is not meant to be a "five-stringed *magadis*" (87). It is clearly a *kithara*.

[167] Convenient summary of approaches in Bieber 1956 and Müller 1994:23–44, 139–141.

[168] Studniczka 1924:89–95 ("das Bildnis einer berühmten Hetäre hellenistischer Zeit"). Gonatas and citharode: Antigonus of Carystus by way of Athenaeus 13.603e; Diogenes Laertius 7.14.

Fannius and the guests at his villa—Room H was probably devoted to convivial gatherings—could thus, like Paul the Silentiary gazing enviously at his painting, notionally compete for her "favor."[169]

According to a more recent interpretation she is Berenice II, wife of the Alexandrian king Ptolemy III, son of Ptolemy II Philadelphus (that lover of Glauce *kitharôidos*), and the girl standing behind her chair is her daughter, Berenice III.[170] The scholar who formulated this theory speculates that Queen Berenice holds the *kithara* as a symbolic token of her homeland, Cyrene, which had a distinguished cult of Apollo. There is every reason to believe that cult statues of Apollo *kitharôidos* had long been displayed in Cyrene, as in other Greek cities, but, even so, this makes for a rather tenuous explanation of the *kithara* in the original Alexandrian images that would have been copied by the Boscoreale painter.[171] If we are indeed looking at Berenice in this image, something grander than mere geographical allusion is likely to be implied by her *kithara*. This "king of instruments," the supreme symbol of ordering harmony, has been drafted into the semiotic arsenal of Hellenistic royal power, and along with it the spectacular allure of the citharode. The intimacy between power politics and citharodic charisma has a long history—Nero, performing in Naples, not far from the villa of Fannius, enacts its *reductio ad absurdum*—but what would set apart the iconographical program behind the Boscoreale painting is gender. It is the queen, not the king, who is imagined as the glamorous citharode. Yet this figuration may not be merely rhetorical, but grounded too in the realities of a contemporary musical culture in which real women were in one form or another involving themselves in the practice of *kitharôidia*.

A significant connection of a Ptolemaic woman from the preceding generation to *kitharôidia* is attested in a fragmentarily preserved epigram of Posidippus (AB 37) that "records the dedication to Arsinoe Philadelphus [wife of Ptolemy II, mother-in-law of Berenice II] by her

---

[169] The gaze of the musician, unlike the front-and-center stare of the girl behind her (an attendant, according to Studniczka 1924:89), is notably awry, and perhaps playfully so. That is, she is forever looking *away* from the viewer who would catch her eye, always showing her favor to another. Cf. Studniczka 1924:88.

[170] Pfrommer 1992:19–23.

[171] An Apollo *kitharôidos* from Cyrene, produced during the reign of Hadrian, now in the British Museum, was based on a Hellenistic model, and probably referred to earlier sculptural images of the god in Cyrene. On the statue, see Flashar 1992:126; cf. Higgs 1994 on its historical context.

temple-keeper ... of a lyre brought ashore by 'Arion's dolphin'."[172] Peter Bing has observed that the epigram not only alludes to the charming story of Arion's dolphin ride to Cape Taenarum, but that it further serves as "modern counterpart" to what became the charter myth of the Lesbian musical tradition, the story that has Orpheus' lyre, along with his head, washing up on the shores of Lesbos (cf. Phanocles fr. 1 Powell), usually at Antissa, the city of Terpander, or, in an alternate tradition preserved in Ovid *Metamorphoses* 11.50, at Arion's native Methymna.[173] The Ptolemies are now, Posidippus is affirming, the undisputed inheritors not only of a prestigious Lesbian lyric and poetic legacy, but of a specifically *citharodic* legacy going back, via Lesbos and Arion, to the mortal source of lyric song, Orpheus himself. As Bing puts it, "The Lesbian lyre has been passed on; today its home is Egypt."[174] Indeed, when Posidippus was writing, third-century Alexandria was fast becoming the premier site for professional *kitharôidia*, and it would remain so through the time of Nero. The Basileia festival instituted by Ptolemy II featured a citharodic *agôn* that attracted international stars such as Nicocles of Tarentum (IG II² 3779). But again, the specific role accorded to Queen Arsinoe in the reception of the Arionic lyre, and in the broader reception of cultural prestige it emblematizes, is noteworthy, and might well reflect a practical interest in string culture at the Ptolemaic court that went beyond mere patronage.[175]

---

[172] Bing 2005:128. AB = Austin and Bastianini 2002. See too the reconstruction and discussion of Puelma 2006.

[173] It is possible that Ovid took his account from a Hellenistic source eager to link the citharodic legacy of Methymna to Alexandria; the two cities enjoyed close political ties in the third century BCE (cf. Bing 2005:130–131, who would locate the Posidippean epigram in this political context). It is notable that one tradition, perhaps of Archaic antiquity, has Terpander bringing the lyre of Orpheus to Egypt (Nicomachus *Excerpts* 1 = T 53b Gostoli). Could this account too have had currency in the Alexandrian culture of *kitharôidia*? The shift of Orphic prestige from Antissa to Methymna, however, may have taken place only after Antissa was destroyed around 167 BCE and its population moved to Methymna (Livy 43.31.14, Pliny *Natural History* 5.139); cf. Graf 1987:93.

[174] Bing 2005:129–130.

[175] Stephens 2004:174 argues that in AB 37 Arsinoe "is imaginatively positioned as the successor of earlier artistic patrons" such as Periander of Corinth, Arion's patron. An epigram of Posidippus from the "Gemstones" series (AB 9) describes the emblem on the famous seal ring of Polycrates of Samos as "the lyre of a singer-man playing the *phorminx*"—another embedded model of lyric patronage (Stephens 2004:173). On possible mythic refractions of Ptolemaic interest in *kitharôidia* in Theocritus *Idyll* 22.24 (the Dioscuri imagined as "citharists and singers") and *Idyll* 18.35–37 (Helen expertly singing hymns to the *lura*), see Part II.10. The latter passage is especially suggestive. If Helen is meant to evoke Arsinoe (Griffiths 1979:86–91), then her expert lyre singing might serve to validate heroically the *kitharôidia* practiced by the Ptolemaic queen.

9. Going Professional

i. *Musica occulta*

We return to Naples. A nervous tension pervades the theater, felt both by the spectators and the performer, who has sung previously only on private occasions to smaller, select groups. Today is Nero's long-awaited public debut. Most citharodes, even the very experienced, suffer pre-performance jitters; a successful reception by each audience they encounter means everything to them.[176] For the Stoic philosopher Epictetus (mid-first to second century CE), the citharode serves as a paradigmatic example of a performer for whom the pressure to please the crowd creates enormous stress: "When he is alone, a citharode sings without anxiety, but when he enters the theater, even if has an excellent voice (λίαν εὔφωνος) and plays the *kithara* well, he is anxious, for he wishes not only to sing well, but also to win acclaim (εὐδοκιμῆσαι), something which is not in his own power" (Arrian *Dissertations of Epictetus* 2.13.1–3). *Suda* s.v. Ἱππαρχίων ἄφωνος and Zenobius 2.35 explain that the proverbial expression *Hipparkhiôn aphônos* 'Hipparchion without a voice' derives from an anecdote about a celebrated citharode, Hipparchion, who was struck dumb with stage fright during the penteteric *agôn* in Syrian Helioupolis.

But the show must go on. As Nero had several times before said to his close friends and confidants, "There is no respect for hidden music" (*occultae musicae nullum esse respectum*, Suetonius *Nero* 20.1). The proverb was a Greek one—Aulus Gellius *Attic Nights* 13.31.3 calls it *verbum illud e Graecia vetus* 'that old saying from Greece'—and by quoting it (in Greek, presumably), the emperor sought to legitimate the controversial publication of his musical enthusiasms by appealing to Greek cultural precedent. As with all of Nero's Hellenic appropriations, however, there is more to his adoption of this rather banal-seeming motto than meets the eye. First, the saying as it is delivered in Suetonius differs slightly yet significantly from the Greek version given in Lucian *Harmonides* 1 (οὐδὲν γὰρ ὄφελος ἀπορρήτου, φασί, καὶ ἀφανοῦς τῆς μουσικῆς 'They say there is no use for secret and unseen music') and a Latin version given by Aulus Gellius (*musicam, quae sit abscondita, eam esse nulli rei* 'Music that has been concealed is worthless'). Nero has reworded the saying to reflect specifically his own

---

[176] Suetonius *Nero* 23.3 describes Nero's performance anxieties on his tour of Greece; cf. Kelly 1979:33–34.

craving for respect and regard (*respectus*) as a musician, and perhaps too his unspoken anxieties about losing respect by bringing his music to the public.

As a well-informed philhellene, he must have recognized that a great deal of respect had in fact been accorded to "hidden music" in Greek antiquity. I refer to the amateur *mousikê* practiced in the socially restricted institutions of the schoolroom and the symposium, which was valorized by elites for the very reason that it was the exclusive possession of the sociocultural aristocracy, notionally "hidden" from the scrutiny of the public. We do not know the provenance of the Greek proverb behind Nero's expression, but it is significant that Lucian puts his version in the mouth of a proudly professional musician, who is, like Nero, eager for popular acclaim. It is notable too how the imagery of secrecy and concealment that runs through its various permutations (ἀπόρρητος, ἀφανής, *occulta*, *abscondita*) negatively figures privately practiced music as something arcane, esoteric, belonging even to the world of the religious mysteries (cf. Aristotle *Nicomachean Ethics* 1111a10), and so forbidden—ἀπόρρητος can mean both 'secret' and 'forbidden'—to all but the initiated few. Could the proverb have begun life as a popular musician's critique of the aristocratic valorization of amateur music making, implying that it, unlike the public, "democratic" activity of the professional, benefits neither members of a general audience, who take pleasure in music, nor the performer himself, who enjoys the audience's acclaim?[177] Be that as it may, Nero's strategic deployment of the expression reflects his acute awareness of the tensions between public and private, professional and amateur musical performance involved in the Greek cultural traditions he emulated as well as in the Roman social *mores* he inherited. In this section and the next we will examine some ways in which Nero negotiated these tensions during his citharodic "coming out."

ii. Liminal Naples

Some thought had been put into the choice of Naples as the site for the emperor's debut. Naples (Neapolis) was a thoroughly Hellenic *polis* at the upper reaches of a region, Magna Graecia, where, unlike in Rome, *kitharôidia* had long been cultivated and appreciated. Arion of Methymna legendarily promoted the art in this area around the end of

---

[177] Cf. n27 above for the critique of elite musical ideology by Stratonicus, the professional's professional.

the seventh century BCE (Herodotus 1.24; Ovid *Fasti* 2.93–94). Citharodes from Hellenic Italy and Sicily are well represented at festival contests throughout Greece from as early as the sixth century BCE; we have one first-century BCE prize inscription (IG IX 2.534) from the Eleutheria at Larisa recording the victory of a Neapolitan citharode. Naples likely had been holding musical contests from an early point, probably in connection with its ancient festival devoted to the Siren Parthenope, the divine patroness of the city. In 2 BCE the grand festival of the Sebasta (full name: Italica Romaea Sebasta Isolympia), modeled upon the penteteric "sacred" festivals of Greece, was instituted in the city at the initiative of the Roman Senate and the Neapolitans in honor of Augustus, who had restored the city after it was damaged by earthquake and fire; *mousikoi agônes* were added to the roster of athletic contests soon after his death, probably in 18 CE.[178] These were likely held in an odeion, a roofed music hall, which had been constructed, like the famous Odeion in Athens, right alongside the theater.[179] By Nero's time the citharodic *agôn* at the Sebasta had attained the rank of a world-class, prestige event, attracting major talent from Greece (cf. Strabo 5.4.7). The honorary inscription in Argos for the early-second-century CE star citharode M. Ulpius Heliodorus of Thessalonike prominently records his two victories in Naples alongside victories at the most prominent interstate and regional festival *agônes* in Greece (IG IV 591).

Although every citharode is first and foremost an *agônistês*, a competitive professional, neither Suetonius nor Tacitus provide indications that Nero is a competitor in an *agôn*, as he would be in Greece two years later, and indeed the details of their accounts speak against this notion.[180] It is tempting to speculate that Nero would have been especially drawn to the opportunity to make his debut at the Augustan *agônes*: the symbiosis of traditional Greek musical culture and Roman imperial power represented by this institution would make it an auspicious and symbolically appropriate launching point for his peculiar

---

[178] See Geer 1935; Arnold 1960:246–247; Caldelli 1993:28–37. Cf. Gouw 2006:220–221 on the appropriateness of Naples as the site of these first Greco-Roman games.

[179] Statius *Silvae* 3.5.91–92. It is possible that Nero sang at some point in this odeion, but both Tacitus and Suetonius indicate that Nero made his debut in the open theater, which was a larger structure.

[180] Cf. Geer 1935:214–215. The quinquennial schedule of the Sebasta would also seem to make a performance at them in 64 impossible, though Nero would later—sacrilegiously—alter the festival calendar in Greece to accommodate his own touring schedule, as well as, perhaps, the date of his own second Neronia (Suetonius *Nero* 23.1; 21.1).

career.[181] But we should imagine, rather, that this is a non-competitive public concert recital, a format that seems to have become increasingly common during and after the Hellenistic period, when celebrated citharodes saw the recital as an auxiliary opportunity to meet the public demand for their music and to supplement incomes earned in the more traditional venue of the *agônes*, most of which, like those of the Sebasta, for example, were chrematitic rather than purely stephanitic.[182]

But for Nero the recital format, as well as the choice of Naples, suggests a transitional strategy, designed to mediate a rite of passage from amateurism to competitive professionalism, to the career-making stages at the festival *agônes* in Greece, where star citharodes such as Terpnus competed before mass crowds for glory, fame, and fortune (Tacitus *Annals* 15.33.2). The culturally liminal space occupied by Naples is crucial to the mediation of this passage. Naples was indeed *quasi Graeca urbs*, as Tacitus calls it, but one comfortingly close to Rome; it was a place where, as Statius puts it, "Roman *honos* 'dignity' and Greek *licentia* mix together" (*Silvae* 3.5.94). It offered the convenient prospect of a Hellenic *polis* qua theme park for many vacationing Roman elites of the late Republic and early Empire, who regularly went there to don Greek garments and play out for a brief time Grecian fantasies before returning safely to their civic identities and duties in Rome.[183] For Nero, however, the experience in Naples inaugurated a permanent vacation from the demands of Roman *civilitas*, a "Greek holiday" that did not cease upon his return to Rome, where he would make his first formal agonistic entrée as *citharoedus* several months later at the second Neronia of 65 CE. Naples would again offer itself to Nero as performative gateway between the Roman and the Greek world. It is possible that he participated in the citharodic *agôn* at the Sebasta in 66 as a first stop on his agonistic tour of Greece.[184] We are told that Naples was the first stop on his triumphant return from that tour, as it had sentimental value "because he had first debuted his art there" (*quod in ea primum artem protulerat*, Suetonius *Nero* 25.1). Dio Cassius 63.26.1–2 indicates that when Nero was informed of the revolt

---

[181] Augustus had attended the Sebasta soon before his death in the summer of 14 CE (Dio Cassius 55.10.9, 56.29.2; Suetonius *Augustus* 98.5).

[182] See e.g. Athenaeus 14.623d: Amoebus, a famous citharode of the third century BCE, earned one Attic talent for each public recital he gave in the theater at Athens.

[183] Strabo describes how both Greek intellectuals working in Rome and Roman citizens alike enjoyed ἡ ἐν Νεαπόλει διαγωγὴ ἡ Ἑλληνική 'the Hellenic lifestyle of Naples' (5.4.7). Further sources discussed in Bowersock 1965:81–84.

[184] Thus Geer 1935:215.

of Vindex, he was in Naples, attending to his voice, his songs, and his *kithara* playing. Perhaps another concert series there was in the offing.

Suetonius includes a significant detail in his account that further underlines the liminality of the first Naples appearance. In the days after the initial performance, when, encouraged by his success, Nero put on encore concerts, he had arranged for banquets to be laid out in the orchestra of the theater, where he would dine while the *populus* sat in the seats above him looking on. When he had finished eating, he would stand up and announce to the crowd—in Greek—his intention "to ring out something packed full [of sound]" (*aliquid suffer[t]i tinniturum*) for them after he had some wine (20.2).[185] With this put-on informality in this contrived convivial setting, it is as if Nero were attempting for the time being to underplay, with the narcissistic *grotesquerie* that characterized all his cultural endeavors, his professional ambitions by playing the role of an amateur lyre player, spontaneously singing for his peers over his cups. That is, Nero effects a "theatrical" casting of the theater—the open site of professional, public *citharodic* spectacle—as the symposium, which was in Classical Greek tradition the closed site of intimate, conventionally amateur *lyric* performance, what Nero himself calls *musica occulta*. (The literary and visual evidence suggest that symposiasts or their hired entertainers in Archaic and Classical Greece, at least in Athens, did not regularly play the *kithara*, as they did the smaller, more manageable lyre and *barbitos*.)[186] This travesty of a public as a private, a popular as an elite musical institution, draws its symbolic force from the deep ethical, political, and socioeconomic distinctions, going back to the fifth century BCE, between the demotic theater and the aristocratic symposium, even as, in typically Neronian fashion, it confounds and perverts those distinctions.

---

[185] On the emendation *sufferti* (for *sufferi*), see Borthwick 1965:252. Borthwick proposes yet another emendation, *se suffritinniturum*, which, he argues, would represent the Greek ὑποτερετίζειν used by Nero, presumably quoting a Greek poetic source, perhaps a sympotic song. The verb describes the singing of the cicada.

[186] At Xenophon *Symposium* 2.1, the verb *kitharizein* is used to describe the performance of a handsome boy at a drinking party. It is often translated as 'play the *kithara*', but Xenophon probably intends it to mean, as often, 'play the lyre' (see Maas and Snyder 1989:80–81). There were exceptional convivial events, however, at which *kitharai* could be heard. At the monarch's or tyrant's symposium, professional citharodes could provide entertainment, or symposia attended by sophisticated musical enthusiasts, some of whom would be sufficiently competent to play the *kithara* (see Power 2007). The citharode Amoebus—the namesake of the famous third-century BCE citharode—performs for fellow *mousikoi* and *literati* at the symposium that is the setting for Athenaeus' *Deipnosophistae* (14.623d).

The fusion of *kitharôidia* and symposium does find precedent in the courts of the Greek tyrants and monarchs who enticed star citharodes and citharists to provide entertainment at their private banquets, thereby conspicuously appropriating what would normally be a public cultural commodity for their personal consumption. Nero himself had, immediately upon assuming the principate, night after night summoned the great Terpnus to sing for him after dinner, while he sat close by (Suetonius *Nero* 20.1).[187]

It was this close study of Terpnus, Suetonius suggests, that led Nero, unlike Greek potentates before him, to move from being patron to performer, to begin his own formal training in *kitharôidia*. Even before his debut in Naples, the emperor had allowed his professional musical ambitions to be publicized abroad. He made appearances in full citharodic *skeuê* before select audiences, including the elite corps of knights called the Augustiani, at his Juvenalian Games, inaugurated in 59 BCE and held in consecutive years thereafter (Tacitus *Annals* 14.14–15; Dio Cassius 61.19–20), but these were exclusive, relatively small-scale events (*Annals* 15.33.1).[188] Otherwise, Nero confined himself to the liminal role of a "convivial citharode." Suetonius *Nero* 22.3 reports the following practice adopted by Nero:

> The cities in which *musici agones* were accustomed to be held had made it a rule to send all the crowns for *citharoedi* to him.[189] These he received so graciously that, not only did he grant an immediate audience to the envoys who brought them, but even invited them to his private table (*familiaribus epulis*). When he was asked by some of them to sing after dinner and received effusive applause, he declared that the Greeks were

---

[187] Under the Empire, however, other wealthy individuals likely retained cithaodes for their private entertainment as well. A character in the "Plutarchean" *On Music* (written around the second century CE), a rich man named Onesicrates, who hosts the symposium that the treatise narrates, pays a salary (*suntaxis*, 2.1131c) to Lysias, a χειρουργῶν κιθαρῳδός 'practicing citharode' (43.1146d).

[188] On Nero's Juvenalia, see Morford 1985:2019–2020. Nero did not take the stage alone at these events; members of the Roman aristocracy were encouraged (or forced) to participate in dramatic and musical (solo and choral) performances. But—important to note—Nero was the only performer who took the stage as a citharode. Dio Cassius describes Nero's performance as the climax of the event: he appears on stage in full *skeuê* and sings the *Attis* (or *Bacchae*) to the rapturous shouts of the Augustiani, who acclaim him a Pythian Apollo. But Dio also emphasizes amateurish details—Nero's advisors Seneca and Burrus prompting him from the wings and the weakness of his voice.

[189] Dio Cassius 61.21.2 says this custom began after the first Neronia of 60 CE.

the only ones who knew how to listen [to music] and that they
alone were worthy of his talents.

Note how the blurring of lines between the public culture of the *agônes*
and the enclosed world of the drinking party, would-be professionalism
and amateur enthusiasm, Greek and Roman, prefigures, with some
inversion, the semiotics of the Neapolitan performance event. There
the public theater takes on the trappings of an "intimate" convivium/
symposium; at Rome the emperor's private feast (*familiaribus epulis*)
becomes a quasi-theater in which he safely, invisibly plays at making
a spectacle of himself, singing to an audience of appreciative Greeks—
representatives by extension of the mass agonistic audience of their
polis, which has already awarded him the prize of victory.

iii. Roman performance anxieties

Nero's long delay in bringing his "hidden music" before the public at
large has been explained as a consequence of his awareness of others'
and his own internalization of aristocratic Roman prejudices against
public performance and professional performers in general. The
private or domestic cultivation of music or dramatics was largely unob-
jectionable, but an appearance in a public entertainment was a transgression against ancestral *mores*, a compromise of the integrity and
good standing, the *dignitas*, of the well-born citizen.[190] As writers both
ancient and modern observe, however, the strong proscription against
public performance could engender a dialectic of shame and titillation,
acting as both curb and incentive for "decadent" aristocrats such as
Nero bent on scenic adventure.[191] Tacitus *Annals* 14.15.1 believes that
Nero's personal sense of shame initially kept him out of the *publicum
theatrum*, but that over time, aroused by his own *evulgatus pudor* 'public
exposure' and psychologically liberated by the death of his controlling mother (*Annals* 14.13–14), his shame eroded and he became more
bold in making appearances on the *promiscae scaenae*, the "promiscuous," public stages of the city (*Annals* 15.33.1; cf. 14.14.2: a younger
Nero drove his chariot in a concealed area of the Vatican valley, *haud
promisco spectaculo* 'with the spectacle closed to a general audience').

---

[190] See Beacham 1999:208–211, 237–238.
[191] For representative modern views, see e.g. Champlin 2003:66–67 and Edwards 1994,
who argues too that transgressive stage play is empowering—a demonstration of the
individual's ability to transcend society's rules.

That Nero's performative debut was as a citharode, however, a relative novelty in Rome in his time, deserves special consideration when
we assess the contemporary reception of his stage career. Though few
would have been Roman citizens to begin with, there is no evidence
that *citharoedi* were officially subject to social and legal *infamia*, as were
actors and mimes, as well as prostitutes, with whom actors and mimes
were elided in the Roman cultural imagination.[192] Although many in
Rome, mass and elite, are likely to have conceptually and aesthetically
assimilated the citharode to more familiar *scaenici*, the actor and singer
(*histrio* and *tragoedus*), the fact that citharodes did not completely
submerge their identities in mimetic play was probably a factor in a
moral calculus differentiating them from actors. Acting by definition
aimed at total illusion and deception, the manipulation of perception
and reality, yet however much the citharode assumed mimetic postures
while singing and playing his songs, audiences, even inexperienced
ones, never lost sight of the grandiose persona of the virtuoso musician, possessed of an Apollonian *gravitas*, commanding the stage.

For a certain class of Roman cultural conservatives, however, the
public display of *kitharôidia* was just as egregiously immoral as acting; it
was a *foedum studium* 'debased pursuit', as Tacitus *Annals* 14.14.1 puts it,
that would disgrace anyone who undertook it, especially the emperor.
Thus the stern praetorian tribune Subrius Flavus, a member of the
anti-Neronian conspiracy of 65 BCE, equates the disgrace (*dedecus*)
of the emperor's *kithara* singing with that of the tragic singing once
performed by the conspiracy's leader, Gaius Calpurnius Piso; both men,
he suggests, have forfeited their right to lead, indeed to live, as a result
of their respective scenic engagements.[193] For Juvenal, the *citharoedus*

---

[192] See Edwards 1994:83–86 and 1997 on actors, prostitutes, and the social and legal
stigmas involved in *infamia*. We may note that practitioners of Nero's primary
athletic pursuit, chariot driving, were similarly exempt from *infamia* (Tertullian *On
Spectacles* 22). Chariot racing was, however, less objectionable than singing to the
kithara. Seneca and Burrus had encouraged a young Nero to drive his chariot (in a
semi-private setting in the Vatican valley) to distract him from pursuing his citharodic ambitions (Tacitus *Annals* 14.14.2).

[193] Tacitus *Annals* 15.65: "In terms of the disgrace, it made no difference if a citharode
were removed and a tragic singer succeeded him, because, as Nero sang to the *cithara*,
so Piso sang in tragic costume." It is possible that when Flavus later tells Nero that he
began to despise him when Nero "became a chariot driver, a *histrio*, and an arsonist"
(*Annals* 15.67.2), he means *histrio* not as a literal description of the emperor's acting,
but as a denigrating metaphor for his citharodic persona—Nero *citharoedus* was no
better than common *histrio* 'actor' (cf. *Annals* 15.59.2, where Flavus imagines Nero as
a cowardly *scaenicus*). Dio Cassius 62.24.2 alternately has Flavus telling Nero that he
could not endure being a slave to a κιθαρῳδός (no mention of acting). Cf. Woodman
1993:125.

princeps had so lowered standards of social decorum that the spectacle of a nobleman playing in one of the lowest of entertainments, the mime, was now *res haut mira* 'a sight hardly surprising' (8.198–199); the satirist goes so far as to figure the citharode as a prostitute (6.380 and 8.25–26). According to the hard-line conservative reaction to Nero's institution of the Neronia, even listening as a connoisseur (*perite*) to the *fractos sonos et dulcedinem vocum* 'effeminate strains and sweet voices' of agonistic musicians fatally compromises the political fitness of the Roman citizen (Tacitus *Annals* 14.20.5).[194]

However, among others more liberally inclined to appreciate the Hellenic performing arts, some of whom, like the sometime-*tragoedus* Piso, themselves cultivated lyre playing (though probably never full-blown public *kitharôidia*), it was surely accorded a respect commensurate to that which it enjoyed in Hellenic culture, at least in the abstract.[195] Nero's attempt to legitimate his professional ambitions by appealing to the statues of Apollo *kitharôidos* that stood both in Greek cities and in Roman temples (Tacitus *Annals* 14.14.1), thereby assimilating them to a prestigious (and Augustan-ratified) musico-symbolic continuity between the two cultures, may be read as a rhetorical ploy designed to appease just these philhellenic connoisseurs. Seneca's early attempt in the *Apocolocyntosis* to valorize Nero's lyric enthusiasms by having a *cithara*-playing Apollo announce to the Fates that Nero would be his "equal in song and voice" (*nec cantu nec uoce minor*, 4.1) may have been intended to make an analogous impression on this discerning audience

---

[194] Tacitus seems to voice this conservative Roman reaction within a conservative Greek discursive frame: the ethos theory of music, which goes back, via Plato, to the Athenian sophist Damon of Oa. The theory holds that musical sound can actually shape the character of its auditor for better or worse. See Anderson 1966. The ethical danger of "effeminizing" music is a recurring preoccupation of ethos theory, both in its vernacular and intellectual expressions (e.g. Aristophanes *Women at the Thesmophoria* 130–145; Plato *Republic* 398e–399a, *Laws* 802d; Aristides Quintilianus *On Music* 2.16; cf. Csapo 2004:230–232). Its proponents argued too that music could effect changes in the body politic as well as the individual, which is the argument Tacitus is channeling here. There is Damon's famous credo, quoted by Socrates in Plato *Republic* 424c: "Nowhere are the styles of music altered without change in the greatest laws (*nomoi*) of the *polis*."

[195] Piso's lyre playing is the subject of fourteen fascinating lines in the poem known as the *Praise of Piso* (163–177; on the poem, see Griffin 1984:148). The anonymous poet is careful to specify that Piso plays the amateur's tortoise-shell lyre (*testudo, chelys, lyra*) rather than the *cithara*, and that he does so "without shame" (169, 171), following the example of Achilles, whose musical interests complemented his martial glories. That so large a chunk of the panegyric is devoted to the lyre, however, suggests that Piso took seriously his lyric culture, and may even have harbored quasi-professional ambitions similar to Nero's, if not as grand.

as well. But the success of such transparent propagandizing was surely limited, for the combination of the emperor's seemingly feckless abdication of political responsibility with his embarrassingly open turn to music professionalism offended not only conservative Romans, but even more open-minded elites, those, like Piso, well versed in the protocols of Greek lyric culture, who themselves dabbled in trying on public musical personae, if less visibly and so less transgressively than the emperor.[196]

Traditional Roman severity did no doubt play a part in shaping Nero's "performance anxiety," but there is something psychologically and culturally reductive about applying to him the shame/titillation dynamic—a bashful yet overstimulated Nero tests the waters of tolerance little by little in his increasingly brazen quest to flaunt corrupt Greek manners. In some instances there is clearly an element of wishful thinking to it, an ideologically satisfying affirmation of the inveterate power of strict Roman *mores* to censure even Nero's cravenly Greekish perversity. Such framing of Nero's public *kitharôidia* within a tension between Greek id and repressive Roman superego informs one interpretation of the motive for Nero's command that the Roman general Corbulo, an axiom of ancestral *virtus*—Nero calls him *pater* 'father', an appropriately Oedipal touch—be slain immediately upon his arrival in Corinthian Cenchreae, where the emperor, preparing for his agonistic tour of Greece, had summoned him. "Some say," reports Dio Cassius 63.17.5, that Nero, who was about to appear as a citharode, could not bear to be seen by the military man while he was wearing his citharodic costume (the long, straight chiton, or ὀρθοστάδιον), and so had Corbulo killed before he could witness the embarrassment. This conflicted Nero simultaneously wants to show off for and yet must still keep his music "hidden" from the judgmental paternal eye of Corbulo. For Tacitus, by contrast, Nero's initial inability to perform was a symptom of his mother complex (*Annals* 14.13.3–14.14.1). Only after the murder of Agrippina in 59 did he feel psychically unencumbered to

---

[196] Champlin 2003:66 probably goes too far in saying that "Nero [qua performing musician] could count on considerable sympathy among the [artistically inclined] leaders of society." Another senatorial opponent of Nero, Thrasea Paetus, like Piso, *tragico ornatu canebat* 'sang in tragic costume' (Tacitus *Annals* 15.65.2; Dio Cassius 62.26.3 says the occasion was a local festival in Thrasea's native Patavium, not the professionally tainted spectacle games in Rome). His fatal refusal to indulge Nero's *kitharôidia* may have been as much an ethical resistance to irresponsible *mousikê* as irresponsible politics. Cf. Beacham 1999: "Thrasea infuriated the emperor because, far from being ignorant or dismissive of the fine arts, he was actually something of a connoisseur; it was Nero's art that he disdained" (242).

indulge *omnis libidines* 'all his desires', musical and otherwise. In reality, however, Nero's dedication to *kitharôidia* was hardly, for him, an irrational, guilty pleasure or a seductive taboo, the illicit thrill of defying societal prohibition—acting or dancing would have better satisfied the craving for self-debasement. We might argue instead that it represents a far more thoroughly considered and seriously studied aspect of his complex engagement with Greek culture than the almost uniformly hostile ancient sources acknowledge. As such, we might better explain his reticence in making his public (and professional) debut against the deeper background of Greek ideology concerning musical performance rather than as a conditioned response to Roman moralism alone.[197]

10. Popular Music and its (Greek) Discontents

As a close reader of Hellenic musical traditions, Nero was surely aware of a distinctly Greek tradition of elite bias, going back to the later Classical period, not against *kitharôidia* per se, but against the "vulgarity" of its star performers, and indeed music celebrities of every stripe, which would have problematized his own desire to emulate those very performers.[198] This bias first emerged as a reaction to the rise of the hyperprofessionalized "star system" that drove popular musical culture in democratic Athens, although it continued to inform upper-class Greek attitudes toward musicians long after that historical moment. Certain educated aristocrats resented the celebrity and influence of virtuoso *tekhnitai* of indiscriminate social and ethnic background, who were, in collusion with their unrestrained demotic audiences, responsible for precipitating a crisis of the traditional spiritual and civic values of public *mousikê*, in particular the venerated, Apollonian medium of *kitharôidia*—or so went the elitist narrative, which is most furiously plotted in Plato's account of what he calls

---

[197] His reticence had a practical rather than ideological basis as well, but one again defined by Greek rather than Roman considerations: Nero, for all his apparent self-delusion and bouts of musical megalomania (e.g. Suetonius *Nero* 41.1), was serious about his *tekhnê*. He knew what professional achievement in it sounded like, and he could have simply been reluctant to perform in public alongside professionals before he felt fully confident to compete at that level. (Recall that the Naples performance was non-competitive.) Cf. Bradley 1978:124.

[198] Romans did not always recognize this Greek bias, but sought rather to distinguish "us Romans" from "those Greeks" with respect to just this proscription of public performance. See the classically reductive contrast in the prologue to Cornelius Nepos *Lives* (5).

theatrokratia in *Laws* 698a–701b. By this account, the "*aristokratia* in music" (701a) that held sway in Athens down until the Persian Wars weakened as the fifth century drew on and the *polis* became increasingly democratized; the power of the uneducated mass of theater spectators in determining the value of and so ultimately affecting the form of competitive musical events accordingly grew, as did popular musicians' interest in meeting (and shaping) the tastes of this lowest common denominator.[199] For Plato's Socrates, the agonistic *kitharistikê* and *kitharôidia* of his day—as practiced by opportunistic professionals such as the citharode Meles, the father of the populist composer of "new dithyramb," Cinesias, a *bête noire* of the musically conservative elite (and singled out by Socrates for criticism, *Gorgias* 501e)—are thus no better than tragedy and dithyramb, those Dionysian genres fundamentally identified with the ignoble Athenian democracy. Like these, they aim solely at producing sensual pleasure (*hêdonê*) rather than goodness in the *okhlos* 'mob' of spectators; they are nothing more than forms of *kolokeia* 'pandering' (*Gorgias* 501e–502c).

Later writers such as Aristotle in turn endorse a politicized, class-based segregation of the experience of the "vulgar" agonistic musician (a *banausos*, literally 'manual laborer'), who plays in the public spaces of music halls and theaters for the common *hêdonê* of the "low audience made up of *banausoi*, hired workers (*thêtai*), and the like," from music used for education, amateur recreation, and relaxation, i.e. sympotic or paideutic lyric, played at home or in the schoolroom by the "free and educated" (ἐλεύθερος καὶ πεπαιδευμένος). The *kithara*, a *tekhnikon organon*, has no place in proper *paideia*, and virtuoso posturing (τὰ θαυμάσια καὶ περιττὰ τῶν ἔργων 'marvelous and excessively elaborate devices'), at home in the *agônes*, brings dishonor to the discreet gentleman *mousikos*. The days before and immediately after the Persian Wars, when aristocrats in Athens and Sparta would attempt to display their *aretê* 'excellence' in public performance, playing instruments alongside trained professionals, were now unimaginable. The noble form, the *kalokagathia*, of the aristocrat was now seen to be at odds with the entertainer's gross, "banausic" body, deformed as it was through his attempts to satisfy the gaze of the equally debased

[199] Cf. "Plutarch" *On Music* 12.1135c, probably quoting Aristoxenus: "[The New Music composers] Crexus, Timotheus, Philoxenus, and the composers who were their contemporaries were excessively low-brow (φορτικώτεροι) and attached to novelty, pursuing the style that is nowadays called crowd-pleasing (φιλάνθρωπον) and money-making (θεματικόν)." On the latter term, referring to valuable prizes won at "thematic" contests, see Pollux *Onomasticon* 3.153, with Barker 1984:218n95.

masses.[200] Indeed, even the hallowed image of Apollo *kitharôidos*, once the supreme symbol of aristocratic excellence and mastery, became ideologically problematic for Greek elites of the later fifth and fourth centuries BCE who sought to distance their own lyric culture from the professionalized milieu of *kitharôidia*; the god's *kithara* and elaborate *skeuê* now carried undesirable socioeconomic connotations. An amateur's lyre and a simple himation were more in order.[201]

Aristotle's student, Aristoxenus of Tarentum, refers to the music performed in the theaters of his time as πάνδημος μουσική, which we may take to mean something along the lines of 'music belonging to the *dêmos* as a whole, meeting public taste indiscriminately', but which also implies "prostituted music" (fr. 124 Wehrli by way of Athenaeus 14.632a–b).[202] Recalling Aristotle's strict partitioning of public and private musical practice, Aristoxenus idealizes a group of embattled elites who cling to the symposium and its old-fashioned musical protocols as a last defense against this pandemic music of the *theatra*,

---

[200] I summarize here the arguments in Aristotle *Politics* 8.1339a–1342a; cf. already Aristophanes *Clouds* 967–972. Aristotle's critique of the "banausic" professionalism of *mousikoi agônes* is illuminated by *Rhetoric* 1.9.1367a32-33. Ober 1989:277 paraphrases: "A man not carrying on a banausic trade (*tekhnê*) was shown to be a free man (*eleutheros*) because he need not 'live for the sake of another'." Both the agonistic performer and his audience are people "living for the sake of another," and so each complements the other. The Damonian ethos theory of music (cf. n194 above), maintained in various forms by Plato, Aristotle, and Aristoxenus, provided the intellectual justification for such snobbery—musical sound was politically and ethically *dangerous* if left uncontrolled by the elite. Ford 2004 is a valuable discussion of Aristotle's conception of the place of *mousikê* in elite *paideia*.

[201] See Sarti 1992. It is important to note that there is no Classical use of the term lyrode, *lurôidos* 'lyre singer' attested, and the term very likely was not used during the Classical period at all (cf. Winnington-Ingram 1988:250). This is no doubt because a certain incompatibility was felt between the connotations of expertise and professionalism that would attend *lurôidos* (cf. *kitharôidos*) and the amateur practice and ideology of the lyre.

[202] For the implications of prostitution in the term, see Gulick 1937:411, who sees an allusion to the "vulgar" Eros or Aphrodite of Plato *Symposium* 180e, 181a. On the fragment, see Meriani 2003:15–48. Aristoxenus alludes as well to the neutral phrase δημώδης μουσική 'popular music' at Plato *Phaedo* 61a7, which Socrates uses to describe his recent settings to the lyre of some *logoi* 'tales' of Aesop and a *prooimion* to Apollo. He deploys this language in a typically ironic fashion, however, deprecating his own humble efforts through mock self-aggrandizement. Despite the fact that he is preparing what amounts to a traditional cithadoric performance—a *prooimion* to Apollo, followed by a sung narrative *logos*—Socrates is of course no cithadore making music for the people; his lyric *mousikê* is truly amateur and will remain apocryphal, hidden away from the *dêmos* at large. At the same time, he uses the phrase with some derision: Socrates' true art, the rarified practice of philosophical dialectic, which to his mind is the ultimate form of *mousikê* (μεγίστη μουσική, 61a3–4), implicitly stands at the opposite pole from the "real" δημώδης μουσική his lyric dabblings parody.

which he claims have been "utterly barbarized" (ἐκβεβαρβάρωται). The popular musician is thus, by implication, socially, ethnically, and sexually "othered" in the strongest possible terms, as barbarian and prostitute. This is an extremely reactionary view, far from the admiration and respect shown by mass and elite alike to career musicians, especially citharodes, in early Greece—paradigmatic is Odysseus' high praise of the professional *aoidos* Demodocus in *Odyssey* 8.437–438—and it is unlikely to have been held in anything like this absolutist form by Aristoxenus' peers, and probably not even always by Aristoxenus himself. But it does reflect, in distorted form, a more pervasive and less ideologically motivated stereotyping of citharodes (not to mention auletes and other music professionals) as soft, effeminate, vaguely immoral, given over to excessive luxury, notionally, if not actually, "foreign."

Traces of these attitudes are to be found throughout Old and New Attic comedy—indeed, comic discourse must have been enormously influential in shaping popular perceptions of the citharode. Such stereotyping, along with reflexive suspicions of their wealth and cosmopolitan lifestyle, worked to stigmatize career musicians, making them to some extent outsiders and deviants in their own communities—a status their itineracy and the "eastern" flair of their *skeuê* only invited—even as their extraordinary talents and glamorous personae won them fame, prestige, the devotion of a wide fan base, and the intimate patronage of kings and tyrants.[203] In his fragmentary comedy *Kitharistês*, Menander dramatizes, and complicates, prevalent Athenian notions about the otherness of music professionals. The rich, world-traveling, and presumably famous citharist Phanias—he has spent considerable time making money in the Greek East—is criticized by another character,

---

[203] Relevant here are the negative characterizations of the Hellenistic *tekhnitai* of Dionysus ("Aristotle" *Problems* 30.10; Theopompus FGrH 115 F 2 *ap.* Athenaeus 6.254b), and their own repeated attempts at self-legitimation. See Lightfoot 2002:218–219. I take this opportunity to note that citharodes do not seem to have been prominent members of the various guilds of Dionysian Artists. A review of the 200-plus post-Classical citharodes listed in Stephanis 1988 yields only five who are explicitly connected to a guild (nos. 15, 1023, 1025, 1661, 2071). Ma 2007:231, 241 argues reasonably that the Phocaean citharode Demetrius son of Menippus (Stephanis no. 636), mentioned in two Tean victor lists from the third and second centuries BCE, was an official in the *Koinon* of the Artists of Ionia and the Hellespont, although we cannot be sure of this, as the inscriptions do not make it clear. Perhaps citharodes were generally in a better position, economically and politically, to operate as free agents than the primarily dramatic and choral-based performers who assembled in the guilds. The obviously Dionysiac character of the genres and performances put on by the artists may also have acted to exclude the notionally Apollonian citharodes.

probably his upper-class neighbor, for "making a life study of luxu-rious excess" (εἰς τρυφήν τε παυδεύεσθ' ἀεί, fr. 5.2 Körte)—this despite the fact that, outside of his rather exotic career, Phanias seems to be a rather sober, conventional Athenian citizen, a member of the Attic deme Euonymon (and not of the tribe of Euonymeans in faraway, deca-dent Ephesus, as the conservative neighbor first thinks, 96–98).[204] Nine Middle and New comedies entitled *Kitharôidos* are attested.[205] Though fragments are lacking, it is a fair guess that these plays similarly capi-talized on the ambivalent fascination with the star citharode in fourth- and third-century BCE Athens, dramatizing stereotypes both positive and negative.[206] We will examine further the ambivalent representa-tion of citharodes in Old Comedy in Part IV.

For the majority of higher-status Greeks of the later-Classical through Imperial periods an idealization of traditional, aristocratic musical *paideia*, the *musica occulta* of schoolroom and symposium, and a concomitant wariness toward the popular music culture could have coexisted alongside a demotic fascination with "vulgar" musical celeb-rities (although the idea of actually training to become an agonistic musician was in either case well beyond the pale, socially unimagi-nable). For instance, Dio Chrysostom—an oratorical "pop star" in his own right—is able to condemn snobbishly the theater audiences of Alexandria for their slavish devotion to supposedly unmusical, "canine" citharodic stars, and to remind them of the moral and aesthetic supe-riority of the bygone *arkhaia mousikê* (32.61–62), while in another

---

[204] Cf. Arnott 1979:139. The neighbor's recognition that Phanias is not so very different from himself may have been integral to the play's ending, in which, the fragments suggest, the neighbor's son Moschion was permitted to marry Phanias' daughter. The daughter was herself a victim of a misconception, being initially identified as an Ephesian rather than Athenian (and so unmarriageable). The suture of socioeco-nomic difference and the righting of culturally conditioned misperceptions about character are features of New Comedy's "philanthropic" mission; cf. the conclusion of the *Dyskolos*.

[205] By Alexis, Anaxippus, Antiphanes, Apollodorus, Clearchus, Diphilus, Nicon, Sophilus, and Theophilus. Cf. Cooper 1920:52; Arnott 1996:292.

[206] Ambivalent attitudes toward professional musician as other, subaltern, or deviant, yet enviably talented, sexually attractive, and socially indispensable are well attested cross-culturally in the anthropological and ethnomusicological literature. See e.g. the classic work of Merriam 1979 and 1964:123–144 on musicians among the Basongye of Zaire ("[T]he attitude toward musicians among the Basongye is ambiva-lent; on the one hand, they can be ordered about, and they are people whose values and behavior do not accord with what is proper in the society; on the other hand, their role and function in the village are so important that life without them is incon-ceivable," 1964:136); Becker 1951, on American jazz musicians; Leppert 1993:153–187, on the representation of the musician as effeminate, ethically dubious outsider in nineteenth-century European art and literature.

speech professing his own admiration for modern-day citharodes who whip crowds into frenzy (19.1–4). We might see this Greek ideological ambivalence, rather than a monolithic case of Roman "performance anxiety," being negotiated in Nero's schizoid play with sympotic and professional musical identities in Naples, before a largely Greek audience, or in his theatrical after-dinner performances before the Greek emissaries at his Roman court.

Dio Cassius 62.21.2–3 reports an anecdote that, even if apocryphal or, as it certainly is, exaggerated, reflects Nero's insistence on maintaining a fictive amateur status, even when his musical practice had long since crossed the publicly acknowledged line into the realm of the professional musician. It foregrounds the critical issue of remuneration in status differentiation, an issue that is as much Greek as Roman.[207] After his return to Rome from the triumphant tour of Greece, the emperor is approached by a wealthy Lydian named Larcius, who offers him one million sesterces to give a citharodic concert. Nero rebuffs the Lydian's miscalculated flattery, as "he disdained doing anything for pay (*misthos*)." Larcius is allowed to live, but only after he pays the million sesterces to Nero's freedman Tigellinus as restitution for the dishonor. Nero goes on to give (gratis) citharodic and tragodic performances in the city. On the one hand, this little drama plays as critique, giving the lie to Nero's claims to amateur status, and suggesting that his de facto professionalism, even if not explicitly remunerated, is in line with the crass avarice that mars his principate. On the other, it could be read (the Tigellinus sequel aside), and was perhaps originally circulated to serve, as a demonstrative vindication of Nero's commitment to amateurism, from a distinctly aristocratic Greek vantage point. Larcius is, notably, a Lydian.[208] The (exploitable) accident of his ethnicity evokes a bit of musical lore recorded in Herodotus 1.155.4. The historian indicates that the Lydians, traditionally thought to be the inventors of coinage, early on conflated music making and commercial professionalism, to

---

[207] See Nagy 1989:135 on the problem of *misthos* 'wage' for poets and musicians, with Will 1975.

[208] The name A. Larcius Lydus is epigraphically attested in Rome (inscribed on a water-pipe); the Roman senator Larcius Macedo, whose violent death at the hands of his slaves is related in Pliny *Letters* 3.14, was probably his son. See Bradley 1978:134, who argues that the elder Larcius is the praetor mentioned in a variant of Dio's anecdote recorded in Suetonius *Nero* 21.2, though this seems unlikely (see Champlin 2003:290). In the Suetonian version, an unnamed praetor offers Nero a million sesterces to perform *inter scaenicos* 'among the stage players' in a *spectaculum* he was organizing. In contrast to Dio's account, here Nero does not reject the offer outright, but considers accepting it.

negative effect; Croesus had encouraged Cyrus to render the once-manly Lydians soft and compliant by having them teach their sons "to play the *kithara*, pluck the harp, and *kapêleuein* 'practice retail trade'." The aetiology of musical show business is thus conveniently displaced onto the morally suspect ethnic other. Nero's refusal of the fee—offered by the Lydian, for whom such transactions are "natural"—speaks to his desire to keep his own *kitharôidia* out of this corrupting sphere of monetary exchange, even as he rewards favorites such as the citharode Menecrates with enormous *misthos* (Suetonius *Nero* 30.2), or, more insidiously, if the account is true, as he pays Roman nobles to disgrace themselves on the public stage as mimes and actors (Tacitus *Annals* 14.14.4).[209]

Contempt for musical professionalism worked its way too into the Hellenistic and Imperial discourse on kingly *paideia*, which has specific relevance to Nero's experience. Aristotle *Politics* 8.1339b8 supplies the grounding precedent: "In poetry Zeus does not himself sing and play the *kithara*." Thus the anecdotal traditions about a young Alexander's (that tutee of Aristotle) being given free rein by his *kitharistês*, since strict lyre lessons benefitted one who planned to play the *kithara* as his *tekhnê*, not one who would be king (Aelian *Historical Miscellanies* 3.32), or, alternately, being chastised by his father Philip ὅτι δεξιῶς τε καὶ ἐμμελῶς ἐκιθάρισεν 'because he played the lyre too skillfully and tune-fully'; according to Philip, it was "shameful for the noble-born man to make a show of himself among the rabble for the purpose of winning acclaim" (Nicephorus Gregoras *Roman History* 1.454). Nicephorus is late, but the story is ancient. Plutarch *Life of Pericles* 1.5–6 has Philip reproach Alexander when he comes upon his son playing the lyre ἐπιτερπῶς ... καὶ τεχνικῶς 'too charmingly and skillfully', "Are you not ashamed to pluck the lyre so well?" (Plutarch uses the verb ψάλλειν 'to pluck', which typically denotes harp playing; its force here is probably less technical than ethical, underlining the inappropriate excess of Alexander's lyre playing by assimilating it to the harp, which was not as a rule played by aristocratic male amateurs in Greece.) Kings, Philip

---

[209] Nero had for the first time instituted contests in *tragôidia* and *kitharôidia* at Olympia in 67 CE, a highly controversial move. Philostratus' Apollonius of Tyana, scandalized at this, scoffs that at Olympia there was neither theater nor stage, only a natural stadium and naked athletes (*Life of Apollonius of Tyana* 5.7), thereby drawing an implicit contrast between this true aristocratic amateurism and the pomp and finery associated with the professionalized *mousikoi agônes* at chrematitic festivals. But perhaps we could view Nero's musical intervention at the Olympic Games not as a thoughtless act of cultural disrespect, but as a deliberate (yet incidentally disrespectful) attempt to invest competitive musicality with the amateur ethos of Olympic sport.

reminds his son, are more fit to be auditors and spectators of *agôn-istai*.[210] Philip himself is implicated in a series of anecdotes in which he too earnestly debates a professional harpist (*psaltês*) on a technical matter, only to have the harpist remind him that, as king, the matter is well beneath his dignity (Plutarch *Moralia* 67f, 179b, 334c–d, 634d). Similarly, the citharist Stratonicus of Athens cuts short a debate with King Ptolemy over *kitharistikê*, admonishing him that "It is one thing to hold the *skêptron* 'scepter'," and leaving him to fill in the rhyming phrase, "another to hold the *plêktron*" (Athenaeus 8.350c).

In these (apocryphal) stories it is the subaltern musician who must remind the king of music's proper place in the social hierarchy— a good reflection of how reflexively ingrained the ideological distinction between professionalism and noble amateurism had become. Just as Nero surely appreciated that in Greek myth and history political power and the *kithara* had long kept company—Alexander himself was, as his father legendarily advised, an adept spectator and auditor, and a dedicated patron of professional musicians, above all the famous citharode Aristonicus (*On the Fortune of Alexander* 334d–335a)—and that citharodic music had long served as a traditional symbolic resource for the articulation of political power and organization, so must he also have realized that his flamboyantly performative conflation of *skêptron* and *plêktron*, remunerated or not, was extraordinarily transgressive, an utter confounding of proper social and symbolic order and identity, in terms not only of Roman attitudes, but of elite Greek musico-political thought as well.[211]

---

[210] Legend has it that Alexander possessed the instrument of his idol Achilles, the paradigmatic aristocratic lyric amateur (Plutarch *On the Fortune of Alexander* 331d; cf. *Life of Alexander* 15.9; cf. Veneri 1995:129). Dio Chrysostom *On Kingship* 2.28 imagines Alexander saying that he wants only to learn the *lura* or *kithara* well enough to sing hymns to the gods and passages of Homer. (Could the unexpected inclusion of the *kithara* in Alexander's decidedly amateur curriculum be Dio's subtle swipe at Nero?) Alexander's real-life lyric skill, however, was apparently negligible, or at least such was the gossip; Demosthenes made mean jokes about it in Athens (Aeschines *Against Timarchus* 169). The general lyric incompetence of the (constitutionally uncultured) Macedonians forms the basis of a humorous anecdote involving the witty citharist Stratonicus and his inept Macedonian student (Athenaeus 8.351b).

[211] Cf. Edwards 1997:90. See Section 14 below.

11. Nero *Citharoedus* in Rome

i. Neronia

In 60 CE Nero took a significant step toward making his honorary agonistic victories abroad a reality at home. In the most demonstratively Hellenizing act of his principate to date, he instituted for the first time in Rome athletic and musical *agônes* modeled after the major quinquennial games of Greece.[212] These Neronia featured of course a contest in *kitharôidia*, which was the city's first formal venue for professional cithardic performance, and, we may suppose, was the primary *raison d'être* for the festival itself—it would provide a legitimating "Greco-Roman" stage for the emperor's *tekhnê*. However, although Nero was honorarily awarded the first prize in the contest by the unanimous verdict of the judges, a body of ex-consuls whom he had appointed, he did not perform, choosing instead to sit among the senators and follow the proceedings as a spectator.[213] His Roman debut would take place several years later, at the second Neronia, not long after the dry run in Naples. Suetonius and Tacitus offer variant accounts of the circumstances of the debut.[214] Suetonius *Nero* 21 says that Nero, "considering it of great importance to sing in Rome" as well as in Naples, held the Neronia in the summer of 64, before its appointed date in 65. (Nero would reschedule the sacred contests during his grand tour of Greece as well, a sacrilegious disregard for tradition that betrays the self-serving agenda behind his grandiose philhellenism.) At the games, the *vulgus* clamored for the emperor's "divine voice," but he initially demurred, promising he would sing for those who wished to hear him *in hortis*, presumably in the same private gardens where he had performed at the Juvenalia—again, an awkward attempt at a compromise between the amateur and the professional, private and public. Then, in what looks like a prearranged ruse, the praetorian guard added to the entreaties. At this he acquiesced; *sine mora* 'without delay' he had his name registered as a contestant, and, in a characteristically overdone

---

[212] Suetonius *Nero* 12.3; Tacitus *Annals* 14.20–21. On the games, see Caldelli 1993:37–43; on their Hellenizing ambience, see Champlin 2003:72.

[213] Suetonius *Nero* 12.3, who says that Nero dedicated the crown to Augustus (see discussion below). Dio Cassius 61.21.2 offers a more hostile, and probably less reliable account: the citharodes' contest was entirely canceled and the crown automatically awarded to Nero. Dio adds too the colorful detail that Nero wore his *skeuê* when he went to the gymnasium to have his *faux* victory officially recorded.

[214] Cf. Champlin 2003:74–75; Bolton 1948.

gesture of "fairness," cast his lot along with the others' into the urn that randomly determined the order of performances.[215] Nero entered the theater with a grand retinue, his *kithara* carried by the praetorian prefects, and performed at great length a piece called the *Niobe*. After his own performance, however, Nero deferred the awarding of the citharodic prize, and the other contests, until the next year, *ut saepius canendi occasio esset* 'that there might be further occasions for singing'.

Tacitus *Annals* 16.4 says nothing about this advance performance, and indeed it is hard to square with his account, which has the second Neronia taking place as scheduled and strongly implies that Nero had not previously made any sort of public appearance as citharode in Rome. Tacitus emphasizes the emperor's definitive crossing of the line between the private and public spheres, although on this occasion too there is a simulated informality to the debut that suggests still a deliberate negotiation of amateur and professional musical personae. Tacitus reports that the emperor at first seemed willing only to recite a *carmen* from the stage, without musical accompaniment. Nero had presented such poetic recitations in the theater on previous occasions, although not in competition.[216] But recitation was not enough; he was rallied by the crowd to perform competitively as a citharode. The *vulgus* loudly demanded *ut omnia studia sua publicaret* 'that he make public display of all of his talents' (Tacitus reports the crowd's exact words). Not surprisingly, conservative forces in the Senate had tried to forestall Nero's public performance by preemptively awarding him the crown of victory in *kitharôidia*, as had happened at the first Neronia, "in order

---

[215] Timaeus FGrH 566 F 43b *ap.* Strabo 6.1.9 indicates that the first slot in the order was the most desirable, and that disputes and special pleading could arise over its assignment. At the Pythian contest, Timaeus has it, the citharode Ariston of Rhegium demanded that he go first, despite his second-place draw, because Rhegium had been a Delphian colony. The proverbial phrase "After the Lesbian Singer" derived from the tradition in Sparta, established to commemorate Terpander of Antissa, of honorarily according citharodic competitors from Lesbos the lead positions in the line-up at the Carneian *agôn* (Aristotle fr. 545 Rose). Why the lead-off slot was considered best by citharodes is unclear; perhaps it was merely a question of prestige. By contrast, at the Athenian dramatic contests it seems to have been seen as a liability to a play's success. Aristophanes *Assembly Women* 1161–1162 warns the judges not to forget his comedy, which was staged first, in the manner of "bad prostitutes" who recall only their latest clients.

[216] Suetonius *Nero* 10.2. The poem that Nero recited at the Neronia could have been an excerpt from his Latin epic, *Troica*, which Dio Cassius 62.29.1 says he recited at a public festival in 65. Cf. Champlin 2003:290n78. The public recitation of poetry was less objectionable than public music making, as Fantham 1996:156 notes: "[I]t seems very likely that he resorted to the poetry of recitation and the book only until he felt free to practice the less dignified and more exciting musical art of the singer."

that the unseemliness of his participation in the games might be veiled over" (*ut ludicra deformitas velaretur*).[217] But on this occasion, Nero, no doubt buoyed by his successful run in Naples—rejecting the preemptive offer of the prize by boasting he was now *aequum adversum aemulo* 'equal to his rivals'—would not accommodate senatorial austerity. His *musica* would no longer remain *occulta* in Rome, performed only in the private setting of the Juvenalian Games, a venue too restricted for "so great a voice" (*tantae voci, Annals* 15.33.1). The emperor would have his official "coming out" as a Greek-style agonistic *citharoedus* in the heart of the *urbs*.[218] Tacitus indicates that Nero played this long-deferred role as if born to it: as he sings, he follows all the rules of the contest, as a seasoned competitor would; then, while awaiting the verdict of the judges on bended knee, *ficto pavore* 'with pretended anxiety', he salutes the audience with his hand, an admirably dramatic touch that is met with appropriately dramatic, and musical, rounds of applause: "And the common people of the city, who were accustomed to encourage the gestures even of actors, began to resound with measured rounds of rhythmic applause. You would think they were pleased, and perhaps they were pleased, in their lack of concern for public disgrace."[219]

Despite Tacitus' reflexive cynicism—all is pretense, dissimulation, etc.—the mass audience viewing the Neronia probably was quite pleased, and uncynically so, with the emperor's performance; the insistent demands to witness it certainly seem genuine enough.[220] Indeed, the historian feels compelled to underplay the positive reaction of the urban *plebs* by reminding us that this crowd is accustomed to celebrate with similar enthusiasm every gesture of the actors, *histriones*. The passing remark carries a double critical charge: first, that the favor of the rabble comes cheap and indiscriminately; and second, that Nero, despite his claims to the Hellenic prestige of *kitharôidia*, is essentially a common *histrio*, merely play acting at being a citharode—a theme that recurs elsewhere in the anti-Neronian discourse—and so deserving

---

[217] Tacitus *Annals* 16.4. Suetonius *Vitellius* 4 has the future emperor Vitellius, who is supervising the games, intercede directly with Nero as an "envoy of an insistent *populus*" to persuade him to perform in the theater as a citharode. Cf. Beacham 1999:230.

[218] For the elitist counterclaim that Nero should have kept his music hidden, see Philostratus *Life of Apollonius of Tyana* 5.6.2.

[219] Tacitus *Annals* 16.4.4: *et plebs quidem urbis, histrionum quoque gestus iuvare solita, personabat certis modis plausuque composito. crederes laetari, ac fortasse laetabantur per incuriam publici flagitii.*

[220] Cf. Bartsch 1994:29, who notes that Tacitus does not qualify this initial enthusiasm.

of this worthless acclaim.[221] But Tacitus hits incidentally on a social reality. The Greek culture of *kitharôidia* had before Nero's principate made few solid inroads at Rome; although the professional citharode had long thrilled Greek audiences, to the majority of Roman citizens his presence was marginal and his charisma foreign. Nero's comment to the Greek emissaries at his table, that "the Greeks were the only ones who knew how to listen [to music] and that they alone were worthy of his talents" (*solos scire audire Graecos solosque se et studiis suis dignos*, Suetonius *Nero* 22.3), sounds like an idle boast by way of cheap flattery, but if, as it seems, Nero means that in his time only Greeks were true connoisseurs of citharodic music, it stands as a more or less accurate assessment. A passage of Tacitus suggests that at the first Neronia the *plebs* showed little enthusiasm for the musical contests (which prominently featured citharodes), since their beloved pantomimes were barred from the official program (*Annals* 14.21.4). Five years later, the *plebs* presumably had enjoyed more exposure to the music of the citharode thanks to Nero's support of it, but it is likely that many Romans still perceived the impressively costumed citharode, so iconically himself in the Greek cultural imagination, through their own cultural frame of reference as another kind of *histrio*. The "histrionic" style of citharodic performance in Nero's time (on which more below) would have only prompted this tendency—Nero's bended knee and deferential salute were probably stock-in-trade gestures for his agonistic rivals as well. Even the "pretended anxiety" that Tacitus implies was a characteristically Neronian affectation could have been proper to the routine self-presentation of citharodes as they awaited judgment.[222]

ii. New Music: The *cithara* and the *urbs*

It is worth dwelling a little on the novelty involved in the public institution of *kitharôidia* in Rome, and by extension the relative unconventionality—his position as emperor aside—of Nero's own citharodic practice there. Despite the (significant) lack of clear evidence for them, concert recitals by itinerant citharodes in late Republican and early Imperial Rome were probably not unheard of, and *ad hoc* citharodic contests may have been irregularly held. Citharodes might, for instance, have participated in the musical games offered to inaugurate Pompey's theater in

---

[221] Cf. n193 above; Section 22.iii below.
[222] Although a supreme confidence is more typical of the citharodic persona in performance. See e.g. Plutarch *How to Praise Oneself Inoffensively* 1.539c (= Timotheus PMG 802).

55 BCE (Dio Cassius 39.38.1; Plutarch *Pompey* 52.4), which would later host the contests of the Neronia (Pliny *Natural History* 37.19). But Rome was hardly the center of citharodic culture it would become under Nero and later emperors. Before Nero, the popular musical culture of Rome was monopolized by dancers, pantomimes, actors, *tibicines* (players of the *tibiae*, the Roman equivalent of the Greek reed pipes, the *auloi*), and singers.[223] One star, the virtuoso singer and *tibicen* Tigellius Hermogenes, a Sardinian by birth, earned massive adulation, as well as plenty of *invidia*, among *plebs* and nobles alike; his wealth and fame brought him into close company with luminaries such as Cicero, Caesar, Cleopatra, and Augustus.[224] Another celebrity singer, Apelles, enjoyed a close, if at times volatile, relationship with Caligula, who nurtured his own dreams of appearing in public as a *cantor atque saltator* 'singer and dancer'.[225] No citharode is on record as having reached anywhere near this pinnacle of popular success or having gained such coveted entrée into elite social and political circles until the Neronian principate, when suddenly Terpnus was installed at the young emperor's side, and, later, another citharodic confidant of Nero, Menecrates, was given property and a residence equal to that of men who had celebrated triumphs (Suetonius *Life of Nero* 20.2). Menecrates returned the favor to Nero: in early 66 CE he arranged a victory celebration in the Circus after Nero had won in a citharodic *agôn*, probably against Menecrates himself. (It is unclear on what occasion or pretext this *agôn* was held.) Dio Cassius 63.3.1 calls Menecrates Nero's *didaskalos* 'teacher' in his report of these events, although Suetonius assigns that role to Terpnus. In any case, these two citharodes, along with a third, Diodorus, apparently formed a sort of clique around Nero, acting as his mentors and (compliantly "lesser") competitors in Rome and Greece (Dio 63.8.4).[226] Even at the beginning of Nero's reign, however, *kitharôidia* did not immediately

---

[223] In 115 BCE the censors banned all performance arts in the public games (*artes ludi-crae*) except those of the "Latin *tibicen* with *cantor* 'singer'" and the native Italian song-and-dance show called the *ludus talarius* (Cassiodorus *Chronica* from 639). Wille 1967:219n107 thinks that the xenophobic ban reflects the growing popularity of *kithara* playing. But that is far from the only implication. Other second-century Roman conservatives are more openly concerned with the popularity of Greek harp (rather than *kithara*) players and dancers. Cf. Comotti 1989:51.

[224] Testimonia collected in Wille 1967:331–334.

[225] Suetonius *Life of Caligula* 54. Apelles: Dio Cassius 59.5.2; Suetonius *Caligula* 33; Philo *On the Embassy to Gaius* 203–206; cf. Beacham 1999:172. The pre-Neronian anecdotal tradition is full of stories of prominent men and women falling in love or lust with actors, singers, mimes, and dancers—not citharodes. See Edwards 1997:80.

[226] Cf. Cizek 1972:208. See Suetonius *Nero* 23.2 on Nero's fraught intimacy with his citha-rodic rivals.

become a popular sensation. Recall Tacitus' droll implication that the *plebs* passed over the citharodes for the pantomimes. The prospect of the emperor's own involvement at the second Neronia of 65 CE seems to have been the factor that truly galvanized widespread interest in the medium.

This is not to say that Greek stringed instruments, lyres, *kitharai*, and harps, were unfamiliar to Romans before Nero. They were familiar, especially to the philhellenic aristocracy, some of whom, following the example set by the educated Greek elite, themselves took up the instruments as amateur players.[227] Images of lyres or *kitharai* leave their mark, typically as accoutrements of Apollo, on Republican coinage as early as the second century BCE.[228] The leading men who minted these coins were on one level simply appropriating a common motif in the Greek numismatic iconography surrounding Apollo, but they must also have appreciated the fundamental ideals of sociopolitical harmony and cultural prestige that were symbolized specifically by the stringed instruments.[229] Augustus' conspicuous deployment of statues of Apollo *citharoedus* in the building program of the Palatine shows that he did as well. Nevertheless, both the material and literary record suggests that Republican and Augustan Romans had limited first-hand experience of professional citharodes. Prose writers and poets of the time occasionally refer to amateur lyre playing, but never to contemporary citharodes or public citharodic performances. The citharodes or citharode-analogues who do appear in their pages (Apollo, Calliope, Orpheus, Arion, et al.) are distinctly "literary" figures, drawn from Greek myth and (legendary) history; and, although Roman authors could be sensitive to the nuanced cultural and political meanings of *kitharôidia* in its traditional Greek contexts, there is little sense that their attention to these figures involves an indirect engagement with the real-life practice and place of *kitharôidia* in the experience of their own city, as is almost inevitably the case

---

[227] See various testimonia collected in Wille 1967:211–218. Cicero *Tusculan Disputations* 1.2.4 recognizes that singing to the lyre (*nervorum vocumque cantus*) represented the peak, the *summa eruditio*, of traditional Greek *paideia*.

[228] Cf. n57 above.

[229] From an early point a significant etymological relationship between the Latin meanings of *fides* as 'trust, good faith' and 'lyre/kithara' was probably recognized (wrongly: musical *fides* probably comes from σφίδη, which Hesychius glosses as χορδή 'string'). According to Festus (s.v. *fides*), whose lexicon epitomizes *On the Significance of Words* by the Augustan-era Verrius Flaccus, the *cithara* is called *fides* because the tuned strings resemble the way good faith establishes social harmony among men. Hardie 2007 discusses the musico-political symbolism (viz. "musical harmony as a model for reconciliation and political concord," 551) of the figure of the lyre-playing Hercules Musagetes, attached to the cult of the Muses in Republican and Augustan Rome.

with Greek writers and poets, living as they did surrounded by a vibrant living culture of string music, professional and amateur.[230]

A story told in Varro *On Agriculture* 3.13.2–3 expresses the literary, mythicized distance at which Late Republican elites held *kithar ôidia*. During a Thracian-themed banquet at his game-preserve, the wealthy orator Quintus Hortensius "ordered 'Orpheus' to be called out. When he appeared in his *stola* and with his *cithara*, and was commanded to sing, he blew a horn (*bucina*)," at which "a crowd of stags, boars, and other animals" was released among the banqueters. This stylized tableau of citharodic myth could not be further from the "real thing." Indeed, the very sound of the *cithara* is represented by the Roman horn; we may assume that Hortensius' "Orpheus" is an actor rather than an actual citharode.

It is only when we come to Neronian and Flavian literature that we see indications, clear ones, of sustained Roman interest in real-world citharodic music, and not only in Nero's, although there can be little doubt that it was his efforts as performer, as well as promoter, of the art that cemented the popularity of *citharoedi* among Romans of the most diverse classes and backgrounds.[231] With his personal patronage of citharodes such as Terpnus and Menecrates, however, and his establishment of the Neronian *agônes*, Nero provided the financial incentives, institutional infrastructure, and even the political-ideological climate to make Rome into a world-class destination for star citharodes, as the Peisistratids had done for Athens and the Ptolemies had done for Alexandria. Terpnus was likely imported by Nero from Alexandria. In Rome he conceivably served not only as the emperor's personal entertainer and trainer, but also as a self-interested advocate for the formal integration of his *tekhnê* into the city's lucrative regime of spectacles.[232] It is indeed possible that in his engagement of Terpnus

---

[230] For example, Wilson 1999/2000 shows how Euripides' dramatic treatments of the mythical citharodes Amphion and Euneus reflect issues in the contemporary string culture of Athens. The *citharoedus* in Horace *Ars Poetica* 355–356 who "always plays the wrong note" is a wholly generic figure, and is probably, like the other musical exemplars mentioned by Horace in the poem, derived from some Greek anecdotal or proverbial source.

[231] Cf. Champlin 2003: "Nero the performer is inseparable from Nero the patron, the giver of games" (68).

[232] Nero's Terpnus is likely to be the same as the Flavius Terpnus, a κιθαρῳδὸς Ἀλεξανδρεύς, commemorated in a second-century CE funerary inscription from Rome (IG XIV 2088). The Flavian praenomen could indicate an accommodation to the post-Neronian political scene. See Wille 1967:322, but cf. Stephanis 1988, no. 2398, who notes problems in dating. Even if this Flavius Terpnus is not Nero's Terpnus, could it be his son or student?

Nero was consciously following a semi-historical "script," the well-known story of Terpander's musico-political intervention in Archaic Sparta. Terpander, like his partial namesake Terpnus the most famous citharode of his day, was summoned by the Spartan authorities from his home in Lesbos to a socially troubled Sparta, where he undertook the first *katastasis* 'establishment' of music, founding (and winning) the first citharodic *agôn* at the Carneia festival.[233] Of course, as performer, Nero himself "played the role" of Terpander as much as did Terpnus.

The earliest indication that *citharoedi*—Nero aside—had taken their place in the popular musical culture of Rome comes by way of a scene in the *Satyricon*, which was probably written by Petronius during Nero's reign. In the baths, the wealthy freedman Trimalchio drunkenly "tears apart (*lacerare*) the *cantica* of Menecrates" (73.3). This Menecrates is almost certainly the same Menecrates *kitharôidos* favored by Nero—a Neronian dating for the *Satyricon* is indeed based in part on the strong probability of this identification. These *cantica* were not old-time classics, but popular "hits" of the day. The scene registers the new enthusiasm in Rome for the citharodic music of Menecrates, and presumably other citharodes as well, while at the same time staging a critique, in the novel's playful manner, of the perceived cultural debasement involved in its Roman reception. Trimalchio, the embodiment of Imperial excess and vulgarity, who otherwise claims he enjoys only the low-brow entertainments of acrobats and horn players (*cornices*, 53), mutilates beyond recognition these products of the "high" Greek citharodic tradition, as earlier (59), among the kitschy dramatizers of epic, the *Homeristae*, his ridiculous exegeses of Homer made a travesty of epic myth and performance. It is tempting to see as well in Trimalchio's drunken, solipsistic singing a gross parody, aesthetic and political, of Nero's own citharodic aspirations.

By the time of Juvenal and Martial, citharodes had become icons of the pervasively Hellenized post-Neronian cultural landscape of Rome, now a *Graeca urbs*, as the self-exiled Roman speaker of Juvenal 3.63 has it, and as competitive a center of *kitharôidia* as any actual Greek *polis*. Domitian's Capitoline Games included a citharodic *agôn* (Juvenal 6.388–389), which was held in the newly constructed, Greek-style odeum in the Campus Martius (Suetonius *Domitian* 5), an impressive structure later restored during Trajans's rule (Dio Cassius 69.4.1). Hadrian counted among his intimates the Cretan citharode and composer Mesomedes.[234]

---

[233] "Plutarch" *On Music* 9.1134b–c, with Hellanicus FGrH 4 F 85 *ap.* Athenaeus 14.635e.

[234] *Suda* s.v. Μεσομήδης, with the sensible emendation proposed by Whitmarsh 2004:382.

Although his state pay (*salarium*), no doubt quite considerable, was supposedly reduced after Hadrian's death by Antoninus Pius (*Historia Augusta, Life of Antoninus* 7.7), Caracalla would later erect a cenotaph for Mesomedes, because he, the emperor, "was learning *kitharôidia*" (Dio Cassius 77.13.7). Hadrian also may have made a practice of *kitharôidia*, if that is what is meant by the phrase *psallendi et cantandi scientia* in *Historia Augusta, Life of Hadrian* 14.9. Domitian's Capitoline *agôn* at Rome came to be ranked prominently among the major Greek *agônes* in the circuit of the professional citharode. On a monument from Smyrna, the two Roman victories of the winningest citharode of the Severan period, C. Antonius Septimius Poplius, are listed at the top of an impressive catalogue of successes at the most prestigious sites across the Empire, only after those at the Smyrnean Olympia and Hadriania.[235]

Entertainers as wealthy and adored as any actor, singer, dancer, or *tibicen*, citharodes became targets of moralizing satire and the poets' own invidious critique. We have already looked at Juvenal's take on the sexualized cult of celebrity surrounding stars such as Pollio and "Hedymeles." Martial 5.56.9–10 cynically advises a father to steer his son away from rhetoric and poetry and toward the "money-making métiers" (*pecuniosae artes*) of the *citharoedus* or the *choraules*, a Greek-style *tibicen* who specialized in providing music for choruses, including reworked excerpts from Athenian tragedies. The citharode had become the match of the long-admired *tibicen*.[236] In another epigram, Martial, biding his time in Imola, asserts facetiously, but with genuinely rueful envy nonetheless, that he would return to Rome only when he had become a *citharoedus* (3.4.7–8); living there as a *poeta*, he enjoyed considerably less love and money than did these stars of the musical stage, one of whom, Pollio, amassed a fortune that is mentioned by Martial in another epigram from Book 3 (3.20.18; cf. Juvenal 7.176–177).[237]

---

[235] IGR IV 1432 = Stephanis 1988, no. 2121. The catalogue of festivals is a vivid testimony to the geographical expanse of Imperial citharodic culture: Smyrna, Rome, Puteoli, Naples, Actium, Argos, Nemea, Pergamon, Delphi, Ephesus, Epidauros, Athens, Sardis, Tralles, Miletus, Rhodes, Sparta, and Mantinea. Bowie 1990a:89 is surely right in saying that Mesomedes was "the tip of an iceberg. There must have been many citharodes whose songs gave pleasure to Antonine Greeks" (and Romans, we should add).

[236] The *choraules* seems to have become a popular figure in Flavian Rome. See West 1992:93n63 and 377; Strasser 2002. Juvenal 6.76–77 imagines that the citharode Echion, the *choraules* Ambrosius, and the *tibicen* Glaphyrus have fathered children with aristocratic Roman *matronae*. Trimalchio perversely commands his *choraules* to 'sing in Latin' (*Latine cantare*), that is, to accompany singing in Latin rather than the usual Greek (*Satyricon* 53).

[237] The epigraphical record also reflects this post-Neronian focus on the citharode. Wille 1967:322 counts six Roman epitaphs for *citharoedi* (and one for a *citharoeda*, Auxesis,

The money to be made by cithârodes in Rome was no satirical exaggeration. Menecrates, we saw, became wildly rich thanks to Nero's largesse; even the thrifty and conservative Vespasian (Suetonius *Vespasian* 16.1, 19.2; Tacitus *Annals* 3.55), whose personal interest in *kitharôidia* seems to have been minimal—he supposedly once either walked out of the theater or fell asleep while Nero was singing in Greece—read the winds of popular enthusiasm and awarded the hefty sum of 200,000 sesterces each to Terpnus and Diodorus for performing at the games to celebrate the dedication of the restored Augustan Theater of Marcellus.[238] A *tragoedus* also performed at the games for a fee of 400,000 sesterces.[239] But the cithârodes' paydays were still enormous; to put the amount in perspective, a Roman legionary made only 900 sesterces *per annum*. That these famously close associates of Nero continued to thrive professionally and win imperial patronage in Rome well after the end of his disastrous reign, and despite the corrective stance taken toward Neronian excesses by Vespasian, indicates just how irrevocably Nero had embedded *kitharôidia* in Roman cultural and political life, and how effectively he secured the star status of its leading virtuosos in the eyes of Roman citizens.

But if Vespasian realized that the public dispensation of citharodic music was now a necessary part of Imperial cultural politics, as a Neronian legacy it was nevertheless tainted by association. It is possible that, as in the visual realm, where statues of Nero were re-carved in the likeness of the new emperor, so in the musical realm Vespasian at once inherited, yet also essayed a creative *damnatio memoriae* of his predecessor's groundbreaking patronage of citharodic diplays.[240] Indeed, Vespasian's renovation of the Theater of Marcellus and his presentation of musical events there for the first time read as blatant attempts to erase Neronian influence from recent cultural memory. Nero had used the Theater of Pompey for his own public performances, including

---

CIL VI 10125). Some of these cithârodes were free, some slaves to wealthy families, such as the auspiciously named Amphion, property of one C. Salarius Capito (CIL VI 10124B). Such slaves were probably not competitors at *agônes*, but rather kept for private entertainment.

[238] Suetonius *Life of Vespasian* 19; walking out/falling asleep: 4; Tacitus *Annals* 16.5.3, who has Vespasian dozing off at the second Neronia.

[239] The MSS. name him Apellaris, which many take as a corruption of Apelles. This Apelles was perhaps the same Apelles who enjoyed fame in the time of Caligula. If so, he would have been quite old when he sang at Vespasian's games. Perhaps it was a deliberately politicized choice to bring this star from the days before Nero back into the spotlight.

[240] See Varner 2004:52–55 on Vespasian's appropriation of Neronian statuary. On Vespasian as a patron of the arts, see Suetonius *Vespasian* 17.

those of the Neronia; the Theater of Marcellus, however, does not seem to have been a focal point of Neronian musical culture. Its innocence in this respect, as well as its association with nostalgized Augustan culture—parts of the *Ludi Saeculares* were presented there (CIL VI 32323.157)—no doubt made it an appealing venue at which to inaugurate a new era of Roman performance politics.[241] The musical events also seem to have been similarly framed. Suetonius writes, "For the games, Vespasian had revived the old musical entertainments as well" (*ludis ... vetera quoque acroamata revocaverat*). This does not mean that for the first time since the death of Nero citharodes and tragic singers gave performances in Rome; we hear, for instance, that Vitellius presented a citharodic spectacle in 69 BCE (Suetonius *Vitellius* 11.2). It is more probable that this musical "revival" was a purely rhetorical construct of Vespasianic propaganda. The performance genres with which Nero was most closely identified would thus have been purged of Neronian associations and re-presented as *vetera acroamata* 'ancient musical entertainments' under the exclusive auspices of Vespasian (a man of "archaic dress and diet," according to Tacitus *Annals* 3.55).[242] As with the restoration of the theater, Vespasian is generating new cultural capital by remaking the past on his own terms; he has appropriated Nero's citharodes, and cast them in a new—that is, old—light.[243] We can be sure that on this occasion Terpnus and Diodorus did not perform ("revive") the music of their old patron. Perhaps in the spirit of these *vetera acroamata* they played an archaizing program of uncontroversial, old-time citharodic classics.[244]

---

[241] On the history of the theater, see now Sear 2006:61–65.

[242] Latin writers sometimes use *acroama* to refer to an entertainer rather than an entertainment (e.g. Suetonius *Life of Augustus* 74). Even if Suetonius is using it here in that sense, my interpretation of the symbolic force of Vespasian's act is essentially the same—he is ostentatiously redeeming these "old-time entertainers" from the previous regime by re-presenting them under his own cultural aegis.

[243] If Jones 1973 is correct in dating the *Alexandrian Oration* of Dio Chrysostom to the reign of Vespasian, then we might see a reflex of such propagandizing in Dio's contrast between Nero's "excessive involvement in and enthusiasm for" *kitharôidia* and the *paideia*—the word evokes a re-engagement with the Classical tradition—promoted by the current *arkhôn*, Vespasian (32.60).

[244] "Archaic revival" recitals had occasionally been presented by citharodes in Greece. A second-century BCE proxeny decree from Delphi honors Thrason and Socrates, brothers from Aegira, who presented concerts featuring "lyric compositions [*lurika sustêmata*] of ancient poets." The *lura* that is carved into the stone alongside the inscribed decree (FD III 1 no. 49) suggests not that these brothers literally played lyres, but that they were citharodes reperforming, as the decree indicates, the works of the old-time lyric poets in their own professionalized, citharodic concert versions.

By contrast, Vitellius, eager to capitalize on the popularly mandated citharodic politics of the Neronian principate to shore up his own rule, publicly sanctioned the revival of the *Neroniana cantica* at a citharodic performance he had arranged early in his short reign to commemorate Nero's death: "He openly urged the citharode, who was entertaining the crowd at the feast, to 'perform something too from the master's work', and, when the citharode began to sing the songs of Nero, he was the first to jump up and applaud."[245] Vitellius here reprises his role as Nero's model fan, one he had savvily played when he was supervisor of the *certamen* 'contest' (presumably the citharodic one) at the second Neronia of 65 CE. While Nero was leaving the theater, (seemingly) reluctant to join in the contest, Vitellius interceded directly, as an "envoy of an insistent *populus*," to persuade him to return and perform on stage (Suetonius *Vitellius* 4).

iii. Playing to the *plebs*

To sum up: the fact that the star citharode becomes a standby of post-Neronian Roman culture should not blind us to Nero's pioneering contributions toward that development. As patron and performer, he was the prime instigator of a process of cultural, musical, even political and ideological translation, a kind of mass-market *paideia*—making the Hellenic language of *kitharôidia* legible and lovable to Romans. This process of enculturation is made audibly and performatively manifest in a detail of Tacitus' account of Nero's reception at the second Neronia: after his performance, the crowd *personabat certis modis plausuque composito* 'began to resound with measured rounds of rhythmic applause' (*Annals* 16.4.4). These plaudits significantly echo the enthusiastic response of the audience, a mix of Campanian locals, members of Nero's claque from Rome, and Alexandrians from a nearby fleet, to the concert in Naples. Suetonius *Nero* 20.3 singles out the positive reaction of the latter group. The presence of this sizable contingent of Alexandrians in Naples is a lucky coincidence for Nero—suspiciously lucky perhaps—since the inhabitants of Alexandria, as we already have several times observed, are known to be great connoisseurs of music, not least of *kitharôidia*.[246] Alcides, an Alexandrian *mousikos* who

---

[245] Suetonius *Life of Vitellius* 11.2: *convivio citharoedum placentem palam admonuit, ut aliquid et de dominico diceret, incohantique Neroniana cantica primus exsultans etiam plausit.*

[246] It would not have been unusual for Alexandrians to be in Naples, given that the Egyptian grain ships came to port at nearby Puteoli (Bradley 1978:127). But could their arrival have been deliberately timed to coincide with the concert in Naples

is among the symposiasts in Athenaeus' *Deipnosophistae*, claims that at citharodic performances in his city "even the lowest-class (*eutelestatos*) and illiterate (*analphabêtos*) layman is accustomed to criticize mistakes in striking notes as soon as they occur" (4.176e).

It was before these discerning spectators that Nero daydreamed of making a living from his citharodic τέχνιον. Their presence at and approval for his public debut would go some way toward legitimating the emperor's endeavors in the Greek art of *kithara* singing. That approval would have been audibly, *musically* expressed in waves of rhythmically marked applause distinguished, like song, across different *genera*. Suetonius mentions three types, whose names reflect the method of clapping or the sound produced by the clappers' hands: "buzzings," "roof-tiles," and "bricks." Suetonius seems to indicate that these various *modulatae laudationes* 'musical approbations' came not only at the end of the performance, but were interspersed throughout Nero's singing (*cantanti*), perhaps at customary pauses in the junctures between the sections of his song. The effect of this is remarkable indeed: the enthusiasts in the audience themselves become active participants in the performance—"actors in the audience," as Shadi Bartsch would put it—imprinting their own rhythmic soundmaking on the sonic texture of the musical event as it unfolds.[247]

Clappers might even have engaged in a kind of meta-occasional musical *agôn* among themselves, arranged as they were into factions. "Captivated" by the manual performance of the Alexandrians—Suetonius' *captus* cannily implies the subjugation of the *imperator* to its affective power, perhaps alluding to Horace's *Graecia capta ferum victorem cepit* (*Epistles* 2.1.156)—Nero organized his own Roman claque, the Augustiani, who had been charged with leading the acclaim for his musical efforts since the first Juvenalian performance of 59 (Tacitus *Annals* 14.15.4; Dio Cassius 61.20.3–4), into *factiones*, each of which would learn one of the Alexandrian *genera* of applause. Suetonius includes the

---

(or vice versa)? Suetonius *Nero* 20.2 says that after the Neapolitan debut, Nero did expressly summon more Alexandrians to supplement his "official" claque. We may note, however, that in his archly critical account, Tacitus mentions that the audience was composed of Neapolitans and "those whom the *fama* surrounding the event had drawn from the nearby *coloniae* and *municipia*" (*Annals* 15.33.3). Is Tacitus consciously suppressing mention of the Alexandrians just because their response to Nero was "genuinely" positive? From another angle, however, one would expect Tacitus to expose Nero's shameless self-promotion if he had deliberately stacked the audience with Alexandrians.

[247] Bartsch 1994. On Greek theatrical audiences as "performers," see Wallace 1997, with discussion in the following section.

significant information that the equestrian corps of the Augustiani was augmented by 5,000 young men recruited from the *plebs*, as well as by Alexandrian citizens who were expressly summoned, Suetonius implies, to teach their native cheerleading techniques to the Romans. The issue of these lessons, transmitted via the exemplarily combined plebeian and elite ranks of the Augustiani, can surely be heard in the "measured rounds of rhythmic applause" that met Nero's Roman debut at the second Neronia (although Tacitus does not name the Augustiani explicitly, he does note at *Annals* 16.5.1 that soldiers stationed in the seats forced reluctant spectators to maintain the incessant *clamor* despite their fatigue and "unpracticed hands").[248] Colorfully partisan theater claques and factions had long existed in Rome—especially around the pantomime troupes—and so had stylized expressions of *acclamatio* (cf. Ovid *Art of Love* 1.113), but Nero seems to have been intent on Hellenizing Roman spectatorship, recreating in the *urbs* the vigorous citharodic fan culture of the Alexandrian *polis* at the levels of sound and spectacle.[249] The rhythmically synchronized crowd at the Neronia is actively implicated in the realization of the emperor's phil-hellenic fantasy: a dynamic, musical bond of sorts forged between *princeps* and *populus*, performer and audience.[250]

12. "Bad" Citharodes, Tough Crowds

Audiences could signal displeasure with citharodic performance through a far less "collaborative" variety of sonic participation. An anecdote concerning Timotheus of Miletus tells how the citharode was hissed by Athenian audiences who were baffled by his novel style (Plutarch *Whether an Old Man Should Engage in Public Affairs* 23.795d).[251]

---

[248] Cf. Bartsch 1994:29.

[249] See Cameron 1976:191–229 and Slater 1994 on theatrical factions in Rome. Earlier in Nero's principate factions attached to the pantomimes had rioted in the theater (Tacitus *Annals* 13.25.3), as they had under Tiberius (e.g. *Annals* 1.77; Suetonius *Tiberius* 37.2).

[250] Cf. Cizek 1972: "Such a program [the formation of the Augustiani and the institution of the Neronia] was the consequence of the emperor's limitless passion for art and athletics and at the same time of his concern to create an adequate social and ideological context [for them]" (124). Cf. Bradley 1978:127–128.

[251] See Wallace 1997:105 on hissing; Csapo and Slater 1994:290 on the repertoire of crowd noises in the Athenian theaters. Timotheus *Persians* 209–212 evokes the hostile reaction to his music in Sparta: "The people (*laos*) buffets me, flaming, and drives at me with fiery blame, that I dishonor the older Muse with my new songs."

The Alexandrian concertgoers described by Alcides surely voiced their criticisms of technical faults as readily (and loudly) as they offered their plaudits to virtuoso accomplishments (Athenaeus 4.176e). There are suggestions too of more violent reactions from displeased crowds, but these merit skepticism. In an anecdote recorded by the third-century BCE humorist Lynceus of Samos (*ap.* Athenaeus 6.245d), a parasite, Corydus, comments drolly to his fellow dinner guest, a citharode named Polyctor, who has bitten into a stone mixed in with his lentil soup, "You poor man, even your soup pelts you." Machon, the Alexandrian humorist, has κιθαρῳδός τις, ὡς ἔοικε σφόδρα κακός 'a certain citharode, a really bad one as it seems' joking wryly that at his next performance he will amass more than enough stones to build a house (fr. II Gow, also by way of Athenaeus 6.245d; Gow conjectures that the citharode is again Polyctor). A point is in order here: infamously "bad" professional citharodes are above all creatures of comic fantasy and witty anecdote. While there were winners and losers in the *agônes*, and technical and performance skills naturally varied from performer to performer and performance to performance, the competitive structure of the citharodic field as a whole would have prevented truly subpar musicians from achieving any sort of sustained career, just as the modern-day business of Classical music would not permit the existence of an objectively unskilled concert pianist. As was indicated in the discussion of Lucian's hapless citharode Evangelus, it is unlikely that anyone, even Nero, would have been able to take the stage at an *agôn* even once, unless he possessed the considerably demanding prerequisite talents and skills.

"Badness" was thus situational, relational, and, above all, a conveniently reductive term of occasional invective or deprecating fun. Neophyte citharodes could have had rough going at times, especially against more experienced competitors, and been called "bad." Even star virtuosos could flub notes, commit a gaffe, or otherwise fail to meet the exacting standards of merciless audiences such as the ones in Alexandria. Fans of one citharode would surely be quick to disparage those cheered by others, regardless of their actual abilities or achievements.[252] Musicians themselves could mobilize harsh attacks against

---

[252] The scholia on Aristophanes *Acharnians* 13–14 ("At another time I felt joy, when Dexitheus came onstage after Moschus to sing the Boeotian *nomos*") seem to preserve traces of such disagreements over the quality of the two popular citharodes mentioned by the play's protagonist Dicaeopolis, or at least how variant opinions of them were refracted in Old Comedy. One scholiast *ad loc.* says that Moschus was a φαῦλος κιθαρῳδός 'poor citharode', because he sang ἀπνευστί 'without taking a

their rivals, as is well evidenced, albeit in stylized, semi-fictional form, in the abundant anecdotal tradition devoted to the withering comments made by the fourth-century citharist Stratonicus of Athens on the abilities of his professional contemporaries.[253] With few exceptions, every musician he comes across he dismisses as incompetent, untalented, "bad." An exemplary story: "After Stratonicus was victorious over his rivals in Sicyon, he dedicated in the Asclepieion a trophy with the inscription: 'Stratonicus, from the spoils of those who play the *kithara* badly'" (νικήσας δ' ἐν Σικυῶνι τοὺς ἀνταγωνιστὰς ἀνέθηκεν εἰς τὸ Ἀσκληπιεῖον τρόπαιον ἐπιγράψας· Στρατόνικος ἀπὸ τῶν κακῶς κιθαριζόντων, Athenaeus 8.351f). The kind of all-or-nothing critical displays of which Stratonicus was a past master were strategic to the musician's self-marketing, the rhetorical performance of his professionalism—he is the star, others are most certainly not—but as such should in no way be taken as communicating objectively valid assessments of musical skill.

A performer's appearance or physique could draw invective that shaded easily into aspersions on his skill. A citharode who was disparaged by audiences for his large size was comically "praised" by Diogenes the Cynic for singing to the *kithara* instead of turning to brigandage (Diogenes Laertius 6.47). Stratonicus said "riddlingly" of the Rhodian citharode Propis, who was "big in size, but bad (*kakos*) in *tekhnê* and inferior to [the great size of] his body," that he was οὐδεὶς κακὸς μέγας ἰχθύς, meaning "first of all, that he is οὐδείς 'a nobody'; secondly, that he is κακός 'bad'; and, in addition, that he is μέγας 'big', and ἰχθύς 'a fish', on account of his having no voice (*aphônia*)."[254] Timotheus' red hair may have similarly been exploited as a mark against or stain upon his musical skill. In Pherecrates *Cheiron* fr. 155.24 K-A, Music disparages him as Μιλήσιός τις Πυρρίας 'a certain Pyrrhias from Miletus'; Pyrrhias, or "Red," was a nickname commonly reserved for slaves.[255]

---

breath'. Another, however, reports that some (*tines*) have it that Moschus was so called after the calf (*moskhos*) that he won as a victor in a contest—a sign of success. Similarly, this scholiast says that Dexitheus was an ἄριστος κιθαρῳδὸς καὶ πυθιονίκης 'star citharode and Pythian victor', but notes too that "others say" he was *psukhros* 'frigid'.

[253] The anecdotes are collected in Athenaeus 8.347f–352d. See Gilula 2000; Wilson 2004:289–292.

[254] Clearchus *On Proverbs* fr. 80 Wehrli = Athenaeus 8.347f. Wilson 2004:292 notes the class-based assumptions here; Stratonicus invokes "a persistent élite ideal of a perfect conformity between body-type, voice, and ability." We should note that Stratonicus, as a citharist, was himself literally "without a voice." He criticizes just that which makes *kitharôidia* a more prestigious medium than *kitharistikê*.

[255] Cf. Austin 1922:73.

Stylistically innovative or idiosyncratic citharodes such as Timotheus, although not objectively poor musicians, stirred such intense animosity in some listeners that accusations that they were simply "bad" were inevitable; these accusations could in turn inform comic representations, or vice versa. Thus the innovative fifth-century BCE citharode Phrynis of Mytilene was derided in Old Comedy as γύννις καὶ ψυχρός 'effeminate and frigid [i.e. flat, unimpressive]' (scholia to Aristophanes *Clouds* 971b). But if he left some cold, he excited many others—he was victorious at the Panathenaia of 446 BCE. In Pherecrates' comedy of 420 BCE, *Wild Men* (fr. 6 K-A), one character asks another, "Who was the worst citharode ever born?" (κιθαρῳδὸς τίς κάκιστος ἐγένετο;). The reply: Meles son of Peisius. Meles is also ridiculed by Socrates in Plato *Gorgias* 502a as one who "pained" (*aniân*) his audiences, so defying, pathetically, the essential "pleasure principle" of the medium. But for Plato and Pherecrates, the fact that Meles was the father of the objectionably modern dithyrambist Cinesias, who was routinely abused by the comedians and by Plato himself (*Gorgias* 501e), is surely what has (retroactively) made him "bad."[256] In any case, stoning, as the humorous tone of the anecdotes suggests, was more fiction than fact. In reality, neither were audiences so aggressively disposed nor citharodes so aesthetically "bad" or morally offensive as to allow for more than impassioned, noisy criticism of a disagreeable performance. Fabricated or exaggerated too are reports such as Lucian's mention of whip-bearers at the Pythian games, whose job it

---

[256] See the harsh characterizations of Cinesias among the testimonia collected in Campbell 1993a:41–59. Meles' own stylistic predilections are left vague—he is never explicitly counted among the New Musicians—but we may assume that the apple did not fall far from the tree. In Pherecrates fr. 6 the second worse citharode is said to be Chaeris. This Chaeris is a tough nut to crack, as the ancient testimony for his activity and identity—aulete and/or citharode?—is confusing (cf. n274 below). But if the Chaeris mentioned at Aristophanes *Acharnians* 15–16, who "stooped sideways" (παρέκυψε) onto the stage to play the Orthian *nomos* in the *agôn*, is Pherecrates' citharodic Chaeris, as seems likely, then his "badness" was a comic *topos*: Aristophanes' Dicaeopolis says that he "almost died and was in torture" when he saw Chaeris come onstage. It is likely that Chaeris either once contorted his body in some unfortunate fashion while performing, ironically, the "upright" (*Orthios*) *nomos* (cf. Platter 2007:61), perhaps at the Great Panathenaia of summer 426 BCE, the year before *Acharnians* was produced (cf. Olson 2002:70), or, more likely, that his "stooping" was an intentional histrionic effect (see further discussion of this possibility below). Either scenario could explain why Chaeris was unfairly tarred by the comedians as a "torturous" performer. Despite the satire, however, the fact that he was even among the select ranks of festival agonists in Athens indicates that he was highly competent. A proverb, "Chaeris singing the *Orthios*" (Χαῖρις ᾄδων ὄρθιον) was applied to those who sang well (*Paroemiographi Graeci* I, Appendix to Centuria V, 21; *Suda* s.v. Χαιριδεῖς).

was to scourge "bad" citharodes to the point of drawing blood (*The Uncultured Book Collector* 9), or the stories of Spartan ephors forcibly cutting the strings from the *kitharai* of Timotheus and other innovators.[257] A mid-fourth-century Paestan bell krater by Asteas (Salerno, Museo Archeologico Provinciale Pc 1812) shows what seems to be a violent confrontation, perhaps based on a scene from Eupolis' comedy *Demes*, between a citharode labeled Phrynis and a fiery, white-haired old man labeled Pyronides, who attempts to seize either the recalcitrant citharode or his instrument.[258] Pyronides holds a staff; perhaps he is meant to be acting in the capacity of a judge. Full-blown assaults such as these, by either outraged judges or scandalized spectators, belong above all to the realm of comic or anecdotal fantasy.

Judges did penalize musicians for disobeying the rules of the *agôn*, which no doubt were taken very seriously (Plato *Laws* 700c; "Plutarch" *On Music* 37.1144f). We will see below that a strict sense of propriety and conservatism attended the performance of the contest pieces, *nomoi*—*nomos* means, in its non-musical sense, 'law' or 'regulation', a coincidence not lost on ancient audiences—by citharodes and other solo agonists. Tacitus *Annals* 16.4.3 records that Nero compulsively observed the rules (*leges*) whenever he performed. While we never hear exactly what sort of penalties could be levied, presumably they would involve disqualification, demotion in ranking, or perhaps monetary fines rather than actual physical punishment. It is conceivable that minor infractions committed during performance might have prompted judges to issue "mild corrections," perhaps with their staffs or wands, but these would have been a far cry from the savage floggings occasionally administered at athletic *agônes* by the rod- and whip-bearing officials, whom Nero made a great show of fearing at Olympia (Philostratus *Life of Apollonius of Tyana* 5.7.10). Although *kitharôidia* could be an intensely physical experience, the vigorously corporeal atmosphere of the athletic games nonetheless essentially differed from that of the *mousikoi agônes*.[259]

---

[257] Cicero *On the Laws* 2.15.39; Pausanius 3.2.10; Dio Chrysostom 33.57; Boethius *On Music* 1.1; Athenaeus 14.636e–f; Plutarch *On Advancing in Virtue* 13.84a, *Agesilaus* 10.4 (Phrynis has two strings cut off his nine-string *kithara*), *Laconian Institutions* 17.238c (Terpander censured for adding eighth string; ephor cuts away Timotheus' extra strings at the Carneia). See further Wilamowitz 1903:69–70; Palumbo Stracca 1997.

[258] Cf. Taplin 1993:42 (with fig. 16.16); Storey 2003a:117 (with fig. 1), 130, 169–170.

[259] See Crowther and Frass 1998, although their contention (p61) that flogging was common at dramatic and musical contests seems to me based on a superficial reading of the testimonia. "Mild corrections": Herington 1985:17. I would disagree with his contention (p226n30), however, that Aristophanes *Frogs* 1024 (Dionysus, acting in

13. Factional Dramas

Citharodic *agônes* involved competition not only between the *agôn-istai*, but among the audience members, who formed fan factions—devoted hordes of what Xenophon *Memorabilia* 1.7, speaking of auletic fan culture, calls ἐπαινέται 'praisers'—and actively played favorites. Nero used his authority to organize ersatz *factiones* on the Alexandrian model, which were nothing more than cooperative claques whose energies were "harmonized" for the narcissistic purpose of amplifying his glory alone. The genuinely felt enthusiasms (σπουδαί) of authentic factions, however, would have been far less harmonious and far more volatile. The cultural history of the public audition of *kitharôidia* in Greece and Rome is difficult to write with any precision, but, as with dramatic audiences, it is safe to say that listening and spectating behaviors were as much socially and politically as aesthetically determined and oriented.[260] Relevant accounts suggest that, before an *agôn*, fans might engage in aggressive politicking meant to sway the verdict of the judges for a favorite, and, after the contest, partisans could erupt into violent conflict. Dio Chrysostom 32.59–60 berates the *stasis*-prone Alexandrians for acting like reveling bacchants and satyrs in their inappropriate craze for Apollonian *kitharôidia*, or even worse, like combatants: "If you merely hear a *kithara* string, as if you had heard the war trumpet (*salpinx*), you are no longer able to keep the peace. It isn't the Spartans you are emulating, is it? They say that in the old days the Spartans made war to the *aulos*, but you make war to the accompaniment of the *kithara*." The comparison with Sparta, which recurs elsewhere in the speech (67, 69), is loaded. It was to a strife-ridden Sparta that Terpander legendarily brought social harmony with his *kitharôidia*; by contrast, the Alexandrians, overstimulated by their wild devotion to star citharodes, enact a parody of the legend, perverting the cosmic, ordering mandate of the *kithara* with their unruliness.

The interlocutors of Plutarch's *Dialogue on Love* flee the city of Thespiae, "as if from a hostile land," for the peace and safety of the country-side around Mt. Helicon, "close by the Muses," while a "troublous

---

the capacity of judge of the *agôn* between Euripides and Aeschylus, tells the latter to "take a beating," τύπτου, because his *Seven Against Thebes* made the Thebans more warlike) reflects the reality of *mousikoi agônes*.

[260] For testimonia on the behavior of dramatic audiences in Greece and Rome, see Csapo and Slater 1994:301–317. Wallace 1997 puts the Greek testimonia in context and deals with *mousikoi agônes* as well. The notoriously unruly pantomime factions in Rome have been studied by Slater 1994. For a rich study of the active listening culture at operas and concerts in early modern Paris, see Johnson 1996.

agôn of citharodes, fraught with factional machinations and (rival) enthusiasms" (ἀργαλέον ἀγῶνα κιθαρῳδῶν, ἐντεύξεσι καὶ σπουδαῖς προειλημμένον) is being held at the city's Erotideia festival (749c). In that charged partisan environment, the narrator relates, Thespiae and, ironically, its festival of Eros, were no place for harmonious philosophical discussions, least of all about Love, or for communing with the Muses. (Thespiae also hosted a Mouseia, the city's main venue for *mousikoi agônes*, which was closely connected to the Erotideia; the two festivals were combined at least once during the Imperial period.)[261] Plutarch seems intent on constructing a scenario that dramatizes the Platonic valorization of philosophical dialogue as the "greatest *mousikê*" above and against the mundane popular music, *dêmôdês mousikê*, heard in the civic *agônes* (*Phaedo* 61a), but the roiling partisanship from which his characters retreat was no doubt a common feature of the actual festival contests in Thespiae and in other cities as well. We might detect too a class- or status-based discomfort implicit in the scene of the citharodic *agôn*. Plutarch's sociocultural elites are only too eager to leave to the partisans the music and its attendant commotion, in which they seem to have no interest. We are reminded of Aristoxenus' "barbarized" theaters and Aristotle's distinction between the "free and educated" and the vulgar audience of the *agônes*.

Aelian *Historical Miscellanies* 3.43 records a relevant anecdote set in the Italian city of Sybaris; the events it relates are meant to take place slightly before 510 BCE, when Sybaris was conquered by neighboring Croton. While a citharode was singing in the local *agôn* devoted to Hera, "the Sybarites fell into rioting on his account, taking up weapons against each other" (στασιασάντων ὑπὲρ αὐτοῦ τῶν Συβαριτῶν καὶ τὰ ὅπλα λαβόντων ἐπ' ἀλλήλους). The fearful citharode caught in the middle took refuge at the altar of the goddess, still in his costume, but "some" (οἱ δέ) of the Sybarites, presumably members of an opposing faction, nevertheless murdered him in cold blood. As divine vengeance for the perverted sacrifice of this "*therapôn* of the Muses," the city as a whole was destroyed by the Crotonites. The Sybarites, with disastrous consequences, had failed to heed the wisdom contained in the warning given by the singer Phemius to Odysseus: "There will be upon you here-

---

[261] On the Erotideia and Mouseia, see Graf 2006:191–195; cf. Bonnet 2001. We have epigraphical evidence for citharodic victors only at the Mouseia: IG VII 1762 (Epicrates of Boeotia, two-time victor, third century BCE); IG VII 1760 (Demetrius of Aeolic Myrine; around 85 BCE); IG VII 1773 (Aulus Clodius Achilleus of Corinth, second century CE); SEG III 334.48 (Memmius Leon of Larisa, third century CE).

after grief, if you slay me, an *aoidos*, who sings for gods and humans."[262] Aelian's anecdote takes its place in a series of lurid tales that treat the downfall of wealthy Sybaris through its hubristic decadence.[263] Again, as with Dio's Alexandria, Sparta is the implicit *comparandum*: whereas Terpander's *kitharôidia* produced tears of joy and political reconciliation among the troubled Spartan populace (Diodorus Siculus 8.28 *ap.* Tzetzes *Chiliades* 385–392), in Sybaris, a city at the opposite end of the politico-ethical spectrum from Sparta, *kitharôidia* is a destructively hedonistic exercise; it divides the self-indulgent, excessive citizens, promoting rather than preventing *stasis*, and precipitates impiety and the ruin of the *polis*. But, moralizing agendas and narrative exaggerations aside, the anecdote must draw on real-life incidents in which fans' exuberance, abetted by festival license, spilled out from the theater into the city to become full-blown civic disturbance. It is possible that performers could have been caught up too in the rivalrous disorder, although they would surely not have been murdered, much less at altars.[264]

14. *Theatrokratia,* Fantasy and Reality

According to Plato's narrative of the rise of *theatrokratia*, the boisterousness of Greek theater audiences was a later Classical phenomenon

---

[262] *Odyssey* 22.245–246: αὐτῷ τοι μετόπισθ' ἄχος ἔσσεται, εἴ κεν ἀοιδόν | πέφνῃς, ὅς τε θεοῖσι καὶ ἀνθρώποισιν ἀείδω. The story of Arion contains a similar moral (don't harm singers, or else!) and we could imagine that it and the Sybaris tale—there are significant parallels between them—were both propagated in some form by citharodes with the intent of insuring occupational safety during their travels, or perhaps even during partisan flare-ups such as the one dramatized in the Aelian anecdote. Cf. Svenbro 1984:169–172.

[263] On this tradition, see Ampolo 1993.

[264] One would like to know what sort of intrigue and drama might have attended the Great Panathenaic citharodic *agôn* of 402/1 BCE, the first one held in the wake of the political turmoil following the end of the Peloponnesian War. The gold crown for the winner of the citharodic contest in that year was not in fact awarded, but dedicated by the *polis* (i.e. not the victor) to Athena. This may have been due to a tie for first place, but since we do not know how many judges assessed the Panathenaic *mousikoi agônes*, we cannot be sure that such ties occurred (Lucian *Harmonides* 2 refers to "seven or five" judges at a *mousikos agôn*). Cf. n268 below. Some more politically fraught disagreement over the contest and the competitors might rather have been the cause. This same crown appears in the inventories of the goddess until 385/4 BCE. For the inscriptional evidence, see Kotsidu 1991:86–87, although her contention that different crowns were being dedicated through these years is improbable; cf. Shear 2003:95n33.

(*Laws* 700a–701b). In times past, the Archaic and early Classical period, when, "under the old laws (*nomoi*), the *dêmos* was master of nothing" (*Laws* 700a), audiences, mass and elite alike, would listen to musical performances in silence, "not daring to judge by *thorobos* 'clamor'" (700d), and let qualified judges evaluate their worth. Performers were above pandering to audiences and maintained instead the aesthetic and ethical standards of purity they knew the elite authorities valued. In time, however (i.e. from around the middle of the fifth century BCE), the *okhlos* 'mob' increasingly felt at liberty (*eleutheria*) to make its own opinions known through "hissing" (*surinx*, literally 'panpipe'), "unmusical shouting" (*amousoi boai*), and applause (*krotoi*)—a cacophony that matched the *amousos paranomia* 'unmusical lawlessness' of the professional musicians on stage (700d). The authority of judges was undermined by the crowd's assertiveness. In Sicily and Italy, *theatrokratia* had advanced so far that in Plato's time judges were completely absent; the spectators alone decided the winners in musical contests through applause (659b).

This schematic vision of an orderly Golden Age overtaken by a period of noisy, populist degeneracy influenced the thinking of generations of musical conservatives after Plato, but it is nevertheless of questionable historical value, conditioned as it is by the resentment of fourth-century elites toward their own public musical culture, a development that was discussed above. This idealization of "classical music" should be construed on the whole as false nostalgia, the impossible desire to silence assertive contemporary crowds displaced onto the past. Plato's evocation in *Laws* 700c of the "ordering rod" (*rhabdos kosmousê*) that was used to keep "children, their attendants, and the common *okhlos*" quietly under control may well be make-believe or at least greatly exaggerated, but, historical or not, it betrays his nostalgic fantasy of the innocent musical past. Old-time audiences could be loud and unruly; ideological prohibition alone could not (or, from Plato's retrospective point of view, cannot) restrain their ruckus.[265]

Despite his extremely tendentious rhetoric, however, Plato is no doubt right to note that a stylistic change in the reception of agonistic

---

[265] Wallace 1997: "Plato's historical statement about the rod" is "at best misleading" (99). However, the "rod holders" (*rhabdoukhoi*), charged with keeping order (*eukosmia*) among the audience, are attested in Aristophanes *Peace* 734, with scholia. Surely these officials were not there to keep the crowd quiet, as comic audiences were supposed to be voluble and reactive, nor were they there to beat arrogant comic poets, as Aristophanes jokes. The inebriated comic audience might have been in need of special crowd control.

music had been in the works, at least in Athens, since around the middle of the fifth century, and one that did reflect to some extent a "democratization" of the listening experience under Pericles. The aesthetically and ethically restrained receptive disposition of elites gave way increasingly to the more sensational reactions of the demotic audience, reactions that were emotionally keyed to the musicians' more visually and musically sensational performances.[266] In Athenian musical iconography of the late sixth and early fifth centuries BCE, when agonistic music, above all *kitharôidia*, was still felt to be the spiritual possession of aristocratic connoisseurs, we see auditors fixed in poses of deep concentration, in a sense demonstratively "performing" their intense engagement with the music they are hearing. An excellent example is the well-born young man depicted on the reverse of an amphora by the Brygos Painter (Plate 2). Leaning on his staff, forehead pressed to palm, the elegant youth seems wholly enraptured by the music of the citharode, who sings on the other side, yet nonetheless he remains supremely self-controlled. Similarly, seated judges or spectators are consistently shown listening intently to citharodes without audience distraction.[267] Images such as these are no doubt idealized; the uniformly aristocratic auditors and judges are socially decontextualized, isolated in their aesthetic reverie or critical assessment. The *okhlos* never breaks into the tightly controlled frame. Unfortunately, we lack corresponding images of auditors at *mousikoi agônes* from later periods, so instructive contrast is impossible, but the attitude of these represented listeners and the context of their audition, idealized as it may be, does suggest that a more general tone of repose was set at the early *agônes* than at those of Plato's day and after. It may be too that judges felt less pressured by clamorous crowds (or particularly vociferous factions) in delivering their verdicts.

Yet the case for contrast should not be overstated. Judges of late- and post-Classical musical contests were not the ineffectual pushovers, easily swayed by *thorobos*, who are caricatured by Plato (*Laws* 659a). Nero's show of deference to the judges (Tacitus *Annals* 16.4.2) at the second Neronia, contrived as it was, is one indication that they still exercised autonomy, or at least were believed to, even if their verdicts were more often than not in sympathy with the majority opinion,

---

[266] As Wallace 1997 sensibly argues.

[267] Representative is a black-figured pelike with a citharode playing between two seated men, Staatliche Kunstsammlungen Kassel, Antikensammlung T.675; Shapiro 1992:69, fig. 47; Maas and Snyder 1989:74, fig. 5. Maas and Snyder believe that the listening youth on the Brygos Painter's amphora is a judge (61), but this seems to me unlikely.

as they most certainly were in Nero's case.[268] By the same token, Hellenistic and Imperial audience response was more complex than the idiotic sound and fury Plato's pessimistic vision would suggest. The theatrocratic crowd could display both emotive extroversion and aesthetic discrimination; in music-mad Alexandria, "even the most low-class and uneducated layman" expertly criticizes technical mistakes made by the citharode (Athenaeus 4.176e). Indeed, putting to one side the warping effects of factionalism, which could be considerable (recall Plutarch's mention of the aggressive campaigns waged by partisans to influence the judging at the Erotideia), what judges recognized as worthy or unworthy was more often than not what the masses did as well.[269] Lucian, in a text written in the second century CE but set in the fourth century BCE, and implicitly in Athens, takes it for granted that the majority of spectators at *agônes* "will always follow those who are better able to judge" (πάντως ἀκολουθήσουσι τοῖς ἄμεινον κρῖναι δυναμένοις, *Harmonides* 2). Beneath Lucian's elitist "spin," whereby the "vulgar" (βάναυσοι) masses, "ignorant of true quality" (ἀγνοοῦσι τὰ βελτίω), reflexively fall in line with the educated tastes of their betters, the "leading men" (οἱ προῦχοντες), we detect the outlines of an actually existing, class-transcendent consensus between judges and audience. In order to be successful, citharodes, both before and under the regime of *theatrokratia*, must have been compelled to court both judges and the *okhlos*, in all its demographic complexity. According to Epictetus, the agonistic citharode is always apprehensive when he performs in public, because "he not only wishes to sing well, but also to win popular acclaim" (Arrian *Dissertations of Epictetus* 2.13). Although Epictetus belongs to the second century CE, his characterization of the psychology of competitive citharodes as a dual drive to satisfy objective criteria of musical skill and to please the masses no doubt has a diachronic validity, even if the latter tendency took on increasingly extravagant expressions after the fifth century BCE.

---

[268] See Csapo and Slater 1994:160 on dramatic judging and popular sentiment; cf. Wilson 2000:100–102 for political factors. We know next to nothing about the mechanics of judging *mousikoi agônes*. Judges of music, like those of drama and sport, took oaths of fairness (Plato *Laws* 659a–b). Plato prescribes only one judge, over the age of thirty, to officiate and assess the solo musical contests in his ideal state (*Laws* 765a), but this seems abnormal. The Attic vase paintings tend to show two to three possible judges of *kitharôidia*, but we cannot be sure what figures in contest scenes are in fact meant to be judges. Seven citizens judge a Ptolemaic contest of poets in an anecdote told by Vitruvius 7.5.

[269] The anecdotal record has it that judgments in Athens repeatedly went unfairly against Menander and for his less talented rival Philemon, thanks to the latter's influential partisans (Quintilian 10.1.72; Aulus Gellius *Attic Nights* 17.4).

For our Roman sources, Nero's obsessive attention to the acclamation of the *vulgus* in Naples and then in Rome is symptomatic of his moral and political corruption; the bizarre spectacle of the *imperator* simultaneously orchestrating and submitting to a tyranny of *theatrokratia* perfectly emblematizes the Neronian principate in all its excessive, perverse theatricality. Conceivably, Tacitus has Plato's topsy-turvy evocation of *theatrokratia* in mind as he describes the "public disgrace" that was Nero's Roman debut at the second Neronia (*Annals* 16.4–5). The scene plays as Platonic nightmare, with manipulation and debasement all around: the noisy rabble compels the *faux*-submissive citharode to sing, who in turn compels the audience to applaud. The "ordering rod" of Plato's Golden Age, which once kept the crowd docile and silent, has been replaced with thuggish soldiers who beat spectators "wearied with unpracticed hands" into keeping up the incessant *clamor* at top volume. But in his careful solicitation of audible favor, Nero was in a sense simply following the logic of professional musical practice. Applause and acclamation must always have been valued by agonistic performers to one degree or another; they confirmed and communicated mass recognition and fame, which would have been primary goals of every professional musician. And unless we presume some radical disparity between audience response and the verdict of the judges, applause signaled the promise of gain, it was the sound of an imminent prize or fee, which was obviously also a primary goal of professionals, even those of the old school. When the citharist Stratonicus plays a concert recital (*epideixis*) in Rhodes at which no one applauds, he caustically asks how he can expect the Rhodians to make a "contribution" (*eranos*) when they refuse to give "that which costs nothing" (Athenaeus 8.350b).[270] Controlled applause was good for business; a wholly silent crowd was not.

Post-Platonic sources tend to obscure the value of applause to the professional musician. In Athenaeus 14.631f–632a, to support the tendentious claim that "in the old days popularity with the masses (*okhloi*) was a sign of bad music (*kakomousia*)," the following anecdote

---

[270] Stratonicus curiously refers to the wage (*misthos*) he would typically receive for a concert as an *eranos* 'contribution', a word that obscures the monetary reality of the return. But the sarcasm dripping from his remark makes a mockery of such mystification, putting it in tendentious quotation marks, and serving as a reproach to the audience. Their cheapness with applause, which costs nothing, indicates their larger misperception of "how it works," i.e. Stratonicus plays, and audiences reward his virtuosity with money. Stratonicus also called Rhodes a "city of suitors" (Athenaeus 8.351c), alluding to the Ithacan suitors' selfish misuse of the singer Phemius in the *Odyssey*, but also suggesting the Rhodians' unwillingness to "commit" financially.

is mustered: "When a certain aulete once received loud applause, Asopodorus of Phlius, who was waiting offstage, said, 'What's this? Clearly something really bad must have happened!' For otherwise the aulete could not have been so popular with the crowd." Of course, the idea that applause would be or ever was unappreciated by an *agônistês* is pure fantasy. More realistic is the claim of the titular character in Lucian's *Harmonides*, a young, ambitious aulete, that he would never have studied *aulos* playing at all were it not for the popular recognition (ἡ δόξα ἡ παρὰ τῶν πολλῶν) it promised. To which his teacher, Timotheus, advises him to play to the judges, not the crowd: "At the *agônes* the mass of spectators know how to clap at times and to hiss, but the judging is done by seven or five or however many" (2). While the advice to impress the judges is sound, the advice to ignore the audience response sounds far less authentic. Indeed, the historical Timotheus of Thebes was a huge star of the fourth century BCE. As Lucian mentions, he accompanied sensationalistic dithyrambs composed by his still more famous namesake, Timotheus of Miletus, to great acclaim in Athens. As such, he is an ironically hypocritical mouthpiece for the anti-populist ideology propounded in the *Harmonides*. In terms of the socioeconomic logic of professional music making, Harmonides' fascination with celebrity and his concern for audience approval ring truer than the elitist sentiments contrived for Timotheus.[271]

15. Twin Delight: Aesthetics and Techniques of *Kitharôidia*

In Naples the music is about to begin. Nero raises the *plêktron* and strikes the strings, sounding out the first notes of a melody that will serve as prelude to his song proper. The notes become increasingly clear and of a volume sufficient to be heard alongside his voice as it begins to fill the theater.

The balanced integration of the vocal and instrumental or manual components of *kitharôidia* was a critical aesthetic criterion of the performance, which was perceived to be a near-equal symbiosis of

---

[271] Cf. Amphis *Dithyramb* fr. 14 K-A (fourth century BCE), in which a dithyrambic poet (or perhaps an aulete) looks forward excitedly to introducing an exotic instrument called the *gingras*, a small-scale *aulos* of Phoenician provenance, to the *okhlos* at the dithyrambic *agôn*, where he is sure that it will win the prize by "heaving up everything, like a trident, with the applause (*krotoi*) it gets" (cf. Barker 1984:263; Wilson 2000:69–70). The professional reflexively associates applause with victory.

two *tekhnai*, singing and *kithara* playing. Since it delivered the poetic *logos* and carried the main melody, the voice would always possess some degree of symbolic authority over the *kithara*, but the ancient sources suggest that the ideal relationship between the two was one of complementarity rather than mere accompaniment.[272] This combined mastery of skills no doubt contributed to the greater prestige and higher prize amounts enjoyed by citharodes relative to practitioners in other agonistic media such as *rhapsôidia*, solo *aulos* playing (*aulêtikê*), solo *kithara* playing (*kitharistikê* or, often, *psilê kitharisis* or *psilokithar-istikê* 'bare *kithara* playing'), and *aulôidia* 'singing to the *aulos*', all of which involved the display of only one primary skill on the part of the performer. For Quintilian, singing to the *kithara* is the perfect expression of the mind's "swift and nimble" (*agilis ac velox*) natural ability to pay simultaneous attention to several different subjects:

> *An vero citharoedi non simul et memoriae et sono vocis et plurimis flexibus serviunt, cum interim alios nervos dextra percurrunt, alios laeva trahunt continent praebent, ne pes quidem otiosus certam legem temporum servat—et haec pariter omnia?*

> Do not citharodes simultaneously exert their memory and attend to the tone of their voice and its numerous melodic turns, while with the right hand they run over certain strings

---

[272] The verb ὑποκιθαρίζω 'play the lyre/*kithara* in accompaniment' is late and exceedingly rare (see LSJ s.v.) and does not in any case apply to *kitharôidia*. At *Homeric Hymn to Hermes* 54 we find the phrase θεὸς δ' ὑπὸ καλὸν ἄειδε describing the singing of Hermes to the lyre (cf. 502: θεὸς δ' ὑπὸ καλὸν ἄεισεν, describing Apollo's performance). Nagy 1990b:353 translates 'the god sang beautifully, in accompaniment', which would mean that the composer of the *Hymn* conceives of the vocal component of song as secondary to the lyre. But the idea of sung text as subordinate to instrumental music goes against the dominant ideology of early Greek *mousikê*, which accorded symbolic primacy to *testa* over *musica*. (See Pratinas PMG 708.6–7 for a strong affirmation of this mentality in the context of aulodic song, with Gentili 1988:24–27.) Further, none of the examples of ὑπᾴδω cited in LSJ corresponds to the idea of singing in accompaniment to an instrument; the examples that refer to actual musical performance denote rather singing that "accompanies," i.e. plays a role in, the full ensemble of choral song and dance. West 2003:117, 153 takes ὑπό in the opposite sense, translating, 'the god sang beautifully to its accompaniment [that is, to the accompaniment provided by the *kithara*]'. But perhaps we should not read any notion of 'accompaniment' out of ὑπαείδειν at all, and take the phrase to mean simply 'the god sang in addition to' the lyre *that was already sounding*; that is, ὑπό has a temporal as well as spatial sense—the voice emerges 'from under' the layer of lyric melody that is already sounding. Cf. Ovid *Metamorphoses* 5.340: *haec percussis subiungit carmina nervis* '[Calliope] (sub)joined this song to the struck strings'. The parity between lyre and voice is suggested in the *Hymn* by the recurrent conceit of the lyre as singer (39) or having voice (443, 478–485).

and with the left they pull, damp, and release others? Not even the foot is idle, but it keeps strict count of the rhythm. And all this happens at the same time.

Quintilian Institutio Oratoria 1.12.3

Quintilian's citharode is thus the consummate musical "multitasker," effortlessly orchestrating the demands of song and strings: text, melody, rhythm, vocal production, and complex instrumental technique. The preeminent difficulty of *kitharôidia* is attested in the anecdotal and proverbial traditions of Greece and Rome as well. Cicero cites a saying, common among Greek musicians, that those who cannot succeed as citharodes become aulodes (*Pro Murena* 13.29). A scholiast to Aristophanes *Birds* 858 tells of one fifth-century BCE musician, Chaeris, who began his career as a κιθαρῳδὸς ψυχρός 'frigid citharode', but later became an *aulêtês*. This may be an attempt to account for the existence of two later-fifth-century musicians named Chaeris, one a citharode, the other an aulete, but the common assumption that *aulos* playing is less challenging than *kitharôidia* in any case informs the scholiast's comment.[273] (According to "Aristotle" *Problems* 19.9 and 49, it was thought that singing to the lyre was generally a more difficult proposition than singing to the *aulos*, because the fuller sound of the reeds, itself akin to the human voice, disguised the singer's errors, while the thinner-sounding strings left the voice exposed.)

A citharist named Nicostratus wittily acknowledges the preeminence of the citharode—and the inferiority of his own instrumental *tekhnê*—when he belittles the talents of Laodocus, a citharode, with the neat chiasm that the citharode was "small in a great *tekhnê*, but he himself was great in a small one [i.e. *kitharistikê*]" (Aelian *Historical Miscellanies* 4.2).[274] Even the worth of non-musical *tekhnai* could be

---

[273] Confusion reigns in the scholia. A scholiast on *Acharnians* 16 says Chaeris was both a citharode and an aulode, while a scholiast to *Peace* 951 specifies that there were separate auletic and citharodic Chaerises. See Stephanis 1988:456; Olson 2002:71 and Winnington-Ingram 1988:252–253, who think Chaeris was both citharode and aulete. By contrast, another Aristophanic scholion has it that the citharode Phrynis of Mytilene was initially an aulode (*Clouds* 971a). A comic play on this proverb could lurk here, a comment on Phrynis' perceived lack of talent: he woefully inverts the cliché, a failed aulode turned citharode. Another scholiast (*Clouds* 971b) records that Phrynis was called ψυχρός. Alternately, though not exclusively, the joke could play on the influence of the "polychord" *aulos* (cf. Plato *Republic* 399d) on his harmonically expansive *kitharôidia*.

[274] Nicostratus may be an anecdotal by-form of Stratonicus, the name of the historical citharist whose biting wit became proverbial. See further Stephanis 1988:333; Wilson 2004:282n35. It is notable that in the anecdotes collected in Athenaeus 8.347f–352d

magnified when measured against the objectively impressive yardstick of *kitharôidia*. In Diphilus' comedy *Synoris* (*fr. 75 K-A*), a self-important parasite, proud of his so-called *tekhnê*, asks, "Don't you know that the parasite is ranked (κρίνεται) first after the kitharode?" (Diphilus plays on the expression μετὰ Λέσβιον ᾠδόν 'After the Lesbian Singer', prover-bially applied to those who must take second place behind an undis-puted master, but originally referring to the Spartan custom whereby prestigious Lesbian citharodes were given the privilege of singing first at the Carneian *agôn*.)[275]

In a Latin epigram titled "On a Citharode" included in the *Latin Anthology* (102 Kay = 113R), an anonymous poet foregrounds the audi-ence's wonder at a virtuoso citharode's marvelously seamless harmo-nization of voice and *kithara*. The citharode takes the stage,

> that he might please the ears of the *vulgus*. He stands there, supremely capable in both his manual execution and his voice; his hands harmonize with his tongue, united with it in equal expression. For he deploys both with equivalent expertise in balanced proportion and mingles his hands as allies with the art of his mouth in such a way that it is a matter of doubt to you, captivated by the twin delight, whether it is his voice singing or the lyre sounding by itself."[276]

The perfect fusion of instrument and voice inspires a kind of delightful aporia in its perception, a sensation echoed for the reader in the poem's juxtaposed and interlaced order of words describing those functions.[277] This delight is neatly expressed by another late writer, the early

---

Stratonicus more often than not directs his verbal attacks against citharodes rather than citharists, a tendency that could reflect a concerted rhetorical campaign by this practitioner of the "underdog" medium of *kitharistikê* to chip away at the relatively greater prestige enjoyed by citharodes—a campaign conducted entirely offstage, since citharists could not sing their critical and self-promotional agendas in perfor-mance, as citharodes could.

[275] Testimonia assembled and discussed in Gostoli 1990:40–44 and 122–123.

[276] ... *ingreditur, vulgi auribus ut placeat.* | *stat tactu cantuque potens, cui brachia linguae* | *concordant sensu conciliata pari.* | *nam sic aequali ambo moderamine librat* | *atque oris socias temperat arte manus,* | *ut dubium tibi sit gemina dulcedine capto,* | *vox utrumne canat an lyra sola sonet. Latin Anthology* 103 Kay = 114R, another "On a Citharode" epigram, also foregrounds the "twin delight" produced by the citharode's hands and voice. This one has a "tongued thumb" (*linguato ... pollice*, 3), which makes the "singing strings emit a human voice" (*humanum ... chorda canora loqui*, 4); his "voice and fingers sing as one from their different sources" (*unum ex diversis vox digitique canunt*, 10). Cf. Tibullus 2.5.3, *vocales chordae*; Lygdamus (Tibullus 3) 4.41.

[277] Kay 2006:146 speaks of the "emphasis on combination and harmony" in the epigram.

Byzantine Aristaenetus, who describes the reaction of an enthusiastic fan to an outstanding citharode's performance: "Bravo for the voice, bravo for the lyre! How very harmoniously the two sound together in unison! And how attuned is the tongue to the striking of the strings!" (ε γε τῆς φωνῆς, ε γε τῆς λύρας. ὡς ἄμφω μουσικώτατα συνηχεῖ, καὶ πρόσχορδος ἡ γλῶττα τοῖς κρούμασι, *Greek Epistles* 2.5.1–2).[278]

As this last passage indicates, the vocal melody was typically sung in note-for-note unison with the struck *kithara* strings. The term πρόσχορδος, as in Aristaenetus' phrase, πρόσχορδος ἡ γλῶττα τοῖς κρούμασι, designates this procedure.[279] But citharodes could play too secondary melodic and rhythmic figures on the *kithara*, as color counterpoint to the primary melody and rhythm of the vocal line. Plato *Laws* 812d–e describes such figures as examples of ἑτεροφωνία 'the combination of different notes' and ποικιλία 'ornamentation', specifically,

> when the strings sound different tunes (*melê*) from those of the composer's melody, or when performers combine close intervals [on the strings] with wide ones [with the voice], slow with fast notes, high pitch with low (whether at concords or the octave), and similarly when they fit all manner of rhythmic ornamentations (*poikilmata*) to the notes of the lyre.[280]

Although Plato disapproves of these elaborate effects—as a staunch musical conservative he advocates instead the traditional, homophonic mode of lyre playing, πρόσχορδα τὰ φθέγματα τοῖς φθέγμασι—his vivid polemic indicates that by the fourth century BCE, and thus certainly by Nero's time, they were standbys of every competitive citharode's technical repertoire, deployed, judiciously or not, as virtuoso color contrast to delivery *all'unisono*.[281]

---

[278] Cf. Lucian *Imagines* 14.

[279] Cf. "Aristotle" *Problems* 19.9; Pollux *Onomasticon* 4.63. See Barker 1984:191n7; West 1992:67.

[280] See Barker 1984:162–163 and 1995:41–45. It must be emphasized that Greek musicians never developed systematized chordal harmony or polyphonic counterpoint. The devices mentioned by Plato are essentially ornamental. Gerolamo Mei's 1572 letter to Vincenzo Galilei, a fellow member of the Florentine Camerata, remains an important discussion of the monophonic basis of ancient Greek music (Palisca 1989:56–75).

[281] Cf. Barker 1995:44. The citharodes associated with the Athenian New Music were likely the pioneers of these "contrapuntal" effects, to which their innovative polychord *kitharai* were ideally suited. Earlier experiments were probably essayed as well. See e.g. "Plutarch" *On Music* 21.1138b, which refers to the instrumental *poikilia* of old-fashioned music, with comments in Barker 1984:227.

Purely instrumental playing also had an important place in citha-rodic performance. There was the introductory instrumental prelude, which I discuss in detail in Part II.1. Solo *kithara* music also filled in the time between sung verses. In early *kitharôidia* it seems to have been common practice to give the strings a rhythmic strum with the *plêk-tron* at every verse end. Aristophanes thus has Euripides parody the choral songs of Aeschylus, which, Euripides claims, are stylistically indebted to Archaic citharodic music, by exclaiming *to-phlatto-thratto-phlatto-thratt* after each sung line, a mimetic vocalization of a stereo-typical strumming pattern (*Frogs* 1284–1295).[282] The joke here is not only on Aeschylus; it is also on the old-style *kitharôidia* that Aeschylus emulated, which must have sounded tonally and rhythmically monoto-nous to the more sophisticated ears of many in the audience of *Frogs*, who had become attuned to the adventurous stylings of later-fifth-century citharodes such as Phrynis of Mytilene and Timotheus of Miletus, both experimenters with polychord *kitharai*, instruments with more than the traditional seven strings. We will have more to say about these musicians later. It is enough for now to note the good probability that among their innovations was the elaboration of instrumental interludes, a facet of the wider programmatic tendency within the music of the later Classical period to liberate musical sonority from the formal constraints of the poetic text, *melos* from *logos*.[283]

Contemporary testimony for this comes by way of the comic poet Pherecrates, who, like his rival Aristophanes, stages criticism of such innovation. Pherecrates has *Mousikê*, personified as a sexually violated woman, complain that her worst offender, Timotheus, "stripped and undid me with his twelve strings, when he found me somewhere walking by myself" (κἂν ἐντύχῃ πού μοι βαδιζούσῃ μόνῃ, | ἀπέδυσε κἀνέλυσε χορδαῖς δώδεκα, *Cheiron* fr. 155.30–31 K-A). 'Walking by myself' would seem to mean music without voice. Although it is impos-sible to know precisely what musical effects lie behind the sexual innu-endo of ἀπέδυσε κἀνέλυσε 'stripped and undid'—the double entendres in this passage are notoriously difficult to interpret—*Mousikê* must mean that Timotheus, with the rich sonic palette of his "twelve strings," has introduced new levels of complexity, melodic and rhythmic, to the

---

[282] At Aristophanes *Wealth* 290 the slave Cario imitates the strum of the *kithara* with the expression *threttanelo*; the bright ring of struck strings could also be vocalized as *tênella* (Archilochus fr. 324.1W, with scholia *ad* Pindar *Olympian* 9.1). Aristides Quintilianus *On Music* 2.79 says that the letter *tau* "sounds like strings of an instru-ment"; elsewhere he says that the shape of *tau* resembles that of the plectrum (3.130).

[283] Cf. Csapo 2004:222–229; Gentili 1988:30.

solo instrumental portions of his compositions, a complexity that was viewed by his conservative critics as scandalous.[284] At the minimum, it is certain that neither Timotheus nor his progressive rivals and successors, including Nero, maintained the old verse-strum-verse-strum pattern described by Aristophanes, preferring rather to craft more intricate lyric filigree when not singing.

The critical importance of vocal technique should not be underestimated. Citharodes had not only to make their often-lengthy texts consistently intelligible; they had to sustain the aesthetic integrity of the tones, melodies, and rhythms in which they sang them.[285] Citharodic song demanded impressive range from its singers; one of the oldest and most famous *nomoi*, the *Orthios*, was so called because of its characteristically high pitch.[286] As instrumental technique become more complex with the New Music, so must their singing have kept pace, becoming ever more virtuosic, and, as the text of Timotheus' *nomos Persians* suggests, mimetically dynamic. "Lucian" *Nero* 7 vividly describes the immense strain that was put on breath and voice by the intense physical demands of citharodic performance. We saw that the focus of Nero's rigorous training was his voice, whose "small and indistinct" quality supposedly left an early audience at the Juvenalia laughing and crying at the same time (Dio Cassius 61.20.2; cf. Suetonius *Nero* 20.1). In "Lucian" *Nero* 6 his voice is "naturally hollow and low" and "produces a sort of buzzing sound" (βομβεῖ πως), the result of his constricted throat. Citharodes thus practiced under the tutelage of *phônaskoi* 'vocal trainers', who were skilled in improving such physical and technical deficiencies. It is likely, I think, that Terpnus and Menecrates served Nero in this capacity.

The premium placed upon the work of these professionals is attested in two Imperial inscriptions, both of which honor the *phônaskos* alongside the victories of the citharodes they celebrate. In one of them, which details the winning career of C. Antonius Septimius Poplius, the intimately guiding role of his *phônaskos*, P. Aelius Agathemerus, receives extended mention. Himself a "citharode victorious in the sacred games and a distinguished composer (*melopoios*)," the trainer is said to have

---

[284] Cf. Barker 1984:236n203 on ἀπέδυσε κἀνέλυσε: "[B]oth words indicate undressing ... It is a plausible guess that the first refers principally to the breakdown of rhythmic structure (cf. the use of *apolelumena* at Hephaestion *On Poems* 3.3, Aristides Quintilianus 52.12–14), the second to the disruption of melodic forms by frequent modulation."

[285] See West 1992:42–47 on the aesthetics of the singing voice.

[286] Cf. Barker 1984:251.

"been like a father" to the younger citharode (IGR IV 1432).[287] In the other case, training was an actual family affair; the citharode's own brother was his *phônaskos* (IG IV 591). The term *phônaskos* is late, but vocal coaches, like athletic trainers—and the sustained production of the solo voice through a full citharodic performance was nothing if not an athletic endeavor—surely plied their trade as far back as the Archaic period. It is probable that the bearded man on the reverse of a black-figured amphora by the Berlin Painter is meant to be the trainer rather than a judge of the younger citharode who sings on the obverse side (New York 56.171.38, c. 490 BCE).[288] The man holds aloft a forked wand with his left hand and points emphatically with the thumb and forefinger of his right, a gesture seemingly meant to communicate either praise or criticism of the technique of the citharode.

16. Picking and Plucking

Extensive reconstructions of the manual method of lyre and *kithara* playing have already been undertaken by several scholars.[289] I leave discussion of most of the technical details to them, but I feel obliged to register a few essential points of disagreement that have to do with the use of the *plêktron* and the fingers in sounding the strings of the *kithara*, and how both are deployed in relation to singing. I begin with the procedure of damping strings with the left hand, from "behind" the instrument. In the passage from the *Institutio Oratoria* quoted above, Quintilian seems to be describing a technique of *kithara* playing that involves pulling and pressing against, and thereby damping, selected strings with the fingers of the left hand, while striking open strings with the *plêktron* held in the right ("with the right hand they run over certain strings and with the left they pull, damp, and release others").[290] West provides a helpful discussion of the damping technique, although I think he errs in arguing that citharodes would only

---

[287] Agathemerus also served as secretary of the Guild of the Artists of Dionysus in Ephesus (IGR IV 468.19 = Stephanis 1988, no. 15).

[288] Thus Beazley 1922:73; on 74–75 he discusses an interesting set of parallel images from a now-lost Panathenaic-type amphora. Herington 1985:17 thinks that the man with the forked wand is a judge "correcting" some misdeed of the citharode, but this identification seems to me less probable.

[289] See especially West 1992:64–70; Maas and Snyder 1989:63–64; 92–94.

[290] It is worth noting an emendation for *praebent* written into the Bg codex containing this passage from the *Institutio: prement* 'press', which probably derives from a gloss on the damping function indicated by *continent*. See Borthwick 1959:27.

have damped certain strings when they strummed all seven strings with the plectrum, to deaden the sound of unwanted notes. Quintilian's *percurrunt* 'run over' may well indicate strumming, and strumming multiple strings at once to sound a desired chordal cluster—called *sunkrousis* at Ptolemy *Harmonics* 2.12—is a technique that is both textually and iconographically attested. Yet there seems to be no reason that citharodes could not as well strike an *individual* string with the plectrum while damping nearby strings to prevent them from sounding in case they were accidentally struck or sympathetically set to vibrate. Such left-hand presets would clearly facilitate an efficient right-hand technique.[291] A string would only be released and opened when the melody next called for it; to translate literally Quintilian's terms, the player "presents" (*praebere*) it for striking when he no longer need "restrain" (*continere*) it. The struck note would then be cut off by finger pressure to the string to make way for the next note to sound on an open string, making for a cleanly articulated melodic line.[292] In this way, the left hand would be busy indeed, constantly pulling—more on that below—pressing, and releasing in nuanced response to both strumming and single-string picking.

West's views on damping and strumming build on a set of other assertions: that the fingers of the left hand, when not damping strummed strings, plucked out the single notes of the melody line in accord with the voice; that the plectrum was not used to strike strings individually; and, accordingly, that the citharode never sang when he used his plectrum, since the plectrum was used only to strum out high-volume, percussive, cadential clusters of the type described by Aristophanes as *to-phlatto-thratto-phlatto-thratt*. The citharode would thus sing only when he plucked single notes/strings with the left hand, never when he plied the plectrum.[293] Considering simply the acoustical

---

[291] Cf. Anderson 1994: "The true function of the left hand: to damp in advance the strings not meant to sound; so among present-day Nubian tribesmen—and the working principle of the Autoharp today" (176). Note that Greek vase painters tend to show citharodes holding their fingers in damping position even while not playing (e.g. a red-figured calyx crater, c. 430 BCE; Bundrick 2005:169, fig. 99); maintaining this position was clearly habitual for the well-trained performer. It is also the most natural way to hold the left hand as the wrist is braced by the instrument's support strap.

[292] This damping of a struck note was called *katalêpsis* (scholia *ad Clouds* 318; *Suda* s.v. κατάληψις). Borthwick 1959 discusses the term, but his reconstruction of this rather simple procedure makes it into something overly complicated. Also, we need not suppose that it involved creating staccato effects alone (p25); it may have sometimes, but a good player could use damping to create an even legato tone.

[293] West 1992:64–69. Cf. Maas and Snyder 1989:64 and *passim*; Paquette 1984:99–100; Bélis 1995:1048–1050; Wille 1967:212–213 on Roman sources. With the exception of Anderson

environment of public performance on a stringed instrument, however, it seems unlikely that a citharode would deprive himself of the regular use of the plectrum in playing single-note melodies. Notes struck with the plectrum would be brighter, crisper, and project further than those plucked with the finger, surely appealing qualities for a performer who played before (often noisy) audiences of thousands. The force of the plectrum stroke could easily be modulated to match the volume of the singing voice, now soft, now loud.

What about the ancient evidence? At a glance, the sixth- and fifth-century iconography of *kithariôidia* would seem to support West's reconstruction. Most Archaic and Classical artists depict close-mouthed citharodes in the act of sweeping the plectrum across the strings, or, as in the case of the citharode of the Berlin Painter in the Metropolitan Museum, a smaller number show them singing after having just completed what seems to have been a vigorous sweep. Greek vase paintings are not photorealistic documents, however, and we should be wary of building detailed theories about technical practices around them. There can be little doubt that these poses and gestures became conventional because the energy and dynamism they conveyed were aesthetically appealing to both artists and consumers. For what it is worth, however, we should note that a few painters do depict citharodes and lyre players vocalizing while applying the plectrum directly to the strings; a few more show players who seem to strike individual strings, not strum, although these players do not simultaneously sing. Again, it would be unwise to treat these images as entirely reliable photographic evidence for the practices they (seem to) represent, but they must possess some minimal value in reflecting the *realia* of string playing.[294]

1994:176, this view, with various modifications, is the consensus going back to Sachs 1940:132–133. My dissent responds specifically to West, because his *Ancient Greek Music* has become the standard reference for technical matters. Winnington-Ingram 1956:183 holds, as I do, that the player struck individual notes with the plectrum; less convincing is his contention that the right-hand fingers regularly plucked notes.

[294] Three examples: (1) One of the three singing satyr-citharodes depicted on the "Singers at the Panathenaia" bell krater by Polion inserts his plectrum between the two high strings of his instrument; his left hand probably damps other strings as he does this (New York 25.78.66; West 1992, plate 16). (2) On a pelike by the Meidias Painter (New York 37.11.23; Bundrick 2005:55, fig. 32) the legendary citharode Musaeus applies the plectrum to the strings of his *kithara* while apparently damping with left hand. He does not sing. (3) A singing comast applies the plectrum to the strings of his *barbitos* (red-figured skyphos, Louvre G 156; Paquette 1984:185, B21); strumming seems unlikely.

A vivid yet problematic example of the former type is provided by the Brygos Painter, who shows a citharode striking the middle string with the plectrum, while damping the surrounding strings with the fingertips of his left hand—he is not plucking—and tossing his head back in song, all at once (Plate 1). What complicates a straightforward reading of the image, however, is that the citharode is striking the string beneath the bridge, where it would not resonate properly against the soundboard to produce a full tone. This iconographical oddity was explained by Otto Gombosi as illustrating a special technique whereby the *kithara* player inserts the plectrum beneath the bridge and presses it against a plucked string to raise its pitch, a theory which has been generally discredited.[295] Others propose that the painter has merely captured the moment in which the player brings the plectrum back into position to make another outward sweep.[296] But the string is clearly shown bending with the pressure applied by the plectrum. Despite this deliberate touch, has the artist simply demonstrated a lack of precision in another respect, his positioning of the plectrum? Vase painters rarely misrepresent the fundamental mechanics of stringed instruments and playing technique, but perhaps this is just such a rare case. (It is worth noting that the large, chunky bridge on the Brygos citharode's instrument is placed considerably higher on the sound-board than is usual.)[297] Analogous "errors" in plectrum placement may be found elsewhere.[298]

Early Greek verbal descriptions of lyric performance are still less precise in these matters, but the text that offers the most detailed account of string playing, the *Homeric Hymn to Hermes*, contains reasonably explicit testimony that discrete notes were sounded with the

---

[295] Gombosi 1939:116–122. Winnington-Ingram 1956 shows how improbable are this and other theories about "stopping" *kithara* strings to alter their pitch. Cf. West 1992:66n81. Harmonics—the bell-like, high tones produced by lightly stopping struck strings with the finger—were likely part of the citharode's repertoire of techniques, but their use was surely highly occasional, as it tends to be in modern string playing.

[296] Maas and Snyder 1989:64.

[297] Paquette 1984:112, C18 notes other oddities in the appearance of this *kithara*.

[298] A *kithara* player on a mid-sixth-century neck amphora is depicted striking a string or strumming—it is impossible to tell the difference in this case—well below the bridge (London B 260; Shapiro 1992:65, fig. 42b). On the "Singers at the Panathenaia" bell krater the middle satyr-citharode is striking the string closest to him (i.e. the lowest-pitched string) below the bridge, which, as on the Brygos Painter's instrument, is placed very high up the soundboard. He is singing and damping the outer strings as he does this. His "Thracian" *kithara* has eight strings—perhaps another "error," or perhaps Polion's intentional spoof of the polychord *kitharai* with which some citharodes of the later fifth century were experimenting.

plectrum. By way of instrumental prelude to his song, Hermes "tried out [his new lyre] with the plectrum part by part" (πλήκτρῳ ἐπειρήτιζε κατὰ μέρος, 53), which must mean that the god struck each string with the plectrum, one after the other. That is, Hermes plays a melody across the seven strings of the lyre; possibly he strums it out, but that seems unlikely.[299] Admittedly, the *Hymn* does not say which method, single-string picking or plucking, Hermes employs with his singing, although we should note that the text makes no mention of the latter method. At the opposite end of the temporal spectrum, however, Lucian describes a citharode's "*plêktron* keeping pace with her tongue" (*Imagines* 14); a singer to the *barbitos* in a poem of the *Anacreontea*, emulating an agonistic citharode, announces that he will sing while "striking a clear melody with an ivory *plêktron*" (60a.1–7); and the late antique episto-lographer Aristaenetus offers a vivid evocation of a citharode's voice and plectrum-struck strings sounding in unison: πρόσχορδος ἡ γλῶττα τοῖς κρούμασι 'the tongue is attuned to the strings'.

Pre-Roman literary evidence for the role of plucking in *kithara* playing is slim. The left hand plucked strings while the right tuned them, and plucking was deployed as occasional timbral contrast to picking, especially in virtuoso solo *kithara* music (*kitharistikê*), where such effects would offer welcome relief to sonic monotony. However, we cannot be nearly so confident that it was the constant counterpart to the plectrum, and the primary partner to vocal melody in *kitharôidia*. The unmarked word for both lyre and *kithara* playing is κιθαρίζειν, a denominative verb that says nothing about the physical means of producing sound on the instrument. The verb κρούειν 'to strike', however, is used to denote specifically the striking of a string with the plectrum.[300] The second-century CE lexicographer Pollux classifies the lyre, *kithara*, and *barbitos* as ὄργανα τὰ κρουόμενα 'instruments that are struck with a plectrum' (*Onomasticon* 4.9). The verb that means 'to pluck', ψάλλειν, is used in musical contexts in an unmarked sense to

---

[299] Cf. Borthwick 1959:27n3. The same phrase recurs in lines 419 (Hermes again playing) and 501 (Apollo playing), but in both places the manuscripts have κατὰ μέλος for the κατὰ μέρος of line 53. West 2003:116 adopts κατὰ μέλος for line 53 as well, translating it as 'in a tuned scale', which could of course describe a strum. (The open strings of the lyre or *kithara* were tuned to the notes of a specific "scale," or *harmonia*; see Winnington-Ingram 1956:172–173.) Càssola 1994:520, however, argues strongly for κατὰ μέρος as the original reading in all three lines. Of course, the two variants could have coexisted synchronically within the oral performance tradition of the *Hymn*.

[300] LSJ s.v. I.5. The noun κροῦμα may denote a tone struck by a plectrum (e.g. Aristophanes *Women at the Thesmophoria* 120 and Plato *Republic* 333b, both of *kithara* music); by rough analogy it came to denote tones sounded on the *aulos* as well. See LSJ s.v. I.2. Rocconi 2003:26–51 discusses the semantics of κρούειν and ψάλλειν.

describe the playing of some variety of harp (generic name: *psaltêrion*), an instrument whose strings were usually plucked directly with the fingers of both hands rather than with a plectrum (Aristoxenus fr. 99 Wehrli). Herodotus explicitly distinguishes κιθαρίζειν from ψάλλειν, the former meaning 'to play the *kithara*', the latter 'to pluck the harp' (1.155.4).[301] The few times ψάλλειν is applied to the lyre in earlier Greek literature, it is ambiguously, even negatively marked. Its use to describe lyre playing in Ion fr. 32.3 West must be looked at askance, given the contemptuous tone of the line; so too in Aristophanes *Knights* 522 (if lyre or *barbitos* playing is indeed at issue, and not harp playing). Plato *Lysis* 209b, an account of a young man's unsupervised lyre playing, contrasts it with κρούειν, with the likely implication that the latter is good technique, the former undisciplined fooling around. Compare the proverb, "It's as easy as plucking a string!" (ῥᾷον ἥ τις ἂν χορδὴν ψήλειε, Aelius Aristides 26.31). In no case could the verb easily be taken to describe normative lyric practice.[302] One reason for this could be that, since the harp, in Classical Athens at least, was played—plucked—primarily by women, there was a tendency to keep the word ψάλλειν out of the serious technical lexicon of lyre and *kithara* playing, which were largely, although not exclusively, masculine pursuits.[303]

---

[301] In schools on second-century BCE Teos (SIG 578.15) and Chios (SIG 959.10), separate instruction was provided in *psalmos* and *kitharismos*, that is, harp and *kithara* playing. Cf. West 1992:74n115.

[302] Discussion in Power 2007:198–199. Still more problematic is the compound epithet] οψάλακτος used by the satyrs of Sophocles' *Ikhneutai* to describe the *ompha* 'voice' of Hermes' new lyre (329). Lloyd-Jones' χερ]οψάλακτος 'plucked by hand' would obviously suggest finger plucking, but the first element of the compound may have been something else entirely, and the epithet may have had less literal implications. Again, the context—the satyrs are reacting to an instrument they have never before heard—discourages our taking the epithet as a straightforward description of normative practice. The (fourth-century BCE?) writer of a diatribe against the music theorists called *harmonikoi* that is transmitted in the Hibeh Papyrus 1.13 seems to use *psaltai* and *psallein* (coll. 1.7 and 2.7) in an unmarked sense to cover all stringed instruments, plucked and picked (thus Barker 1984:185n12). This would be unique. But at col. 2.14 we learn that the *harmonikoi* themselves demonstrate their theories on the *psaltêrion*, a plucked string instrument of some sort, and this has probably influenced the writer's overall word choice. Similarly, *psallein* consistently has a "theoretical" rather than practical application in "Aristotle" *Problems* 19. In a few late texts, *krouein* and *psallein* are used indiscriminately, e.g. Plutarch *Moralia* 67f; Lucian *On the Parasite* 17. Musical terminology in general becomes less precise in Imperial literature. Some authors of the period, however, apply *psallein* to lyre playing with derogatory implications, e.g. Plutarch *Life of Pericles* 1.5; Philostratus *Life of Apollonius of Tyana* 5.10.

[303] See West 1992:71–75 and 1997:48–50 on harps. Attic vase paintings show that another stringed instrument played exclusively by women in the fifth century, the *phorminx*, was also occasionally plucked with both hands *à la harpe* (e.g. a Muse on a white-ground kylix, Louvre CA 483; Kaufman-Samara 1997:287, fig. 3). On the "Italiote"

The invention of one common type of harp, the *pêktis*, was accordingly attributed to Sappho, although male Archaic poets mentioned it as well (Athenaeus 14.635a). Beyond their identification with women, harps preserved the ethnic and ethical character of their Asiatic provenance, which made them still more distinct from *kitharai* in the sociomusical imagination of the Classical period. For Aristoxenus, harps were ἔκφυλα ὄργανα 'alien instruments' (fr. 97 Wehrli *ap.* Athenaeus 4.177f). The very connotations of Eastern luxury, *habrosunê*, surrounding them (e.g. Anacreon PMG 373, ἀβρῶς ἐρόεσσαν | ψάλλω πηκτίδα 'I strum luxuriously on my lovely harp'), which appealed to sybaritic elites of the Archaic period, contributed to their alienation from mainstream lyric culture of the Classical period. This "otherness" too may have been semantically policed through the strict marking of ψάλλειν. But even so, if left-hand pizzicato was the systematic practice it has been made out to be by West and others, we should expect to find for it some other, less problematic terminology in fifth-century literature.

Visual evidence for left-hand plucking has been sought in fifth-century vase paintings with somewhat better luck, but here again interpretive certainty is elusive. Those who are predisposed to see plucking will of course see plucking, but to a less biased eye things are not so clear-cut. In most images of *kithara* players the left hand is depicted in a position not easily taken to represent plucking; the thumb and fingers of the left hand, or the fingertips, are held flush against the strings, in better position for damping than plucking.[304] Other images, mainly produced after 475 BCE or so, portray players of various stringed instruments whose thumb and fingers, held crooked, or, with wrist rotated outward, splayed laterally against the strings, more readily suggest plucking action.[305] But such digital contortions are perhaps better taken as the artists' "realistic" attempts to capture the dexterous busywork of left-hand damping and releasing. By comparison, renderings of harp players' hands more clearly evince defined plucking traits: hands arched, thumb and fingertips slightly curled round the strings.[306] Occasionally, a lyre or *kithara* player is carefully shown pulling a string

---

    kithara, occasionally plucked like the harp, see n163 and n165 above. One would like to know more about the social context of the *psaltinx*, which Hesychius s.v. calls a *kithara*, but whose name suggests a hybrid of (plucked) harp and *phorminx*.

[304] Cf. Anderson 1994:176.

[305] On the dating, see Maas and Snyder 1989:93.

[306] See e.g. the Muse playing a *pêktis* on a red-figured amphora (London E 271; West 1992, plate 21).

between thumb and index finger.[307] The clearest example is visible on a red-figured fragment (Florence 128): two youths are performing (practicing?) the maneuver in a schoolroom.[308] Plucking is but one interpretation, however. Even West wonders "whether [the player] is not retracting it [the string] from the plectrum's path (Quintilian's *trahunt*), rather than plucking it."[309] The connection West draws between Quintilian's *trahere* 'pull' and the gesture recorded in the vase paintings seems entirely valid. If Quintilian had wished to refer to left-hand plucking, the verb *carpere* would have been the obvious choice; *trahere* would be unparalleled in this sense.[310] Accordingly, we should understand *trahere* and *continere*, 'pulling' and 'damping', to refer not to sequential but to parallel modes of ensuring that strings do not sound when the plectrum is applied to the instrument.

We must look to other Latin texts of the Augustan and later Imperial periods for explicit references to lyric pizzicato. Although there are quite a few, their evidentiary value for the thesis that citharodes traditionally sang and plucked is problematic. Vergil, Ovid and the elegists, Persius, Statius, and other authors have amateur players of the lyre as well as citharodes using fingers or thumb to "strike" or to "test" the strings (but never, it is worth noting, to "pluck" them). The use of the thumb in particular is a commonplace in these poetic descriptions of string playing, e.g. the "tongued thumb" (*linguato ... pollice*) of a citharode in *Latin Anthology* 103.3 Kay.[311] This recurrent emphasis on the digital manipulation of strings may reflect not a technique traditional to Greek lyric and citharodic culture, but rather a distinctly Roman approach to lyre playing that encouraged the use of both hands, not only the left, to pluck notes, as if the lyre were a harp. It is important to keep in mind that when the Romans were first exposed to Greek string music it was harps and female harpists, *psalteria* and *psaltriae*, rather than lyres or *citharae*, that fascinated them. Livy 39.6.8 speaks of the novelty surrounding imported *psaltriae* and *sambucistriae*, players of the *sambuca*, a type of arched harp that came to popularity in the Hellenistic period, at Greek-style *convivia* in the early second century BCE. Juvenal 3.63–64 counts the *chordae obliquae* 'slanted strings' of the

---

[307] To my knowledge only one image clearly shows a *kithara* player pinching a string: an Apulian krater, Adolphseck 178; Paquette 1984:115, C21.

[308] Plate 18 in West 1992; Maas and Snyder 1989:111, fig. 26, with discussion on p93.

[309] West 1992:69. Another, less likely interpretation of this gesture could be that the player pulls the string to loosen slightly its tension and so lower its pitch—tuning on the fly.

[310] A point made by Borthwick 1959:26.

[311] Cf. West 1992:67n83, with references; Wille 1967:212–217.

sambuca, along with players of the *tibiae* (i.e. *auloi*), among the very first wave of corrupting Eastern exotica to have washed up in Rome.[312] As in Greece, in the early Republic both foreign prostitutes and the wives and daughters of elite citizens cultivated the harp, as did, it seems, some boys and men, although conservatives such as Scipio Aemilianus were scandalized by the thought of freeborn boys and girls going to school to learn the harp "among effeminates" (*inter cinaedos*).[313]

The lyre and *kithara* were eventually taken up too by elite Roman amateurs, but the plucking technique appropriate to the harp seems to have carried over to these normally "struck instruments." Roman wall paintings dating to the late Republic suggest that, while the plectrum was certainly known and used, players of lyres and *kitharai*, especially women, often dispensed with it and plucked two-handed, as if they were harpists.[314] Thus the Latin verb *psallere* possesses an unmarkedness that Greek ψάλλειν generally does not: it can denote either the playing of the harp (e.g. Horace *Odes* 4.13.7; Aulus Gellius *Attic Nights* 19.9.3) or the lyre (Caesius Bassus fr. 1 Courtney *ap*. Priscian 2.527).[315] Harp-style plucking of the lyre is implicit in Ovid *Amores* 2.4.27: a girl *habili percurrit pollice chordas* 'runs over the strings with her skillful thumb'. The verb *percurrere* better suits the action of right-hand playing than left-hand plucking, as we see in Quintilian's *alios nervos*

---

[312] On the *sambuca* see West 1992:77. Cf. further Wille 1967:211–212, 214. Romans long continued to be fascinated by harps. An Alexandrian player of the *trigônos* inspired widespread *mousomania* 'music madness' when he gave a public recital in Imperial Rome (Athenaeus 4.183e).

[313] Macrobius *Saturnalia* 3.14.5. Playing *psalteria* remained a controversial activity for Roman women and girls, though surely not a rare one, even in Quintilian's time (1.10.31).

[314] See Wille 1967:213–214. A female citharist plucking both an "Italiote" *kithara* and a *sambuca* on a wall painting from Stabiae exemplifies the (generally female) bridge between harp and lyre culture in Rome. Cf. n163 above. A painting from the Casa del Citarista reflects a gendered distinction between picking and plucking: a bearded, seated citharist plays with a plectrum, a younger, standing woman plucks a lyre. See Richardson 2000:64–65.

[315] Sometimes it is impossible to tell which is meant by *psallere*. Sallust *Bellum Catilinae* 25.2 says that the aristocratic Sempronia knew how "to *psallere* and dance more charmingly than was fitting for a respectable woman (*proba*)." Was it the *lyra* or the harp she played too well? In either case, Sallust probably wants the word to evoke the louche world of the professional *psaltria* (see e.g. Philodemus of Gadara *Epigrams* 1.1, 3.3, 4.5, 6.1), and so underline the impropriety of Sempronia's (Greek) cultural enthusiasms. Suetonius says that Emperor Titus was good at *psallere* (*Life of Titus* 3); *Historia Augusta, Life of Hadrian* 14.9 says that Hadrian prided himself on his *psallendi et cantandi scientia* 'skill in singing and *psallere*'. One thinks immediately of lyre playing, especially in the latter case, but harp playing should not be ruled out. Notably, Suetonius never uses *psallere* to refer to Nero's citharodic activity.

dextra percurrunt. Unless the girl is a harpist rather than a lyre player, which seems unlikely, she is strumming her lyre strings with her right thumb, without a plectrum. The hypallage in expressions such as "ivory fingers" (Propertius 2.1.9) and "ivory thumb" (Statius *Silvae* 5.5.31)—the Latin poetic plectrum is usually ivory (e.g. Vergil *Aeneid* 6.647, *pectine ... eburno*)—also suggests that the right-hand fingers have taken the place of the plectrum.[316]

Other texts, however, while focusing on the player's application of thumb or fingers to strings, nevertheless imply or describe the alternating use of plectrum and left-hand thumb or fingers that West and others posit as standard procedure.[317] Most of these are best read as poetic idealizations of singing to the lyre or *kithara* in which a distinctly *Roman* preference for finger plucking is foregrounded—a culturally specific conflation of harpist and singer-to-the-lyre. We may note too the significant lack of corresponding descriptions by Greek authors of the Empire, who tend rather to put the focus on the plectrum.[318]

At the same time, however, it should not be denied that Greek citharodes had, well before the time these writers were working, broadly integrated pizzicato techniques into their performances, and that this practical development may have been promoted into the Latin literary topos of finger-struck *kithara* strings. The most explicit ancient testimony for coordinated left-hand plucking/singing and right-hand plectrum strumming is the ecphrasis in Apuleius *Florida* 15 of an Archaic statue in the Samian Heraion of a *kithara*-playing youth, whose "left hand, fingers spread apart, sets the strings going (*nervos molitur*),

---

[316] This seems to me a better reading than to conjecture a "practice of attaching picks to the individual fingers" (West 1992:67n83). Martial 14.167 advises a lyre player, who has presumably been using his right thumb to pluck, to use a plectrum if he wants to avoid blisters. Cf. scholia *ad* Persius 6.5.

[317] E.g. Vergil *Aeneid* 6.647: Orpheus, as lyric accompanist to the eternal choral performances in Elysium, alternately uses his fingers, then the ivory plectrum to strike the seven strings of his instrument (*iamque eadem digitis, iam pectine pulsat eburno*); Ovid *Metamorphoses* 11.168–170: in an idealized citharodic context, Apollo "strikes (*sollicitat*) the strings with skilled thumb," but also clutches a plectrum in his right hand; Persius 6.5: in an amateur lyric context, Caesius Bassus, the poet, uses his "respectable thumb," although he also holds a *pecten* 'plectrum' (2). Cf. too Lygdamus (Tibullus 3) 4.39–40; Venantius Fortunatus 7.1.1.

[318] I leave Philostratus *Imagines* 1.10 out of account here, an ecphrasis of a painting of a seated Amphion playing the lyre. Philostratus says that Amphion plucks (ψάλλει) the strings with his left hand and strikes (παραπλήττων) with his right (4), but there is some potential confusion here with harping. Amphion's lyre is alternately called a *magadis* (2) and a *pêktis* (3). Perhaps this is only *variatio* for the sake of color, a cavalier disregard for organological accuracy that we sometimes encounter in Imperial writers. Nonetheless, we should approach Philostratus' ψάλλει with caution.

while his right hand, with the gesture of one playing a stringed instrument (*psallentis*), moves the plectrum (*pulsabulum*) toward the *kithara*, as if prepared to strike, when the voice has rested in the song" (15.9). Leaving aside the small red flags raised by *psallere*, which evokes the plucking of the harp, yet is unexpectedly applied to the citharode's *picking* hand, and the singular oddity of the word *pulsabulum*, which is textually problematic to boot, the description seems a sufficiently clear account of citharodic performance.[319] But its synchronic descriptive value is not necessarily diachronically valid. There is every possibility that Apuleius is subjectively projecting a practice that he had himself witnessed contemporary citharodes performing onto the Archaic sculptural image—it dates to the time of the sixth-century BCE Samian tyrant Polycrates—whose left hand, as in so many vase paintings, may represent only string damping. (Note the lack of specificity in the verb *molitur*.) And even at that, the passage does not serve to indicate whether pizzicato playing was routine method or occasional effect in Apuleius' own time.

Telling is a bare-bones anecdote recorded in "Plutarch" *Sayings of the Spartans* 233f about a foreign musician, a *psaltês* 'harpist', who was fined by the Spartans "because he played the *kithara* with his fingers" (ὅτι δακτύλοις κιθαρίζει). Apocryphal or not, the anecdote works on the assumption that plucking the *kithara* was not a traditional technique. In Sparta, a center of old-school lyric culture (cf. Alcman PMG 41), it seemed especially transgressive. In light of other stories like this one, the musician in question is almost certainly supposed to be a citharode, a competitor at the famously conservative musical *agôn* attached to the Carneia festival, where, we should note, there was no contest for harpists. He is catachrestically tagged a "harpist" because of his harp-like plucking technique, which has offended the judges. The Spartans, legendary "saviors" of *arkhaia mousikê* from decadent novelty (Athenaeus 14.628b), are said to have similarly punished at the Carneia other innovative citharodes of the later fifth century BCE, but for *polukhordia*, the addition of supernumerary strings to the heptachord

---

[319] On the ambiguity of *psallere*, see n315 above. The word perhaps alludes here to Anacreon's own musico-sympotic frame of reference, which prominently features Eastern harps. Apuleius argues that the statue represents Bathyllus, one of the boys beloved by the Tean poet, and that Bathyllus is singing one of Anacreon's songs. It could be that Apuleius is viewing the statue through an appropriately sympotic lens, figuring the citharode as an Anacreontic harper. But *psallendi* is used of Pythagoras later in the speech in the more neutral sense of "string playing."

kithara.[320] The anecdotal variant preserved in *Sayings of the Spartans* could reflect the fact that pizzicato was, like *polukhordia*, at least in the Classical period a novel innovation practiced mainly by progressive virtuosos, who were intent on pursuing all sorts of musical *poikilia*, the elaborate complexity of texture, melody, and timbre that character-ized the aesthetic program of the Athenian New Music. Latin authors suggest that in post-Classical and Imperial *kitharôidia* plucking had become more commonplace, but even then it likely remained a means of producing special effects meant to accent the established core prac-tice of striking (individual and multiple) strings with the plectrum.[321]

As I suggested above, solo *kithara* players, whose music relied on colorful sound effects, were likely the earliest dedicated experimenters with pizzicato, well anticipating, and presumably influencing, the New Music citharodes with their innovations. Juba II, first-century BCE king of Mauretania and author of the *Theatrical History*, a valuable reposi-tory of organological exotica and arcana, says that a sixth-century BCE citharist, Epigonus of Sicyon, "being a musician of the greatest skill, plucked by hand, without a plectrum" (μουσικώτατος ὢν κατὰ χεῖρα δίχα πλήκτρου ἔψαλλε, fr. 84). Unfortunately, Athenaeus, who reports Juba's testimony (4.183d), does not indicate what instrument Epigonus plucked. Epigonus was also the inventor of a zither-like, polychord instrument, the *epigoneion*, which was most certainly plucked with both hands—Athenaeus calls it a *psaltêrion*.[322] Perhaps it was only this instrument that Epigonus plucked without a plectrum, but the distinc-tion Juba accords to his plucking implies that it was the traditionally plectrum-struck *kithara* as well. Epigonus is elsewhere credited with pioneering a style of playing the *kithara* called *enaulos kitharisis*, an emulation of the timbral and harmonic color of the *auloi* that prob-ably featured pizzicati and harmonics (Menaechmus FGrH 131 F 5 = Athenaeus 14.637f–638a).[323] We hear too of a special type of *kithara*

---

[320] E.g. the account of the Spartans' punishment of the citharode Timotheus preserved in Artemon of Cassandrea FHG IV 342 = Athenaeus 14.636e. There, Timotheus is also figured as a player of a harp called a *magadis*, not because he plucks, but because his *kithara*, like a harp, has more than seven strings.

[321] The term *epipsalmos* 'plucking in addition', a manual technique of *kithara* playing mentioned in Ptolemy *Harmonics* 2.12, may describe one such special effect. For Barker 1989:341–342 the term indicates an "accompaniment adding decorative figures" around the main melody articulated by voice and plectrum. It is easy to see how *polukhordia*, pizzicato, and *heterophônia* (see Plato *Laws* 812d) could all three have been mutually reinforcing developments.

[322] Barker 1984:270n46. Pollux *Onomasticon* 4.59 says that the *epigoneion* had 40 strings.

[323] Barker 1982; Barker 1984:300 and 2001:19–20. West 1992:341–342 offers a different interpretation of the phrase *enaulos kitharisis*.

called either the *Puthikon* or the *daktulikon* (Pollux *Onomasticon* 4.66). The first name suggests that it was used by virtuoso citharists to perform the *Puthikos nomos*, the famed contest piece essayed by competitors at the Delphian *agôn* in *kitharistikê* (introduced in 558 BCE according to Pausanias 10.7.7), which recounted through purely musical mimesis Apollo's slaughter of the Pythian serpent. The different sections of the piece called for all sorts of extraordinary techniques to portray sonically the narrative details.[324] Strabo 9.3.10 says that one section was known as *daktuloi*, which he takes to refer to dactylic rhythms (another section is called *iamboi*), but perhaps it should be taken literally as "fingers," a reference to the string plucking, with either left hand or both hands, that characterized the episode. (The corresponding auletic *Puthikos nomos*, it is worth noting, did not have this section.) The alternate name for the *Puthikon kithara*, the *daktulikon*, could derive from the suitability of this customized instrument for pizzicato playing.

The commentator on Cicero *Verrine Orations* 2.1.53 known as "Asconius" offers interesting testimony for citharistic plucking technique, but it is wrapped up in some misdirected comments about *kitharôidia* made apropos of a well-known expression, *omnia intus canere* 'to sing everything inside', which was proverbially applied to someone who does something in his own interest (cf. Cicero *Against Rullus* 2.26). According to Cicero, it was originally said of the appearance of a famous statue of an anonymous *citharista* in the Pamphylian city of Aspendos. Verres removed this statue while he was quaestor in Asia and hid it away in his house at Rome (*in intimis suis aedibus*), a misappropriation of public property—a monumental symbol of Aspendian civic *mousikê*—for private pleasure, which, Cicero implies, crassly outdid the statue's own proverbial self-centeredness. Cicero does not describe the statue, but "Asconius" explains how the expression referred, by way of the technical jargon of *kitharôidia*, to a specific sort of playing style exhibited by the sculpted musician:

> When *citharistae* sing (*canunt*), they make use of both hands. The right hand uses the plectrum, and that is "to sing outside" (*foris canere*); the left hand plucks (*carpit*) the strings with the fingers, and that is "to sing inside." However, it is difficult to do what the Aspendian citharist was doing: not using singing

---

[324] Cf. Barker 1984:52n17. There was also an auletic *Puthikos nomos* (Pollux *Onomasticon* 4.84). Citharists no doubt felt compelled to compete with the expressive devices the auletes deployed in their *nomos*.

voice and both hands, but managing everything [*omnia*], that is, the entire musical piece, "inside" and only with the left hand.

"Asconius" on Cicero *Verrine Orations* 2.1.53

These comments should not inspire too much confidence, for they are premised upon a fundamental confusion of citharodes and citharists; the latter do not sing. Cicero, however, surely knows the difference between *citharistae* and *citharoedi*.[325] His choice of the former designation for the Aspendian statue must reflect the way the Aspendians themselves viewed their famous statue, as a mute κιθαριστής rather than a singing κιθαρῳδός, and how it became conventionally known abroad. A distinction made between inside and outside *singing*, and their attendant manual techniques, would certainly not be one observed by citharists. Such a distinction probably represents nothing more than a creative inference drawn from a literalizing interpretation of the phrase *intus canere*, which in turn became the basis for the reconstruction of the Aspendian's stunt. A one-handed display of virtuosity is entirely imaginable; it would be in line with the gimmicks deployed by citharistic showmen, and no doubt some citharodes as well.

But it is likely that *omnia intus canere* originally had no technical or citharodic connotations at all, but was merely a clever way of expressing the performative affect of the citharist—especially an inanimate one—who, unlike the citharode, figuratively "sings entirely on the inside." It could be too that something in the manner of the sculptural representation of the Aspendos *citharista*, some strong visual indication of soulful introversion, of "feeling," made the expression particularly apposite.[326] Alternately, it is possible that the sculptor merely posed the musician in such a way that he seemed not to play his instrument at all; that is, he did not appear to be producing any audible instrumental or vocal music. The Aspendian citharist and his *intus canere* were subject to other interpretations, neither more nor less convincing than that of "Asconius."[327]

---

[325] Cf. Coleman-Norton 1948:19n97.

[326] See Coleman-Norton 1948:6n16.

[327] *Scholia Bobiensa* to Cicero *Verrine Orations* 2.1.53 says that the Aspendian citharist strikes the strings "not with thrust-out hand, but with very obscure motions," but offers nothing specific about singing, the left hand, or plucking. Zeno Myndius *ap.* Zenobius 3.161 offers the most fanciful gloss on *intus canere*. No longer is the statue the point of reference, but real Aspendian citharists, who are known for their introverted style of playing; they make no outward gestures, concentrating entirely on their instruments (but again, Zeno makes no mention of plucking). Given the basic acoustical demands of open-air performance on the *kithara*, the existence of an

17. The Performative Body: Marching and Mimesis

We do not know the title of the song that Nero performed at his first concert in Naples. Suetonius indicates its genre, however: he calls it, using the Greek word, for it remained still a thoroughly Hellenic form in Nero's time, a *nomos*. This type of song had long been the premier genre of *kitharôidia*, its formalization going all the way back the putative founder of the medium, Terpander, whom the biographical tradition dated to the early seventh century BCE. As is detailed in Part IV, although the *nomos* had considerably evolved from its "Terpandrean" origins by the first century CE, in critical respects the one performed by Nero would have resembled those produced in the later fifth and fourth centuries BCE, the era of the New Music, when traditional genres such as the *nomos* were given revolutionary musico-poetic makeovers. It is even possible that Nero had in his repertoire *nomoi* that had been composed by the leading light of the New Music, Timotheus of Miletus, whose works, after an initial period of controversy, achieved the status of classics, reperformed for centuries after his death.[328] In this section, however, we are concerned not with the form and content of citharodic song, but with its performative enactment. Specifically, what can be said about the physical comportment of Nero and the citharodes before him as they stood on the stage or on the agonistic platform, the *bêma*, bringing their *nomoi* to life?

It is evident from both literary and visual sources that the body of the citharode, already theatricalized in its elaborate costume, was in its spectacular gesture and movement as integral to his performance as his musical expression. Phillis of Delos, a Hellenistic writer on music history, claims that the early (*arkhaioi*) citharodes—Phillis presumably has in mind those of the Archaic and earlier Classical eras—executed few expressive "movements of the face" (κινήσεις ἀπὸ τοῦ προσώπου); the somatic component of their performances consisted more in "movements of the feet, ἐμβατήριοι καὶ χορευτικαί 'march and dance steps'."[329] A number of sixth- and fifth-century BCE Attic vases that depict citharodes in performance tend to support his claim, the most

---

entire school of dedicatedly introverted, audience-disregarding citharists seems highly unlikely, but that is exactly what West 1992:68n88 believes: "[T]he citharists of Aspendos ... were proverbial for playing in an introvert way, as if only to themselves, without the grand flourishes with the plectrum."

[328] Cf. Part IV.12.

[329] Phillis of Delos *ap.* Athenaeus 1.21f. Cf. Herington 1985:16–17 on the passage.

famous of which is the Berlin Painter's citharode, who steps forward
with knees bent, perhaps dancing in some decorously stylized fashion,
while he plays and sings, back held straight and head tipped back in
song, his garments slightly billowing out behind him. Equally vivid is
an earlier depiction of a citharodic performance on a red-figured eye
cup of c. 520 BCE by Psiax (Plate 7a), in which the painter has captured
perfectly a citharode in the middle of a march-like dance step. One of
the dandyish admirers by his side is shown gaily imitating this elegant
footwork; the rhythm is infectious.[330] Both this image and the testimony of Phillis recall the dynamic pose of Apollo *Mousagêtês* that is
captured near the beginning of the Pythian section of the *Homeric
Hymn to Apollo*:

> αὐτὰρ ὁ Φοῖβος Ἀπόλλων ἐγκιθαρίζει
> καλὰ καὶ ὕψι βιβάς· αἴγλη δέ μιν ἀμφιφαείνει
> μαρμαρυγαί τε ποδῶν καὶ ἐυκλώστοιο χιτῶνος.

> Phoebus Apollo plays the *kithara*, stepping high and hand-
> somely, and a radiance shines about him, even the gleaming of
> his feet and well-spun chiton.

Homeric Hymn to Apollo 201–203

Later in the *Hymn*, Apollo similarly accompanies the performance of
the first paeanic chorus at Delphi καλὰ καὶ ὕψι βιβάς 'stepping high
and handsomely' (516). In both cases, Apollo's orchestic high stepping
is a function of his role as lyric accompanist (the *kitharistês*) to a dancing
chorus, not strictly as a solo *kitharôidos*, although that break-out role
seems already incipient here.[331] What this might suggest is that the
"march and dance steps" attributed by Phillis to the *arkhaioi* citharodes
were vestigial traces of their own evolutionary origins as accompanists
to choral processional and dance.[332] In performing his *Persians*, a *nomos*
of the later fifth century BCE, Timotheus of Miletus might have paid
homage to this "ancient" *alla marcia* style, and obliquely acknowledged
the choral origins of his own medium, as he sang of, and very likely
physically imitated, the chorus of Greeks singing and dancing a paean

---

[330] A similar dance pose is struck by the youthful citharode depicted on a roughly
contemporary black-figured olpe, a small vessel for pouring oil and wine (Wilson
College; Pinney and Ridgway 1979:56–57, no. 25).

[331] See Lawler 1951:67–68 on the Minoan-Mycenaean antiquity of choral high stepping.
The *Hymn* knows Apollo as a solo musician as well (182–184).

[332] See further Part II.3. On the orchestic movement of chorus-accompanying auletes, cf.
Wilson 2002:60–61.

to celebrate their victory at Salamis: ἐπεκτύπεον ποδῶν ὑψικρότοις χορείαις 'They beat the ground with the high-stomping dance movements of their feet' (199–201).[333] In this moment, the citharode reverts to his primordial role of *kitharistês*, high stepping alongside an imaginary chorus.

For Timotheus and the cithardodes who came after him, however, the old style was not the default setting, as it were, but one of many possible physical mannerisms and mimetic modes. The theatricality of musicians' self-display in general became increasingly pronounced with the popularization of the New Music of the later fifth and fourth centuries BCE. The linguistic and sonorous intensities of its texts and scores, brimming with melodramatic effect and affect, invited ever more mimetically sensational bodily expressions. This period witnessed the full-blown "emergence of the actor in music," to use a well-known phrase of Nietzsche from *The Case of Wagner* (section 11). Nietzsche was both horrified and fascinated by the tendency in the musical culture of his time toward the dramatic bombast of Wagner and the virtuoso performative histrionics of Liszt, which he viewed as undermining the proper ethical authenticity and social and moral authority of music.[334]

Athenian cultural conservatives were likewise profoundly disturbed by the histrionic turn in the performance practice of the New Music, and it is in their critiques of its theatrics that we not only hear echoes of the sonic experimentation of the New Music, but also catch oblique visualizations of the moving bodies of its producers. Aristophanes has Dicaeopolis, the hero of his *Acharnians*, mock the citharode Chaeris for the way in which he "stooped sideways (παρέκυψε) onto the stage to play the *Orthios nomos* (ὄρθιον)" at the Panathenaia (16). While the joke here may be on an accidentally comic lapse in posture once committed by Chaeris during a performance, it is as likely that his "stooping" is indicative of a deliberate program of somatic histrionics, which seems ridiculous to the conservative sensibilities of audience members such

---

[333] I follow Herington 1985: "There is much mimesis here, I imagine, recalling the 'marching movements' which an ancient source [Phillis] attributes even to the earlier kitharodic performances" (158).

[334] Cf. Kramer 2001:80–81; Smart 2004 on novel mimetic synchronizations between somatic and musical gestures in nineteenth-century opera, a trend criticized by Nietzsche, for whom Wagner was the most exemplary "mimomaniac" (*Nietzsche Contra Wagner*, 1968:665). In the latter part of the fifth and the beginning of the fourth century BCE, popular stage actors were themselves increasingly "theatricalizing" tragedy, exploring new mimetic modes of "mannerism" and "realism" in their bodily and vocalic self-presentation, which must have offered enticing models for emulation by auletes and cithardodes. See Csapo 2002 and Valakas 2002.

as Dicaeopolis (and Aristophanes). Chaeris' intentional stoop defies the iconic image of the Archaic and early Classical performing citharode, who always stands and moves with erect carriage and with head held high. "Bad posture," as the mannered pose seems to its critics, offends against traditional musical decorum as well, as the word play between παρέκυψε and ὄρθιον indicates: a stooping citharode is no match for the demands of the old-fashioned *Orthios nomos*, whose name indicates not only its high-pitched melodies (cf. scholia *ad* Acharnians 16a), but also suggests the need to stand straight and upright (*orthios*) while singing it.[335]

In a passage from Plato's *Republic*, Socrates provides a vivid depiction of the over-the-top mimeticism of a typically *phaulos* 'vulgar' exemplar of the contemporary popular music:

οὐδὲν ἑαυτοῦ ἀνάξιον οἰήσεται εἶναι, ὥστε πάντα ἐπιχειρήσει μιμεῖσθαι σπουδῇ τε καὶ ἐναντίον πολλῶν, καὶ ἃ νυνδὴ ἐλέγομεν, βροντάς τε καὶ ψόφους ἀνέμων τε καὶ χαλαζῶν καὶ ἀξόνων τε καὶ τροχιλιῶν, καὶ σαλπίγγων καὶ αὐλῶν καὶ συρίγγων καὶ πάντων ὀργάνων φωνάς, καὶ ἔτι κυνῶν καὶ προβάτων καὶ ὀρνέων φθόγγους· καὶ ἔσται δὴ ἡ τούτου λέξις ἅπασα διὰ μιμήσεως φωναῖς τε καὶ σχήμασιν.

He will think nothing unworthy of him, so that he will make great efforts, before large audiences, to imitate (*mimeisthai*) everything, including the things which we have just mentioned—thunderclaps, and the noises of winds and hailstorms and axles and pulleys, and the voices of trumpets and *auloi* and pan pipes and instruments of every kind, and even the sounds of dogs and sheep and birds; and his diction will consist entirely of imitation (*mimêsis*) by vocalisms and gestures.

Plato *Republic* 397a–b[336]

---

[335] Olson 2002:70–71 offers a different interpretation of παρέκυψε: Chaeris "pokes his head out" from the side of the stage "with a view to performing the *Orthios nomos*." Other instances of the verb *parakuptein* in Aristophanes support this interpretation, but in this case, the meaning "stooping sideways" (LSJ s.v.) while performing certainly makes for a richer comic scene. On Chaeris as a "bad" musician, i.e. a New musician, see n256 above.

[336] Translation based on Barker 1984:128. Cf. *Laws* 669e, where the instrumental imitation of animal noises is derided.

Plato has Socrates link in his critique the musician's heavily mimetic score and "diction," i.e. the text, to his physically mimetic *skhêmata* 'gestures' (or even 'postures'); the musico-poetic and somatic elements of this phantasmagoric performance are thus complementary. Plato seems to have in mind here primarily virtuoso citharodes rather than auletes, as it would make little sense to say that auletes imitate the sound of the *aulos*.[337] But it was probably the auletes, both as agonistic soloists and dithyrambic choral accompanists, who took the lead in introducing novel bodily *skhêmata* into musical performance. To the old guard this trend represented a debasement of the ethical and somatic propriety of traditional *mousikê*, appealing to an audience of the lowest common denominator.[338] The comments of Aristotle are typical:

> ὁ γὰρ θεατὴς φορτικὸς ὢν μεταβάλλειν εἴωθε τὴν μουσικήν, ὥστε καὶ τοὺς τεχνίτας τοὺς πρὸς αὐτὸν μελετῶντας αὐτούς τε ποιούς τινας ποιεῖ καὶ τὰ σώματα διὰ τὰς κινήσεις.

> The listener, being a low-class man (*phortikos*), tends to alter (*metaballein*, with a play on *metabolê* 'harmonic modulation') the music, so that he makes the musical professionals (*tekhnitai*) who play for him become like himself in character and in respect to their bodies, through the movements (*kinêseis*) that they make.

Aristotle *Politics* 8.1341b15–19

The context of this passage strongly suggests that Aristotle is referring primarily to auletes, but citharodes are *tekhnitai* as well, and may be a secondary target of his critique. Pausanias 9.12.4, surely channeling an older, perhaps Peripatetic anti-populist source, says that Pronomus, a famous Theban aulete of the fifth century, whose playing was "most seductive to the masses" (ἐπαγωγότατα ἐς τοὺς πολλούς), "afforded an excess (*perissôs*) of pleasure (*terpsis*) to the theaters by means of his facial expression and the movement of his entire body" (λέγεται δὲ

---

[337] Arguably the passage could represent a composite of various musical media. But note that Plato specifically attacks citharodic imitation of auletic music in *Laws* 700d.

[338] Cf. Plutarch *Alcibiades* 2.4: Alcibiades claimed that lyre playing suited a free man because it did not affect his noble *skhêma* 'bearing' and *morphê* 'appearance', while the *aulos* distorted the features and so was unfitting for the free man. Athena supposedly rejected the *aulos* for the same reason (Aristotle *Politics* 8.1341b1–6). This ideological investment in the non-mimetic, subdued aspects of lyre playing—a gentleman could "be himself" while he played the lyre—surely contributed to old-guard anxieties surrounding the theatralization of *kitharôidia*: citharodes were beginning to look more like auletes when they performed.

ὡς καὶ τοῦ προσώπου τῷ σχήματι καὶ ἐπὶ τοῦ παντὸς κινήσει σώματος περισσῶς δή τι ἔτερπε τὰ θέατρα).[339] Looking beyond the critical frame of these comments, we gain objective insight into the intimate dynamic between music and body in performance. The corporeal hyperkinesis of the aulete "embodies" the sonic lability of the New Music, which was (in)famous for its modulations (*metabolai*) from one *harmonia* 'mode' to another. Pronomus actually designed a pair of *auloi* that would allow him to modulate *harmoniai* in the same composition without changing instruments (Pausanias 9.12.4, Athenaeus 14.631e; citharodes would later achieve similar effects by adding strings to the *kithara*).[340] At the same time, the moving body of the musician produces its own powerful *terpsis*, so powerful, Pausanias' source suggests, that it threatens, in its visual "excess," to transcend its supplemental role and overwhelm the primary pleasure of musical audition. If this theatralization of musical experience worried reactionaries, it was nevertheless, as Pausanius puts it, "most seductive to the masses" in the theaters.

We may suspect that in the wider context of his remarks Phillis of Delos was concerned to draw an invidious comparison between the relatively restrained movement of the old-time citharodes and the gestural excess of his performing contemporaries in the Hellenistic period.[341] His

---

[339] Theophrastus fr. 92 Wimmer *ap.* Athenaeus 1.22c attributes the innovation of rhythmic body movement in *aulêsis* to one Andron of Catana, perhaps a player of the generation before Pronomus. On the mimetic body of the aulete, cf. Csapo 2004:213; Wilson 2002:61.

[340] For Plato the *aulos* is the model "panharmonic" instrument (*Republic* 399d). To appreciate the relationship between mode and movement, it is important that we should understand *harmonia* not merely syntactically, as a systematized collection of intervallic relationships—*harmonia* is hypothetically a discrete tuning of the seven-stringed lyre—but also processually, with each differentiated mode involving its own "fuzzy" parameters outside of pure harmonic syntax, such as pulse, tempo, tessitura, timbre, mood, performative dispositions, those affective, non-structural stylistic elements that add up to what a jazz musician might call a "vibe" or a "feel," and what Greek writers on music call an *êthos*. (For syntax versus process, see Feld and Keil 1994:96; on *êthos*, see Anderson 1966.) Collectively, these elements carry class, gender, sexual, and ethnic connotations. To change *harmoniai* thus means to enact a variety of socioculturally inflected schemata whose characteristics may be represented visually on the body of the performer.

[341] Phillis, like most other music historians of the late Classical and Hellenistic periods, was very probably nostalgic for old-time music, and thus was likely biased against the "new" citharodes. His qualification of the old citharodes' march-style movements as *embatêrioi* may be meant to evoke the famous military marching song of the Spartans, the *embatêrion*, which, for those opposed to new musical trends, "stood for old-fashioned simplicity and good order" and "offered a brilliant antithesis to New Music and all that it symbolized" (Csapo 2004:242). The *embatêrion* was accompanied by the *aulos* (Polybius 4.20.1–6), but Phillis may have in mind the connections between early *kitharôidia* and the Spartan Carneia.

observation that old-time citharodes did not allow many facial movements is loaded; it suggests that a younger generation of citharodes *did* indulge these, as did auletes such as Pronomus, whose "facial *skhêma*," singled out by Pausanius, must have been renowned. Given that the *auloi* and the strap that held them in place, the *phorbeia*, already occupied the player's mouth, lips, and cheeks (for a memorable image of this see Dio Chrysostom 78.32), we should probably assume that his eyes, brows, and forehead carried the expressive burden; citharodes were freer to register emotion and character on their faces.[342] We saw that by Plato's time citharodic music and performance were both mimetically charged affairs. Besides the passage from *Persians* just discussed, the textual fragments of Timotheus' *nomoi* certainly suggest any number of opportunities for robust, full-body gesticulation. An anecdote about Timotheus' first performance of the *Nauplios*, a piece that probably found its way into the repertoire of Nero centuries later (Suetonius *Nero* 39.3), indicates that the piece featured a tour-de-force tonal simulation of a sea storm (Hegesander *Memoirs ap.* Athenaeus 8.338a = FGH IV 416). It is easy to imagine that the dramatic effect of the music was visually enhanced through bodily synchronisms; recall that the "winds and hailstorms" mentioned by Plato came with mimetic *skhêmata*. The main narrative section of *Persians*, with its heaving descriptions of the sea battle at Salamis and its various laments of suffering barbarians, their bodies grotesquely abused and violated, clearly offered wide scope for extraordinary musical and bodily mimesis.[343] In light of Phillis' remarks on facial *kinêsis*, it is notable that the text of *Persians* repeatedly isolates images of the dying barbarians' faces and mouths, sucking in seawater and gnashing teeth (64–70, 85), spitting up teeth (91–93), contorting to sputter imprecations in pidgin Greek (146–149). Timotheus certainly scripted mimetically active "roles" for the auletes who accompanied the dithyrambic choruses for which he composed. In his *Scylla* (PMG 793–794), the eponymous monster was apparently portrayed by the aulete with an extraordinary degree of histrionic physicality, which scandalized the conservatives in the audience. Aristotle *Poetics* 26.1461b30–32 compares tragic actors who overdo their gestures to

---

[342] Aristophanes *Assembly Women* 102 (with scholia) suggests that Pronomus wore a great, bushy beard, but the joke is probably that Pronomus was clean-shaven, the better to display his facial mannerisms. A smooth, "effeminate" look may have been cultivated by the stars of the New Music; compare Agathon in *Women at the Thesmophoria* 191–192. Cf. n123 above; Part IV.10n279.

[343] Cf. Part IV.11.

"the vulgar (*phauloi*) auletes who drag around the *koruphaios* 'chorus leader' if they are playing (the) *Scylla*."[344]

As citharode, Timotheus himself impersonated the eponymous monster of his *Cyclops*, a *nomos* (PMG 781). The inherent irony of this "casting," the notionally Apollonian citharode imitating the lawless, uncultured Polyphemus, inspired a dithyrambic parody by Philoxenus, in which the Cyclops was depicted incongruously singing to the *kithara* (PMG 815–827).[345]

The performance of the citharodic *nomos* is unlikely to have become less gestural and histrionic in the Hellenistic and Imperial periods, but rather more so. Indeed, Nero's other great artistic pursuit, *tragôidia* 'tragic acting plus solo singing', was probably not so far from *kitharôidia* in its performative techniques and modes of self-presentation. As *nomoi* such as *Persians* suggest, tragic and citharodic *mousikê* had become increasingly assimilated since the later fifth century BCE. Nero is said to have himself composed a citharodic *Oresteia* and an *Antigone*; he performed an *Attis* or *Bacchae* at the Roman Juvenalia in 59 BCE.[346] Tragic costume significantly left its mark on citharodic *skeuê*. Dio Cassius 63.22.4 says that as *citharoedus* Nero wore the high platform shoes called *kothurnoi* that were favored by tragic actors. This would seem to be a post-Classical innovation, as citharodes depicted on Attic vases of the fifth century either go barefoot or are shod in low slippers. A variant of a late Aesopic *logos* has a thieving fox finding a tragic mask among the *skeuê* not of an actor (*hupokritês*), as other versions have it, but a citharode (Perry 27). We should not imagine a masked Nero *citharoedus*, but the interchangeability of citharode and actor in the Aesopic tradition reflects a more general conflation of the two *tekhnai*.

---

[344] Conservatives' anxieties about the revolutionary nature of the "new dithyramb," its privileging of the mimetic over the diegetic, music over text-centric *mousikê*, aulete over chorus (cf. Pratinas PMG 708), are almost absurdly realized in the gesture memorialized with distaste by Aristotle. The aulete actually *attacks* the *koruphaios* during the performance: an iconic moment of transgression of the earlier social and aesthetic hierarchy of professional accompanist and amateur citizen chorus.

[345] Cf. discussion in Power 2011 (forthcoming).

[346] Philostratus *Life of Apollonius of Tyana* 4.39; Dio Cassius 61.20.2. On the Imperial *tragoedus* 'actor-singer', see Hall 2002 and Kelly 1979.

18. The Athletic Citharode

In the "Lucianic" dialogue *Nero* there is an extended assessment of Nero's performance style, which stands, in fact, as our most detailed account of the normative aesthetic and practical protocols of citharodic performance, at least in the Imperial period. It indicates how significant a contribution dramatically timed physical movement and the spectacular deployment of the body made to the performer's success. One of the interlocutors, Musonius, explains that Nero offset the weakness of his voice not only by skillful *kithara* playing, but also by knowing "the right moment (*kairos*) to walk, stand, change position, and to match the swaying of his head to the melodies (*melê*)" (καιρὸς βαδίσαι καὶ στῆναι καὶ μεταστῆναι καὶ τὸ νεῦμα ἐξομοιῶσαι τοῖς μέλεσιν, 6). No dance steps per se here, but what Musonius describes amounts to a fairly sophisticated choreographed "routine" synched to the rhythmic and melodic contours of the music.[347] Nero invites derision from the audience, however, "if he should imitate his betters" (εἰ δὲ μιμοῖτο τοὺς κρείττονας, 7), not so much by emulating their musical pyrotechnics, but when he overestimates his histrionic prowess by attempting to strike and hold one of the more challenging poses of which the virtuosos are capable. An exemplary misstep is described:

> νεύει μὲν γὰρ τοῦ μετρίου πλέον ξυνάγων τὸ πνεῦμα, ἐπ' ἄκρων δὲ διίσταται τῶν ποδῶν ἀνακλώμενος ὥσπερ οἱ ἐπὶ τοῦ τροχοῦ. φύσει δ' ἐρυθρὸς ὢν ἐρευθεῖ μᾶλλον, ἐμπιπραμένου αὐτῷ τοῦ προσώπου· τὸ δὲ πνεῦμα ὀλίγον, καὶ οὐκ ἀποχρῶν που δή.

> Drawing in his breath, he sways his head more than is appropriate, and stands, feet apart, on tiptoe, with his body arched back, like men on a *trokhos* 'wheel of torture'. Although his natural complexion is ruddy, he reddens still more as his face burns up; his breath becomes short and not at all sufficient.

> "Lucian" *Nero* 7

The writer presents us with an image of Nero being tortured, figuratively and literally; given that the emperor's sadistic cruelty is

---

[347] Macleod 1967:515 translates τὸ νεῦμα ἐξομοιῶσαι τοῖς μέλεσιν as 'swaying his head in time to the music', which I have followed in Section 2 above. The phrase does seem to refer primarily to the rhythmic coordination of head and music, but the verb ἐξομοιῶσαι literally means 'to liken, assimilate', which may suggests too some stylized synching of head movement to the ethical character of the *melê*.

elsewhere discussed at length (8–9), it has probably been chosen for its ironic value. But the sort of hyperextended, balletic pose that Nero is made to strike no doubt carried real mimetic significance vis-à-vis an actual text that was being sung by the citharodes of the day, if not by Nero himself.

This image suggests too the extent to which the dramatic posturing expected of citharodes could augment the already great physical challenge of executing flawless musical expression both on the *kithara* and in the vocal component of the song. In this way, *kitharôidia* was truly as much an athletic event as a musical display. It was an all-consuming physical labor like that experienced by agonistic sportsmen, testing to the limit the performer's mental acuity and physical endurance. The athleticism of the citharodes may in part have motivated the recurring image of Heracles *kitharôidos* that we see on later-sixth-century Attic vessels (see Plate 6); in his stunning mastery of severe physical labors, Heracles could stand as both paradigmatic athlete-warrior and paradigmatic citharode.[348] Analogously, the citharode shown exerting himself on the eye-cup of Psiax mentioned above is visually echoed on the reverse of the cup by a powerful warrior shown falling on one knee, seemingly overcome by the extremes of battle (Plates 7a and b). The harsh training regimen of diet and exercise undertaken by Nero seems entirely justified in light of the athletic demands of performance. Some citharodes, such as the infibulated Hedymeles of Juvenal 6.379–380, practiced, or at least made a show of practicing, sexual abstinence. Aelian *On the Nature of Animals* 6.1 relates that the famous Hellenistic citharode Amoebus, who reputedly was paid a whole talent to play a concert in Athens (Athenaeus 14.623d), refrained from sexual intercourse with his wife "during the entire period of time leading up to his competition in an *agôn*" (παρὰ πάντα τὸν χρόνον, παρ' ὃν

---

[348] Although we have no preserved *epinikion* for a citharodic victor, Pindar's *Pythian* 12, for Midas of Acragas, an auletic victor at the Pythian *agônes*, does draw parallels between the heroic labors (18) of Perseus—his slaying of Medusa, which precipitates Athena's very invention of the *auloi*, and his return to Seriphus—and the agonistic experience of Midas. It is not surprising that we should have an epinician commemoration of an auletic victory, as auletes could not "speak for themselves." Citharodes could, however, celebrate their own past victories in their *prooimia* or in the *sphragis* sections of their *nomoi*. We have such an embedded auto-epinician, Timotheus PMG 802, in which the citharode boasts of a victory over an older rival, Phrynis. Another "mute" instrumentalist, the citharist Stratonicus, relied on the extra-performative medium of the epinician inscription to commemorate his victories (although some citharodes did this as well). See n70 above.

ἀγωνιούμενος).[349] The anecdote clearly resembles stories about the celibacy of famous athletes. Another telling of it in *Historical Miscellanies* 3.30 is notably adjacent to an account of the abstinence practiced by one Iccus, an Olympic pentathlete.[350] True or not, what the Amoebus anecdote reflects is the conflation in the cultural imagination between agonistic athlete and musician, both of whom are able to exhibit almost superhuman physical and mental discipline. The conspicuous detail that Amoebus' wife was *hôraiotatê* 'utterly gorgeous' only emphasizes the enormity of his self-control, while also hinting at the sexual glamour that is the flip side of this star's vaunted celibacy.

John Herington has estimated that a Timothean *nomos* would have taken between 35 and 40 minutes to perform.[351] It is indeed difficult to overestimate the grueling demands put upon the citharode's vocal purity, manual dexterity, rhythmical evenness, psychological concentration, and corporal stamina during this long and intense interval, with all its bravura turns of bodily exertion, such as the one that so tortured Nero. The sheer weight of the *kithara*, which citharodes are occasionally depicted showily hefting upwards in the vase paintings (Plates 1 and 10), must by itself have caused enormous strain, even with the assistance of the support strap. Yet the citharode was expected to maintain perfect composure throughout the performance. Roman sources indicate that both audience and judges evaluated competitive citharodes not only on their musical execution, but also on their ability to project an aesthetically pleasing image of bodily self-control. The performance of a consummately untalented citharode sketched in *Rhetorica ad Herennium* 4.60 is marred as much by the "exceedingly

---

[349] Other competitive musicians practiced and/or advertised sexual abstinence. See the references collected by Kay 1985:230, who is commenting on Martial 11.75.3, where the practice of infibulation is associated with citharodes. Galen *De locis affectis* 8.451 claims that both young athletes and singers who refrain from sex risk premature genital shriveling.

[350] See Scanlon 2002:227–236 on stories of athletes' abstinence. As he points out, total abstinence rather than sexual moderation was probably the exception, never the general rule for training athletes.

[351] Herington 1985:275n25 bases his timing on the estimated total length of Timotheus' *Persians* (around 700 lines, some 240 of which are preserved), "allowing ... for considerable variations in tempo and perhaps even pauses for miming." This estimate may even be too low. Nero's penchant for marathon performances should be kept in mind here. Suetonius *Nero* 21.2 emphasizes the great length of his version of the *nomos Niobe* at the second Neronia. Since the *nomos*—in particular, the more open-ended Terpandrean *nomos*—was not simply the sum of its text or its melody, but rather the framework for an improvised performance event (see Part II.5), its duration could vary quite a bit depending on the citharode's approach to the material, as Herington recognizes.

graceless movement of his body" as his harsh voice (*vocem mittat acer-bissimam cum turpissimo corporis motu*). Tacitus provides rather specific indications of what constituted the graceful somatic comportment demanded of citharodes in his description of Nero's first appearance at his eponymous games in Rome; again, we get a visceral sense of the grueling physical requirements of agonistic performance: "He enters the theater, obeying all the rules of the *cithara* [i.e. the citharodic contest]: that he not sit down when tired, that he only wipe off perspiration with the garb that he wore for his outfit, and that he not allow the audience to see any unseemly discharge from his mouth or nostrils" (*ingreditur theatrum, cunctis citharae legibus obtemperans, ne fessus resideret, ne sudorem nisi ea, quam indutui gerebat, veste deterget, ut nulla oris aut narium excrementa viserent*, Annals 16.4.3).[352] Apparently, citharodes were not permitted to make use of a handkerchief while they performed, as it was not officially part of the *skeuê* (here called the *indutus*). For those performing outdoors, in Mediterranean heat and in full concert attire, perspiration control must have been a serious issue, one that the rules of the *agôn* did not make any easier to handle.

Here we should note the emphasis on the integrity of the citharode's head and face, which are privileged objects of attention in the remarks of Phillis and "Lucian" as well. In late Archaic and early Classical vase paintings, the faces of performing citharodes tend to show ecstatic yet decorously controlled expressions, with the head tilted back and the mouth open in song. The Berlin Painter's citharode provides an excellent example, as does the Brygos Painter's (Plate 1). So iconic was this "sublime" *skhêma* that, as the anecdotal tradition reported, the reputed founder of agonistic *kitharôidia*, Terpander, actually met his death frozen in it: while performing at the Carneia festival, Terpander, "singing and with mouth agape in song" (ᾄδοντος καὶ κεχηνότος πρὸς τὴν ᾠδήν), choked on a fig hurled by someone in the audience—presumably not a hostile gesture meant to show displeasure, as produce tossing sometimes is, but the misguided attempt of the audience member to reciprocate symbolically his pleasure in Terpander's "sweet song."[353] The controlled, artful presentation of head and face was presumably all the more critical after the Classical period, when, as

---

[352] Cf. Suetonius *Nero* 24.1: *in certando vero ita legi oboediebat, ut numquam excreare ausus sudorem quoque frontis brachio deterget* 'In competition he so thoroughly obeyed the rules that he never dared to clear his throat and he even wiped the sweat from his brow with his arm."

[353] *Suda* s.v. γλυκὺ μέλι καὶ πνιξάτω = T 16b Gostoli; cf. *Palatine Anthology* 9.488 = T 16a Gostoli.

we saw, the dramatic play of facial expressions became an increasingly integral effect of citharodic performance. After the mimeticizing turn of the New Music, citharodes would have allowed themselves to put on a variety of stylized faces, even outlandish ones, but with that freedom came the need for still greater discipline and measure. Overdone gestures made a bad impression, as "Lucian" illustrates with Nero's inappropriate head swaying; even in the intensely histrionic citharodic culture of the Empire, there was a limit (*to metrion*) that could be easily overstepped, taking the performer from the sublime to the ridiculous or the grotesque.

19. Neronian Citharodic Politics

Let us return to the more fundamental question of the peculiar logic of Nero's desire to pursue, specifically, a citharodic career. It will not suffice to discount that desire as but one more expression of Nero's excessive *popularitas*, his pathological rage for universal recognition (Suetonius *Nero* 53). It was that in part, but other, more established performance arts would have offered surer means of satisfying his narcissism, in Rome at least—acting, of course, or singing and dancing, which an earlier self-obsessed exhibitionist, Caligula, had planned to practice professionally (Suetonius *Caligula* 54). Nero eventually tried his hand at all of these, but *kitharôidia* was his self-professed τέχνιον from beginning to end. Rather, we should understand Nero's practice of *kitharôidia* as a multivalent expression of his complex relationship to Greek culture.[354] On the one hand, it was driven by an immature, make-believe version of philhellenism, as was his early interest in chariot racing (Tacitus *Annals* 14.14); his dream was to dazzle discerning festival audiences in Greece, like the star virtuosos he idolized, a dream he realized in typically over-the-top fashion by undertaking his tour of the Achaean *agônes*. On the other hand, it was born of a more profound understanding of the political resonances of the art in Greek history and myth, its intimate relations to power and social order, which Nero was intent to exploit in the making of his own principate. Not surprisingly, any such musico-political sophistication is occluded or distorted by the ancient sources, for whom Nero's citharodic endeavors represented at best a tyrant's aberrant whim, at worst a lunatic perversion of his status and his office. Modern scholarship has generally followed

---

[354] On Nero's unique brand of philhellenism, see Griffin 1984:208–220.

these sources without due criticism.[355] While it would be misguided to rationalize too deeply the obviously mixed motives that led Nero to stages in Naples and beyond, the cultural political tradition of *kitharôidia* nevertheless provides a valid lens through which to detect some method to his apparent musical madness. That tradition offered the young emperor, as both patron and performer, an eclectic range of mythical and historical role models to emulate and scenarios to recreate as he formulated his personal vision of a "citharodic politics." Neronian citharodic politics were, of course, self-serving—the augmentation of "real" imperial power by the cultural star power of the citharode—but also, I would argue, genuinely communal in intent, an attempt, unintentionally ironic as it might have been, to bring Rome and the Empire to order through the ancient Apollonian-Orphic-Amphionic potential of *kitharôidia* to effect social harmony and good government.

As to the latter design, Nero's summoning of Terpnus to Rome was, as argued in Section 11.ii, a conscious reenactment of the mythico-historical scenario of Terpander's summons to Sparta, where he ended civic discord with his *nomoi*. More obviously, an essential component of Nero's political self-fashioning was his identification with Apollo *kithar-ôidos*, the divine exemplar of musical ideals both aesthetic and sociopolitical, and the deity whom a mortal citharode such as Timotheus could implore to bring peace, prosperity, and *eunomia* to the city in which he performed his *nomoi* (*Persians* 237–240).[356] Seneca promotes this identification, with its full freight of political, even cosmological connotations, as early as the *Apocolocyntosis*, his satire of Claudius, probably composed around 54 BCE, in which Apollo sings to the *cithara* of the coming of Nero while the Fates, figured as Muses—Lachesis wears a wreath of "Pierian laurel"—spin out the Golden Age that will be his principate:

> The sisters were amazed at their material. The common wool was changed to a precious metal; a Golden Age spun down on the beautiful thread. There was no end to it ... Phoebus was present and, assisting with his singing and delighting in

---

[355] Champlin 2003 is a notable exception. Although not particularly relevant to Nero's musical enthusiasms, Alcock 1994 is an exemplary attempt to recover a viable geopolitical agenda behind his Grecian tour, one of his supposedly "madcap antics."

[356] On Nero's complex Apollonism, see Champlin 2003:112–116. See most recently the insightful discussion of citharodic Apollo in Bundrick 2005:142–150. Her comments on his guardianship of cities are especially relevant: "Apollo was honored as a god who brings not only *sophrosyne* and *harmonia* but also *dike*, a god who continues to protect the city and its interests" (146).

the times to come, now joyously moved his plectrum, now joyously handed them their wool. He kept them focused on his singing and distracted them from their toil. And while they praised highly their brother's *cithara* and his songs (*carmina*), their hands spun more than usual and their work, praised [by Apollo], transcended human destinies. "Take nothing away, Fates," said Phoebus. "Let him surpass the temporal limits of mortal life, he who is like me in looks and like me in grace, and inferior to me in neither song nor voice. He will offer an age of happiness to the weary and he will break the silence of the laws (*legumque silentium rumpit*) ... Such a Caesar is at hand, such a Nero will Rome now behold. His radiant face gleams with a gentle brightness and his comely neck with flowing hair.

Seneca *Apocolocyntosis* 4.1[357]

Seneca has the god himself do the panegyric heavy lifting. Apollo both prophesies and ratifies the new world order that will come to pass under Nero, while anointing him to be his earthly semblant, his uncanny equal in physical aspect and "song and voice," that is, in *kithar-ôidia*. Appropriately, these ordinances take the form of *carmina* sung to the *cithara*. Apollo thus sets a practical model for Nero's praiseworthy performance of citharodic song even as he cosmically grounds and divinely authorizes it. The phrase *legum silentium rumpit* 'he will break the silence of the laws' refers primarily to the fact that Claudius "had seriously encroached on normal legal activities," a situation that Nero promised to rectify.[358] But in the word *leges* 'laws' we may hear too an allusion to the common Greek play on the meanings of *nomos* as 'law' and as the main genre of song performed by citharodes. The politico-legal and the musical are thus implicitly conflated. As *princeps*, Nero will give new "voice" to the laws; as *citharoedus*, he will more literally give voice to *nomoi* in Rome, where previously they have been "silent," i.e. not heard and appreciated. It is likely, I think, that Seneca initially suggested the prestigious Hellenic cultural precedents in which his young charge could clothe his naked yearning for the concert stage in legitimacy, social responsibility, and even sublimity.

---

[357] I follow in part the translation of Eden 1984:33–35. See the general discussion of the passage as Neronian propaganda in Schubert 1998. I see no compelling reason to view these lines as a late insertion into the satirical text, as does Champlin 2003:116. Seneca is laying the groundwork for programmatic themes that would emerge more openly in Nero's principate in the 60s.

[358] Eden 1984:78.

It must be significant too that the poet of the *Praise of Piso*, a pane-gyric of the charismatic, philhellenic anti-Neronian conspirator Gaius Calpurnius Piso, is at pains to emphasize the Apollonian mandate behind Piso's own accomplished, yet amateur lyre playing:

> sive chelyn digitis et eburno verbere pulsas,
> dulcis Apollinea sequitur testudine cantus,
> et te credibile est Phoebo didicisse magistro.

> Or, if you strike the lyre (*chelys*) with fingers and ivory plec-trum, a sweet song follows on the Apollonian lyre (*testudo*), and one would believe that you learned [lyric music] with Phoebus as your teacher.

Praise of Piso 166–168

The praise is bold: Apollo himself was Piso's *magister* (168); his lyre is Apollo's (167; cf. 171). It is likely also tendentious. This figuring of Piso as Rome's premier Apollonian lyre player would seem to be a deliberate challenge to his rival Nero's own outsized claims to identification with Apollo *kitharôidos*. The poet also compares Piso's (privately, modestly practiced) lyric enthusiasms to those of Achilles, who, secluded in his tent, sang to his lyre in between battles (*Iliad* 9.184–191). The implica-tion is that Piso knows how to balance the martial and the musical, while Nero, singing in public to the *cithara*, does not.

As further subtext to the Piso-Achilles identification, we might read a swipe at Nero's own attempts to rehabilitate Paris as a model epic hero. Such rehabilitation may have had a rhetorical purpose specifi-cally concerned with the emperor's own *kitharôidia*. In the *Iliad*, Paris is notoriously hedonistic, indolent, and given too much to music making. His brother Hector warns him that his *kitharis* 'lyre playing' will not assist him in battle (3.54). Probably as early as the Classical period, the lyre of Paris had become a symbol of effeminate and immoral musical culture, the ideological other to Achilles' manly, virtuous lyre.[359] In Nero's epic *Troica*, however, Paris appears as the *fortissimus* 'bravest' of the Trojans, who "defeated everyone in an agonistic competition

---

[359] Discussion in Veneri 1995. For the implicit critique of musical professionalism involved the praise of Achilles' and Piso's lyre, cf. n195 above. Tradition had it that Alexander the Great followed the noble example of Achilles in enjoying music, even claiming to possess the hero's lyre; cf. n210 above; Veneri 1995:128–131. Alexander's legendary rejection of the lyre of Paris as effeminate and morally corrupt (Plutarch *On the Fortune of Alexander* 331d, *Life of Alexander* 15.9, Aelian *Historical Miscellanies* 9.38) is worth noting in view of Nero's praise of Paris.

at Troy (*in Troiae agonali certamine*), even Hector himself" (Servius *ad* Vergil *Aeneid* 5.370). Nero was likely following the account presented in the *Alexander* of Euripides, in which Paris returns unrecognized to Troy 20 years after Priam had him exposed. As the Hypothesis to that play relates, he returns just as the *agônes* that Hecuba had established in his honor two decades before are being celebrated. Participating incognito in his own *agônes*, Paris is the victor in the racing and pentathlon competitions (and probably boxing as well), and thus angers the aristocratic Deiphobus, who threatens to kill him. (According to Servius, Nero chose the more melodramatic option of making Hector the violently aggrieved sore loser; in Euripides fr. 62a.11–12 it is Hector who attempts to calm a hot-headed Deiphobus.)

Nero's attraction to Paris was surely multifaceted.[360] But two parallels stand out: one, Paris was a lyre player; two, he competed successfully at his own *agônes*, as Nero did at the Neronia in 65 BCE. It is probable that Nero both recited excerpts from the *Troica* at this festival—perhaps even the part dedicated to Paris—and made his Roman debut as a citharode (Tacitus *Annals* 16.4, with Dio Cassius 62.29.1). Did these two exemplary aspects of Paris' *vita* overlap in the *Troica*? Although Paris does not seem to have participated in *mousikoi agônes* in the Greek tradition, nor does Servius make any explicit reference to it, could Nero have made Paris into an exemplary citharodic *agônistês*? Nero was probably not the first to do so. Tourists to Troy in the time of Alexander the Great, and probably still in Nero's day, were given the opportunity to view the *lura* of Paris (Plutarch *On the Fortune of Alexander* 331d, *Life of Alexander* 15.9), a fact that suggests that the lyric persona of this problematically glamorous hero had assumed a star quality that transcended Hector's brief, derogatory mention of his *kitharis* in the *Iliad*, as well as the later defamation of it by culturally conservative elites.[361]

---

[360] See Sullivan 1985:92–93, followed by Champlin 2003: "Paris the hero ... was chosen to reflect the paradoxes of Nero's own character, with its combination of sensual living and careful training" (82–83).

[361] Something of this star quality, in this case auletic rather than citharodic, is captured by Euripides *Iphigenia at Aulis* 576–578, in which the chorus imagines Paris, still an oxherd on Mt. Ida, "playing barbarian tunes on his *surinx*, blowing (?) *mimêmata* 'imitations' of the *auloi* of Olympus on his reeds." Despite his humble surroundings and rustic *surinx*, Paris emulates the glamour and virtuosity of professional auletes, who in Euripides' time would still have played the *nomoi* attributed to their exemplar, the legendary Phrygian piper Olympus (on whom cf. "Plutarch" *On Music* 7.1133d–f). In Judgment of Paris scenes in sixth- and fifth-century BCE Attic vase painting, the pastoral Paris fetchingly plays the tortoise-shell lyre, the image of an attractive, well-born Athenian youth (see Bundrick 2005:65–66). In a late rendering of the Judgment,

20. Augustan Antecedents

As a new *princeps*, Nero had claimed that he would follow the example of Augustus in his rule (Suetonius *Nero* 10.1). Accordingly, his emulation of Apollo *kitharôidos* found an intermediary model in Augustan *Kulturpolitik*. Recall his claims that *cantus Apolloni sacros* '[citharodic] songs were sacred to Apollo' and that statues of citharodic Apollo *adstare non modo Graecis in urbibus sed Romana apud templa* 'stood not only in Greek cities but also in Roman temples' (Tacitus *Annals* 14.14.1). The rhetoric of this latter claim is savvier than Tacitus acknowledges. Nero legitimates his musical practice by appealing to the grounding role of Apollo *kitharôidos* in the organization of the Greek *polis* as well as in the symbolic repertoire of Hellenizing cult in Rome (in both cases a role made materially manifest as statuary, which is how a majority of Romans would be most familiar with the culture of *kitharôidia*). The *Romanum templum* Nero must surely have had foremost in mind was the Augustan temple of Apollo Palatinus, dedicated in 28 BCE, in whose cella was installed the impressive statue of Apollo *citharoedus* attributed to Scopas, an image that stood at the heart of the Augustan building program as a conspicuous monument to the divinely favored political stability and consonance supporting the ascendant imperial order.[362] Propertius had likely interpreted this statue as a symbol of the

---

however, Paris, seated in a columnated structure holding a princely scepter in one hand, the lyre in the other, transcends the role of the humble country lyrist—he is a star (cup by the Painter of Berlin, Berlin F 2536; Maas and Snyder 1989:104, fig. 9). *Pace* Maas and Snyder 1989:226n18 the figure with the *kithara* in the (pre-)Judgment scene on a red-figured amphora in Brussels (A 3089, CVA Belgium III, pl. 120) is Apollo, not Paris.

[362] On the statue, cf. n58 above: it may not actually have been Scopas' work, but I will continue to refer to it as such. Miller 2000:409–410 notes the symbolism of Nero's triumphal procession to the Palatine temple after his victorious musical tour of Greece: "The lyre-playing god greeted the lyre-playing emperor, and vice versa." This *triumphus* was a parody of a conventional military triumph, complete with a "captive" citharode, Diodorus, whom he had bested in the contests (Dio Cassius 63.20.4). See further Miller 2000:416–417. Suetonius *Nero* 39.2 records an anonymous *graffito* that cleverly connects Nero's failure of leadership to his fascination with Apollo in his musical, rather than martial, aspect: *dum tendit citharam noster, dum cornua Parthus, | noster erit Paean, ille Hecatebeletes* ("While our leader tunes his *cithara* and the Parthian bends his bow, ours will be [Apollo] Paean, theirs will be [Apollo] Far-shooter"). Champlin 2003:116 suggests, however, that Nero chose to sing the *Niobe* at his first appearance in Rome at the Neronia because the myth shows Apollo in his most martially relentless aspect: "to sing the woes of Niobe was to sing the fearsome power of Apollo." We know nothing about the content of the *Niobe*, but we might speculate that Apollo's *kitharôidia* was somehow thematized in the *nomos*. Niobe's husband was Amphion, whom one tradition made an antagonist of Apollo for jeering, presumably along with his wife, at Leto and her children (Pausanias 9.8.4).

peaceful harmony that Rome would enjoy thanks to Octavian's victory at Actium and the definitive conclusion of civil war: *bella satis cecini: citharam iam poscit Apollo | victor* 'Enough have I sung of wars; now victorious Apollo demands the *cithara*' (4.6.69–70).[363]

But there was another statue of Apollo, this one holding the lyre, in the portico before the temple, its maker unknown. It is possible that this Apollo bore some physical resemblance to Augustus.[364] This is highly speculative territory, but it is worth exploring a little more, for if Augustus had—at the purely symbolic level, of course—conspicuously identified himself with the musical Apollo, he would have provided a richly significant exemplar with which Nero would have in turn strongly identified, in all his characteristic excess.[365] The statue is described by Propertius in the same poem in which he describes the Scopas statue in the cella: *hic equidem Phoebo visus mihi pulchrior ipso | marmoreus tacita carmen hiare lyra* ("And there [in the temple's portico] I saw one who seemed to me more beautiful even than Phoebus himself, a marble figure with parted lips as if singing to his silent lyre," 2.31.5–6).[366] The ecphrasis is enigmatic. Is Propertius merely expressing the rhetorical conceit that this splendid artifice is even more beautiful than the real thing? Or is the implication that this is Octavian represented in the guise of musical Apollo, and as such, Apollo is made even more beautiful than usual? A scholiast to Horace *Epistles* 1.3.17 says that in the Palatine library Octavian "had erected an effigy of himself in the garb and stature of Apollo" (*sibi posuerat effigiem habitu ac statura Apollinis*). Could this be the same statue that Propertius sees now in the portico? Or is the latter modeled on the library statue? We cannot be sure what connection, if any, existed between them.[367] In any case,

---

But their antagonism had a properly musical dimension as well; that Amphion was a protégé of Hermes rather than Apollo may have played a part in its genesis. In the *Niobe*, then, Apollo's fierceness as a citharodic agonist—thus we see him in the myth of his contest with the aulete Marsyas—as well as an archer may have been at issue. The combination of musical and martial prowess was something Nero himself tried to project, as his triumph illustrates.

[363] Cf. Tibullus 2.5.1–2, probably also referring to the Scopas statue in light of Actium: "Phoebus, come here with your *cithara* and your songs" (*Phoebe ... huc age cum cithara carminibusque ueni*). See Murgatroyd 1994:165–170.

[364] Not entirely certain, but still open to the possibility is Camps 1967:205–206; cf. Barchiesi 2005:284–285, who notes that the "iconography of Apollo had been converging with the official image of Octavian long before 28 BCE."

[365] On Augustan emulation of Apollo as an inspiration for Nero, see Champlin 2003:142.

[366] Translation of Camps 1967:205.

[367] Camps 1967:205 suggests that we might read *quidam* for *equidem* in Propertius 2.31.5, which, while still vague, would make the case clearer that the statue is meant to represent a "certain somebody" (Augustus) in the guise of the god. Servius on Vergil

the Horatian scholiast indicates that Octavian did in fact promote the visual identification of himself with Apollo within the privileged space of the Palatine; further, the word *habitus* might suggest that this was Apollo wearing some version of his familiar citharodic raiment.

We do not hear whether Nero ever had a statue of himself as citharode erected publicly in Rome, although Suetonius *Nero* 24 suggests that he probably did so in Greece. After his return from Greece in 67 BCE, it was said that Nero placed in his bedchambers (*in cubiculis*) the crowns he had won as well as statues of himself in *citharoedicus habitus*—monuments of victory he had presumably collected during his winning tour (Suetonius *Nero* 25.2). Given Nero's eagerness by the middle of the 60s to publicize his cithardic persona, it is curious that he kept these statues stored away as personal souvenirs in private rooms, out of the public gaze he habitually courted. It is true that such intimate hoarding of self-congratulatory images seems to express neatly the pathological self-obsession we associate with Nero, but perhaps too neatly—the story could be nothing more than a gossipy comment on his narcissism.

Yet Suetonius claims that Nero had coins struck with the likeness of these statues, which, if true, would mean that Nero had devised a way to disseminate his winning citharodic image further and more effectively than if he had simply displayed the statues in the *urbs*. We do not, however, have any Roman coins bearing the explicit image of Nero *citharoedus*. Suetonius might have mistaken Nero for Apollo *citharoedus*, who does appear on a number of Neronian coin types between 62 and 65 BCE. Of course, such confusion was no doubt the effect intended by the design of coins such as those showing on the obverse Nero wearing a radiate crown, evoking Apollo the Sun god, and Apollo *citharoedus* on the reverse, an arrangement which easily invites the assimilation of the two figures.[368] Hellenic coinage of the time immediately following Nero's liberation of Greece in 66 more directly conflates Nero and Apollo *citharoedus*. For instance, the city of Nicopolis in Epirus, which was founded by Augustus to commemorate his Actian victory of 31 BCE (Dio Cassius 51.1.3) and refounded by Nero as Nerononicopolis, minted coins showing "Nero Apollo the *Ktistês* 'Founder'" playing the *kithara*.[369]

Eclogues 4.10 mentions, but does not locate, a statue of Augustus *cum Apollonis cunctis insignibus* 'with all the insignia of Apollo'.

[368] See e.g. Griffin 1984, fig. 31. On the pairing of the radiate crown and the *kithara* in Nero's Apollonian self-fashioning, see Champlin 2003:116–118. On Nero's triumphant return from the Greek tour in 67, he was publicly lauded as "Nero Apollo" (Dio Cassius 63.20.5; cf. Suetonius *Nero* 53).

[369] RPC 1371 and 1376. Other examples discussed by Champlin 2003:117.

As the caption indicates, the Greek citizens of Nicopolis possessed the cultural heritage to appreciate and indeed the semiotic *savoir-faire* to articulate verbally and visually the ideological bridge between Nero's musical and political interventions in Achaea. That nuanced appreciation is signaled as well by the reverse images of the two preserved examples of these coins. One shows Nike, in commemoration of the emperor's citharodic victories in Greece (and an allusion to the name of the city); the other shows Eleutheria 'Freedom', in commemoration of the liberation of Greece. These coins neatly condense the expansive ideological underpinnings of Nero's citharodizing in Greece: his victorious *kitharôidia* brings with it an Apollonian mandate to restore a "foundational" order and prosperity to the liberated cities of Imperial Greece, in particular to the refounded city of Nicopolis itself.[370]

A curious piece of anecdotal testimony preserved in Suetonius *Nero* 12.3–4 also suggests Nero's conscious emulation of a "lyric Augustus." When Nero was honorarily awarded the crown of victory in *kitharôidia* at the first Neronia in 60 BCE, he ordered it to be carried off to a statue of Augustus (*ferrique ad Augusti statuam iussit*). Suetonius does not say what statue of Augustus this is, but the one in the portico may be our best candidate.[371] It would certainly be the one most likely to be adorned with a citharodic crown, however incongruent such a crown may have been with the statue's original symbolic ethos. If so, we may further speculate on the significance of Nero's gesture. First, it plays

---

[370] It is worth noting that Nicopolis hosted the Augustan-founded Actian Games for Apollo, which included *mousikoi agônes*, and surely citharodic *agônes* at those. Nero does not seem to have competed at the Actian Games, but the refoundation of their host city does seem to have been a bid to engage with a significantly Hellenic facet of Augustus' post-Actian politics. For the possible overlap between Apollo *Ktistês* and *Kitharôidos* in the Greek cultural imaginary, see Franklin 2006b:382, with reference to the refoundation of the Sicilian city of Camarina in the later 460s BCE, in which the strings of the lyre provided the symbolic structuring coordinates for the reorganization of the citizen body. See Cordano 1994; Wilson 2004:280–281. Plutarch *Life of Aratus* 2.1 registers an interesting inversion of the association between lyric *harmonia* and civic organization. In Sicyon, when the old Doric aristocracy gave way to demagoguery and factionalism, it was as if the *harmonia* of the city—we presume the Dorian *harmonia*—had been put out of tune. The implicit lyrico-political ideology here is properly elitist: the *polis* as *lura* is imagined as the possession of the aristocracy, for whom the "real" lyre would have served as a marker of social privilege and distinction.

[371] Champlin 2003:142 identifies this statue as that of Augustus-Apollo in the Palatine library. His observation, "[Nero] was surely paying the tribute of one citharode to another," is one with which I would partially agree, but which needs to be nuanced along the lines I explore below.

as political theater, a conspicuous bid to legitimate his own controversial investment in the popular music culture of Greece by linking it to the "white marble," classicizing Hellenism of the Augustan past and the more sober program of cultural politics in which that Hellenism played a critical role, one so well embodied in the image of Augustus as a restrained Apollo—the epitome of all that is cultured, moderate, harmonious—holding not the professional's *kithara*, but the noble amateur's lyre, and a gracefully *silent* one at that.[372] Indeed, Propertius seems determined to overdetermine the obvious fact that the statue is mute: the *lyra* is *tacita*, the player's lips are parted (*hiare*), but the *carmen* has not yet begun. The music here is entirely potential, symbolically pure, undefiled by the base facts of sound and performance.

By contrast, Propertius in the same poem writes that the statue of Apollo *citharoedus* within the temple, the one supposedly sculpted by Scopas, "in his long vestment sounds out his songs" (*in longa carmina ueste sonat*, 2.31.16). In these differing representations as interpreted by Propertius we may detect a reflex of long-standing ideological distinctions made by Greek elites between the string music of professional citharodes, who play the *kithara* in public, and cultured amateurs, who play the *lura* in private (Nero's *musica occulta*). It is acceptable that Apollo still be represented in the traditional manner of a performing citharode, but a musically figured "Augustan Apollo" should be shown only in his "lyric" aspect, and in a heavily abstracted, symbolic style at that.

At the same time, in light of his stormy history of familial psychodrama, it is difficult to resist interpreting Nero's seemingly deferential coronation of Augustus as a gesture of profound Oedipal ambivalence. Is Nero the filial son seeking to win the approval of Augustus the *pater durus* 'strict father' for his own musical ambitions? Or is he provocatively flaunting his Greek "decadence" before him? Or, and this may be the most likely scenario, is he passive-aggressively remaking the lyric Augustus in his own image, literalizing, and so vulgarizing, making a travesty of, his purely symbolic musicality, casting him in the model role of the real-world competitive citharode he himself aspires to be?[373]

---

[372] In terms of the literary-poetic expression of Augustan cultural politics, we may note how far the emulation of consecrated Hellenic poetic canons—Homeric epic, Aeolic monody, Alexandrian learned poetry—practiced by Horace and Vergil lie from Nero's promotion of the relatively vulgar, professionalized, gaudy culture of *kitharôidia*.

[373] A related *détournement* of Augustan material culture occurs on Nero's return to Rome from his victorious tour of the Greek games: Nero appropriates for his "musical" triumph the same chariot that had carried a militarily triumphant Augustus into the *urbs* (Suetonius *Nero* 24–25; Dio Cassius 63.20).

21. Evolving Models of Patronage

Augustus offered no model patronage of *kitharôidia.* As we have seen, it is Nero who deserves the credit for introducing the medium on a mass scale to Rome. Nero does take his place, however, in a long line of autocratic Greek patrons of *kitharôidia.* Since the early Archaic period, tyrants and leading men had sought to "possess" the illustrious medium in order to bolster their own cultural prestige and that of the cities under their control, as well as to foster order and docility among their citizens. The earliest and most famous tyrannical cultivator of *kitharôidia* was Periander of Corinth, whose patronage of Arion of Methymna, both "a citharode second to none of the citharodes in his day," and a composer of dithyrambs (Herodotus 1.23), was the stuff of legend. Herodotus seems to imply that Arion served as a public organizer of musical culture in Corinth, as Terpander had in Sparta; in other narrative traditions Arion is figured as a highly remunerated private entertainer to the tyrant. In the words of Lucian, "Periander enjoyed Arion and often sent for him to perform on account of his *tekhnê,* and Arion became a rich man thanks to the tyrant" (ἔχαιρεν αὐτῷ καὶ πολλάκις μετεπέμπετο αὐτὸν ἐπὶ τῇ τέχνῃ, ὁ δὲ πλουτήσας παρὰ τοῦ τυράννου, *Dialogues of the Sea Gods* 5.2). One scholar has argued that Nero may have "tried to reinvent publicly a significant part of his private life in the image" of Periander, a deeply ambivalent figure, renowned as a wise and cultured leader as well as a violent, amoral transgressor of law and custom.[374] The Corinthian tyrant may have thus presented to Nero a special model of citharodic patronage. Nero privately enjoyed the music of Terpnus at dinner (Suetonius *Nero* 20.1), while also encouraging the public performance of *kitharôidia* in the city by favorites such as Menecrates, on whom he lavished riches (*Nero* 30.2). As a performing musician, however, Nero would have identified with Arion, who remained a byword for virtuoso *kitharôidia* well into the late Empire (e.g. Julian *Oration* 3.111).[375]

The Hellenistic age offered models of more intimate, indeed eroticized, relationships between royal powers and star citharodes; the gap between patron and celebrity musician, which Nero would

---

[374] Champlin 2003:107.

[375] We may note that one aspect of his Neapolitan debut recalls the story of Arion's seaborne adventure. Nero, like Arion, played to an audience made up (largely) of sailors, if considerably less hostile than Arion's Corinthians. This was probably a coincidence, and very improbably a deliberate set-up, but Nero may have appreciated the fact that it added a certain mythic resonance to his performance.

radically close, was beginning to narrow. As we saw in Section 6.ii, the Macedonian king Antigonus II Gonatas romantically pursued the citharode Aristocles (Athenaeus 8.603e). We looked too at the possible ties between the female musician Glauce and Ptolemy II Philadelphus of Alexandria, whose wife, Arsinoe Philadelphus, is celebrated in Posidippus AB 37 as a patron of the ancient Lesbian citharodic tradition—essentially a new Periander. And Berenice II, if that is her likeness in Boscoreale, cannily appropriated the visual glamour of the citharode to enrich her own royal persona.

During the late Classical and Hellenistic periods, citharodes themselves became more adept at negotiating volatile, shifting interstate politics, and at marketing their services, musical and otherwise, to rulers established and aspirant who understood the benefits of strategically deploying their star power.[376] The trendsetter in this was Aristonicus, an Olynthian citharode, whose career was distinguished by a remarkable series of high-level patronal engagements and exploits; he was a kind of Zelig of fourth-century geopolitics. When we first hear of Aristonicus he is working in the service of the Rhodian mercenary general Memnon in 353 BCE, using his talent and celebrity to gather critical tactical information for his patron (cf. Section 6.iii):

> Memnon decided to make war on Leucon, the tyrant of the Bosporus. He wanted to assess the size of Leucon's forces and the population of the country, so he sent Archibiades of Byzantium on a trireme as his ambassador to Leucon, on the pretense of arranging a friendly alliance with him. And with him he sent the Olynthian citharode Aristonicus, the most celebrated of all the citharodes at that time among the Greeks, in order that wherever they landed on their journey, when the citharode put on a public concert (*epideixis*) and the inhabitants excitedly crowded to the theaters to hear him,

---

[376] A model for this arrangement may already be suggested by the story of Arion's Western tour (Herodotus 1.24). Schamp 1976:118 has posed the question, "Would Arion have been a sort of ambassador in the service of Periander's politics of prestige?" Beyond sheer cultural prestige, however, his patronage of Arion conceivably represented a savvy "business" investment for the tyrant and his commercially oriented city of Corinth (cf. Thucydides 1.13.5). Corinth "had intense contact with the West, the direction in which its colonial and commercial interests primarily lay from early in its history" (Munn 2003:197). Arion's itineracy in southern Italy and Sicily may have served as an advertisement in these lucrative markets for Corinthian exports. The notion of Arion's *kitharôidia* as a "luxury export" (from the Eastern Aegean, with its Lydian cachet, via Corinth) is reinforced by his transport on a Corinthian merchant vessel (Herodotus 1.24.2).

the size of the population would become perfectly clear to the ambassador.

Polyaenus Strategems 5.44.1

There is no reason to doubt the veracity of the story; Memnon is cleverly following in a tradition of capitalizing on citharodic charisma. But the idea of a citharode's serving officially as the international goodwill ambassador of a powerful man, or indeed as his "secret agent," is unheard of before Aristonicus. The next we hear of Aristonicus, he is playing alongside the famous aulete Dorion at the public festivities in Macedon celebrating Philip's victory at Chaeroneia in 338 BCE (Theopompus FGrH 115 F 236 = Athenaeus 10.435b); he has traded up for a new and more powerful patron. That Aristonicus hailed from Olynthus, a city that Philip had razed ten years earlier, indicates the way that lucrative musico-political alliances transcended ethnic loyalties in this cosmopolitan age of commodified celebrity. Most strikingly, we last find the citharode out on campaign with Alexander in Asia in 328, where he is killed fighting for his life as a soldier in a battle at Zaraspia, having unwisely moved too far from his true vocation in music. As Arrian *Anabasis* 4.16.6–7 puts it, Aristonicus died "not as you would expect of a citharode" (οὐ κατὰ κιθαρῳδόν), but as a "noble warrior" (ἀνὴρ ἀγαθός). Alexander later honored him with a statue erected at Delphi that portrayed the citharode holding both a spear and *kithara* (Plutarch *On the Fortune of Alexander* 2.334f)—a fitting tribute to this ambitious social and musical operator, whose career was so long intertwined with those of great military men.

While his career may have been particularly illustrious, Aristonicus' exploits were not unique. Antigonus I, following the example of his Macedonian predecessors, employed the greatest citharode of his day, Amoebus, whose performance at a wedding in Corinth served to distract the citizens while Antigonus seized control of their city (Polyaenus *Strategems* 4.6.1). From the second century BCE we have fascinating epigraphical evidence of a citharode named Menecles serving quite literally as a musical ambassador from Teos to the Cretan cities of Knossos and Priansos. Menecles, accompanied by one Herodotus, who does not seem to have been a musician, visited Crete with the intention of requesting Cretan recognition of the *asulia* 'inviolability' of Teos.[377] In honorary decrees set up in Teos, the magistrates

---

[377] The relevant inscriptions are I.Cret. I viii 11 (Knossos) and xxiv 1 (Priansos). Teos was a major center of the Artists of Dionysus, and Aneziri 1997:96–97 and others

and citizens of Knossos and Priansos praised Menecles' public perfor-mance μετὰ κιθάρας 'with the *kithara*' of (once controversially inno-vative, now indisputably classic) *nomoi* by the New Music citharodes Timotheus and Polyeidus, as well as works by "our ancient poets," presumably canonical Cretan composers.[378] Strategic concert program-ming, this—Menecles knew how to please the patriotic sensibilities of local audiences, as well as how to wow them with the virtuoso music of the prestigious classics. The success of his citharodic diplomacy is well attested by the two inscriptions.[379]

Another politically engaged citharode of note, closer in time to Nero, was Anaxenor of Magnesia on the Maeander, whose fame was such that he was honored with a bronze statue in the Magnesian theater, its inscription lauding his "epic" talent: the man has the "godlike voice" of a Demodocus (Strabo 14.1.41; cf. Section 5 above). Anaxenor's celebrity led him to develop a close relationship with Nero's great-grandfather, Mark Antony:

Ἀναξήνορα δὲ τὸν κιθαρῳδὸν ἐξῆρε μὲν καὶ τὰ θέατρα, ἀλλ' ὅτι μάλιστα Ἀντώνιος, ὅς γε καὶ τεττάρων πόλεων ἀπέδειξε φορολόγον στρατιώτας αὐτῷ συστήσας.

The theaters exalted Anaxenor the citharode, but Antony exalted him most of all, since he even appointed him revenue collector from four cities, arranging a bodyguard of soldiers for him.

Strabo 14.1.41

---

understandably assume that Menecles (who is called "son of Dionysius") belonged to the organization. But it is notable that no mention of it is made in either decree. Cf. n203 above. In the Knossian decree Menecles is complimented as an ἀνὴρ πεπαιδευμένος 'cultured gentleman', but that need not mean that he was a musical amateur, as Bélis 1999:45 would have it.

[378] Menecles also "brought in (εἰσήνεγκε) a historical cycle (*kuklos*) about Crete and the gods and the heroes born in Crete, creating his compilation from many poets and historiographers." What may be described here is a piece in the "patchwork" or medley style associated with the fourth-century citharode Polyeidus ("Plutarch" *On Music* 1138b); cf. Hordern 2002:12–13, who thinks of "a collection of otherwise unre-lated poems on the same general theme."

[379] Chaniotis 1988 argues that two other Cretan decrees from the second century BCE indicate that ambassadors from Mylasa performed songs by the Cretan classic Thaletas. Thaletas is mentioned in the inscriptions, but unfortunately there is no clear mention of performance, nor whether the Mylasians were musicians. Thaletas was known as a choral composer, but certainly the Mylasians could have performed cithardic adaptations, as Menecles probably did of the "ancient poets" of Crete. Here, I would note a third-century CE honorary decree from Crete for the citharode Eubius of Messene, awarded *proxenia* and citizenship (I.Cret. I xxiv 4A).

Anaxenor had parlayed his theatrical successes into something more than lucrative patronage; Antony made him into a quasi-autonomous mini-potentate overseeing Imperial business across an interstate network of cities. Indeed, one would imagine that his political responsibilities overshadowed his musical career. (Or did he somehow combine tribute collecting and concertizing?) Strabo says that in his home city of Magnesia the citizens "clad him in purple as one consecrated to Zeus Sosipolis (the 'City-Savior'), as the γραπτὴ εἰκών 'painted image' in the agora shows." That elaborate monuments to Anaxenor commanded prime real estate in both the theater and the agora demonstrates how deeply the city was invested in this citharode's prestige, enhanced as it was by his intimacy with Antony; so too does his being adorned in the purple of Zeus Sosipolis, whose cult was among the most important in Magnesia. There was probably a citharodic *agôn* attached to the local festival of this deity, but the painting would seem to commemorate the appointment of Anaxenor to some distinct honorary position within the cult rather than the mere recognition of a festival victory. (Could his association with Zeus Sosipolis reflect his own reputation as a city-savior? The ideal of the citharode as a musical protector of the *polis* goes back to Terpander and the accounts of his rescuing Sparta from destructive strife.) There is no question that Antony's exuberant, wide-eyed philhellenism—his direct participation in living Greek culture(s) high and low, in contrast to the idealized Hellenizing of an Octavian—was an important model for Nero; his ancestor's political manipulation of citharodic prestige in the case of Anaxenor might well have nourished his own vision of an Imperial politics of *kitharôidia*.[380]

Finally, worthy of mention is another politically active musician of the Antonian period, Theomnestus, a *psaltês* 'harper', who was a rival for power to Nicias, a tyrant of Cos. Strabo 14.2.19, which is our only mention of him, supplies no further details about his activity, but the fact that at least some of the citizens of Cos endorsed the prospect of a tyrant-harpist suggests how receptive Greeks, especially those in the East, where Anaxenor too held sway, would have been toward a *princeps citharoedus*.

---

[380] Cf. Champlin 2003:173–176. As with Nero, Antony's citharodic associations raised Roman eyebrows. His intimacy with Anaxenor is cited in Plutarch *Life of Antony* 24.2 as a sign that he had "gone native" in Asiatic Greece.

22. Nero's Catastrophic *Kitharôidia*

i. Trojan music

Nero never made it to the Greek East—where two of his revenant impostors would, however, make their rounds—nor to his romanticized Alexandria, another haunt of Antony. By all accounts, however, the Greek masses in Naples and Achaea, like the urban *plebs* in Rome, eagerly applauded Nero's appearance before them in his grand *skeuê*, neither knowing nor caring that they were witnessing a "public disgrace" (Tacitus *Annals* 16.4.4). But despite all attempts to legitimate and ennoble his activity by appeals to validating precedents from myth and history, Roman and, still more so, Greek intellectuals and cultural elites who knew and appreciated the myth and history of *kitharôidia* reacted with horror to the idea of the citharodic emperor. For them, Nero not only transgressed standards of Roman decorum and compromised his principate with his show business; more so, what seemed to them his crass bid for citharodic stardom at the utter expense of his political authority also denigrated the classic ideal of *kitharôidia* itself as a force for civic order and stability. Nero had wanted to claim this ideal for himself. These informed critics in their turn used exemplary models of sociopolitically normative *kitharôidia* to undercut the viability of any such claim, figuring Nero as a citharodic anti-ideal.

A rich expression of such critique is to be found in Dio Chrysostom's oration delivered to the Alexandrian populace (32.60). Dio asks the Alexandrians, who are notorious both for their devotion to citharodes and their political volatility, if they "want to be seen as having the same disease (νόσος) as Nero." The orator continues, "His excessive involvement (ἡ λίαν ἐμπειρία) in and enthusiasm (σπουδή) for this [the music of the *kithara*] did not profit that man at all. Indeed, how much better would it be to imitate the present ruler, who is attentive to culture (παιδεία) and reason (λόγος)? Will you not disregard that shameful and immoderate lust for popular acclaim (φιλοτιμία)?" Dio's comparison of the Alexandrians qua spectators/citizens to Nero qua citharode/emperor flatters neither. Both are wildly devoted to *kitharôidia*, but in its lowest, most sensationalistic form, one that sacrifices the spiritual nobility of the music to the base φιλοτιμία of its practitioners. Accordingly, Dio suggests, in both cases the traditional alliance between the *kithara* and political order, which goes back to myths of Amphion in Thebes and legends of Terpander in Sparta, curing the Spartans of their

debilitating *stasis*, has been traumatically ruptured; the purely spectacular dimension of *kitharôidia* has overridden its cosmic ordering function. Nero, citharode and king, suffered from disease, νόσος; Dio may
be ironically alluding to a variant of the Terpander story in which the
civil strife of the Lacedaemonians is figured as illness or plague (Aelian
Historical Miscellanies 12.50; Boethius *On Music* 1.1), with the implication that Nero, compromised both politically and musically, could not
cure himself of his own corruption in either respect. Likewise, the
Alexandrians, obsessed by a star-driven, spectacular citharodic culture
with little respect for *nomoi* (musical and political) are, as audiences,
"gluttonous listeners" (32.62), and, as a civic body, are lacking of discipline (*eutaxia*), gentleness (*praotês*), social concord (*homonoia*), and civic
order (*kosmos politeias*, 32.37). These were the very goods guaranteed by
the healthy citharodic culture of ancient Sparta, with which the orator
explicitly contrasts unruly, present-day Alexandria (32.60; cf. 32.67,
69).[381] By way of cure, Dio urges the populace to emulate the current
emperor, probably Vespasian, who successfully balances good culture
in the Classical tradition, *paideia*, with rational government, *logos*.[382] It
is possible that Dio has in mind too Nero's irrational wish to surrender
his rule and ply his *tekhnê* in Alexandria (Dio Cassius 63.27.2); the
combination of political irresponsibility and "immoderate φιλοτιμία"
expressed by it resonates perfectly with the orator's critical vision of
the Alexandrian *polis* and the Roman emperor.

Implicit in a dramatic event prominently placed in both the
Tacitean and Suetonian accounts of the Naples performance is another
critical resonance of citharodic myth. Suetonius writes, "Even though
the theater was suddenly rocked by the tremor of an earthquake, Nero
did not cease singing until he completed the *nomos* he had begun"
(*Nero* 20.1). Tacitus, somewhat less dramatically, has it that the theater
collapsed after the completion of the performance, when audience and
performer had gone: "There an event occurred, which many thought
ill-omened, but which he took to be a sign of providence and divine
favor: after the people who had been in attendance exited, the theater

---

[381] Dio 32.70 reminds the Alexandrians that a leader from their own recent history
presaged the travesties of Nero: Ptolemy XII (80–51 BCE), nicknamed *Aulêtês*, was, like
the Roman emperor, a would-be musician who "busied himself with *aulos* playing"
while his city fell into violent factionalism. Dio imagines Alexandria in its last days
of pre-Roman autonomy gripped by a self-consuming *danse macabre*: "In the end, he
with his *aulos* playing and you with your dancing destroyed the *polis*."

[382] Vespasian: Jones 1973, who connects the oration to an outbreak of *stasis* in Alexandria
mentioned by Eusebius, probably in 74/5 CE (p307).

collapsed, empty and without harming anyone."[383] Putting to one side questions about the exact timing and details of the earthquake, southern Italy is geologically unstable, and a serious tremor probably did occur at some point around the time Nero played in the Neapolitan theater, perhaps even during his engagement there. But in the traditions hostile to Nero on which Tacitus and Suetonius both draw, the earthquake could only have been seen in a meaningfully negative light. Specifically, it presented a distorted reflex of two primal citharodic myths, that of Orpheus and Amphion. Nature's apparent response to Nero's performance and the destruction of the theater's walls invert respectively the myths of these exemplary proto-citharodes. Whereas Orpheus uses his music to control and cultivate wild nature, Nero's serves as a sort of provocation to it, paradoxically rousing its irrational, violent force; whereas the sounds of Amphion's lyre move the stones that will form the walls of Thebes, his music making serving as the founding act of political *kosmos*, the *kithara* of the *princeps*, who should stand as master of the political order in the Imperial world, instead precipitates the disorderly ruin of walls, of edifice, of that which symbolizes civic structure and political integrity.[384] That Nero so radically misinterprets the event—to him it is not a bad omen, as the majority of people (*plerique*) would have it, but an act of divine providence—even commemorating the "lucky" event in song, as Tacitus records, only reinforces the mythopoetic irony of his situation. There was also the historical coincidence, whose incidental symbolism may have been exploited by hostile critics, that Augustus had once restored an earthquake-damaged Naples; the penteteric games of the Neapolitan Sebasta had been instituted in honor of this service. Augustus had built the city up, structurally and culturally; Nero, by contrast, brought it again to ruin.

Dio Chrysostom, in the same speech discussed earlier in this section, similarly deploys the myths of Orpheus and Amphion to criticize what he sees as the debased citharodic culture of Alexandria, with its rabid fans and star citharodes "born of *Amousia* herself" (32.61). Of the latter performers he says:

---

[383] Annals 15.34.1: *illic, plerique ut arbitra[ba]ntur, triste, ut ipse, providum potius et secundis numinibus evenit: nam egresso qui adfuerat populo vacuum et sine ullius noxa theatrum collapsum est.* The story about the total collapse of the theater is not known to Suetonius, who places Nero back in the theater in the days after his debut, playing to an audience.

[384] Amphion: Hesiod fr. 182 M-W = Palaephatus *On Unbelievable Tales* 41; Pindar fr. 194 S-M, "the golden foundations [of Thebes] have been made to sound with holy songs," evoking the Amphionic foundation (cf. Nagy 1990b:145). See Rocchi 1989:47–56.

ὁ μὲν οὖν Ἀμφίων πρὸς τὸ μέλος, ὥς φασιν, ἤγειρε καὶ ἐπύργου
τὴν πόλιν· οὗτοι δὲ ἀνατρέπουσι καὶ καταλύουσιν. καὶ μὴν ὅ
γε Ὀρφεὺς τὰ θηρία ἥμερου καὶ μουσικὰ ἐποίει διὰ τῆς ᾠδῆς·
οὗτοι δὲ ὑμᾶς, ἀνθρώπους ὄντας, ἀγρίους πεποιήκασι καὶ
ἀπαιδεύτους.

Amphion to the accompaniment of his music, as the story
goes, built up and fortified the walls of his city, but these citharodes overturn and destroy theirs. And surely Orpheus tamed
the wild beasts and made them musically cultured through his
song, yet these here have made you—human beings!—savage
and uncultured.

Dio Chrysostom 32.62

Dio does not explicitly enlist Nero in this gang of politically deleterious
citharodes, but his name, as we saw, is invoked as a paradigm, indeed
an object of imitation for such perversely destructive music making.

We see a related casting of Nero *citharoedus* as an anti-Amphion in
Dio Cassius' telling of the infamous *rumor*, as Tacitus *Annals* 15.39.3 calls
it, that Nero sang while Rome burned in 64 BCE:

πάντων δὲ δὴ τῶν ἄλλων οὕτω διακειμένων, καὶ πολλῶν καὶ
ἐς αὐτὸ τὸ πῦρ ὑπὸ τοῦ πάθους ἐμπηδώντων, ὁ Νέρων ἔς τε
τὸ ἄκρον τοῦ παλατίου, ὅθεν μάλιστα σύνοπτα τὰ πολλὰ τῶν
καιομένων ἦν, ἀνῆλθε, καὶ τὴν σκευὴν τὴν κιθαρῳδικὴν
λαβὼν ᾖσεν ἅλωσιν, ὡς μὲν αὐτὸς ἔλεγεν, Ἰλίου, ὡς δὲ
ἑωρᾶτο, Ῥώμης.

While everyone else was in such state [of panic], and many, in
their extremity, were jumping into the fire itself, Nero went
up to the roof of the palace, from which there was the best
view of most parts of the conflagration, and donning his citharodic *skeuê*, he sang the *Capture of Troy*, as he himself called it,
though as it was viewed by the spectators, it was the Capture
of Rome.

Dio Cassius 62.18.1

Dio clearly wants to dramatize the fatal link between the emperor's
political irresponsibility and the musical activity that he feels is so
unbefitting his office. His Nero, adorned in full citharodic *skeuê*, climbs
to the top of the Palatine Hill to watch the city burn to the ground as he
performs, for a very unsettled audience, a composition of his own, the

Capture of Troy (*Halôsis Iliou* in its properly Greek title). That this piece was likely a *nomos* is an added level of implicit irony—as rumor had it, and as Dio believes (62.16), it was Nero who had ordered the fires to be set, an act of radical disrespect for custom and law, *nomos*.

Suetonius *Nero* 38.2, setting the scene in the Tower of Maecenas on the Esquiline, captures an iconic image of Nero, decked out in his stage apparel (*scaenicus habitus*), just as he sings a section from the *Halôsis* describing the "beauty of the flame" that consumes Troy. As Tacitus writes in his brief account of the episode, Nero's song "likened present misfortunes to ancient calamities" (*praesentia mala vetustis cladibus adsimulantem, Annals* 15.39.3). The emperor's Hellenizing *kitharôidia* transforms Rome into Troy. To the critical eye, the warped relationship between the narcissistic, self-absorbed "creative" activity of the *princeps* and the civic destruction taking place all around, which he views from an aesthetically autistic distance, resonates powerfully against the normative cultural image of the citharode as founder and Apollonian healer of cities. Indeed, we may see in the hostile narrative tradition of Nero's performance of his *Capture of Troy* a latent identification with Apollo in his musical aspect—and again, as with the Amphion comparison, a highly ironic one, full of meaningful inversions. The specific point of reference here may be an obscure version, but one not unknown in Rome, of the myth of the founding of Troy that has Apollo building that city's walls, Amphionically, with the magic of his lyre.[385] Ovid alludes to the myth in *Heroides* 16.179–180: "You will behold Ilium and its walls, fortified with high towers, built with the song of Phoebus' lyre" (*Ilion adspicies firmataque turribus altis | moenia, Phoebeae structa canore lyrae*). Martial 8.6.6 follows: *muros struxit Apollo lyra* 'Apollo built the walls with his lyre'. Nero emerges from the fire anecdotes, then, as a perverted incarnation of this constructive Apollo. Standing not far from the Palatine temple that contained Scopas' rendering of the musical god as supreme emblem of peace and order, Nero sings his song about the destruction of the city that Apollo's own music built, as a soundtrack to the cinematic inferno consuming the city below him.

But if we are to assume that this performance, or at least one somewhat like it, really did take place, we may wonder whether Nero saw things in a different light. Even if he did not plan the Fire of 64,

---

[385] The version related in Homer *Iliad* 7.453 has Apollo and Poseidon building the walls, with no mention of music; cf. 21.446 (Poseidon alone). Kenney 1996:107 thinks the "Amphionic" version is an "Ovidian embroidery." But it need not be; Apollo also built, alongside Alcathous, the walls of Megara with his *kithara*: "Vergil" *Ciris* 107–109; Pausanius 1.42.2; *Palatine Anthology* 16.276.

the catastrophe offered him an opportunity to rebuild the city on his own terms.[386] While it may be no more than a bit of gossip spoofing Neronian philhellenic excess, it is worth noting that Suetonius *Nero* 55 has Nero speaking of his decision to rename Rome Neropolis, a name that recalls his beloved Naples (Neapolis), and that might point to some grander plan, or dream, for a Hellenizing refoundation of the city.[387] What would seem then to be a macabrely inappropriate performance to most, and no doubt was exaggerated and distorted by hostile reports to seem all the more so, might have been, according to Neronian logic, one that very much followed Apollonian and Amphionic mythical scripts. The destruction of the old *urbs* portended the birth of a new *polis*, midwifed by the music of the imperial *kithara*. It is worth noting that in his epic poem *Troica* Nero mentioned Apollo Cynthius as a founder of Troy (Servius *ad* Vergil *Georgics* 3.36), perhaps an indication that the lyric foundation of Troy was treated in that lengthy work in some detail.

The hostile reception of Nero *kitharôidos* as a musical destroyer of cities may find a comic expression, in a distinctly Greek context, in a satirical ("skoptic") epigram by Lucillius:

Ἑλλήνων ἀπέλυε πόλιν ποτέ, δέσποτα Καῖσαρ,
εἰσελθὼν ᾆσαι Ναύπλιον Ἡγέλοχος.
Ναύπλιος Ἕλλησιν ἀεὶ κακὸν ἢ μέγα κῦμα
<νηυσὶν ἐπεμβάλλων> ἢ κιθαρῳδὸν ἔχων.

Once, Lord Caesar, Hegelochus freed a city of the Greeks when he came to sing the *Nauplios*. Nauplios has always meant disaster for the Greeks, whether hurling a great wave against their ships (?), or with a *kitharôidos*.

Lucillius *Palatine Anthology* 11.185[388]

Given the difficulties involved in dating Lucillius himself, we cannot with certainty identify the figures referred to in this poem. But there are good reasons to assume that Hegelochus the *kitharôidos* is meant to

---

[386] Champlin 2003:178–209, defending the ancient tradition of Nero's arson, argues that Nero did plan the destruction of Rome, with a view to rebuilding it as his dream city. Griffin 1984:132 rejects the tradition, but see her discussion of Nero's ambitious urban planning (130–131).

[387] McGlew 1993:22 suggests that Nero's (possibly) literal destruction of Rome recalls Greek colonists' "symbolic destruction" of their cities in order to "exert political control over their own refoundation."

[388] The translation follows that of Nisbet 2003:119.

be Nero. Suetonius *Nero* 39.3 tells us that the emperor had a citharodic song called the *Nauplios* in his repertoire, which was perhaps a revival of an old classic, the *Nauplios* by Timotheus of Miletus (PMG 785). Nero conceivably performed this *Nauplios* on his tour of the Greek *agônes*, during which he conspicuously granted freedom to the cities of Achaea (Suetonius *Nero* 24.2). Lucillius has wittily conflated the "disaster" caused by the main character in the *nomos*, Nauplios, whose false beacons destroyed the Greek ships returning from Troy, with the musical "disaster" visited on Greek audiences by the citharode who sings the *nomos*, Nero.[389] The obvious joke is about Nero's aesthetically disastrous *kitharôidia*. "Hegelochus," the name of a proverbially inept actor who mispronounced his lines (Aristophanes *Frogs* 303; scholia *ad* Euripides *Orestes* 279; *Suda* s.v. Ἡγέλοχος), insinuates that Nero is only pretending to be a citharode, and doing a bad job of it at that.

Beneath the easy joke, however, sounds a more serious political critique. The imperial citharode, far from genuinely liberating the Greek cities, threatened them rather with civic chaos and destruction, conditions that are, again, perversely at odds with the customary structuring and ordering politics of *kitharôidia*. Relevant is an observation made by Dio Cassius in connection to the Grecian tour, that Nero "inflicted untold disasters (*kaka*) on many cities" (κακὰ ἀμύθητα πολλὰς πόλεις εἰργάζετο, 62.21.3). Who then is the Caesar addressed in the first line of the epigram? Vespasian is a good candidate, on account of his general hostility to Nero, against whose excesses his own persona and policies stood in stark contrast. In particular, Vespasian had repealed the autonomy granted to the Greek provinces by Nero (Suetonius *Vespasian* 8.4), and there are indications too that he critically engaged the legacy of Neronian musical politics (cf. Section 11.ii above). He would thus have been an appreciative audience for Lucillius' satire.[390]

---

[389] Cf. Nisbet 2003:122–123. Lucillius is perhaps picking up too on an anecdote in which Timotheus' performance of his *Nauplios* was mocked by the aulete Dorion for its bathetic imitation of a sea storm (Hegesander FHG IV 416 *ap.* Athenaeus 8.338a).

[390] Aubreton 1972:262 argues for Vespasian. Longo 1966 argues that the poem is addressed to Nero: Lucillius flatters him by suggesting that even a Greek citharode could not sing the *Nauplios* as well as the emperor. But see rebuttal in Nisbet 2003:121–123.

ii. Negative exemplars

Classically negative models of musical behavior were also attached to Nero. The author of the pseudo-Lucianic *Nero* implicitly figures the emperor as Thamyris, who challenged the Muses in song and was punished by them for his hubris (*Iliad* 2.594–600): Nero went to Achaea convinced that not even the Muses could "prelude (*anaballesthai*) more sweetly than he" (2). The comparison underlines Nero's self-delusional hubris, which informs too his decision to cut a canal across the Isthmus. Even more provocatively, Nero is made to claim at Delphi that not even Apollo would dare to compete against him in *kithara* and song—intimations of Marsyas, whose agonistic boldness also ended badly for him.

As was set out in Section 10, Greek cultural elites under the Empire often, if not always, maintained a hostile front toward the popular music of their time, including contemporary *kitharôidia*. The expression of such hostility in writers of the Second Sophistic such as Plutarch, Philostratus, Dio Chrysostom, and Lucian tends to be stylized and self-consciously archaizing; indeed, what we hear in it is the music critical idiom of the later Classical period, when the innovations of the New Music drew fire from the Athenian cultural conservatives. By any measure, the controversies generated by the New Music had long since lost their relevance; Timotheus and his ilk had centuries earlier been safely canonized. What drew the Second Sophistic to this discourse was not its timeliness but rather its ossified Classical prestige—this was the opinionated language of Aristophanes, Plato, Aristoxenus, and other worthies—as well as its usefulness in defining a nostalgic ideal of elite Hellenic cultural identity that could stand up against the indiscriminately consuming forces of mass culture under the Empire.

Thus when Dio Chrysostom scolds the second-century CE Alexandrians for their unruly obsession with popular entertainers, he has recourse to the fifth-century BCE attacks on the New Music. He criticizes the virtuoso citharodes beloved in Alexandria for "having perverted and shattered the majesty of song and in every way defiled *arkhaia mousikê*," that is, the "classical music" already nostalgized by Classical Greeks (διαθρύψαντες <γὰρ> καὶ κατάξαντες τὸ σεμνὸν τοῦ μέλους καὶ πάντα τρόπον λωβησάμενοι τὴν ἀρχαίαν μουσικήν, 32.61). These so-called musicians produce nothing noble, only "women's songs and tunes for dancers and drunken excesses of monsters" (ἀλλὰ ᾄσματα γυναικῶν καὶ κρούματα ὀρχηστῶν καὶ παροινίας τερετισμάτων, 32.62). Fitting the overall invective brio of the oration, the language and metaphors vividly recall the conservative vitriol heaped upon New

Musicians by the poets of Attic Old Comedy, in which the "unmanning" of music is a recurrent *topos*, as is its coincident opposite, the charge of sexual excess and perversion.[391] Phrynis the citharode was thus repeatedly mocked in comedy for making the manly art of *kitharôidia* effeminate (scholia *ad* Aristophanes *Clouds* 971a, b). Dio's image of the Alexandrian citharodes "defiling *arkhaia mousikê*" alludes above all to the passage in Pherecrates *Cheiron* (fr. 155 K-A by way of "Plutarch" *On Music* 30.1142e) in which Phrynis, Timotheus, and others are accused of inflicting λώβη 'sexual defilement' on a personified *Mousikê*. The curious inclusion of "drunken excesses of monsters" on the list of musical misdeeds also probably harks back to some fifth- or fourth-century criticism of Timotheus, whose *Cyclops* indeed starred a drunken monster (PMG 780–783). The piece may well have been performed still in Dio's day, but it was unlikely to have continued to shock anyone, including Dio himself, whose outrage at musical "transgression" is entirely stylized, a literary posture.

Not surprisingly, this antiquarian critical discourse, with its full freight of Attic cultural prestige, could be turned against Nero, as we see in a passage from Philostratus' *Life of Apollonius of Tyana*, in which the Gallic aristocrat, Roman senator, and political agitator Julius Vindex exhorts his troops to revolt against the emperor. Vindex foregrounds his disgust at Nero's *kitharôidia*:

> ἐπὶ Νέρωνα ἐν Ἀχαΐᾳ ᾄδοντα τὰ ἔθνη τὰ ἑσπέρια λέγεται κινῆσαι Βίνδιξ ἀνὴρ οἷος ἐκτεμεῖν τὰς νευράς, ἃς Νέρων ἀμαθῶς ἔψαλλε, πρὸς γὰρ τὰ στρατόπεδα, οἷς ἐπετέτακτο, λόγον κατ' αὐτοῦ διῆλθεν, ὃν ἐκ πάνυ γενναίας φιλοσοφίας ἐπὶ τύραννον ἄν τις πνεύσειεν· ἔφη γὰρ Νέρωνα εἶναι πάντα μᾶλλον ἢ κιθαρῳδὸν καὶ κιθαρῳδὸν μᾶλλον ἢ βασιλέα.

> While Nero was singing in Achaea, Vindex, a man capable of cutting off the strings that Nero was boorishly plucking (ἀμαθῶς ἔψαλλε), is said to have rallied against him the peoples in the West. For he delivered to the troops in his command a speech against Nero, one such as a man out of the noblest thought (*philosophia*) might express toward a tyrant.

---

[391] For remarks on the "ancient" Greeks' anxieties about effeminate music, cf. 33.57, from Dio's speech to the Tarsians. A still later example is to be found in an oration of Themistius to the citizens of Constantinople (c. 350 CE), in which Themistius praises Aristoxenus for having "attempted to give a manly vigor to music that had been made womanly" (364b = Aristoxenus fr. 70 Wehrli). Commentary in Visconti 1999:131–132.

> He declared that Nero was anything rather than a citharode,
> and a citharode rather than a king.
>
> Philostratus *Life of Apollonius of Tyana* 5.10

Philostratus draws on Classical citharodic lore to characterize the antagonism Vindex holds toward the emperor, specifically, the series of anecdotes about Spartan ephors who cut off (ἐκτεμεῖν) with knife or adze the excess, "unlawful" strings from the polychord *kitharai* that foolhardy citharodes dare to play at that bastion of musical traditionalism, the Carneian *agôn*. (Any *kithara* with more than the seven strings first standardized by Terpander qualifies as an outlawed polychord instrument.) Most of these anecdotes involve the New Music celebrity Timotheus, whose own account of his "creative differences" with Spartan authorities is preserved in his *Persians* (202–212). Other versions have Phrynis, an older rival of Timotheus, or even Terpander himself submitting to the grim censure of the ephors.[392] The anecdotal tradition, however, speaks above all to the concerns of those critics opposed to the New Music, and it is to them we should source it. The ephors violently enact what among culturally conservative Athenian intellectuals such as Plato and Aristoxenus remains a romantic lost cause, a purely utopian fantasy: the preservation of *arkhaia mousikê* against the pernicious inroads of musical innovation and still more against the extramusical effects, i.e. social degradation and moral corruption, that lurk in the Trojan Horse of such novelty.[393]

Thus, through the lens of this loaded storyline, Vindex is appropriately cast into the ephoric role of conservative, incorruptible guardian of social and musical rectitude, while the lawless tyrant Nero is the decadent, "Timothean" transgressor deserving of censure for his willful corruption of traditional citharodic culture in its most ancient stronghold, Sparta, a city that, significantly, had never fallen to tyranny. As was suggested above, Nero likely had Timothean *nomoi* in his repertoire. But that is not really at issue, as these compositions were now familiar classics. Rather, Nero is Timotheus as he is forever fixed in the cultural imagination, an eternal scandal despite the post-Classical canonization of his work. The iconic conflict between ephor and the citharodic transgressor offers validating cultural historical depth to the musico-political critique of Nero *kitharôidos* and *turannos*

---

[392] See Wilamowitz 1903:69–71; Hordern 2002:7–8. Cf. n257 above, with references.

[393] Csapo 2004:244 discusses the displacement of conservative Athenian fantasies about the violent repression of New Music onto fiercely traditional Sparta.

offered by Philostratus through the aristocratic Vindex. Similarly, Dio Chrysostom enjoins the Alexandrians to emulate the Spartan ephors in checking their addiction to decadent, "Timothean" citharodes and so restoring order to their troubled *polis* (32.67; cf. 33.57, where the anecdote serves a more humorous point). Dio Cassius relates a relevant anecdote: when Nero toured Greece, he chose not to participate in musical contests in Sparta, "on account of the *nomoi* 'laws' of Lycurgus being opposed to his *prohairesis* 'intentions'" (62.14.3). The real reasons for Nero's passing over Sparta are unclear; probably the citharodic *agôn* of the local Carneia, once so prestigious, in his own day lacked the glamour of the so-called periodic festivals.[394] But the anecdotal excuse must allude to the legendary conservatism of the citharodic culture there, the strict *nomoi* governing the execution of musical *nomoi*, which would not tolerate the bad "intentions," aesthetic and moral, of the emperor.[395]

The phrase ἀμαθῶς ἔψαλλε deserves further comment. The proper way to sound the strings of the *kithara* is with the *plêktron*, not the fingers. Finger plucking (ψάλλειν) is more appropriate to the harp, an instrument whose distinctly Asiatic provenance and association with female players, both citizen wives and prostitutes, diminished its sociocultural status in comparison to the normatively male-played, Hellenic-identified lyre and *kithara* (see Section 16 above). It is unlikely that Philostratus/Vindex is really taking to task Nero, who surely used a plectrum, for inappropriate playing technique. One inference to be drawn is that Nero's engagement with citharodic culture makes him no better than a lowly harp girl. The charge of effeminacy is implicit here, as it is explicitly in Boudicca's abuse of Nero in Dio Cassius 62.6.4–5. But, as an allusion to the old Athenian musical conservatism, the comment implies not that Nero is disgraced by his *kitharôidia*, but rather that it is he who debases and feminizes—recall the charges that were brought against Phrynis—the noble, manly art of the *kithara* through his boorishness, *amathia*, just as Timotheus had disgraced it with his extra

---

[394] Kennell 1988 argues for Nero's focus on establishing himself as a *periodonikês* 'periodic victor'; followed by Champlin 2003:98, 295n32. (The periodic *agônes* entered by Nero were six in number: the Olympics, the Pythia, the Nemeia, the Isthmia, the Actia, and the Argive Heraia.) Other views presented in Alcock 1994:105; Arafat 1997:144–145.

[395] Dio reports that Nero avoided another one-time capital of citharodic culture, Athens, "on account of the story of the Furies," a fictive excuse similarly involving an allusion to Classical Greek culture. The Panathenaia of the first century CE had fallen far from its Classical glory: Kennell 1988:244–245.

strings.[396] Again, Vindex is made into a righteous guardian of *arkhaia mousikê.*

iii. *Citharoedus scaenicus*

The passage from *Life of Apollonius* concisely articulates the intertwined ethical, musical, and political grievances against Nero *citharoedus* held by learned Greeks of the Empire such as Philostratus. On the one hand, Nero's musical practice is a moral and status issue, loaded with real sociopolitical ramifications, as it is too, still more severely, for the Roman elite: the ideological embarrassment at the fundamental inappropriateness, even the obscenity of the *princeps* pursuing in the theaters the career of a professional musician. On the other hand, and at the same time, the way that anti-Neronian invective makes him resonate dissonantly against normative citharodic models or, alternately, aligns him with negative musical exemplars of the past, signals fundamental respect for the age-old traditions of *kitharôidia.* Here the problem moves beyond social *mores* and becomes a musico-political issue that is deeply rooted in the symbolic authority of lyric music in Greek society. That is, the problem may be not so much that the emperor is publicly taking up the *kithara*, but that, despite his self-serious artistic intent, in the end he is merely *playing* the part of a citharode, grotesquely parodying it; it is his own bad ethics and politics that are at fault. As such he can never truly master the ancient, constructive sociopolitical energy latent in *kitharôidia* that goes back to Apollo, Orpheus, Amphion, and Terpander; he instead distorts it to negative effect. Philostratus' Vindex goes further than the lapidary snobbery of Dio Cassius, who claims that by winning crowns in *mousikoi agônes*, Nero lost his imperial crown (63.9.2). The Philostratean Nero represents a deeper "philosophical" paradox, one that indicates a concern for both traditional Roman propriety and an appreciation of the proper politics of traditional Greek *kitharôidia.* This Nero performs a travesty of both emperor and citharode, and each "role," at least as he plays it, precludes the possibility of the legitimacy and effectiveness of the other. For Philostratus, the normally beneficial association between

---

[396] It is worth recalling the story that the Spartan ephors once censured a *psaltês* 'harpist' because he "played the strings (*kitharizein*) with his fingers" ("Plutarch" *Sayings of the Spartans* 233f). Here "harpist" is likely a derogatory name for a *kithara* player. The additional strings on Timotheus' *kithara* led to the mistaken impression that he was a harpist, a player of the polychord *magadis* (Artemon of Cassandrea FHG IV 342 = Athenaeus 636e).

the citharodic and political is paradoxically annulled in the obscenely excessive identity of the two in the person of Nero: "Nero was anything rather than a citharode, and a citharode rather than a king."

If, as Pliny has it (*Panegyricus* 46.4), Nero was an *imperator scaenicus*, in the double sense of an "actor-emperor" and "one acting at being emperor," then he was also a *citharoedus scaenicus*, one merely pretending to genuine *kitharôidia*. Like everything else in Nero's purview, political and cultural, the art was reduced to an empty simulation of the real thing, an act. Other Greek writers of the time pick up on this idea. "Lucian" *Nero* thus criticizes Nero's failed "imitation" (*mimeisthai*) of the performance style of "real" citharodes (7); despite his best attempts, not only his skills, but his ethical inauthenticity betrayed him.[397] Dio Cassius 63.12.2 notes the bitter irony that Helius, a freedman left in charge of Rome as Nero toured Greece, "emulated Caesars" (Καίσαρας ἐζήλου), while Nero, a descendant of Augustus, emulated cithar odes and tragic singers—all is simulation, at the expense of good government and good music.

iv. Nero on Lesbos

Let us conclude by looking at a passage from Lucian's *The Uncultured Book Collector* that relates a tale of the transgression and punishment of an earlier anti-Orpheus:

> It would not be out of place to tell you also a Lesbian tale (*mûthos*) that happened long ago. They say that when the Thracian women tore Orpheus to pieces, his head and his lyre, falling into the river Hebrus, were carried out into the Aegean Sea, and that the head floated on top of the lyre, the head singing a dirge for Orpheus, as the story (*logos*) goes, and the lyre sounding all by itself as the winds fell upon the strings. And thus, with the accompaniment of song, they came ashore to Lesbos to the sound of music, and the people there, having taken up the head, buried it where now stands their temple of Dionysus (*Bakkheion*), and they hung up the lyre in the temple of Apollo, where it was preserved for a long time. Later, however, Neanthus, the son of Pittacus the tyrant, heard the reports about the lyre, how it charmed animals and plants and stones, and produced music even after the death of Orpheus

---

[397] "Lucian" may be Philostratus; see Whitmarsh 1999.

without anyone's touching it. He fell in love (*erôs*) with the idea of possessing the object (*ktêma*) and, after corrupting the priest [of Apollo] with a great sum of money (*megala khrêmata*), he persuaded him to substitute another, similar lyre and to give him the one of Orpheus. After he took it, he thought it unadvisable to make use of it in the city during the daytime, but, holding it under his cloak, he went out into the suburbs (*proasteion*) at night and, putting his hand to it, he struck and jangled the strings, unskilled and unmusical boy (*atekhnos kai amousos neaniskos*) that he was, hoping that the lyre would produce the marvelous melodies with which he could charm and enchant everybody, and indeed that he would become truly blessed (*makarios*), an inheritor of the music of Orpheus. But eventually the dogs—there were many of them in that place—brought together by the noise, tore him apart; in that, at least, his experience was like that of Orpheus, but only the dogs were called together to him. At that point it became abundantly clear it was not the lyre that was able to enchant, but the *tekhnê* and the song of Orpheus, which were the only outstanding things he possessed through inheritance from his mother [the Muse Calliope]. The lyre was just another piece of property (*ktêma*), no better than the other *barbitoi*.

Lucian *The Uncultured Book Collector* 11–12

Lucian is no doubt tailoring this story to suit the anti-materialist message of his essay, the debilitating commodification of culture at the hands of *nouveaux riches* grasping after social legitimacy by hoarding cultural artifacts. As we saw in Section 3, in the same essay Lucian elaborates the story of the contest between the citharodes Evangelus and Eumelus to express, rather tendentiously, a similiar theme. But it is worth looking beyond this superficial agenda to see the more profound ideological assumptions involved. Like the story of the contest, the tale of Neanthus might not be a Lucianic invention. The backstory to it, the *logos* of Orpheus' head and lyre floating to Lesbos, likely dates to the Archaic period. It is tempting to take Lucian at his word that he is working from a local oral account of some real antiquity, a Λέσβιος μῦθος πάλαι γενόμενος 'Lesbian tale (*mûthos*) that happened long ago'.

Indeed, it is tempting to trace the roots of the *muthos* as far back as the Mytilenean aristocratic faction of Alcaeus, with whose cultivation of lyric music and anti-tyrannical politics its plot certainly resonates. Neanthus is named only here, a *hapax* that could arguably be an antiquarian detail inserted by Lucian to make his tale seem more authentic, or one that could point to the genuine antiquity of the story.[398] Arguably, even if the story was not based on actual anti-Pittican propaganda circulated among the sympotic-political circle of Alcaeus, and even if it is Lucian's fiction, it nevertheless represents a concise narrative reflex of elitist ideology in Mytilene as encoded in the lyric poetry of Alcaeus, an ideology that took for granted the aristocratic "possession" of lyric *mousikê*. The final, rather unexpected comparison of the Orphic lyre to the *barbitos*, the baritone lyre that was a signature musical resource for both Sappho and Alcaeus, works as a kind of "tag," distinctly evoking the aristocratic symposium that was the main performative context of Alcaean monody.[399]

This instrument appears in a fragment of a lyric song of Alcaeus that recalls the story of Neanthus in that it places the *barbitos*, here called the *barmos*, in inappropriate hands, notionally those of Pittacus.[400] The fragment imagines a symposium attended by the companions of Pittacus, who are celebrating his accession to power in Mytilene.[401] The first preserved stanza contains this striking personification of the *barmos/barbitos*:

ἀθύρει πεδέχων συμποσίω . [
βάρμος, φιλώνων πεδ' ἀλεμ[άτων
εὐωχήμενος αὔτοισιν ἐπα[

[I]t makes merry, taking part in the symposium ... the *barmos*, feasting lavishly with vain braggarts, (is pleasing to) them.[402]

Alcaeus fr. 70.3–5

Alcaeus' invective figures the *barmos* as one of the symposiasts celebrating alongside Pittacus, and, being a member of such bad company,

---

[398] I note that the Hellenistic historian Neanthes of Cyzicus wrote on the invention of the *barbitos*, ascribing it to Anacreon (FGrH 84 F 5 by way of Athenaeus 4.175e); Lucian mentions the *barbitos* at the end of his account. Could Neanthes have referred to our *mûthos* in the presentation of his antiquarian research, inspiring somehow the Neanthus in Lucian?

[399] The *barbitos* remained a primary signifier of the Lesbian lyric tradition well after the Archaic period. Cf. Part III.15.

[400] For *barmos* cf. Sappho fr. 176; West 1992:58.

[401] Page 1955:235–237.

[402] I translate Liberman's supplement in line 5, ἐπα[νδάνει 'it is pleasing'. On the meaning of φίλων as 'braggart', see Kurke 1994:73n11. Stehle 1997:235 notes the pun on φίλων 'friends' (in the genitive plural form).

it performs with an appropriate lack of decorum.[403] This *barmos* "feasts lavishly," pleasing its fellow symposiasts, and in its gluttony it resembles Pittacus himself, whom Alcaeus would damningly have "devour the *polis*" (δαπτέτω πόλιν, 7), yet who manages to win the confidence of the populace and god-granted κῦδος ἐπήρ[ατ]ον 'the glory he craves' (12–13).[404] At the same time, Alcaeus conflates the *barmos* with the other symposiasts, those "vain braggarts," thereby suggesting both the aesthetic and ethical debasement of the instrument's "voice." Alcaeus' contention: as in the public political sphere, so in the private sympotic sphere. In the proper aristocratic symposium, the instrument acts as a decorous prop to good poetic and ethical order, *kosmos*, and as a graceful musical complement to the politically just discourse circulated there. But as a possession of the Pittacan symposium, it is made to perform a travesty of these noble roles, taking on the character of its déclassé, morally deficient players and auditors. The bad politics of the tyrant are mirrored in his bad lyric culture.[405] In music and government, Pittacus is a "ridiculous, incongruous pretender."[406]

Neanthus' offenses are far more severe. The boy misappropriates a Lesbian national treasure, the lyre of Orpheus, on account of which "songs and dances and lovely *kithara* playing pervade the island, and of all the islands it is the one most known for song (ἐκ κείνου μολπαί τε καὶ ἱμερτὴ κιθαριστύς | νῆσον ἔχει, πασέων δ' ἐστὶν ἀοιδοτάτη, Phanocles fr. 1.21–22 Powell). The true inheritor of the Orphic lyre and its attendant prestige was generally recognized to be Terpander of Antissa. In

---

[403] On the issue of decorum in this fragment, see the discussion of Kurke 1994:73–75. Cf. Stehle 1997:234–236.

[404] On the semantics of gluttony in *daptô*, see Page 1955:167.

[405] Fifth-century populist politicans in Athens would find themselves victims of similar elitist sociomusical critique. Aristocratic Cimon attacks the *amousia* of Themistocles (Plutarch *Themistocles* 2.4–5, Cicero *Tusculan Disputations* 1.4; cf. Harmon 2003). The demagogue Cleon is unsurprisingly derided as a bad lyre player by the chorus of old-school elites in Aristophanes *Knights* 989–990. Sappho may attack the combined lyric and moral-ethical decorum of her aristocratic rivals by claiming that they use dildos (*olisboi*) instead of plectra to play their lyres (fr. 99.5 L-P), but the fragmentary nature of the text makes that interpretation uncertain. Cf. n130 above. In fr. 55, however, Sappho explicitly attacks a wealthy rival for her lack of musical culture. Williamson 1995:86 observes, "If poetic skill was a badge of aristocratic accomplishment for aristocratic women as it certainly was for men, then this poem [fr. 55] may be as intimately bound up in the politics of Lesbos as any of Alcaeus' tirades, pitting aristocratic culture against mere wealth."

[406] "Pittakos has revealed himself to be base—and yet, he is now ruler of Mytilene, elected by the equally degraded *damos*. Alkaios exposes him for what he is, brands him as a ridiculous, incongruous pretender." This is Kurke 1994:85, on Alcaeus fr. 129, whose themes dovetail with those of fr. 70.

one account, it becomes the personal possession of Terpander after it washes up at Antissa and is conferred upon him gratis by the fisherman who finds it; this inherited lyre is the idealized material symbol of the Terpandrean citharodic tradition's spiritual legacy from Orpheus.[407] It is this prestige that Neanthus too lusts to win for himself—he wants to become an "inheritor (*klêronomêsanta*) of the *mousikê* of Orpheus"—but, unlike Terpander, he does so with dubious motives and through dubious means. For Neanthus the Orphic lyre qua material object of possession, *ktêma*, represents a medium through which to access limitless, even divine power, to "charm and enchant everybody"—a hubristic, tyrannical ambition.[408] And he is willing to spend a great sum of money and tamper with Apollo's priest to acquire this *ktêma*.

If the seeds of the story of Neanthus do belong to Alcaean circles, however, we might expect its original subtext to have been that it is Alcaeus and his friends who are the proper inheritors of the Orphic lyre/*barbitos* and its attendant prestige. It is possible that in fr. 45, which opens with a hymnic invocation of the river Hebrus, Alcaeus related how Orpheus' lyre and head floated down the Hebrus to be received in Lesbos. The poem breaks off after the second stanza, leaving us no evidence of this, but, as Page puts it, "the invocation of Hebrus would probably suggest at once the story of Orpheus."[409] Yet that story need not have included Terpander. Alcaeus may not have been sympathetically disposed to the Terpandrean *kitharôidia* of his native island; he may have viewed it as a threat to his own musical prestige. Indeed, given the nexus of Lesbian *kitharôidia*, tyranny, and money that is limned in accounts of Alcaeus' rough contemporary, Arion, at Periander's Corinthian court (cf. Herodotus 1.23–24), we might even see in the Neanthus tale the faint reflex of an Alcaean critique of Pittacus' own patronage of citharodic culture, perhaps with a view to creating a musically populist counterbalance to the elitist *mousikê* cultivated by

---

[407] Nicomachus *Excerpts* 1 = T 53b Gostoli.

[408] His wish to become "truly blessed," *makarios*, may contain a punning reference to Macareus or Macar, the first settler and ruler of Lesbos (*Iliad* 24.543–545, with scholia). Macar ruled the island as a whole before the advent of its separate city-states, so it is as if Neanthus is angling to become tyrant not only of Mytilene, but of all of Lesbos. Might the same pun lie behind Timotheus' claim that he, a Milesian, was *makarios* when his victory against the *Lesbian* citharode, Phrynis of Mytilene, was announced (PMG 802)?

[409] Page 1955:288, who acknowledges that this reconstruction is entirely speculative. If the anonymous lyric text from the Cologne "Sappho Papyrus" (P.Köln col. II, 9–21) in any way draws upon Sapphic themes (cf. Gronewald and Daniel 2005), then its mention of the magical lyre of Orpheus (19–20) could suggest that Sappho knew and related the story of its transit to Lesbos.

Alcaeus. Yet we can say nothing certain about the social ideology of *kitharôidia* on Archaic Lesbos, and we should probably not push this line of interpretation too far. In fact, a respectful, even emulative coexistence between Alcaean monody and the citharodes is as likely to have been the case as antagonism.[410] In any case, generic subtleties are not essential to Lucian's telling of the tale, which is concerned with tyrannical perversion of lyric music *tout court*.

As with Alcaeus' vision of his father Pittacus, the lyre in the hands of this *atekhnos kai amousos neaniskos* becomes debased, an instrument of aesthetic, political, and moral corruption. He plays badly, in a socially disembedded context (on the darkened fringes of the *polis*) that stands in striking contrast to the nodes of sociopolitical integration in which both sympotic lyric and public *kitharôidia* traditionally operate. Here, ironically, Neanthus wins his audience, the pack of dogs, drawn together not by music, which he is incapable of making, but by the unmusical noise produced by the lyre. The act of violence perpetrated by the dogs mirrors the aesthetic disorder of the boy's *amousia*, the symbolic violence he himself perpetrates against the lyre. What Neanthus tragically misrecognizes is something that is abundantly clear to Alcaeus and Lucian: *mousikê* is a spiritual property that resists misappropriation; it cannot be objectified, bought or sold, and "put to use"; it does not inhere in any material *ktêma*.[411] Orpheus' instrument is "no better than the other *barbitoi*," but in the hands of the deserving, be it Alcaeus and his friends or Terpander (reputed in one tradition to be the inventor of the *barbitos*, Pindar fr. 125 S-M), that is, those who possess the proper ethical and political orientation to practice true *mousikê*, *barbitoi* do become extraordinary instruments; they become animated with the cosmic potential that the unmusical Neanthus fails to elicit from the Orphic lyre.

---

[410] We will return to this question in Part III.11.

[411] Lucian's account would seem to reflect an Alcaean assumption that, as aristocratic excellence inheres in the blood, so does the essence of lyric musicality, and its transmission from generation to generation, heirloom-style, presumes wealth but necessarily transcends it. Thus the *tekhnê* and the song of Orpheus are the only riches he inherited "from his mother [the muse Calliope]." This idea is implicit in Pindar, e.g. *Olympian* 1.14–15, *Nemean* 4.13–16. On the mentality of essentialism in Archaic lyric, see Kurke 1994:83. For Alcaeus, that Pittacus supposedly is κακοπατρίδαις 'base born' (fr. 348.1) surely makes him unmusical as well. Of course, this is pure slander. We should expect Pittacus, who was ranked as one of the Seven Sages of Greece, to have been "in real life" just as much a *mousikos* as any other Mytilenean elite, despite the critique of his musicality presented in fr. 70, and to have used music and poetry, as Alcaeus did, to further his political goals. *Suda* s.v. Πιττακός says that elegiac verse was attributed to him.

Nero is not an explicit object of the satire in Lucian's text, but, as with Evangelus, the citharodic pretender exposed at the Pythian *agôn*, so Neanthus and his failed attempt to hijack the lyric tradition inevitably evoke the memory of Nero's citharodic ambitions, in the former case as spectacular comedy, in the latter as political malfeasance. The main themes of the Neanthus tale, the tyrannical misappropriation of *kithar-ôidia* and the problem of musical imposture, clearly recall the concerns of the anti-Neronian musico-political discourse we have examined in this section. Again, the tale itself may not go back before Lucian, but it does display a familiarity with the musical political ideology of Archaic Lesbian lyric. As such, it suggests the profundity of the tradition of elitist counter-culture through which the learned critics of Nero could frame and elaborate their own ideological antipathy toward the *princeps citharoedus*. As Nero could play the role of a citharodic culture hero, an Apollo, Orpheus, or Terpander, so could his cultured detractors assume the oppositional roles of Spartan ephors, Classical Athenian reactionaries, even Mytilenean aristocratic symposiasts.

Part II

Anabolê, Prooimion, Nomos:
Form and Content of Citharodic Songs

1. Prelude/*Anabolê*

I N THEIR DESCRIPTIONS of Nero's performance in Naples, neither Tacitus nor Suetonius says anything about an instrumental lead-in, but a prelude to the song proper, typically called the *anabolê*, was a standard element of citharodic performance, and so would most likely have been performed by Nero in Naples. The proto-cithardic Homeric bards Demodocus and Phemius both play *anabolai* on the *phorminx* before beginning the vocal component of their performances (ὁ φορμίζων ἀνεβάλλετο καλὸν ἀείδειν 'He struck up on the *phorminx* an *anabolê* to his beautiful song', *Odyssey* 1.155, 8.266; cf. 17.262). Ovid describes Orpheus making exploratory runs on the strings of his *cithara* before "moving his voice in song" (*Metamorphoses* 10.145–147). Similarly, the Muse Calliope *praetemptat* 'tries out' the strings of her *cithara* before beginning her song (5.339–340).[1] Such preludes have a practical function. They provide the citharode a chance to limber his fingers and a final opportunity to check the instrument's tuning; the latter function is clearly indicated in the former Ovid passage: *et sensit varios, quamvis diversa sonarent, | concordare modos* ("And Orpheus heard that the various notes, although they produced different sounds, were in tune with one another"). If a *kithara* player is accompanying a chorus, the instrumental prelude meets the additional task of calling the rhythm and tune for the choral song and dance (e.g. Pindar *Pythian* 1.1–3).

But the "deferral" (*anabolê* in its non-technical sense) of song proper also plays an important psychological role in the ritualized performance event. Beyond simply alerting the audience that the performance is beginning, it mediates the transition from the quotidian phenomenal world to the emotionally heightened, ritually marked experience of song that, ideally, both performer and listeners share.[2]

---

[1] See discussion and further examples in West 1981:122. In Lucian *The Uncultured Book Collector* 9 a nervous citharode breaks three strings during his prelude because he applies the *plêktron* too forcefully.

[2] See Nagy 1990b:31–33 for the ritual "markedness" of song. See too the brief discussion of the practical function of the aulete's *proaulion* in Aristotle *Rhetoric* 3.14.1414b19–24. Aristotle emphasizes the importance of establishing harmonic and thematic

There is a quasi-erotic dimension to this mediation as well: preludial deferral—foreplay—stokes the desire for the song to come. This process of musico-erotic seduction is well captured in the aetiological citharodic performance described in the *Homeric Hymn to Hermes*. Hermes is playing the newly invented lyre before an initially recalcitrant audience of one, Apollo, whose resistance quickly dissolves upon hearing the notes of the *anabolê*:

> λαβὼν δ' ἐπ' ἀριστερὰ χειρὸς
> πλήκτρῳ ἐπειρήτιζε κατὰ μέρος· ἣ δ' ὑπὸ χειρὸς
> σμερδαλέον κονάβησε. γέλασσε δὲ Φοῖβος Ἀπόλλων
> γηθήσας, ἐρατὴ δὲ διὰ φρένας ἤλυθ' ἰωὴ
> θεσπεσίης ἐνοπῆς καί μιν γλυκὺς ἵμερος ᾕρει
> θυμῷ ἀκουάζοντα. λύρῃ δ' ἐρατὸν κιθαρίζων
> στῆ ῥ' ὅ γε θαρσήσας ἐπ' ἀριστερὰ Μαιάδος υἱὸς
> Φοίβου Ἀπόλλωνος, τάχα δὲ λιγέως κιθαρίζων
> γηρύετ' ἀμβολάδην, ἐρατὴ δὲ οἱ ἕσπετο φωνή.

[Hermes], taking the lyre up on his left arm, tried it out with the *plêktron* string by string. At his touch it made an awesome sound. And Phoebus Apollo laughed with joy; for through his heart went the lovely sound of its marvelous voice and sweet desire took hold of him in his spirit as he listened. And playing on the lyre in lovely fashion the son of Maia, encouraged, stood to the left of Phoebus Apollo; soon, while playing the lyre brightly, he began to vocalize in the manner of a prelude (ἀμβολάδην), and a lovely voice attended him.[3]

Homeric Hymn to Hermes 418–426

The *anabolê* was traditionally brief, as it seems to be here. Some formally adventurous musicians of the fifth century BCE, however, expanded it into a showcase for instrumental virtuosity, to the consternation of critics such as Democritus of Chios, who said, parodying Hesiod *Works and Days* 265–266, "A man who contrives evils for another contrives evils for himself, but the long *anabolê* is the greatest evil for its composer" (Aristotle *Rhetoric* 3.9.1409b26–30). Aristotle says that Democritus was

---

continuity between prelude and the main composition. Also relevant are the remarks on preluding in European classical music traditions in Goertzen 1996.

[3]   For the preludial theme of musical seduction, cf. Alcman PMG 27, a request to the Muse to "put desire," *himeros*, in the *humnos*; *Homeric Hymn* 10.5 (the singer asks Aphrodite to grant him an ἀοιδὴ ἱμερόεσσα 'song that stirs desire'); Hesiod *Theogony* 104.

criticizing Melanippides, a dithyrambic composer, who enlarged the preludial role of the *aulos* in his choral songs. But developments in *kitharôidia* and dithyramb kept close pace in the fifth century, so we could expect that citharodes too experimented with this controversial innovation.[4]

2. The *Prooimion*: Necessary Introductions

Hermes moves from his seductive instrumental prelude, pregnant with *erôs*, to another prefatory performance, sung ἀμβολάδην 'in the manner of an *anabolê*'. This secondary *anabolê*, this time a sung prelude (its content is indirectly described in lines 427–433 of the *Hymn*), came, by at least the first part of the fifth century, to be called a *prooimion*.[5] *Prooimia* are hymns (*humnoi*)—the two terms were occasionally used interchangeably—typically composed ἐν ἔπεσι ("Plutarch" *On Music* 4.1132d), that is, in dactylic hexameters or quasi-hexametrical dactylic measures, in which singers "dedicated themselves to the gods as they wished (πρὸς τοὺς θεοὺς ὡς βούλονται ἀφοσιωσάμενοι)." After this hymnal dedication, citharodes would "move immediately (ἐξέβαινον εὐθύς) to the poetry of Homer and other poets," that is, to the narrative song that was the main event of the performance, the piece that came to be called the citharodic *nomos* (*On Music* 6.1133c).[6] With the *prooimion*, then, citharodes "begin from" the divine before embarking on the *oimê* 'song', with its typically mortal themes, that follows.[7] The

---

[4]   On Democritus of Chios, see Wilamowitz 1903:96n3, who thinks Democritus was a citharode. If so, his critique of the dithyrambist should not indicate that certain contemporary citharodes, including Democritus, did not also perform elaborate *anabolai*; his specific focus on their use in dithyramb indeed suggests that they did. A spirit of competitiveness likely informs the comments, as Democritus was himself a notorious innovator (Aristophanes fr. 930, Eupolis fr. 91 K-A).

[5]   The term *prooimion* appears first in Stesichorus (probably), Pindar, and Aeschylus, who uses the contracted form *phroimion* (e.g. *Agamemnon* 31, 829, 1216); see Koller 1956:187–194 on its history. Later, *prooimion* could be used as an umbrella term for introductory musical material. Anonymous Seguerianus *Art of Rhetoric* 4 uses *prooimion* to cover both the instrumental *anabolê*, which the author calls *anakrouma* (cf. Lucian *The Uncultured Book Collector* 9), and sung prelude; similarly, Plato *Laws* 722d conflates sung prelude and instrumental prelude (*anakinêsis*) under the term *prooimion*.

[6]   Cf. Clay 1996b:494–495 on the coincidence of *humnos* and *prooimion*; in Philostratus *Life of Apollonius of Tyana* 4.39 the citharodic *prooimion* is called a *humnos*. As Clay notes, however, *humnos* could also be used more generally for 'song' of any genre.

[7]   For the proemial idea of "beginning from" a god, see *Odyssey* 8.499, Pindar *Nemean* 5.25. Cf. Ford 1992:41–43, with previous bibliography, on the spatialized semantics

shorter *prooimia* collected among the *Homeric Hymns* served an analogous function in rhapsodic performance, a medium closely connected to *kitharôidia*. For example, the performer of *Hymn* 31, addressing Helios, declares, "After beginning (ἀρχόμενος) from you, I will celebrate the line of mortal heroes" (18–19; cf. 32.18–19, to Selene).

Indeed, at least some of the *Homeric Hymns* could have been derived from or even common to the repertoire of citharodes. Rhapsodic and citharodic *prooimia* were more morphologically and phraseologically alike than different; they shared, after all, the same generic DNA.[8] A partial dactylic verse, κύκνος ὑπὸ πτερύγων 'the swan to the accompaniment of his wings', is identified by the Alexandrian scholar Aristarchus as the ἀρχή 'beginning' of a work by the citharode Terpander, presumably a *prooimion* rather than a *nomos* (fr. 1 Gostoli = SLG 6). The same phrase occurs in the first verse of *Homeric Hymn* 21, to Apollo, in which the speaker hymning Apollo, implicitly describing himself as a citharode, compares himself to the singing swan: "Phoebus, of you the swan also sings clearly to the accompaniment of his wings ... And of you the *aoidos* holding the clear-toned *phorminx* with his sweet verse always sings first and last" (21.1–4).[9] Perhaps Aristarchus knew *Hymn* 21, or some close version thereof, as a citharodic *prooimion*. Another dactylic phrase, ἀλλά, ἄναξ, μάλα χαῖρε, is cited by Aelius Dionysius as the ἀρχή of an ἐξόδιον κιθαρῳδικόν, which we may take to mean the lead-off verse (ἀρχή) of the concluding section of the *prooimion* rather than of the song proper, the *nomos* (*Attic Lexicon* 76). Such χαῖρε-formulas mark

---

of *oimê*, which specifically means 'theme for heroic song', as 'path of song'. From an early point the word was conceptually assimilated to *(h)oimos* 'path' (*Hymn to Hermes* 451). In Callimachus *Hymn to Zeus* 78 citharodes are thus designated as those who "know well the ways (*oimoi*) of the lyre." Cf. too Quintilian 4.1.2–3. On the sense of *pro-* in *prooimion*, see Nagy 1996:63: "[T]he pro-*oímion* is literally the *front*, or, better, the *starting end* of the song." Cf. Koller 1956:191. Nagy, however, argues for understanding *oimê* as the 'thread of song', based upon a "verb-root meaning 'sew'," which would play into a wider metaphoric of songmaking as weaving.

8 Thus Weil and Reinach 1900:19n45; van Groningen 1955:191; Koller 1956, who defends the "singability" of hexameter verse (164–165) and argues the priority of citharodic to rhapsodic *prooimia*; Bowra 1961:23; Pavese 1972:237. (Beware Böhme 1953:44, who argues that the long *Homeric Hymns* are citharodic *nomoi* rather than *prooimia*. This entails, among other problems, a misleading confusion between *prooimia* and *nomoi*.)

9 Another source cited in the same commentary, preserved in P.Oxy. 2737 fr. 1 i 19–27 (= SLG 6), says that the phrase derives from the works of Alcman, who composed lyric *prooimia* to choral songs in Sparta. It would not be surprising if the same phrase recurred in the *prooimia* of choral accompanists, the citharodes, and the rhapsodes, as all three media are intrinsically related. The poetic imbrication of lyre, singer, and swan has a long history, finding early material expression in the Minoan-Mycenaean swan-neck *kitharai*. See Vorreiter 1975, with Egyptian parallels.

the conclusion of most of the *Homeric Hymns* (e.g. 21.5, 31.17), when the rhapsode bids farewell to the hymned god before moving to the heroic song.[10]

It is notable, however, that, for Plato, writing in the fourth century BCE, *prooimia* belong first and foremost to *kitharôidia*.[11] He several times evokes the traditional sequencing of *prooimion* and citharodic *nomos* as a metaphor for the logical exposition of political theory. (The metaphor is prompted in part by the long-standing play on *nomos* as "song genre" and as "law," e.g. *Laws* 722e.) Thus in *Timaeus* 29d Socrates tells Timaeus, who has begun expounding on the divine creation of the physical world, "We have welcomed, then, your *prooimion* with wondrous admiration (θαυμασίως), but, following the sequence (ἐφεξῆς), begin to perform for us the *nomos*."[12] Socrates' casting of Timaeus as a hymn-singing citharode indeed begins with his earlier, punning injunction to Timaeus to "invoke the gods according to custom (κατὰ νόμον)." The latter does indeed call upon the "gods and goddesses" at the beginning of his discourse, in the customary manner of the proemial hymn (27b–c).[13] We should assume that in actual practice the divinities hymned by citharodes were usually those honored in the broader context of the festival or celebratory occasion on which the citharode performed. Accordingly, in the retelling of Arion's performance aboard a ship at sea in Plutarch *Banquet of the Seven Sages* 18.161d, the citharode appropriately "strikes up a prefatory invocation of the sea gods" (τινα θεῶν πελαγίων ἀνάκλησιν προανακρουσάμενος) before moving on to the rest of his performance. Occasional appropriateness did not always determine the choice of hymned god, however. The

---

[10] Cf. Gostoli 1990:54; van Groningen 1955:187.

[11] See above all *Laws* 722d: καὶ δή που κιθαρῳδικῆς ᾠδῆς λεγομένων νόμων καὶ πάσης μούσης προοίμια θαυμαστῶς ἐσπουδασμένα πρόκειται ("Indeed, there are before us *prooimia*, wondrously elaborated, to the compositions of citharodic song called *nomoi*, and of every type of music.") *Prooimia* are explicitly "marked" here as citharodic. Cf. *Republic* 531d, 532d, with Koller 1956:183–184.

[12] Cf. Nagy 2002:36–69, who uncovers allusions to Panathenaic rhapsodic performance practice in the *Timaeus*.

[13] Socrates' expression of θαῦμα, wonder and admiration, at the *prooimion* recalls the phrase προοίμια θαυμαστῶς ἐσπουδασμένα 'prooimia wondrously elaborated' in Laws 722d. We are reminded that *prooimia*, although functionally subordinate to the song proper, were nevertheless themselves objects of aesthetic appreciation, able to be enjoyed and criticized independently of the song proper. There is a relevant anecdote in Athenaeus 8.350a. The citharist Stratonicus, while listening in Byzantium to a performance by a citharode who "sang well the *prooimion*, but blundered the rest of the performance" (τὸ μὲν προοίμιον ᾄσαντος εὖ, ἐν δὲ τοῖς λοιποῖς ἀποτυγχάνοντος), stood up and announced to the audience that he would give a thousand drachmas to whoever could "reveal the man who sang the *prooimion*."

189

vocationally appropriate Apollo and the Muses, through whom "singer men and citharists populate the earth" (ἄνδρες ἀοιδοὶ ἔασιν ἐπὶ χθόνα καὶ κιθαρισταί, Hesiod *Theogony* 95)—ἄνδρες ἀοιδοὶ καὶ κιθαρισταί is clearly a hendiadys for "citharodes"—were no doubt reliably supra-occasional hymnic subjects.[14]

The complete sequence of *anabolê* to *prooimion* to song proper is neatly represented in the description of the citharodic performance of Orpheus in Ovid *Metamorphoses* 10.145–155. Orpheus begins with an instrumental prelude (145–147), transitions to a *prooimion* (begun *ab Iove* 'from Zeus', 148–154), and then to the main event, a medley of love stories about Ganymede, Hyacinth, and other mortals, which continues through the rest of Book 10. A passage in Philostratus' *Life of Apollonius of Tyana* (4.39) confirms that Nero, and other real-life citharodes of his day, followed this traditional sequencing as well. Philostratus describes the three-stage performance of an impersonator of Nero, who, dressed in citharodic garb, faithfully recreates the emperor's "act" in the unlikely confines of a Roman inn. The impersonator starts with the "customary" instrumental *anabolê* (ἀναβαλόμενος οὖν, ὅπως εἰώθει), then sings a brief proemial *humnos* that had been composed by Nero (βραχὺν διεξελθὼν ὕμνον τοῦ Νέρωνος), then finally "adds on" to these introductory segments a medley of Nero's songs, *melê*, that constitutes the main focus of the performance (ἐπῆγε μέλη).

Nero presumably followed this traditional sequencing at his Neapolitan performances as well. Tacitus *Annals* 15.34.1 mentions that, in response to an earthquake that damaged the Neapolitan theater but hurt none of the spectators, Nero composed and performed a song of thanks to the gods (*per compositos cantus grates dis ... celebrans*). Tacitus has Nero singing this song—the plural *cantus* would seem to describe multiple melodic elements artfully arranged together, *compositi*, into a single song—before he left Naples. It sounds like it was a *humnos*, and we might imagine that he incorporated it as a *prooimion* into his routine there or soon after at his public appearances in Rome. Tacitus says too that in the song Nero "celebrated the good fortune that attended the recent downfall" (*ipsam recentis casus fortunam celebrans*). This detail, which implies self-reference or self-dramatization, could also point to a *prooimion*. Given the paucity of firm textual evidence it is difficult to say with certainty, but citharodes seem to have used the *prooimion* as a space in which to engage in some form of self-referential discourse, in

---

[14] For the phraseology cf. *Homeric Hymns* 25.3 and Hesiod fr. 305.2 M-W; Koller 1956:165. See Böhme 1970:133; Maas and Snyder 1989:31.

most cases, however, probably more generic than the more personally specific tenor of Nero's song of thanksgiving: requests for divine inspiration and audience favor, vaunting, self-promotional commentary about their musical art or expressions of their own hopes for victory.[15] A two-line hexametrical fragment from what is perhaps a citharodic *prooimion*, in which the singer boasts of singing new songs to a seven-stringed *kithara*, suggests this (fr. 4 Gostoli = PMG p363). There is musico-poetological commentary too in the *prooimion* sung by Orpheus in Ovid *Metamorphoses* 10.148–154.

Quintilian *Institutio Oratoria* 4.1.2 attests to the related rhetorical function of the *prooimion* as a *captatio benevolentiae*: "οἴμη is a song, and citharodes have given the name *prooemium* to those few words that they sing for the sake of winning favor before they enter on the contest proper" (οἴμη *cantus est et citharoedi pauca illa, quae, antequam legitimum certamen inchoent, emerendi favoris gratia canunt, prooemium cognominaverunt*). Quintilian's *favor* means not only divine favor, but that of the audience and judges as well, as the context of the passage makes clear—Quintilian is comparing oratorical to citharodic *prooemia*. The critical role of the *prooimion* in favorably disposing audiences to the citharode is dramatically attested by the story, probably apocryphal, in which Euripides shows his support for Timotheus of Miletus, unpopular in Athens because of his innovative style, by composing for him the *prooimion* to the *nomos Persians*, "with the result that Timotheus won the prize and ceased to be despised" (Satyrus *Life of Euripides* T 4.24 Kovacs).[16] An anecdote concerning Nero suggests that citharodes might directly address their audience, but this could be no more than a literary distortion. In his account of Nero's first, semiprivate appearance as a citharode at the Juvenalian festivities of 59 BCE, Dio Cassius 61.20.1–2 records that, before singing to the *kithara* his showpiece, *Attis* or *Bacchae*, "the emperor said, 'My lords, give me a favorable hearing,'" (κύριοί μου, εὐμενῶς μου ἀκούσατε, εἶπεν ὁ αὐτοκράτωρ). We are reminded that Quintilian says *prooimia* were brief (*pauca illa*), but this

---

[15]   For self-reference and self-promotion in the *Homeric Hymns*, see e.g. 3.166–176; 21.3–4, 25.2–5; 30.18; 6.19–20, where the rhapsode prays for victory in the present *agôn*. Cf. Wilamowitz 1903:91–92; Bowra 1961:23; Korzeniewski 1974:38; Nagy 1990a:54. The closing section of the cithardic *nomos*, the *sphragis*, likewise offered the citharode an opportunity to speak *in propria persona*—closing arguments, as it were. The "I" of the *sphragis*, the "signature" of the poet, however, may have been more personal and less generic than that of the *prooimion*.

[16]   This *prooimion* is lost. The attempt of Hansen 1990 to identify the anonymous "Prayer to the Fates" (PMG fr. adesp. 1018b) as the *Persians* prologue is unconvincing; cf. Hordern 2002:127.

preface seems too minimal to qualify as a *prooimion*; further, it is spoken rather than sung. While it is certainly possible that Nero, and citharodes more generally, offered a preliminary greeting before any music began, it is likely that Dio has compressed a more extensive proemial rhetoric of ingratiation into a "one-liner," the better to dramatize the (to his mind) grotesque irony of an αὐτοκράτωρ deferring, in the obsequious manner of the entertainer, to an audience of his subjects (cf. Philostratus *Life of Apollonius of Tyana* 5.7).

The *prooimion* could also have provided the opportunity for more extensive praise of the citharode's host city. Such praise forms the subject of two hexameters attributed to Terpander, which celebrate the martial, cultural, and political excellence of Sparta:

> ἔνθ' αἰχμά τε νέων θάλλει καὶ Μῶσα λίγεια
> καὶ Δίκα εὐρυάγυια, καλῶν ἐπιτάρροθος ἔργων.

> Where the spear of the young men (*neoi*) blooms, and the
>   clear-voiced Muse,
> and Justice who goes along the wide avenues, a helper in
>   noble deeds.

Terpander fr. 5 Gostoli = PMG p363[17]

While it is possible that these lines come from a narrative song that would constitute the bulk of the *nomos*, a *prooimion* seems a better bet. Such a *prooimion* would be a traditional piece intended for performance in Sparta, that important market for early *kitharôidia*, a piece perhaps handed down specifically by the Lesbian line of citharodes "descended" from Terpander, those recurrent winners at the *mousikoi agônes* at the Carneia.[18] The conclusion of the Delian portion of the

---

[17] Plutarch *Lycurgus* 21 has epic-Ionic Μοῦσα; Arrian *Tactica* 44.3 has Laconian Μῶσα, which Gostoli prints. Both forms are, however, "authentic" variants in terms of the evolution of the citharodic performance tradition. Because I assume that these lines were meant to be sung first of all in Sparta (although subsequent diffusion was likely; see below), I hesitate to translate ἔνθα as 'there', which potentially complicates the situation of the text's performance within Sparta, preferring instead the relative 'where'. Cf. *Homeric Hymn to Apollo* 147, discussed below.

[18] Pindar fr. 199 S-M, probably from a choral work performed in Sparta (at the Carneia?), reworks this traditional citharodic text, or some variant iteration of it. Cf. Janni 1965:93; Gostoli 1990:141, although her alternative hypothesis that "Terpander" and Pindar were independently drawing on "motivi tradizionali della poesia e dell' etica spartana" is not compelling. It was, after all, the ancient Terpandrean citharodic poetry that first and famously articulated those motifs. Pindar is implicitly augmenting his praise of Spartan culture by taking a hypotext from that prestigious tradition, so fundamentally associated with Sparta's early history.

Homeric Hymn to Apollo, in which the singer links his praise of the god with praise of the Ionians assembled at the Delian festival of Apollo and the local maiden chorus that also sings there (146–178), offers a sense of the wider proemial context, and the still wider festal context of performance, in which the encomiastic rhetoric of fr. 5 Gostoli might have found place. It is worth noting that the praise of Delos in the *Hymn* (as preserved in Thucydides 3.104) is introduced by phraseology that echoes the language of the Terpandrean lines:

> ἀλλὰ σὺ Δήλῳ, Φοῖβε, μάλιστ' ἐπιτέρπεαι ἦτορ,
> ἔνθά τοι ἑλκεχίτωνες Ἰάονες ἠγερέθονται
> αὐτοῖς σὺν παίδεσσι γυναιξί τε σὴν ἐς ἄγυιαν·
> οἱ δέ σε πυγμαχίῃ τε καὶ ὀρχηθμῷ καὶ ἀοιδῇ
> μνησάμενοι τέρπουσιν ὅταν στήσωνται ἀγῶνα.

> But in Delos, Phoebus, you most of all delight in your heart,
> where (ἔνθα) the Ionians in trailing chitons gather
> with their children and wives on your avenue.
> And with boxing, dancing, and song
> they call you to mind and delight you, when they settle into
> their assembly.

> *Homeric Hymn to Apollo* 146–150

Like the rhapsodic performer of these lines at Apollo's festival on Delos, the citharode at the Carneia festival may similarly have sung fr. 5 by way of fusing praise of the hymned god with the here-and-now Apollonian virtues on display in Sparta and in particular in the festal program of the Carneia.

It is significant that not only was the Carneia an occasion for competitive lyric music, it was more functionally a "*mimêma* 'imitation' of military training" (Demetrius *Marshaling of the Trojans ap.* Athenaeus 4.141e), a frame for rituals, such as a footrace for youths (*neoi*), that were aimed at the "integration of initiates to the adult life of the soldier and the citizen."[19] Indeed, the fragment comes into clearer focus when read against the backdrop of the festival. If the "clear-voiced Muse" refers to the agonistic practice of *kitharôidia*, which "blooms" (θάλλει) each time the Carneia is celebrated, so too the "spear of the *neoi*" could allude to the festival's quasi-militaristic contests, which seasonally represent the "blooming" of Spartan martial valor from year to year;

---

[19] Calame 1997:203, following analyses of Jeanmaire 1939 and Brelich 1969. Further bibliography in Calame 1997:202n347. See too Robertson 2002:36–74.

both music and the spear in turn ensure the flourishing of Justice, that is, political order, in the city.[20] Yet the transmission and performance of the *prooimion* to which these lines belong surely transcended the original occasion of the Carneia. The idealized Spartan setting, graced by the music of Terpander, could be re-evoked by later citharodes singing the *prooimion* in any number of places. Plutarch and Arrian, both writing during the time of Hadrian, cite the lines. Arrian quotes them (without naming, however, Terpander as their author) at the very end of his treatise *Tactica*, claiming that "these *epê* seem to me to suit much more the current kingdom (*basileia*), which Hadrian has ruled for twenty years, than ancient Lacedaemon" (44.3). In light of both Hadrian's classicizing philhellenism and his patronage of *kitharôidia*, it is possible that Plutarch and Arrian knew the verses from the living culture of *kitharôidia* under Hadrian, which was seeing a revival of the Terpandrean classics.

On the comparative basis of the shorter rhapsodic *Homeric Hymns*, we may conjecture that citharodic *prooimia* by and large had a highly generic, recyclable character, and thus were fit to be reperformed on appropriate occasions, regardless of the content of the main song. Cicero *De oratore* 2.80 says that the citharodic *prooemium* is "joined to" (*adfictum*) the song proper, without the coherent thematic connection that the oratorical *prooemium* has with the speech it prefaces. Given the exiguousness of the fragments, we cannot be too specific about the form and content of citharodic *prooimia* beyond their probably considerable overlaps with the *Hymns*. The invocational formula ἀμφί 'about' + the name of the hymned subject seems to have been a consistent generic signature, at least in an early period. The formula introduces four of the *Homeric Hymns* (7, 19, 22, 33), presumably on the model of the citharodic practice.[21] Hermes begins the very first hymn performed to the lyre by singing ἀμφὶ Δία Κρονίδην καὶ Μαιάδα καλλιπέδιλον 'about Zeus the son of Cronus and Maia of the beautiful sandals' (*Hymn to Hermes* 57); the divine subjects of Demodocus' proto-citharodic *humnos* of Ares and Aphrodite are also indicated by ἀμφί

---

[20] On the synecdoche of αἰχμά 'spear' for martial valor, see Gostoli 1985. If we accept the attractive theory of Robertson 2002:70–72, that the Carneia was originally called the *Kraneia* (*hiera*), meaning 'Spear (rites)', because the young warriors at the festival carried spears of cornel wood (*kranon*), then the "spear of the *neoi*" would take on still richer local resonance.

[21] Clay 1996b:493. The formula appears in Aristophanes *Clouds* 595 (ἀμφί μοι αὖτε Φοῖβ' ἄναξ, a parody) and Euripides *Trojan Women* 511–513, by way of making allusion to citharodic performance. See Gostoli 1990:129–130 for further examples.

(*Odyssey* 8.267). The best-known iteration of the ἀμφί formula was a dactylic verse attributed to Terpander:

ἀμφ' ἐμοὶ αὖτις ἄναχθ' ἑκατηβόλον ἀειδέτω φρήν

About the far-shooting lord once more let my heart sing.[22]

Terpander fr. 2 Gostoli = PMG 697 (fr. 1)

The line or some close variation was the highly traditional *incipit* of a proemial hymn to Apollo. So common was it that by the fifth century BCE citharodes had earned the nickname *amphianaktes*, and a verb was coined, ἀμφιανακτίζειν, that was used synonymously with προοιμιάζεσθαι.[23] The temporal adverb αὖτις 'once more' (in some versions rendered as αὖτε) announces, "from the top," the recursiveness of the *prooimion*, the cyclicality of its inaugural function, and dramatizes the serial reenactment of the persona of its legendary composer, Terpander of Lesbos, by the citharodes who assume the "I"of his *prooimion*.[24] Just as common-repertoire rhapsodic *prooimia* were attributed collectively to a single author, Homer, who was emulated by generations of rhapsodes, so were traditional citharodic *prooimia* attributed collectively to Terpander ("Plutarch" *On Music* 4.1132d,

---

[22] On the meter (four dactyls with closing iambic sequence), see van Groningen 1955:189, who argues, perhaps rightly, that ἀειδέτω was originally scanned as ἀΐδέτω, thus yielding a hexameter; West 1982:130. Gostoli 1990:129, following Gentili 1977:35–37 (= 1995:38–41; cf. Danielewicz 1990:136), analyzes the line as *kat' enoplion*, an alcmanic + reizianum, which in her view would liken it to Stesichorean metrical patterning. See, however, reservations in Campbell 1993b:71.

[23] *Suda* s.v. ἀμφιανακτίζειν. Gostoli 1990:49–50 collects the testimonia on the terms *amphianaktes* and *amphianaktizein*. Euripides alludes to the stereotypical use of *amphi anax* in citharodic *prooimia* to Apollo when in his *Antiope* he has Hermes, the first divine citharode, address Amphion, the first mortal citharode, as Ἀμφίων ἄναξ 'lord Amphion' (fr. XLVIII.97 Kambitsis). Cf. Wilson 1999/2000:446n72, who suggests that the allusion serves to foreshadow ironically Amphion's future antagonism with Apollo. I discuss below (Section 9.ii) the proemial use of *amphi* in a hexameter inscription (PMG 938e) on a red-figured cup by Douris.

[24] For αὖτις/αὖτε as 'encore', the audience's injunction to repeat a performance "from the top," see Xenophon *Symposium* 9.4; cf. *Homeric Hymns* 31.1. At Stesichorus fr. 193.9, δεῦρ' αὖτε θεὰ φιλόμολπε 'come hither once more goddess who loves choral song and dance (*molpê*)', αὖτε is used in the context of a choral proem. A two-line proemial invocation of Zeus in spondaic pentameters attributed to Terpander thematically imbricates its own performative function as "this beginning (*arkha*) of *humnoi*" with the eternally inceptive status of Zeus, the "beginning of everything" (fr. 3 Gostoli, Ζεῦ πάντων ἀρχά, πάντων ἀγήτωρ, | Ζεῦ, σοὶ πέμπω ταύταν ὕμνων ἀρχάν 'Zeus beginning of everything, leader of everything, Zeus, to you I send this beginning of song').

6.1133c), the model citharode.[25] Terpander set a model for such performative emulation by emulating classic models in his own musical and performative practice. The second-century BCE scholar Alexander Polyhistor captures this dynamic: Terpander himself "emulated (*ezêlôkenai*) the epic verse (*epê*) of Homer and the melodies (*melê*) of Orpheus" (FGrH 273 F 77 *ap.* "Plutarch" *On Music* 5.1132f).

There is no mention of an Alexandrian edition of the Terpandrean *prooimia*, and there probably was not one.[26] It is possible, however, that traditional *prooimia* ascribed to Terpander were transmitted orally and reperformed well into and perhaps well after the Hellenistic period, not necessarily in the form of absolutely fixed texts, but rather as scripts open to the kind of creative "recomposition" that many Homerists have argued informed rhapsodic reperformance of traditional *epos*.[27] Aristarchus, as we saw, claims familiarity with a proemial verse of Terpander, which he may have known from live performance rather than from a book. But already in the fifth century composer-citharodes such as Timotheus were producing custom *prooimia* to *nomoi* they had also composed; these *prooimia* in turn entered the common citharodic repertoire, eventually becoming classics (*Suda* and Stephanus of Byzantium s.v. Τιμόθεος). Philostratus *Life of Apollonius of Tyana* 4.39 attests that Nero composed his own *prooimia*, which, like those of Terpander and Timotheus, also achieved canonical status in reperformance. We should presume they were transmitted as part of the "Master's Collection" that we hear about in Suetonius *Life of Vitellius* 11.

We have the text, as well as the musical notation, of a *prooimion* attributed to Mesomedes, a Cretan citharode and composer who enjoyed the patronage of Hadrian:

Καλλιόπεια σοφά, Μουσῶν προκαθαγέτι τερπνῶν
καὶ σοφὲ μυστοδότα, Λατοῦς γόνε, Δήλιε Παιάν,
εὐμενεῖς πάρεστέ μοι.

---

[25] Cf. Wilamowitz 1903:91–92. See Capponi 2003 on the reenacted "I" in the *Homeric Hymns*; Nagy 1996:61 on the rhapsode as mimetically "recomposed performer" of Homer.

[26] Cf. Gostoli 1990:127.

[27] See Nagy 1990a:38–40 and Collins 2001 on rhapsodic reperformance of Homer. The scant remains of the Terpandrean texts collected in Gostoli 1990 show lexical and dialectal variants that could reflect creative variation in the performance tradition rather than "mistakes" in textual transmission.

Wise Calliope, leader of the pleasure-bringing Muses,
and wise giver of mysteries, child of Leto, Delian Paean,
stand kindly beside me.

Mesomedes 1*b* Heitsch[28]

The first two lines are hexameters in "Doric" melic dialect, to which is appended a short trochaic verse. The melody is harmonically and rhythmically simple; word accent coincides with melodic pitch throughout, and there are no melismatic figures.[29] The *prooimion* presumably prefaced the citharodic *nomoi* for which Mesomedes was known, and was probably transmitted along with them by performing citharodes (Dio Cassius 78.13.7; Eusebius 2.2160; *Suda* s.v. Μεσομήδης). The "brief *humnos*" performed by Philostratus' Nero impersonator could have sounded something like it, at least verbally. Styles of music, however, may well have changed from the time of Nero to Hadrian, and the simple tune of Mesomedes perhaps reflects the broader archaizing trends, literary and visual, that developed under Hadrian. Of course, the musical settings of citharodic *prooimia*, even in the wake of the New Music, might always have been relatively straightforward and unadorned, characterized by a restrained, hymnic solemnity that stood in contrast to the greater degree of sonic elaboration that would characterize the following *nomos*.

[28] A separate proemial text, also with musical notation (1*a*), is transmitted along with 1*b*. See Bowie 1990a:85. It is an apostrophe to the Muse in two iambic tetrameters (or four dimeters) and Ionic dialect: "Sing, Muse dear to me, and lead off my song (*molpê*), and let the breeze from your groves stir my thoughts." The term *molpê* often denotes choral song and dance; this *prooimiom* might thus have prefaced a choral performance. See Wilamowitz 1921:606 and Whitmarsh 2004:383–385 for possible choral scenarios. Wilamowitz detected another *prooimion* in the first (spondaic) six lines of poem 2, the *Hymn to Helios* (1921:604). Wilamowitz 1903:97 doubts Mesomedes' authorship of the *prooimia*, viewing them rather as anonymous products, late but formally "traditional," of living citharodic practice, to which Mesomedes has simply set his own music.

[29] Transcription and analysis in West 1992:303–304. The piece is notated in the Lydian *tonos* 'key', although it sounds in the Dorian octave species, which may correlate with the old Dorian *harmonia* 'mode'. See Solomon 1984:250–251. If so, this modal setting would be a traditional stylistic element. Clement *Miscellanies* 6.748 says that one of the Terpandrean *prooimia*, the stately fr. 3 Gostoli, to Zeus, was sung in the Dorian mode. A couple of late sources characterize the Lydian *harmonia* as especially proper to *kitharôidia* (Proclus *ap.* Photius *Bibliotheca* 320b.21, Michael Psellus [?] *On Tragedy* 5). Westphal (see Severyns 1938:162), however, would read Aeolian (= Hypodorian; see Heraclides of Pontus *ap.* Athenaeus 14.625a on the equivalence) for Lydian in Proclus, as the Aeolian/Hypodorian mode is closely associated with the citharodic *nomos* in "Aristotle" *Problems* 19.48, which calls the Hypodorian μεγαλοπρεπὲς καὶ στάσιμον 'magnificent and stable' and thus most suited to *kitharôidia*. Cf. Rutherford 1995:357n17.

It is possible that a difference in complexity between *prooimion* and *nomos* was thematized in two hexameters attributed to Terpander, Gostoli fr. 4 = PMG p363. Strabo quotes the lines in the course of his survey of Lesbian geography, when he has occasion to mention Methymna's most famous musical son, Arion:

οὗτος μὲν οὖν κιθαρῳδός. καὶ Τέρπανδρον δὲ τῆς αὐτῆς μουσικῆς τεχνίτην γεγονέναι φασὶ καὶ τῆς αὐτῆς νήσου, τὸν πρῶτον ἀντὶ τῆς τετραχόρδου λύρας ἑπταχόρδῳ χρησάμενον, καθάπερ καὶ ἐν τοῖς ἀναφερομένοις ἔπεσιν εἰς αὐτὸν λέγεται

σοὶ δ' ἡμεῖς τετράγαρυν ἀποστέρξαντες ἀοιδάν
ἑπτατόνῳ φόρμιγγι νέους κελαδήσομεν ὕμνους.

1 ἀποστρέψαντες Strabo: ἀποστέρξαντες Cleonides *Introduction to Harmonics* 12

This man [Arion] was a citharode. They say that Terpander too was a practitioner (*tekhnitês*) of the same type of music and was of the same island, the first man to make use of the seven-stringed lyre instead of the four-stringed lyre, as is stated in the hexameter verses (*epê*) that are attributed to him:

> For you we will, loving four-voiced song no more, sing new songs to the heptatonic *phorminx*.

Strabo 13.2.4 = fr. 4 Gostoli = PMG p363[30]

It is tempting to read these verses as Terpander's own manifesto of musical innovation, anticipating the modernist claims of New Music composers such as Timotheus PMG 796, which begins, "I sing not the old songs, for my new ones (*kaina*) are better."[31] But we might do better to understand their significance within the specific context of the citharodic performance ritual.[32] If the verses come from a *prooimion*,

---

[30] Strabo cites the lines completely in Ionic dialect. Page and Gostoli "restore" presumably earlier Doric-Aeolic forms in the first verse of the fragment. But there is no reason to believe that Ionicisms were imposed on citharodic proemial texts only in their late (and limited) written transmission. The incursion of Ionic elements into an Aeolic fundament likely goes back to the intersection of epic *kitharôidia* and Ionic *rhapsôidia* on Archaic Lesbos and in the Aeolis; cf. West 2002b:217–218. Bergk's thoroughgoing Laconization of the text (e.g. νέως ὕμνως) constitutes nothing less than a reinvention of Terpander as parochial Spartan poet in the mold of Alcman.

[31] Wilamowitz 1903:64n1 assumes that the verses are a late "forgery" inspired by such claims.

[32] This is not to say that certain citharodes, at least, could not have made explicit the modernizing rhetoric implicit in these lines. Discussion in Part III.5.

which seems likely—the σοί 'you' must refer to a hymned divinity—
they might belong at its conclusion, signaling a transition to the song
proper, the *nomos*, which is referred to cataphorically, and in the poetic
plural, as *neoi humnoi*.[33] The rhetorical intent, if not the precise phraseology, recalls a transitional formula recurrent in the *Homeric Hymns*,
μεταβήσομαι ἄλλον ἐς ὕμνον 'I will shift to another *humnos*' (5.293, 9.9,
18.11), with which the rhapsode (or citharode), after bidding farewell
to the hymned divinity, signals that he is ready to move on from the
prooimion to the heroic *epos*.[34]

In the case of the Terpandrean fragment, the *nomos* would be
"new" in multiple senses. First, as we will see in the following section,
the semi-improvisatory framework of the *nomos*, in contrast to the
more fixed format of the *prooimion*, guaranteed that in each performance it would be new vis-à-vis its own previous iterations. Within
the endophoric logic of the performance, however, it would be new
(i.e. different) relative to the *prooimion* that the citharode was currently
singing. Finally, it would be new compared to the *prooimion* in terms of
the musical *tekhnê* and stylistic complexity involved in its execution.
That is, the proemial *humnos* would have been sung to an old-fashioned
four-note scale (τετράγαρυς ἀοιδά) as once upon a time defined by the
limited range of the now-obsolete tetrachord lyre, while the *nomos*
would exploit the fuller harmonic range allowed by the technologically advanced heptonic *kithara* that the citharode actually employed,
the instrument whose prototype Terpander legendarily invented along
with the *nomoi* themselves.[35]

The *kithara* is figured, not unusually, as the "heroic" *phorminx* (cf.
Pindar *Pythian* 1.1). With the notable exception of Euripides (*Alcestis* 568,
Ion 881, *Heracles* 348), Archaic and Classical poets prefer the archaizing
poeticisms *lura*, *phorminx*, and *kitharis* to *kithara*; perhaps the technical
and professional connotations of the latter word acted as a disincentive
(and, for that reason, as an incentive for the more "realist" Euripides).[36]

[33] My reading owes something to West 1971:307–308, although his conclusions are
     different from mine.
[34] Or, 'I will shift now to the rest of the song', the rendering of Nagy 1990b:353–354 and
     359. Nagy follows Koller 1956:177 in taking *humnos* as referring to "the totality of
     performance."
[35] Strabo 13.2.4; "Plutarch" *On Music* 30.1141c; Pliny *Natural History* 7.204.
[36] The noun *kithara* makes an exceptional appearance, and its first, in an elegiac hymn
     included in the Theognidea (773–782) and probably composed around 480 BCE. The
     poet, whom West 1992:18n22 tentatively identifies as the Megaran Philiadas, calls on
     Apollo to protect the *polis* of Megara from the invading Medes, "so that the people
     (*laoi*), in festive high-spiritedness (*euphrosunê*), when spring comes, may send you
     glorious hecatombs, taking pleasure in the *kithara* (*terpomenoi kitharêi*) and in the

Even the modernist Timotheus, in a self-dramatizing passage from his *Persians* that alludes to these lines, uses the Homeric archaism *kitharis* to ennoble his recently introduced eleven-stringed *kithara* (*Persians* 231; cf. Ion fr. 32.1 West, a "hendecachord *lura*"). But perhaps too *phorminx* is a nod of verisimilitude toward the great antiquity of Terpander, whom one tradition puts *before* the development of the concert *kithara* proper, which is dated to the time of Terpander's student Cepion ("Plutarch" *On Music* 6.1133c, compared to Duris FGrH 76 F 81, who attests Terpander's invention of the *kithara* itself). Indeed, Terpander's "invention" of the *nomos* and his "invention" of the seven-stringed lyre (or *kithara*) are cognate themes in the history of *kitharôidia*.[37] The performing citharodes who sing these verses thus reenact these foundational acts of invention or renewal, their own identities merging across time with that of their famed primogenitor. We may note the force of the first-person plural pronoun ἡμεῖς 'we' in underlining this effect.[38] At least in this case, the movement from melodically simple *prooimion* to complex *nomos* recapitulates the historical development of *kitharôidia* itself.

---

lovely feast and the choruses and cries of paeans around your altar" (776–779). The poet is likely describing the festival of Apollo Pythaieus, which offered athletic games (scholia *ad* Pindar *Nemean* 3.147), choral performances, and, as the marked use of *kithara* in the poem seems to indicate, a contest of *kitharôidia*. (The participle *terpomenoi* might be meant to evoke the spirit of the model agonist, Terpander himself.) Local tradition had it that Apollo helped the hero Alcathous rebuild the walls of Megara—the Theognidean poem opens by invoking the myth (773–774)—and the music of the god's *kithara*, like that of Amphion's at Thebes, was significantly involved in the construction. Pausanias 1.42.2 says that the stone on which Apollo placed his instrument still makes the sound of a *kithara* string when struck with a pebble; cf. "Vergil" *Ciris* 107–109, Ovid *Metamorphoses* 8.15–16. Could the *kitharôidia* at the festival have been thought to commemorate the civic (re-)foundation of Megara by Apollo *kitharôidos*? (The aetiology propounded by Pausanias, that Apollo momentarily "put down" his *kithara* on the stone so he could help Alcathous erect the walls by hand, sounds like a late rationalization of the magical, Orphic/Amphionic power of lyric music to bring the city into being; we detect in it the underlying theme that the stones themselves are animated by the god's music (cf. Cordano 1994:426n35). (Similarly, the story in Philostratus *On Heroes* 11.10 that the walls of the Lesbian city of Lyrnessos echo the sound of Orpheus' lyre may also "echo" a lyric foundation.) The Theognidean hymn resembles, rhetorically and formally, a citharodic *humnos*, but its elegiac meter, combined with its length, points away from public citharodic performance and toward the symposium.

[37] Cf. Nagy 1990b:88–90, and discussion below.

[38] Cf. Dyer 1975:121, arguing that ἡμεῖς in *Homeric Hymn to Apollo* 174 includes "Homer and all the Homeridae."

3. Hymnic and Choral Origins of *Kitharôidia*

Proemial performance was not always "in sequence," as the *Homeric Hymn to Hermes* shows. After his instrumental *anabolê*, Hermes begins to sing (ἀμβολάδην) his *prooimion*, which is essentially a self-legitimating cosmo-theogonic hymn (also theogonic is the abbreviated hymn to his parents, Zeus and Maia, that he performs earlier, at 57–61), by honoring Mnemosyne, mother of the Muses, "for she had received the son of Maia [in his capacity as lyre singer] as her lot" (430). He goes on to sing, still in proemial mode, the other immortal gods κατὰ κόσμον 'in perfect order', until he is interrupted by Apollo, who is desperate to question Hermes about his new musical art (426–435). But at this point the expected transition to the song proper is indefinitely deferred. The fact that Hermes' performance is "all prologue" perhaps carries a self-referential, meta-formal charge, in keeping with the playful self-reflex-iveness of the text as a whole. The *Hymn to Hermes* was itself notionally a *prooimion*, but, as with the other long, presumably rhapsodic texts included among the *Homeric Hymns*, its great length would probably have completely deferred the narrative *epos* that normally followed the recitation of the *prooimion*.[39] As Quintilian's *pauca illa*, Philostratus' βραχὺν διεξελθὼν ὕμνον, and Mesomedes 1*b* indicate, the typical *prooimia* of citharodes tended to be brief and functional, at least in the Imperial period. It may be, however, that citharodes performed too longer, freestanding *prooimia* in the style of the monumental *Homeric Hymns*, which served no introductory purpose. Indeed, such pieces may have played an important evolutionary role in the early history of *kitharôidia*, and it is possible that they continued to be performed alongside the fuller ensemble of *prooimion* plus *nomos* that became the norm for agonistic *kitharôidia* by the fifth century BCE.

Here it is worth recounting, and fine-tuning, the reconstruction of the generic and performative archaeology of the *prooimion* proposed by Hermann Koller, which in turn relates to the early development of *kitharôidia*. The *prooimion*, Koller argues, was originally sung by a lyre player, the *kitharistês*, as lead-in to the song of the chorus of singer-dancers he accompanied.[40] In Pindar's *Odes* we encounter paradigmatic

---

[39] Even if they maintain the fiction that they are functionally preludial. See Nagy 1990a:54–55.

[40] Koller 1956, followed in part by Nagy 1990b:353–361. Calame 1997:49–53 is a helpful complementary discussion. Choral citharists are depicted on a number of Geometric vases; see e.g. Maas and Snyder 1989:19, fig. 5b, 20, fig. 7a, 22, fig. 11. The instrument played by these accompanists is the four-stringed *phorminx*, which would give way

scenes of citharist-accompanied choral lyric performances that follow the scheme of instrumental prelude–*prooimion*–song proper discussed above; their ancestral relation to *kitharôidia* is clear. Pindar *Pythian* 1 begins with a stylized proemial introduction, a compressed description of a performance by Apollo and the chorus of the Muses in which Apollo's golden *phorminx* strikes up ἁγησιχόρων ... προοιμίων ἀμβολαί 'instrumental preludes to chorus-leading *prooimia*'; these "chorus-leading *prooimia*" are sung preludes that in turn preface the main body of the choral song (1–4).[41] In *Nemean* 5.21–26, the epinician chorus evokes the same divine ensemble's performance at the wedding of Peleus and Thetis: Apollo played a prelude on the *phorminx*, after which the Muses ὕμνησαν ἀρχόμεναι Διός 'sang a *humnos*, beginning from Zeus' (25), before celebrating the heroic exploits of Peleus. In these scenes it is the chorus that sings the *prooimion*, but "the picture ... of a prooimion *as if* performed by the chorus [and not by the *kitharistês*] is idealized."[42] This idealization may be intended to reflect the actual performance of epinician songs, self-contained compositions in which the chorus seemingly handled all proemial responsibilities, such as they were.

The four hexameter lines of Alcman PMG 26 represent the inheritance of an older and more pervasive choral lyric performance mode. They probably come from a *prooimion* sung solely by the *kithara* player, explicitly called the *kitharistês* in PMG 38.2, and probably to be identified with Alcman himself (cf. PMG 39.1), who accompanied the choral song and dance of the Spartan *parsenikai* 'girls' addressed in the first line of the fragment.[43] Another hexameter verse of Alcman, PMG 107, is

---

to the heptatonic *kithara* of the Archaic citharodes and the more complex musical settings enabled by it.

41 Cf. Calame 1997:50.

42 See Nagy 1990b:356–357 on the "stylized prooemia in Pindar." But cf. n49 below on Apollo's (literary) non-singing.

43 Cf. Bowra 1961:23–25; Nagy 1990b:357. In a stylized fashion, the Chian *aoidos* who addresses the chorus of Delian Maidens in the *Homeric Hymn to Apollo*, a rhapsodic *prooimion* (Thucydides 3.104.4–5), assumes the traditional persona of the Alcman-type citharist who sings solo *prooimia* to the maiden chorus he accompanies (165–176; cf. Bethe 1914–1927[I]:49). The *Hymn* thereby acknowledges its own origins as lyric *prooimion* to choral song, and the rhapsode his "citharodic" lineage. The "traffic in praise" between chorus and singer articulated in the *Hymn* indeed finds a significant correlation in Alcman PMG 38, in which such praise is scripted by the poet for the chorus to sing: ὅσσαι δὲ παῖδες ἁμέων ἐντί, τὸν κισαριστὰν αἰνέοντι 'and all the younger girls among us praise the *kitharistês*'. A newly reconstructed Sappho poem (fr. 58), in Aeolic distichs, similarly locates Sappho in the role of singing citharist addressing the girls she accompanies; the poem is (or imitates) a lyric *prooimion*. If West's supplement, or something like it, is correct, Sappho directs the girls (*paides*)

likely also derived from a *prooimion*: Πολλαλέγων ὄνυμ' ἀνδρί, γυναικὶ δὲ Πασιχάρηα 'Speak-a-lot is the man's name, Pleased-with-all is the woman's'. Aelius Aristides, who quotes the line in *Oration* 45.32, understands it to mean, "Let the man say much, and let the woman be happy with whatever she hears." It is tempting to read the line as a meta-performative, "allegorical" statement of Alcman's traditional proemial practice: the (male) citharist sings while the (female) chorus waits in silence for its turn to begin the song proper.[44] We may note, however, that the fragmentary remains of Alcman suggest that his choruses did in their turn perform abbreviated proemial invocations, condensed "speech acts" to mark the start of their own singing ("Come, Muse ... begin a μέλος νεοχμόν 'new song' for girls to sing," PMG 14; cf. PMG 27, 29). These secondary choral *prooimia*, as PMG 14 shows—the *melos* is not only absolutely "new," but new in relation to the song that went before it—are self-consciously distinct from the preceding "citharistic" *prooimia*. (Pindar, we saw, entirely neglects the latter.) A rather enigmatic paraphrase of a Stesichorean verse by Aelius Aristides (33.2 = PMG 241), μέτειμι δὲ ἐπὶ ἕτερον προοίμιον 'I will switch over to a different *prooimion*', may be explained in reference to this proemial stacking. The phrase resembles the stereotypical transitional formula μεταβήσομαι ἄλλον ἐς ὕμνον 'I will shift to another *humnos*', but the Stesichorean variant of this formula, whatever its original wording and meter, could have been voiced by the *kitharistês* to indicate the passage from his traditional role as singer of the solo *prooimion*, which he is now performing, to that of accompanist to the *prooimion* infixed in the choral song itself, called here the ἕτερον προοίμιον.[45]

---

to "be zealous for" (σπουδάσδετε], 2) the φιλάοιδος λιγύρα χελύννα 'song-loving, clear-sounding tortoise-shell lyre' that she presumably plays—shades of Alcman PMG 38 and the *Hymn*. Further, Sappho's dramatization of her geriatric infirmities recalls the laments about aging in Alcman fr. 26. Needless to say, these self-referential comments should not be taken as autobiographical statements. The conceit of the singers' weakened limbs in both texts—Sappho (5–6) and Alcman (1–2) can no longer dance—must thematize the fact that the citharist typically moves less actively than the choral dancers he accompanies. (But some dance gestures were likely typical; the quasi-orchestic movement of early citharodes bears the traces of them. Cf. Part I.17.) In *Odyssey* 8.262 Demodocus sings and plays ἐς μέσον 'in the middle' of the dancers around (ἀμφί) him (Apollo *Mousagêtês* also stands ἐν μέσαις in Pindar *Nemean* 5.23; cf. further examples in Calame 1997:36).

[44] Cf. Bowra 1961:24–25. Cf. McKay 1974, who thinks that the line comes from a wedding song, and that the speaking names belong to generic caricatures of a husband and wife. It is possible that Alcman humorously metaphorizes the performative relationship between citharist and chorus as a marriage.

[45] Cf. Clay 1996b:498, who compares Stesichorus fr. 241 to the "stringing together of hymns" in rhapsodic performance. Proemial stacking is implicit too in the *Homeric*

In time, some citharists transcended their limited roles as accompanists, taking center stage as virtuoso soloists, as citharodes.[46] This process of performative differentiation is mythicized in an aetiological account of agonistic *kitharôidia* at Delphi, preserved by Proclus, which we looked at in Part I.4 in connection to the dramatically transformative effect of citharodic costume:

Χρυσόθεμις ὁ Κρὴς πρῶτος στολῇ χρησάμενος ἐκπρεπεῖ καὶ κιθάραν ἀναλαβὼν εἰς μίμησιν τοῦ Ἀπόλλωνος μόνος ᾖσε νόμον, εὐδοκιμήσαντος δὲ αὐτοῦ διαμένει ὁ τρόπος τοῦ ἀγωνίσματος·

Chrysothemis the Cretan, wearing conspicuous raiment and taking up the *kithara* in reenactment (*mimêsis*) of Apollo, was the first man to sing by himself a *nomos*; and since he won acclaim, this style of competitive performance persists to this day.

Proclus *Chrestomathia ap.* Photius *Bibliotheca* 320b.1–4

The definitive moment is captured in which Chrysothemis, elsewhere attested as the victor of the first Pythian musical contest (Pausanias 10.7.2), emerges into the spotlight, resplendent in his Apollonian garb, as a citharode. The background from which he emerges is implicitly choral, for the oldest medium of lyric song at Delphi was the paeanic chorus, whose model incarnation, comprised of the Cretans who first settled at Delphi, was led at the founding of the Pythian shrine by Apollo *kitharistês* himself (*Homeric Hymn to Apollo* 514–519). The father of Chrysothemis, Carmanor, was said to have purified Apollo on Crete after the god's slaying of the serpent (Pausanias 2.7.7; 2.30.3; 10.7.2); according to the implied mythical chronology, then, his son would have belonged to that pioneering group of paean singers. Strabo 9.3.10 records that citharodes at the legendary "ancient *agôn*" of the Pythia used to compete in singing paeans for Apollo, a claim that would seem to conflate the solo performance of competitive *kitharôidia* at the historical Pythia with its protomorphic origins in choral performance. While it has been argued that the testimony of Strabo and Proclus reflect late attempts by Peripatetic eidographers to posit a historical

---

Hymn to Apollo: the blind Chian's proemial *humnos* to Delian Apollo is taken up by the proemial *humnos* to Apollo sung by the Delian Maidens (158).

[46] Cf. Bethe 1914–1927(I):49.

basis for a perceived correlation between the monodic *nomos* and choral paean, the two genres most closely associated with Apollo, it is entirely possible that both writers (or their sources) had access to the local musical lore of Delphi, as Pausanias, who makes clear that he is reporting local Delphian accounts, certainly did (10.7.2).[47] Conversely, it was related that Philammon, the second victor at the Pythian *agôn* after Chrysothemis, "seemed to have been the first to establish choruses of *parthenoi* 'girls'" at Delphi (πρῶτος ἐδόκει χοροὺς συστήσασθαι παρθένων, Pherecydes FGrH 3 F 120 = scholia MV to *Odyssey* 19.432; cf. "Plutarch" *On Music* 3.1132a). In the musico-mythical economy of Delphi, both Chrysothemis and Philammon thus alternately play the archetypal roles of solo agonistic citharode and integrated choral *kitharistês* serving the interests of the local cultic community.[48] In the *Homeric Hymn to Apollo* Apollo himself alternates between solo performance, playing his *phorminx* on the way to his Pythian shrine (180–185), and his role as *Mousagêtês*, the *kitharistês* to the chorus of the Muses on Olympus (186–206).[49]

We might detect too a curious reflex of citharode/chorus differentiation in the fate of Philammon's son, Thamyris, the third Pythian victor in *kitharôidia* according to the Delphian tradition recorded in Pausanias 10.7.2. As the version of events related in the *Iliad* has it,

---

[47] For the eidological theories, see Rutherford 1994/1995.

[48] On parallels with the musical culture on Archaic Lesbos, famous for its paeans and its *kitharôidia*, see Part III.11. We may note that Arion of Methymna operated both as an itinerant, agonistic solo citharode and as the first choregete of dithyramb in Corinth (Herodotus 1.23), although it is unclear whether he was imagined to have accompanied his dithyrambic choruses with the *kithara* or with the *aulos*, the instrument that accompanied the Classical Athenian dithyramb. Koller 1962 argues for the former, although the *aulos* was certainly used in Lesbian songmaking (Sappho fr. 44.24; Alcaeus fr. 307b). But it is true that Corinthian, Laconian, and Attic vase paintings of the Archaic period show the lyre or *kithara* in Dionysiac quasi-choral or comastic contexts. See Stibbe 1992 on the Laconian musical iconography; he makes the good point that *kitharai* and *auloi* easily coexisted "in der Welt der Komasten und Satyroi" (143).

[49] As the iconographical and literary record suggest, at both Delphi and on Delos Apollo *Mousagêtês* was earlier and better established than Apollo *kitharôidos* (cf. Solomon 1994:44–45). The priority of the former figure reflects the historical secondariness of *kitharôidia* to choral performance. It may be that as a consequence of Apollo's relatively early "subordination" to the choral Muses he is not made to sing in Archaic poetry. Calame 1997:50n126 observes that, even as a choral *kitharistês*, Apollo is never explicitly described as singing *prooimia*, but only as playing *anabolai*; the Muses alone sing. The case in visual depictions is different, however; the earliest image of lyric Apollo shows him singing along with the Muses (Melian amphora from third quarter of the seventh century BCE; Athens NM 911, Maas and Snyder 1989:42, fig. 2). And in later fifth-century poetry Apollo *kitharôidos* does sing, e.g. Euripides *Ion* 897–906.

Thamyris boasted that he could defeat the Muses in a song contest, and was subsequently punished by them at Messenian Dorion with the loss of his singing (*aoidê*) and his *kithara* playing (*kitharistus*), that is, his *kitharôidia*:

> Δώριον, ἔνθά τε Μοῦσαι
> ἀντόμεναι Θάμυριν τὸν Θρήϊκα παῦσαν ἀοιδῆς
> Οἰχαλίηθεν ἰόντα παρ' Εὐρύτου Οἰχαλιῆος·
> στεῦτο γὰρ εὐχόμενος νικησέμεν εἴ περ ἂν αὐταὶ
> Μοῦσαι ἀείδοιεν κοῦραι Διὸς αἰγιόχοιο·
> αἳ δὲ χολωσάμεναι πηρὸν θέσαν, αὐτὰρ ἀοιδὴν
> θεσπεσίην ἀφέλοντο καὶ ἐκλέλαθον κιθαριστύν.

> ... Dorion, where the Muses met Thamyris the Thracian and put an end to his singing, as he was journeying from Oechalia, from the house of Eurytus the Oechalian: for boasting he vaunted that he would win, even if the Muses themselves were to sing against him, the daughters of Zeus the aegis-bearer; but in their wrath they maimed him, and took from him his wondrous singing, and made him forget his *kithara* playing.

> *Iliad* 2.594–600

While the mythos surrounding Thamyris is complexly overdetermined, involving multiply layered accretions of commentary on real-world musico-poetic developments of the Archaic and Classical periods, at a most basic level the Iliadic episode deals with the intimate relationship between citharode and chorus, which here takes an antagonistic turn; the former's detachment from the latter is made problematic, indeed catastrophic.[50] It is notable that some writers identify Thamyris as a citharist (Plato *Ion* 533b–c; Dio Chrysostom 12.21; Pliny *Natural History* 7.204) rather than a citharode, echoing perhaps an implicit sequel to the contest in which Thamyris is forcibly subordinated to the chorus as a "mute" accompanist, his hopes for a solo career irrevocably dimmed.[51]

---

[50] Cf. Koller 1956:161; Nagy 1990b:376, who contrasts this scene with the respectful encounter between the blind Chian, "Homer," and the Deliades in *Homeric Hymn to Apollo* 165–176. "Homer" is able to engage with the "local quasi-Muses, the Deliades," yet also detach from them as "a Panhellenic personality."

[51] Wilson 2009, which the author was kind enough to share with me prior to its publication, offers some intriguing speculation on the recuperation of Thamyris by citharists as a model exponent of their voiceless *tekhnê*. Cf. Cillo 1993:216, 241. Citharistic appropriation of Thamyris would likely have been a later Classical development, in times when "critical research" into early musico-poetic *tekhnê* was hitting its stride with Glaucus of Rhegium and then the Peripatetics (see Zhmud 2006:26, 76). We

The adjective πηρός in *Iliad* 2.599 was taken by ancient interpreters to mean that he was made 'lame' as well as 'blind', 'dumb', or 'mad'. Could we not then understand too the physical incapacitation of Thamyris by the Muses in light of the subtext of the aborted differentiation, as a symbolic curtailment of the Panhellenic aspirations of the itinerant, agonistic citharode—Thamyris significantly meets the Muses while traveling from one professional engagement to another—and his notional containment within the local horizons that define choral performance culture?[52] The Panhellenically ambitious rhapsodes primarily responsible for the oral composition and transmission of the *Iliad* may have been particularly drawn to the myth for the way in which it puts the citharode, a potential rival, back in his place, as it were.

These themes register obliquely in a first-century BCE epigram by the poet Honestus of Corinth, which was attached to a statue of Thamyris that had been dedicated two centuries earlier by one Philetaerus, son of Eumenes of Pergamon, in the Valley of the Muses at Mount Helicon in Boeotia, then controlled by the city of Thespiae: "Look at me, one who was overbold in music, now voiceless in song. (Why did I come against the Muses in contest?) Here I sit, Thamyris the Thracian, with my *phorminx*, lame [or blind, πηρός]. But, goddesses, to your music do I listen."[53] Honestus connects the metaphorical implications of the statue's emplacement at the sanctuary with the metaperformative subtext of the Iliadic story: Thamyris is posed with his *phorminx*, immobile and

---

could perhaps detect the cunning hand of the fourth-century citharist Stratonicus of Athens, who elsewhere brings Homer into the critical discourse of the music of his time (Athenaeus 8.350a, 8.351c).

[52] On the punishment of Thamyris, see Brillante 1991:431–432, 449. For the idea that blindness could exempt a performer from agonistic *kitharôidia*, see Pausanias 10.7.3, where Homer is said not to have competed in the Pythian *agôn* because "even though he had learned how to play the lyre, his learning was of no use to him thanks to the accident that befell his eyes." Pausanias himself discounts the story about Thamyris' blinding by the Muses, and believes instead that his blindness, like Homer's, was caused by disease (4.34.1).

[53] [τ]ὸν θρασὺν ἐς μολπὴν ἄφθογγον νῦν μ' ἐς ἀοιδήν | λεῦσσε. τί γὰρ Μούσαις εἰς ἔριν ἠντίασα; | [π]ηρὸς δ' ὁ Θρῆξ Θάμυρις φόρμιγγι πάρημαι· | ἀλλά, θεαί, μολπῆς δ' ὑμετέρης ἀίω (XX Gow-Page). It is unclear whether the statue to which Honestus added his poem is the same one that Pausanias reports seeing in the Valley of the Muses, which shows Thamyris blind (*tuphlos*) and "grasping his broken *lura*." If so, then we might translate φόρμιγγι πάρημι as 'I sit beside my *phorminx* [which lies broken on the ground?], blind'. Cf. Roesch 1982:140–142. Another reading: In view of the phrase ἄφθογγον νῦν μ' ἐς ἀοιδήν 'voiceless now in song', it is possible that with the Iliadic adjective πηρός Honestus alludes to its interpretation by Aristarchus to mean "lame of song" (τῆς ᾠδῆς πηρόν), that is, "dumb."

without the ability to sing, subordinated musically and spatially to the local Muses of Helicon, whose choral identity is explicitly acknowledged by Honestus in another statue-base epigram from the sanctuary (XXI Gow-Page, in which the sculpturally represented Roman noblewoman, Augusta, is called a σύγχορος 'chorus-mate' of the Heliconian Muses).[54] The properly choral identity of the Muses may be indicated in the Thamyris epigram by a word I have twice translated generically as 'music', *molpê*, but which often specifically denotes the combination of song and dance that constitutes choral *mousikê*. If it has that meaning here, we might understand the poem's opening phrase [τ]ὸν θρασὺν ἐς μολπήν to mean 'the one who was insolent toward choral song and dance', and the closing phrase addressed to the Muses, μολπῆς δ' ὑμετέρης ἀίω, to mean 'I hearken to your choral song and dance'.

The figure of Thamyris may in fact have been directly implicated in ritual *khoreia* in the Valley of the Muses. The evidence is highly suggestive, if entirely circumstantial. One scholar has suggested that the Θαμυρίδδοντες 'Thamyrists', officials whose existence, if not their precise duty, is attested in a Boeotian inscription of the fourth century BCE (SEG 32.503), served as organizers of competitive choral performances for Thespian youths, the παίδων ὀρχήσεις 'boys' dances' mentioned by a local historian, Amphion of Thespiae (Athenaeus 14.629a = FGrH 387 F 1), and perhaps instituted in connection with a hero cult for Thamyris in the Valley of the Muses, which the Thamyrists apparently managed.[55] These performances likely had an initiatory function, for which the suffering of Thamyris at the hands of the Muses—a failed rite of passage, broadly speaking—could have served as a mythic anti-model. It is tempting to speculate that the Thamyrists not only supervised the ritually recurring performances of the cult, but

---

[54] See the discussion of Honestus and the Thespian epigrams in Gutzwiller 2004:11–13. Honestus' work elsewhere reveals his interest in recondite themes of early poetic and musical history (e.g. VIII Gow-Page, on the invention of satyr drama in Sicyon; III and VI, learned meditations on the foundation of Thebes by Amphion's lyre versus its destruction to the sound of the *aulos*).

[55] Brillante 1991:444–445. Roesch 1982:138–142 argues plausibly that the Thamyrists were charged with overseeing the hero cult of Thamyris. For the appropriateness of Thamyris' cult in the shrine of the Muses, see Nagy 2005: "The sacred space assigned the hero in hero cult could be coextensive with the sacred space assigned to the god who was considered the hero's divine antagonist" (87). Linus, who, like Thamyris, was punished by a divinity (Apollo) for his superhuman citharodic talents, also received hero cult in the Valley of the Muses (Pausanias 9.29.6; cf. Calame 1996:45). At least by the time of the reorganization of the Mouseia festival in the third century BCE, and probably earlier, Hesiod was honored as well with hero cult at Helicon. See Calame 1996:48–54; cf. Fantuzzi and Hunter 2004:52.

actively participated in them, mimetically reenacting their eponym in some fashion, perhaps as lyric choral accompanists.[56]

The formal complement to the performative differentiation of citharode from chorus was the detachment of *prooimia* from the choral songs they once introduced, and their subsequent repurposing as preludes to the extended heroic narratives framed by the monodic *nomos* that replaced the strophic choral song, such as the one Chrysothemis sings in the "breakout" performance described by Proclus. We will examine the formal and contentual aspects of the *nomos* in the following sections. In a parallel development, however, citharodic *prooimia* also evolved beyond their introductory role into long, stand-alone narrative *humnoi* of the kind collected among the *Homeric Hymns*. While these latter *humnoi* may have been rhapsodic, we should nevertheless imagine that formally analogous *humnoi* were sung melodically to the *kithara* as well.[57] We ought to consider the public performance of the bard Demodocus in the agora in Scheria as a symptom of this latter development. Standing in the midst (ἐς μέσον) of a chorus of Phaeacian youths, who danced but did not sing, Demodocus "struck up on the *phorminx* an *anabolê* to a beautiful song about the love of Ares and Aphrodite of the fair crown" (αὐτὰρ ὁ φορμίζων ἀνεβάλλετο καλὸν ἀείδειν | ἀμφ' Ἄρεος φιλότητος ἐϋστεφάνου τ' Ἀφροδίτης, *Odyssey* 8.266-267). The lengthy tale sung by Demodocus (268-366) has its roots in the *prooimion*, as the telltale incipit ἀμφί indicates. While the context remains ostensibly choral, it is now the chorus that is the "mute" accompanist; the *kitharistês* has emerged as solo *kitharôidos*, elaborating his functional *prooimion* into a self-sufficient *humnos*. Some have sought, inconclusively, to locate the inheritance of

---

[56] Bonnet 2001:55 imagines the Thamyrists to be a "compagnie d'artistes vraisemblablement chargée de l'organisation des fêtes en plus spécifiquement cultuelles qui avaient lieu dans le sanctuaire."

[57] Koller 1956:203-206 credits the development of the longer *humnoi* to Ionian rhapsodes, who, he thinks, correspondingly expanded the diegesis of the *prooimion* to shape the narrative form of hexameter heroic epic. But why should citharodes, who, after all, sang hexameters as well as other melic rhythms (cf. Koller 1956:163), not have taken a role in either of these developments? Koller rationalizes, "Die Begleitung durch Kithara wurde überflüssig, ja störend, sobald das Prooimion nicht mehr Einleitung zur Kitharodie war" (206). This rationalization entails a broader flaw in Koller's reconstruction, his totalizing (and technically inaccurate) identification of choral lyric with *kitharôidia*. Koller seems not to recognize that the latter form was as robust and ambitious a solo medium as *rhapsôidia*, nor does he take into proper account the internal evidence in Homeric epic for the singing of heroic saga to the lyre by the bard. It seems logical that citharodes would have played a major part in expanding the parameters of the *prooimion* to make long hymns, as well as in elaborating narrative *epê* in the *nomos*. Cf. Wilamowitz 1903:87; Nagy 1990b:359.

this arrangement—citharode plus "mute" chorus—in the performance of Stesichorean song.[58] It is better to view Demodocus' performance, lodged as it is between the choral and the monodic, as representing a liminal stage in the evolution of *kitharôidia* from its supporting role in choral song, *khorôidia*.[59] For Heraclides of Pontus, the compiler of a fourth-century BCE history of *kitharôidia*, what he calls Demodocus' *Marriage of Aphrodite and Hephaestus* counts as a proto-citharodic song (fr. 157 Wehrli = "Plutarch" *On Music* 3.1132b). The "G-rated" title is in line with the streak of cultural conservatism and religious piety that runs through Heraclides' scholarship on music, which, like the musicology of his Academic forerunner Plato, is concerned to distinguish the "good old days" of lyric music from the notional decadence of the *kitharôidia* in the fourth century.

Finally, we may note that, while the performance of Demodocus and the dancers is not explicitly competitive—no musical performance

---

[58]   E.g. Wilamowitz 1913:238; West 1971:309; cf. Nagy 1990b:362, *contra*. Athenaeus 1.15d calls the Phaeacian song-and-dance show a *huporkhêma*, which was a performance mode (rather than a fixed song genre) that involved the orchestic mimesis of events narrated in a sung text, but whose exact form and occasion remain uncertain. *Huporkhêmata* do not seem to have always involved a "mute" chorus (Athenaeus 14.631c). See Calame 1997:80n217 on the vagueness of the term. Nagy 1990b:351–353 and Mullen 1982:13–17 propose performance scenarios. While the *Iliad* and *Odyssey* stage other scenes of *phorminx* players accompanying choruses, in none is it clear that the dancers are "mute," and, in many, the presence of the word *molpê*, which typically indicates combined song and dance, strongly suggests choral singing (see survey of passages in Barker 1984:19–32). For instance, at *Odyssey* 1.155, Phemius, acting as choral *kitharistês*, "struck up on the *phorminx* a beautiful song" (~ 8.266), which precedes the μολπή τ' ὀρχηστύς 'song and dance' that the suitors crave (1.152), and presumably help produce. Phemius also acts as *kitharistês* of a singing chorus in 23.133–152, leading the μολπῆς τε γλυκερῆς καὶ ἀμύμονος ὀρχηθμοῖο 'sweet song and blameless dance' (145). In *Iliad* 18.567–572 a boy sings to the *phorminx* the Linus Song, and a chorus "follows," stamping feet, singing (*molpê*), and shouting. In this case, the Linus Song might constitute a *prooimion* to the choral *molpê*. Cf. Hesiod fr. 305 M-W: "Linus ... whom all mortal singers and citharists bewail at festivals and choral performances; they call on Linus as they begin and as they leave off (*arkhomenoi de Linon kai lêgontes*)." The language of "beginning" and "leaving off" evokes the *prooimion*; cf. Böhme 1970:430n3. Linus himself is called a *kitharistês* by Clement of Alexandria *Stromateis* 1.4.25; Heraclides of Pontus makes Linus one of the original cithar odes (fr. 157 Wehrli).

[59]   D'Alfonso 1994:42–44 notes that the Odyssean text gives no sure indication that the Phaeacians dance while Demodocus sings. She proposes that first the dancers dance (262–265), then Demodocus sings (266–366), then expert dancers dance once more (370–384). Her reading is tendentious to be sure, but her point that the *terpsis* felt by Odysseus and the gathered Phaeacians after Demodocus' song is described in purely aural terms is entirely valid; there is no mention of visual pleasure in the dance, as there is at 264–265 and 382–384. The choral background is overshadowed by the foregrounded citharode.

in the *Odyssey* is—traces of formalized competition nevertheless show through in this episode, subtle reminders of the festal agonistic contexts in which real-world citharodic performance eventually would be instituted. Nine *aisumnêtai kritoi dêmioi* 'publicly selected umpires' prepare the *agôn*, which here has the meaning 'place for contests' (8.258–260), where the music making will take place.[60] These civic officials presumably attend to regulating and assessing the dance—one of their tasks is to "make smooth the dancing-place" (260)—but, just as Demodocus here embodies the transformation of the choral *kitharistês* into the citharode, so these umpires might prefigure the judges of agonistic *kitharôidia*. Visually and situationally, this scene is the most "citharodic" of any performance scene in the *Odyssey*.[61] Unlike those set within the halls of the *basileus*, where the *aoidos* performs, sitting down, for a restricted group of elites, here we see the *aoidos* standing up, in the open space of the agora, to sing to his instrument for a socially diverse mass audience.

Traces of long-form *humnoi*, without chorus, are elsewhere detectable at the level of proto-citharodic legend. Pausanias 10.7.2 reports a local tradition of Delphi that the oldest citharodic contest at the Pythian festival was in the singing of a *humnos* to Apollo. Strabo 9.3.10 calls this hymn a paean, which suggests its origins in choral performance; we may recall the remarks of Proclus on the self-differentiation of the "first" citharode, Chrysothemis, whom Pausanias records as the first Pythian victor in hymn singing (although in Proclus Chrysothemis is imagined as already having advanced to singing competitively a *nomos*). Heraclides of Pontus says that another legendary citharodic victor at the Pythia, the Delphian music hero Philammon, "set forth in songs (δηλῶσαι ἐν μέλεσι) the wanderings of Leto and the birth of Artemis and Apollo." Heraclides may simply be projecting the rhapsodic *Homeric Hymn to Apollo* back onto the mythical citharode, but it is possible that he knows as well a tradition of citharodic hymns to Apollo treating the same subject matter as the rhapsodic hymn, transmitted as the work of Philammon.[62] Similarly, Heraclides' claim, made in the same passage, that the legendary Boeotian citharode Anthes

---

[60] See the insightful discussion of the language and meaning of this passage in Ford 1992:115–116.

[61] The appearance of Thamyris in the *Iliad* offers us a different perspective on proto-citharodic performance. Discussion above in this section; cf. Section 8 below.

[62] Fr. 157 Wehrli = "Plutarch" *On Music* 3.1132a. Heraclides also claims that Philammon "was the first to establish choruses at the temple of Delphi," making him a sort of double of Chrysothemis: both performed as *kitharistês* and as *kitharôidos* (cf. FGrH 3 F 120 = scholia MV *ad Odyssey* 19.432).

of Anthedon composed *humnoi* could reflect a citharodic tradition of *humnoi* ascribed to this mythical musician, perhaps one localized in Boeotia, as the obscurity of the musician Anthes, who is mentioned only here, might suggest.

The Hesiod of *Works and Days* claims that he won a tripod at the funeral games of Amphidamas in Euboean Chalcis with a *humnos* (657). This *humnos* might better be imagined as proto-citharodic song than as *rhapsôidia*.[63] The Panhellenic persona and practice of Hesiod was, at least by the Classical period, by and large rhapsodic; the image of a rhapsodic Hesiod was widely thought to be inscribed in the *Dichterweihe* scene at *Theogony* 30–32, in which Hesiod receives the *skêptron* 'staff' from the Muses, rather than a lyre.[64] Yet, remarkably, the manifestation of Hesiod as a citharode persisted at the local Boeotian level. Pausanias 9.31.3 reports that the victory tripod from Chalcis, which Hesiod claimed to have dedicated to the Muses at Helicon who "first set [him] on the path of *aoidê* 'song'" (*Works and Days* 658–659), was still present in the Valley of the Muses below Mount Helicon, a site steeped in citharodic culture and lore. Here, by the tripod, there was a statue of Hesiod seated and holding a *kithara*—"inappropriately," a surprised Pausanias notes—rather than the rhapsode's staff.[65] In proximity to this statue were images of the citharodes Thamyris, Arion, and Orpheus, as well as a sculptural group of Apollo and Hermes struggling over possession of the lyre (9.30.1–3). Also situated in the area was a grotto devoted to the prototypical citharode and citharist Linus, the musical rival of Apollo, who received hero cult in conjunction with the Muses (9.29.6).

We saw that the *Homeric Hymn to Hermes* imagines Hermes' first lyric performance before Apollo as a self-contained cosmo-theogonic

---

[63] As Koller 1956:166 argues.

[64] See Pausanias 9.30.2; cf. 10.7.2; Plato *Republic* 10.600d, *Ion* 531a. Nicocles FGrH 376 F 8 calls Hesiod the first rhapsode, no doubt because of the iconic transfer of the staff in the *Theogony*.

[65] Pausanias 9.31.4 makes the surprising claim that the inhabitants around Helicon have a tradition that Hesiod composed nothing other than the *Works and Days*. Could this rejection of the *Theogony* have been prompted, at least in part, by the rhapsodic implications of the *Dichterweihe* scene of the proem, which might have contradicted the localized citharodic persona of Hesiod? Pausanias mentions too that the locals do not accept the ten-line proem to the *Works and Days* as authentic. It is curious to note in this regard that in Plutarch *Sympotic Questions* 736e, one of the classicizing characters, Erato, performs a lyric rendition (πρὸς τὴν λύραν) of the *Works* that begins (τὰ πρῶτα) with line 11; the proem is passed over. The same Erato later sings to the lyre "the Hesiodic verses about the birth of the Muses" (743c)—a citharodic version of the *prooimion* to the *Theogony*? For a full discussion of the local consecration of the *Works and Days* at Helicon, see Calame 1996.

song that is reminiscent of the Hesiodic *Theogony*. The original divine *kitharôidia* as conceived in the *Hymn* is thus hymnic. Another primal cosmogonic *humnos*: in Euripides' *Antiope*, Amphion makes his initial entrance singing to the lyre, before an audience of Athenian shepherds who comprise the chorus. He sings a hexameter, Αἰθέρα καὶ Γαῖαν πάντων γενέτειραν ἀείδω 'Heaven and Earth the begetter of all things I sing' (fr. VI Kambitsis). The verse would appear to be the *incipit* of a *humnos* that likely continued for several more lines. What Euripides is staging here is a primal cithorodic scene that recapitulates Hermes' hymnic performance before Apollo in the *Hymn to Hermes*, which similarly begins from the origins of the "immortal gods and the dark earth" (426). (There may also be a reference to the proemial invocation attributed to Terpander [fr. 3] that begins Ζεῦ πάντων ἀρχά 'Zeus, beginning of all things'.) The first mortal citharode plays to an amazed crowd on the lyre of Hermes (fr. IV; XLVIII.96–97) a cosmo-theogony with distinctly Hesiodic overtones.[66] Significantly, Euripides has Amphion characterize his *tekhnê* not as *kitharôidia*, but as *humnôidia* 'hymn singing' (fr. V).[67] The primal musical form chimes with its primal content, the evocation of the first cosmic principles, Earth and Sky. The hymnic evocation itself foreshadows Amphion's "Orphic" dominion over nature, which is guaranteed by Hermes at the end of the play (fr. XLVIII.92–94, "Charmed by your music, solid rocks will follow you and trees will leave their seats in their mother [i.e. Earth])."

Evidence for the continued performance tradition of cithorodic *humnoi* in the Classical period is to be found in the *Suda* entry on Timotheus, which says that the Milesian produced 36 *prooimia* and 21 *humnoi*, yet only 19 *nomoi*. Neither these numbers nor these generic designations should be taken at face value—*humnos* in particular could

---

[66] And perhaps "Orphic" ones as well. For the possible absorption of Orphic cosmotheogonic material into the hymnic repertoire of professional citharodes by the fifth century BCE, see Part III.8. The hymnic cosmogony and theogony that Apollonius of Rhodes has Orpheus sing in *Argonautica* 1.496–511 may reflect to some extent the "Orphic" content of real cithorodes' proemial hymns.

[67] Wilson 1999/2000:441, following Wilamowitz, argues that Euripides fr. 911 N ("Golden wings are about my back and the winged sandals of the Sirens fit me, and I will go on high to the vast aether to visit Zeus") "may preserve part of the *khoros*' reaction to their first experience" of *kitharôidia*, and that, further, this language evokes the (high-flying) ethos and aesthetic of the New Music. The superimposition of archaic and modern, mythical and contemporary is entirely Euripidean. The time-warp effect would be underlined if Amphion were attired in the costume of a contemporary citharode, as fr. IX.3 suggests: Zethus tells Amphion, "You are conspicuous by your womanly appearance" (γυναικομίμῳ διαπρέπεις μορφώματι), a possible allusion to the elaborate *skeuê* worn by the actor portraying Amphion.

serve as a catch-all term for any sort of composition attributed to Timotheus, even a dithyramb or *nomos*—but at least some of the pieces called *humnoi* (and perhaps *prooimia*) were likely stand-alone pieces, unattached to *nomoi*.[68] By the time of Timotheus, the *nomos* served as the regular contest piece; the typical context of hymnic performance must therefore have been cultic and civic celebration, which may or may not have had a competitive dimension, rather than festival *agônes* per se. Timotheus' *Artemis*, although it is named without generic designation by the *Suda*, seems to have been a *humnos*. The Hellenistic poet and historian of poetry Alexander of Aetolia tells, in elegiac verse, the story that the Ephesians commissioned, for a fee of golden shekels, Timotheus, "skilled in *kithara* and melodies (μελέων)"—the phrase qualifies the citharode as both performer and composer—to "hymn" (ὑμνῆσαι) Artemis; the occasion, according to Macrobius' paraphrase of Alexander, was the rededication of her temple in Ephesus (fr. 4 Powell *ap.* Macrobius *Saturnalia* 5.22.4–5).[69] An anecdote recorded by Plutarch has Timotheus reperforming the *Artemis* in Athens, where its exotic evocation of the goddess as "thyiadic, frantic, maenadic, fanatic" (θυιάδα φοιβάδα μαινάδα λυσσάδα) was supposedly so shocking that not even the avant-garde dithyrambist Cinesias could keep from standing up to voice his outrage.[70] If the anecdote is not totally apocryphal, however, then the context of the Athenian performance is unclear. Had Timotheus repurposed his *humnos* for a suitable cultic occasion in Athens? Or had he perhaps adapted it as a supra-occasional agonistic *prooimion*, fit to be sung in Athens—touchy audiences aside— or, for that matter, in any other contest-hosting city?

Nero composed his own self-contained *humnoi*. "Lucian" *Nero* 3 says that the emperor inaugurated, on site, his ambitious project to cut an Isthmian canal by singing an occasionally appropriate *humnos* to Amphitrite and Poseidon, followed by a "short song" (ᾆσμα οὐ μέγα), presumably also a hymn, to the local sea divinities Melicerte and

[68] The relative brevity of Timotheus' nomic *prooimia* is suggested by Stephanus of Byzantium s.v. Τιμόθεος, who says that Timotheus composed 8,000 lines of *nomoi* and 1,000 lines of "*pronomia*." The exact numbers of lines cannot be accurate, but their differential is nonetheless telling. On *pronomia*, see Hordern 2002:10.

[69] See discussion of Brussich 1990, who dates the hymn to 397–395 BCE; the performance could have taken place at the Great Artemisia. Wilamowitz 1903:80n4 imagines that the priests of Ephesus made the hymn a permanent feature of cultic performance there, to be continually reperformed "an den Festtagen von Kitharoden." Hordern 2002:101, however, thinks that Macrobius misunderstands the poem of Alexander.

[70] Cinesias shouts, "May you have a daughter like that!" PMG 778 = Plutarch *On Superstition* 10.

Leucothea. Suetonius *Nero* 22.3 records that Nero marked the beginning of his tour of contests in Greece by singing (*cantare*) at the altar of Zeus Casios immediately upon his arrival in Cassiope on Corfu. The song he sang, which Suetonius does not name, was presumably a *humnos* to Zeus, which would have made an auspicious *prooimion*, begun *ab Iove* 'from Zeus', to the "path of song" through Greece that was to follow. Mesomedes, who, we saw, composed *nomoi* and *prooimia*, also produced *humnoi*. These are not as short as the *prooimia*, nor are they especially lengthy. The hymns to the sun (2) and to Nemesis (4), for which we have text and musical notation, are both around 20 lines. The performance context for these pieces is entirely uncertain. Hadrian's symposia are one possibility—Mesomedes' other poems, such as the short, preciously witty ecphrastic works on a sponge (9) or a gnat (11), indeed read more like ludic sympotic lyric than public *kitharôidia*—although actual cultic or celebratory occasions should not be ruled out.[71] At the same time, their middling length would not preclude them from serving as *prooimia* to *nomoi*.

Martin West argues that the musical notation accompanying a hexametrical hymnic text preserved on a third-century CE inscription from Epidaurus indicates that the hymn, which might be dated as early as the third century BCE, was performed citharodically.[72] Addressed to Asclepius, it was probably sung on some important ritual occasion, like Timotheus' hymn to Artemis. We may note, however, that the Epidaurian Asclepieia festival included *mousikoi agônes* by the later fifth century BCE (Plato *Ion* 530a); this *humnos*, or ones like it, dedicated to the patron god of this festival might have served the citharodic competitors there as an occasionally appropriate *prooimion* to their contest pieces.

4. The Rule of *Nomos*: What's in a Name?

The word *nomos* in its primary sense belongs to the realm of the social and the political: 'local custom, law, rule, regulation'. The musico-generic application of *nomos* presumably grew out of a more general

---

[71] Cf. Whitmarsh 2004:383. *Suda* s.v. Μεσομήδης mentions a now-lost ἔπαινος εἰς Ἀντίνοον (*Praise of Antinous*), composed for Hadrian's deified beloved. This song was probably a *humnos*; the "εἰς ... titular element," as Whitmarsh points out (p381), suggests as much.

[72] West 1986. Unlike the through-composed score of the Mesomedes hymns, each verse of this hymn was sung to the same melody.

musical application of the word, the semantics of which Gregory Nagy describes as follows:

> In generalized references to song within song, *nomos* has the general sense of 'localized melodic idiom' (as in Aeschylus *Suppliants* 69); such a usage meshes with the basic meaning of *nomos*, which is 'local custom'. Just as *nomos* as 'local custom' refers to the hierarchical distribution or apportioning of value within a given society (root *Nem-*, as in *nemô* 'distribute'), so also *nomos* as 'localized melodic idiom' refers to the hierarchical distribution or apportioning of intervals within the melodic patterns of song.[73]

From this primary, generically unmarked musical sense of *nomos* developed a secondary, generically marked use, that denoting the contest pieces performed by citharodes, auletes, aulodes, and citharists, pieces that deployed, in systematic fashion, harmonic and rhythmic elements drawn from a number of regional and occasional musical idioms, *nomoi* in the primary sense. Inasmuch as the competitive performers of early *nomoi* were expected to observe certain structural and musical "rules" in their performance of these pieces, however, the name was particularly, if coincidentally apt. A passage in "Plutarch" *On Music*, almost surely derived from Heraclides of Pontus, indeed argues that the old-time citharodic *nomos* took its name just because of its strictly regulated musical character:

> οὐ γὰρ ἐξῆν τὸ παλαιὸν οὕτως ποιεῖσθαι τὰς κιθαρῳδίας ὡς νῦν οὐδὲ μεταφέρειν τὰς ἁρμονίας καὶ τοὺς ῥυθμούς· ἐν γὰρ τοῖς νόμοις ἑκάστῳ διετήρουν τὴν οἰκείαν τάσιν. διὸ καὶ ταύτην <τὴν> ἐπωνυμίαν εἶχον· νόμοι γὰρ προσηγορεύθησαν, ἐπειδὴ οὐκ ἐξῆν παραβῆναι <τὸ> καθ' ἕκαστον νενομισμένον εἶδος τῆς τάσεως.

> It was not permitted in the old days to compose citharodic songs as they do now or to modulate modes (*harmoniai*) and rhythms. For in each of the *nomoi* they would maintain the arrangement (*tasis*) that was proper to it. Therefore the *nomoi* had the name they do: they were called *nomoi* since it was not

---

[73] Nagy 1990b:88; cf. Smyth 1900:lviii–lix. Nagy cites Alcman PMG 40, "I know the *nomoi* of all the birds," in which *nomoi* makes the best sense as a reference to birdsong, a "localized melodic idiom" (cf. PMG 39).

permitted to deviate from the type of arrangement (*tasis*) laid down by custom/law (*nenomismenon*) for each *nomos*.[74]

"Plutarch" On Music 6.1133b

The etymology proposed by Heraclides is surely off the mark, as it completely disregards the meaning of *nomos* as 'melodic idiom' in favor of a direct derivation from the original sense of 'law, custom'. There is little doubt that a reality-distorting ideological agenda is at work here. Like most Athens-based, post-Platonic cultural historians, Heraclides has a tendency to overplay the "lawful" conservatism of the old-time music, *arkhaia mousikê*, that he sets off against the supposed musical decadence of his own day, decadence that portends or entails political, moral, and religious disorder—an idea that goes back, via Plato and Socrates, to the sociomusical theories of the sophist and Periclean cultural advisor, Damon of Oa, that "nowhere are the styles of music altered without change in the greatest laws (*nomoi*) of the *polis*" (οὐδαμοῦ γὰρ κινοῦνται μουσικῆς τρόποι ἄνευ πολιτικῶν νόμων τῶν μεγίστων, Plato *Republic* 424c).[75] But the point Heraclides makes nonetheless has some objective validity: the citharodic *nomos* was inherently conservative in form, content, and execution.[76] According to "Plutarch" *On Music* 6.1133b, "On the whole, the *kitharôidia* of the time of Terpander continued in a quite simple form until the time of Phrynis," that is, for a span of over 200 years, from the early seventh century BCE, when Terpander supposedly established the first citharodic *agôn* in Sparta.[77]

---

[74] On the likelihood that the source is Heraclides, see Barker 1984:211n42. The term *tasis* has the specific meaning 'pitch' (so Barker 1984:211 translates it). But Heraclides seems to be using *tasis* here in a more general sense, to cover not only pitch (the range of notes characteristic of each *nomos*), but also rhythm and tuning (or harmonic mode, *harmonia*). Thus my noncommittal "arrangement." Cf. Wilamowitz 1903: "τάσις … die Spannung und Stimmung sowohl der Saiten wie der Stimme, oder, wie es in einem andern Auszuge heisst, Sangesweise, Tonart und Takt" (89); Bartol 1998:305.

[75] Damon remains an enigmatic figure. Our impression of him is inevitably skewed due to his appropriation by Plato and his followers to give "scientific" authority to their prescriptively conservative sociology of musical practice. Anderson 1955:94–95 makes the argument that Damon was not the musical conservative Plato was, i.e. his statements about music are to be taken as descriptive, not prescriptive. Wallace 2004, however, argues that Damon may have at least been perceived by the Athenians as intervening in the musical politics of city, and was ostracized as a result.

[76] Cf. Fleming 1977:223; Barker 1990:53–55; Borthwick 1994:22; especially Bartol 1998.

[77] Proclus *Chrestomathia ap.* Photius *Bibliotheca* 320b closely resembles the account in "Plutarch" (perhaps derived from Heraclides of Pontus or an earlier historian of music, Glaucus of Rhegium), although it adds that Arion of Methymna "considerably augmented" (οὐκ ὀλίγα συναυξῆσαι, 320b7) the *nomos*. This could reflect the fact that

This generic inertia was grounded primarily in the agonistic system, which required a relatively homogeneous formal basis for judging musical performance, and thus discouraged excess innovation in the *nomos*; severe punishments for infractions of the sort of musical rules alluded to by Heraclides are recorded in the anecdotal tradition. Judges could act as umpires at *mousikoi agônes*, enforcing basic codes of performative conduct. It is possible too that at some festivals, authorities prescribed the content of the poetic texts to be sung by the citharodes.[78] But Heraclides' presumption of a formal set of rules stipulating exactly what sort of musical techniques citharodes were permitted or forbidden to employ is a late, tendentiously literalizing way of understanding the organically self-regulating conventionality of early citharodic contest culture as whole, and the *nomos* in particular. That is, an ideology of conservatism, acting in concert with the institutional practicalities of the *agôn*, informed the "horizon of expectations" of judges and audiences at *mousikoi agônes*. Archaic and Classical citharodes intent on success in the *agônes* were compelled to meet and negotiate these expectations by working within the unwritten "laws" of the *nomos*.[79] After all, to deviate excessively from the accepted musical and performative conventions could mean loss in the contests—the worst fate for an agonistic citharode who relied both on prize winnings and popular acclaim to sustain his livelihood. Yet such compulsion was surely not felt as an oppressive, external restriction on free expression, as the late Classical musicologists romanticize it, but rather took the

---

some traditional *nomoi* were attributed to this semi-legendary later-seventh-century citharode, made famous by his mention in Herodotus 1.24; cf. Herington 1985:20. *Suda* s.v. Ἀρίων says that he composed both *aismata* 'songs' and two books of *prooimia*. The former may refer to Arion's Corinthian dithyrambs (Herodotus 1.23), but the latter claim could indicate that some citharodes attributed their *prooimia* to Terpander's younger countryman. More likely, Proclus (or his source) is merely speculating that Arion made significant contributions to the repertoire. Of course, the statement in "Plutarch" is reductive. Anonymous citharodes must have experimented to some degree with nomic forms before Phrynis.

78 But we have no real evidence of this practice for *kitharôidia*. On the Panathenaic Rule determining *rhapsodic* performance at the Panathenaia, see n147 below. Of course, citharodes would have gravitated to certain texts for their *nomoi* based on the local circumstances of performance; such considerations could constitute in some cases a de facto prescription or censorship.

79 For the term "horizon of expectations" (*Erwartungshorizont*), defined broadly as the conventional set of cultural and generic expectations that meet a work at the historical moment(s) of its reception, see Jauss 1982:3–45. Cf. the remarks in McClary 1991: "Genres and conventions crystallize because they are embraced as natural by a certain community: they define the limits of what counts as proper musical behavior" (27).

form of a systemic orthodoxy maintained unreflexively by performers and audiences alike. This does not mean, of course, that experimentation and innovation did not take place before Phrynis in the later fifth century BCE; the claim made to that effect in *On Music* is clearly exaggerated. The *nomos* was in fact a form entirely open to individual creativity, albeit within well-defined limits. (And those limits would surely have been differently defined in different contexts and locales, say, at the Athenian Panathenàia versus the Spartan Carneia.) When successfully introduced and received, innovations would have become naturalized, legitimated conventions, and could model other such innovations in turn—the essential "lawfulness" of the *nomos* perseveres; tradition accommodates and integrates the new. Consider the verse fragment attributed to Terpander, probably belonging to a *prooimion* rather than a *nomos* (although perhaps referring to the musical setting of the *nomos*), in which the singer boasts, "We will sing new songs to the seven-toned *phorminx*" (Gostoli fr. 4 = PMG p363). As was proposed above, the verse acts as a kind of legitimating speech act, channeling the model citharode as an authorizing model of innovation-in-tradition for the citharode who sings it. Conservative musicologists of the fourth century and after accordingly recognized that Terpander introduced new harmonic and rhythmic devices in his own time, although they were quick to stress that he did so with a "dignity and propriety" lacking in the self-consciously progressivist stance of later Classical musicians (*On Music* 28.1140f; cf. 12.1135c).

Puns on *nomos* as civic law and strictly disciplined musical genre were not uncommon (e.g. Plato *Laws* 700a–b, 722d, 734e, 799e–800a; Athenaeus 8.352b). Although this punning generally dates from the fourth century BCE, it reflects earlier mentalities about the traditional propriety of the musical form, as well as age-old associations between the *kithara* and *kitharôidia* and social order.[80] Timotheus of Miletus provides a case in point. Resistance to the radical musical and formal innovations, often referred to collectively as *kainotomia*, introduced by Timotheus into his art led to charges of *paranomia* 'musical lawlessness' being brought against him (Plutarch *Whether an Old Man Should Engage in Public Affairs* 795d; cf. "Plutarch" *On Music* 4.1132e). His public response to these charges is preserved in the final section of *Persians*, a *nomos*, which concludes with the suggestion that his *kitharôidia*, far from being

---

[80] Cf. Smyth 1900:lviii–lx ("Nome and law alike were distinguished by a prescribed and well defined character"); Koller 1956:173–177; Zimmermann 1993:46; Bélis 1995:1056n99.

"lawless," in fact promotes, through the intercession of Apollo, an *epik-ouros* 'auxiliary' to the citharode's songs (204–205), *eunomia* 'good civic order' in the *polis* (240). The political "spin" that Timotheus puts on his citharodic *nomos*—the implicit contention that it is lawful—demonstrates how fluidly the musico-aesthetic sense of *nomos* could shade into the sociopolitical. The oscillation between music and politics, which moves beyond the realm of the poetic and metaphorical and into the real of the social imaginary, was at home above all in the "cosmic" ideology attached to *kitharôidia*. And this ideology, even if only explicitly articulated at its late Classical twilight, after Minerva's owl had flown, as it were, must have long acted as a stabilizing influence on the *nomos*, as a sort of generic superego, making it especially resistant to *kainotomia*. For as much as *kitharôidia* was popular entertainment, an agonistic spectacle, it still carried on some level its fundamentally conservative extra-aesthetic charge to put in order disordered states, to bring about normative social structure and harmony, as exemplified in the myths of Amphion and Orpheus, of lyric purifications at Delphi by Apollo (*Homeric Hymn to Apollo* 514–519, actually a proto-citharodic paean), and in the accounts of Terpander's musico-political intervention in Sparta. Plato asserts the "naturalness" of this condition when he imagines that οἱ παλαιοί 'the men of old' named the citharodic *nomos* after *nomos* 'law, custom' because they unselfconsciously recognized, "as if in a dream," its inherent political potential (*Laws* 799e–800a); both political and musical *nomoi* are dedicated to the maintenance of good social order, and both should be violated only on the pain of penalty.[81]

The intimacy between *kitharôidia* and Apollo must also have colored the ethical disposition of the *nomos*, even though the *nomos* itself was not, like the Classical choral paean to which it was often linked, solely dedicated to the god. Proclus *Chrestomathia ap.* Photius *Bibliotheca* 320a34–35 preserves a popular etymology of *nomos* that derives it from Apollo's epithet *Nomimos*, thus linking the musical form

---

[81] "Aristotle" *Problems* 19.28 seems to connect *nomos* qua melodic pattern to *nomos* in its sociopolitical sense without any explicit reference to the citharodic *nomos*: before people knew writing, they would sing their laws (*nomoi*) so as not to forget them. However, we may detect an implicit reference to *kitharôidia* in the last sentence of this *Problem*: "Therefore people gave the same name to the first of their later songs that they had given to their first songs" (καὶ τῶν ὑστέρων οὖν ᾠδῶν τὰς πρώτας τὸ αὐτὸ ἐκάλεσαν ὅπερ τὰς πρώτας). The weak wordplay on *prôtos* 'first' has caused some confusion, but the writer may mean by "the first of their later songs" the citharodic *nomos*—"first" is used qualitatively ("most important") rather than temporally (cf. Barker 1984:198n58). By the time the *Problems* were written, *nomos* was used in its musical sense more of contest pieces than "tunes" in general, and the citharodic *nomos* was the most prominent member of the former group.

specifically to the Apollonian ideal of lawful order and social equilibrium.[82] (Proclus in fact seems to make the argument that Apollo has taken his epithet from the name of the genre, but it is probable that he or Photius has confused the more commonly held derivation.) This divine ideal is manifest at the formal-aesthetic level as well: the *nomos* "on account of the god [Apollo] rises in orderly and magnificent fashion; it is calm in its rhythms and uses grandiose language."[83] This restraint stands in marked contrast to the tenor of the Dionysian dithyramb, which is hypothesized as the sonically tumultuous, emotionally excessive aesthetic-ethical "other" to the *nomos* (320b12–30). Proclus' source for this is probably a fourth-century writer on music; Heraclides is a likely candidate.[84] What this source is describing is almost certainly not the contemporary *nomos* of the fourth century BCE, which had significantly assimilated the style of the dithyramb, but rather the *nomos* in its old, Terpandrean aspect. The description is certainly idealizing, and the Apollonian/Dionysian distinction reductive, but, again, there is no good reason to think that the testimony in Proclus does not reflect preconceptions surrounding the *nomos* in the Archaic and Classical periods.

[82] Apollo was even made the inventor of citharodic *nomoi* (*Etymologicum Magnum* 607.1). Severyns 1938:137 contends that Proclus wrote not *Nomimos* but *Nomios*, which is an epithet of Apollo elsewhere attested (but cf. Gostoli 1990:108 for keeping *Nomimos*). *Nomios* alternatively means 'god of Law' (Cicero *On the Nature of the Gods* 3.23.57, with Severyns 1938:139) and 'Pasturer', a reference to Apollo's service to Admetus (e.g. Callimachus *Hymn to Apollo* 47–49). Servius *ad* Vergil *Georgics* 3.2 registers the pastoral and conflates the legal and musical meanings: "[Apollo] is called *Nomius* either ἀπὸ τῆς νομῆς, i.e. from pasturing, or ἀπὸ τῶν νόμων, i.e. from the law of strings (*a lege chordarum*)." Euripides in the *Alcestis* seems to make a similar musical/legal/pastoral pun, evoking an image of "Pythian Apollo of the lovely *lura*" (570) Orphically charming animals with his *kithara* "in the *nomoí* 'pasture lands'" of Admetus (574, with Pierson's ἐν νομοῖς for received ἐν δόμοις). One might hear in *nomoí* too the *nómoi* 'rules' prescribed for Apollo by Admetus.

[83] ὁ νόμος ... διὰ τὸν θεὸν ἀνεῖται τεταγμένως καὶ μεγαλοπρεπῶς καὶ τοῖς ῥυθμοῖς ἀνεῖται καὶ διπλασίοις ταῖς λέξεσι κέχρηται. I follow the text (which is problematic), translation, and analysis of Severyns 1938:45, 156–157. "Aristotle" *Problems* 19.48 observes that the Hypodorian mode is "most citharodic" because it is "magnificent and stable." Cf. n29 above.

[84] Cf. Rutherford 1995:360–361. Rutherford argues, with some merit, that the *nomos* has taken the place of the choral paean in post-fifth-century eidographical accounts; Proclus' incorrect classification of the *nomos* as a song in honor of the gods reflects this confusion. But that does not necessarily mean that the conservative ("Apollonian") tenor that late writers ascribe to the *nomos* is misapplied. Paean and *nomos* were already conceptually linked in the generic imaginary of the fifth century BCE, as Timotheus *Persians* 202–205 strongly suggests; cf. Part IV.11.iv. On *nomos* and dithyramb, see Power 2011 (forthcoming).

Andrew Barker sees the semantic development of *nomos* from the general, as melodic idiom, to the specific, as contest piece, taking place only in the later fifth century, at the initiative of historians and theorists of music, who were then beginning attempts at a scholarly systematization of musical genres. For them it served as a "scholar's term of art."[85] It is true that the incidental legal semantics of *nomos* appealed to their conservative views on civic *mousikê* and *kitharôidia* in particular. But the literary record suggests that the properly generic sense of the word was already known by the early Classical period, and coexisted alongside the generalized usage. In Sophocles' *Thamyras*, probably produced around the middle of the fifth century BCE, a character speaks of being drawn to the "place of assembly" (*eira*) to listen to the eponymous lyre singer "under the compulsion of the *lura* and of the *nomoi*, with which Thamyris makes outstanding music" (fr. 245). The semantics of *nomoi* here are dual: in the mythical world of the drama, the word has its primary, unmarked sense of 'tunes', but, in the unmistakably proto-citharodic context of the public lyric performance that is described, to the here-and-now audience it carries too its marked, generic sense. The latter meaning would come across all the more clearly if Sophocles (or another actor) did in fact play the role of Thamyris equipped with a *kithara*, as several sources report (*Life of Sophocles* 24; Athenaeus 1.20e–f; Eustathius *Commentary on the Iliad* 381.8 van der Valk). That Thamyris already in *Iliad* 2.594–600 appears as an itinerant, self-promoting, agonistic singer-to-the-*kitharis* rather than a subservient *Haussänger* like the other Homeric bards surely eased his assimilation to the persona of the contemporary professional citharodes, who perform *nomoi*. Another connotation may be in play as well. The mythographer Conon preserves a tradition that has the Scythians making Thamyris their king because of his great skill in *kitharôidia* (FGrH 26 F 1 [7]); Strabo 7 fr. 35 says that he ruled over the Thracians in Acte, on the slopes of Mt. Athos. It is possible that in Sophocles' play Thamyris was similarly made king of the Thracians. If so, *nomoi* in fr. 245 would carry not only its generic sense, but also its legislative one: the citharode-king acts as musico-political "nomothete" in the Thracian assembly-place, calling the populace to order with his *lura*.[86]

---

[85] Barker 1984:255; cf. 250n263: "The poets provided the word, with its general ambience: it was the music historians who took it over and converted it into a technical term." Cf. West 1992:216.

[86] Sophocles perhaps puns on the etymology of the hero's name, which "is evidently related to the old Aeolic word θάμυρις meaning 'assembly, gathering of the people'" (West 1999b:376, following Durante 1976:195–202, who conjectures a hereditary group

A more explicit case is presented by Herodotus, who, composing his *Histories* not later than c. 430 BCE, refers to the ὄρθιος νόμος of Arion as a way of describing the generic character of the "swan song" performed by that famous citharode before his leap into the sea (1.24.5). Herodotus' Arion is not singing a 'high-pitched melody', but *the* famous citharodic *nomos* called the *Orthios*, which was traditionally attributed to Terpander.[87] Much earlier, Pindar, in an ode for a musical victor in the Pythian auletic contest of 490 BCE, mentions the κεφαλᾶν πολλᾶν νόμος (*Pythian* 12.25). This again is a technical, generic use of *nomos*: not a 'melody of many heads', but a well-known contest piece, the *Polukephalos nomos*, the 'Many-headed *nomos*', is what Pindar means.[88] This *nomos* is an auletic one, but given that auletic, aulodic, and citharistic *nomoi* were thought to be secondary, both historically and in relative prestige, to the citharodic *nomos*, the Pindaric reference is *a fortiori* evidence that the songs performed by citharodes were from an early point known generally as *nomoi*.[89] One could even say that *nomos* in its generic sense has as its "unmarked" referent the citharodic *nomos*;

---

of Thamyrids, 'i cantori delle riunioni festive'; cf. Nagy 1979:311 on the agonistic implications of θάμυρις). The musical and political may thus be already intertwined at the very inception of the Thamyris myth: he is a cosmically endowed lyre singer, capable of mustering a political community into being through his music. Fleming 1977 argues persuasively that the musical and political meanings of *nomos* are made to overlap in Aeschylus' *Oresteia*, so much as to constitute a thematic motif running through the trilogy.

[87] Cf. Bergk 1883:240. I suggest too that in this passage Herodotus is playing on the double sense of *nomos* as song genre and law. The Corinthian sailors who would rob and kill Arion are drawn to his *nomos* by the sheer *hêdonê* 'pleasure' it brings them, but their lawlessness makes them immune to its "lawfulness." The sociomusical ineffectiveness of Arionic *kitharôidia* in this context is highlighted by the fact that Herodotus has Arion play the *Orthios nomos* to his hostile audience. This *nomos* was known also as the *Terpandreios nomos*, and it is tempting to think that Herodotus assigned this *nomos* to Arion in part for its Terpandrean associations (cf. *Suda* s.v. ἀμφιανακτίζειν, with Gostoli 1990:49–50). Arion's surely skillful, yet socially inert rendering of this *nomos*, his failure to bring order to the anomian Corinthian sailors, who can only experience selfish pleasure, would thus resonate against the idealized image of Terpander in Sparta harmonizing the community with his song.

[88] On the *Polukephalos nomos* see "Plutarch" *On Music* 7.1133e, where it is said that Pratinas of Phlius, roughly contemporary to Pindar, also mentions this *nomos*, attributing it to the younger Olympus. Even if this *nomos* is a playful invention of Pindar (or Pratinas)—the title might allude to the multitudes thronging the Pythian games, where the *Puthikos nomos* was the name of the most famous auletic contest piece, and could be what the victor, Midas, really played there—my point still stands. Pindar does, however, use *nomos* to mean simply 'melodic idiom' at *Nemean* 5.25, where Apollo leads the Muses in singing "all sorts of *nomoi*." There the idealized divine performance is universal in scope, encompassing every melodic idiom.

[89] E.g. "Plutarch" *On Music* 4.1132d; Barker 1984: "Reputedly the most ancient and certainly the most respected class was the kitharodic" (250).

the other types are always "marked." Thus Plato in his well-known discussion of Classical song genres in *Laws* 700b equates *nomoi* with citharodic *nomoi* alone.[90]

5. What's in a (Terpandrean) *Nomos*?

By the fifth century BCE at least seven or eight of the *nomoi* routinely performed as contest pieces at citharodic *agônes* across Greece had achieved canonical status. These were generally attributed, as were the common-repertoire citharodic *prooimia*, to Terpander. The attribution is bound up with two other legendary accounts of Terpandrean "inventions," both of which register the circumstances, technical and institutional, that shaped the emergence of the citharodic *nomos*. First, Terpander's seven-stringed lyre, prototype of the concert *kithara*, whose expanded range enabled the synthesis of harmonically simple local melodic traditions, *nomoi*, into a Panhellenically comprehensive, harmonically complex repertoire of agonistic *nomoi* that went under the idealized authorship of Terpander.[91] The second cognate "invention" is Terpander's "first *katastasis* 'establishment'" of musical culture in Sparta, which featured prominently his victory at (and probably foundation of) the oldest and most prestigious citharodic *agôn*, supposedly attached to the Carneia festival in Sparta, period 676/3 BCE.[92] The competitive setting of the Carneia is where he was envisioned to have developed and canonized his *nomoi*; Heraclides says that he performed his *nomoi* "in the *agônes*" (*On Music* 3.1132c), as was the practice of historical citharodes. The establishment of the *agôn* at this Apolline festival also provided the background for the sociopolitical significance attributed to the citharodic *nomos*. For Terpander's agonistic *nomoi* were not merely delightful showpieces, but served to bring harmony to the fractious Spartans who listened to them. This exemplary conflation of the musical and the political is rendered literally in late sources such as Clement of Alexandria, who writes that Terpander "set to music (*emelopoiêse*) the *nomoi* of the Lacedaemonians" (*Stromateis* 1.16.78). The

---

[90] Cf. Fleming 1977:224.

[91] Thus Nagy 1990b:88–89. On the specific harmonic innovations attributed to Terpander, formulated in the theoretical terms of later Classical musicology, see "Plutarch" *On Music* 28.1140f; "Aristotle" *Problems* 19.32. Cf. Barker 2001.

[92] Carneian *agôn*: Hellanicus FGrH 4 F 85 *ap.* Athenaeus 635e, with Sosibius FGrH 595 F 3 for the dating. For the *katastasis*, see "Plutarch" *On Music* 9.1134b, with Barker 1984:214n65; Gostoli 1990:XIV, 71–72, 84–85.

thinking behind this claim finds an earlier expression in the synchronization of Terpander's activities in Sparta with the political activity of the Spartan lawgiver Lycurgus in the early eighth century BCE, which is presented by Hieronymus of Rhodes in his *On Citharodes* (fr. 33 Wehrli *ap.* Athenaeus 14.635f). Hieronymus, a disciple of Aristotle, was presumably trying to forge an explicit identity between citharodic and civic *nomoi*; on this view, it is as if Terpander served as the lyric accompanist to that famed lawgiver, their organizing musical and political discourses performed in a duet of *eunomia*.[93] Similarly, Plutarch *Agis* 10.6 says that Terpander "by singing accomplished the same things as Lycurgus," although he does not make him a coeval of Lycurgus. Hieronymus' synchronic rationalization may be relatively idiosyncratic, but it likely reflects a more mainstream recognition of a conceptual affinity, no doubt promoted by both the citharodes and the Spartans, between Terpander's musical ordering of *stasis*-ridden Spartan society, an operation thought to have been mandated by no less than Apollo's oracle in Delphi, and his foundational *katastasis* of musical culture at Sparta, including the Carneian *agôn*, where the *nomoi* were sung—a paradigmatic dovetailing of the political and the aesthetic, the cosmic and the spectacular.

We will return to the musical, historical, and political implications of the Terpandrean biographical tradition in Part III. What follows in this section is rather an account of the musical form and poetic content of the Archaic and Classical ("Terpandrean") *nomos*, much of which will be perforce impressionistic and speculative. There is no other ancient

---

[93] Cf. Gostoli 1990:77, 106; van Wees 1999:7–8. Solon supposedly sang his laws (Plutarch *Solon* 3.5), a tradition that conflates in practical terms his poetic and political activities, which of course were conceptually and intellectually coterminous. On the vexed relationship between Tyrtaeus' elegiac *Eunomia* and the Spartan "Great Rhetra," see now van Wees 1999, who argues that a hexameter line attributed to Tyrtaeus by Bergk (ἁ φιλοχρηματία Σπάρταν ὀλεῖ, ἄλλο δὲ οὐδέν 'The love of money will destroy Sparta, nothing else', Diodorus Siculus 7.12.6) belongs rather, because of its mixed Doric-Ionic dialect, to a citharodic *nomos* attributed to Terpander and sung by Lesbian citharodes in Sparta (p4). The practice of singing laws in pre-literate Archaic communities is elsewhere attested, and, in some cases, probably has some historical basis in early Indo-European culture. "Aristotle" *Problems* 19.28 claims that the primitive Thracian Agathyrsi still (in the fourth century BCE) sing their laws—living proof of the old ways. At Hesiod *Theogony* 66–67 the chorus of the Muses sings the *nomoi* 'ordinances' of the gods. Gostoli 1990:106 lists further examples; see too Franklin 2004:244. Martianus Capella 9.926 claims that "the laws of many Greek cities and public decrees used to be recited to the *lyra.*" This is likely a generalization of the tradition recorded by Clement that has Terpander singing laws, but it could reflect the broader (ancient) perception that *kitharôidia* served to maintain law and order in the *polis*.

song genre as culturally central as the *nomos* that remains so mysterious to us in its particulars. This, as we will see, is not only due to the alternating generality and obscurity of our meager testimonia, but is also the result of a certain constitutive vagueness in the genre itself.

In the mostly late sources, Terpander is alternately said to have composed (*poiein*), written (*graphein*), or invented (*heuriskein*) the *nomoi* to which his name is attached; he is in any case assumed to be their author.[94] Heraclides of Pontus, our fullest authority on early *kitharôidia*, presents more complex testimony, however. In one place, he calls Terpander a "*poiêtês* 'composer' of citharodic *nomoi*," and says that he first gave them names (*onomata*) (fr. 157 Wehrli *ap.* "Plutarch" *On Music* 3.1132c). But in another passage from his scholarship excerpted in *On Music*, Heraclides is more circumspect in his attribution of authorship to the old master:

> οἱ δὲ τῆς κιθαρῳδίας νόμοι πρότερον <οὐ> πολλῷ χρόνῳ τῶν
> αὐλῳδικῶν κατεστάθησαν ἐπὶ Τερπάνδρου· ἐκεῖνος γοῦν τοὺς
> κιθαρῳδικοὺς πρότερος ὠνόμασε Βοιώτιόν τινα καὶ Αἰόλιον
> Τροχαῖόν τε καὶ Ὀξὺν Κηπίωνά τε καὶ Τερπάνδρειον καλῶν,
> ἀλλὰ μὴν καὶ Τετραοίδιον.

> The *nomoi* of *kitharôidia* were established in the time of Terpander, not long before the aulodic *nomoi*; that man first gave names to the citharodic ones, calling them Boeotian and Aeolian, *Trokhaios* and *Oxus*, *Kêpiôn* and *Terpandreios*, and finally *Tetraoidios*.[95]

"Plutarch" On Music 4.1132d

Here Terpander is not the composer, but merely the namer of *nomoi*, which have come into being without the agency of a composer. The indeterminateness of this formulation may reflect the fact that, in actual practice, these *nomoi* did not exist as the closed-off, totalized creations of one individual author. Rather, they functioned more like open-ended structures that, despite the totalized regulation suggested by their name, allowed citharodes considerable leeway in their choice of texts to be sung as well as some room for improvisation and elaboration within the traditional musical guidelines. Heraclides, in the passage from *On Music* quoted in Section 4, stresses the careful observance of a specific *harmonia*, rhythm, and *tasis* 'arrangement' honored

---

[94] See the relevant testimonia in Gostoli 1990:16–28.
[95] For the attribution of this testimony to Heraclides, see Gostoli 1990:92–93.

by performers of early *nomoi*; Photius s.v. νόμος similarly emphasizes the "established *harmonia* and (pre)determined rhythm" (ἁρμονία τακτή, ῥυθμὸς ὡρισμένος) of the *nomos* (cf. *Suda* s.v. νόμος). We should note, however, that structural articulation, rhythm, and mode, as well as the other epiphenomena of the appointed mode (tessitura, tempo, dynamic range, and ethical quality), are rather broad areas, each open to interpretation. A citharode could make a personalized mark on a traditional *nomos* by playing creatively within the assigned rules, in particular by crafting unique melodic variations on the source material.

There is no indication that any one pre-composed melody (*melos*) or set of melodies defined the Terpandrean *nomoi*, in contrast to the songs of Sappho or Pindar, which, at least ideally, possessed rigidly distinct melodic identities.[96] Photius in fact calls the *nomos* a "style or manner of melodizing" (τρόπος τῆς μελῳδίας; cf. "Plutarch" *On Music* 28.1140f), a definition implying that each *nomos* was ultimately a format for melodic improvisation based upon prescribed motival elements.[97] Indeed, it must be the case that a certain tension was built into the performance of these *nomoi*, a dialectical tension between the careful preservation of the traditional elements characteristic of the *nomos* and the necessary introduction of original interpretive touches, and that a successful citharode was one who knew how to keep this tension between strange and recognizable in a balance that would be most amenable to the particular audience before whom he appeared.[98]

---

[96] Pindar *Nemean* 4.13–16 imagines the victory song (*humnos*), reperformed in a monodic, sympotic context, as sung to the same tune (*tode melos*) it has in its choral form. In practice, many lyric texts could have been set to new music in reperformance, as indeed texts themselves were recomposed (cf. Fabbro 1992; Currie 2004:53). But Cratinus fr. 254 K-A indicates that even drunken symposiasts were usually careful to sing poems to their original tunes.

[97] Cf. Vetter 1936: "By *nomoi* we should understand not actual musical works of art, but rather merely melodic patterns (*Muster*) for the epic performance of the citharode" (col. 786). Sophocles fr. 966 suggests that *nomoi* had characteristic arcs of expressive intensity: "When someone sings the Boeotian *nomos*, leisurely (*skholaion*) at first, but then intensely (*entonon*)."

[98] See Griffith 1990:188–189 for this tension in dramatic contests. Specific details about the musical setting of the Terpandrean *nomos* are few and hardly reliable. Late sources claim that the Lydian or Hypodorian (i.e. Aeolian) modes were typical of *kitharôidia* (see n29 above), but these could represent mere assumptions based on Terpander's Lesbian/Aeolic origins, and the proximity, geographical and cultural, of Lesbos to Lydia. Cf. Reinach 1903:82n1. "Aristotle" *Problems* 19.48 observes that the Hypodorian mode is "most citharodic" because it is "magnificent (*megaloprepes*) and stable." That a tone of *megaloprepeia* 'magnificence' characterized early *kitharôidia* seems entirely probable, but we should also remember that our post-fifth-century musicological sources are almost all ideologically motivated to romanticize the dignified simplicity of archaic music as a tonic to the decadent excess of the New Music of Timotheus

In terms of Western musico-generic ontology, then, we might think of the Terpandrean *nomos* as being more akin to a classic jazz standard, which may be subject to considerably diverse interpretations by different performers through time, than a classical sonata or *Lied.* As one writer on jazz puts it, "Ideally, a new version of an old song is virtually a recomposition and this labile relation between composition and improvisation is one of the sources of jazz's ability to constantly replenish itself."[99] However, even a standard possesses a more fixed melodic identity than would a *nomos.* A better comparandum might be the classical Indian *rāga,* which is defined not by set melodies, but by modal prescriptions, "designation of a particular scale ... pitch ranking, characteristic ascent and descent patterns, motives, use of ornaments, performance time, and emotional character."[100]

Clearly, then, musical performance in action, as process, was the definitional aspect of early *kitharôidia,* not the objective, reified, static musico-poetic "work of art."[101] The Terpandrean *nomos* had no unitary, fixed identity before it was realized in performance; it was a template to be filled in by the citharodes, who were "performers and singers above all," but were nevertheless, even if in a restricted sense, creative artists—absolute distinctions between performative fidelity and compositional creativity are especially out of place here.[102] Heraclides' characterization of Terpander as a "*poiêtês* of citharodic *nomoi*" may thus be

---

et al. The claim probably made by Aristoxenus *ap.* "Plutarch" *On Music* 20.1137e that the music of the *kithara* employed the chromatic genus "from the start" is surely incorrect. (The genus is the intervallic division of the base tetrachord in each *harmonia;* there were three, diatonic, enharmonic, and chromatic. The chromatic genus is generally viewed as being later than the enharmonic, but Aristoxenus tendentiously places the former before the latter.) As Barker 1984:225n132 notes, Aristoxenus likely has in mind not the fixed chromatic genus per se, but *khroai,* harmonic "colorings" that deviate from normal scalar intervals, which came into fashion with the New Music of the fifth century.

99 Dyer 1997:86.

100 Cf. West 1992:216–217. Quotation from *The New Harvard Dictionary of Music* s.v. *Rāg(a).* See too Gerson-Kiwi 1980:182–210 for the analogous role of rule-bound creative improvisation in Middle Eastern classical music: "Playing in the cultured regions of the Orient means continual re-creation at the moment of performing, and learning to play means learning to compose" (202).

101 On the history of the idea of the permanent musical "work of art" in the Western tradition, see Goehr 2007. Although she overlooks the *nomos,* her characterization of the processal aspect of ancient Greek *mousikê* is apposite, if perhaps too reductive of the general picture: "Musical activities of Antiquity were expressive performances rather than productive or mechanical ones. Their expressive potential was directed toward producing not a physical construction or product but the activity or performance itself" (124).

102 "Performers": Wilamowitz 1903:103.

intended not to mean that he was *the* sole and original composer of the canonical *nomoi*, but that he was a prototypical agonistic composer-in-performance, who "in each *nomos* set *melê* to his own verses (*epê*) and those of Homer and sang them in the *agônes*" (fr. 157 Wehrli)—a generic description of the creative elaboration of traditional material every agonistic citharode was expected to demonstrate in performance. Similarly, "Plutarch" *On Music* 5.1133b cites another, unnamed source that "ancient Philammon of Delphi constructed (*sustêsasthai*) some of the citharodic *nomoi* composed (*pepoiêmenôn*) by Terpander." In this scenario, Terpander, whom one probably related account makes into a four-time Pythian victor (*On Music* 4.1132e), is cast in the role of the generic creative performer, "composing" the *nomoi* that were "constructed"—the verb *sunistasthai* here suggests a broader-stroked, less detail-oriented assemblage than a formal composition (*poiein*)—by his predecessor Philammon, here filling the role played by Terpander in more mainstream traditions. Thus at *On Music* 3.1132c Terpander's fundamental contribution to *kitharôidia* is compared to that made to *aulôidia* by Clonas of Tegea (or Thebes; cf. *On Music* 5.1133a), "the first to construct the aulodic *nomoi*" (τὸν πρῶτον συστησάμενον τοὺς αὐλῳδικοὺς νόμους).

However, it is reasonable to assume that certain historical citharodes could, in a strong sense, make this or that *nomos* their own, that is, they could produce a definitive version of a *nomos* that indelibly bore their own authorial stamp, performing it repeatedly over time to the same melodies and texts. Such successfully "composed" renditions of the traditional *nomoi* could conceivably have been reperformed by successive citharodes. Timotheus, whose own nomic compositions we will discuss below, at some point, perhaps early in his career, likely performed his own versions of the Terpandrean *nomoi*. *Suda* s.v. Τιμόθεος mentions eight διασκευαί 'adaptations' in a catalog of his works, which Wilamowitz sensibly understands to be "reworkings of old *nomoi*."[103] Pollux *Onomasticon* 4.65 lists eight *nomoi* in the Terpandrean canon, so it stands to reason that these adaptations were renditions of the classics that took on the status of quasi-original "works" attributed to Timotheus qua composer.

Just as *nomoi* were forms open to different musical content, so they were receptacles for various texts. No one *nomos* seems to have been tied to any one particular text. Significantly, *nomoi* were named

---

[103] Wilamowitz 1903:81n3; cf. Hordern 2002:10; also Veyne 1978 for *diaskeuai* as remakings of Classical dramas.

not according to their poetic content, which could have changed from performance to performance, but rather after the regional affiliations of their musical styles, their purported inventor, or some distinctive characteristic of their rhythmic, structural, or harmonic profile.[104] The case with the aulodic *nomoi* is similar (*On Music* 4.1132d). We may conclude that texts were chosen at the citharode's discretion. Presumably the choice was influenced in part by occasional factors, but there seems not to have been any citharodic *nomos* whose referential content was thematically predetermined by a specific festival or cultic-ritual context, as was the case with the auletic and citharistic *Puthikos nomos*, a program piece performed at the Pythian festival that drama-tized in music Apollo's foundational slaying of the serpent at Delphi (Pollux *Onomasticon* 4.84; Strabo 9.3.10; Pausanias 10.7.7).[105]

Could we be more specific about what texts were sung? Yes and no. That the early citharodes preferred to sing heroic narratives is clear from the sources. Alexander Polyhistor says that Terpander "emulated (*ezêlôkenai*) the epic verse (*epê*) of Homer and the melodies (*melê*) of Orpheus" (FGrH 273 F 77 *ap.* "Plutarch" *On Music* 5.1132f). Plutarch *Laconian Institutions* 17.238c calls Terpander an ἐπαινέτης ἡρωικῶν

---

[104] "Plutarch" *On Music* 4.1132d lists seven Terpandrean *nomoi*. There are the Boeotian and the Aeolian *nomoi* (regional affiliation); the *Trokhaios* (rhythmic) and *Oxus* (tessitural); the *Tetraoidios* ("Four-songed": structural/harmonic); the *Terpandreios* and the *Kêpiôn*, said to be named after a disciple of Terpander, who at *On Music* 6.1133c is associ-ated with the development of the concert *kithara*. (Wilamowitz 1903:90n1 argues that the *Kêpiôn* actually took its name from a cropped hairstyle called the *kêpos* 'garden', which some formal or sonic feature of the *nomos* conceptually evoked; one wishes he had gone into more detail in making this argument.) Pollux *Onomasticon* 4.65 lists eight canonical *nomoi*. His eighth *nomos* is the famous *Orthios*, probably named after its high pitching rather than its meter (cf. Barker 1984:251). Whether the individual titles given by Heraclides and Pollux are totally "authentic" is moot. See the debates about their relative historicity in Barker 1984:250–255 and Gostoli 1990:XVI–XVIII. The important point is the generic one: the old citharodic *nomoi* were not titled after their poetic content.

[105] The sole reference to a citharodic *Puthikos nomos* is in Plutarch's version of the Arion story, where it seems to be a figment of the writer's literary imagination. Plutarch's telling of the tale is radically different from Herodotus' in its religious sensibility, its explicit emphasis on the piety of Arion and Apollo's divine guidance. Arion conceives the idea to give his shipboard performance "through a kind of divine impulse," and when he does sing (the *Puthikos nomos*, instead of Herodotus' *Orthios nomos*), he does so piously, to request the *sôtêria* 'salvation' of himself, the ship, and the sailors (*Banquet of the Seven Sages* 18.161c). The *Orthios nomos*, however, may have been especially at home in Apollonian contexts. The Terpandrean proemial invocation of Apollo, PMG 697 (fr. 1) = fr. 2 Gostoli, was closely associated with the *Orthios*. See testimonia in Gostoli 1990:49–50.

πράξεων 'praiser of heroic deeds'.[106] One biographical tradition makes him into a descendant of Homer, which likely speaks to the content of his *nomoi*; according to perhaps the same tradition he was from Cyme, where Homer had, some claimed, been a native (*Suda* s.v. Τέρπανδρος).[107]

Other testimonia make the more explicit claim that Terpander set Homer's actual verse to music. "Plutarch" *On Music* 6.1133c says that after the *prooimion* citharodes went on to sing "Homer and other poets." Heraclides of Pontus is more specific. After rehearsing a list of legendary proto-citharodes, which depends on a Sicyonian inscription (*anagraphê*, FGrH 550 F 1) that treated the history of music, including a section on legendary *kitharôidia*, the music historian describes the compositional process of Terpander:[108]

Ἡρακλείδης δ' ἐν τῇ Συναγωγῇ τῶν ἐν μουσικῇ
<εὐδοκιμησάντων> τὴν κιθαρῳδίαν καὶ τὴν κιθαρῳδικὴν
ποίησιν πρῶτόν φησιν Ἀμφίονα ἐπινοῆσαι τὸν Διὸς καὶ
Ἀντιόπης, τοῦ πατρὸς δηλονότι διδάξαντος αὐτόν. πιστοῦται
δὲ τοῦτο ἐκ τῆς ἀναγραφῆς τῆς ἐν Σικυῶνι ἀποκειμένης,
δι' ἧς τάς τε ἱερείας τὰς ἐν Ἄργει καὶ τοὺς ποιητὰς καὶ τοὺς
μουσικοὺς ὀνομάζει. κατὰ δὲ τὴν αὐτὴν ἡλικίαν καὶ Λίνον
τὸν ἐξ Εὐβοίας θρήνους πεποιηκέναι λέγει, καὶ Ἄνθην τὸν ἐξ
Ἀνθηδόνος τῆς Βοιωτίας ὕμνους, καὶ Πίερον τὸν ἐκ Πιερίας τὰ
περὶ τὰς Μούσας ποιήματα· ἀλλὰ καὶ Φιλάμμωνα τὸν Δελφὸν
Λητοῦς τε <πλάνας> καὶ Ἀρτέμιδος καὶ Ἀπόλλωνος γένεσιν
δηλῶσαι ἐν μέλεσι, καὶ χοροὺς πρῶτον περὶ τὸ ἐν Δελφοῖς
ἱερὸν στῆσαι· Θάμυριν δὲ τὸ γένος Θρᾷκα εὐφωνότερον καὶ
ἐμμελέστερον πάντων τῶν τότε ᾆσαι, ὡς ταῖς Μούσαις κατὰ
τοὺς ποιητὰς εἰς ἀγῶνα καταστῆναι· πεποιηκέναι δὲ τοῦτον
ἱστορεῖται Τιτάνων πρὸς τοὺς θεοὺς πόλεμον· γεγονέναι δὲ καὶ
Δημόδοκον Κερκυραῖον παλαιὸν μουσικόν, ὃν πεποιηκέναι
Ἰλίου τε πόρθησιν καὶ Ἀφροδίτης καὶ Ἡφαίστου γάμον·

---

[106] Nagy 1979:98 shows that the verb *epaineô* 'praise' is the "technical word used by *rhapsôidoi* for the notion of 'recite Homer'." Cf. Nagy 2002:27–28. The agent noun *epainetês* is used of the rhapsode Ion twice in Plato *Ion*, 536d3, 542b4. Plutarch's application of it to Terpander reflects the tradition that citharodes sang Homer to the *kithara*.

[107] Homer the Cymean: Ephorus of Cyme *ap. Vita Plutarchea* 1.8–11. Ephorus may be the *Suda*'s source too for the Cymean Terpander (although not necessarily his inventor); this fourth-century historian may have related accounts of Terpander's activity in Sparta (cf. Kiechle 1963:200). The Cymean birthplace may, however, belong to an alternative tradition that makes Terpander a descendant of Hesiod, whose father was from Cyme; cf. Welcker 1865:142; Wilamowitz 1903:88n2.

[108] On the Sicyonian *anagraphê*, see Jacoby FGrH II B Kommentar, p443 and III B 550 Kommentar, p536. Cf. Gostoli 1986:112n19 and Griffin 1982:160.

ἀλλὰ μὴν καὶ Φήμιον Ἰθακήσιον νόστον τῶν ἀπὸ Τροίας μετ'
Ἀγαμέμνονος ἀνακομισθέντων ποιῆσαι. οὐ λελυμένην δ' εἶναι
τῶν προειρημένων τὴν τῶν ποιημάτων λέξιν καὶ μέτρον οὐκ
ἔχουσαν, ἀλλὰ καθάπερ <τὴν> Στησιχόρου τε καὶ τῶν ἀρχαίων
μελοποιῶν, οἳ ποιοῦντες ἔπη τούτοις μέλη περιετίθεσαν· καὶ
γὰρ τὸν Τέρπανδρον ἔφη κιθαρῳδικῶν ποιητὴν ὄντα νόμων,
κατὰ νόμον ἔκαστον τοῖς ἔπεσι τοῖς ἑαυτοῦ καὶ τοῖς Ὁμήρου
μέλη περιτιθέντα ᾄδειν ἐν τοῖς ἀγῶσιν.

Heraclides in his *Collection of [Famous] Musicians* says that
Amphion the son of Zeus and Antiope was the first to conceive
of *kitharôidia* and citharodic poetry; clearly, it was his father
who instructed him.[109] This is attested by the inscription
preserved in Sicyon, from which Heraclides derives the names
of the priestesses at Argos and the names of poets and musicians. Around the same time Linus of Euboea was composing
thrênoi 'dirges', Anthes of Boeotian Anthedon *humnoi*, and
Pierus of Pieria poems about the Muses, while Philammon of
Delphi told of the wanderings of Leto and the birth of Artemis
and Apollo, and was first to establish choruses at the temple in
Delphi. Thamyris, by birth a Thracian, sang with such better
voice and so much more tunefully than anyone alive in his
time that, as the poets have it, he entered into an *agôn* with
the Muses. It is said that Thamyris composed a *War of the Titans
Against the Gods*. Demodocus of Corcyra was also a musician of
old, who composed a *Sack of Ilion* and a *Marriage of Aphrodite
and Hephaestus* while Phemius of Ithaca composed a *Return
from Troy of Agamemnon and His Company*.[110] The arrangement
of words (*lexis*) in the poems by the aforementioned [citha-
rodes] was not "free" (*lelumenê*) and lacking meter [as it was in
the citharodic poetry of Heraclides' day], but was like that in
the poetry of Stesichorus and the melic composers (*melopoioi*)
of old, those who composed *epê* and set *melê* 'melodies' to
them. Heraclides also said that Terpander, being a composer

---

[109] As Barker 1984:207 notes, the title of Heraclides' treatise could have been simply
Collection of Musicians (literally, *Collection of Those in Music*) or even *Collection of Facts
about Music*. I prefer to retain Jacoby's supplemental <εὐδοκιμησάντων>.
[110] In line with his treatment of Homeric myth as history Heraclides identifies Phaeacia
as Corcyra. Cf. Aristotle fr. 512 Rose.

(*poiêtês*) of citharodic *nomoi*, in each *nomos* set *melê* to his own *epê* and those of Homer and sang them in the contests (*agônes*).

Heraclides of Pontus fr. 157 Wehrli = "Plutarch"
On Music 3.1132a–c

The crucial question presented by this passage is how we are to take the meaning of *epê*, which in turn would better indicate what is meant when we hear that Terpander set Homer to music for performance at musical contests. Were Terpander's Homeric *epê*, and his own, dactylic hexameters, as Alexander Polyhistor seems to employ the word, or as Proclus *Chrestomathia ap.* Photius *Bibliotheca* 320b5–6 assumes when he writes, "By using heroic meter, Terpander seems to have been the first to perfect the *nomos*" (δοκεῖ δὲ Τέρπανδρος μὲν πρῶτος τελειῶσαι τὸν νόμον ἡρῴῳ μέτρῳ χρησάμενος)? Or by *epê* does Heraclides mean also some other variant of lyric dactyls? The latter interpretation is prompted by the mention of Stesichorus, who composed heroic narratives arranged in strophic units of various dactylic cola rather than in the stichic hexameters of the Homeric epics.[111] But is Heraclides directly equating citharodic *nomoi* with the poetry of Stesichorus and the Archaic *melopoioi*? Those who think so have used this passage to support the idea that Stesichorus was himself a citharode.[112] Bruno Gentili has argued that the *epê* employed by both Terpander and Stesichorus represent an early lyric stage of dactylic rhythms that eventually underwent a "normalizzazione omoritmica" to become the dactylic hexameter.[113] Indeed, we saw that a one-line fragment ascribed to Terpander is in a quasi-hexametrical iambo-dactylic rhythm that shares characteristics with Stesichorean metrical cola (fr. 2 Gostoli = PMG 697).[114] The verse introduces a *prooimion*, not a *nomos*, but we learn at *On Music* 4.1132d that Terpander's *prooimia*, which seem to be known in some versions even to the late compiler or at least his source

---

[111] Russo 1999: "'Lyrical dactyls' is a more accurate equivalent to ἔπη in this context, since it suits the realities of Stesichorus' metrical forms" (346). Cf. Bowra 1963:145–146; Gentili 1995:39n78. On the triadic structure of Stesichorus' songs, see *Suda* s.v. τρία Στησιχόρου, with D'Alfonso 1994:21–40, who emphasizes the orchestic function of the triad.

[112] Arguments and bibliography condensed in Gostoli 1998.

[113] Gentili 1995.

[114] Gostoli 1990:129. Gentili 1995:39–40 also points out that fr. 3 Gostoli = PMG 698, a two-verse fragment from a Terpandrean *prooimion*, is in a spondaic pentameter that accords rhythmically with the Stesichorean pentameter. The meter occurs also in the parodos of Aeschylus' *Agamemnon* (106), which perhaps shows the influence of the citharodic *nomos*; cf. n119 below.

(cf. 6.1133c), were also composed in *epê*. Two other fragments attributed to Terpander (frs. 4 and 5 Gostoli = PMG p363) are in perfect hexameters, however.

6. Stesichorus and the Citharodes

Before examining further the meaning or meanings of *epê*, we should consider more closely the reason for which Heraclides brings Stesichorus into his discussion of the early citharodes. The latter were not, as far as we can tell, designated as *melopoioi*. Terpander is called a *melopoios* only once, by the Byzantine chronicler George Syncellus (T 11 Gostoli). The term was reserved for canonical "lyric" poets, choral and monodic, with whom Stesichorus is usually grouped, Pindar, Simonides, Sappho, Alcaeus, and Anacreon (cf. Dionysius of Halicarnassus *On Composition* 19 and 24), and for tragedians (Aristophanes *Frogs* 1250, the earliest use of the word), that is, poet-composers whose socioeconomic status and production of reified "works" distinguish them from the itinerant, agonistic citharodes, virtuoso re-elaborators of traditional musical and textual material. Inversely, Stesichorus, save for one highly dubious mention of a Stesichorus the *kitharôidos* in *Suda* s.v. ἐπιτήδευμα, is never explicitly identified as a citharode in the ancient literary record. Heraclides does not call him one here, nor does Heraclides, or anyone else, call his compositions *nomoi*.[115] Quintilian's oft-cited characterization of Stesichorus in *Institutio Oratoria* 10.1.62 as "singing of great wars

---

[115] See West 1971:309. The *Suda* entry is impossible to take literally. "Stesichorus the citharode" is mentioned alongside an "Aeschylus the aulete" as victim of the robber and murderer Hicanus. The story is of a type with that of Arion and the sailors or Ibycus and the bandits (*Suda* s.v. Ἴβυκος). But there must be some kind of witty "point" to this story that has been lost. Surely we are to think that this Aeschylus is *the* Aeschylus (who spent time in Sicily) and this Stesichorus is *the* Stesichorus. But no one would argue that Aeschylus was an aulete. One reading of this anecdote is that both Aeschylus and Stesichorus have undergone "downgrades" from the status of poet or *melopoios* to that of itinerant professional musician. The poet of aulodic tragedy becomes, fittingly, an aulete, and the poet of citharodic choral poetry becomes a *kitharôidos*. The testimony of Philodemus *On Music* 1, fr. 30.31–35, p18 Kemke (= PMG 281c), is also liable to misinterpretation. In it Stesichorus is figured as a solo singer-to-the-lyre who sings a "song of exhortation" during a period of internal hostilities in an unnamed city. His *melos* brings the two factions to peace. I would suggest that in the narrative economy of the anecdote, the sociopolitical complexity of Stesichorus' choral interventions in Himera is simplified to the iconic image of the monodic performer harmonizing the community with his song. Terpander in *stasis*-torn Sparta, whom Philodemus mentions in the same passage, is the obvious model; cf. Nagy 1990b:428.

and heroic leaders and sustaining on the lyre the weight of epic song" (*maxima bella et clarissimos canentem duces et epici carminis onera lyra sustinentem*) has been taken to mean that Quintilian knows Stesichorus as a citharode, but the statement really says nothing about performance. In fact, Quintilian knows very well what a *citharoedus* is and does (e.g. 1.12.3), and we should expect him to designate Stesichorus as such if he thought him to have been one. The Himeran poet is but another one of the nine canonical "lyric" poets, *lyrici*, like Alcaeus, whose achievement on the lyre Quintilian also emphasizes.

Although over the past four decades a number of scholars have sought to reclassify Stesichorus as a citharode, performing with or without a mute chorus, I remain attached to the older consensus view, recently strengthened by a number of energized "choralist" responses to the "monodist" claims, that he—not to mention Ibycus, Pindar, and Bacchylides—was, as his speaking name suggests, by and large a composer and arranger of choral songs accompanied by a *kitharistês*. While this arrangement early on served as a template for the emergence of *kitharôidia*, and could include monodic song by way of *prooimia*, it was not *kitharôidia* properly speaking.[116] It is true, as one "monodist" puts it, that the "epic content and narrative manner of [Stesichorean] compositions, and the almost epic scale of some of them seem to fit more neatly into what we know of the earlier kitharodic tradition than into the practice of any other so-called lyric poet."[117] But

---

[116] Choral Stesichorus: Burkert 1987:51; Burnett 1988; Nagy 1990b:362, 422; D'Alfonso 1994; Cingano 1990, 1993, and 2003. Stesichorus *kitharôidos*: Wilamowitz 1913:238; Pavese 1972:243; Herington 1985:19–20; Gostoli 1998; Russo 1999; Barker 2001. Willi 2008:76–82 is a convenient summary of the debate over Stesichorean performance (Willi is himself a "choralist"). Note that in the article that energized the "monodist" movement, West 1971, West, implicitly acknowledging Stesichorus' status as a *melopoios*, initially does not commit to calling Stesichorus a citharode: "[O]ne reason for [Heraclides'] bringing in Stesichorus ... might be that he was thought to be, not indeed a 'citharode', for a 'citharode' sang other people's verse, even in Terpander's time, but something analogous, a singing poet" (309); on p311, however, Stesichorus is called a citharode with no hedging. Gostoli 1998 argues that Stesichorus was primarily a solo citharode, but that, like Arion, who composed dithyrambs, he "potesse comporre anche canti propriamente corali" (152). While I agree in principle that Stesichorus worked in multiple media, I would argue that *khorôidia* was his primary medium—the triadic nature of the fragments strongly suggests this—and that occasional monodic lyric, although not full-blown citharodic *nomoi*, was secondary. Such was the case for other *melopoioi*, we assume, such as Pindar, Bacchylides, and Simonides. Cf. Cingano 1990:209–211; Davies 1988 (although the distinction between chorality and monody seems to me to have been more fundamentally recognized in antiquity than Davies would have it). Burnett 1988:139n108 speculates that the erotic songs attributed to Stesichorus were intended for solo performance; a sympotic context seems likely.

[117] Herington 1985:19–20.

why should this resemblance, objective as it is, amount to anything other than the influence of a solo performance medium on a choral one? The claim made in *Suda* s.v. Στησίχορος, that Stesichorus "first established a chorus with (or to) *kitharôidia*" (πρῶτος κιθαρῳδίᾳ χορὸν ἔστησεν), need not mean, as Wilamowitz first suggested, that he sang monodically while a mute chorus danced in pantomime (as Demodocus does for the Phaeacian chorus in *Odyssey* 8). Rather, it communicates, in reductive terms, the fact that Stesichorus had "choralized"—or, given its distant origins in choral song and dance, "rechoralized"—the *kitharôidia* of his day. That is, he was among the first to marry the ambitious musical techniques, including the use of a technically advanced concert *kithara*, as well as the more Panhellenically oriented, long-form heroic narratives of the citharodic *nomoi* to the triadic song-and-dance format of choral *mousikê*, which previously had drawn largely from epichoric heroic and cultic traditions, as we see in the fragments of Alcman.[118] What Stesichorus created was a choral lyric adaptation of heroic sagas—including those attributed to "Homer," alongside whom ancient critics as early as Simonides tend to set Stesichorus (PMG 564)—not as they were recited by the rhapsodes, but as they were sung by the citharodes. The observation of the Peripatetic scholar Chamaeleon in his treatise *On Stesichorus* that Homer's verses were "melodized" (μελῳδηθῆναι) is cited without context by Athenaeus (14.620c = fr. 28 Wehrli), but it may have been made in the context of a discussion about the practice of Stesichorus' citharodic models.

At a later time, Aeschylus would, if we trust the retrospective assessment of Aristophanes, similarly borrow from the rhythms and tunes of the *kitharôidikoi nomoi* of his day in composing his choral songs, such as the parodos to the *Agamemnon* (*Frogs* 1281–1300).[119] Aeschylus

---

[118] Stesichorean lyric may assume a localized perspective, but always with a stylized, self-conscious tenor, as if "in the process of making a bid for Panhellenic status" (Nagy 1990b:422). See further Burnett 1988 on the interactions of Panhellenic and local perspectives in the choral performance culture of Archaic Magna Graecia. Burkert 1987 offers a vivid reconstruction of the Panhellenic enterprise behind Stesichorus' choral activity. Kleitias, the painter of the sixth-century BCE François Vase, may have known Stesichorus' songs and alluded to him by labeling the Muse otherwise named *Terpsikhorê* 'she who delights in the chorus' as *Stêsikhorê*. See Stewart 1983:56.

[119] According to a scholion to *Frogs* 1282, the first-century BCE scholar Timachidas of Rhodes said that Aeschylus' specific model was the *Orthios nomos*. But we should be wary about taking Aristophanes' claim too literally, and trying to reconstruct the exact metrical profile of a Terpandrean *nomos* from either the parody presented by Euripides/Aristophanes in *Frogs* or from the parodos of *Agamemnon* itself (as Wilamowitz 1903:101–102 almost does), although both do show a preponderance of lyric dactyls, which is what we might expect from the *nomos*, in particular the

would have grown up listening to citharodes sing *nomoi* above all at
the Panathenaic festival *agônes*. Stesichorus would have been a young
man during Arion's tour of Italy and Sicily as related in Herodotus 1.24,
which represents an idealized narrative condensation of an objectively
historical process, the spread of *kitharôidia* to culturally receptive
Western markets in the late seventh and early sixth century BCE. By
contrast, there is testimony that it was not until the very end of the
sixth century that the Chian rhapsode Cynaethus, one of the Homeridai,
first recited Homeric verses in Syracuse (Hippostratus FGrH 568 F 5).[120]
This could indicate the late entry of professional *rhapsôidia* into those
same markets, or at least into Sicily, and in turn bolster the notion that
the Homer Stesichorus experienced, at least initially, was sung to the
kithara rather than chanted by the rhapsodes.[121]

Orthios ("Plutarch" *On Music* 7.1133f). Cf. Fraenkel 1918:321–323 = 1964:202–204 on
the Aeschylean combination of dactyls and iambics, which we see also in PMG 697
(fr. 1) = fr. 2 Gostoli; on the spondaic "Terpandrean" meter of *Agamemnon* 106, cf.
n114 above. Despite superficial semblances, Aeschylean songs, like Stesichorean
ones, are triadic and more metrically diverse than the stichic *nomoi* (cf. Danielewicz
1990:141). What Aeschylus took from the citharodes, I believe, was less a consistent
rhythmical patterning and more a grand, expansive manner of heroic narration, as
well as a general tone of stateliness and magnificence, *megaloprepeia*, the quality that
was ascribed to the old *nomos* ("Aristotle" *Problems* 19.48; cf. Proclus *Chrestomathia
ap.* Photius *Bibliotheca* 320b17). For audiences accustomed to the punchy, labile new
nomoi of Phrynis and Timotheus, as the spectators of *Frogs* were, the style of both
the old *nomoi* and Aeschylean melic seemed slow and monotonous, an impression
emphasized by Euripides' incessant "refrain" of *phlattothratto*, imitating a strummed
kithara, repeated after each sung verse. Thus Dionysus asks Aeschylus whether he
got his ἱμονιοστρόφου μέλη 'rope-hauler's songs'—these being proverbially boring
and repetitive—"from Marathon," a place lost in time, its associations with the "old
days" firmly fixed in the Athenian imagination (1296–1297; I remain unconvinced by
Borthwick 1994:23–25 that the expression evokes the patter of fairground hustlers).
There may be a reference too to the Herakleia festival at Marathon, which probably hosted a citharodic *agôn*, as an inscription on a pelike by the Epimedes Painter
suggests (Plate 13); perhaps the contest maintained a conservative ethos. Cf. Dover
1993:349. Aristophanes, however, has Aeschylus present his borrowings from *kitharôidia* as, in their own time, an innovation in Athenian tragedy (1298–1300). Aeschylus
certainly knew Stesichorean poetry; perhaps he emulated too Stesichorus' choral
emulation of *kitharôidia*.

[120] See Burkert 1979:54–56 for the probable validity of Hippostratus' notice, which finds
remarkable support in the archaeological record: the remains of a sixth-century
statue base inscribed with the name of its dedicator, Cynaethus, presumably the
celebrated rhapsode.

[121] The arguments here for a choral reception of *kitharôidia* are complemented by Cassio
2005:20–21, who argues that the Lesbian citharodes profoundly influenced the
Aeolic-based dialectal composite of choral melic poetry on the mainland and in the
West. Bowra 1961:82–83 argues for the influence of Arion on Stesichorus, but specifically in the former's role as a dithyrambic choral composer.

Stesichorus' expansion of choral form had models too in earlier generations of innovative Italian *melopoioi*. Xenocritus of Locri, who took part in the second-wave institution (*katastasis*) of musical contests at Sparta, composed choral paeans that were later classified as dithyrambs because they so markedly contained "heroic themes" ("Plutarch" *On Music* 10.1134e). Xenocritus was surely acquainted with the agonistic *kitharôidia* that constituted the first *katastasis* of musical culture in Sparta, and perhaps borrowed material from its *nomoi* for his choral songs. But he seems to have been known (or remembered) primarily as an aulodic composer: Pindar fr. 140b S-M indicates that he devised a "*harmonia* for the *auloi*," i.e. the Locrian mode, in which to sing a paean for Apollo and the Graces.[122] A curious passage from Glaucus of Rhegium *On Ancient Poets and Musicians* (by way of *On Music* 7.1133f) connects Stesichorus with the music of the *aulos*. Glaucus asserts that he "imitated neither Orpheus nor Terpander nor Archilochus nor Thaletas, but Olympus, since he employed the *Harmateios* 'Chariot' *nomos* and the dactylic species of rhythm, which some say comes from the *Orthios nomos*." Glaucus should not be taken to mean that Stesichorus exclusively composed for the *aulos* rather than for the *kithara*, although it is entirely possible that he did, like Xenocritus, occasionally compose aulodic songs.[123] Rather, Glaucus, who maintained the seemingly minority view that the first composers of *aulôidia* were anterior to Terpander, and, presumably, to *kitharôidia* itself (*On Music* 4.1132e–f), is concerned to counter the *communis opinio* that Stesichorus emulated lyric poets, and to show instead how his music emulated the earliest musician and inventor of the Chariot *nomos*, the ur-aulete Olympus.[124]

---

[122] Pindar mentions only a "Locrian," but a scholion to *Olympian* 10.17 specifies that this is Xenocritus. One would like to know more about Xanthus, a *melopoios*—his provenance, date, and his specific genre(s)—from whose treatments of the Oresteia and Heracles saga Stesichorus supposedly borrowed, according to the Peripatetic scholar Megaclides (*ap.* Athenaeus 12.512e = PMG 229). It could be that Xanthus was, like Xenocritus, a choral poet from Magna Graecia. Cf. West 1992:338; Bowra 1961:82.

[123] Cf. Burnett 1988:130–131. A fragment from the *Oresteia* (PMG 210), in which a plural singing subject, probably indicative of a chorus, refers to *damômata* 'hymns composed for public delivery by choruses' that are sung in a "Phrygian *melos*," suggests an auletic accompaniment, since the Phrygian *harmonia* was most closely associated with the *aulos*. (Olympus was a Phrygian.) Alternatively, the fragment could exemplify Stesichorus' borrowing of auletic styles for his choral lyric. I follow the interpretation of *damômata* in Smyth 1900:266.

[124] This passage from *On Music* is controversial, since at 4.1132d, probably drawn from Heraclides, it is asserted that citharodic *nomoi* are older than aulodic ones. Weil and Reinach 1900:21 thus emend *aulôidia* to *aulêtikê*, while Gostoli 1990:74 suggests that Glaucus refers to Archilochus rather than Terpander. But we maintain consistency within the textual farrago of *On Music* only at the risk of distorting Glaucus' actual

He also makes the tendentious argument that Stesichorus' preference for dactylic rhythms does not reflect his dependence on the
nomic tradition of *kitharôidia*, but rather his adaptation of *aulos* music,
specifically the *Orthios nomos*, best known in its Terpandrean citharodic
version, but here, presumably, a pre-citharodic, aulodic (or auletic)
version devised by Olympus.[125]

This confusing testimony prompts several interrelated points.
First, the *communis opinio* that Glaucus criticizes is no confirmation that
Stesichorus was viewed as a solo citharode, since neither Archilochus
nor Thaletas were viewed as citharodes. Archilochus composed for
dithyrambic and paeanic choruses; Thaletas of Gortyn was a composer
of choral paeans, renowned for his activity alongside, or slightly
before, Xenocritus of Locri at festivals in Sparta, Arcadia, and Argos
(*On Music* 9.1134b–c; Glaucus dated him earlier than Xenocritus, *On
Music* 10.1134f). Unlike Xenocritus, however, Thaletas seems to have
specialized, as did Stesichorus, in lyre-accompanied *khorôidia*.[126] It is
significant, then, that elsewhere in his *On Ancient Poets* Glaucus seeks to
"aulodize" Thaletas in the same manner he does Stesichorus, claiming
that the paeonic and cretic rhythms employed by the Cretan composer
were inherited from Olympus rather than from Archilochus, Orpheus,
or Terpander (*On Music* 10.1134e–f). The parallelism is clear. In Glaucus'
view, like Thaletas before him, Stesichorus was a composer of choral
lyric who imported *aulos*-based musical devices into his *kithara*-based
settings. Again, Glaucus has a pro-*aulos* agenda, as it were, and we
should be suspect of his claims about influence. The *communis opinio*
surely had it right that Stesichorus "imitated" the citharodes, represented, as often, by Orpheus and Terpander, as well as the techniques
of older choral lyric composers such as Thaletas and Archilochus.
Nonetheless, Glaucus may well have identified something distinctly
auletic in the Stesichorean lyric scores with which he was familiar.[127] It
would not be surprising if Stesichorus merged in a distinctive fashion
material borrowed from the nomic repertoire of the *aulos*, perhaps by

---

views. At 5.1132f we read that "aulodic poets" lived before Orpheus himself, a contention that is immediately contradicted at 1133a, where it is said, perhaps again by
Heraclides, that Terpander lived *before* Clonas, the first composer of aulodic *nomoi*.
The former claim has been attributed to Alexander Polyhistor (FGrH 273 F 77), but it
likely represents a reiteration of the chronology proposed first by Glaucus.

[125] On the aulodic/auletic *Orthios nomos,* see "Plutarch" *On Music* 10.1134d, Pollux
Onomasticon 4.71, and scholia *ad* Aristophanes *Acharnians* 16; cf. Barker 1984:253.

[126] Cf. Barker 1984:214n66, 215n75; West 1992:336.

[127] See Barker 2001 for some interesting speculation on these matters. Cf. n123 above on
the Phrygian modal setting of the *Oresteia*.

way of aulodic predecessors such as Xenocritus, with that appropriated from citharodic *nomoi.*

In view of this possibility we might consider an odd story preserved in Himerius *Oration* 22.5 concerning Ibycus, who composed choral lyric on the Stesichorean model, if on a less ambitious scale. Ibycus, the story goes, was on his way from his hometown of Catana in Sicily to nearby Himera when he fell from his chariot (*harma*) and broke his wrist; "for some time after, he was out of tune (ἀπῳδός), but did not dedicate his *lura* to Apollo [i.e. he did not cease to compose music]." In Himerius' stripped-down, contextless rendering, the precise significance of the obviously metaphorical subtext of this anecdote is obscure. But its details, impressionistic as they are, conspire to suggest a commentary of some sort on Ibycus' reception of the distinctive lyric music of Stesichorus, whom Himerius mentions immediately before recounting it. Ibycus is traveling to Himera, the city of Stesichorus; the chariot recalls the Chariot *nomos* (*Harmateios*) that Glaucus associates with Stesichorus; Ibycus plays the lyre "out of tune" as a result of the chariot incident—all this might amount to a narrativization of Ibycus' stylistic debt to his Himeran predecessor, its original context now lost.[128]

Let us return to the testimony of Heraclides. Stesichorus and the other *melopoioi* who treated epic material melodically are cited not because they were citharodes, but because their compositional process offers an instructional comparandum for early citharodic song-making. We need not think that Heraclides means to say, however, that Terpander and the early citharodes sang strophic songs as Stesichorean choruses did, nor even that he is referring to the technical affinities in the metrical patterning of their *epê*. The formal basis of the comparison is more general even than that. The rhythmic regularity and discipline characteristic of early citharodic *nomoi* and Stesichorean songs are what unite them, each in their own way, against song that employs λελυμένη λέξις καὶ μέτρον οὐκ ἔχουσα "diction that is 'free' and lacking meter." Heraclides elsewhere emphasizes the rhythmic predictability of the *nomos* ("Plutarch" *On Music* 6.1133b), which, in both its old and new forms, was stichic, not strophic.[129] We should keep in mind that

---

[128] Cf. Bowra 1961:242.

[129] "Aristotle" *Problems* 19.15 offers clear evidence for an essential distinction between stichic *nomos* and choral response: "Why were *nomoi* not composed antistrophically, while other songs, those for choruses, were? Is it because *nomoi* were pieces for competitors, and since they were able to perform imitatively and to sustain lengthy exertions, their song became long and multiform? Like the words, then, the melodies followed the imitation in being constantly varied" (trans. Barker 1984:192). As Barker 1984:192n16 recognizes, the writer of the *Problem* must have the old *nomoi* in mind,

Heraclides was writing in the later fourth century, by which time a new, freer style of *kitharôidia* had become dominant and the Terpandrean style had largely fallen away. As the old *nomoi* of Terpander increasingly disappeared from the repertoire of citharodes, they left no significant traces in the textual record, because they had no fixed textual identity; they were open musical structures waiting to be filled, in performance, with a diverse range of narrative poetry, little of which would have been preserved in a dedicated written transmission independent of performance practice.[130] This "song loss" is indicated by an indirect proof employed later in the *On Music*, for which Heraclides is probably still the source: "That the citharodic *nomoi* of old consisted of *epê*, Timotheus made clear. He sang his first *nomoi*, at least, in *epê* while mixing in dithyrambic diction (ὅτι δ' οἱ κιθαρῳδικοὶ νόμοι οἱ πάλαι ἐξ ἐπῶν συνίσταντο, Τιμόθεος ἐδήλωσε· τοὺς γοῦν πρώτους νόμους ἐν ἔπεσι διαμιγνύων διθυραμβικὴν λέξιν ᾖδεν, 4.1132d–e).[131] That is, Heraclides must resort to the *nomoi* of Timotheus, which he would know both as written and performed compositions, to make the argument for a now "lost" Terpander. The case with Stesichorean song was different. Stesichorus composed autonomous musico-poetic texts that could be and were preserved under his name. Their language, metrical structure, and perhaps even their musical scores—traditionally affiliated with *kitharôidia*—would still have been familiar to the readers of Heraclides.[132] The Terpandrean nomic practice, however, once practically, performatively obsolescent, would have existed almost entirely as

---

even if the emphasis on imitation (*mimêsis*) and verbal/melodic variation as determining factors in the development of the *nomos* reflects the aesthetic of the later Classical *nomos*.

[130] As I discuss below, however, there are some minor traces in the textual record of the traditional citharodic narratives sung in *nomoi*. The case with the traditional *prooimia* ascribed to Terpander is different from that of the *nomoi*. These shorter texts, which had a more formally reified status than the *nomoi*, may have enjoyed reperformance after the Terpandrean *nomoi* themselves had ceased to be performed, and were more likely to have been textually circulated (even if in non-Alexandrian, "unofficial" versions). See Wilamowitz 1903:91–92; Nagy 1990b:359.

[131] See Gostoli 1990:97–98 for the probably Heraclidean sourcing. On the relevant ethnomusicological notion of "song loss," see Nettl 1983:350–351.

[132] The lengthy allusion to Stesichorean song, including his *Oresteia* (PMG 210), at Aristophanes *Peace* 775–796, from a choral ode, could suggest a familiarity not only with the poetry, but also with the music of Stesichorus. Classical Athenian symposiasts were still singing Stesichorean songs (Eupolis frs. 148 and 395 K-A; scholia *ad* Aristophanes *Wasps* 1222; Ammianus Marcellinus 38.4). These were probably shorter, monodic pieces, but adapted excerpts from the lengthy choral pieces should not be ruled out. Eupolis fr. 148 indeed names Stesichorus alongside two *melopoioi* best known for choral works, Simonides and Alcman. For monodic lyric reperformance of choral melic, see discussion in Nagy 1990b:107.

a cultural memory. In a sense, Stesichorus serves a purpose analogous to that of Timotheus, to attest to what is no longer heard (or read).

It is no coincidence that the citharodes of the Lesbian school, so dominant in the *agônes* of the Archaic and earlier Classical periods, who had once been the main proponents of the repertoire attributed to Terpander, pass from the scene by the end of the fifth century. Phrynis of Mytilene, who won a Panathenaic victory at mid-century, is the last citharode of the Lesbian line of whom we have certain evidence. As a formal innovator, however, he must have been largely responsible for the decline of the Terpandrean style that he himself inherited. (According to the scholia to Aristophanes *Clouds* 971a, which also record the Panathenaic victory, his teacher was Aristocleitus, a direct descendant of Terpander.) "Plutarch" *On Music* 6.1133b claims that *kitharôidia* remained "simple" from the time of Terpander until the time of Phrynis, and Proclus *Chrestomathia ap.* Photius *Bibliotheca* 320b8–10 specifies that it was Phrynis who fundamentally renewed it, introducing harmonic and rhythmic *kainotomia* (ἐκαινοτόμησεν): he employed a polychord *kithara* and "attached hexameter to 'free verse'" (τό τε γὰρ ἐξάμετρον τῷ λελυμένῳ συνῆψε). This metrical mixture prefigures the mixing of *epê* and dithyrambic diction practiced by Timotheus, who "brought the *nomos* to its current form (*taxis*)." Phrynis' "free verse" (*lelumenon*) is probably something like what Hephaestion *On Poems* 3.3 calls *apolelumena*, "verse written at random (*eikê*) and without defined meter," for which are adduced the *nomoi* of Timotheus as examples. (Hephaestion's language notably echoes that of Heraclides in *On Music* 4.1132d–e.) These metrical and lexical changes introduced by Phrynis and Timotheus were inextricable from their properly musical innovations, which are well attested in other musicological sources as well.[133]

There is no reason to believe, however, that late- and post-Classical notions of the Terpandrean style were entirely suppositional. The Terpandrean *nomoi* were maintained on a Panhellenic scale at festival musical contests until at least the second half of the fifth century, in some places, such as Sparta, perhaps later (for Athens, see Aristophanes *Acharnians* 13–16; *Knights* 1278-1279, with scholia *ad loc.*; cf. *Suda* s.v. Λοιδορεῖσθαι τοὺς πονηρούς). Heraclides and scholars of music after him, although they may not have had first-hand experience of the performance of Terpandrean *nomoi*, at the very least would have been familiar with the work of later fifth-century writers who did, such as

---

[133] Cf. Hordern 2002:29. For Timotheus' emulation of Phrynis, see Aristotle *Metaphysics* 1.993b15.

Glaucus of Rhegium. Thus they are presumably reliable when they say that the melodizing of *epê* was a feature of the early *nomos*.

7. Terpander's Homer

But what about the claim that Terpander set Homeric poetry to music? Does Heraclides mean that Terpandrean *nomoi* dealt with (some of) the same material the Homeric rhapsode did, but in "Stesichorean" form, in lyric dactyls rather than hexametrical *epê*? Or should we take his account more literally to mean that the *nomoi* incorporated Homeric hexameters? The answer to both these questions is yes, which makes sense if we do not think of the Terpandrean *nomoi*, like the *prooimia*, as a body of works that are synchronically the products of one master poet-composer, but rather the mutable frameworks of an Archaic citharodic performance tradition that evolved diachronically and could accommodate different models of textual presentation side by side as its Panhellenic perspectives widened. Terpander came to stand as the hypostasis of this tradition. That is, an ancient practice of singing heroic and divine exploits in pre-hexametrical melic cola, cultivated above all by Aeolic *aoidoi*—perhaps this is what Heraclides calls "Terpander's own *epê*"—coexisted alongside and interacted with the singing of the hexametrical *epê* that we have come to associate primarily with the recitations of the Ionian rhapsodes. Both the rhapsode and the citharode were offshoots of the *phorminx*-playing singer of the Dark Age, who, in addition to his monodic performance of heroic *epos*, played the part of the *kitharistês* for the melic chorus as well.[134] The poetic patrimony of the Archaic and Classical citharode was thus metrically heterogeneous, including both the hexameter and "irregular" *epê* such as we see in Terpander PMG 697 and refracted in Stesichorean song, as well as a range of traditional narratives to suit each. Certain *nomoi*

---

[134] As West 1981:124 puts it, "In the 8th century the bard always 'sang', and normally accompanied himself on the four-stringed phorminx. The spread of the cithara in the following century caused a schism. Some adopted it, and evolved a more elaborate, heptatonic style of vocal melody to go with it. Others ... persevered in the traditional style. [These, who would become rhapsodes] retained the loyalty of the public interested in the narrative rather than in musical virtuosity." I would disagree, however, with West's contention that hexameter *kitharôidia* was historically anterior to a "separate style of lyric epic, mainly dactylic but not in regular hexameters," such as we see reflected in Stesichorean lyric (125). As Gentili 1995:38–40 demonstrates, the latter was likely the older style, from which the homo-rhythmic hexameter evolved (cf. Nagy 1990b:439–464).

had rhythmic profiles that doubtless called for predominantly non-hexametrical texts; the Trochaic *nomos* would seem to be such a one.[135]

But hexameter may have been prevalent even in the early *nomoi* of the seventh century BCE. Some indirect evidence for this presents itself. *Suda* s.v. Ἄλκμαν contains the odd datum that Alcman was the first poet to compose *melê* without hexameters (τὸ μὴ ἐξαμέτροις μελῳδεῖν). Broadly speaking, the claim is incorrect for two reasons: first, non-hexametrical melic was of course composed before Alcman; second, Alcman himself sang hexameters! However, the sheer erroneousness of the testimony should give us pause. Could it be rather a clumsy expression of some historically and generically reductive, yet still essentially valid belief that Alcman was the first "citharode" to perform extensively non-hexametrical lyric, i.e. metrically varied choral lyric, in Sparta, where previously citharodes, the Lesbian line most prominently, were known for melodizing epic hexameters at the Carneia festival?[136] It is also a striking coincidence that our one reference to *kitharôidia* by a Lesbian poet, πέρροχος ὡς ὅτ' ἄοιδος ὁ Λέσβιος ἀλλοδάποισιν ("Outstanding, like the Lesbian singer against foreign rivals," Sappho fr. 106), with its evocation of the "Lesbian Singer" who is unbeatable in contests abroad—we are to think primarily of Terpander and his descendants at Sparta—is a hexameter line, and so perhaps involves a playful allusion to the preferred metrical expression of the Lesbian citharodes.

By the fifth century BCE, hexameter texts almost certainly dominated the performance of the citharodic *nomos*, likely a result of the influence of the rhapsodes in defining Panhellenic ideals of epic form, thanks especially to their prominent role in standardizing the texts of the *Odyssey* and *Iliad* at the Panathenaic festival in Athens.[137] It is telling that two representations of citharodic song in fifth-century tragedy are perfectly hexametrical, Sophocles *Thamyras* fr. 242 and Euripides *Antiope* fr. VI, although the latter, at least, probably represents a *humnos*

---

[135] The *Orthios nomos*, traditionally linked with the "irregular" dactylic PMG 697, could have been another.

[136] Cassio 2005:21n27 reviews earlier, ultimately unnecessary attempts to make sense of the testimony, which include inserting μόνον 'only' after μή 'not', or removing the μή.

[137] See Nagy 2002 on this process. The standardizing influence of *rhapsôidia* on *kitharôidia* is detectable too in the dialectal composite evident in the proemial fragments attributed to Terpander, a mixture of Aeolic, Laconian, and epic-Ionic elements, sometimes apparent within variants of the same line (e.g. the first hexameter of PMG p363 = fr. 4 Gostoli, with discussion in Gostoli 1990:XLIII–XLVI). Cf. Nagy 1990b:418; Cassio 2005:20–21.

rather than a *nomos*. Proclus attests that Phrynis mixed "free" verse with hexameters. According to "Plutarch" *On Music* 4.1132e, Timotheus composed part of his "first *nomoi*" (ἐν ἔπεσι) with dithyrambic language (and presumably meters). This description *epê* surely refers foremost to hexameters, as we have one invaluable hexameter verse from a *nomos* of Timotheus, the *Persians*, probably the initial line of the work (PMG 788): κλεινὸν ἐλευθερίας τεύχων μέγαν Ἑλλάδι κόσμον ("Fashioning a glorious and great adornment of freedom for Greece"). We saw above that in this same passage of *On Music*, which is probably derived from Heraclides, Timotheus' *epê* are adduced to show that Terpander too used *epê*. This would imply that what Heraclides has uppermost in mind when he speaks of citharodic *epê* are hexameters, although his use of the word in connection to Stesichorus clearly shows too that he is aware of its broader applications for *kitharôidia*.

What then does Heraclides mean when he says that the citharodes performed Homer? For a mid-fourth-century inhabitant of Athens such as Heraclides, "Homer" meant above all the *Iliad* and *Odyssey* as they were performed by rhapsodes at the Panathenaia.[138] We do in fact have literary evidence for the citharodic performance of episodes from these Homeric epics. Athenaeus preserves this intriguing testimony:

Τιμόμαχος δ' ἐν τοῖς Κυπριακοῖς Στήσανδρον λέγει τὸν Σάμιον ἐπὶ πλεῖον αὐξῆσαι τὴν τέχνην καὶ πρῶτον ἐν Δελφοῖς κιθαρῳδῆσαι τὰς καθ' Ὅμηρον μάχας, ἀρξάμενον ἀπὸ τῆς Ὀδυσσείας.

Timomachus in his *History of Cyprus* says that Stesander of Samos greatly augmented the *tekhnê* [of *kitharôidia*] and was the first at Delphi to perform citharodically the battle scenes in Homer, starting from the *Odyssey*.

Athenaeus 14.638a = Timomachus FGrH 754 F 1

Stesander is difficult to date with accuracy, but a date in the later sixth or early fifth century BCE is possible.[139] Timomachus, probably

---

[138] As Wilamowitz 1884:353 observed, "Um 500 [BCE] sind alle Gedichte von Homer; um 350 [BCE] sind von Homer im wesentlichen nur noch Ilias und Odyssee." Cf. West 1999b:372n23. For Aristotle, the poems of the Epic Cycle—he names the *Cypria* and the *Little Iliad*—were non-Homeric (*Poetics* 23–24.1459a37–b16).

[139] Cf. Barker 1984:300n208; Pavese 1972:247. It is tempting to connect Stesander's Homerizing *kitharôidia* to the Samian tyrant Polycrates, whose vigorous patronage of Homeric *rhapsôidia* played a key role in his imperially ambitious cultural politics, which included Delphi as well as Delos in its purview (evidenced by his "Delian-Pythian

writing in the earlier fourth century BCE, seems to imply that Homeric narrative had been sung by citharodes before Stesander, perhaps even at Delphi, and presumably at the Pythian *agônes* there; the Samian's innovation was to focus on citharodizing the most dramatic episodes from the tradition, the better to show off his cutting-edge *tekhnê*. (Although Timomachus mentions only the *Odyssey*, Stesander's singing of Homeric "battle scenes" certainly points to the *Iliad* as well.) It is worth noting a lyric hexameter in Alcman fr. 102 Calame = PMG 80 that resembles, yet differs slightly from *Odyssey* 12.47: καί ποκ' Ὀδυσσῆος ταλασίφρονος ὦατ' ἑταίρων | Κίρκα ἐπαλείψασα 'And once Circe anointing the ears of the companions of long-suffering Odysseus'. Alcman, who himself played the role of the *kitharistês*—the lines perhaps come from a *prooimion*—could be drawing on a tradition of "Homeric" *kitharôidia* that was known at Sparta through the *agôn* at the Carneia.[140]

This fragment suggests as well that citharodic *Odysseys* or, more likely, collections of citharodic Odyssean episodes were performed alongside rhapsodic versions, overlapping with them in some ways—the Samian Stesander, for example, would have been particularly intimate with the Homeric *rhapsôidia* that flourished in Ionian Greece—but differing in others, be they metrical and dialectal features, or, as we see in Alcman's verses, phraseology and narrative detail.[141] At the metrical level, we might expect citharodes to have been less consistently rigid in their deployment of the hexameter, to have sung some "pre-Homeric" melic cola alongside a majority of hexameters, the rhythmic flexibility determined by the expressiveness of the melodic lines.[142] It may be worth interpreting in this light the claim made in Athenaeus 14.632d that "because Homer set to music (*memelopoiêkenai*) all of his poetry" metrical anomalies persist in its transmission, specifically the substitution of shorts for longs in beginning, middle, and end of the hexameter

---

games" on Delos). See Burkert 1979:59–61; Aloni 1989. Apuleius *Florida* 15.6–12 describes a statue of a youthful citharode that was supposedly dedicated by Polycrates (*a Polycrate tyranno dicata*) in the temple of Hera on Samos. In Apuleius' time, the story went that the statue represented Bathyllus, one of Anacreon's beloveds. This identification is suspect, but the statue's Archaic antiquity may well have been real. If so, such a conspicuous dedication might reflect Polycrates' interest in *kitharôidia*.

[140] Cf. Wilamowitz 1903:87n2 and Fraenkel 1918:323 = 1964:204, who argues that Alcman "in der Tradition der lesbischen, 'terpandrischen' Kitharodie" at Sparta, sang epic episodes to the *kithara*. Alcman's treatment of the Sirens episode here recalls the evocation of the Sirens qua competitive chorus in his first *Partheneion*, PMGF 1.95–97.

[141] On the dynamic interplay between rhapsodic and citharodic production, cf. Bethe 1914–1927(II):378.

[142] Cf. Pavese 1998:64, who speaks of early citharodic verse as "heterometric 'ma non troppo'."

verse. By contrast, the hexameters of the Archaic elegiac poets, who "did not set their poems to melodies," are more metrically consistent than those of Homer. Rather than dismissing this testimony as "the desperate theory of some metrician or philologist," we might see it in it a recognition that melodized citharodic texts of Homer were known for taking certain musical liberties with the fixed schemata of the hexameter line.[143] Of course, such a view is anachronistically warped. It is not that citharodes were consciously "breaking the rules" of hexameter composition. Rather, their metrical freedom was a natural, organic function of their musical renderings of heroic narrative, distinct from the tightened constraints of rhapsodic recitative.

As far as we can tell, at the Archaic and Classical Pythian *mousikoi agônes*, *rhapsôidia* was not a competitive event. Delphi and Sparta were better known as centers of agonistic *kitharôidia* than *rhapsôidia*, so perhaps it is telling that a citharodic Homer is attached to these places. In Athens, however, it was the Ionian rhapsodes who exerted authority over the texts of the *Iliad* and *Odyssey*, an authority supposedly guaranteed to them by the Peisistratid tyrants in the latter half of the sixth century BCE.[144] It has been argued that, as a result of this state of affairs, citharodes would have been unlikely to perform "any part of the Homeric epics, since the *rhapsodic* performances of them were by then well established."[145] On this view, citharodes in Athens would, for instance, have cultivated the less proprietary, non-Homeric epic material from the Cycle. (And indeed there were citharodic settings of Cyclic narratives, as we will see in Section 9 below.) But, of course, the very opposite view could be taken, that the increasing popularity of the

---

[143] "Desperate theory": Herington 1985:180. Athenaeus or his source presumably had access to texts of Homer containing more such anomalous verses than do ours. Could some of these verses have been drawn from a citharodic performance tradition? For instance, a variant of *Iliad* 19.189, μιμνέτω αὖθι τέως ἐπειγόμενός περ Ἄρηος, analyzable as a hemiepes plus an enoplian colon, resembles exactly a line of Stesichorus that occurs in a longer sequence of lyric hexameters, αὐτίκα μοι θανάτου τέλος στυγεροῖο γένοιτο (PMGF 222b.213; cf. discussion in Steinrück 2005:484–485). Given Stesichorus' affiliation with the citharodic tradition, the resemblance is highly suggestive. Rather than viewing the variant as a vestigial trace of pre-Homeric melic *epê* that has been innocently preserved in the metrically normalized rhapsodic tradition, it might be better construed as a reflex of Homeric *kitharôidia* in the Classical period that has worked its way into written transmission.

[144] On the tyrants and the rhapsodes, see the indispensable studies of Aloni 1984, 1989, and 2006; cf. Davison 1955, Shapiro 1993.

[145] Herington 1985:20.

rhapsodic Homer would have encouraged citharodes to present their own competing versions of Iliadic and Odyssean narratives.[146]

In any case, we need not think that a rhapsodic monopoly on the performance of the Homeric epics in Athens came into being, either by custom or by official enforcement, with the Peisistratidai. As will be argued below, the tyrants probably did promote the citharodic performance of certain non-Homeric epic narratives, but we hear nothing about restrictions placed upon Panathenaic citharodes' choice of material, as we do for rhapsodes, who were supposedly compelled by the so-called Panathenaic Rule to recite only episodes from the *Iliad* and *Odyssey*, in fixed sequence.[147] The imposition of this rule, or at least the belief that once upon a time such a rule was imposed, indicates that rhapsodes were held to a higher calling at this festival, to compete yet also to collaborate in reproducing the texts of the two epics in their complete measure, practicing what Nagy has called a "communalization of repertoire."[148] Unencumbered by any such requirements, citharodes were presumably free to select scenes from these traditions, perhaps even ones adapted from the familiar rhapsodic texts themselves, to fit into their *nomoi*; Stesander's method of presenting only maximally sensationalistic battle scenes exemplifies this selective freedom. Such virtuoso settings of the material would obviously have offered an emotional, sensual, and spectacular *terpsis* that stood in contrast to the more affectively prosaic, yet cognitively satisfying sequenced renditions of the rhapsodes—the pleasures of the ear and eye versus the pleasures of the text, to put the distinction in reductive terms.

Attic vase painting offers some tentative clues to the citharodic performance of Homer in Athens, at least in the sixth century BCE. On a black-figured lekythos from around 580, now in Heidelberg, a musician wearing impressive garb, a long, red himation flowing over a decorated chiton, is depicted singing to a large instrument, ostensibly

---

[146] Thus Wilamowitz 1920:314.

[147] The Panathenaic Rule is attributed to the Peisistratid Hipparchus in "Plato" *Hipparchus* 228b–c; cf. Lycurgus *Against Leocrates* 102. Diogenes Laertius 1.57 attributes it to Solon. Definitive commentary in Nagy 1996:80–82 and 2002:9–16. For Nagy the rule is a fictional reflex, projected onto early lawgiver figures, of a traditional principle of equal distribution of Homeric poetry amongst Panathenaic rhapsodes. Compare my comments on the etymological fiction that the citharodic *nomos* was so called because of the official "rules" imposed upon its musical execution (Section 4 above). For more historicist views on the Panathenaic Rule, see Davison 1955, who proposed the term; Skafte Jensen 1980:145–149.

[148] Nagy 1996:82.

a tortoise-shell lyre, but which may be the painter's approximation of a *kithara*.[149] Indeed, the flashy dress suggests that the musician is a citharode rather than an amateur lyre player, one who would sing on some pre- or proto-Panathenaic performative occasion. He stands flanked by two large sirens. These sirens may have a purely symbolic function, signifying the enchanting appeal of the song. But might they also allude to the content of the song itself, the Sirens episode that would form part of our *Odyssey* 12, and which Alcman's lyric verse also treats?[150] It has been suggested, however, that the painting depicts a scene from the saga of the Argonauts, a life-or-death song contest between Orpheus and the Sirens, traces of which are to be found in the *Argonautica* of Apollonius of Rhodes.[151] We will return to this interpretation below.

An eye cup by Psiax, produced around 520 BCE, during the reign of the Peisistratidai, when Homeric rhapsodes had been introduced to the Panathenaic festival, might point toward Iliadic *kitharôidia*. It shows on one side a citharode in the midst of a performance, flanked on either side by rapt spectators. On the matching reverse side, a heroic warrior, wearing a horse-hair helmet, is shown collapsing to one knee in agony (Plates 7a and b). On the one hand, the paired images invite a valorizing comparison between the spectacular exertions of the citharode and those of the warrior—a virtual heroization of the musician, expressing the high esteem in which his *tekhnê* was held. On the other hand, and not exclusively, the pairing might reflect the content of the citharode's song. It has been argued that the warrior on this cup is meant to be none other than Hector, and that the singer's "theme is surely not just some run-of-the-mill combat scene, but the critical duel which seals the fate of Troy."[152]

---

[149] For the image, see Gropengiesser 1977:583, with discussion; Maas and Snyder 1989:50, fig. 14d. Maas and Snyder discuss the "unusual" aspects of the instrument, its large size and the knobs on its crossbar (p37); both are features of the *kithara*.

[150] Along with the Sirens, the Polyphemus episode is the only iconographical representation of the *Odyssey* before the middle of the sixth century BCE (see Snodgrass 1998:130). Timotheus composed a *nomos* called *Cyclops* (PMG 780–783). Could it have been his fresh take on a much longer-standing citharodic engagement with this narrative?

[151] Gropengiesser 1977:607–610.

[152] Schefold 1992:257. On a black-figured neck amphora by the Painter of Munich 1410 (ABV 319, 10), the obverse shows a citharode in performance, the reverse shows Ajax with the body of Achilles, perhaps the theme of the citharode's song. On an amphora by the Andokides Painter (Louvre G 1; c. 525 BCE), an image of a citharode playing atop a *bêma* is paired with a scene of Athena and Hermes watching two dueling warriors, one holding a Boeotian shield, the other a shield painted with a scorpion.

8. Rhapsodes Versus Citharodes

The relationship between the citharode and rhapsode was indeed far more complicated than Homerists and other scholars of Archaic poetry have recognized. The two were proximal others, treating in distinct fashions similar, even identical narrative subjects (Homer primarily, but also other epic traditions) and generic forms. It is likely that this close relationship resulted in a professional rivalry between them—given their shared roots in Dark Age bardic performance, a sibling rivalry. For, although they were not in direct competition at the *agônes*, they did compete extra-agonistically for cultural prestige, not to mention for popular attention and economic "market share" at agonistic festivals where both performed, in particular at the Great Panathenaia, which by the end of the fifth century BCE had become the most important stage in all of Greece for both *rhapsôidia* and *kitharôidia*.[153] Although rhapsodes in a sense gained leverage in Athens by taking control of the textualization of the prestigious Homeric epics, the iconographical evidence suggests that *kitharôidia* generated far more popular enthusiasm than *rhapsôidia*. We have over 90 depictions of citharodes (and citharists) on Attic vases from the middle of the sixth century to the end of the fifth; over the same period, we have only a handful of images of rhapsodes.[154] It may be that "with no fancy costume or distinctive

---

Cf. Webster 1972:161. This scene, like the first, is probably from the Cycle. See discussion below.

[153] It would be enlightening to know the relative prize amounts awarded to citharodes and rhapsodes in Athens. Unfortunately, the fourth-century BCE inscription IG II^2 2311 recording prize amounts for Panathenaic victors does not include prizes for rhapsodes (the prize for the winning citharode is the highest of the categories listed). Some have speculated that rhapsodic prizes were recorded in a now-missing top piece of the inscription (lines 1–3); if so, the initial placement would probably reflect that their prestige and value were greater than those of the citharodes. But we cannot be at all sure of this (cf. Shear 2003:91; Davison 1958:37, who is doubtful). We may note that at the Artemisia in Euboea first prize in *rhapsôidia* was only 120 drachmas, versus 200 in *kitharôidia* (IG XII ix 189). Plato *Ion* 530d suggests that winning Panathenaic rhapsodes received a golden crown, perhaps equal in value to the crown won by citharodes, but, curiously, Ion is made to say that he "deserves to be crowned with a gold crown by the Homeridai." This is probably meant figuratively—I am so talented a rhapsode that the Homeridai themselves would give me a golden crown—but could he mean that representatives of the Homeridai acted as judges at the Panathenaia, and perhaps even as underwriters of the rhapsodic contest? This could explain the absence of civically funded prizes for rhapsodes in IG II^2 2311. Cf. Allen 1907:135 on the *Ion* passage: "The Sons of Homer then have a position which authorises them to reward persons who honour their parent. They are not private individuals."

[154] Shapiro 1993 discusses the paucity of representations. Depictions of citharodes also far outnumber those of auletes and aulodes. See Vos 1986.

instrument, the rhapsodes tended not to catch the artist's eye."[155] But the artist's eye nevertheless focalized the enthusiasms and desires of the spectators at the *agônes*. The citharode was the showman par excellence, and the numerous depictions demonstrate how deeply audiences appreciated and wanted to commemorate that showmanship. He made a more compelling spectacle of himself than the rhapsode did, or could; his performance of text and music was more embellished, sensationalistic, visually and acoustically enchanting.[156]

Plato's Ion evokes a scene of rhapsodic performance at the Panathenaia that suggests the way a talented and dramatic rhapsode could keep a mass audience spellbound in pleasurable suspense (*Ion* 535e). But Ion is of course touting the aesthetic and psychagogic force of his chosen medium, and we should leave some room for exaggeration when he describes the violent emotional transport he creates in his audience. It is also conceivable that by Ion's time, the later fifth century BCE, rhapsodes had begun to imitate not only the histrionic delivery of tragic actors (532d), but also the grandiose self-presentation of the citharodes, who themselves were increasingly theatricalizing their acts at this time. Plato emphasizes the brilliant *skeuê* worn by Ion, and his golden crown (530b, 535d). Such rich costume is at odds with the relatively unadorned garb worn by rhapsodes in Archaic and early Classical depictions, and accords more with the showy costume of the citharode.[157] Attempts to dress up *rhapsôidia* had limited effect in making it as sensationally compelling as *kitharôidia*, however. At

---

[155] Shapiro 1992:73.

[156] Burkert 1987:211–212 has posited an analogous rivalry between "old epic singers" and the choral lyric epic of Stesichorus, which, possessing "a more emotional, even larmoyant appeal" with its music and dance components, "swept the lonely singer from the marketplace." In turn, Burkert reasons, rhapsodes rose to prominence at the *agônes* by exploiting the "power of the spoken word," the pleasures of narratives cohesively authored by Homer. Stesichorean "oratorium" was in turn eclipsed. There is a pleasingly Hegelian logic to this elegant arrangement, but it is flawed in its reductive diachronism and neglect of the historical role of the citharodes. It was the citharode and the rhapsode together who put the old *phorminx*-playing *aoidos* out of business (if we wish to put it that way; cf. the formulation of West 1981:124), and who evolved in synchrony. As was argued above, Stesichorus represents a choral reception of an already developed citharodic tradition of mythic-epic narrative. But that reception was too specialized and too late a phenomenon—even if it did, as seems likely, have the Panhellenic exposure Burkert would confer upon it—to have inspired the rhapsodic invention of Homer. Rhapsodes may have tightened their hold on a fixed version of "Homer," however, in response to the ongoing professional threat posed by the musical charms of the citharodes, and perhaps to a lesser degree those of epic choral lyric as well.

[157] Cf. Herington 1985:14.

Plato *Laws* 658d the Athenian Stranger speculates that of all the practitioners of agonistic entertainments a rhapsode reciting the *Iliad* and
Odyssey and Hesiodic excerpts would most appeal to conservative older
men (*gerontes*) such as the Stranger and his interlocutors. This geriatric demographic suggests that *rhapsôidia*, contrary to the claims of
Ion, was not the most exciting display of show business on offer at
the *agônes*.

If we look closely, oblique expressions of a rivalry between the
two media reveal themselves. Attempts to connect Terpander genea-
logically to Homer—essentially making him a Homerid—could simply
reflect the fact that citharodes were singing Homeric texts, but they
could as well represent the promotion of a citharodic Homer by the
citharodes in their biographical manipulations of Terpander (*Suda* s.v.
Τέρπανδρος). A passage from Plato's *Ion* seems to capture something
of the rhapsodic counter-rhetoric to such tendentious genealogizing
(533b–c). Socrates, in conversation with Ion, imagines that practitioners of *aulos* playing, *kithara* playing, *kitharôidia*, or *rhapsôidia* would be
able to "provide explanations" (*exêgeisthai*) about—presumably about
the *lives* of—model exponents of these media, Olympus, Thamyris,
Orpheus, or "Phemius the Ithacan rhapsode."[158] Socrates flatteringly
implies that, just as Ion, as a competent rhapsode, would be able to
discourse knowledgeably on Phemius, so another competent rhapsode would be able to speak authoritatively on Ion. This suggests that
for a rhapsode such as Ion, the singer Phemius (and we may presume
Demodocus as well) was figured as a model rhapsode; rhapsodes thus
retrojected their own practice into the Homeric world they represented in performance. So Homer himself is imagined as an agonistic
rhapsode in the *Contest between Homer and Hesiod* (cf. Hesiod fr. 357
M-W) and in the *Lives*.

By contrast, cithardoic lore, as refracted in the musical historical
scholarship of the fourth century BCE, claimed Phemius and Demodocus
as proto-citharodes. Both are included in Heraclides' catalogue of early
citharodes ("Plutarch" *On Music* 3.1132b). According to Demetrius of
Phalerum, Demodocus, who is made a native of Laconia, the heartland
of early *kitharôidia* in continental Greece, was the winning competitor
at the early Pythian cithardoic *agôn*, where an impressed Agamemnon
engaged him to be his court singer.[159] Demetrius' scenario, a tendentious

---

[158] See Martin 2001:24 on this passage.

[159] Fr. 144 Fortenbaugh and Schütrumpf = scholia *ad Odyssey* 3.267. Demetrius identifies Demodocus as the unnamed *aoidos* appointed by Agamemnon to watch over
Clytemnestra, who is referred to at *Odyssey* 3.267. After his exile by Aegisthus,

imposition of historical citharodic culture onto the mythical past, builds on earlier antiquarian research on citharodic history, which in turn, I suspect, registered the Homerizing propaganda of the citharodes themselves.[160] Demetrius was clearly sympathetic to the practice of a citharodic Homer, which represented the conjunction of conservative cultural and political ideals dear to him: Homer, the ultimate in poetic prestige, and *kitharôidia*, long recognized for its ability to bring societies to good order (as Laconian Demodocus was to keep order in an Agamemnon-less Mycenae, and as Terpander later brought harmony to unstable Sparta). There was a nostalgic tone to his research, as there was to other Academic and Peripatetic scholarship on *arkhaia mousikê* (cf. "Plutarch" *On Music* 3.1131f). In his own time, the Classical practice of singing Homer to the *kithara* had largely disappeared from Athens, having been overtaken by the performance of new, dramatically loaded nomic texts, some dealing with Homeric episodes, but not confined by epic meter, diction, or tone, which were introduced a century earlier by Timotheus.

However, in his practical capacity as ruler of Athens, Demetrius is said to have "introduced into the theaters" a specialized class of performers, the Homeristai, who "set the poems of Homer to music" (ἐμελῴδουν τὰ τοῦ Ὁμήρου).[161] The relation of the Homeristai—if that is what Demetrius called them—to the Panathenaic rhapsodes is not entirely clear, nor do they seem to have been citharodes. Some kind of dramatized setting of Homer, poised in between the narratival sensibility of *rhapsôidia* and the musical sensation of *kitharôidia*, was perhaps what these Homeristai presented in the *theatra*.[162] But we might wonder

---

Demodocus would have found his way to Scheria and the court of Alcinous. Demetrius makes Demodocus the pupil of one Automedes of Mycenae, who composed *epê* about "the battle of Amphitryon against the Teleboans and between Cithaeron and Helicon." Automedes himself was student of Perimedes of Argos, who taught also Licymnius of Bouprasion, Sinis the Dorian, Pharidas of Laconia, and Probolus the Spartan. Demetrius has uncovered a whole secret history of pre-Homeric Peloponnesian *kitharôidia*; the focus on Sparta and Laconia reflects Demetrius' interest in the political prestige enjoyed by the art there. Cf. Wilson 2004:269–271. Licymnius of Bouprasion is an intriguing figure. Nestor speaks of competing in games in Bouprasion for the dead king of the Elians, against whom he had waged war (*Iliad* 23.629–631; 11.669–761). Was Licymnius perhaps an *aoidos* character embedded in Pylian heroic tradition, unearthed and transformed into an agonistic citharode by Demetrius?

[160] See Gostoli 1986:105–107 on the relevant music scholarship available to Demetrius.

[161] Eustathius *Commentary on the Iliad* 14.482 van der Valk; cf. Athenaeus 14.620b (= frs. 55A and B in Fortenbaugh and Schütrumpf).

[162] Wilson 2004:271–272 imagines rhapsodes being compelled by Demetrius to sing Homer to the "noble lyre." Perhaps, but I would imagine the lyre (or *kithara*) to be

whether this promotion of a melodized Homer, clearly an attempt by Demetrius to sell his conservative, antiquarian cultural politics to audiences devoted to theatrical entertainments, also entailed a related revival of citharodic settings of the *Iliad* and *Odyssey* at the Panathenaia, at least for the ten years in which Demetrius held power (317–307 BCE).

The most striking reflex of citharodic-rhapsodic antagonism may be hiding in plain sight, embedded in the (rhapsodic) *Iliad* itself. I refer to the cameo of Thamyris that has made its way into the Messenian section of the Catalogue of Ships, in a passage we have already had occasion to consider (*Iliad* 2.594–600). Although Homeric poetry acknowledged the status of the *aoidos* as a wandering professional *dêmioergos* 'worker for the community', "summoned all over the boundless earth" (*Odyssey* 17.382–385), it is Thamyris alone who appears as a musical free agent, moving from one local engagement, as retainer to the house of King Eurytus in Oechalia, to another. As the historicizing research of Demetrius imagines Demodocus to be a Panhellenically competitive Pythian *kitharôidos* in between his royal appointments, so Thamyris in his itineracy is drawn in the *Iliad* as a citharodic *agônistês*, his contest with the Muses—alluded to, but not actually described— a prototype of institutionalized *mousikoi agônes* such as those of the Pythia.[163] According to local Delphian lore, Thamyris was in fact a winning competitor at one of the earliest Pythian citharodic *agônes* (Pausanias 10.7.2). The description in lines 599–600 of Thamyris' musical art suggests a gloss on *kitharôidia*: the Muses "took from him his wondrous singing (*aoidê*), and made him forget his *kithara* playing (*kitharistus*)."[164] The word *kitharistus* seems marked. Used only here in early Greek poetry, it is, according to the scholia vetera *ad loc.*, an Aeolic formation (ὁ σχηματισμὸς τῆς λέξεως Αἰολικός); as such, it might constitute a deliberate dialectal allusion to the Aeolic origins of *kitharôidia*. Significantly, the word is used only once elsewhere, by the learned Hellenistic poet Phanocles (fr. 1.21 Powell), to describe the famed *kithara* playing on Lesbos, the cradle of competitive *kitharôidia*,

---

played by accompanists rather than by the performers themselves, or else we would expect our sources to call the Homeristai citharodes. Nagy 1996:156–190 sees a stronger continuity between the Homeristai and the rhapsodic Homeridai and the Panathenaic rhapsodic tradition, arguing, however, that by the Imperial period, the Homeristai had developed a full-blown mimetic, spectacular approach to Homeric performance. Cf. Collins 2001:153–155, 2004:207–213.

[163] Cf. Ford 1992:97 for the Thamyris tale's offering a "negative *aition* for the 'normal' epic competitions of the eighth century."

[164] Compare the hendiadys of Hesiod *Theogony* 95: ἄνδρες ἀοιδοὶ καὶ κιθαρισταί 'singer men and *kithara* players'. Cf. n14 above.

that was the legacy of another Thracian proto-citharode, Orpheus. It is significant too, of course, that Thamyris is working and traveling in Aeolic Thessaly (Oechalia is located in Thessaly at *Iliad* 2.730).

Other scholars have noted the metapoetic implications of the Thamyris narrative, arguing that Thamyris stands for rival, pre-Homeric poetic traditions, whose instability and ultimate failure vis-à-vis the Iliadic tradition are reflected in the Thracian's hubris and grim fate.[165] But the narrative serves too as a metaperformative critique, an undercutting of the celebrated status of agonistic citharodes by the rhapsodes who stood behind the textualization of the *Iliad*, and a de facto affirmation of the superiority of their own *tekhnê*.[166] After his encounter with the Muses, the Panhellenic aspirations of itinerant Thamyris are deflated, as are his musical pretensions, and this divinely wrought diminution of his confidence and abilities subordinates him (and the citharodes he prefigures) to the rhapsode who narrates his fate. After all, the Catalogue of Ships into which the Thamyris tale is subsumed stands as a bravura display of the rhapsode's mastery of Panhellenic poetic traditions, yet one that is introduced by an elaborately humble and pious invocation of the Muses, who authorize its performance (2.484–486: "Tell me now, Muses who have dwellings on Olympus—for you are goddesses and are at hand and you know everything, whereas we hear only tell of things and know nothing—who were the rulers of the Danaans and their lords"). At the same time, the *Iliad* passage, by stripping Thamyris of his singing and his *kithara* playing, that is, of his *kitharôidia*, implicitly renders him ... a rhapsode. It is as if the Muses, in correcting the musical excesses of the citharode,

---

[165] For Ford 1992:97, Thamyris "stands for preceding poets, and his contest shows that mere temporal earliness is not enough to guarantee a strong transmission of song if the Muses are not honored." Martin 1989:229–230 sees in Thamyris' journeying from Oechalia an allusion to the *Sack of Oechalia*, an older epic rival to the *Iliad*: "When Homer says that a poet returning from Oikhalia was deprived of his art, he can hardly be more explicit: this is a claim that the Herakles tradition is faulty, that it suffered a break in historical transmission from the event itself. By contrast, Homer in Book 2 makes it clear that his narrative has a continuity with the past which is guaranteed by Homer's own contact with the Muses (2.484–86)" (230). Cf. Martin 2001:30.

[166] Wilson 2009 (cf. n51 above) comes to a somewhat similar conclusion. I would approach, however, the representations of the Thamyris myth as determined not by individually abstracted generic forces, "a clash between two musical traditions that expressed themselves ultimately in different generic performance-types of hexameter epic and kitharodic lyric" (p58), but as rhetorical expressions of the professional rivalry, with its full course of institutional and practical causes and effects, between the practitioners of those performance-types, rhapsodes and citharodes.

have revealed *rhapsôidia* to be the natural state of epic performance, the mode most genuinely suited to the transmission of heroic *kleos*.

There are, however, indications of a corresponding citharodic recuperation of Thamyris, a promotion of his (ethically transcendent) status as an outstanding exemplar of the art.[167] As was discussed above, in the citharodic lore attached to the Pythian Games (where rhapsodes did not compete), Thamyris, as local culture hero (the son of Philammon), was remembered not for his infamous defeat, but for his agonistic success. It was conceivably in friendly citharodic traditions too that Thamyris was made the deviser of foundational musical resources for *kitharôidia*, the *Orthios nomos* and the Dorian *harmonia*.[168] Heraclides of Pontus, in the discussion of early *kitharôidia* in his *Collection of [Famous] Musicians* (fr. 157 Wehrli = "Plutarch" *On Music* 1132b), which draws on encomiastic citharodic lore preserved in the Sicyonian *anagraphê*, does not hesitate to rank the Thracian among the most celebrated of legendary citharodes, even to assert his superiority over them, saying that Thamyris "sang with better voice and more melodiously than anyone else in those days." And while Heraclides acknowledges the story that Thamyris challenged the Muses to an *agôn*, he notably distances himself from it, and says nothing of the outcome; the story is "told by the poets" (κατὰ τοὺς ποιητάς).[169] We might detect some ambivalence too in his mentioning that "Thamyris is recorded (*historeitai*) to have composed a *War of the Titans against the Gods*." It is possible that Heraclides detected a critical tendentiousness in the attribution of the "appropriately early and hubristic theme, the Titanomachy" to the supposedly hubristic citharode, and so treated it with some circumspection.[170] Alternatively, however, the attribution may not be a complete fiction. Titanomachy narratives may have circulated under the name of Thamyris, supplying the texts for actual citharodic *humnoi* or *nomoi*.

---

[167] For the cultic-ritual recuperation of the Thamyris myth at Thespiae, see Section 3 above. For citharists' adoption of the "mute" Thamyris as mythical exemplar, see Cillo 1993:216, 241; Wilson 2009:77–78. Plato *Ion* 533b–c refers to citharists' providing exegetical accounts of Thamyris.

[168] The attribution of the *Orthios nomos* appears in a gloss in the *Lexis Herodotou* A *ad* Herodotus 1.24 (Latte and Erbse 1965:197). Dorian *harmonia*: Pliny *Natural History* 7.207; Clement *Stromateis* 1.16.76; Eustathius *Commentary on the Iliad* 297.38 van der Valk (*ad* 2.594). See discussion in Wilson 2009:58n48.

[169] There may have been active attempts to valorize Thamyris' challenge to the Muses, refuting its stigma of hubris: *Suda* s.v. Θάμυρις μαίνεται records a proverb, "Thamyris is mad," which is used of someone who appears to act irrationally, yet in reality is acting *kata sunesin* 'with full understanding'.

[170] Quotation from Ford 1992:96n9.

Relevant is the claim made in *Suda* s.v. Θάμυρις that he composed a *Theologia* (that is, a *Theogony*) of 3,000 lines in length. A Titanomachy could certainly have fit into the frame of this theogonic narrative. Such "Hesiodic" material likely made up a respectable portion of the citharodic repertoire. From a more skeptical point of view, however, this *Theologia* may be no more than a late, written "sacred text" foisted on Thamyris after he had been adopted as founder of a mystery cult, perhaps that at Andania in Messenia. Similar religious pseudepigrapha were attributed in the late Classical period and after to other mythical citharodes attached to telestic cults, Orpheus and Musaeus.[171]

Finally, we may note the conspicuous trend of "Thracian chic" in the outfitting of competitive citharodes and citharists during the second half of the fifth century in Athens, as illustrated by the vase paintings of the time.[172] Thamyris was as likely to be the model for such role-playing as the other famous Thracian singers, Orpheus or Musaeus. The infamy attached to Thamyris clearly did not dissuade agonistic musicians from emulating his exotic glamour—only enhanced by his treatment in Athenian dramatic and dithyrambic productions of the fifth century—as well as his outsized confidence.

9. Terpander and "Other Poets"

The poetic content of the early *nomoi* was by no means limited to episodes drawn from Iliadic and Odyssean traditions. Heraclides says that Terpander sang his own *epê* as well as Homer's in the *agônes*. "Plutarch" *On Music* 6.1133c says that citharodes used to sing "the poetry of Homer and others." Neither the content of these Terpandrean *epê* nor the identity of these "other" poets is made explicit in our

---

[171] For Thamyris at Andania, see n323 below. Pseudepigrapha: West 1983.

[172] And the related iconographical rendering of Thamyris as a concert citharode. See Cillo 1993:215 and discussion in my Part I.6.iii. Cillo argues that the "giovane e bel Trace" provided an apposite model for younger competitors at the Panathenaia, as it is typically youthful musicians who are depicted with the Thracian or Thamyris *kithara* (238); cf. Maas and Snyder 1989:146. The bulk of these may be boy or young adult citharists, appropriately so, in light of traditions that made Thamyris a "voiceless" citharist (see n51 above). The bell krater by Polion of three men costumed as satyrs playing Thamyris *kitharai* and labeled "Singers at the Panathenaia" (New York 25.78.66) suggests to me, however, that the instrument (and its namesake) had broader appeal among the *agônistai* than the preserved iconography indicates. Maas and Snyder *loc cit.* note two representations of older players, who may be citharodes. Wilson 2009:76–77 argues that his boldness made Thamyris an icon for the iconoclastic New Musicians.

sources.[173] We can, however, make some reasonable guesses about the range of mythopoetic traditions beyond the Homeric *Iliad* and *Odyssey* that informed the nomic texts presented to audiences by the Archaic and Classical citharodes.

i. Lesbian lyric epic and the Epic Cycle

It has usually been the assumption, implicit or explicit, that rhapsodes were solely responsible for creating and transmitting the poems of the Epic Cycle.[174] Yet it makes little sense not to assume that citharodes too, from an even earlier point in some cases than the rhapsodes, played a key role in the production and performance of a range of Cyclic narratives, although these need not have mapped onto the neat segmentations of the Cycle as it is summarized in Proclus' *Chrestomathia*.[175] There can be general agreement about the existence, from at least the tenth century BCE, of a pre-Ionian (and pre-rhapsodic) Aeolic epic tradition located on and around Lesbos that treated myths relating to the Trojan War, myths that were the cultural patrimony of the Boeotian and Thessalian settlers in the region. The proximity of Lesbos and neighboring Aeolic settlements to the Troad would obviously have encouraged their cultivation of this body of myths. The old Aeolic phase evident in Homeric diction, which is marked by specifically Lesbian dialectal forms, attests to the foundational status of this tradition in the evolutionary history of Trojan epic.[176] What has been little recognized, however, is that the famed citharodes of Lesbos, the "Lesbian Singers" who followed the lead of Terpander, must have been primary inheritors and elaborators of their native heroic oral poetry. They would have expanded the simple music of its old bardic performance in accord with the widened

---

[173] Our sources, all post-fifth-century, were themselves probably only vaguely aware of the full extent of the early citharodes' poetic repertoire, as the practice of nomic composition had by their time changed from the old Terpandrean epic to the newer Timothean dramatic style. One would like to know whether Classical citharodes actively attributed non-Homeric poetic material to Terpander, or whether Heraclides' claim that Terpander set his own *epê* to music is merely his own catch-all way of describing non-Homeric, "other" citharodic poetry.

[174] See now Burgess 2004, with previous bibliography.

[175] For the synthetic reductiveness of late accounts of the Cycle, see Burgess 2001:22–35; cf. Dué 2002:27, on the fluidity and multiformity of the oral Archaic Cycle, and Holmberg 1998.

[176] See West 1973:191, 2002b. Aloni 1986 and Dué 2002:59–60 consider possible refractions of the Lesbian tradition in the *Iliad*. For a review of scholarship on the Aeolic phase, with a view to both Homer and Lesbian *kitharôidia*, see now Cassio 2005:13–19; cf. Bowie 1981:49–60

harmonic and melic scope of the new heptatonic *kithara*, while keeping its subject matter relatively intact. This inheritance, then, would have yielded sophisticated citharodic treatments of episodes that fell within the parameters of what would become the *Iliad*, and of ante- and post-Iliadic episodes as well. Yet scholars have overlooked the citharodic reception of the Lesbian epic tradition; it is as if the epic patrimony of Aeolic Lesbos, passing over the island's native singers, went directly to the Ionian rhapsodes.

Thus, in a recent study of the reception of heroic epic, Iliadic and Cyclic, by Sappho and Alcaeus, Martin West mentions neither Terpander nor the citharodes. The Lesbian poets, he asserts, used "Ionic models, representing an Ionian tradition," and these were what their audiences knew as well: "The implication is that rhapsodes were performing regularly at public or private gatherings on Lesbos."[177] There can be no doubt that by the end of the seventh century BCE itinerant Ionian rhapsodes would have established a firm "footprint" in Lesbian performance culture, and that Sappho and Alcaeus were familiar with their renditions of epic material. But what about the local pride of Lesbos, the *kitharôidoi*? West does argue that a "popular tradition of some kind" was perpetuated by "epic singers" on Lesbos even as *rhapsôidia* was beginning to define the form and content of Trojan epic.[178] Although not identified as such by West, these popular performers would have been above all the native-born citharodes, who were by Sappho's time making their name Panhellenically as well, as Sappho fr. 106 directly attests. West adduces a relevant morphological detail in the poetic dialect of the Lesbian *melopoioi* as evidence of their familiarity with this epichoric tradition:

> [My observation] concerns the dialect forms of Priam's name that Sappho and Alcaeus use, Πέρραμος [Alcaeus fr. 42.2] and Πέραμος [Sappho fr. 44.16]. Πέρραμος shows a regular Lesbian development from Πρίαμος, while Πέραμος is a metrical accommodation that presumably originated within a Lesbian hexameter tradition: in any formulae involving Priam's name the first syllable had to be kept short. Now, where did Sappho

---

[177] West 2002b:217–218.

[178] West 2002b:218, following in part Liberman 1999:xiv. Liberman posits that Ionian epic held a certain sociocultural cachet that Lesbian aristocrats such as Alcaeus and Sappho would have prized above any ("lower status," West) local tradition. But I would note here that Sappho fr. 106 shows that Sappho, at least, held the Lesbian Singers in high regard.

and Alcaeus hear these forms, if the Lesbian line of tradition about the Trojan War had completely petered out and given way to the Ionian tradition?[179]

West's answer to the last question is that Sappho and Alcaeus heard these forms from "epic singers." I would specify that they heard them sung at concerts or *agônes* of citharodes, on the same festival occasions on which rhapsodes too might have presented their accounts of Trojan myth. The interactions between the performance traditions of rhapsodes and citharodes, both rivalrous and emulative, afforded by such occasions would be the most logical background against which to understand the introduction of the Πέραμος form: the citharodes were gradually bringing their older lyric cola, to which Πέρραμος was suited, in line with the hexametrical rhythmicization of the increasingly standardized rhapsodic treatment of Trojan epic.[180] (We should recall that Sappho's praise of the "outstanding Lesbian Singer" in fr. 106 is itself expressed in a hexameter line.) It is important to recognize, however, that such formal and linguistic accommodation by citharodes of *rhapsôidia* does not signal their own obsolescence; their creative, musical engagement with rhapsodic practice would, as we have seen, continue until the end of the fifth century BCE, with no dimming of their cultural relevance and popularity.

Sappho was clearly attuned to both media. Significantly, she uses the Πέραμος form in fr. 44, The Wedding of Hector and Andromache, her most explicitly "epic" poem in content, narrative style, and form. It is sung in stichic, dactylically expanded glyconics (× × – ◡ ◡ – ◡ ◡ – ◡ ◡ – ◡ –), the Aeolic meter that "most resembles the dactylic hexameter in its effect."[181] This poem has been viewed by many not only as an indication of Sappho's familiarity with Ionian hexameter poetry, but, more remarkably, as an expression of her reception of a living Lesbian-Aeolic epic tradition. Again, however, it is a properly citha-

---

[179] Cf. West 1973:191.

[180] Bowie 1981:10–14 singles out Old Smyrna, an Aeolic city close to Lesbos that fell to Ionians at the end of the eighth century BCE, as a crucial site of interaction between Aeolic and Ionian traditions. Our earliest representation of a seven-stringed *kithara* is on a sherd from Old Smyrna (Maas and Snyder 1989:42, fig. 1), which points to the early flourishing of citharodic culture there. For Lesbos itself, we might imagine that the federated sanctuary of Messon (modern-day Mesa) was the site of Pan-Lesbian festival *mousikoi agônes* at which Sappho and Alcaeus could hear rhapsodes and citharodes performing side by side. See Nagy 1993; Dué 2002:60. Cf. Cassio 2005:19 for epic-lyric traffic on Lesbos.

[181] West 1973:191. Cf. Nagy 1974:118–139.

rodic manifestation of that tradition that Sappho engages.[182] Indeed, in the closing lines of the poem, which describe a song-within-a-song, a paeanic-cum-hymeneal choral performance by the men of Troy, there are potential allusions to the citharodic medium Sappho is emulating:

πάντες δ' ἄνδρες ἐπήρατον ἴαχον ὄρθιον
Πάον' ὀνκαλέοντες ἐκάβολον εὐλύραν,
ὕμνην δ' Ἔκτορα κ'Ανδρομάχαν θεοεικέλο[ις.

And all the men sang out a lovely high-pitched melody (ὄρθιον), calling on Paon [Apollo] the far-shooter, the one skilled at the lyre [or, the one with a fine lyre], and they celebrated in song Hector and Andromache the godlike.

Sappho fr. 44.32–34

While ὄρθιον could be taken adverbially ("at high pitch"), it is more likely an adjective with an unstated object noun such as *melos*, or even *nomos* 'tune, melody' ("a high-pitched melody"; cf. Aristophanes *Acharnians* 16). Either way, it is arguable that ὄρθιον comes loaded with an anachronistic reference to the citharodic *Orthios nomos*, which was supposedly devised by Terpander and cultivated by citharodes of the Lesbian line such as Arion of Methymna (Herodotus 1.24.5), a contemporary of Sappho. The reference would be anachronistic inasmuch as Sappho would be cannily mingling the modes of the mythical choral performance with the "modern" solo songs to the *kithara* that she had heard.[183] This argument assumes that the technical-generic meaning of *nomos* was already known in the seventh century BCE, at least on Lesbos, but, given that the island was a hotbed of Archaic citharodic culture, it seems reasonable that the Terpandrean *Orthios nomos* would have been a familiar entity there from an early point. The Trojans' invocation of Apollo may contain two further generic allusions. First, while Apollo's epithet ἐκάβολος 'far-shooter' is common enough, it is notable that Apollo is invoked with the variant form ἑκατηβόλος in the Terpandrean *prooimion* that was traditionally associated with the *Orthios nomos*, fr. 2

---

[182] A similar conclusion might be reached about the *humnoi* of Alcaeus and Sappho. West 2002b:217 observes that the "parallelisms are such that we must at least say that the melic and the hexameter hymns [the *Homeric Hymns*] stand in a common tradition." But rather than conjecture scenarios of one form's exclusive influence on the other, we should factor in the mediating role of the citharodic *humnos*, which served as common model to both rhapsodes and the Lesbian *melopoioi*.

[183] And perhaps acknowledging the originally choral matrix of the latter. Lesbos, like Delphi, had a famed tradition of paean singing, as Archilochus fr. 121W indicates.

Gostoli = PMG 697 (fr. 1).[184] Second, there is the epithet εὐλύρας 'skilled at the lyre' or 'with fine lyre', which is purely melic; it will not fit into Homeric hexameter, but we do not find the metrically suitable variant εὔλυρος in Homer, either. Could Sappho have borrowed the word from the traditional diction of (pre-rhapsodic) citharodes, for whom it served to figure the god as a model citharode?[185]

Of course, it should not be assumed that fr. 44 is an exact facsimile of Lesbian citharodic epic. Sappho is creatively adapting this expansive, virtuosic, public mode to her smaller-scale, more intimate, lyric performative context and style. There is a good chance that fr. 44 was composed for performance at a wedding, an event poised between the public and the private.[186] The stichic format suggests a monodic rather than choral delivery. The accompanying instrument would probably have been the *khelus*-lyre or the *barbitos* rather than the concert *kithara* (although one cannot rule out the *aulos*, which is mentioned in the narrative at 44.24). A song such as fr. 44 was thus *virtually*, not practically citharodic.[187] But the pre-Iliadic subject, focused on heroic

---

[184] On the Ionic dialect of the proemial fragment, see n30 and n137.

[185] The epithet is attached to Apollo in his specifically citharodic aspect in melic passages in Euripides *Alcestis* 570 and Aristophanes *Women at the Thesmophoria* 969; cf. Limenius *Paean* line 4, p149 Powell.

[186] Despite the (to us) questionable auspiciousness of the mythic subject. See Lardinois 2001:79–80, with previous bibliography in 80n21.

[187] Although Sappho is most often depicted with the amateur's *barbitos* in Attic iconography, which reflects the primarily elite, sympotic contexts in which her songs were reperformed in Athens, she may occasionally have been portrayed with a *kithara* in later-sixth-century BCE imagery. See Yatromanolakis 2001:161n16. It is possible, however, that "quasi-citharodic" poems such as fr. 44 prompted the assimilation of Sappho to the image of the concert citharode. Although it is very late, it is worth noting too a passage in Himerius *Oration* 9, in which the orator imagines that Sappho "went to the bridal chamber after the *agônes*" (εἰσῆλθε μετὰ τοὺς ἀγῶνας εἰς θάλαμον). As Nagy 2007a:252 argues, "[T]he reference to the *agônes* 'contests' in which she supposedly competes seems to be a playful anachronistic allusion to the monodic competitions of *kithara*-singers at the festival of the Panathenaia. It is as if Sappho herself were a monodic singer engaged in such public competitions." Himerius' intriguing collocation of Sapphic hymeneal poetry and citharodic *agônes* could be a distant echo of a much earlier mentality of reception surrounding fr. 44 and similar poems, in which Sappho's identity as a wedding singer is implicitly conflated with her virtual citharodic identity. It is significant that some of Sappho's wedding poems seem to have been partly composed in hexameters, e.g. frs. 105 and 106, with its reference to the Lesbian citharodes (cf. Part III.11n174). Could these fragments perhaps come from solo lyric *prooimia* to epithalamic choral songs? If so, Sappho's reference to citharodes in fr. 106 would conceivably have underlined the quasi-citharodic nature of the performance of the proemial lyric dactyls. (Perhaps the dactylically cast fr. 44 was also performed as a *prooimion* to an epithalamic choral song.) An important point, however, should be made. It seems unlikely to me that Sappho's songs would have been routinely performed by Archaic and Classical citharodes at

adventures in and around Lesbos and the Aeolic Troad—Hector escorts Andromache to Troy from her native city of Aeolic Thebe (44.6), on the west coast of the Troad—is of a type that Lesbian citharodes might also have treated, perhaps even in their renditions of the *Orthios nomos*.[188] It has been convincingly argued that Thessalian Achilles loomed large in Aeolic epic, his experiences in the lead-up to and during the early years of the Trojan War the subject of multiple narrative traditions.[189]

In view of the probable citharodic reception of those epic traditions, we might note the significance of the *phorminx* that Achilles is playing when the ambassadors dispatched by Agamemnon come to persuade him to return to battle:

> τὸν δ᾽ εὗρον φρένα τερπόμενον φόρμιγγι λιγείῃ
> καλῇ δαιδαλέῃ, ἐπὶ δ᾽ ἀργύρεον ζυγὸν ἦεν,
> τὴν ἄρετ᾽ ἐξ ἐνάρων πόλιν Ἠετίωνος ὀλέσσας·
> τῇ ὅ γε θυμὸν ἔτερπεν, ἄειδε δ᾽ ἄρα κλέα ἀνδρῶν.

And they [the embassy] found him delighting his heart with
    a clear-sounding *phorminx*,
beautiful and cunningly wrought, and there was a silver
    bridge on it.
He won it from the spoils after he destroyed the city of
    Eëtion.
Now he was delighting his heart with it, and he was singing
    the glorious deeds of men.

Iliad 9.186–189

This *phorminx* is no ordinary instrument, but one of those auratic artifacts whose wondrous craftsmanship and mythically resonant provenance, although only briefly alluded to in the Iliadic narrative, indicate that they played some far more meaningful role in a para-Iliadic

---

major festivals of the Classical period such as the Panathenaia (cf. Nagy 2007a:243 and 2004). Unless we conjecture long medleys, the relative brevity of Sapphic songs (as well as those of Alcaeus and Anacreon) would not have lent them to filling out the structural framework of the citharodic *nomos*. As for Pindaric (Nagy 2007a:235–236, 243) and Stesichorean (Herington 1985:20; Shapiro 1992:69) choral songs, they are longer, but we lack any evidence that these strophic compositions were adapted to normally stichic *nomoi* by early Classical citharodes. Medley-style performances of old lyric songs may, however, have been a feature of post-Classical citharodic culture; cf. Part I.11.iin244.

[188] On political ties between Thebe and Lesbian Mytilene, see Aloni 1986:51–67.

[189] West 1973:189–190, 2002b:210; Nagy 2007b:36–37; Dué 2002.

tradition.[190] In this case, that tradition is a distinctly Aeolic one, devoted to romantic accounts of Achilles' sacking of cities on Lesbos and across the Troad, accounts that would have been cultivated originally by *aoidoi* in these areas and then inherited by the Lesbian citharodes.[191] It is entirely reasonable to assume that in singing Achilles' exploits citharodes would have taken a particular interest in foregrounding and expanding his lyric persona, in linking his heroic glory to the famed *kitharôidia* of Lesbos and environs by telling of his recovery and possession of a lyre with meaningful attachments to local Aeolic place lore.[192] Like citharodic Apollo in Sappho fr. 44.33, this Achilles is εὐλύρας.[193] Such self-regarding inclusion of charismatic "heroic citharodes" (or quasi-citharodes) in citharodic epic narrative is a phenomenon that, we will see, is elsewhere attested. However, in the rhapsodic *Iliad* we catch only a glimpse of the elaborately characterized lyric Achilles. As Nagy has argued, the scene in *Iliad* 9, in which Achilles sings while Patroclus "waits for whatever moment the Aeacid would leave off singing" (191), is specifically imagined in terms of the late Archaic and Classical "esthetics of rhapsodic sequencing," the relay-style performance of the *Iliad* from one rhapsode to the next that was formalized above all by the

---

[190] Cf. Minchin 2001:121 on the evocative power of such objects, including the lyre of Achilles; also, Gernet 1981:73–111.

[191] See Leaf 1912:242–243, 397–399 and Burgess 2001:151–152, who discusses the relation of these accounts to the Cyclic *Cypria*. Cf. Nagy 1979:140–141 on traces of these local accounts in the *Iliad*: "This emphasis on Achilles is especially striking in the case of Lesbos; the *Iliad* says that Achilles himself captured *all* Lesbos (IX 129, 271), and the significance of such a heroic deed seems to have less to do with the epic fate of nearby Troy and far more to do with the here-and-now of a Homeric audience in the eighth or seventh century B.C." (I would underline, however, the critical role of the properly *citharodic* audience on Archaic Lesbos.) Dué 2002:63–64 offers further discussion and bibliography.

[192] Stories about Achilles' youthful lessons in lyre playing with the Centaur Cheiron surely figured into the elaboration of an Achilles *lurikos*, although at a later time they became ideologically paradigmatic for the lyric enculturation of aristocratic youths. Indeed, the *Iliad*'s iconic image of Achilles singing to the lyre would, by the fifth century BCE, become detached from the professionals who originally propagated it and was adopted as a symbol of elite antagonism to musical professionalism, with its connotations of effeminacy and ethical turpitude. As early as Pindar *Pythian* 4 (462 BCE), the skilled amateur aristocrat Damophilus plays a *daidalea phorminx* at a symposium (296). Cf. "Plutarch" *On Music* 40.1145e–1146a; Plutarch *On the Fortune of Alexander* 331d; Dio Chrysostom 2.28–31. See discussion in Veneri 1995. A Roman reflex of this aristocratic appropriation of "Achilles' lyre" is to be found in the *Praise of Piso* 163–177, in which Piso's Achilles-like amateur dedication to the lyre is (implicitly) set against the professional ambitions of Nero.

[193] On the implicit assimilation of lyric Achilles to Apollo, see Nagy 2007b:37–38.

Panathenaic Rule in Athens.[194] The description of the *phorminx* nevertheless betrays its importance to the heroic experience of Achilles in the Aeolic tradition. The *Iliad* says that Achilles selected it from the spoils that were the possessions of King Eëtion of Thebe (cf. 6.414–418, 23.826–829), a city of the Troad at the nexus of key pre-Iliadic myths.[195] It was the home of Andromache, the daughter of Eëtion, and it is clear from the frequent references in the *Iliad* that Achilles' capture of it had been the subject of lavish narration.[196]

In another account, preserved by Diodorus Siculus 5.49, Achilles took possession of the lyre after sacking the nearby city of Lyrnessos, where he won another crucial prize, Briseis.[197] This lyre, according to Diodorus, came with a remarkable pedigree. It was no less than the first lyre of all, that invented by Hermes, who gave it as a wedding gift to Cadmus and Harmonia. After his foundation of Thebes, in which this lyre of Hermes was presumably involved—the secondary lyric foundation of Thebes by Amphion, to whom Hermes more typically presents his lyre, has seemingly informed the earlier Cadmeian establishment—Cadmus brought the lyre to Lyrnessos, where it remained until Achilles captured the city. In an alternative tradition preserved by Philostratus *On Heroes* 11.10, it was the lyre of Orpheus that came to Lyrnessos, which Philostratus seems to place on Lesbos rather than on the coast of the Troad. This lyre "imparted sound to the rocks" that naturally surrounded the city. Even in his own day, Philostratus reports, the sea around Lyrnessos "resounds with the song of the rocks." The story has the marks of an ex post facto lyric foundation myth, with the Orphic lyre playing the part of that of Amphion (or Cadmus) in Thebes; it recalls as well the tradition that Orpheus' lyre was recovered at Lesbian Antissa by Terpander (Nicomachus *Excerpts* 1).[198] Since Philostratus tells the story of the lyre in the midst of a discussion of Achilles' martial exploits on Lesbos, including his sack of Lyrnessos, we are entitled to assume that in the account upon which he relies it was this very

---

[194] Nagy 1996:72–73, with Ford 1992:115n31. On the "diachronic skewing" involved in such envisioning of epic lyric performance as rhapsodic, see Nagy 2003:39–48.

[195] Rocchi 1980 is a useful discussion of narratives involving the lyre of Achilles, but it treats them as socioculturally abstracted emanations of "Greek myth" rather than sourcing them to actual performance traditions.

[196] See Burgess 2001:152.

[197] Lyrnessos and Thebe were significantly confused. Aeschylus fr. 267 makes Lyrnessos the home of Andromache; Dictys of Crete *Chronicle of the Trojan War* 2.17 makes Eëtion king of Lyrnessos.

[198] Follett 2004:235 suggests that Lyrnessos may have been associated with Antissa ("in the neighborhood of Antissa") in the source from which Philostratus is drawing.

Orphic lyre that Achilles took from Lyrnessos.[199] Rather than viewing the testimonia of Diodorus and Philostratus as late, learnedly fanciful elaborations of Homeric myth, we should see in them genuine traces of ancient citharodic variations on the lyric Achilles. In both versions, Achilles is made the inheritor of an instrument otherwise associated with important proto-citharodic figures, Orpheus and Terpander, or Hermes, Cadmus, and Amphion. Further, in both these cases, the pedigreed lyre is implicitly heptachord, and as such a suggestive precursor to the seven-stringed *kithara* played by the citharode. The superfine, "daedalic" manufacture of the *phorminx* as it appears in the *Iliad*—indeed, no other *phorminx* in Homer is so lavishly constructed—may also reflect accounts of its technical advancement.

Finally, we might ask ourselves the reason for the variation in the backstory of Achilles' lyre as related by Diodorus and Philostratus. Could the two versions represent distinct, perhaps rival strains of citharodic lore, each making claim on the lyric Achilles, the one followed by Philostratus based in the northeastern Aegean and the Aeolis, tracing inventions in the field back to Orpheus and Terpander—a reflex of which is to be found in Timotheus *Persians* 221–231—the other followed by Diodorus a variant of "mainland" traditions that commemorated either Cadmus or Amphion as mortal founding fathers of the lyre? Nicomachus *Excerpts* 1 might preserve another such (seemingly

---

[199] The extent in *On Heroes* to which Achilles and Trojan epic are "lyricized" is remarkable. Philostratus describes a young Achilles studying the lyre with Cheiron and praying to Calliope to grant him musical skill (45.6–7); at Troy, Achilles composes a lyric song called "Palamedes," presumably on the lyre taken from Lyrnessos (33.36); a post-mortem Achilles and his wife Helen on the White Island "sing their desire for one another, Homer's *epê* about Troy, and Homer himself" (54.12). Philostratus includes a representation of such a song in 55.2–3, a hymn to Echo, which is a condensed lyric "echo" of the *kleos* of Homeric epic. The song is short—it is indeed praised for its brevity, which Philostratus' Phoenician interlocutor views as proper to lyric songs (55.4)—and thus seemingly suited to an intimate sympotic context rather than a citharodic one (cf. 45.7; 54.12). On such elitist reclamation of lyric Achilles see n192 above. But Philostratus is nevertheless elaborating on an older performance tradition in which Achilles was fundamentally associated with the lyre, and that tradition was likely to have been maintained by the citharodes. Indeed, the insistence of the Phoenician that "it is *sophon* 'a mark of taste and skill' not to stretch out these matters [epic narrative] in lyric songs or to perform them in extended fashion" has a tendentious ring to it, suggesting that Philostratus knows that Homer had been so performed to the *kithara* (Philostratus was, it should be noted, a native of Lemnos, close to Lesbos). It could even be that citharodic settings of Homer had come back into style in his day. Achilles Tatius, a rough contemporary, describes a wealthy girl singing to a *kithara* a scene from *Iliad* 16, the "fight between the boar and the lion" (*Leucippe and Cleitophon* 2.1); the setting is domestic, but it could reflect the fashion in the public performance culture.

competitive) difference in the mythical claims of these traditions, although he tries, rather awkwardly, to resolve it. Nicomachus relates that Hermes gave his seven-stringed lyre to Orpheus, from whom it passed to Terpander; as a result, "Terpander is said to have invented the heptachord lyre. But," he continues, Terpander brought the lyre to Egypt, from where "they say the Achaeans received it from Cadmus son of Agenor." The catalogue of legendary citharodes offered by Heraclides of Pontus, which draws from lore recorded in the Sicyonian *anagraphê*, also seems to hew to "mainland" traditions focused on Boeotia and Delphi. The figures mentioned are all Boeotian (Amphion, taught by Hermes, is the earliest; Pieros of Pieria is a Boeotian creation, as Pausanias 9.29.2 shows); or they are Euboean (Linus), Delphian (Philammon and Thamyris, a Thracian absorbed into Delphic myth), or Homeric (Phemius and Demodocus); Orpheus, despite his origins in Pieria and Thrace, does not make the list.[200]

ii. Lesches and the (citharodic) *Little Iliad*

Post-Iliadic Trojan Cycle narratives also received citharodic treatments. Again, we should look first of all to the epic-lyric activity of the early Lesbian citharodes. The predominant attribution of the *Little Iliad* to Lesches of Mytilene is highly significant in this regard.[201] As it appears in the summary of Proclus, this poem, narrating events from the award of Achilles' arms to Odysseus to the admission of the Horse into Troy, occupies the place in the Cycle after the *Aethiopis* and before the *Iliou Persis* (*Sack of Troy*), both poems attributed to Arctinus of (Ionian) Miletus. However, as the fragmentary remains indicate, in the living performance culture of the Cycle the *Little Iliad* of Lesches covered more extensive ground, including narrative events alternately treated in the *Aethiopis* and especially in the *Iliou Persis*.[202] In view of the

[200] Although there is a possibility that Terpander was mentioned in the *anagraphê*: Gostoli 1990:99. Pliny *Natural History* 7.204 records a difference in opinion about the inventor of the *cithara* (some say Amphion, others Orpheus, others Linus), which could be rooted in the divergent regional traditions I am positing.

[201] Lesches was also said to hail from Pyrrha (scholia to Aristophanes *Lysistrata* 155; IG XIV 1284 i 10 = Tabula Iliaca A (Capitolina) p29 Sadurska). Other poets, including Homer, Thestorides of Phocaea, and Cinaethon of Sparta, were attributed the composition of the *Little Iliad* (scholia *ad* Euripides *Trojan Women* 822). On the Homeric attribution in particular, see Nagy 1990b:78.

[202] See Holmberg 1998: "The *Little Iliad* appears to share many incidents and episodes with both the *Aethiopis* and the *Iliou Persis*; this coincidence has led a number of scholars to conclude that the *Aethiopis*, the *Little Iliad*, and the *Iliou Persis* were originally one undifferentiated poem called the *Little Iliad*" (466). Pausanias' attribution to

proximal and even overlapping subjects treated in the epic traditions represented by Lesches and Arctinus, we should not be surprised to find preserved by Phaenias, a Peripatetic historian of music and poetry, the significant fiction of a contest between the two legendary poets (fr. 33 Wehrli *ap.* Clement *Stromateis* 1.131.6). Nagy offers a valuable analysis of the story as a reflection of the "historical relationship" between the two traditions:

> As we look at the narrative coverage of the *Little Iliad* as attributed to Lesches, this poet from the island of Lesbos, it seems at first to be an intrusion into the narrative of Arctinus of Miletus. But it would be more accurate to say that the narrative of Arctinus envelops the narrative of Lesches at both ends, almost engulfing it. Just as the Epic Cycle is built around the Homeric *Iliad* and *Odyssey*, so also, within the Cycle, the repertoire of Arctinus seems to be built around that of Lesches. There seems to be a stratification here, as if an earlier repertoire represented by Lesches of Mytilene were being enveloped by a later repertoire represented by Arctinus of Miletus.[203]

At least in the version of the story that Phaenias tells, Lesches emerges as the winner of the contest (διημιλλῆσθαι δὲ τὸν Λέσχην Ἀρκτίνῳ καὶ νενικηκέναι). Although this outcome may seem to be at odds with the diminished place in the Cycle assigned to the *Little Iliad*, it may simply be a matter of patriotic pride—Phaenias was from Eresos, a city of Lesbos— or, less personally, a reliance on local Lesbian accounts. Geographical biases aside, however, Nagy sees a more complex dynamic at work in this narrative condensation of the Cycle's formation: "As long as a given tradition can somehow survive after losing to another tradition, the loser can be presented as the winner." While keeping intact the essential terms of Nagy's valuable analysis, I would contend that the anecdotal contest between Lesches and Arctinus assumes a historical

---

Lesches (whom he mistakenly calls Lescheos), son of Aeschylinus of Mytilene, of the *Iliou Persis* that inspired the murals of Polygnotus in the Cnidian Lesche (club house) at Delphi suggests that Lesches (i.e. the *Little Iliad* tradition) was as closely associated with narratives of the sack as Arctinus was (10.25.5). I would note the obvious similarity between the word *leskhê* 'club house' and the name *Leskhês*. This is probably coincidental, but it is possible that the latter was somehow derived from the former—Lesches was the poet whose work Polygnotus famously illustrated in the Cnidian Lesche; biographical details (such as the name of his father, Aeschylinus) were fleshed out later.

[203] Nagy 1990b:76.

tension not only between successive poetic traditions but between rival performance traditions as well. That is, the epic tradition represented by Lesbian Lesches is a citharodic tradition, while that by Ionian Arctinus is a rhapsodic one, which largely succeeded, yet did not make entirely obsolete the older citharodic one.[204]

Predictably, direct evidence for a citharodic *Little Iliad* is nonexistent. But there are several clues worth considering. First, it is significant that Phaenias mentions Lesches in close conjunction with Terpander of Lesbos (fr. 33 Wehrli), whom he emphatically dates after Lesches. It is unclear what criteria Phaenias is using for this chronological arrangement, but it might be based on an inference from the poetic repertoire of the old Terpandrean *nomoi*: because these *nomoi* used to be filled out with episodes from the *Little Iliad*, Lesches was therefore one of the "other poets" whose *epê* Terpander supposedly melodized (to use Heraclides' formulation), and was thus obviously older than his citharodic countryman.

Next, we have two intriguing bits of text that could represent traces of a citharodic *Little Iliad*. Clement *Stromateis* 1.104.1 (= fr. 9 Bernabé) quotes as follows a verse from the *Little Iliad* that describes the night on which Troy was captured: νὺξ μὲν ἔην μεσάτα, λαμπρὰ δ' ἐπέτελλε σελάνα ("It was the middle of the night, and the bright moon was rising"). The same verse was also known, more widely it seems, in the dialectally variant form νὺξ μὲν ἔην μέσση, λαμπρὰ δ' ἐπέτελλε σελήνη. In this version, the epic-Ionic forms μέσση and σελήνη stand in place of the Doric or Aeolic form μεσάτα and the Doric σελάνα preserved in Clement's version. The word λαμπρά, which appears in both versions, has the long final alpha characteristic of melic Doric-Aeolic dialect.[205] Benedetto Bravo has recently argued that the verse cited by Clement is a concoction of a learned grammarian, who, "knowing that Lesches was a Lesbian poet (from Mytilene or Pyrrha), fabricated an edition of the *Little Iliad* that arbitrarily modified its Ionic dialect form so as to give it the greatest possible Aeolic *coloratura*."[206] Bravo's theory is ingenious, but it complicates a simpler and more probable scenario, which is that the two versions represent two related but variant *Little Iliad* traditions. Specifically, the Doric-Aeolic verse cited by Clement represents a textual "capture" of the original, citharodic performance transmission of the *Little Iliad*, while the Ionicized version captures a

---

[204] Cf. already Flach 1883:189.

[205] On the dialect forms, see Bravo 2001:82, quoting Martin Peters (*per litteras*), who notes that Aeolic σελάννα could originally have occupied the place of Doric σελάνα.

[206] Bravo 2001:83.

secondary performance transmission of the same narrative material, which became the mainstream tradition.[207] This tradition was primarily rhapsodic, but it should be noted that λαμπρά, a distinctly non-Ionic form that could easily have been changed to λαμπρή, remains. We may recall that the fragments of the Terpandrean *prooimia* show a juxtaposition of epic-Ionic and melic-Doric-Aeolic forms, so perhaps even the Ionically inflected νὺξ μὲν ἔην μέσση, λαμπρὰ δ' ἐπέτελλε σελήνη is a verse a fifth-century citharode would have sung (and a rhapsode would have recited). In an epic fragment preserved on a later-fourth- or third-century BCE papyrus (P.Oxy. 2510), which Bravo has persuasively argued belongs to the *Little Iliad*, we find the non-Ionic genitive singular μάχας instead of the metrically equivalent Ionic form μάχης (line 11). This is unlikely to be a copyist's error, and, given the relatively early date of the papyrus, it is still more unlikely that the work of a literary counterfeiter lies behind it.[208] Again, we are probably looking at a melic remainder in a rhapsodic (or mixed-use) text of the once-dominant citharodic performance tradition of the *Little Iliad*. It is worth noting that the same verse that contains μάχας also contains a metrical anomaly, a rare breach of Hermann's Bridge, the constraint against word break after the fourth-foot trochee. Such a violation need not be indicative of musical performance of the hexameter, but in conjunction with the Doric-Aeolic form, this metrical freedom may point to an originally melodic setting.[209]

Fifth-century Attic vase painting presents us with what appears to be another textual "capture" of a citharodic rendition of material from the Cycle. In the schoolroom scene on a red-figured cup of Douris from around 490–480 BCE (Antikensammlung, Staatliche Museen zu Berlin, Preussischer Kulturbesitz F 2285), a boy—not one playing a lyre, but standing in the company of lyre players—studies a scroll

---

[207] A related argument is made in West 1971: "[C]ould [Clement's] source have used a citharode's text?" (308n3). (But West 2002b:218n46, arguing that Lesches "composed his epic in Ionic, not Lesbian," does not mention the possibility.) Cf. Nagy 1990b:77, who speaks of an "Ionic layer ... superimposed on the arguably Aeolic traditions represented by Lesches of Mytilene." Even if Bravo's theory were correct, it would still be possible that the learned fabricator of an Aeolic *Little Iliad* (or at least of this one verse) was trying to recreate textually what he knew to be the citharodic prehistory to the rhapsodic *Little Iliad*. Similarly, when the Peripatetic scholar Dicaearchus of Messana (fr. 90 Wehrli) and Zopyrus of Magnesia (FGrH 494 F 3) claim that the *Iliad* should be "read in Aeolic dialect" (*ap. Vita Romana* 32.25 Wilamowitz), they may have in mind the recovery of a notionally "original" citharodic *Iliad*.

[208] Another non-Ionic form probably appears in line 5 of the fragment, ἄιξαν (for ἤιξαν); cf. Bravo 2001:60.

[209] See Bravo 2001:69 for other metrical oddities in the fragment.

containing a hexameter verse: ΜΟΙΣΑ ΜΟΙ | ΑΦΙ (ἀμφὶ) ΣΚΑΜΑΝΔΡΟΝ | ΕΥΡΩΝ (ἐύρροον) ΑΡΧΟΜΑΙ (ἄρχομ') | ΑΕΙΝΔΕΝ (ἀείδεν) 'Muse, for me, I begin to sing about wide-flowing Scamander' (PMG 938e). The Aeolicism Μοῖσα suggests that the verse, although grammatically and orthographically garbled in Douris' depiction, belongs to a citharodic setting of a non-Homeric Trojan War episode.[210] The presence of ἀμφί further suggests its specifically proemial function. As Cicero *De oratore* 2.80 indicates, however, citharodic *prooimia* avoided mention of the thematic content of the narrative poems they prefaced. The verse might then be meant to represent a secondary *prooimion* sung in the introductory section of the *nomos* proper, the *arkha* (see discussion below), stating the subject of the song text, and thus comparable to *Iliad* 1.1. Alternatively, its ungainly construction might indicate that it is the artist's idiosyncratically reductive conflation of a typical hymnic *prooimion*, signaled by the signature features *Moisa moi amphi*, and an epic theme typical of the nomic song that would follow it—the "wide-flowing Scamander" stands as metonym for the entire Trojan Cycle.[211] In either case, the image provides valuable evidence for the circulation of at least some written copies of citharodic texts among practicing musicians—the *kitharistês* who owned the scroll was perhaps a profes-sional citharode as well—in the fifth century BCE, even if their main avenue of transmission was oral.

Ernst Diehl included the melic hexameter from the Douris cup in his *Anthologia Lyrica Graeca* as Stesichorus fr. 26.[212] Although fifth-century schoolboys did learn to sing Stesichorean songs monodically to the lyre (e.g. Eupolis fr. 395 K-A), the attribution in this case remains highly uncertain. Still, if it is true that Stesichorus' choral compositions were fundamentally influenced by *kitharôidia*, then we might see in the Troy-related titles of his works—the *Iliou Persis*, *Wooden* (or *Trojan*) *Horse*, *Nostoi*, *Helen*, and *Oresteia*—a reflection of the poetic repertoire of the cithardoic *nomoi*.[213] Similarly, there is something to the fact that

---

[210] Cf. West 1971:308 and Palumbo-Stracca 1994:121, 126–128.

[211] On the verse as a pastiche cf. Palumbo-Stracca 1994:124–125; Ford 2003: "Hence, though the school scroll on the Douris cup ... is inscribed with words that may be construed as an awkward hexameter, they may simply be a melange of two incompat-ible epic incipits" (25). Cf. Euripides *Trojan Women* 511, discussed below.

[212] Diehl 1936; cf. Beazley 1948:338.

[213] See the résumé in Gerber 1997:238–239. Citharodic *Sacks* had a parallel in (or may have inspired) treatments of the same themes in the contemporary agonistic medium of *aulôidia* 'singing to the *aulos*'. Athenaeus 13.610c says that Sacadas of Argos composed an *Iliou Persis* (the text is corrupt, but we should read Σακάδα τοῦ for the MSS σακατου, as Casaubon first realized). Sacadas, active in the early sixth century BCE, produced *melê* for choruses, but, more probably, this *Iliou Persis* was a monodic

Aeschylus, who, according to Aristophanes *Frogs* 1281–1282, borrowed from the citharodic *nomoi* in the composition of his choral songs, also drew so much poetic material from the Cycle. In a well-known anecdote preserved in Athenaeus 8.347e, Aeschylus claims that his plays are "slices from the banquet of Homer" (i.e. the Cycle), and the citharodically marked parodos in the *Agamemnon*, which treats pre-Iliadic Cyclic material, must be a prime example of what he means.

Euripides' own *Trojan Women* attests to a citharodic tradition of singing Cyclic narrative. In the first stasimon of the play, the chorus of captive Trojans recounts the ill-fated welcome of the Horse into their city—an episode known from the *Little Iliad* of Lesches—beginning as follows:

> ἀμφί μοι Ἴλιον, ὦ
> Μοῦσα καινῶν ὕμνων,
> ἄεισον ἐν δακρύοις
> ᾠδὰν ἐπικήδειον·
> νῦν γὰρ μέλος ἐς Τροίαν ἰαχήσω.

Sing for me about Ilion, Muse of novel *humnoi*, a song of lamentation amidst tears; for now I will raise a melody for Troy.

Euripides *Trojan Women* 511–515[214]

The dactylic incipit ἀμφί μοι Ἴλιον unmistakably references citharodic music. As with the verse inscribed on the Douris cup, it may be meant to represent either the phraseology of the secondary proemial introduction to the narrative section of the citharodic *nomos*, or it may be Euripides' conflation of typical proemial *humnos* and nomic narrative. In either case, Euripides looks to Classical *kitharôidia* as the most obvious model for a melic account of the fall of Troy such as he is composing. In so doing, however, he self-consciously creates a novel fusion of citharodic song and the women's song of lament (ᾠδὰν ἐπικήδειον) that his tragic chorus is made to sing. Such a generic fusion, which involves the melodramatic intensification of the old *nomos* and its epic contents, is redolent of the Athenian New Music, and very likely reflects the theatrical transformations of the *nomos* that citharodes such as Timotheus of

---

elegy fitted to the framework of an aulodic *nomos*, a genre for which Sacadas was also known, and which was typically performed by aulodes at *mousikoi agônes* ("Plutarch" *On Music* 8.1134a; Sacadas himself was a three-time Pythian victor). Cf. Bowie 2007:53.

[214] I observe the punctuation of Biehl's Teubner text (1970), which makes Μοῦσα καινῶν ὕμνων into a single noun phrase.

Miletus were at the time introducing into their art (*Trojan Women* was produced in 415 BCE). Indeed, the Μοῦσα καινῶν ὕμνων 'Muse of novel *humnoi*' invoked by the chorus might contain an allusion to the *sphragis* section of a *nomos* in which Timotheus claims to reject the "Old Muse" (Μοῦσα παλαιά) in favor of the καινά 'novel songs' that he prefers to compose instead (PMG 796).[215]

The attributions of *Nostoi* to Phemius and a *Sack of Troy* ('Ιλίου πόρθησις) to Demodocus by Heraclides of Pontus are surely prompted by the depiction of these singers in the *Odyssey* (fr. 157 Wehrli = "Plutarch" *On Music* 3.1132b), but, to give this scholar a bit more credit, it is possible that Heraclides was aware that these Cyclic epics had been in the repertoire of Archaic and Classical citharodes. There are indications too that the episodes of the *Little Iliad* and *Iliou Persis*, excellent opportunities for narrative and musical sensationalism, continued to attract citharodes long after the Classical period. A victor list from second-century BCE Teos records that a Phocaean citharode, Demetrius son of Menippus, sang to the *kithara* (ἐκιθαρῴδει), probably as a solo performance, a dithyramb called the *Horse* at a festival contest sponsored by the Guild of the Dionysiac Artists based on Teos.[216] Nero's composition of a citharodic *Capture of Troy* was perhaps a traditional gesture, a conscious emulation of the popular treatment of *Iliou Persis* scenes in Classical *kitharôidia*. The inclusion of a *Niobe* and a *Nauplios* in Nero's repertoire nodded to past classics as well, but to those of a later period, the post-Terpandrean, dramatically inflected *nomoi* introduced by Timotheus.[217]

---

[215] See Kranz 1933:254 on the influence of the New Music on this stasimon. Croally 1994:245 offers a less culturally specific (vis-à-vis later-fifth-century Athens) reading: "The newness of what the chorus say consists in two points. First, their song now compares unfavourably with the happy songs which were being sung in Troy before its destruction (529–30, 544ff.); second, this treatment of war is quite different from epic treatments because it is seen almost entirely through the eyes of women." Of course, from the most basic point of view, the chorus' song is a *kainos humnos* because no one has ever before sung of the fall of Troy.

[216] The inscription is presented and discussed in Ma 2007:232–245. "Citharodic dithyramb" was a Hellenistic phenomenon, and probably rare, perhaps even exclusive to the repertoire of Demetrius of Phocaea; cf. Part IV.9. On Demetrius, see Stephanis 1988, no. 636.

[217] Cf. Part IV.12. Although we may speculate too that the Timothean *Nauplios* (PMG 785) itself represented a continuity with Classical citharodic *Nostoi*.

10. *Argonautica Citharoedica*

The roots of Argonautic myth in Aeolian Thessaly make it a good candidate for early reception and elaboration by Lesbian citharodes.[218] Although tales of the Argonauts would eventually, by the later sixth century BCE, make their way into the rhapsodic repertoire, in poems such as the *Carmen Naupactium*, which was widely attributed to a Milesian poet (Pausanias 10.38.11), the primary, seventh-century oral source for them—and thus the source engaged by the *Odyssey* (12.69–72)—was likely to have been citharodic.[219] The prominent inclusion of Orpheus in the ranks of the Argonauts, which seems to have occurred no later than the seventh century, adds credence to this scenario: the mythical figurehead of the Lesbian line of citharodes has been elevated to the level of the questing heroes of the Argo.[220] In other words, the image of the citharodic performer has been gloriously inscribed within the frame of the performed tradition by its very performers.

It is remarkable that our oldest representation of Orpheus, sculpted alongside the Argonauts Castor and Polydeuces on a metope of the Sicyonian Monopteros, a square pavilion at Delphi whose construction is datable to the reign of the tyrant Cleisthenes of Sicyon or shortly thereafter (Cleisthenes ruled from around 600 to 560 BCE), shows him holding what appears to be a *kithara* (rather than a lyre) and dressed in the long chiton of the agonistic citharode (Plate 8).[221]

---

[218] Cf. West 1973: "The Aeolian colonists who settled around Lesbos were the obvious people to transmit this Thessalian mythology to the Ionians" (189).

[219] See West 2005:40 on the mystery shrouding the early history of the Argonautica ("we cannot identify any Argonautica of this period [seventh century] that was available to later readers").

[220] West 2005:46–47 argues compellingly for a seventh-century Argonautic Orpheus, whose role in the tradition seems already well established by the sixth century. In addition to the Sicyonian Monopteros image discussed below, there are poetic reflections. Ibycus, whose songs treated Argonautic material (PMG 292, 301, 309), mentions an ὀνομάκλυτον Ὀρφήν 'famous Orpheus' in PMG 306, presumably from an Argonautic narrative. Simonides PMG 567 describes a singer, probably Orpheus on board the Argo, charming birds and fish with his song. Other fragments of Simonides confirm that he treated the quest for the Fleece in various poems (PMG 540, 544–548, 568, 576). I would argue that Ibycus, who probably spent time in Cleisthenic Sicyon (Barron 1964:224, Griffin 1982:57–58), and Simonides received their Argonautic myth from the citharodes, adapting it for choral performance. Cf. discussion of Pindar *Pythian* 4 below.

[221] See La Coste Messelière 1936:82–95; Griffin 1982:57; Parker 1994; and Knell 1998:22–23 on the dating and planning of the Monopteros, with the bibliographies compiled in the latter two; cf. too Neer 2007:245–246, who reaffirms the building's Sicyonian rather than Sicilian (as some have argued) identity. Vojatzi's view (1982:42) that Orpheus holds a *khelus*-lyre does not fit the visual profile of the instrument held by

---

It is not easy to resist linking this Orpheus and the other Argonautic scenes from the Monopteros metopes with the report in Herodotus 5.67.1–68.1 that, during a period of open hostilities between Sicyon and Argos, Cleisthenes banned rhapsodic competitions of Homeric epic because he objected to what he understood as its pro-Argive content.[222] Herodotus mentions only that Dionysian "tragic *khoroi*" were established in place of the rhapsodic contests, but it is a reasonable assumption that *agônes* of predominantly Aeolic citharodes, singing an Aeolic-based epic tradition, could have been promoted by the tyrant as a politically and culturally suitable substitute for the Homeric rhapsodes and the Argive heroic *kleos* that they perpetuated.[223] In his civic promotion of *kitharôidia*, Cleisthenes would have had models (and rivals) in the Archaic Peloponnese, Sparta, which had been hosting citharodic contests at the Carneia, dominated above all by the Lesbian virtuosos, since the early seventh century, and Corinth, where Periander had enlisted the musical services of Arion of Methymna—testimony that surely condenses a wider-based engagement with citharodic as well as dithyrambic culture on the part of the Corinthian tyrant.

Citharodic Argonauticas found receptive audiences elsewhere. On the metope of the Sicyonian Monopteros at Delphi, Orpheus is shown standing next to another figure holding a *kithara* and wearing a chiton. Although not identified by a legible inscription, as is Orpheus (labelled Ορφας), this citharode is most likely meant to be the Delphian music hero Philammon. According to Pherecydes of Athens (FGrH 3 F 26), who is presumably drawing from Delphian lore, it was Philammon who participated in the voyage of the Argo, not Orpheus.[224] We may thus imagine citharodes appeasing local sensibilities at Delphi, above all at the Pythian *agônes*, by making Philammon, a legendary Pythian victor (Pausanias 10.7.2), their avatar in the Argonautic narratives they sang there. The conspicuous pairing of Orpheus and Philammon on the Sicyonian metope at Delphi might represent an attempt on the part of Cleisthenes to harmonize, as it were, the variant, even rivalrous traditions, and to visualize the notion of a continuity of prestige between the citharodic cultures nurtured at Delphi and Sicyon, where

---

Orpheus; it is clearly a square-based *kithara*. On the probable death of Cleisthenes shortly before or in 560/59, see Barron 1964:226.

[222] See Herington 1985:83–84; Irwin 2005b:288. Cingano 1985 argues that the rhapsodic poem Cleisthenes objected to was the *Thebais*, which at an early time was assigned to Homer, but Irwin does well to remind us of potentially objectionable Argive content in the Trojan Cycle as well.

[223] See the related arguments in Böhme 1953:15–19; 1991:130–131; Schefold 1992:184.

[224] See Robert 1920:416n6, followed by Vojatzi 1982:44, with further bibliography.

Cleisthenes had instituted his own Pythian Games (scholia *ad* Pindar *Nemean* 9, title), a likely setting for *kitharôidia* in Sicyon.[225] Of course, it is possible that citharodes themselves had at some point begun to accommodate both the Orphic and local Delphian traditions by making the two citharodic heroes into a dynamic duo of sorts, perhaps on the model of other heroic pairs on the Argo, the Dioscuri and the Boreads.

Depending on how we interpret the image on another artifact, the black-figured Attic lekythos from the time of Cleisthenes (c. 580 BCE) that was discussed above in connection to a citharodic Odyssey, we could have oblique evidence for the citharodic performance of Agonautic saga in Athens. The musician shown singing and playing between two sirens may be a citharode performing the Odyssean episode of the Sirens. Alternatively, we may be looking at a scene from an Argonautica in which Orpheus counters the deadly singing of the Sirens with his own song.[226] The lyric *aristeia* of Orpheus was probably an ancient feature of the Argonautica tradition, and not coincidentally a heroizing reflection of its primary performance medium, *kitharôidia*. (As on the Sicyonian metope, Orpheus, if it is he, is depicted as a professionally accoutered citharode on the Attic vase.) The episode is treated at some length by Apollonius of Rhodes in his *Argonautica* (4.891–919), with sufficient distinction in mythological detail to suggest that it had

---

[225] See Power 2004 for more on the role of *kitharôidia* in the cultural politics of Cleisthenic Sicyon. Traces of either traditional doubling or rivalry (or both) between Orpheus and Philammon appear in Hermesianax fr. 7 Powell, transposed to the erotic register. The Hellenistic poet makes Argiope (or Agriope) the wife of Orpheus (1–2), but that name is otherwise given to the nymph with whom Philammon conceived Thamyris (Conon FGrH 26 F 1 [7]; Pausanias 4.33.3; Apollodorus 1.3.3). Even if this is an innovation of Hermesianiax, it most likely reflects a preexisting tension between the two proto-citharodes. Dio Chrysostom 77/78.19–20 says that Orpheus would be happy above all to have his music praised by Philammon, which would also seem to speak to some rivalry between them. Note that a "haughty" Orpheus, more mystagogue than performing musician, did not participate in the Pythian *agônes* according to local Delphian accounts, while Philammon and his son Thamyris were celebrated early victors there (Pausanias 10.7.2). There are possible intimations here of a divide between an Aegean-Aeolic (Orphic) and a "mainland" citharodic tradition, the latter encompassing Delphic musical culture. Given that an Orpheus *kitharôidos* was known in Archaic Sicyon, it is curious, however, that he seems to go unmentioned by the Sicyonian *anagraphê*, which provided information for the "mainland" citharodic catalogue of Heraclides of Pontus. But it is unclear to what extent or in what sense the *anagraphê* (datable to the late fifth century BCE: Griffin 1982:159) reflected a Cleisthenic musico-cultural agenda. Cf. Power 2004:430–432. For the possibility that Terpander's Pythian victories were mentioned in the *anagraphê*, see Gostoli 1990:99. Elsewhere Heraclides acknowledges Orpheus as "the greatest of all mortals in the *tekhnê* of *kitharôidia*" (scholia *ad Rhesus* 346 = fr. 159 Wehrli).

[226] Gropengiesser 1977:607–610.

enjoyed a long-standing autonomy and was not merely a late fantasia derived from the *Odyssey*.[227] However, Argonautic and Odyssean Siren episodes could have been developed more or less in tandem as narrative resources in the nomic repertoire of the early citharodes.

Citharodes likely continued to perform Argonautic narrative through the fifth century. Pindar, like Ibycus and Simonides before him, treated the adventures of Jason and the Argonauts in his poetry, most extensively in *Pythian* 4. Although it has been argued that this triadic song, composed for a chariot victory of Arcesilas IV of Cyrene in 462 BCE, was sung monodically (that is, citharodically) on account of its considerable length and "epic" style, there is, as in the case of the long Stesichorean compositions, no compelling reason to discount its performance by a trained chorus.[228] Certainly, Pindar emerges from the biographical tradition as an even less likely citharode than Stesichorus. But, like Stesichorus, Pindar was familiar with the citharodic *nomos*. The lengthy, epicizing narrative of *Pythian* 4 could represent a "Stesichorean" attempt to emulate that genre, which remained strongly identified with Argonautica, in the choral medium.[229] Pindar emphatically includes Orpheus in his catalogue of the Argonauts, describing him as the ultimate proto-citharode: "And from Apollo came a *phorminx* player, father of songs, renowned Orpheus" (ἐξ Ἀπόλλωνος δὲ φορμικτὰς ἀοιδᾶν πατὴρ | ἔμολεν εὐαίνητος Ὀρφεύς, 176–177).[230] The epithet εὐαίνητος 'renowned' is notable. It is a relatively rare word, used only here in this form; a variant, εὐαίνετος, appears only twice, at Bacchylides 19.11, where it modifies *merimna* 'poetic fantasy',

---

[227] Cf. West 2005:45–46. Meuli 1975:593–676 argues that the Sirens episode, which motivated Orpheus' inclusion in the epic, belonged to the earliest stages of Argonautic mythos, and antedated the Odyssean episode.

[228] For monodic performance, see Davies 1988:56, with further references.

[229] At the end of *Pythian* 4, Pindar imagines Damophilus, a political dissident recalled from exile by Arcesilas, "raising his wondrously wrought (*daidalea*) *phorminx*"—note the redemptive allusion to the daedalic *phorminx* that Achilles plays while still alienated from King Agamemnon (*Iliad* 9.186–187)—at a peaceful, rift-healing symposium, held significantly by the spring of Apollo, god of civic order, and attended by the now-friendly King Arcesilas and his elite political peers, the *sophoi politai* (294–297). Of course, Damophilus was no professional citharode; the sympotic context rather points to a monodic reperformance of the choral ode (cf. *Nemean* 4.13–16; *Olympian* 1.15–19), which here, given the length of *Pythian* 4, may be more of a notional conceit than an actual prospect. But the connection between lyric music and political stability may reflect wider beliefs held by the Cyreneans about the harmonizing potential of Apollonian *kitharôidia*. See further discussion immediately below.

[230] The idea of Orpheus as "father of songs" finds a significant echo in a citharodic *nomos* of Timotheus, *Persians*, in which Orpheus is said to have first "begotten" (ἐτέκνωσεν, 222) the "tortoise-shell lyre with its intricate music."

and in Antimachus 32.2 Wyss, where it describes a winning horse in a chariot race. It has been suggested that Pindar is alluding to an earlier evocation of Orpheus by Ibycus, presumably in an Argonautic narrative, in which Orpheus is called ὀνομάκλυτος 'famous' (PMG 306).[231] But another allusion may be at work here, a punning reference to the Lesbian citharodes who traced their musical practice back to Orpheus through Terpander. Among the most famous of the Lesbian *apogonoi* 'descendants' of Terpander was the presciently named Euainetidas, who hailed from Antissa, Terpander's home city (Hesychius s.v. Λέσβιος ᾠδός). The existence of this citharode has been all but lost to us, but so well regarded in antiquity was Euainetidas that some claimed that he as much as Terpander had claim to the title of the superlative "Lesbian singer" of the proverb μετὰ Λέσβιον ᾠδόν 'After the Lesbian Singer' (Eustathius *Commentary on the Iliad* 741.15 van der Valk; Hesychius s.v. Λέσβιος ᾠδός), which referred to the preeminence of the Lesbian citharodes at the Spartan Carneia. To an early-fifth-century audience, εὐαίνητος, in the context in which it is used in *Pythian* 4, might well have evoked the name of this legend of *kitharôidia.*

Indeed, a Cyrenean audience was perhaps especially able to appreciate the allusion. The expression 'After the Lesbian singer' originally *referred* to the supremacy of the Lesbian citharodes at the Spartan Carneia, but Dorian Cyrene, where *Pythian* 4 was performed, also celebrated a festival of Apollo Carneius. In *Pythian* 5, composed for the same victory of Arcesilas IV as *Pythian* 4, Pindar's Cyrenean chorus in fact celebrates the glorious Spartan cultural heritage that is represented by the Carneia of its own city (72–80). We know nothing about what sort of *mousikoi agônes* were attached to this festival in the fifth century BCE, but if the Spartan Carneia were a model in this respect, we would expect *kitharôidia* to have been prominently featured.[232] (And we might speculate further that the citharodes competing there found

---

[231] Braswell 1988:257.

[232] Bibliography on the Cyrenean Carneia is collated in Dougherty 1993:119n27; cf. too Malkin 1994:143–168. Ceccarelli and Milanezi 2007 consider tragic and dithyrambic contests in Cyrene. Tarentum, an ancient Spartan colony, also celebrated a Carneia, which presumably featured citharodic *agônes* on the model of the Spartan Carneia. Significantly, Tarentum is the last stop on Arion's travels in Magna Graecia, as related in Herodotus 1.24.2. Might we see this as a reflex of a Tarentine effort to attract westward the Lesbian Singers famously hosted at the Spartan Carneia? Tarentum in later years must have become an important center of *kitharôidia*. The star citharode Nicocles (third century BCE) was Tarentine, as is the fictional Evangelus, who tries to compete at Delphi in Lucian *The Uncultured Book Collector* 8–11. For the citharodes Lycon (second century BCE) and Heracleides (first century BCE) of Tarentum, see Stephanis 1988, nos. 1082 and 1570.

that Argonautic narratives successfully complemented local accounts of Cyrene's heroic past, just as Pindar did.) It is significant that in *Pythian* 5.65 Pindar, enumerating Apollo's gifts to mortals, foregrounds that the god, who was essential to the foundation of the Cyrene, "gave them the *kitharis*" (πόρεν τε κίθαριν), that is, the music of the *kithara*. This *kitharis*, allied with the Muse, is in turn appropriately conducive to *eunomia* 'good civic order' (67). As in Timotheus *Persians* 240, *eunomia* would seem to evoke secondarily the civic ordering brought about by the citharodic *nomos*, an effect most famously demonstrated in Terpander's sociomusical pacification of the fractious Spartans at the Spartan Carneia. Just as Terpander's intervention was metaphorized as a healing of a diseased populace (Aelian *Historical Miscellanies* 12.50; Boethius *On Music* 1.1), so Pindar depicts Cyrene as a city sick with *stasis*, in need of healing that will come not only from its ruler, Arcesilas, but from Apollo's lyric music, which is presented as an extension of his healing arts (*Pythian* 4.271–274; *Pythian* 5.63–65).[233]

The metaphorical constellation of political order, healing, and the *kithara* is surely meant to valorize first and foremost the performance of Pindar's own (choral lyric) song, which may have been integrated into the very proceedings of the Carneia festival.[234] But Pindar could nevertheless be responding to the local ideology surrounding the musical culture of the Carneia. That is, the Cyreneans might have followed the Spartan model not only in establishing citharodic contests at its Carneia, but also in investing them with the same potential to effect a cosmic and political catharsis conducive to *eunomia* in their city. The colossal marble Apollo *kitharôidos* that was installed in the temple of Apollo in Cyrene during the reign of Hadrian is a late yet nonetheless significant indication of the city's long-standing investment in the symbolic power of *kitharôidia*. Although based formally on a Hellenistic model, as a conspicuous emblem of the civic and cultural revival in Cyrene initiated by the archaizing Hadrian the statue surely reflected a much older Cyrenean tradition of imagining the city's archegete as

---

[233] Cf. Marshall 2000. Pindar accentuates Arcesilas' own musical skill (*Pythian* 5.114).

[234] On the choral performance of *Pythian* 5 at the Carneia, see Krummen 1990:97–116. At *Pythian* 5.102–103 it is said that Apollo *khrusaôr* should be invoked "in the *aoida* of young men," who are presumably the chorus singing the present song. The epithet probably means 'of the golden lyre' as well as 'of the golden sword'; in fr. 128c.12 S-M Pindar mentions Ὀρφέα χρυσάορα, and here the epithet must refer to Orpheus' lyre. Cf. Ceccarelli and Milanezi 2007:197n23. The epithet thus posits another implicit link between Pindar's epinician and the citharodic culture of the Carneia.

kitharôidos, probably going back as far as the god's seventh-century BCE temple.[235]

There is another possible point of continuity, at the level of song content, between the citharodic cultures at the Spartan and Cyrenean Carneia festivals. The figure in question is Alcestis, whose status as the Thessalian daughter of Pelias notably brings her into the orbit of Argonautic myth and poetry (Hesiod fr. 37.16–22 M-W). She was depicted on the Chest of Cypselus among scenes from the Funeral Games of Pelias, in which Argonautic characters prominently figured (Pausanias 5.17.9–11).[236] The chorus of Euripides' *Alcestis* makes an intriguing mention of the performance at the Spartan Carneia of lyric songs commemorating Alcestis:

> πολλά σε μουσοπόλοι
> μέλψουσι κατ᾽ ἑπτάτονόν τ᾽ ὀρείαν
> χέλυν ἔν τ᾽ ἀλύροις κλέοντες ὕμνοις,
> Σπάρτᾳ κυκλὰς ἁνίκα Καρνεί–
>   ου περινίσεται ὥραμηνός, ἀειρομένας
> παννύχου σελάνας,
> λιπαραῖσί τ᾽ ἐν ὀλβίαις Ἀθάναις.
> τοίαν ἔλιπες θανοῦσα μολ–
>   πὰν μελέων ....

Often shall the servants of the Muses sing of you to the seven-toned mountain tortoise, and in lyreless songs (*humnoi*), celebrating your fame, at Sparta when the circling season of the month of Carneius comes around, while the moon is raised high the whole night long, and in shining, prosperous Athens. Such a musical theme (*molpa*) do you leave by your death for singers of songs (*melê*).

Euripides Alcestis 445–454

The "lyreless *humnoi*" must refer to the *aulos*-accompanied choral songs of Athenian tragedy—as such the expression is an apposite bit of choral self-reference. What about the songs at the Carneia? Choral

---

[235] Cf. Part I.8.iiin171. On Hadrian's interest in the early culture of Cyrene, see Boatwright 2002:177.

[236] Cf. Bowra 1961:120, who suspects the influence of the Stesichorean *Games for Pelias* on the Chest. But if the Chest does date to the time of Cypselus (before Stesichorus' *floruit*), or even if it was produced somewhat later, cithardic hypotexts may well be at issue instead. Periander's engagement of Arion signals a broader Corinthian interest in *kitharôidia*.

performance could be indicated by μέλψουσι and μολπάν (446, 454), both of which tend to denote singing and dancing together, but these words could more properly belong to the Athenian aulodic-choral milieu.[237] The "Muses' servants" in Sparta might then be the citharodes, above all the Lesbian *apogonoi* of Terpander, for whom the Carneian *agônes* were most famous.[238] Indeed, with the term μουσοπόλοι, which occurs in Sappho fr. 150.1, Euripides would appear to be alluding specifically to the Lesbian musicians who made the Carneia such a conspicuous center of *kitharôidia*.[239] The extended description of the lyre (the "seven-toned mountain tortoise"), which sequentially accords with Sparta as the "lyreless *humnoi*" accord with Athens, strongly supports the interpretation that it is citharodes who sing of Alcestis.[240]

Apollo plays no small part in the *kleos* of Alcestis, and Euripides may have known of a citharodic song tradition popular at the god's festival in Sparta, one perhaps annexed to a broader citharodic Argonautica tradition, that recounted the story of Alcestis. Further, it has been suggested, on the basis of iconographical evidence from fifth-century BCE Cyrene (two funerary reliefs depicting Alcestis), that either Euripides' *Alcestis* was reperformed in Cyrene, or that the story of Alcestis formed the subject of an "Apollonian" dithyramb sung and danced at the Cyrenean Carneia.[241] But a third, not necessarily exclusive scenario presents itself: Alcestis was citharodically hymned in Cyrene as she was in Sparta, again, in line with a locally conditioned Cyrenean interest in Argonautic-related characters and episodes.

---

[237] Cf. Dale 1954:90.

[238] Choruses likely did perform at the Spartan Carneia, but we have no explicit testimonia for them, as we do for the Hyacinthia and Gymnopaidiai festivals, whose choruses were renowned (see Calame 1997:202–204). There is, however, iconographical evidence for mixed-gender choral dancing at the Tarentine Carneia (see Ceccarelli and Milanezi 2007:200, fig. 19b); for Cyrene, see Callimachus *Hymn to Apollo* 85–87. The mention of "Carneius, a Trojan" in Alcman PMG 52, perhaps from a choral song, is also worth noting.

[239] Thus Hardie 2005:14, who speculates that *mousopoloi* was an "East Greek coinage applied to professional musicians."

[240] Cf. Binney 1905:99. Euripides' emphatic reminder of the organic, vital origins of the lyre in the periphrasis "seven-toned mountain tortoise" (ἑπτάτονος ὀρεία χέλυς) is thematically appropriate to the consolatory rhetoric for Alcestis, whose death will provide "life" for song. Similarly, the tortoise's death is musically redeemed: though voiceless in life, it emits a voice after death as the lyre (*Homeric Hymn to Hermes* 37–38; Sophocles *Ikhneutai* 300; Nicander *Alexipharmaca* 560–563). See the discussion of the silent tortoise/speaking lyre paradox in Borthwick 1970 and Svenbro 1992.

[241] Laronde 1987:140 for reperformance of the *Alcestis* (he reproduces images of the funerary reliefs on 138–139, plates 36–37); for dithyrambic performance, see Ceccarelli and Milanezi 2007, especially 198–203.

Before leaving Argonautic myth and *kitharôidia* in Sparta, it is worth considering the implications of a curious passage in Theocritus *Idyll* 22, the hymn to Castor and Polydeuces, in which the speaker asks in the rhetorical style of a *prooimion*:

> ὦ ἄμφω θνητοῖσι βοηθόοι, ὦ φίλοι ἄμφω,
> ἱππῆες κιθαρισταὶ ἀεθλητῆρες ἀοιδοί,
> Κάστορος ἢ πρώτου Πολυδεύκεος ἄρξομ' ἀείδειν;

> The both of you, who assist mortals, who are both dear to them,
> horsemen, citharists, athletes, singers,
> Whom first shall I begin to sing, Castor or Polydeuces?

Theocritus Idyll 22.23–25

Line 24 clearly alludes to a traditional hendiadys for "citharodes," ἄνδρες ἀοιδοὶ καὶ κιθαρισταί, which appears in early hexameter poetry, most notably Hesiod *Theogony* 95. But, although the Dioscuri were associated with an armed dance at Sparta (Plato *Laws* 796b), the characterization of them as singers-to-the-*kithara* is unique to this passage. Has Theocritus invented it?[242] If so, we might see it as a projection onto the twins of the cultural enthusiasms of the apotheosized royal sibling couple of Ptolemy Philadelphus and Arsinoe (the *Theoi Adelphoi*), who may be the implicit recipients of the hymnic praise directed toward the Dioscuri in the poem.[243] Similarly, in *Idyll* 18, the "Epithalamium for Helen," Helen is uniquely praised for her ability to play and sing to the lyre (35–37: "Surely no one is as skilled as Helen at striking [*krotêsai*] the *lura* and singing of Artemis and broad-breasted Athena").[244] The praise could again reflect the lyric interests exhibited by Arsinoe, whose marriage to Philadelphus the poem, some have argued, indirectly

---

[242] Thus Sens 1997:94, who sees a "special literary point" in the "association of poet and honorands."

[243] Sens 1997:23 discusses echoes between the Dioscuri and the Ptolemies. See Part I.8 above for the Ptolemies as patrons and practitioners of *kitharôidia*.

[244] Helen's musical talents are better attested than those of her brothers. She was imagined in Spartan cult as a chorus leader of young girls (Aristophanes *Lysistrata* 1296–1321; cf. Calame 1997:191–192), and the mention of Artemis and the choral setting of *Idyll* 18 as a whole recall that role. It is possible that the girls (*parthenikai*, 2) who notionally sing *Idyll* 18 are recalling the days when Helen served as lyric accompanist (*kitharistês*) to their chorus (cf. Sappho fr. 58), and sang the *humnoi* that prefaced their choral songs. But Theocritus may as well envision a solo lyric performance, a transcendent extension of Helen's "prima donna" role in the choral dance (on which cf. Nagy 1990b:345). For the transformation of *kitharistês* into *kitharôidos*, see Section 3 above.

celebrates.[245] But if the *Idyll* 22 passage is a crypto-encomium of the Ptolemies, this need not entail that the lyric Dioscuri represent a Theocritean innovation. Theocritus may rather be performing some virtuosic musico-poetic archaeology, uncovering a traditional motif in citharodic poetry: the assimilation of the athletic twins to the image of the agonistic citharodes who sing their heroic exploits—note the pointedly asyndetic intertwining of the athletic and the musical in ἱππῆες κιθαρισταὶ ἀεθλητῆρες ἀοιδοί.[246] Such a motif would have been rooted at the Spartan Carneia, but was conceivably at home in other festal contexts in cities in which the divinized Dioscuri were honored, including Athens.[247] The Dioscuri also received cult on Archaic Lesbos— Alcaeus composed a hymn to them (fr. 34)—a fact that is notable in light of the predominantly Lesbian provenance of the citharodes at the Carneia; perhaps they brought these lyricized Dioscuri with them to Sparta.[248] Given that Theocritus' poem as a whole plays with the form of the Archaic *humnos*, and the passage in question is markedly proemial, the citharodic casting of the Dioscuri may have originally figured in proemial evocations of the brothers in locally relevant *humnoi* that prefaced the performance of *nomoi*.[249] But it could as well have been elaborated in one of the epic narratives featuring the Dioscuri that constituted the text of a *nomos*, e.g. the voyage of the Argo, the Calydonian boar hunt, the battle against the Hippocoontidae, or the

---

[245] See Griffiths 1979:86–91; cf. Hunter 1996:163.

[246] Cf. the remarks on the lyric Achilles above, the citharodic Heracles below. The musical skill of the Dioscuri, married to their martial and athletic prowess, might also have heroically validated the lyric enthusiasms of Spartan aristocrats (cf. Alcman PMG 41, with Plutarch *Lycurgus* 24), perhaps even their occasional participation in the Carneian citharodic *agônes* alongside the professional Lesbian singers. Aristotle *Politics* 8.1341a33–34 supplies the relevant information that, around the time of the Persian Wars, a Spartan *khorêgos* himself played the *aulos* for his chorus, which may be indicative of a wider dabbling by non-professionals in musical contests in early Sparta. Cf. Wilson 2000:131.

[247] The twins in Athens: Pausanias 1.18.1; Plutarch *Life of Theseus* 31–33. See Shapiro 1989:149–154.

[248] Dioscuri on Lesbos: Shields 1917:78–79.

[249] Hunter 1996:52–57 discusses the intertextual play between *Idyll* 22 and the (rhapsodic) *Homeric Hymn (33) to the Dioscuri*. Leutsch 1856:342 thought that a hymnic invocation preserved in Dionysius of Halicarnassus *On Composition* 17, ὦ Ζηνὸς καὶ Λήδας κάλλιστοι σωτῆρες 'O finest saviors, born of Zeus and Leda' (fr. dub. 9 Gostoli), was from a Terpandrean composition. The attribution to Terpander was prompted by the spondee-heavy meter, classified by Dionysius as a Molossian, which is loosely similar to fr. 3 and fr. dub. 8 Gostoli, the latter of which was called Terpandrean by Bergk also because of its spondaic make-up. See West 1982:55–56 and Gostoli 1990:151. Perhaps the verse did belong to a citharodic *humnos*, but there is no way to be sure; the meter is not a reliable guide.

brothers' rescue of Helen from Theseus and Perithous, a story treated chorally by Alcman (fr. 21) and in the Cycle (*Cypria* fr. 13 Bernabé). A lyric Helen might similarly have made an appearance in any number of citharodic epics performed in Sparta. The scholia to *Idyll* 18 report that "some things" (τινα) in Theocritus' poem were derived from the *Helen* of Stesichorus.[250] One of those things was perhaps the image of Helen singing hymns to her *lura*. In view of Stesichorus' debt to *kitharôidia*, however, we might further speculate that a citharodic exemplar, localized in Sparta, stood behind his lyric Helen.[251]

Although no literary trace of the lyric Dioscuri exists outside of *Idyll* 22, Attic vase painting offers a possible reflex of the theme, significantly in close connection to the image of a citharode. On the shoulder of a red-figured hydria from c. 430–420 BCE the Kadmos Painter has depicted a scene of *theoxenia*, a sacred feast set by mortals for the divinized Dioscuri, who are shown approaching on horseback a column-framed hall in which a table covered with offerings and a couch have been prepared for them.[252] Propped upright against cushions on the couch are two identical lyres, looking somewhat like anthropomorphized prefigurations of the twins who will notionally recline there to play them. While the lyres and couches in an interior setting imply sympotic music making, the painter has depicted in the foreground of the image the characteristically unsympotic figure of a bearded citharode in full *skeuê*, playing a grand concert *kithara* and wearing an ankle-length, elaborately decorated robe and a victory wreath. A brightly checked cloth hangs from the back of the *kithara*, as we see in many images of festival *agônistai*. The precise relation of this citharode to the represented setting of the *theoxenia* is unclear. The inscription that runs above his head, *komos*, is not much help; it merely indicates that the citharodic music celebrates the triumphant return of the twins. Are we to think that he is a mythical figure contemporary with the Dioscuri, prepared to entertain them at this idealized, exemplary *theoxenia*? Paul Veyne has made the interesting argument that the musician is Tyndareus, the twins' father.[253] If so, his depiction in

---

[250] Cf. Hunter 1996:149–151.

[251] For the possibility that Stesichorus was active in Sparta, see Bowra 1961:106–115.

[252] Plovdiv, Departmental Archaeological Museum 298; Maas and Snyder 1989:74, fig. 7, with their comments on p57. The connection between the hydria and *Idyll* 22.24 was first made in Chapouthier 1935:134n3.

[253] Veyne 2000:11, who also argues that the unidentified woman shown standing across from the citharode with her arms raised in surprise or delight is Leda. What Veyne is essentially arguing is that the Kadmos Painter is imagining the original *theoxenia*, the twins' once-upon-a-time homecoming to Sparta.

citharodic costume would seem to reflect a tradition that *kitharôidia* was a Tyndarid family affair (recall Helen's lyric panache). Or are we looking at a snapshot of an actual *theoxenia* festival, and is this a real-life citharode providing musical entertainment for the notionally visiting divinities, presumably by singing their own *kleos* to them?[254] In either case, the constellation of citharode, Dioscuri, and the lyres that "sit in" for them must reflect the implication of the brothers in citharodic poetry, and possibly their occasional characterization in that poetry as practitioners of *kitharôidia*.

It is worth noting too that on the Argo metope of the Sicyonian Monopteros in Delphi, the horse-mounted Dioscuri are shown closely flanking the two citharodes, Orpheus and (probably) Philammon (Plate 8). Could the sculptor have reflexively grouped these Argonauts together because the twins' exploits—martial, athletic, and perhaps musical as well—were an especially popular theme for citharodic songs? The Dioscuri were worshiped in Sicyon; Pausanias 2.7.5 mentions their sanctuary there. A panel on a different wall of the Monopteros that is devoted to another one of their deeds, cattle rustling in Arcadia, also points to their importance in Sicyon. The sculptural program of the Monopteros might thus reflect a particular emphasis placed upon the Dioscuri in Sicyonian citharodic culture.[255]

11. Heracles *kitharôidos*

A rich vein of iconographical evidence points to the cithardic performance of Heraclean epic in Athens. I refer to the numerous depictions, on a range of Attic ceramic vessels produced from around 530 BCE until the end of the sixth century, of Heracles playing the part of an agonistic citharode, holding a concert *kithara* as he mounts or stands on the festival *bêma*, ready to perform for a divine and occasionally

---

[254] This seems to be the interpretation of Maas and Snyder 1989:226n23. Cf. Chapouthier 1935:133-134, who thinks that the musician is a priest and the woman a priestess. Veyne 2000:11-12 notes parallels for the performance of theoxenic music meant to entertain "feasting" gods. If the Kadmos Painter is showing us a "real" *theoxenia*, it is still unclear whether it is set in Sparta or Athens. There was a festival for the Dioscuri at Athens, the Anakeia, but we know nothing about its musical aspects (Parker 1996:97; 2005:157). A Spartan setting is possible: Burn 1987:25 argues that later-fifth-century vases with Spartan-themed paintings were commissioned by pro-Spartan Athenian aristocrats.

[255] Cf. Boardman 1978a:16. For a more politically oriented reading of the composition of the Argo metope, see Neer 2007:245-246.

mortal audience that almost always includes, but is not always limited to his and Athens' patroness, Athena. Plate 6, from a black-figured amphora by the Andokides Painter, is a representative scene: Heracles, characteristically attired as adventurer and warrior, with his lion skin and quiver, steps onto the *bêma* as he tunes up the grand *kithara* in his arms; an expectant Pallas Athena, in helmet and with spear, looks on.[256] John Boardman has sought to contextualize such scenes within a broader propagandistic deployment of Heraclean myth and imagery by the Peisistratid regime; in particular, he argues, the images may be meant to reflect the Peisistratids' own "heroic" efforts at fostering musical arts on the civic level, above all their active involvement in the Panathenaic *mousikoi agônes*.[257]

It is possible that the figure of Heracles *kitharôidos* existed solely as a visual expression of themes in Peisistratean *Kulturpolitik*. Alternatively, it could be the artists' visual conflation of medium and message—Heracles imagined as one of the citharodes who sing his *kleos* in Peisistratean Athens. But a specific poetic counterpart to the image, also responsive to the tyrant's interests, and also localized at the Panathenaia, is entirely conceivable.[258] Besides an intriguing reference in Theocritus *Idyll* 24.109–110 to Heracles' being taught to play the "boxwood *phorminx*," i.e. the *kithara*, by the Eleusinian priest Eumolpus— here called the son of Philammon of Delphi, a conspicuous citharodic pedigree—there is, however, no explicit trace of a poetic account of Herakles *kitharôidos* in the literary record. We find no indication that

---

[256] Heracles' posture and gesture—stepping up to the *bêma*, tuning the *kithara*—are typical of citharodes/citharists on late Archaic and early Classical vases; cf. the identical schema on an early-fifth-century pelike by the Pan Painter (New York, Solow Art and Architecture Foundation; Bundrick 2005:167, fig. 98).

[257] Boardman 1975:10–11; cf. 1972:69. (Boardman oddly suggests, however, that the images refer to the Homeric recitals, by which he must mean the rhapsodic recitals, in Athens.) Schauenburg 1979 follows up, demonstrating in detail the iconographical derivation of the Heracles *kitharôidos* scenes from those of mortal agonists shown competing at the Panathenaia. Cf. Kotsidu 1991:113–115, with the helpful bibliography provided at p216nn29–33; Shapiro 1992:69; Bundrick 2005:160–161.

[258] Cf. Beazley 1964: "This new conception of Herakles must be due to a poem that has not come down to us, in which he was depicted as not only brave ... but the friend of the Muses as well" (76). Cf. Schauenburg 1979:75. Dugas 1944 had earlier conjectured the vase painters were illustrating "an episode from the life of Heracles" in which the hero sang to the *kithara* for his divine audience (62). This would seem to presume a poetic tradition. Dugas' theory that this episode reflected a Pythagorean interest in the lyre is interesting (70), but ultimately unconvincing. The glamorous agonistic citharode is far from the meditative realms of the Pythagorean. And although Heracles is shown on some later-sixth-century vessels playing the lyre or *barbitos*, he generally does so in exuberant comastic milieux—again, territory not conducive to deep Pythagorean speculation.

it appeared in the Heracles epics attributed to Peisander of Rhodian Cameirus or Panyassis of Halicarnassus (although it may have appeared somewhere in either or both). Indeed, on fifth-century Attic vessels it is the *amousia* of Heracles that is illustrated, in scenes in which the young hero assaults his lyre teacher, Linus.[259] But the Theocritean clue, to which we will return below, is significant; we think of Theocritus' analogous recovery in *Idyll* 18.24 of recondite citharodic lore, namely the submerged tradition in which the Dioscuri were figured as citharodes. And we might expect that, just as the citharodic Heracles disappears from the visual record shortly after the fall of the tyrants, so might the corresponding poetic accounts also fade from performers' repertoire, more gradually perhaps, but still leaving few traces, after the demise of the tyrants' cultural-political program.[260]

The iconographical record shows beyond doubt that citharodes were performing prominently at the Panathenaic *agônes* under the Peisistratids; indeed, the vase painters based the visual character of their Heracles upon these real-life musicians.[261] If we do posit a poetic source for the Heracles *kitharôidos* images, then the nomic texts sung by the Panathenaic citharodes would be a logical place for it to have been elaborated—the citharodes were themselves singing Heracles after their own image, and thus embedding a heroic exemplar for their own art within their songs.[262] Rhapsodes were, after all, mostly,

[259] E.g. a red-figured cup by Douris from c. 480 BCE, on which Heracles bludgeons Linus with a stool (Munich, Staatliche Antikensammlungen und Glyptothek 2646; Bundrick 2005:73, fig. 44). The story of the attack is variously related in late literary sources, e.g. Aelian *Historical Miscellanies* 3.32, in which Heracles stabs Linus with his *plêktron*; Apollodorus 1.14.2, 2.63.4; Diodorus Siculus 3.67 (Linus bludgeoned with the lyre itself); Pausanias 9.29.9. Cf. discussion in Bundrick 2005:72–74.

[260] Heracles *kitharôidos* continues to make rare appearances, however, in late Classical (on one Apulian vase) and Imperial iconography; see Schauenburg 1979:53. Also notable is a fragment from a red-figured vessel of around 430 BCE that shows a youth holding a *kithara* and mounting a *bêma* in front of a shrine of Heracles (Bucharest 03207; CVA Bucharest 1, plate 32, 1). The image could refer to the *mousikoi agônes* at the Herakleia in Marathon (cf. n119 above), where perhaps the memory of the citharodic hero was kept alive. In any case, we would expect that citharodes competing at the Herakleia would sing Heraclean narratives.

[261] Cf. Schauenburg 1979: "Ohne Zweifel ist das Schema des Herakles auf dem Bema von den Bildern mit Agonen Sterblicher abzuleiten, die, wenn lokalisierbar, mit den Panathenäen zu verknüpfen sind" (73). Bundrick 2005:160 notes apropos of the Panathenaic localization of Heracles *kitharôidos* that Hermes, who is often depicted alongside Athena in Heracles' audience, may, as Hermes Agoraios, "serve to set the scene in the Athenian Agora, which may have been the locale for the *mousikoi agones*" in the sixth century BCE.

[262] For Heracles as a model of the athleticism involved in cithardic performance, see Part I.18.

if not entirely, focused on reciting the Homeric *Iliad* and *Odyssey* at the festival, as per the policy of Hipparchus himself. This left the citharodes free to perform episodes from the rich store of Heraclean narratives, among which the *ad hoc* scene of the hero's citharodic performance may have been inserted. But at what point? Mount Olympus, after the hero's apotheosis, seems unlikely.[263] The allusion to Eumolpus as Heracles' music teacher points to the story of the hero's initiation into Eleusinian cult, which Eumolpus was said to have overseen; the initiation episode was in turn subordinated to the larger epic narrative of Heracles' journey to the Underworld (*katabasis*) to fetch Cerberus. But the scene depicted by the artists is itself clearly not an initiation, nor is it a lesson with Eumolpus, nor is there any hint of the Underworld. It is rather a proto-Panathenaic agonistic occasion of some sort, on which Heracles plays the part of a virtuoso competitor. I would propose instead that the scene is set shortly after the Gigantomachy, in which both Athena and Heracles, the latter expertly deploying his mighty bow, played critical roles in assuring the gods' victory. A relevant textual witness to traditions about the aftermath of that battle is Euripides *Heracles* 179–180. Amphitryon recalls how Heracles, "after piercing the Giants through the sides with his winged arrows, sang in a revel (*kômos*) with the gods the *kallinikos* song" (Γίγασι πλευροῖς πτήν᾽ ἐναρμόσας βέλη | τὸν καλλίνικον μετὰ θεῶν ἐκώμασεν). First, we may note the strong possibility of a muted allusion to the lyric Heracles in Euripides' use of ἐναρμόσας, a participle from the verb ἐναρμόζειν, which means 'to fix in, pierce', but which has also distinct applications to the musical phenomena related to *harmonia* 'tuning, mode'. At Aristophanes *Knights* 989, for instance, the verb (in the middle voice) describes the tuning of the lyre.

Euripides may have in mind the metaphorical association between the lyre and the bow, articulated most famously in the detailed simile of *Odyssey* 21.404–411, in which Odysseus, stringing his bow, is compared to a singer expert at stringing and tuning his *phorminx*. There the symbolic force of the metaphor is clear: Odysseus will restore harmony to his house and island, currently in a state of disorder thanks to the suitors, through the violent deployment of the bow. Similarly, in the Euripidean vision of Giant-slaying Heracles—a vision that is, it should be said, likely picking up on representational themes in traditional accounts of the Gigantomachy known in Athens—the hero wields his bow as a sort of lyre, his archery aiming to suppress the cosmic

---

[263] Cf. Dugas 1944:62.

disorder threatened by the Giants and to guarantee harmony in the world.[264] (In images such as our Plate 6, the empty quiver on Heracles' back invites us to view his *kithara* as a transfigured bow; visual and conceptual echoes of his sometime antagonist, Apollo, who also keeps order with bow and *kithara* in alternation, are surely intended.)[265] In Euripides' play, the performance of the victory revel-song (*kallinikos kômos*) by Heracles and the gods gives musical expression to that newfound harmonic order.[266]

Indeed, on a number of vases from the same period that sees the clustering of images of Heracles *kitharôidos*, Heracles is depicted playing either the lyre or the *auloi* in the midst of a high-spirited *kômos*, surrounded by satyrs (who had assisted Dionysus in fighting the Giants); sometimes other gods are present as well.[267] Heracles' more restrained performance as agonistic *kitharôidos* represents an occasionally *ad hoc* variation of the *kallinikos kômos*, a stylized formalization of its exuberant, free-form musical energy.[268] A citharodic Gigantomachy localized in Peisistratean Athens is a logical source for this shift in musical setting and characterization. In such a musico-poetic performance tradition the theme of Heracles *kitharôidos* would function as a sort of self-aggrandizing *mise en abyme*. Citharodes sing a Gigantomachy, whose heroic protagonist in turn sings to the *kithara* not a simple *kallinikos*, but a more poetically refined and musically elaborate commemoration of his exploits alongside the gods—that is, he sings his own Gigantomachy. And inasmuch as that song symbolizes the restoration of cosmic order within the represented world of myth, its reenactment, as it were, implies that the real-life citharodic song that frames

---

[264] In Pindar *Pythian* 1.13–14 the noisy, grotesque Giants are made to exemplify all that is irreconcilable with the cosmically stabilizing lyric music of Apollo and the Muses, which is perfectly in tune with the Olympian divine order (1–12).

[265] Likewise, the comparison of Odysseus as he strings his bow to a lyre singer implicitly figures him as Apollo, enforcing law and order in an inharmonious Ithaca. Apollonian intimations are only strengthened since Odysseus' revenge is set against the backdrop of the festival of Apollo (*Odyssey* 20.275–278, 21.267–228, 338). Cf. Wilson 2004:270. On the structural and symbolic relation between Apollo's bow and lyre, see Monbrun 2001, with n269 below. On Heracles' quiver as a visual reminder of his *aristeia* in the Gigantomachy, see Mackay 1995:293.

[266] On the *kallinikos* song in Heraclean myth and cult, see Lawler 1948.

[267] Examples and discussion in Schauenburg 1979:54–55.

[268] The two variant forms of celebration are linked on a privately owned amphora discussed in depth in Schauenburg 1979 (figs. 1–2 on p50). The obverse shows Heracles *kitharôidos* stepping onto the *bêma* along with Athena, who plays the *auloi*— the image clearly is meant to prefigure the *mousikoi agônes* of the Panathenaia; the reverse, only partly preserved, shows a comastic scene, with a lyre-playing Hermes leading a procession of Dionysus and silens.

it might have an analogous symbolic effect in the Athenian here-and-now.[269] Further, the ordering interventions of hero and citharode may have been thought to echo the sociopolitical "harmony" guaranteed by the tyrants, who identified themselves with Heracles and were, of course, the primary patrons of civic *mousikê*.[270] That patronage prominently included the Panathenaic citharodic *agôn*, for which Heracles' auto-epinician citharodic turn before Athena likely served as *aition*.[271]

This latter scenario would be of a piece with the aetiological account of the Panathenaia as a whole that is recorded in Aristotle fr. 637 Rose, according to which the festival was founded "following the slaying of the Giant Asterios by Athena."[272] Gloria Ferrari has made compelling arguments that the popularity of other scene types featuring Athena and Heracles on sixth-century Attic vases specifically reflects the currency of this foundation legend in the years following the reorganization of the Panathenaic festival in or around 566 BCE.[273]

---

[269] Like Heracles *kitharôidos*, Apollo slays an earth-born monster (the Pythian serpent) with his bow and later celebrates his victory with the *phorminx* (*Homeric Hymn to Apollo* 356–374, 514–519). This sequence of events, god battles monster/god celebrates new order with music, was represented in compressed form in the auletic and citharistic *Puthikos nomos* performed at Delphi (Pollux *Onomasticon* 4.84; Strabo 9.3.10; cf. West 1992:212–214). At Athens, a Heracles-focused Gigantomachy narrative, capped by the hero's musical performance, was perhaps presented in a nomic framework modeled on these Pythian *nomoi*. Cf. Bundrick 2005:161 on the possible rivalry between Pythia and Panathenaia: "One could even say that Herakles in a sense usurps Apollo's position; might the depictions of Herakles proclaim Athens as a new rival to Delphi in in the realm of *mousikoi agones*?" In one tradition, Apollo sang a citharodic song to celebrate Zeus' victory over the Titans, a direct parallel to Heracles *kitharôidos* in the Gigantomachy (Seneca *Agamemnon* 332–334; cf. West 2002a:116n28 for related passages, and n277 below on the Titanomachy).

[270] Irwin 2005a:82 speculates on the political subtext of a Peisistratean Gigantomachy: it might have alluded to Peisistratus' definitive victory over his Alcmaeonid-led elite opponents at the Battle of Pallene. Thracian Pallene was also known as the site of the final defeat of the Giants (Diodorus Siculus 4.15). The Giant-slayer Heracles would thus figure Peisistratus in his fight against the hubristic elite of Athens. Indeed, Gigantomachy scenes become more common in the later 540s, after the Battle of Pallene; cf. Watrous 1982:165.

[271] Heracles was also made the founder of the athletic *agônes* at Olympia (see sources and bibliography in Nagy 1990b:119n16)—a significant precedent for his connection to the Panathenaia. The performance of the *kallinikos* song was traditionally associated with Heracles as exemplary Olympic victor (Pindar *Olympian* 9.1–4, alluding to Archilochus fr. 324W) as well as Giant-slayer. Cf. Lawler 1948:254; Ferrari 1994/1995:222.

[272] For the aetiological link between Gigantomachy and Panathenaia, see Pinney 1988:471; Schefold 1992:55–56; Shear 2001:31–37. Scenes from the battle were woven into the peplos presented to Athena at the Panathenaic festival.

[273] Pinney 1988 and Ferrari 1994/1995, in which she links the scene type of Athena and Heracles in a chariot to the *kallinikos kômos*. This latter article is critical of the theory of Boardman (cf. Boardman 1972, 1975) that the vase painters took their cues from

Her interpretation of the significance of the common scene of a striding, spear- and shield-equipped Athena on Panathenaic amphorae parallels the interpretation of Heracles *kitharôidos* that was offered above: "[I]t illustrates an *aition* of the Festival with an image, not of the battle, but of the goddess' victory dance, which becomes, in turn, the *aition* of the pyrrhic competition," that is, the *agôn* in the *purrikhê*, the armed dance.[274] A still more direct parallel is provided by a red-figured Panathenaic-shaped amphora by the Nikoxenos Painter, on which an armed Athena appears playing the kithara before a flaming altar placed between two cock-topped columns, traditional markers of a Panathenaic setting (Plate 11); a mortal agonistic citharode is represented on the reverse. Athena is usually depicted as an eager supporter of Heracles *kitharôidos*. Her appearance here as *kitharôidos* surely represents a variation on the Heraclean theme, and probably carries the same aetiological significance vis-à-vis the Panathenaic citharodic *agôn* as the musical Heracles does.[275] Since the amphora was produced around 500 BCE, not long after the fall of the Peisistratids, the image might reflect a reactionary turning away, at least on the part of some Panathenaic performers and audience members, from the tyrannical musical and festal politics with which the figure of Heracles *kitharôidos* was closely associated. It is now the divine patroness of the democratic city as a whole who models and founds the citharodic contest at her own festival.[276]

While there are many preserved visual representations of scenes from the Gigantomachy, poetic fragments, testimonia about composition and performance, and authorial attributions are lacking. It goes unmentioned in Homer and in the Hesiodic *Theogony*. The very

---

Peisistratean propaganda in producing images of Heracles. For Ferrari, it is simply Heracles' connection to the Panathenaia that motivates the images. As she notes, however (225–226), the Peisistratids maintained a keen interest in the festival, and, even if Peisistratus himself played no part in the reorganization of 566 (but this is uncertain; cf. Herington 1985:85–86), the Heraclean agenda of the tyrants conspicuously overlapped with the artists' celebration of the festival's charter myth, the currency of which in turn notably coincided with the tyrants' reign. Certainly, Heracles *kitharôidos* appears only at a point when the Peisistratids had been long established in power; it is thus difficult not to see in this figure a deliberate fusion of the glamour and prestige of festival, tyrant, and agonistic citharode.

[274] Pinney 1988:471, citing testimony of Dionysius of Halicarnassus *Roman Antiquities* 7.27.7 that links Athena to the armed dance and the Gigantomachy. Parker 2005:257n19 is skeptical of the interpretation, presumably because Athena is not explicitly depicted in a dance posture. An aetiological reading of Heracles *kitharôidos* is obviously less problematic in this respect.

[275] For Athena as a model aulete, cf. n268 above.

[276] Cf. Bundrick 2005:164.

elusiveness of an epic Gigantomachy could be a consequence of its status as a predominantly citharodic tradition, which, although widely diffused in performance—we can presume that citharodes sang versions of this Panhellenically appealing story at festivals across Greece, adding locally relevant elements such as the proto-Panathenaic Heracles *kitharôidos* where appropriate—nevertheless escaped uniform textualization and written transmission.[277] Besides the implicit evidence of Heracles *kitharôidos* already discussed, Attic vase painting may provide other indications that citharodes sang the Gigantomachy in sixth-century Athens, and continued to do so into the fifth century as well. A black-figured neck amphora from a painter of the Leagros Group, produced under the Peisistratids, has on one side a citharode mounting the *bêma* before a seated judge and standing spectators; on the reverse, Athena is shown about to deliver the *coup de grâce* to a kneeling Giant, either Enkelados or Asterios.[278] This latter image may be an illustration of the song the citharode will sing when he begins his performance.[279] Similarly, on one side of the neck of a red-figured volute krater by the Altamura Painter (London E 469, c. 470 BCE), a victorious citharode is depicted, attended by two Nikai; the body of the krater is taken up entirely by scenes from the Gigantomachy, which might illustrate the subject of the citharodic song. Alternatively, however, the Gigantomachies on both vases could allude more broadly to the Panathenaia itself, at which we may presume the depicted citharodes perform.[280]

This latter interpretation may be supported by a black-figured pelike from around 520 BCE (Dunedin E 48.226), which resembles the

---

[277] Vian 1952:184–222 reconstructs the narrative of a seventh-century BCE epic Gigantomachy, but does not speculate about performance medium. I note the attribution of a citharodic Titanomachy to Thamyris that is recorded by Heraclides of Pontus (*ap.* "Plutarch" *On Music* 3.1132a–b)—Titanomachies and Gigantomachies were often conflated, as Vian shows.

[278] London 1926, 6–28.7. See Maas and Snyder 1989:75, fig. 11, with discussion on p61.

[279] This is suggested by Webster 1972:161; cf. Shapiro 1989:41–42, who identifies the Giant as Enkelados.

[280] Cf. Webster 1972:161–162; Bundrick 2005:168. While the scene of the citharode's victory on the Altamura Painter's krater could well be the Panathenaia, it is notable that Triptolemus, mythical priest of Demeter at Eleusis, is depicted opposite the citharode on the neck of the vessel. Might the citharode have been a competitor at the Eleusinia festival, which, certainly in the third century BCE, and probably earlier, included musical as well as athletic and equestrian contests. See Parker 2005:210, 328; Simms 1975; on the antiquity of the festival, Aelius Aristides *Panathenaicus* 13.189.4–5; on its athletic games, Pindar *Olympian* 9.99, 13.110, *Isthmian* 1.57, with Kyle 1987:47. Of course, the inclusion of Triptolemus might allude to a separate victory at the (less prestigious) Eleusinia; thus the two Nikai surrounding the citharode.

roughly contemporary neck amphora in London. A bearded man, apparently a rhapsode, stands in declamatory posture atop a *bêma* before a seated judge; the reverse has a Gigantomachy scene featuring Athena.[281] If the rhapsode is performing at the Panathenaia, we would expect that he is reciting Homer and that the reverse image accordingly refers to the festival context of the performance rather than the rhapsode's poem. Of course, the contest need not be Panathenaic, and, even if it is, the vase might attest some *ad hoc* exception to the Panathenaic Rule, an occasion on which the Gigantomachy was recited.

12. Heracleia and Hesiodica

Other episodes from the life of Heracles were probably narrated in early citharodic *nomoi*, but the evidence is especially indirect. Richard Martin has argued that the *Iliad*, in having Thamyris journey from the house of Eurytus in Oechalia on his way to the fatal clash with the Muses near Dorion (2.596), alludes agonistically to the *Sack of Oechalia*, a rival epic poem from the Heraclean cycle of myths.[282] Thamyris, we saw above, is imagined in this scene as an agonistic citharode, and thus as an implicit rival to the rhapsode. While a *Sack of Oechalia* was performed by rhapsodes—it belonged in the repertoire of the Samian rhapsodic clan of the Creophylids—it would seem more likely that the Iliadic allusion is to a cithardic tradition of singing the *Sack*.[283] As was argued above, Thamyris is imagined in the *Iliad* as a proto-professional citharode. And since we are probably to assume that it was Heracles' attack on Eurytus that terminated Thamyris' engagement in Oechalia and precipitated his wandering, it would make sense that the *Sack* would be thought his (and thus cithardic) property—he experienced it firsthand, after all.

Attic iconography points to the cithardic setting of other Heraclean adventures, but, again, the evidence, such as it is, involves the problematic assumption that a mythical scene on one side of a vase visualizes the subject of the song a singer is depicted singing on the other. An amphora of Group E from 550–540 BCE has on the reverse a citharode standing between two cock-topped columns, which, despite the absence of a *bêma*, suggest that the performance is set at the Panathenaia. On the obverse, Heracles battles the Nemean

---

[281] See Shapiro 1989, pl. 22 b and c, with discussion on p46; cf. Shapiro 1993:98.
[282] Martin 1989:229–230.
[283] On the rhapsodic *Sack of Oechalia*, see Burkert 1972.

lion, a tableau also centered between two columns. This image could be intended as a metaphorical expression of the competitive struggle that the agonistic citharode endures, or it could more generally refer to the Heraclean propaganda of the Panathenaia's tyrannical patrons. But it could, not necessarily to the exclusion of these possible meanings, reflect the theme of the citharode's song.[284] A somewhat later red-figured amphora by the Andokides Painter (c. 525–520 BCE) similarly pairs an image of Heracles' bout with the Lion opposite a scene of an aulodic performance, an arrangement that might also indicate that the aulode is singing the hero's exploits.[285] An Archaic tradition of Heraclean *aulôidia* at *mousikoi agônes* is suggested too by Pausanias, who says that in Thebes the sixth-century Arcadian aulode Echembrotus dedicated a bronze tripod to Heracles that he had won "singing for the Greeks melodies and elegies" at the Pythian *agôn* of 586 BCE (10.7.6).[286]

Finally, we might consider those compositions of Stesichorus devoted to specific exploits of Heracles, such as the *Geryoneis*, the *Cerberus*, and the *Cycnus*, to be products of the (choral) reception of an established tradition of *kitharôidia* treating such episodes. Accordingly, we might reframe the view that the numerous Archaic vase paintings and sculptural representations of these adventures were influenced by performances of Stesichorean lyric epic—a not entirely feasible scenario.[287] The source for at least some of these images, especially for those that predate Stesichorus, may rather be the same itinerant

---

[284] Cf. Shapiro 1992:65. For plates of both sides of the amphora (San Antonio 86.134.40), with interpretive discussion, see Picon and Shapiro 1996:86–89. See now Stansbury-O'Donnell 2006:89–127 for the concurrent depiction of performance and theme of performed song in Archaic vase painting.

[285] Basel BS 491; cf. Shapiro 1992:67, with fig. 45; Schauenburg 1961, figs. 1 and 2. The fight with the lion would make suitable material for a *nomos* on the model of the *Puthikos*, in which Apollo's slaying of the serpent was represented. Lachmann 1929 observes remarkable structural and narrative-mimetic similarities between a programmatic Tunisian flute piece describing a battle with a lion, which was still performed by Bedouin musicians in the early twentieth century, and the *Puthikos nomos*. Cf. West 1992:213n53.

[286] Cf. discussion in West 1974:4–5. Bowie 1986:34 discusses the possibility of Heraclean elegiac-aulodic narrative poetry by Archilochus. A calyx krater by Euphronius (Louvre G 103; c. 510–500 BCE) has a concert scene on the obverse, with an aulete, named Polykles, mounting the *bêma* before an audience; on the reverse, Heracles wrestles Antaeus, perhaps the mimetic subject of Polykles' instrumental auletic *nomos*. Cf. Webster 1972:49; Shapiro 1989:42–43 (who notes that a Polykles is also depicted as a citharode on a contemporary oinochoe, Villa Giulia 20839–40); Bundrick 2005:163–164.

[287] See Robertson 1969 for Stesichorean influence on images of the Geryon encounter; on the *Cycnus* as model for Attic vase paintings of the battle between Cycnus and Heracles, see Shapiro 1984:524.

citharodes who influenced the narrative and musical content of Stesichorus' songs.[288] It is worth making a few observations and suggestions in this regard, even if they must remain highly speculative.

For Stesichorus' *Cycnus* we could imagine a citharodic predecessor in the form of a lyric counterpart to the presumably rhapsodic version of the *Shield of Heracles* that we now have, which has been dated to the first quarter of the sixth century BCE, while Stesichorus was composing his own works.[289] Surely something like the "pulp epic" sound and fury that distinguishes the narrative of the mortal combat between Heracles and the barbaric Cycnus (backed by his father, Ares) in the *Shield* would have suited the musically virtuosic setting of a *nomos*.[290] In Hypothesis A to the *Shield* (PMG 207) Stesichorus is said to have attributed the poem as he knew it to Hesiod, presumably in his *Cycnus*. As Bowra notes of this attribution, Stesichorus either used "'Hesiod' in a generic sense as early writers used 'Homer'," or he knew the poem "in a slightly different form" from the (rhapsodic) *Shield* we have.[291]

Did Stesichorus know a "Hesiodic" *kitharôidia*? Hesiod is mentioned alongside Homer by the Peripatetic scholar Chamaeleon (fr. 28 Wehrli = Athenaeus 14.620c) as a poet whose works used to be sung as well as recited.[292] *Suda* s.v. Τέρπανδρος records a tradition that Terpander

---

[288] Cf. Brize 1980:28–29 for the argument that both Stesichorus and the artists were influenced by preexisting oral traditions, not only of Heraclean saga, but also Trojan narrative.

[289] On traces of rhapsodic performance in the text of the *Shield*, see Martin 2005:166–167; Janko 1986:39–40.

[290] On the "pulp epic" qualities of the rhapsodic *Shield*, see Martin 2005. One thinks of the "pulpiness" of our one preserved text of a citharodic *nomos*, the *Persians* of Timotheus, with its baroque descriptions of violent combat and the lurid suffering of the defeated. Such excess is largely attributable to the sensationalist aesthetic of the New Music in general, but it may as well have been an extension of certain preexisting tendencies in the texts of the Classical *nomos*.

[291] Bowra 1961:80. Cf. Janko 1986:59 on competing variants of the *Cycnus* narrative in the early sixth century BCE. As Janko and Bowra (80–81) both demonstrate, there are at least two significant differences between the Stesichorean *Cycnus* and our *Shield* (in the former, Heracles initially retreats from Ares and Cycnus is said to make a shrine to Apollo from the skulls of travelers; neither of these details is to be found in the latter). These divergences could be explained as Stesichorus' creative innovations on the myth as recounted in the *Shield*, but we might also conjecture that Stesichorus was following an altogether separate version of the Cycnus-Heracles battle. We may also note that in sixth-century Attic vase painting the battle is depicted in ways that are distinct from the *Shield* narrative (see Shapiro 1984). Again, we could explain the divergences as the vase painters' creative interpretations of the myth, or we might imagine a separate musico-poetic (citharodic?) source of inspiration for the images.

[292] Chamaeleon mentions Archilochus, Mimnermus, and Phocylides as other poets who were sung, but with these aulodic performance is probably at issue. On the citharodic performance of Hesiod, see too Koller 1956:165; Böhme 1970:135–138. Nagy

---

was a descendant (ἀπόγονος) of Hesiod, and that he was born not in Lesbian Antissa, but in either Boeotian Arne or Aeolian Cyme, the native home of Hesiod's father. As with Terpander's genealogical links to Homer, these putative Hesiodic affiliations may reflect the historical practice of setting "Hesiodic" texts to "Terpandrean" *kitharôidia*, which was perhaps cultivated above all at Boeotian festivals.[293] Perhaps there were even attempts made within Boeotian citharodic culture to make the Lesbian citharode, like Hesiod, a transplanted local. Terpander was said to have invented a *nomos* called the Boeotian (scholia *ad* Aristophanes *Acharnians* 13). He was attributed a student, Cepion or Capion (as Pollux *Onomasticon* 4.65 has it), who, some claimed, invented the concert *kithara*, and whose name was given to one of the canonical Terpandrean *nomoi*.[294] Capion is attested as a Boeotian name, and so may represent a Boeotian incursion into the Terpandrean *diadokhê*.[295]

We saw in Section 3 that in his native Boeotian manifestation at the Heliconian shrine of the Muses Hesiod was imagined as a citharode (Pausanias 9.30.2), his statue placed alongside those of other famous citharodes honored at the site, including that of Arion of Methymna, a member of the Lesbian-Terpandrean line of citharodes. The very tripod (it was said) that Hesiod had won at a song contest in Chalcis and dedicated to the Heliconian Muses was also on display here (*Works and Days* 650–659). Hesiod's own lineage could be traced back to legendary citharodes such as Linus, Pierus of Pieria, and Orpheus (*Contest Between Homer and Hesiod* 4).[296] At Helicon, Hesiod received hero cult alongside those for the citharodes Linus and Thamyris. It is notable that a text evoking citharodic and choral commemorations of Linus was ascribed to Hesiod (fr. 305 M-W: "Linus … whom all mortal singers and citharists

---

1990b:27–28, who is interested in distinguishing modes of performance for "poetry" and "song," however, would discount Chamaeleon's testimony as a retrojection of post-Classical musical settings of rhapsodic or recited verse onto an earlier time.

[293] So Stesichorus was made a son or grandson of Hesiod (Philochorus FGrH 328 F 213; Cicero *Republic* 2.20; Tzetzes *Life of Hesiod* 18). Cyme was also said to be Homer's native city, so his supposed birth there might rather speak to Terpander's Homeric affiliations; cf. n107 above.

[294] Invention of *kithara*: "Plutarch" *On Music* 6.1133c; Douris FGrH 76 F 81; *nomos*: Pollux *Onomasticon* 4.65.

[295] The name Capion is attested in Boeotian inscriptions; see Vollgraff 1901; cf. Flach 1883:207n1. However, Wilamowitz 1903:90n1 thinks that the name Cepion/Capion derives from the *nomos* called the *kêpiôn*; cf. n104 above.

[296] Cf. Calame 1996:54 and *passim* for the myth-historical ties between Helicon and the citharodically seminal regions of Pieria and Thrace. On Pierus of Pieria as a mediating figure between the citharodic cultures of Pieria and Helicon, see Pausanias 9.29.2.

bewail at festivals and choral performances"); one is tempted to place it in the context of this Heliconian musical hero culture.

There were *mousikoi agônes*, including both *kitharôidia* and *rhapsôidia*, attached to the Mouseia festival at Helicon, which were reorganized by the city of Thespiae in the Hellenistic period.[297] As the reorganization suggests, however, the *agônes* must have boasted a longer prehistory. Inscriptional evidence shows that the contests were changed through the third-century BCE reorganization from thematic (cash and valuables prizes) to stephanitic, so it is reasonable to assume that musical *agônes* had previously been held at the festival, perhaps going back as far as the Archaic period.[298] The Mouseia, or its festal predecessor, is then one possible site at which citharodic and rhapsodic Hesiodica may have been performed side by side and exerted mutual influence upon one another. The *Shield*, however, has been persuasively connected to the performance context of the Theban Herakleia (or Iolaeia), another Boeotian festival that could have featured citharodic as well as rhapsodic renditions of "Hesiodic" texts.[299] Boeotia, although famous for star auletes such as Pronomus and Antigeneidas, must also have been an important region for *kitharôidia*. Plutarch attests to the overwhelming popular enthusiasm for *kitharôidia* at the Thespian Erotideia festival (*Dialogue on Love* 749c). We may presume that similar excitement attended the citharodic events at the Thespian Mouseia as well. The city of Orchomenus hosted the Charitesia festival, whose citharodic *agônes* are attested by second-century BCE inscriptions, but must have been established considerably earlier; the Amphiaraia

---

[297] On the musical contests of the Hellenistic Mouseia, see Bonnet 2001.

[298] Cf. Jamot 1895; on the reorganization, see now Knoepfler 1996. Lamberton 1988:496–497 argues that the musical contests of the Mouseia (as well as the cult of Hesiod) were established by the Thespians only in the Hellenistic period, since the archaeological record yields no definitive traces of earlier activity at the site. But this view seems too extreme (cf. Calame 1996:51–52, 54; Veneri 1996:81n30). We may note, for instance, that Pausanias 9.30.1 mentions statues of the Muses there by Classical sculptors such as Strongylion and Cephisodotus; these could be later dedications imported from elsewhere (as was Myron's Dionysus, dedicated by Sulla), but they could as well have been original installations.

[299] On text-internal evidence for Theban performance of the *Shield*, see Janko 1986:48, who puts forward the Herakleia/Iolaeia as the site of the poem's first performance. Larsen 2007:51 speaks of the *Shield* more generally as an "archaic Boiotian literary production and ... a potentially important source for the Boiotian collective in the archaic period." Of course, Herakleia festivals proliferated across Classical Greek cities, so Heraclean *kitharôidia*, despite any local factors, would have been a supralocally mobile and marketable commodity.

at Oropus included a citharodic contest in the Classical period.[300] And Thebes was a city built, after all, on the citharodic music of Amphion. There too, as at Helicon, Linus received hero cult (Pausanias 9.29.9). Indeed, the city's cultivation of lyric song dates back to the Mycenaean period. A Linear B tablet attests to the official role of lyre players in Theban palatial culture.[301]

Indeed, it would not be surprising if there were Boeotian traditions of citharodic song dealing with not only Heracles, but also the local hero Amphion. Pausanias 9.5.8 records that in the "*epê* about Europa" it is said that "Amphion was the first to use the lyre, with Hermes as his teacher," and that the poet of this epic narrated how Amphion "led the rocks and the animals (λίθων καὶ θηρίων) by his singing." Was this *Europia* originally citharodic, or at least indebted for its musical lore to Boeotian-based citharodic sources? (This latter question could also be asked of Stesichorus' *Europia* [PMGF 195], although there is no explicit indication that the poem mentioned the lyric foundation of Thebes.) A *Europia* was also attributed to the Corinthian lyric and epic poet Eumelus, but this is not necessarily the poem to which Pausanias refers.[302] However, lyric settings of Amphionic myth may well have had a place in the citharodic cultures of Corinth and Sicyon, the latter a city that seems to have claimed Amphion as its own (Pausanias 2.10.4; we may note too the inaugural role of Amphion in the account of early *kitharôidia* in the Sicyonian *anagraphê*).[303]

---

[300] Charitesia: documentation in Schachter 1981:140–144; an Athenian citharodic victor is attested at the fourth-century BCE Amphiaraia (IG VII 414).

[301] Aravantinos 1996, with Franklin 2006a:56, who speculates that lyric accounts of Amphion's construction of Thebes could be grounded in the Mycenaean musical culture of the city.

[302] Scholia D to *Iliad* 6.131; cf. West 2002a:126–128.

[303] Pausanias 9.5.8 mentions another epic in which Amphion was treated, the *Minyas*, but there it is Amphion's punishment in Hades, for "insulting" Leto, Apollo, and Artemis (presumably in connection with his wife, Niobe); the *Minyas* also mentioned the underworld punishment of the hubristic Thamyris (cf. 4.33.7). Pausanias 4.33.7 names as author of the *Minyas* Prodicus of Phocaea, an Ionian city on the southern edge of the Aeolis. If the *Minyas* that Pausanias knew came out of a firmly Ionian rhapsodic tradition, then the negative representation of the citharodes could reflect the sort of anti-citharodic attitude that implicitly informs the representation of Thamyris in *Iliad* 2.594–600. But perhaps the traces of a properly "metacitharodic" rivalry are preserved in the *Minyas*, an antagonism between "mainland" traditions of *kitharôidia*, whose mythical exponents include Theban Amphion and Delphian/Thracian Thamyris, and an Eastern Aeolic one, headed by Orpheus. We may note the near-Aeolic provenance of Prodicus. There are indirect indications that the *Minyas* presented Orpheus in a favorable light. First, a *katabasis* of Orpheus was attributed to a Prodicus of Samos, probably the same as the Phocaean (Clement *Stromateis* 1.21.131; see Robertson 1980:281). The attribution might be based upon the presence

Amphion's lyric construction of the Theban walls was narrated too in the Hesiodic *Catalogue of Women*, introduced, presumably, into a section on Amphion's mother, Antiope.[304] The attractive suggestion has been made that a dactylic sequence appearing in a catalogue of mythical lyre singers by Nicomachus (*Excerpts* 1), ἑπταπύλους τὰς Θήβας ᾠκοδόμησεν 'he constructed seven-gated Thebes', may be a partial verse from a Hesiodic Amphion episode.[305] Again, we might posit a citharodic source or parallel for this narrative. There is a relevant passage in the *Protesilaus* of Anaxandrides, a poet of Middle Comedy, which describes the performance of an Athenian citharode, Cephisodotus of Acharnae, at the lavish wedding ceremony of the Athenian general Iphicrates and the daughter of the Thracian king Cotys in 380 BCE:

καὶ κιθαρίζειν
Κηφισόδοτον τὸν Ἀχαρνῆθεν,
μέλπειν δ' ᾠδαῖς
τοτὲ μὲν Σπάρτην τὴν εὐρύχορον,
τοτὲ δ' αὖ Θήβας τὰς ἑπταπύλους
τὰς ἁρμονίας μεταβάλλειν.

---

of Orpheus in the *Minyas*. Second, in Pausanias' description of Polygnotus' *Nekyia* painting in the Cnidian Lesche, which he thinks was influenced in part by the *Minyas* (10.28.2), we read that Orpheus was depicted in Greek garb singing to his *kithara* for an appreciative audience of prestigious heroes, while Thamyris was pictured nearby, blind and abject, standing above his broken *kithara* (10.30.6–9). Polygnotus obviously intended to draw out a contrast between the two, and Martin 2001:30 reasonably speculates that an older poetic rivalry lay behind it. Again, I would contend that that rivalry, as expressed in both the painting and the *Minyas* that perhaps influenced it, was specifically between traditional schools of *kitharôidia*. (Plato *Republic* 620a also mentions Orpheus and Thamyris side by side in an account of the Underworld, but here the undertones of rivalry are muted: the soul of Orpheus assumes the life of a swan, Apollo's bird, that of Thamyris the life of a nightingale, a bird whose song was appropriately associated with sorrow and lament.) Polygnotus depicted Thamyris too in the Stoa Poikile in Athens, but not, it seems, in the Underworld; there the influence was said to be the *Thamyras* of Sophocles (*Life of Sophocles* 24).

[304] Frs. 181, 182 M-W. According to Palaephatus *On Unbelievable Tales* 41 (= fr. 182 M-W) Hesiod said that Amphion and Zethus together built the walls (ἐτείχισαν) with the *kithara*, but we cannot be certain whether this means the brothers were both represented as citharodes in the *Catalogue*, or this is merely the mythographer's tendentious or mistaken reading (he claims rather improbably that both were star citharodes, κιθαρῳδοὶ ἄριστοι). Amphion's marriage to Niobe was also treated in the *Catalogue* (fr. 183 M-W).

[305] Franklin 2003:303.

> And Cephisodotus of Acharnae played the *kithara* and sang in
> his songs now of Sparta with its broad dancing places, now of
> Thebes again, the seven-gated, modulating the modes.

Anaxandrides Protesilaus fr. 42 K-A

There seem to be two layers of humor here. The first is extramusical. The citharode's switching between Spartan and Theban
themes, and between *harmoniai* 'modes', is surely a "reference to the
Spartan seizure of the [Theban] Kadmeia in 382 and its liberation in
379 B.C."[306] The second likely involves a jab at the harmonically mercu-
rial style of the "new *kitharôidia*" practiced by Cephisodotus (τὰς
ἁρμονίας μεταβάλλειν). While we know nothing else of Cephisodotus,
Anaxandrides names two other, better-attested performers at the
wedding: Antigeneidas, the famously innovative Theban aulete, and
Argas, who is mentioned, alongside one Telenicus of Byzantium, by the
late-fourth-century BCE Peripatetic scholar Phaenias as a composer
of μοχθηρὰ ᾄσματα 'worthless songs' that paled in comparison with
the classic *nomoi* of Terpander and Phrynis.[307] Apparently, then, Argas
was a citharode, and a notably progressive one at that—by contrast
to his *nomoi*, even those of the once controversial Phrynis are classics. Cephisodotus must have also been a distinctly "new" citharode
to be placed in this company. The themes of the songs through which
Anaxandrides has him cycle seem to be, however, classic ones; this
is presumably part of the joke. One song is devoted to Σπάρτην τὴν
εὐρύχορον 'Sparta with its broad dancing places'; the phrase has an
epic weight that evokes Archaic Terpandrean *kitharôidia*, which was
fundamentally tied to Sparta (cf. the praise of Sparta's Δίκα εὐρυάγυια
'Justice who goes along the wide avenues' in Terpander fr. 5 Gostoli =
PMG p363). The other celebrates Θήβας τὰς ἑπταπύλους 'Thebes the
seven-gated', which recalls the dactylic ἑπταπύλους τὰς Θήβας that
we read in Nicomachus. The phrase may be a shorthand reference to a
well-known nomic text dealing with Amphion's foundation of the city,
a theme with relevant political symbolism in light of the liberation of
Thebes from Spartan occupation in 379 BCE.

A fragment from Sophocles' *Thamyras* suggests that citharodes
sang, in lyric hexameters, the sort of genealogical poetry we see assembled in the Hesiodic *Catalogue of Women*:

---

[306] Webster 1953:30.

[307] Phaenias fr. 10 Wehrli by way of Athenaeus 14.638c. On Antigeneidas and Argas, see
West 1992:367 and 372.

ἐκ μὲν Ἐριχθονίου ποτιμάστιον ἔσχεθε κοῦρον
Αὐτόλυκον, πολέων κτεάνων σίνιν Ἄργεϊ κοίλῳ.

She had at her breast a son by Erichthonius,
Autolycus, plunderer of many goods in hollow Argos.

Sophocles Thamyras fr. 242

The nursing woman is Philonis, mother, with Hermes (here called Erichthonius), of the master thief Autolycus and, with Apollo, of the citharode Philammon, and so the paternal grandmother of Thamyris, son of Philammon.[308] Thamyris is almost certainly singing these hexameter lines, which perhaps belong to one of the citharodic *nomoi* mentioned by another character in the play (fr. 241). Like Hermes in the *Homeric Hymn to Hermes*, who sings to the lyre a hymnic account of his own birth from Zeus and Maia (57–61), Sophocles' Thamyris sings his own prestigious genealogy. We find this same parentage detailed in the *Catalogue of Women*:

]δῖα Φιλων[ίς
ἣ τέκεν Αὐτόλυκόν τε Φιλάμμονά τε κλυτὸν αὐδήν,
τὸν μὲν ὑποδμηθεῖσα ἑκηβόλῳ Ἀ]πόλ[λ]ωνι,
τὸν δ' αὖθ' Ἑρμάωνι μιγεῖσ' ἐρατῇ] φιλ[ό]τητι
Αὐτόλυκον τίκτεν Κυλληνίῳ Ἀρ]γεϊ[φ]όντ[η.]

> godly Philonis,
> who bore Autolycus and Philammon, renowned for his
> voice,
> the latter after she was overcome by far-shooting Apollo,
> the former after she lay with Hermes in loving intercourse;
> Autolycus she bore to the Cyllenian Argus-slayer.

Hesiod fr. 64.14–18 M-W[309]

Sophocles may simply have adapted hexameter poetry on Thamyris' family from the rhapsodic *Catalogue* tradition for the *kithara*, which he himself supposedly played onstage in the role of Thamyris (or which he at least may have mimed playing).[310] But it is as likely that he drew upon a separate citharodic tradition of heroic genealogy, in particular,

---

[308] Hermes as Erichthonius: *Etymologicum Magnum* s.v. Ἐριχθόνιος.

[309] The *Catalogue* also treated Thamyris' encounter with and punishment by the Muses (fr. 65 M-W), presumably in the course of the same genealogical narrative to which fr. 64 M-W belongs.

[310] See Wilamowitz 1903:101.

the genealogies of mythical musicians, that was variously reflected as well in the Hesiodic *Catalogue*. As we have repeatedly seen in the preceding review of the possible material developed in the citharodic *nomos*, citharodes seem to have liked to sing about *kitharôidia* and its practitioners, not exclusively, of course, but often enough to constitute a pattern. Sophocles would thus have had his mythical citharode singing poetry of the sort that his dramatic audience heard integrated into the *nomoi* of contemporary citharodes, where genealogies framed narratives or provided digressions within them.[311] With a twist, of course: this citharodic hero celebrates in song his own glorious descent from Apollo and Philonis (whose relationship with Hermes, the inventor of the lyre, redounds significantly to his glory as well) and then, we should presume, through Philammon and the Parnassian nymph Argiope.[312] Again, compare Hermes in his *Homeric Hymn*: the first divine lyre singer sings what is recognizably a citharodic *humnos* about himself. We might detect a trace of such genealogizing in the *Persians* of Timotheus. In the closing section of this *nomos*, the *sphragis*, Timotheus praises "Orpheus, son of Calliope," and imagines "Aeolian Lesbos" (Λέσβος Αἰολία) as the mother of Terpander, who "bore him (γείνατο), destined for fame, in Antissa" (221–228).[313] We will examine in more detail citharodes' biographical commentary on their predecessors in Part III.

The existence of a citharodic version of Heracles' *katabasis*, his quest to retrieve Cerberus from Hades, or at least some parts of the story, is suggested by Theocritus *Idyll* 24.109–110, lines that I have already argued reflect the Hellenistic poet's awareness of Archaic traditions of Heraclean *kitharôidia* in general: "And he made him a singer and shaped both his hands to the boxwood *phorminx*, Eumolpus, son of Philammon" (αὐτὰρ ἀοιδὸν ἔθηκε καὶ ἄμφω χεῖρας ἔπλασσε | πυξίνᾳ ἐν φόρμιγγι Φιλαμμονίδας Εὔμολπος). *Idyll* 24, the *Little Heracles*, concerns the early life of Heracles, and, in the passage from which these lines are drawn (103–134), Theocritus assembles a wide range of traditional

---

[311] Cf. Martin 2005:173–175 for the integral relationship between catalogue and narrative in *rhapsôidia*.

[312] On Argiope cf. n225 above. Others made Thamyris' mother a Muse (e.g. Scholia D *ad Iliad* 10.435).

[313] For the conceit of Lesbos as mother, cf. *Persians* 234–235, where Timotheus says that Miletus "nurtured" him; cf. Hordern 2002:243. The text of lines 223–224 of *Persians* is corrupt, but it likely included an honorific for Calliope, such as κόρας | Διός 'daughter of Zeus' (M.L. West's *exempli gratia* supplement, recorded by Hordern 2002:241). It is notable too that Orpheus is assigned a metaphorically paternal role vis-à-vis the lyre that he invents: "he begot (ἐτέκνωσεν) the lyre of intricate music" (221–222).

accounts about the training of the young hero, in warcraft as well as in arts and letters. Theocritus was, however, unlikely to have found an earlier account in which an adolescent Heracles took lessons in *kitharôidia* from Eumolpus—the "boxwood *phorminx*" is surely an archaizing description of the *kithara* he plays in Archaic Attic vase painting.[314] Multiple literary and Classical iconographical sources have it that Linus was Heracles' music teacher, and not a teacher of the *kithara*, but of the tortoise-shell lyre, the proper instrument for an aristocratic youth (e.g. Apollodorus 2.4.9). Their lessons were known, as early as the fifth century BCE, to have been famously unsuccessful, ending in the violent death of Linus. Theocritus instead has Linus teaching Heracles to read (105–106).[315] I suspect that he may have replaced Linus with Eumolpus and the lyre with the *kithara* to flatter the interest in *kitharôidia* maintained by his Ptolemaic patrons.[316] But this does not mean he invented these details *ad hoc*.

The association between Eumolpus and Heracles was traditionally placed in the hero's career, when, in preparation for his *katabasis*, he came to Eleusis to be purified—he was still polluted after his slaying of the Centaurs—and initiated into the Mysteries by their first hierophant, Eumolpus, whose name indicates the primal function of song and dance (*molpê*) in Eleusinian cult (Apollodorus 2.5.12; cf. 1.5.2).[317] Hugh Lloyd-Jones has proposed that the encounter between the two was originally related not in Stesichorus' *Cerberus*, but in an epic poem on or at least including the Heraclean *katabasis* composed around the middle of the sixth century BCE, "probably [by] an Athenian or a person belonging to the orbit of Athenian culture."[318] Boardman has

---

[314] Cf. Apollonius of Rhodes *Argonautica* 1.538–540 for the synonymy of *phorminx* and *kithara* (here describing the instrument of a proto-citharodic Orpheus). The epithet "boxwood" is likely also a stylized touch of the archaic. Philostratus *Imagines* 1.10 describes a primitive *lura*, made before the days when fancy materials such as ivory were used, as partially constructed from boxwood. Cf. Hunter 1996:141n9.

[315] In an anonymous epigram cited at Alcidimas *Odysseus* 24, Orpheus is said to have taught (ἐξεδίδαξεν) Heracles. Presumably the subject of instruction was reading and writing rather than music, as Orpheus in the epigram is said to have first discovered writing. Cf. Linforth 1931; 1941:15–16.

[316] On the likely Ptolemaic context of *Idyll* 24, see Griffiths 1979:94–95.

[317] Further sources discussed in Robertson 1980:275–276; cf. Boardman 1975:6–7. The earliest preserved account would seem to be Pindar fr. dub. 346 S-M. See Lloyd-Jones 1967. Heracles' battle with the Centaurs may itself have been the subject of citharodic song. In the *Orphic Argonautica*, Cheiron, engaged in a musical contest with Orpheus, takes the battle as his theme (415–418). This poem is late Imperial, but it evinces a familiarity with song traditions much older (cf. Nelis 2005).

[318] Lloyd-Jones 1967:226–228. Robertson 1980 argues that the initiation episode was included in the Hesiodic *Aegimius*, which may in fact have been the case. But this

appealingly contextualized the poem conjectured by Lloyd-Jones within a "nexus of manoeuvres involving Peisistratos, Herakles, and Eleusis," that is, the Tyrants' strategic attempts to integrate Eleusis and the Mysteries into the realm of Athenian civic culture through the mediating figure of Heracles, with whom they closely identified.[319]

We have already examined the figure of Heracles *kitharôidos* both as a character in a citharodic Gigantomachy and as a sociopolitically reso-nant symbol of the Peisistratean investment in the citharodic culture of the Panathenaia. While it is possible that Theocritus knew a version of Heracles' early life in which Eumolpus was merely a doublet of Linus, no more than a *kitharistês*, this seems unlikely, given the prominence of their encounter at Eleusis. Theocritus' poem, I suggest, refracts rather an Archaic narrative about the training of Heracles by Eumolpus in *kitharôidia* that was once attached to the story of the *katabasis*. Such a narrative would not only have provided a satisfying back story to the hero's triumphant citharodic turn in the Panathenaic Gigantomachy, it also would have forged, under the sign of the tyrants, as it were, an effective mythical link between the festal, musical, and cultic spheres of Athens and Eleusis, where the figure of Eumolpus and his sacred music had long been enshrined, as the *Homeric Hymn to Demeter* attests (154, 474–475).[320] Citharodic accounts of Orpheus' *katabasis*, which were probably circulating contemporaneously in sixth-century BCE Athens, may have inspired this narrative—Heracles prepares for his journey to the Underworld by learning, Orpheus-like, to play the *kithara*.[321] Some

---

view little affects arguments for a sixth-century Athenian *katabasis* epic featuring Eumolpus.

[319] Boardman 1975:10; cf. Parker 1996:98.

[320] On the Eleusinia festival at Eleusis, which likely included *mousikoi agônes* from an early point, see n280 above. Note that the krater of the Altamura Painter discussed there includes references to two citharodic victories, possibly at the Panathenaia and the Eleusinia, in significant conjunction with scenes of the Gigantomachy and of Eleusinian Triptolemus—perhaps a legacy of Peisistratean musical/festal politics.

[321] On Archaic citharodic treatments of Orphic myth, see Part III.8. Lloyd-Jones 1967:228 tentatively suggests that the Heraclean *katabasis* was related in an epic circulated under the name of Musaeus, the "Attic Orpheus," who represents "a link between Orpheus and the Eleusinian cult." Cf. Graf 1974:146. In the sixth century BCE a collec-tion of oracles went under his name (Herodotus 7.6.3), but Musaeus' musico-poetic persona and his connection to Eumolpus (his son) and Eleusis were more fully devel-oped only in the later fifth century: West 1983:39–41. Musaeus is depicted as a full-fledged concert citharode in the company of his wife Deiope, his infant son Eumolpus, the Muses, and Aphrodite on a late-fifth-century pelike by the Meidias Painter (New York, Metropolitan Museum of Art 37.11.23). In Diodorus Siculus 4.25.1 it is Musaeus, the son of Orpheus (and father of Eumolpus), who initiates Heracles—presumably a secondary tradition. In light of the connection between Heracles *kitharôidos* and

now-unknown role of the lyre (or *kithara*), perhaps administered by the priestly clan of the Eumolpidai, the descendants of Eumolpus, in the real-world initiation rituals of the Eleusinian Mysteries may also (or alternatively) lie behind it. It is true that in sixth-century vase paintings of the *katabasis* Heracles is not shown with a *kithara*, but it is also important to note that there are no images at all of Heracles with Eumolpus; the musical component of the story may have extended only through the initiation episode.

It may be the case that the meeting of Heracles and Eumolpus was first invented by citharodes in Peisistratean Athens, and indeed that the poem in which it took place was originally a citharodic text. That text may have been a dedicated account of the *katabasis* (such an account, economically told, could easily suit the scope of a *nomos*), or it may have been a "flashback" sequence in a citharodic Gigantomachy, explaining how Heracles had, during a previous adventure, become skilled in *kitharôidia*. Alternatively, we might imagine that the citharodes adapted an older rhapsodic Heraclean *katabasis*, yet perhaps put their own spin on it by elaborating the role of *kitharôidia* in the initiation episode. In any case, Theocritus' description of Eumolpus as the son of Philammon is worthy of note. Eumolpus is usually made the son of the Orpheus-like Musaeus; Theocritus has chosen to follow instead a more "recondite source."[322] Again, that source is likely to have been, ultimately, citharodic. The affiliation to Philammon, one of the legendary early victors of the citharodic *agôn* at Delphi, takes the "good singer" Eumolpus out of the strictly mystic-cultic context of Eleusis, in which he and his music were typically situated (cf. *Homeric Hymn to Demeter* 475–479), and positions him and, by extension, his student Heracles in the grand history of agonistic *kitharôidia*. Eumolpus was said too to have been a victor at the citharodic *agôn* (*Suda* s.v. Εὔμολπος), a tradition that would seem to be connected to that which makes him Philammon's son, a full-fledged citharode. Conversely, Philammon, presumably after the example of his son, was made a mystagogue. Pausanias 2.37.3 reports the claim that Philammon established the

---

the Gigantomachy, it is interesting that Diodorus also records a tradition in which Musaeus assists the gods against the Giants (5.71.3).

[322] Gow 1952:432. On the various parentage assigned to Eumolpus and the late rationalizing construction of multiple Eumolpi, see Williams 1994:140–141. It is to be noted that in one genealogical tradition Eumolpus was said to be son of Poseidon and Chione, whose name is also an alternative name of Philonis, the mother of Philammon.

Eleusinian-style mysteries of Demeter at Lerna, a place, it may be noted, with significant Heraclean associations.[323]

13. Theseus in *Kitharôidia*?

On one side of a red-figured column krater by the Harrow Painter (Harvard 1960.339; c. 480–470 BCE) Theseus is shown in the company of his father, Poseidon, along with Amphitrite, Nereus, and a Nereid. The scene recalls, not without significant variations, however (most conspicuously the presence of Poseidon on the krater), the undersea meeting between Theseus and Amphitrite that is described in a contemporary choral song composed for performance on Delos, Bacchylides *Dithyramb* 17 (lines 97–116). Webster has suggested that the youthful citharode who is depicted on the other side of the vessel is meant to be singing a solo rendition of that same choral song ("an Athenian revival ... of foreign choral poetry").[324] He explains the image's marked divergences from the Bacchylidean narrative as reflective of a separate Theseus epic, also familiar to the vase painter, which, he imagines, had been circulating in Athens since the last quarter of the sixth century. I would propose an alternative scenario. The citharode on the column krater is singing not a citharodic version of the choral dithyramb, but an episode from the longer-established epic *Theseid* itself, which, I suggest, was known in Athens predominantly through citharodic rather than rhapsodic performances, and which was likely to have influenced Bacchylides' song.[325] The argument has long been made, based on the

---

[323] For Eleusinian influence on the Lernaean Mysteries, see Farnell 1907:200. Wilson 2009:54 speculates that Thamyris, brother of Eumolpus from their father Philammon, was connected to the mystery cult at Messenian Andania (which was linked with another key place-name of Heraclean myth, Oechalia, in this case located in the Peloponnese rather than Thessaly). Again, the model for Thamyris at Andania would likely be Eumolpus at Eleusis. In the later fifth and fourth centuries Eleusis itself diversified its roster of prestigious lyric poet-founders, integrating, alongside Eumolpus, Musaeus and then Orpheus into its early myth history, and incorporating a body of texts (not necessarily citharodic or lyric) ascribed to them into its sacred poetic canon. See Graf 1974; West 1983:1–44, 281.

[324] Webster 1972:162; cf. Gentili 1954.

[325] One might presume that Theseus' underwater dive to the halls of Poseidon was a popular episode from the epic-citharodic *Theseid*, and was thus taken up by Bacchylides. (One depiction of the episode, on a cup by Onesimos [Louvre G 104, c. 500–490 BCE], predates Bacchylides 17, as Webster 1972:162 notes.) For the probable reliance of Bacchylides 18 on a *Theseid*, see Mills 1997:20–21. An earlier choral lyric reworking of the *Theseid* narrative may be Simonides' treatment of the Cretan adventure, of which we have, however, only one line (PMG 550). The *Theseids* referred to

sudden proliferation of Theseus scenes in the late sixth century, that a poetic cycle of Theseus myths, in which the hero was cast as an Attic Heracles, and related visual representations of it were encouraged by the Alcmaeonids, the aristocratic clan opposed to the Peisistratean regime, and in particular by the Alcmaeonid Cleisthenes, who guided the democratic reform of Athens after the fall of the tyranny.[326] If it is true that the Peisistratids' self-serving promotion of Heraclean mythos manifested itself at the cithardic *agônes* of the Panathenaia, as the Heracles *kitharôidos* scenes strongly suggest, it is then conceivable that a "rival" cithardic Theseid might also have gained a foothold in the *agônes*, perhaps through the influence of the Alcmaeonids.[327] It is worth noting in this respect that Theseus, like Heracles, was in one tradition attributed the institution of the Panathenaia (Plutarch *Life of Theseus* 24.3). Others have argued that it was the tyrants who encouraged the creation of a *Theseid* and the vase paintings related to it.[328] If so, it is still likely that a Peisistratean *Theseid* was formalized and performed foremost by the citharodes; after all, Hipparchus had the rhapsodes busy reciting Homer.

It is significant that in Archaic iconography Theseus is conspicuously associated with the lyre. On the François Vase (c. 570–560 BCE) the hero assumes the role of the Apollonian *kitharistês*, leading, in splendid chiton and mantle, the choral victory dance after the slaying

---

in Aristotle *Poetics* 8.1541a19–21, Plutarch *Life of Theseus* 28.1, and scholia *ad* Pindar *Olympian* 3.50b seem to be later written epics. Such a poem is ascribed to a fourth-century BCE poet, Nicostratus, by Diogenes Laertius 2.59.

[326] See Sourvinou-Inwood 1971:97–100, Webster 1972:82–86, Neils 1987:143–151, Parker 1996:85, and Mills 1997:19–29 for further bibliography and discussion of the content and political status of the sixth-century *Theseid*.

[327] This is not to say, however, that cithardic treatments of Theseus myth, certainly of the Cretan adventure (which is the only Thesean subject of Attic vase painting before around 510 BCE), are necessarily younger than those dealing with Heracles. Cf. Shapiro 1989:144–149, who argues that Theseus was seen as an Athenian national hero already in the time of Solon. Indeed, the figure of Heracles *kitharôidos* may be derived from a longer-established figure of lyre-playing Theseus (cf. Mills 1997:24n99), already attested on the François Vase, which antedates the first reign of Peisistratus. (Theseus' lyric identity may in turn have been inspired by the *phorminx*-playing of Achilles.) See the following note.

[328] Thus Shapiro 1989:146, with previous bibliography. In favor of this view is the report in Plutarch *Life of Theseus* 20 that Hereas of Megara (FGrH 486 F 1) said that Peisistratus tampered with the texts of Hesiod and Homer to bolster the image of Theseus. But cf. Parker 1996:85n73, who observes that "one can ... deny Pisistratus' responsibility for the postulated *Theseis* and still acknowledge that he may have taken some interest in the hero (why should he not?)." Walker 1995:35–47 argues against a strong Theseus-Peisistratus connection.

of the Cretan Minotaur.[329] On the roughly contemporary Chest of Cypselus Theseus was reportedly depicted with a lyre, standing by Ariadne, who holds a crown (Pausianias 5.19.1); the hero's lyric skill no doubt added to the glamour which attracts Ariadne to him.[330] In other images, a bystander holds the lyre while Theseus is shown fighting the Minotaur in the labyrinth, as if keeping it in reserve until he is ready to take it up and play, thus marking the restoration of order after the death of the monster (compare Heracles' citharodic turn after the Gigantomachy). On a black-figured cup from the later sixth century BCE, Theseus slays the Minotaur while Athena stands behind him holding a lyre, which is clearly labeled *lura*, a detail that indicates the instrument played a prominent role in the hero's story.[331] A still later expression of the lyric Theseus image, on a calyx krater by the Kadmos Painter from around 420 BCE (Syracuse 17427), has Theseus (or perhaps a companion) holding a lyre as he boards a ship, probably either bound for or departing from Crete. (Note that it is from this ship that, during the voyage from Athens to Crete, Theseus will make his dive, the likely subject of the citharode's song on the krater of the Harrow Painter.)[332]

Collectively, such images suggest two things: first, that in the poetic sources on which the images presumably drew, Theseus was figured as an accomplished lyre player; second, that Theseus' lyre also alludes to the performance medium of those sources, which were themselves lyric, viz. a citharodic *Theseid*.[333] We have seen a similar theme

---

[329] Florence 4209; Maas and Snyder 1989:50, fig. 14c. For debates over the scene's setting—Delos or Crete—see Mills 19997:17n63 and Shapiro 1989:146–147 and 1991:125–126, whose own theory that the hand-holding group of youths led by Theseus is *not* a chorus seems improbable.

[330] Cf. Shapiro 1991:127.

[331] Munich 2243; Shapiro 1991:127, fig. 6; cf. Maas and Snyder 1989:85 for discussion of relevant fifth-century images. Shapiro 1989:147n37 lists other scenes in which a bystander holds the lyre.

[332] The Kadmos Painter also produced an elaborate image of the dive (Bologna 303).

[333] Cf. Maas and Snyder 1989: "Theseus ... seems to have acquired his association with the lyre through accounts (now lost) of this scene [the victory celebration on Delos]" (38). Callimachus presumably knew such accounts, including perhaps the citharodic one I am conjecturing here. In his *Hymn to Delos* 312–313, a victorious Theseus plays *kitharistês* to a *kuklios khoros* on the island: ἐγειρομένου κιθαρισμοῦ | κύκλιον ὠρχήσαντο, χοροῦ δ' ἡγήσατο Θησεύς 'as the music of the lyre (or *kithara*) was raised, they danced in circular formation, and Theseus led the chorus'. According to Hyginus *Astronomica* 2.6, the constellation called *Lyra* was said to belong to a proximal constellation sometimes identified as Theseus, because Theseus "had learned to play the lyre." Hyginus quotes a verse of Anacreon, ἀγχοῦ δ' Αἰγείδεω Θησέος ἐστὶ λύρη 'near Theseus son of Aegeus is a lyre' (fr. 99, Bergk 1882). If Anacreon the Archaic poet is the author, constellations are not at issue. We might expect the line instead to come from a monodic lyric setting of Theseus' Cretan adventure, perhaps as known from a

emerge in the preceding review of possible cithardic epics, that of the "lyric hero," a textually embedded, stylized reflection of the cithardic performer. There can be no doubt that Theseus' *lura*—he is never shown with the concert *kithara*—is the "sign of the well-bred, καλὸς κἀγαθός prince."[334] Athenian elites who regarded the lyric Theseus in text and image would surely have seen in him a heroic validation of their own investment in lyric *mousikê*, as they did in the *phorminx*-playing Achilles. But the aristocratic connotations of the hero's lyre—an instrument at home above all in the elite symposium and schoolroom—need not be exclusive of an iconic allusion to the cithardic setting of the hero's deeds and the cithardes who performed it, nor should we imagine any ideologically informed contrast in play between Heracles' *kithara* and Theseus' *lura*. Ideological distinctions between these instruments, which involved elites' anxieties about populism and professionalism, only came to pass in the later fifth century (cf. Part I.10). In Archaic and early Classical Athens, large-scale festival *kitharôidia* and aristocratic lyric culture kept relatively close company, as we will see in Part IV. Indeed, it is possible that the Harrow Painter's young cithardode is a member of the Athenian elite, the Athenian hero's glorious dive being perhaps not only the subject of his song, but also a mythical model for his success in the *agônes*.

---

currently circulating cithardic *Theseid*. We should think above all of the vase paintings of bystanders holding the lyre in close proximity (ἀγχοῦ) to Theseus as he fights the Minotaur. Anacreon's engagement with the lyric Theseus could support arguments for a Peisistratid patronage of a *Theseid* (Anacreon was famously employed by Hipparchus), but it could as well postdate the tyrants. We know from vase paintings that Anacreon continued to be active in Athens during the decade following the expulsion of Hippias in 510 BCE (cf. Hutchinson 2001:259–260), the same period in which the iconographical record sees a spike in Theseus images. Anacreon was close to the family of Critias (Plato *Charmides* 157e; scholia *ad* Aeschylus *Prometheus Bound* 128). The long survival of his statue on the Acropolis, dedicated in the 440s, perhaps by Pericles, which represented him playing the lyre or *barbitos* (Pausanias 1.25.1), indicates that he had ingratiated himself with the post-Peisistratean aristocratic powers-that-be in democratic Athens, including the Alcmaeonids. Pausanias says that the statue was located immediately alongside that of the Alcmaeonid Xanthippus, father of Pericles, and a passage in Himerius suggests that Anacreon had praised Xanthippus in one of his songs (*Oration* 39.10, with Bowra 1961:301–302). Ridgway 1999 argues against a relationship between Xanthippus and Anacreon and would date the statue to the fourth century BCE, but see Zanker 1995:22–31, who argues that the statue represented an ethically and politically correct, distinctly Periclean refashioning of the poet's decadent image; cf. Shapiro 1996:218. Voutiras 1980:77–91 suggests rather that the statue's erection was undertaken by anti-Periclean oligarchs. Cf. Wilson 2003b:193–194, who speculates on the role of the oligarch Critias. Simonides' treatment of Thesean narrative (PMG 550) might similarly date from the years after his engagement by the tyrants.

[334] Shapiro 1991:126.

14. A Summary of Sections 5–13

Sixth- and fifth-century audiences of *kitharôidia* could expect to hear citharodes singing in their *nomoi* selected episodes from the *Iliad* and *Odyssey*. By the fifth century the citharodes' Homer probably sounded quite a bit like the rhapsodes' standardized Panhellenic Homeric text, and was perhaps in some cases an adaptation of it. But a wide range of epic-heroic material attributed to "other poets," as Heraclides puts it, was also on offer. Under the umbrella of "other poets" we could imagine a store of heroic saga drawn from the Trojan Cycle as well as from traditions not strongly connected to it, such as Heraclean and Thesean epic. The expanse of material covered by Stesichorus, whose works, I argue, represent a choral engagement with *kitharôidia*, reflects the diversity of the citharodic repertoire. Certain "Hesiodic" narrative and genealogical poetry was created or adapted by the citharodes as well. While it may seem that I have cast the net too wide in search of possible content for the Archaic and Classical citharodic *nomos*, it is probably the case that the net has not been cast nearly wide enough. It is conceivable that any oral epic tradition, Panhellenic or local, had a citharodic as well as a rhapsodic manifestation. What rhapsodes, uninhibited by the formal, temporal, and musically technical demands of the *nomos*, could do that citharodes could not, however, was to cultivate in and across performances sophisticated, long-form narrative expressions of epic traditions that yet transcended any one performance occasion, "sewing together" discrete episodes into coherent, sequentially arranged oral texts, whose monumental status encouraged their evolution into, and fixation as, written works.[335] Citharodes treated much of the same traditional material as the rhapsodes, but their poetic treatments did not rise above the level of the discrete episode or episodes that could be fitted into the set framework of the *nomos*. Their medium discouraged the emergence of an extra-occasional, monumental textualization of such episodes. The logic of *kitharôidia* was essentially defined and delimited by performance; the itinerant citharode's poetic repertoire was a collection of associated yet nonetheless discrete narrative episodes (or condensed, "epyllic" sequences of episodes), each one suitable for a single performance occasion. Further, these pieces were presumably open to considerable textual manipulation in performance, depending on place and occasion. As such, written traces of

---

[335] On *rhapsôidoi* as those who "sew together (*rhaptein*) songs" into a monumental text, see Nagy 1996:65–112.

citharodic poetry are predictably few, and what there may have been in the way of scripted texts was most likely eclipsed by those drawn from the rhapsodic tradition.

Another factor behind the lack of preserved texts from the early citharodic *nomoi*, as well as the lack of detailed post-Classical testimonia about their contents, is the rise to prominence of a new style of *kitharôidia* as practiced by the likes of Timotheus of Miletus at the end of the fifth century BCE. As we will see in greater detail in Part IV, the "new *nomoi*" were organic, autonomous works, with text and music composed and fitted together exclusively by the citharode-poet. The creative recombination-in-live-performance of traditional melodic and poetic elements that belonged to the earlier generation of *nomoi* faded from practice, and with it, to a wide extent, the texts that had been developed by the citharodes for oral delivery and perhaps in some cases even set in writing. When citharodes reperformed a new *nomos* of Timotheus, they basically reproduced the work as originally composed and performed, making some variations in the language, no doubt, but probably only minor ones (melodic variation and innovation may have been more common). The citharodic repertoire from the fourth century BCE on consisted largely of these newer "classics," in definitive, often scriptural form, just as fourth-century dramatic companies, for instance, had in their repertoire definitive (if not entirely authentic) written texts of tragic works. The melodies and the textual material of the Terpandrean *nomos*, while conceivably still maintained in some culturally conservative places such as Sparta (and even there probably not for too long after the fifth century BCE), fell into silence.

15. Pollux on Nomic Form

Pollux, writing in the second century CE, records that the Terpandrean *nomos* was divided into seven parts: *arkha* 'beginning', *metarkha* 'after the beginning', *katatropa* 'turn-around' (?), *metakatatropa* 'after the katatropa', *omphalos* 'center' (literally 'navel', presumably the core narrative section of the *nomos*), *sphragis* 'seal', and finally the closing *epilogos* (*Onomasticon* 4.66). This testimony has been met by scholars with skepticism for a variety of reasons: Pollux is simply too late to know how the old *nomoi* were articulated; these seemingly fussy subdivisions smack too much of late rhetorical theory; the very number seven is suspiciously the same as the number of strings supposedly introduced to the lyre by Terpander, as well as the number of canonical *nomoi* attributed to him (although Pollux himself lists eight Terpandrean *nomoi*). Pollux elsewhere in the *Onomasticon* (4.84) enumerates the traditional five parts of the auletic *Puthikos nomos*, a purely instrumental, programmatic set piece in which the story of Apollo's slaying of the Python is expressed through musical mimesis, and it has been thought too that he or a source has awkwardly tried to impose similarly episodic subdivisions on the citharodic *nomos*, where they do not belong.[336]

Wilamowitz argued that, although the older *nomoi* would have been structured in a simple tripartite form, the Polluxian schema does apply to the more elaborate "new" Timothean *nomos*.[337] Indeed, our lengthy fragment of the latter portion of Timotheus' *Persians* contains a concentrated narrative section that could correspond to the *omphalos*—Wilamowitz suggests that the original narrative in the *omphalos* of the new *nomos* took the place of the "borrowed" epic piece that formed the centerpiece of the Terpandrean nomic practice—followed by a *sphragis* section in which Timotheus addresses his audience *in propria persona*, identifying himself and talking about his music and his career, and capped by a brief epilogue, a final prayer to Apollo. Not enough of the earlier part of the *nomos* has survived for us to say whether the *arkha*, *metarkha*, and the rest are clearly articulated sections, nor do we have any good sense of what exact form and character these sections might have had in the piece were they there. Is the *katatropa*, for example, or the *metakatatropa* for that matter, a purely instrumental passage, or does it characterize the sung text in some way, in terms of meter or content or both?[338] One hexameter line preserved from the beginning of *Persians* (PMG 788) might belong to the *arkha* and, if so, would indicate that one aspect of the function of this section would be to introduce the theme of the *nomos*—a kind of secondary proemial function integrated directly into the *nomos*. But beyond that we remain in the dark.

Rudolf Westphal accepted in large part the historical accuracy of the testimony of Pollux. While he went too far in trying to uncover the heptapartite schema in Pindaric odes and Aeschylean choral songs,

---

[336] See Gostoli 1990:XXIII for a bibliography of the relevant scholarship. The *Puthikos nomos* also existed in a citharistic version.

[337] Wilamowitz 1903:96–98. Cf. van Groningen 1955.

[338] Gostoli 1990:XXV notes the possibility that there was rhythmic response between *arkha* and *metarkha* and *katatropa* and *metakatatropa*. But this is purely speculative, not at all guaranteed by the "responsive" terms. In fact, "Aristotle" *Problems* 19.15 specifically indicates that *nomoi* were composed without response.

he nonetheless made a reasonable case for its existence in the *nomoi* of the Archaic and Classical periods, arguing that the Doric terminations in *arkha* and the other structural designations reflect the elaboration of the nomic form in Archaic Sparta, an important musical center closely connected to the famous Lesbian citharodic tradition going back all the way to Terpander's (legendary) activity there in the early seventh century BCE.[339] It is of course impossible to decide between the proposals made by Wilamowitz and Westphal, as both have logical counter-arguments. On the one hand, why should the early *nomoi* have necessarily been structurally simpler than the later versions? Teleological arguments for increasing formal complexity are more often than not fallacious. On the other, could not Pollux be deliberately archaizing in his use of Doric forms to make the terminology seem more authentic?

Without going further into this fruitless debate, I would make two broad observations prompted by the Polluxian testimony about the psychology and pragmatics of the citharodic performance event. First, the names of the first five of the seven parts recorded by Pollux all contain metaphors or images of spatiality, describing a sense of progressive movement or traversal in the cognitive experience of the citharodic *nomos* in performance. The terms seem to mark relative stages on a cognitive map that correspond to a sort of notional journey on the "pathway of song," the *oimê*. The citharode traverses a set course of musico-poetic space in his performance, and the audience follows along.[340] Inasmuch as this metaphoric of spatial movement makes more substantial, vivid, physically "real" the invisible temporality of the musical abstract, we may connect it with the emphasis on the visuality and athleticism of citharodic performance—citharodes do move their bodies, vividly and expressively, during their performances.[341] Second, we might connect the multipartite articulation of the *nomos*

---

[339] Westphal 1869:75; further bibliography in Gostoli 1990:XXIVn90.

[340] I would note that, although *epilogos* in the Polluxian schema contains no clear spatial sense, Aelius Dionysius calls the concluding section of the *nomos* the *exodion*, a term that does belong to the metaphorical realm of travel and movement (*Attic Lexicon* 76). Cf. Wilamowitz 1903:98.

[341] It is coincidentally notable that the most rigorously formalist, "nomic" composer of the twentieth century, Iannis Xenakis, whose quest to express spatiality as well as temporality through musical sound is well known, composed a work for solo cello called *Nomos Alpha* (1966), divided into 24 discrete sections, and clearly inspired by the ancient *nomos*. Xenakis, who trained as an architect under Le Courbusier, was concerned to treat in his music a "conception of time as a representation of physical space, and musical material as a representation of matter"—not a bad way, perhaps, to describe the spatial sectioning of the citharodic *nomos* in performance (Cody 2002).

with its regular status as a competition piece. That is, alongside the evaluative criterion of aesthetic pleasure and admiration produced by the execution of the *nomos* as a whole, the proper observation of the various segments of the *nomos* could have served as a sort of "compulsory element" in the performance, allowing the judges a more nuanced and objective formal basis for comparing the *tekhnê* of citharodes working with different musico-poetic content.[342] (For example, how did this citharode's execution of his *metarkha* compare to that one's?) We should think here of one possible musical-performative application of the non-musical meaning of the word *nomos* ('law, custom'). This is a form that requires its players to "go through the motions," as it were, conforming to the contours of a traditional, deep structure, regardless of the contingent content that fills it out.[343] Suetonius remarks that not even an earthquake stopped Nero from singing his *nomos* to the end during his performance in Naples (*Nero* 20.1). While this detail from one point of view neatly epitomizes Nero's crass self-absorption—he has no concern for the safety and welfare of the audience—from another it reflects his respect for the compulsive force exercised by nomic form.

---

[342] Cf. Griffith 1990:188–189, with 202n15.
[343] Cf. Barker 1984:249.

Part III
Inventions of Terpander

1. Terpander between Myth and History

ANY STUDY OF *KITHARÔIDIA* must reckon closely with Terpander of Lesbos. While figures such as Orpheus, Philammon, and Amphion were routinely put forward as exponents of citharodic music in the mythic *illud tempus*—as Wilamowitz put it, Orpheus was "nothing but a citharode retrojected into the Heroic Age"—Terpander emerges from the ancient sources as its true *prôtos heuretês*, the real-life culture hero single-handedly responsible for developing the formal and performative elements that informed the historical practice of *kitharôidia* from the Archaic period through the time of Nero.[1] As Antonietta Gostoli has written in her essential monograph on this figure, "Terpandro è concordemente presentato dalla tradizione antica come il primo grande esponente ed archegeta della citarodia in epoca storica, cioè post-eroica."[2]

The present chapter uses the ancient testimonia about the life and activity of Terpander as a framework around which to organize a number of interrelated discussions about the production and consumption of citharodic culture, primarily as it was constituted in the Archaic and Classical periods, but also in subsequent eras. It will be useful then to begin with a synthetic account of the major testimonia. First, a word of warning: the "Life of Terpander," as we will see, is a *bricolage* of temporally, generically, even ideologically disparate voices, not always in accord, so it is important to keep in mind that the more or less linear, cohesive narrative assembled below merely presents the illusion of synchronic wholeness. In reality these biographical elements were never brought together at any one point in time, at any one place during antiquity. I do, however, foreground what seem to be the more mainstream, widely recognized elements, and although I

---

[1] Wilamowitz 1903:84. According to Alexander Polyhistor, Orpheus is the primal, *sui generis* citharode, who "imitated no one" (οὐδένα μεμιμημένος, FGrH 273 F 77 *ap.* "Plutarch" *On Music* 5.1132f).

[2] Gostoli 1990:XVI. ("Terpander is unanimously presented by the ancient tradition as the first great exponent and archegete of *kitharôidia* in the historical, that is to say post-heroic period.")

include several idiosyncratic contributions to the tradition, others of a more obscure character will figure in later discussions.

> Terpander was born in the city of Antissa,[3] on the northern coast of Lesbos, sometime during the reign of Midas, king of Phrygia (738–696 BCE).[4] His father was named Derdeneus, which is all we know of him.[5] While Terpander was still residing in Antissa, some fishermen found the lyre of Orpheus, which, along with his head, had floated to the northern coast of Lesbos after the Thracian was torn apart by enraged women, and gave it to Terpander.[6] Terpander modified the lyre by adding three strings to its existing four, giving it its classic heptachord form.[7] Perhaps it was he who invented the so-called Asiatic *kithara*, the large, square-bottomed concert *kithara* played by later Archaic and Classical festival citharodes; others assign its invention to one of his pupils, Cepion (or Capion).[8] Terpander composed citharodic music and poetry in the genres of the *prooimion* and the *nomos*, which he performed at *agônes*. He was known to borrow the poetry of Homer as text for his nomic melodies.[9] If Terpander did not himself invent the *nomos*—though he may have—he did first give the canonical varieties of *nomoi* their

---

[3] E.g. Timotheus *Persians* 239–240; Stephanus of Byzantium s.v. Τέρπανδρος; *Suda* s.v. Τέρπανδρος (= T 46, 23, 24 Gostoli [hereafter G]).

[4] So Hellanicus FGrH 4 F 85b *ap.* Clement *Stromateis* 1.21.131 = T 2 G: Ἑλλάνικος γοῦν τοῦτον ἱστορεῖ κατὰ Μίδαν γεγονέναι. Campbell 1993b:70 has argued that by γεγονέναι Hellanicus must mean 'was born' rather than 'lived' if we want to reconcile this testimonium with the date commonly given to Terpander's first Carneian appearance, 676/3 BCE (Sosibius FGrH 595 F 3 = T 1 G). Perhaps that is true, but perhaps not; Hellanicus is, according to Clement, one of those who "archaize" (ἀρχαίζουσι) Terpander. Terpander's dating was an issue of contention (cf. Shaw 2003 *passim*; van Wees 1999:5), behind which lurked agendas that went beyond the objectively chronological. The Peripatetic scholar Hieronymus of Rhodes is the great archaizer. In his *On Citharodes* he dates Terpander well before the usual seventh-century window, synchronizing him with Lycurgus and the first Olympiad of 776 (fr. 33 Wehrli = T 6 G). Perhaps Hieronymus is following Aristotle's *Constitution of the Lacedaemonians*; in that work Aristotle connected Lycurgus to the first Olympiad (fr. 533 Rose).

[5] Parian Marble FGrH 239 A 34 = T 5 G, where we have only the genitive Δερδένεος. The nominative is likely to be Derdeneus rather than Derdenis: Bechtel 1917:117.

[6] Nicomachus *Excerpts* 1 = T 53b G.

[7] Strabo 13.2.4 = T 48 G, with Terpander fr. 4 G; Pliny *Natural History* 7.204 = T 49 G; Nicomachus *ap.* Boethius *On Music* 1.20 = T 53a G; *Suda* s.v. Τέρπανδρος = T 24 G. Nicomachus *Excerpts* 1 = T 53b G, however, has it that the Orphic lyre inherited by Terpander already had seven strings.

[8] "Plutarch" *On Music* 6.1133c; Duris FGrH 76 F 81 (= T 51a and b G).

[9] Heraclides Ponticus fr. 157 Wehrli = T 27 G; "Plutarch" *On Music* 4.1132d = T 32 G.

names.[10] In addition to cultivating a musical career on Lesbos, Terpander visited Lydia; at the luxurious banquets there he heard the playing of harps, which inspired him to invent the elongated, baritone version of the tortoise-shell lyre called the *barbitos*.[11] Perhaps these Lydian drinking parties also inspired him to invent the *skolion*, the Greek sympotic drinking song, and the Mixolydian *harmonia*.[12] At some point after his career was established, Terpander left Antissa; some say he was exiled from the city because he murdered someone there.[13] Delphi enters the story at this important juncture. Sparta had been suffering from self-destructive civic strife. Spartan emissaries to Delphi, seeking solutions to this domestic crisis, were told by the oracle to send for the "Lesbian Singer." Terpander thus arrived among the Lacedaemonians and quelled their *stasis* with his lyric song.[14] In connection to this act of communal musical therapy, Terpander was said to be the first man to organize civic musical culture in Sparta. A key component of this sociomusical organization, the so-called "first *katastasis*," seems to have been Terpander's foundation of a citharodic *agôn* attached to the festival of the Carneia, in the twenty-sixth Olympiad (676–673 BCE); he was, not surprisingly, also the victor at the very first Carneian contest.[15] At some point during his tenure in Sparta—maybe even before, while he was still a resident of Lesbos—Terpander took to the road in the style of an itinerant *agônistês*, performing at the enneateric

---

[10] Heraclides Ponticus *ap.* "Plutarch" *On Music* 4.1132d = T 28 G. Pollux *Onomasticon* 4.65 = T 38 G lists eight titles in the canon of "Terpander's" *nomoi*: Aeolian, Boeotian, Orthios, Trochaic, *Oxus*, *Tetraoidos*, Terpandrean, Capion; cf. *Suda* s.v. νόμος, ὄρθιον νόμον καὶ τροχαῖον = T 43 and 44 G. Pollux also says (*Onomasticon* 4.66 = T 39 G) that Terpander himself gave the classical *nomos* its characteristic seven-part form. *Suda* s.v. Τέρπανδρος has Terpander as *prôtos heuretês* of "lyric *nomoi*." Scholia *ad* Aristophanes *Acharnians* 13 = T 30 G: Terpander "invented" the Boeotian *nomos*. A probably Hellenistic scholar named Theodorus wrote a treatise called *On Nomopoioi* that began with Terpander (Diogenes Laertius 2.103 = T 41 G).

[11] Pindar fr. 125 S-M = T 45 G.

[12] Pindar *ap.* "Plutarch" *On Music* 28.1140f = T 25 G. Pindar probably ascribed the invention of *skolia* to Terpander in the same poem from which fr. 125 (previous note) is derived. Mixolydian: *On Music* 28.1140f = T 37 G.

[13] Photius *Lexicon* s.v. μετὰ Λέσβιον ᾠδόν = T 60i G.

[14] Many sources make reference to this Delphic-mandated Spartan intervention. Relevant testimonia: 12–15, 17, 19–22, 59–60 G.

[15] Victory at Carneian *agôn* implicit in Athenaeus 14.635e (citing Hellanicus and Sosibius) = T 1 G. The first Spartan musical *katastasis* (ἡ πρώτη κατάστασις τῶν περὶ τὴν μουσικὴν ἐν τῇ Σπάρτῃ) is described in "Plutarch" *On Music* 9.1134b.

Pythian contests, where he won four times in succession.[16] After one such excursion abroad Terpander returned to Sparta to perform at the Carneia, but for the last time: while singing, he choked on a fig and died, *kithara* in hand.[17] Terpander's work as musical culture hero was esteemed so highly by the Spartans that long after his death they continued to honor his memory by granting the right of "first performance" at the Carneia to those Lesbian citharodes who could claim descent from him. The proverbial expression μετὰ Λέσβιον ᾠδόν 'After the Lesbian Singer' grew up around this practice—and the fact that Terpander's Lesbian descendants were so good that they inevitably won the contest; everyone else finished behind them.[18]

Gostoli follows the ancient tradition in treating the Lesbian citharode as if he had been an actually living person. For her the testimonia relevant to the life and activity of Terpander are to be evaluated as either accurate or inaccurate records of what really did occur in the past, and through careful consideration of their historical accuracy, in whole or in part, we may extract from them what we need to reconstruct the life of Terpander as it actually was. Gostoli is certainly not alone among modern scholars in following this line of approach, and with some reason. For, while different scholars may dispute the historical validity of this or that invention or exploit ascribed to Terpander, taken all together the testimonia, both early and late, do conspire to present him as an authentically historical figure rather than a pure figment of legend.[19] Indeed, we see in them notably few of the fantastic events and tendentious eccentricities of biographical detail that mark the Lives of Homer. Nor is Terpander routinely linked by blood or other close association to patently mythical or divine figures, as is his counterpart in musical invention, the seminal aulete Olympus, whom legend made the beloved pupil of Apollo's musical adversary,

---

16   "Plutarch" *On Music* 4.1132e = T 32 G.

17   *Palatine Anthology* 9.488 = *Planudean Anthology* 1a.36.14; *Suda* s.v. γλυκὺ μέλι καὶ πνιξάτω (= T 16a and b G).

18   Testimonia assembled under T 60 G. The earliest certain citation of the proverb is in the comedy of Cratinus entitled *Cheirons* (c. 440–430 BCE): Cratinus fr. 263 K-A = T 60b G. But the preeminence of Lesbian citharodes is already "proverbial" by Sappho's time, as her fr. 106 = T 60a G suggests.

19   Gostoli tends to be far more credulous in her approach to the "facts" presented in the testimonia than, say, Wilamowitz, who, although also a believer in Terpander's historicity, was nonetheless quick to see major episodes in the tradition as fictions (e.g. the account of Terpander's victories at Delphi, or his therapeutic musical intervention in Sparta; see especially Wilamowitz 1903:88).

the satyr Marsyas, not to mention a consort of Silenus and wrestling partner of Pan.[20] Terpander's very early *floruit* necessarily shrouds him in a layer of mist.[21] Yet he nonetheless seems to move more surely than Olympus on the historical side of the myth-history divide, in a familiar ambience of well-attested locales, institutions, and festival occasions, practicing his *tekhnê* much like later, indubitably historical citharodes would. Thus we read in the Pauly-Wissowa encyclopedia entry on Terpander that Olympus is "purely legendary, his name a collective term [*Sammelbegriff*] for the achievements of Mysian and Phrygian auletes," while Terpander stands as the first flesh-and-blood figure of Greek musical history.[22]

The approach to the Terpandrean biographical tradition taken here differs from that taken by Gostoli and others. Rather than attempting to reconstruct the life and deeds of one musician named Terpander who actually lived and worked in the early seventh century BCE by subjecting this or that testimonium to the "truth test," I

---

[20] For Olympus and Marsyas see, for example, "Plutarch" *On Music* 5.1132f, 7.1133d–e; Silenus: Pindar fr. 157; Pan: Pliny *Natural History* 36.35. The ancient tradition, at least as early as the choral poet Pratinas (PMG 713 i), actually posited two Olympuses, one who lived before the Trojan War and invented the enharmonic genus, and another, his descendant, who lived in the time of King Midas. See the entries in *Suda* s.v. Ὄλυμπος 219 and 221 (test. 1 in Campbell 1988). The younger Olympus Pratinas and subsequent authors attribute more specific musical inventions, such as the well-known *Polukephalos* ('Many-headed') *nomos* and the *nomos* of Apollo, which is presumably to be identified with the famed *Puthikos nomos* (see *On Music* 7.1133d–f = test. 3 Campbell). Perhaps this clearly artificial fracture in the Olympus tradition was an attempt to isolate patently fantastic elements from more "realistic" ones, and so to construct a more historically tenable culture hero of *aulos* music. Cf. Campbell 1988:264, West 1992:331. Significantly, the younger Olympus was made to be a (slightly older?) contemporary of Terpander, who, according to Hellanicus of Lesbos (fr. 85b Jacoby), also lived, or, as Campbell 1993b:70 argues, was born (γεγονέναι) in the time of King Midas. Was Olympus synchronized with Terpander—by professional auletes and aulodes themselves—in a gesture of intergeneric rivalry? It is worth noting that at some point someone tried to supplant Terpander himself with this "Terpander of the *aulos*." *Suda* s.v. Ὄλυμπος 220: "Olympus: he who composed and taught the *nomoi* of kitharôidia." Cf. Ritschl 1978:260–261. Marsyas too was reimagined as a citharode; on the iconographical evidence, see Boardman 1956, Wilson 2004:285–287. Hyagnis, sometime father of Marsyas and grandfather of Olympus (*On Music* 5.1132f), in one tradition added the sixth string to the lyre, anticipating Terpander's seventh (Nicomachus *ap.* Boethius *On Music* 1.20).

[21] The only named "lyric poet" whose *floruit* falls earlier than Terpander's is Eumelus of Corinth (middle of the eighth century BCE). This Eumelus supposedly authored both *epos* and *melos*: two lines of his prosodion composed for a Messenian chorus on Delos have been preserved by Pausanias (PMG 696). Although we have rather factual-seeming biographical data about him, his historicity should nevertheless remain in question, as should his authorship of the various works attributed to him. See West 2002a.

[22] Vetter 1934, col. 785.

propose to disregard the very criterion of objective veracity in the hope of recuperating information that is more valuable than inert biographical tidbits pertaining to one individual. We should attempt instead to extract from the testimonia not *the* truth about the specific details of Terpander's life—the search for which keeps us mired in anti-quarian debates—but the refractions of deeper and broader "cultural truths" about the performance genre of *kitharôidia* as a whole, especially in the Archaic period, but in later years as well. We should thus approach the biographical material not as historical documentation (true or false) but as episodes in the history of *representation*. Such a treatment is neither ahistorical nor completely anti-positivist; it just does not aim to establish any certainties about the "real" exploits of one great man named Terpander. Stories about Terpander can provide important insight into how things really were, but they do so by narra-tivizing, particularizing, and idealizing *realia* about the experiences of early citharodes and the development and mechanics of early citha-rodic practice in general.

Perhaps more crucially, by treating these stories as representations, we can be confident that we can recover less concrete, more discur-sive properties from them as well, the traces of beliefs, controversies, agendas, and mentalities, social, political and ethical, surrounding the culture of *kitharôidia*, on the sides of both production and reception, from an early through a late period. To borrow a phrase from Richard Martin, whose analysis of the lives of the Seven Sages is an exemplary effort to transcend the deadlock of biographical positivism, there are "interpretable cultural values" embedded in the Terpander tradition, which we can engage if we read between the lines, asking ourselves why Terpander is represented the way he is.[23]

---

[23] Martin 1993:108. Irwin 1998 and 2005b:132–142, on Archilochus and Solon respec-tively, and Graziosi 2002, on Homer, are also admirable attempts to move past the "did he or didn't he" method of assessing poets' *vitae* (for which see Lefkowitz 1981, a book that hammers home the point that *vitae* are flush with fabrications, mostly based on details found in the poets' own poems). Also of note is the insightful work of Compton 2006, which sees the lives of poets as shaped by archetypal patterns (scape-goat, warrior, hero) rooted deeply in the Indo-European sociocultural continuum. Compton takes for granted the workings of what I would call, borrowing the title of Thomas Schatz's book on the collaborative creation of films in the old Hollywood studios (Schatz 1996), the representational "genius of the system," i.e. the tradi-tional mythopoetic *langue* (in Saussurean terms). What gets shaded over in such a transhistorical, transindividual thematic approach are the idiosyncratic, localized social, political/ideological, even personal factors in the reception history of this or that poet's tradition. The poet's life as the work of *parole* better characterizes the approach taken here.

Thus every Terpandrean testimonium, regardless of its seeming credibility or lack thereof, contains potentially useful information about practices or attitudes relating to citharodic culture. That goes as well for those testimonia that come to us via late sources, as many in fact do. Our reliance on late reports to derive a sense of Archaic and Classical experiences and mentalities is of course always fraught with some risk, but we do well to follow the productive example set by recent scholarship devoted to the explication of the "cultural poetics" of Archaic Greece. An axiom central to this scholarship, which is so characteristically committed to unlocking the wider signifying potential of the "minor" anecdote, is that anecdote-rich late sources (Plutarch, Athenaeus, Aelian, et al.) may well in some cases—and case-by-case evaluation is always the best policy—be considered valid transmitters, even if unaware or incidental ones, of "long-lost" Archaic and Classical traditions.[24] At the same time, because the practice of *kitharôidia* persisted as a living tradition well into late antiquity, it is inevitable that some post-Classical representations of Terpander should also bear the imprint of later, even contemporary stages of citharodic culture and its intercultural contexts.[25] Again, a case-by-case policy is the best one to follow in trying to determine whether multiple levels of temporal reference might be at work in a representation, and what sort. In most cases dependence on definite earlier *Quellen* is impossible to establish with any certainty, so some grounded speculation is unavoidable.

2. Terpander in Gaza

Consider the following example, which stands at the chronological extreme of over one millenium after the supposed *floruit* of Terpander.[26]

---

[24] See for example the essays collected in Dougherty and Kurke 1993, with this programmatic statement in the editors' Introduction: "There is some justification for mining later sources (as we must, given the exiguousness of actual archaic evidence) if we can identify metaphors or systems of signification that correspond to archaic ones and that are often anomalous or obscure within the text in which they are embedded" (6). See too the exemplary treatments of late biographical anecdotes relating to Solon in Irwin 2005b:134–142 and Stehle 1997:61–63.

[25] See Hardie 1983:29 on the comparable way in which late biographies of Homer both look back to the early "biographical work of the rhapsodes" and "represent a view of Homer's life as an itinerant poet held by writers who were familiar with the itinerant poets of later ages."

[26] On the persistence of Terpander's fame well into the late Imperial and early Byzantine periods, see Gostoli 1990:XLVIII.

In an excerpt from one of his *Discourses*, the early sixth-century CE orator Choricius of Gaza expresses the (surely unattainable, markedly "rhetorical") wish to perform his rhetorical displays, *epideixeis*, only before select, educated audiences equipped with the proper learning to appreciate his skill, those he calls the ἐπιστήμονες λόγων 'connoisseurs of speeches'. He cites an unexpected model for such discrimination: Terpander, who, like Choricius in the field of declamation, was uncontested in *kitharôidia*. Choricius attributes to Terpander a curious pre-performance ritual of selection that is otherwise unattested:

μέλλοντος γὰρ κιθαρίζειν ἐκείνου θεράπων μουσικὸς παρὰ τὴν αὔλειον θύραν εἱστήκει, ὅς τις ἀκροᾶσθαι βούλεται Τερπάνδρου· βοῶν, ἅμα τὴν λύραν ἐπιδιδούς, ἔφερε γάρ, ἐκέλευεν ἕκαστον τὴν ἁρμονίαν εὖ μάλα ἐντεινάμενον κρούειν ἢ ἀπαλλάττεσθαι ὡς ἀνάρμοστον ὄντα Τερπάνδρου κιθάρας ἀκούειν.

Whenever Terpander was about to perform on the *kithara* (*kitharizein*), a musical assistant of his (*therapôn mousikos*) stood by the courtyard door and called upon whoever wanted to hear Terpander; handing the willing person a *lura* (for the assistant carried one), he would bid him either to tune it and play it proficiently or to go away, since he was not fit (*anarmostos*, literally 'out of tune') to listen to the *kithara* of Terpander.

Choricius Discourse 9.3²⁷

The idea that Terpander, or any famous agonistic citharode for that matter, employed the services of a "musical assistant" acting in the capacity of a bouncer tasked with the vetting of would-be audience members, should not, of course, be taken seriously. Citharodic culture, not unlike the epideictic oratorical culture developed under the Empire, was, even from an early period, inherently large-scale, indiscriminate, "middling"; citharodes were by and large professional entertainers who relied on establishing mass appeal, on creating broad-based consensus amongst socially differentiated festival audiences, *mousikoi* and *amousoi* alike.

But we should not completely write off this anecdote as a fabrication concocted by Choricius alone. The figure of the lyric gatekeeper restricting public access to the music of Terpander, who remains

---

27 This very late bit of Terpandrea is not to be found in Gostoli's collection of testimonia. See the discussion of Di Marco 1997.

secluded behind doors, may be his own creation. But even if it is—and we cannot be sure that Choricius did not get the notion from some earlier writer—the elitist tone of the anecdote as a whole could nevertheless suggest that we are dealing with a narrative reflex of sociological content, an ideological mindset, from a previous era: specifically, the resentment voiced by some later-fifth- and fourth-century elite factions in Athens at their diminished authority, as creators and connoisseurs, within the civic culture of *mousikê*, not least in the field of *kitharôidia*.[28] The tenor of Choricius' story, if not its exact narrative detail, could well be a distant echo of this reactionary sentiment. This Terpander was cast as a kind of musical oligarch—his close connection to Sparta, whose famously conservative musical life was a source of fascination for sociomusical conservatives in Athens, probably inspired the casting choice—while *kitharôidia* was idealized as an economically disinterested, socially restricted practice, in the manner of old-time sympotic music making, its pleasures open only to the musically educated social elite. That the assistant puts prospective auditors to the test with the *lura*, the gentleman symposiast's stringed instrument, is significant. An aesthetic and ethical "harmony" between amateur proficiency on the lyre and the virtuosity demanded by the *kithara* is implicit; appreciation of the latter is tendentiously made dependent on, even secondary to, the former. The message: cithardic *terpsis* is the exclusive privilege of a lyric elite. Again, this was ideological belief, not the historical state of affairs.

It should be noted that the musical politics that I am arguing form the subtext of this anecdote had long before the time of Choricius become irrelevant; the rhetor may not have even been aware there was originally a subtext. His evocation of this elitist Terpander serves first and foremost his own self-aggrandizing rhetoric—something along the lines of, "I as much as Terpander deserve the most cultured sorts of audiences for my brilliant performances." But this is not to say that Terpander was to Choricius or his audiences a bloodless exemplum, a famous name from the legendary past without any contemporary relevance. The reference in fact must have had more active cultural resonance. To appreciate its impact we must keep in mind that *kitharôidia* continued to be practiced even as late as the reign of Justinian (527–565

---

[28] Choricius does not say that he is borrowing from a Classical source, but elsewhere in his work this Atticizing rhetor is eager to show off his familiarity with fifth- and fourth-century culture. As Di Marco 1997:32 puts it, as a "profundo conoscitore della letteratura del passato, ammiratore di Tucidide, Platone, Demostene, Elio Aristide, egli ama impreziosire i suoi discorsi di citazioni letterarie e di allusioni dotte."

CE). The vibrancy of late antique citharodic music explains why not only Choricius but other Imperial Greek rhetors make repeated reference to citharodes, occasionally putting their oratorical skills, explicitly or implicitly, on the level of the musical prowess of a Terpander, Arion, or Orpheus.[29] Indeed, the performance cultures of *kitharôidia* and epideictic oratory had significant practical and conceptual overlaps. As cosmopolitan, high-earning itinerant performers, citharodes moved in much the same orbit as professional rhetors; both enjoyed considerable celebrity among the enormous crowds they entertained throughout the Greek world; their formidable glamour won them powerful patrons as well. Both cultivated performance styles designed for maximum impact on large civic audiences: highly theatrical, mimetic, gestural, sensationalistic.[30] A certain degree of professional rivalry almost certainly existed between them.[31] We hear of one performer of the third century CE, Aurelius Hierocles, who likely competed in both citharodic and oratorical festival *agônes* in Miletus.[32] Against this backdrop, Choricius' exemplary citation of Terpander is far more than a random show of antiquarian learning. It is a culturally charged act of appropriation whose implications would be well understood by Choricius' contemporaries: a rhetor borrowing for his own practice the prestigious example set by the iconic founder of the rival citharodic tradition.

---

[29] Terpander is once elsewhere evoked as *comparandus* by Choricius, in the charged context of his funeral oration for Procopius, his teacher. Choricius praises Procopius' smooth delivery by claiming that "one could more easily apprehend Arion of Methymna or Lesbian Terpander striking the strings tunelessly than that man saying anything unrhythmically" (*Oration* 8.8). Menander Rhetor advises the praise of "famous lyre-players" such as Orpheus, Amphion, and Arion as a suitable oratorical topic (Russell and Wilson 1981:123). As early as the fourth century the parallel between citharode and rhetor is detectable. Plato compares the enchanting voice of the itinerant sophist Protagoras to that of Orpheus (*Protagoras* 315a5–b2).

[30] See Connolly 2001 on theatricalized performance in Second Sophistic oratory.

[31] Antagonism is suggested in Dio Chrysostom's critique of the Alexandrians' obsession with citharodes (32.61). Elsewhere he expresses sheer amazement at the star power of a popular citharode in the city of Cyzicus (19.2–5), and claims he enjoys listening to citharodes more than to orators, although both professions should be taken with a grain of rhetorical salt.

[32] I.Didyma no. 181.5, with discussion in Section 5 below.

3. Contested Legacies

Terpander emerges from my reading of this anecdote as a figment of his own reception. But what about the "real" Terpander? My view is that even if there was an early Archaic musician from Lesbian Antissa called Terpander, who played the seven-stringed *kithara*, sang at the first Spartan Carneia, etc., the legend nevertheless subsumed the man to such an extent that the legend became more substantial, more "real" than any truths that could be told about the man. We may recall the (appropriately oft-misquoted) dictum of the wise newspaper editor in John Ford's classic Western *The Man Who Shot Liberty Valance*: "When legend becomes fact, print the legend." In other words, if Terpander had not existed, he would have had to be invented; but, even if he did exist, he would still have had to be "invented." It thus seems to me most effective to approach Terpander not as the mortal inventor of *kitharôidia*, but rather as the ongoing invention, a work-in-progress, as it were, of the evolving citharodic tradition itself—"Terpander" as an objective genitive in the title of Part III, "Inventions of Terpander."[33] The tradition has invented its inventor, many times over.

I am not the first to follow this general line. Gregory Nagy has discussed at length Terpander's status as proto- or archetypal lyric composer.[34] Nagy emphasizes Terpander's supposed invention of the seven-stringed lyre, an instrument with which could be readily synthesized, for the first time, the various melodic idioms (*nomoi*) and modes (*harmoniai*), which characterized the once-distinct local musical

---

[33] The title is a nod to Barbara Graziosi's *Inventing Homer*, which traces how the figure of Homer was constructed by performers and consumers of hexameter epic as early as the sixth century BCE. Another reference point is West's 1999 article "The Invention of Homer," in which he argues for the key contribution of the rhapsodic guild of the Homeridai to the creation of "Homer." I offered preliminary views on the "invention" of Terpander in Power 2004, especially 417–420, some of which appears as Section 10 below.

[34] Nagy 1990b:82. Related approaches could be mentioned here as well. Long ago, Wilamowitz (1903:89) gestured toward a "reading" of Terpander that would make him the retrojection of several centuries of citharodic practice, up to the time of the fifth-century BCE innovator Phrynis—Terpander as *Sammelbegriff*, to borrow the expression applied to Olympus by Vetter (n22 above). Campbell 1988:265, while taking a strongly historical view of Terpander, neverthless acknowledges that "Terpander is in some ways ... a convenient symbol for Asiatic musical influence reaching Greece via Lesbos, for the excellence of music and poetry in the island which was to produce Sappho and Alcaeus, and for the artistic life of Sparta before the middle of the seventh century." Most recently, Beecroft 2008 offers an interpretation of Terpander as a metonymical construct of the citharodic tradition, which complements the one offered here and in Power 2004.

traditions of Greek and near-Asian regions. Nagy's Terpander is thus an avatar of the sophisticated Panhellenic lyric *melos* that took shape in the Archaic period. In approaching Terpander's prototypicality I take a somewhat different path. Most critically, it is narrower. Terpander is for me not so much the generically undifferentiated primordial songmaker and lyre player, the embodiment of evolving patterns in the melodic and formal development of lyric song qua macrogenre, encompassing monodic and choral, amateur and professional styles of performance; rather, he is first and foremost a model agonistic *kitharôidos*. His *vita* encodes information that is relevant above all to the practice of one performance genre, *kitharôidia*, which, despite the fact that it shares some important musico-generic DNA with lyric forms such as sympotic monody or choral song and dance, has its own morphologies of practice and its own distinct contexts of performance.[35] In other words, the story of Terpander is not so much the story of "lyric poetry" writ large as it is the story of one distinct variety of it, *kitharôidia*.

Before I turn again to that story, I want to qualify the formulation stated above, "The tradition has invented its inventor." As I see it, Terpander's prototypicality was not some automatic creation of tradition in its anonymous, collective conception, nor was it some transhistorical emanation of the genius of the mythopoetic system. Nor was it monolothic. That is, it was not so much a question of an unmediated emergence from the systematic *langue* of collective tradition as it was the accretive result of more individually differentiated, historically situated acts of *parole*.[36] There must be, as I have already indicated, an essential kernel in the Terpandrean *vita* that constitutes something close to an impersonal, unmediated narrative reflex of typical patterns of formal development and practice in early *kitharôidia*; this hard kernel could indeed reflect the actual experiences of a "real" Terpander on Lesbos and in Sparta. But over and above it, the iconicity of Terpander took a series of more deliberately mediated turns. It was in flux, diachronically and synchronically; it was open to contestation, manipulation, appropriation, not only at the hands of the citharodes, but also, with just as much impact, from a range of non-citharodic agents.

---

[35]   It is worth noting that Nagy 2004 discusses Terpander far more explicitly as a professional citharode than does *Pindar's Homer* (Nagy 1990b). This is not to detract from the invaluable insights into Greek musico-poetic history offered in the latter work. Again, while Terpander justifiably looms large in Nagy's expansive, holistic vision of lyric songmaking in the Archaic period, I opt for a more parochial approach.

[36]   Cf. n23 above.

As such, the repository of cultural capital, specifically citharodic, but, more broadly, musical, that was "Terpander" could serve as a powerful rhetorical resource. The projection of certain inventions, actions, or social postures onto this larger-than-life screen could serve to legitimate or authorize critical positions held by the projector. Claims made about Terpander were hardly ever constative; they were dynamic, often literally performative efforts to make and remake musical history in light of particular agendas in the here-and-now. We will see this clearly in the case of Timotheus' *Persians*. Choricius' engagement with a vision of Terpander that could itself have been a product of later Classical sociomusical rhetoric and the romanticization of early Sparta shows how such tendentious biographizing could be deployed by culture producers, historians, and critics outside the immediate realm of *kitharôidia*. We will see too that Pindar made rhetorical appeal to Terpander in elaborating an authoritative history of the typically non-citharodic song genre of the *skolion* in which he worked. Finally, the oral traditions belonging to certain regions—Lesbos, Sparta, Delphi—that had an interest in promoting (or challenging) prestigious Terpandrean legacies could also produce distinct variations on biographical themes. Herodotus 1.23–24 gives us some indication of this when he reports that the people of Lesbos and Corinth related independent accounts of the seaborne adventures of the celebrity citharode Arion, who had strong ties to both locales. The works of Hellanicus of Lesbos entitled *Lesbiaka* and *Karneonikai* (*Victors at the Carneia*) probably recorded tales of Terpander as told both on Lesbos and in Sparta, where the citharode was assigned a major role in the historical formation of the *polis*.[37] The life of Terpander as we have it is in this way a *bricolage*, and each contribution to its assemblage can tell us something about the different stages of cithAROdic culture as whole, its contexts of production and reception, its *realia* and fantasy images, the various mentalities cohering around it. "Terpander" is ultimately an organizing nexus for this culture and its sundry manifestations, fashionings, and idealizations, past and present.

---

[37] We have two preserved mentions of Terpander by Hellanicus. One, FGrH 4 F 85a = T 1 G, is from the *Karneonikai*; another, FGrH 4 F 85b = T 2 G, is perhaps from the *Lesbiaka*. See discussion of both in Jacoby FGrH I Kommentar, p458 and in Gostoli's commentary *ad loc*. Hellanicus was likely an intermediate source for Herodotus' telling of Arion's famed shipboard performance. We know that the Lesbian historian discussed Arion in his *Karneonikai* (FGrH 4 F 86). Kiechle 1963:200 argues for an oral tradition dedicated to Terpander in Sparta.

Finally, an important corollary to an interpretation of Terpander that sidesteps the deadlocks of historical positivism concerns the six fragments that were attributed to him in antiquity and whose authenticity has long been subject to debate. Most recently, Gostoli, whose credulity in the matter of testimonial objectivity extends to her treatment of the poetry, has accepted as authentic compositions of Terpander all six of the fragments that were attributed to him in antiquity. Far less credulous is Denys Page, who reluctantly acknowledges only two fragments as (possibly) Terpandrean (PMG 697, 698 = frs. 2, 3 G). Wilamowitz had been even more skeptical in his assessment of them, detecting the hand of the "literary forger" in more than one.[38]

But once we give up the quest to recover an actually existing Terpander "out there" and we recognize his immanent function within the very expanse of citharodic culture, we can abandon too the fruitless quest to determine the authenticity or inauthenticity of the fragments.[39] Rather than as the direct pronouncements from the mouth of one citharode named Terpander, they are better understood as installments in the centuries-long invention of Terpander, each possessing a "truth" vis-à-vis the presentation and reception of *kitharôidia*.[40] As was discussed in Part II.2–3, these fragments belonged to proemial compositions that were maintained, alongside a collection of the stereotyped melodic frameworks called *nomoi*, in the traditional (and so "authentic") repertoire of itinerant citharodes; their canonical status went hand in hand with their attribution to the prototypical citharode. Similarly, rhapsodes attributed to Homer the traditional hexameter poetry they performed, both lengthy heroic narratives and *prooimia*, viz. the *Homeric Hymns*. Versions of such citharodic compositions, we saw, dated back to the Archaic period, when Lesbian citharodes—perhaps among them one standout named Terpander—displayed their *tekhnê* at the Carneian *agônes*, and that thereafter they moved into broader Panhellenic circulation, reperformed, and surely reworked, under the name of Terpander, whose iconic persona continued to be brought to life by the citharodes singing "his" verses and melodies.

---

[38] See Robbins 1992:8. Wilamowitz 1903:64n1, 92–93: 3, 4, 5 G late literary forgeries.

[39] Cf. Beecroft 2008, with n34 above.

[40] I leave out of consideration the three fragments that have been attributed to Terpander only by modern scholars, Bergk and Leutsch (frs. dubia 7 and 8, and 9 G, respectively). But these attributions may themselves be viewed as very late installments in the invention of Terpander. On the Medieval and Renaissance reception of Terpander (via the philosopher Boethius), see van Schaik 2004.

4. The Citharodes' Citharode

It is likely that those primarily responsible for the elaboration of Terpandrean biography and the transmission of Terpandrean lore were those also responsible for the transmission of his poetry and music, the citharodes themselves. At the forefront of these dual processes was the διαδοχή 'succession' of citharodes from Terpander's native Lesbos ("Plutarch" *On Music* 6.1133d). These citharodes earned early fame for their preeminence at the Spartan Carneia, whose *agôn* Terpander is said to have established in the early seventh century BCE when he came to save the city from self-destruction with his song and to lay the initial foundation of civic musical culture there (the "first *katastasis*," as it is called in *On Music* 9.1134b). They enjoyed too agonistic success at other points abroad well into the fifth century BCE. Terpander must have been first and foremost their creation, his exploits a synchronic condensation of their own diachronic activities; his prestige and renown accordingly grew in tandem with theirs, as each generation of the *diadokhê* inherited and built upon the legends of its founding member. Some, perhaps all of the Lesbian Singers, as they were proverbially known as early as the seventh century BCE (cf. Sappho fr. 106), claimed to be descendants of Terpander, his ἀπόγονοι, members of his extended family, his *genos*.[41] Indeed, in early Sparta it may have been the case that the Lesbian citharodes competing at the Carneia came to be viewed as "second comings" of Terpander, their identities ritually conflated with that of their ancestor, the archetypal Lesbian Singer.

The *apogonoi* were supposedly granted the right of first performance at the Carneia—the original sense of the proverb μετὰ Λέσβιον ᾠδόν 'After the Lesbian Singer'—"in honor and commemoration of ancient Terpander" (ἐπὶ τιμῇ καὶ μνήμῃ Τερπάνδρου τοῦ παλαιοῦ), who

---

[41] ἀπόγονοι: scholia *ad* Aristophanes *Clouds* 971a; Aristotle fr. 545 Rose; Hesychius s.v. μετὰ Λέσβιον ᾠδόν (= T 56, 60c, 60g G). See Gostoli 1990:XLVIII–XLIX and West 1999b:373–374 on the notional descent of professional groups or guilds from a mythical ancestor. Eustathius and Hesychius say that the Spartans made a distinction between the Lesbian *apogonoi* of Terpander and "other" Lesbian citharodes at the Carneia, but this seems to depend on a tendentious interpretation of the proverb "After the Lesbian Singer." It stands to reason that the majority of Lesbian citharodes would have claimed affiliation to Terpander, certainly as his reputation grew. Of course, we need not think that the Lesbian Singers were a harmonious, mutually cooperative collective. They were, after all, in competition against one another. One or more musicians or groups within the *diadokhê*, especially those from Antissa (such as Euainetidas, according to Hesychius s.v. μετὰ Λέσβιον ᾠδόν), might thus have boasted exclusive descent from the master and contested the claims of others.

was the first performer and victor at the festival.[42] This institution-
ally ritualized commemoration of Terpander suggests that the Lesbian
Singers of the here-and-now were meant to emulate their archetype,
whose *kitharôidia* had brought not only entertainment but also political
salvation to Sparta. The identification between past and present was no
doubt mediated too by the dynamics of *mimêsis*, or reenactment, that
were built into the very performance by the Lesbians of the *prooimia*
and *nomoi* they attributed to Terpander.

Nevertheless, the members of the Lesbian *diadokhê* could emerge as
"name" stars in their own right. Some, such as Euainetidas, Aristocleides
(or Aristocleitus), and Phrynis of Mytilene, achieved such fame in and
beyond Sparta that debate arose as to whether one of these, rather
than Terpander, was the Lesbian Singer referred to in the proverb.[43] We
have the names of other Lesbian Singers. Cepion (or Capion), said to be
Terpander's *erômenos* or student and called by some the inventor of the
concert *kithara*, is probably not historical.[44] Another, Pericleitus, almost
definitely a real person, was remembered for the transitional position
he occupied in the history of the Lesbian *diadokhê*:

> τελευταῖον δὲ Περίκλειτόν φασι κιθαρῳδὸν νικῆσαι ἐν
> Λακεδαίμονι Κάρνεια, τὸ γένος ὄντα Λέσβιον· τούτου δὲ
> τελευτήσαντος, τέλος λαβεῖν Λεσβίοις τὸ συνεχὲς τῆς κατὰ τὴν
> κιθαρῳδίαν διαδοχῆς.

> They say that Pericleitus was the last citharode of the Lesbian
> *genos* to be victorious at the Carneia in Sparta and that when

---

[42] Plutarch *On the Delay of Divine Justice* 13.558a; cf. Eustathius *Commentary on the Iliad*
741.16 van der Valk (= T 60d and c G).

[43] Aelius Dionysius *ap.* Eustathius *Commentary on the Iliad* 741.15 van der Valk = T 60e G:
καὶ τὸν τῆς παροιμίας Λέσβιον ᾠδὸν Τέρπανδρόν φησιν ἢ Εὐαινετίδην ἢ Ἀριστοκλείδην
'Aelius Dionysius also says that the Lesbian Singer of the proverb is either Terpander
or Euainetidas or Aristocleides'. Cf. Hesychius s.v. Λέσβιος ᾠδός, which adds Phrynis
to the mix. The Aristocleides named by Aelius Dionysius is presumably the same musician
as the Aristocleitus named in scholia *ad* Aristophanes *Clouds* 971a (see n46 below). On
Euainetidas, see Part II.10. It is important to note that the debates about the precise
identity of the Lesbian Singer that are played out in our late sources misunderstand
the ritualized logic of reenactment at work at the Carneia. The "Lesbian Singer" was
a role ideally played by Terpander (as Aristotle fr. 545 Rose realizes) and subsequently
replayed by representatives of his *diadokhê*. Cf. Gostoli 1990:123.

[44] Pollux *Onomasticon* 4.65 (*erômenos*); "Plutarch" *On Music* 6.1133c (student). He may be
a Boeotian accretion to the Terpandrean tradition; cf. Part II.12.

he died the unbroken continuity of the Lesbians' tradition (*diadokhê*) in *kitharôidia* came to an end.

"Plutarch" *On Music* 6.1133c

This testimony deserves more detailed discussion, as it has implications for the Panhellenic diffusion of Terpandrean lore beyond Lesbos and Sparta. The writer-compiler of *On Music* (or his source, perhaps Heraclides of Pontus) has presumably gotten his information about Pericleitus from Hellanicus of Lesbos, who dealt with his countrymen's citharodic successes in Sparta in his *Karneonikai*, a work composed in both poetry and a prose versions that recorded the winners at the Carneian *mousikoi agônes* from the time Terpander supposedly established them (676/3 BCE) up to his own time, the later fifth century BCE. The way in which the information is expressed in *On Music* is confusing, however. We know that Lesbian citharodes who could place themselves within the *diadokhê* were in fact still winning contests after the death of Pericleitus, whom we can date to around the middle of the sixth century BCE, or perhaps somewhat later in that century.[45] Aristocleides (or Aristocleitus), another *apogonos* of Terpander, was enjoying fame throughout Greece at the time of the Persian Wars.[46] His student was Phrynis, who won first prize in *kitharôidia* at the Panathenaic *mousikoi agônes* in 446, around the time they were reorganized by Pericles.[47] Phrynis was most likely active in Athens as well as at other *agônes* through the 420s. So what do we make of the report in *On Music* that the "continuous tradition" of Lesbian *kitharôidia* died out with Pericleitus? The passage must not mean that the Lesbian tradition as a whole came to an end before the middle of the sixth century; it means only that the unbroken streak of victories won by the Lesbian Singers at the Spartan Carneia *in particular* was over by this time.[48] Further, it is likely that

---

[45] Pericleitus is said to be earlier than Hipponax in "Plutarch" *On Music* 6.1133d = T 8 G. Hipponax's *floruit* has usually been dated to around 540 BCE (Pliny *Natural History* 36.11; cf. Parian Marble Ep. 42), but see Degani 1984:19 for the probability of a lower date.

[46] Scholia *ad* Aristophanes *Clouds* 971a: ὁ δὲ Ἀριστόκλειτος τὸ γένος ἦν ἀπὸ Τερπάνδρου, ἤκμασε δὲ ἐν τῇ Ἑλλάδι κατὰ τὰ Μηδικά 'Aristocleitus was of the *genos* descended from Terpander and was at the peak of his career in Greece during the Persian Wars'. Cf. *Suda* s.v. Φρῦνις.

[47] Panathenaic victory: scholia *ad* Aristophanes *Clouds* 971a; cf. *Suda* s.v. Φρῦνις. For the 446 date, which involves a minor correction of an archon's name in the scholion's text (Callimachus for Callias), see Davison 1958:40–41. The Periclean reorganization of the Panathenaic *mousikoi agônes*: Plutarch *Pericles* 13.

[48] Thus Gostoli 1990:117.

individual Lesbian citharodes did continue to win Carneian victories after the time of Pericleitus; it was just that they did not win every year.

Why did this happen? The answer lies in two closely interrelated developments. We should first consider that as the agonistic *kitharôidia* that the Lesbians had refined in Sparta increasingly achieved Panhellenic recognition, the supremacy of its Eastern Aeolic pioneers must have been challenged successfully by new waves of cithrodes from regions far and wide, who were mastering the music and technique of the concert *kithara* on their own terms, fusing the Aeolic-Lesbian style with stylemes from their own native lyric traditions.[49] It is significant that the one name we have of a Carneian victor after Pericleitus belongs to an Athenian citharode, Execestides, who won the crown in Sparta around the middle of the fifth century (Polemon fr. 47 Preller). No longer was *kitharôidia* a niche *tekhnê* for the Lesbians, and, as enterprising promoters of their art, spreading its wonders across the Mediterranean, they in a sense had themselves to blame for this development. This last point brings us to the second development. By the middle of the sixth century BCE the preeminence of Sparta as the center of citharodic culture was being challenged by rival states seeking to possess for themselves the cultural and political prestige that the medium of *kitharôidia* brought with it. There was, in economic terms, a diversification of the cultural capital of *kitharôidia* not only at the level of "sellers," i.e. the musicians, but also at the level of "buyers" or "investors."[50] Already in the late seventh century BCE a new range of incentives, financial and honorific, was being offered to enterprising, ambitious musicians by organizers of regional and Panhellenic festivals, and by individual tyrants, who sought to cultivate politically beneficial patronage relationships with them.

This growing decentralization of citharodic culture must have cut into the institutional prestige of the Carneia festival and diminished its ability to maintain a persistent monopoly on the best talent, i.e. Terpandrean *apogonoi*, who were increasingly traveling elsewhere to seek fame and fortune.[51] Most illustrative of this trend is Arion,

---

[49] Cf. the discussion in Nagy 1990b:82–115 of the patterns of Panhellenic synthesis in the formal traditions of Archaic lyric.

[50] We may note a roughly analogous situation in the realm of visual arts. Laconian vase painting peaks in the first part of the sixth century BCE, then production begins to decline around 550 BCE, affected by the competition posed by other states, especially Athens. See Cook 1962:157.

[51] See the catalogue of evidence for Archaic and Classical musical contests assembled by Herington 1985:161–166. The cithorodic *agôn* at the Carneia did not suddenly sink into obscurity after the sixth century; for some time it held its own against the

the Lesbian Singer from Methymna, whose organization of musical culture in Periander's Corinth follows the model of Terpander's first *katastasis* of civic music in Sparta and whose storied tour to Sicily and Italy reflects the more general spread of *kitharôidia* into Western Greece during the Archaic period.[52] In the early to mid sixth century, local festivals founded by tyrants such as Cleisthenes' Sicyonian Pythia and Peisistratus' reorganized Panathenaia must have drawn the best Lesbian citharodes.[53] Aristocleides seems to have been employed by the fifth-century Sicilian tyrant Hieron of Syracuse (Ister FGrH 334 F 50; see Section 15 below).

As the Lesbian *diadokhê* moved into different regions of Greece, working an increasingly Panhellenic circuit of *agônes* and tyrannical courts, we may imagine that they brought with them not only a repertoire of Terpandrean music and poetry, but also life stories of their illustrious ancestor. By the time of the first attestation of his name in preserved Greek literature, in Pindar's early fifth-century encomium for Hieron (fr. 125 S-M), Terpander was no doubt Panhellenically

---

competition for talent from rival cithardic centers. It must have remained an important destination on the itinerary of competitive citharodes, if not for the value of its prizes—about which we know nothing definite, though we may imagine they were considerably less grand than those offered at the aggressively marketed Panathenaia, for instance—then certainly for the honorific value guaranteed by its hallowed reputation. (Tripods were perhaps offered as prizes: *Palatine Anthology* 7.709, with Bergk 1883:205n8.) Although the stories of their violent run-ins with ephors are probably apocryphal, Phrynis and his younger rival Timotheus probably both performed in Sparta. Both were citharodes associated with Athens and the Panathenaia, which had surely eclipsed the Carneian *agônes*, but not yet driven it out of business. In the fifth century the cithardic contest at the Carneia probably still stood alongside those at the Panathenaia and the Pythia as the most prestigious in Greece. The career highlights of the Athenian citharode Execestides are thus reckoned as victories at the Pythia, the Carneia, and the Panathenaia (Polemon fr. 47 Preller *ap.* scholia *ad* Aristophanes *Birds* 11). The vaunted conservatism of the Carneian contest, however, which alienated innovative talents such as Phrynis and Timotheus, was probably its eventual undoing. As the new style of *kitharôidia* became mainstream in the fourth century, contests that remained musically reactionary would have fallen out of touch and had difficulty attracting top talent. Thus by the third century BCE the Carneian contest seems to have been dropped from the itinerary of the professional *agônistês*. A monument (IG II² 3779) from that century listing the contests won by the citharode Nicocles of Tarentum prominently includes the Pythian and the Panathenaic, but the Carneian is not even included among the smaller regional festivals mentioned.

[52] Herodotus 1.24. As a member of the Archaic Lesbian *diadokhê*, Arion was also connected to the Spartan Carneia. He is discussed by Hellanicus in his *Karneonikai* (FGrH 4 F 86 by way of scholia *ad* Aristophanes *Birds* 1403). Another Spartan connection is suggested by the report in the *Suda* s.v. Ἀρίων that Arion was the student of Alcman. Cf. Bergk 1883:239n130.

[53] Cf. Power 2004.

acknowledged as the first mortal exponent of *kitharôidia*, attributed a fixed canon of compositions and exploits—his musical purification of Sparta, his invention of seven strings and the *nomoi*—yet also subject to ongoing revision and reinvention, even resistance. As we will see, Pindar makes him into a pioneer of sympotic lyric, while Delphi mounts an epichoric challenge to the mainstream accounts of Terpander's achievements, offering up local heroes in his place. With the obsolescence of the *diadokhê* by the end of the fifth century BCE—Phrynis is the last Lesbian Singer of whom we hear—Terpander was so well established in that role that non-Lesbian citharodes such as Timotheus claimed his legacy as their own, and customized it to suit.

5. Timotheus' Terpander

In analogous manner it was the early professional rhapsodes who first fashioned and transmitted stories about the notional founder of their art and line, Homer, in order to satisfy the curiosity of their audiences and, through their exclusive access to this ancient lore, to advertise their privileged artistic lineage. At first, at least, these rhapsodes were members of the Chian rhapsodic guild of the Homeridai, who claimed familial descent from Homer, although at a later point non-Homerids such as the world-famous rhapsode Ion of Ephesus, portrayed in the Platonic dialogue named for him, must also have engaged in biographical glossing.[54] Their accounts could be "paratextual," that is, transmitted outside the primary performance of the text, or, thanks to the textual fluidity of orally composed and transmitted *rhapsôidia*, they could be woven into the text itself by its reperformers.[55] As an example of the latter phenomenon we could cite Hesiod fr. 357 M-W, in which an archetypal rhapsodic contest between Homer and Hesiod is described. We could also consider in this light the famous evocation of the blind

---

[54] See Allen 1907 and West 1999b on the Homeridai. Ion, though not a member of the Chian guild, was "crowned by the Homeridae" in recognition of his service to the poet's legacy (*Ion* 530d). Nagy 1990a:51–52 proposes the combined transmission of Archilochean biographical lore and poetry by an authorized body of reciters connected to the poet's hero cult on Paros; cf. Nagy 1979:304–305.

[55] See Isocrates *Helen* 65 for evidence of the Homerids' biographizing. Fuller discussion in Velardi 1992:17, Ford 2002:70–71, and Graziosi 2002:36–37 on what I call, borrowing the term from Genette 1997, "paratextual" performance of Homeric lore. Such paratextual performance could also have a text-exegetical component (which may not have been totally separate from its biographical dimension). This is made clear by Plato *Ion* 530c–d and 533b–c, on which see Velardi and Ford *op. cit.* and Martin 2001:24.

Chian *aoidos* in the Delian *Hymn to Apollo* 172. Of this latter text one scholar has perceptively written,

> The Delian hymn belongs to the Homeridai of Chios, a guild of rhapsodes that traced itself to a founder/ancestor whom they called Homer: the reference in the hymn to the blind bard of Chios is intended to evoke this founder/ancestor, and, whoever the actual poet or poets of the hymn, the hymn's allusion to Homer is in effect the *sphragis* of the guild.[56]

The citharodic *prooimion* is one obvious site for such biographizing-in-performance. The proemial fragment Gostoli fr. 4 = PMG p363 ("For you we will, loving four-voiced song no more, sing new songs to the heptatonic *phorminx*") both records and reenacts Terpander's foundational discovery of the seven-stringed lyre as well as the *nomos* whose performance that lyre enables; citharodes "become" Terpander by way of commemorating his legacy. The concluding *sphragis* section of the citharodic *nomos* would alternately have offered citharodes the opportunity to speak *in propria persona* about themselves and their *tekhnê*.[57] In addition to such self-revelation, it would have provided a fitting textual/performative space for the propagation of the Terpandrean *vita*, as well as ample opportunity for the contemporary singer to associate himself with the glories of his ancestor.

We may detect a startling, if truncated, reflex of such self-interested biographizing in the *sphragis* of *Persians*, a *nomos* composed by Timotheus of Miletus. That this Ionian citharode aligns himself with the founder of the distinctly Aeolic *diadokhê* is a clear indication that citharodes in general, even those not of the Lesbian line, adopted Terpander as their model and contributed to the elaboration of Terpandrean lore. (Compare the authority assumed over the Homeric legacy by the second-generation, non-Homerid rhapsode Ion.) In a passage that renders a heavily edited version of citharodic history, Timotheus makes honorable mention of the seminal accomplishments of Orpheus and Terpander and, passing over in marked silence the Lesbian *apogonoi*, follows up with a celebration of his own new style of *kitharôidia*:

πρῶτος ποικιλόμουσον Ὀρ-
φεὺς <χέλ>υν ἐτέκνωσεν

---

[56] Frame 2006. Gostoli 1990:XLIX discusses similarities between the Terpandrean *apogonoi* and rhapsodic guilds such as the Homeridai, with further bibliography. Cf. Flach 1883:211–212.

[57] Cf. Wilamowitz 1903:64–65.

υἱὸς Καλλιόπα<ς ˘ -
-- > Πιερίαθεν·
Τέρπανδρος δ' ἐπὶ τῷ δέκα
ζεῦξε μοῦσαν ἐν ᾠδαῖς·
Λέσβος δ' Αἰολία νιν Ἀν-
τίσσᾳ γείνατο κλεινόν·
νῦν δὲ Τιμόθεος μέτροις
ῥυθμοῖς τ' ἑνδεκακρουμάτοις
κίθαριν ἐξανατέλλει.

221 ποικιλομουσος pap.: -ον Wilamowitz 222 <χέλ>υν Wil.: <λύρ>αν Jurenka: <τέχν>ην Hutchinson 226 τεῦξε pap.: ζεῦξε Wil.

Orpheus, son of Calliope, first begot a tortoise-shell lyre of elaborate music ... in Pieria. After him Terpander yoked music in ten songs; Aeolian Lesbos bore him to be Antissa's fame. And now Timotheus makes the *kitharis* again spring up with eleven-struck meters and rhythms.

Timotheus *Persians* 221–231

The rhetorical thrust of this priamel-like survey is that Timotheus' contribution to *kitharôidia* is equal to, if not greater than those made first by Orpheus and then by Terpander. Notable here is the way Timotheus boldly reinvents Terpandrean tradition: "Terpander yoked music in ten songs (*ôidai*); Aeolian Lesbos bore him to be Antissa's fame." As Wilamowitz first argued, Timotheus is concerned here to legitimize his own controversial use of the novel eleven-stringed *kithara*, which had made him, or so he claims, *persona non grata* in musically conservative Sparta (*Persians* 206–212; cf. Pausanias 3.12.10, where Timotheus has "excess" strings cut from his polychord *kithara* in Sparta). He does so by attributing "ten songs"—almost certainly a euphemism for or at least a coy suggestion of ten *strings*—to the citharode who was famous for inventing the seven-stringed lyre and who had been an "honorary Spartan" to boot.[58] (Note that Timotheus analogously euphemizes

---

[58] Wilamowitz 1903:27, 68–69; Maas 1938:1333; Aron 1930:33–34. Cf. LSJ s.v. ᾠδή 3, "metonym for *khordê*." Hordern 2002:243 notes that the metaphor of "yoking" recalls the *zugon* 'crossbar' (or, less technically, 'yoke') to which the strings of the *kithara* were attached. Even if *oîdai* 'songs' refer to Terpander's *nomoi* (so Barker 1984:96n16), Timotheus would still be innovating the mainstream tradition, as there were famously only seven (or eight) Terpandrean *nomoi*. The rhetorical effect is similar too if one accepts, as Gostoli 1990:113–114 does, Aron's ἐπὶ τῷδε κατηῦξε μοῦσαν ἐν ᾠδαῖς ("After him Terpander increased/augmented music in his songs/strings"),

his own controversial eleven *strings* as "eleven-struck meters and rhythms," what emerges when the strings are struck.)[59] Terpander is thus cannily figured as an exponent of the New Music *avant la lettre*.

Orpheus too is given the modernizing treatment. Timotheus imagines the primordial Orphic lyre, which he designates with the old-fashioned-sounding metonym χέλυς (cf. Sappho frs. 118, 58.12 V), as *poikilomousos*, an epithet that brings significant ambiguity into the scene.[60] It is clearly intended to echo expressions in Archaic lyric such as Pindar's φόρμιγξ ποικιλίγαρυς '*phorminx* with varied voice' (*Olympian* 3.8; cf. 4.2, 6.87; *Nemean* 4.14). But, rather paradoxically given the traditionalist connotations of χέλυς, it also brings to mind (and how could it not?) the more recent buzzword status of *poikilia*. The New Musicians and their critics both seized on this traditional term to valorize or denigrate the supercharged harmonic and technical complexity and variability

---

which could simply refer to the use of seven strings, but which seems at least to *imply* something more intricate (Orpheus' lyre is already *poikilomousos*, after all). But κατηῦξε is metrically problematic: see Hordern 2002:243. Also problematic, but still appealing, is Seeliger's κα‹ινὰν› τεῦξε μοῦσαν ἐ. ὠ. ("Terpander crafted a new music in his songs"). This reading certainly has the merit of retaining the papyrus' τεῦξε, and it nicely echoes μοῦσαν νεοτευχῆ from earlier in the *sphragis* (203).

[59] Gentili 1993:10 sees the separate mention of meter (qua articulation of *logos* 'text') and rhythm (qua articulation of musical structure) as a boldly innovative programmatic statement: "Significativa è la distinzione tra i metri e i ritmi assunta da Timoteo, prima testimonianza esplicita del divorzio tra metrica a musica." The New Music did free musical expression from the hegemony of the text. But is it fair to say that Timotheus is outright vaunting the "divorce" of his musical rhythms from his poetic *metra*? I would read μέτροις ῥυθμοῖς τε not as a provocative statement but as a totalizing, even pleonastic description of the composition and performance of the *nomos* that links the richness of both the textual meters and the musical rhythms to the eleven-stringed *kithara* (euphemized as "eleven *kroumata*"). On meter and rhythm cf. Privitera 1965:40–42; Janssen 1984:140–141, who argues that by the fourth century at the latest a clear distinction between the two terms was not always apparent.

[60] I accept ποικιλόμουσον (Wilamowitz) against the ποικιλόμουσος of the Abusir (Berlin) papyrus that contains *Persians*. Timotheus claims not that Orpheus birthed *the* lyre, but the "lyre of elaborate music." I follow most scholars in accepting too the ‹χέλ› υν of Wilamowitz rather than Jurenka's ‹λύρ›αν. The former appeals not only textually, but also rhetorically and thematically, in that its primitive simplicity better offsets the epithet. Also, although the true father of the *kithara*, the *phorminx*, is older than the *khelus*-lyre (West 1992:53), there seems to have been the sense, at least by the early fifth century BCE (cf. *Homeric Hymn to Hermes*), that the latter was earlier, no doubt due to the shell, a striking visual reminder of "raw" natural origins, and perhaps due as well to the amateur contexts in which it was played. By comparison, the professional's box *kithara* seems to emerge from a later, more sophisticated stage of artifice and technical manufacture. Timotheus (deliberately?) leaves Terpander's instrument unnamed.

typical of the innovative contemporary style.[61] Orpheus' *poikilomousos* tortoise-shell lyre ideally combines the simple with the complex, the antique with the modern, foreshadowing and so legitimating the same combinations in Timotheus' eleven-stringed *kitharis*—the Homeric term is deliberately chosen to archaize what is very much a cutting-edge concert *kithara*.[62] Citharodes could thus play fast and loose with their representations of citharodic lore to suit their own ambitions, although we may note that Timotheus scripts, and so controls, the terms of his own biographical reenactment, his own "musical myth." Citharodes reperforming *Persians* would, as they sang the sphragic text, forevermore "become" Timotheus as he "makes the *kitharis* again spring up with eleven-struck meters and rhythms." We may compare how the Terpandrean invention of the heptatonic lyre and the *nomos* is forever renewed when citharodes sing the proemial verses of Gostoli fr. 4 = PMG p363 ("For you we will, loving four-voiced song no more, sing new songs to the heptatonic *phorminx*").

If we had more citharodic texts, we would, I suspect, have more such examples of the elaboration of Terpandrean legend in song. We may, however, be able to detect the traces of a Timothean Terpander in later, non-citharodic sources. Indeed, given the success and long-running popularity of works such as *Persians*, we should not be surprised to find that Timotheus influenced later images of Terpander. Plutarch *Laconian Institutions* 17.238c records a tradition, attested only here, that Terpander was censured by the Spartan authorites because he added an "extra string," presumably an eighth, to his *kithara* "for the sake of vocalic *poikilia*" (τοῦ ποικίλου τῆς φωνῆς χάριν)—a phrase that distinctly resonates with the discourse surrounding the Athenian New Music. Insofar as this tale unexpectedly puts Terpander in the position normally occupied by Timotheus in accounts of clashes with reactionary ephors at the Carneia—Plutarch in fact immediately juxtaposes a story in which it is the Milesian's *kithara* from which an ephor's knife cuts "excess" strings—it could well represent an anecdotal reflex of the rhetorical assimilation of Timotheus and Terpander qua

---

[61] Plato equates musical *poikilia* and radical innovation (*kainotomia*), demonizing both (e.g. *Laws* 812d). For Aristoxenus certain compositions of Timotheus were "excessively complicated (τὰ ποικιλώτατα) and had the highest degree of *kainotomia*" (fr. 76 Wehrli). See Csapo 2004:229, 243 for *poikilia* and *polukhordia*. On the use of *poikilia* in Archaic poetry to denote artistic or musical ornamentation not necessarily innovative in itself, see Page 1955:3; on Pindaric musical *poikilia*, see Barker 1995:43–45.

[62] Cf. Hunter 1996:148; Wilson 2004:306. Similar archaism is common in Pindar, who avoids the word *kithara* in favor of the anachronistic *phorminx*: Svenbro 1992:145n54.

citharodic innovators that we encounter in the *sphragis* of *Persians*.[63] Plutarch elsewhere records a variant of the story in which an axe-wielding ephor named Ecprepes cut (ἐκτεμεῖν) two extra strings from the nine-stringed *kithara* of Timotheus' older contemporary Phrynis.[64] Wilamowitz took this version of the anecdote to be the earliest, and as such the source for the later variants involving Timotheus and Terpander.[65] Perhaps, but that could mean that Phrynis, the last big-name Lesbian citharode—he was the protégé of Aristocleitus, an *apogonos* of Terpander (scholia *ad* Aristophanes *Clouds* 971a)—himself anticipated Timotheus in "updating" Terpander to legitimate his own use of a polychord (nonochord?) *kithara*. Timotheus and Phrynis were at one point close rivals (cf. PMG 802); it is conceivable that the younger Ionian and the older Lesbian citharode, whom Timotheus calls, rather oddly in light of his own provenance, an ἰωνοκάμπτας 'bender of Ionian melody' in PMG 802, struggled with one another for control of the prestigious Terpandrean legacy. If Phrynis was already making use of nine strings (and perhaps citing Terpander's eight strings as a precedent), this could explain why Timotheus attributes "ten songs" to Terpander in *Persians*, effectively trumping Phrynis' innovation with that of his Lesbian forerunner and so making the latter a more suitable model for his own use of eleven strings.

There can be no doubt, however, that Timotheus was the most celebrated victim of Spartan severity. Pausanias 3.12.10 says that the Milesian citharode's interdicted *kithara* (or what locals claimed was that *kithara*) was hung up for public display in the *Skias*, the assembly-cum-concert hall in the market place, where the Carneian *mousikoi agônes* were held (*Etymologicum Magnum* s.v. Σκιάς; Athenaeus 4.141f). By this time, the Spartans were clearly exploiting their legendary "Lycurgan" cultural conservatism for the sake of an antiquarian tourist trade, which was taking off by the first century CE.[66] The *kithara* was no

---

[63] Cicero *On the Laws* 2.15.39; Pausanius 3.12.10; Dio Chrysostom 33.57; Athenaeus 14.636e–f; Boethius *On Music* 1.1. See further Wilamowitz 1903:69–71; Hordern 2002:7–8. There is an interesting modern parallel to these string-cutting stories. The story goes that while Bob Dylan was performing his controversial folk rock set at the Newport Folk Festival in 1965, Pete Seeger, an organizer of the festival and the dean of the American folk music revival, became so enraged at Dylan's noisy electric guitars that he threatened to cut the power cables to the amplifiers with an axe. No such thing ever happened (most likely). But the existence of the story shows how quickly the discursive position-takings of musicians (and critics) can crystallize into concrete biographical narrative. Dylan at Newport: Marshall 2006.

[64] Plutarch *Life of Agis* 10.7; *On Advancing in Virtue* 13.84a; *Laconian Sayings* 220c.

[65] Wilamowitz 1903:73.

[66] Cf. Cartledge and Spawforth 1989:207–212.

doubt a must-see on the itinerary of tourists eager to take in relics of the city's romanticized Archaic austerity.[67] But Spartan guides, eager to give their visitors what they came for, were ready to expound not only on Timotheus' run-in with the law, but also that of Phrynis, and even that of the very founder of the Carneian *agônes*, Terpander.

Then there is the entry about Terpander on a now-lost portion of the Parian Marble (364/3 BCE). If Jacoby's reading of the damaged lines is correct (FGrH 239 A 34), Terpander's seminal contribution to music is described in terms also notably reminiscent of Timotheus' late-fifth-century rhetoric of innovation: Τέρπανδρος ὁ Δερδένεος ὁ Λέσβιος τοὺς νόμους τοὺ[ς κιθ]α[ρ]ῳιδ[ικ]οὺς {ΘΑΙΑΥΛΗΤ..} [ἐκαι|νοτόμ]ησε καὶ τὴν ἔμπροσθε μουσικὴν μετέστησεν ("Terpander of Lesbos, son of Derdeneus, made radically new the citharodic *nomoi* ... and he changed the music that came before"). It could be that the Marble simply refers to Terpander's supposed replacement of an old four-stringed *phorminx* by the newer seven-stringed lyre, but the extreme tone of the language suggests the mediation of the New Music; this "revolutionary" Terpander may be, I think, a refraction of the Terpander tradition through the modernizing rhetoric of Timotheus. There is in fact an entry on the Marble devoted exclusively to Timotheus (Ep. 76), and the inscription on the whole evinces the dedicator's familiarity with prominent figures of the Athenian New Music (the "modern" *dithurambopoioi* Melanippides, Telestes, Polyeidus, Philoxenus are each mentioned, Ep. 47, 65, 68, 69).[68]

Kainotomia ([ἐκαινοτόμ]ησε), like *poikilia*, is a keyword of the New Music; compare Timotheus PMG 796, lines probably from the *sphragis* of a citharodic *nomos*: "I do not sing the old songs, for my new ones (*kaina*) are better. The Zeus who is young and new reigns; long ago Cronus ruled. Away with the Old Muse!"[69] We might speculate that Timotheus is alluding to the traditional proemial verses of Gostoli fr. 4, in which "Terpander" claims he "will sing new songs" (νέους κελαδήσομεν ὕμνους), i.e. the *nomos*, to his seven strings, since he "loves no more" (ἀποστέρξαντες, Cleonides *Introduction to Harmonics* 12, p202 Jan) or, in another version of the text, after he has "turned aside"

---

[67] A related tourist attraction was the archaizing Laconian decree, probably produced in the second century CE, censuring Timotheus for his morally corrupting citharodic and dithyrambic innovations (cf. Palumbo Stracca 1997). Somewhat ironically, the Spartans, who had once hounded Timotheus from their city (or so he claims in *Persians* 206–212), were in the Imperial period capitalizing on continued popular fascination with his iconoclastic persona.

[68] Cf. Jacoby 1904:99.

[69] See Wilamowitz 1903:64–65 on the likelihood of a sphragic context.

(ἀποστρέψαντες, Strabo 13.2.4) the song accompanied by the older four-stringed *phorminx*.[70] Wilamowitz thought that these lines were a post-Classical forgery, a projection of a Timothean modernist vaunt onto Terpander.[71] But this is to read "Terpander" through the assimilating prism of Timotheus, who in his own poetry picks up on and exploits rhetorically what is already seemingly progressive in the Terpandrean tradition. It is conceivable, however, that the Terpandrean text was substantively altered in light of its Timothean reception. I refer to the alternation of ἀποστρέψαντες 'turning aside' with ἀποστέρξαντες 'loving no more' as recorded respectively by Strabo and the music theorist Cleonides. The variation need not be a quirk of post-Classical written transmission, but could have long existed within the citharodic performance tradition. Citharodes with more of a stake in asserting a musically innovative stance might have sung ἀποστέρξαντες, which implies a principled, historically self-aware, "Timothean" rejection of the past, more so than the far more neutrally toned (and presumably longer-established) ἀποστρέψαντες.[72]

It is likely too that Timotheus "reinvented" Terpander on a grand scale by recomposing his *nomoi*, presumably in his own contemporary style and with his own texts. According to the *Suda* s.v. Τιμόθεος, he

---

[70] See Part II.2 for how the lines may have referred not only to instrumental innovation, but to the transition between *prooimion* and *nomos*.

[71] Wilamowitz 1903:64n1.

[72] Another possible reflex of a New Music reception of Terpander on the Marble, originating with either Timotheus or one of his contemporary innovators, could be lurking in the garbled sequence ΘΑΙΑΥΛΗΤ. Various solutions to the textual problems involved have been proposed, none satisfactory. What is clear is that in this sequence the inscription makes reference of some kind to the *aulos*, its music or its players, in the context of Terpander's own innovative activity. This association between the master citharode and the *aulos*, however, is made nowhere else in the Terpandrean testimonia, and has irked the likes of Wilamowitz, who rejected the sequence as an interpolation made by John Selden, the seventeenth-century *editor princeps* on whose transcription we must rely for this lost portion of the Marble. Cf. Jacoby 1904:97. The *aulos* was the instrument at the center of the Athenian New Music (see Csapo 2004), and to a great extent innovations in *kitharôidia* such as *polukhordia* are attempts to imitate its range and mimetic capacities. Timotheus composed aulodic dithyrambs, known for their *kainotomia*, as well as *kitharôidia*. Was Terpander similarly fashioned? Of course, the figure of the citharodic composer of dithyramb is at least as old as Arion (Herodotus 1.23), so we may conjecture that from a much earlier point Terpander was viewed as a composer of *aulôidia* and dithyramb (cf. Gostoli 1990:76). The sixth-century CE antiquarian writer Joannes Lydus offers a tantalizing clue when he writes, "Terpander the Lesbian says that Nyssa nursed Dionysus" (*On the Months* 4.51). Does Joannes know of some dithyramb attributed to Terpander? Or was the composition to which he refers a citharodic *humnos* to the god? Since Joannes mentions the *sparagmos* of Dionysus by the Titans, however, it is also possible that the text at issue is an "Orphic" Titanomachy attributed to Terpander. See discussion below.

produced among his other works eight διασκευαί. These "adaptations" go unnamed and their contents go unspecified, but they could very well have been updated versions of the classic Terpandrean *nomoi*, which numbered, at least in the account of Pollux *Onomasticon* 4.65, eight. As was argued at length in Part II, the Terpandrean *nomoi* had throughout the Archaic and Classical periods been subject to extensive recomposition-in performance by the citharodes who sang them. What Timotheus attempted seems to have been of a different order, however. He made fixed, "authored" pieces out of his personal interpretations of the Terpandrean classics—a bold appropriation of the tradition.

By scripting autobiographical elements into his own *nomoi*, Timotheus, as I proposed above, was able to shape the reception of his musical and poetic persona. Yet a citharode whose legacy was as enormous as Timotheus' must have inspired a line of dedicated exegetes of his works and life. A third-century CE inscription from Miletus indicates that there were certain performers, probably citharodes, active at the Great Didymeia festival in that city who were called Timotheastai (I.Didyma no. 181.5). The inscription tells us nothing about the exact nature of the relation of these Timotheasts to their eponym. Were citharodes so designated simply ones devoted to the repertoire of Timotheus' *nomoi*? Or were they members of a Milesian guild who claimed some more privileged connection to Timotheus, even, in the manner of the Chian Homeridai or the Lesbian *apogonoi* of Terpander, lineal descent from the master or quasi-filial pedagogical links to him? In the latter case, the Timotheasts might have further claimed that they and they alone possessed and performed authoritative versions of both the Timothean *nomoi* and life story.

Another Milesian inscription dated roughly one century earlier than the inscription from the Great Didymeia might offer support for this latter scenario (SEG XI 52c). It records the public honors accorded to Gaius Aelius Themison, a Milesian musician, almost certainly a citharode, who won numerous times at *agônes* across Hellas and Asia. The language of the inscription has it that he was "the first and only to set to his own music (*melos*) Euripides, Sophocles, and Timotheus" (μόνον καὶ πρῶτον Εὐρειπίδην Σοφοκλέα καὶ Τειμόθεον ἑαυτῷ μελοποιήσαντα). We may compare Timotheus' own "adaptations" of Terpandrean *nomoi*. The uniqueness and novelty ascribed to Themison's creative revision of classic Timotheus is notable; it leads to the conjecture that more "traditional" renderings of compositions by Miletus' most famous musician were the order of the day, and these we may tentatively attribute to the Timotheasts.[73] The inscription from the Great Didymeia records that the Timotheasts were actually unsuccessful at the festival games, defeated by one Aurelius Hierocles, about whom we know nothing except that he was seemingly a practitioner of both oratory and *kitharôidia*.[74] Perhaps the public enthusiasm that greeted Themison's novel settings of Timotheus decades earlier had marked the beginning of a decline in the popularity and authority of the Timotheasts.[75] It would certainly make for a neat historical irony if the biggest name of the Athenian New Music was centuries later caught up in another "New Music" movement back home in Miletus, this time playing both sides of the fence, as it were, claimed by both the new wave and the old guard.

6. A Simonidean Intermezzo

We might detect the vestiges of a related New Music co-optation of an old-school eminence in the heurematography of the *kithara* compiled by Pliny the Elder: "Amphion invented the *cithara*, although some say Orpheus did, others Linus; Terpander added three strings to the four that were there and first sang to seven strings; Simonides added the eighth, Timotheus the ninth" (*Natural History* 7.204). Like most late catalogues of musical invention this one is a hodgepodge, its elements drawn from a number of generically and temporally disparate sources. The heurematography of the lyre and *kithara* (along with their individual strings) is especially jumbled and conflicting. Hermes, Apollo, and various legendary and historical mortals are named as inventors

---

[73] Themison was surely not the first citharode to adapt these fifth-century classics. The music of Timotheus' *nomoi* had probably also been extensively revised by numerous citharodes, including Nero (see Hordern 2002:77–78; discussion in Part IV.12). But the phrase "first and only" is more than just an honorific formula. It likely echoes the self-promotional rhetoric of this internationally successful musical star, which would have emphasized his innovation and singularity (cf. the vaunts in Timotheus PMG 796). Bélis 1999:174–177, however, offers more detailed speculations on what could have been objectively unique about Themison's adaptation technique; cf. Prauscello 2006:114–116.

[74] Cf. West 1992:382. Hierocles also defeated a group called the Hegesiasts, whose eponym was presumably the third-century BCE orator Hegesias of Magnesia, a famous proponent of the flashy "Asiatic" rhetorical style. Similar questions surround these Hegesiasts as do the Timotheasts: were they simply performers reviving the style of Hegesias or were they dedicated reperfomers of his works? In any case, Hierocles represents a fascinating crossover of *kitharôidia* and epideictic oratory, two media running in close competition in late antique performance culture.

[75] Cf. Hordern 2002:79.

and cultivators, a confusing roll call that echoes a disorderly riot of local oral traditions, rationalizing scholarly researchers in contest with one another, and musicians' own rivalrous metamusical mythologizing.[76] Given that these were the most prestigious instruments of Hellenic *mousikê*, it is not surprising that would-be authoritative versions of their history were so diversely constructed and contested. As with the construction of the life of Terpander, all manner of intellectual, cultural, and professional agendas were at stake. The figure of interest in Pliny's list is neither Terpander, who plays his usual role as inventor of the heptachord, nor Timotheus, although he is more regularly attributed the eleventh than the ninth string.[77] What is notable is Simonides' invention of the eighth *kithara* string, which is attested only here. This oddity could derive from Simonides' own poetry. Theocritus might also be alluding to a reference to *polukhordia*, or some phrase that could be construed as such, in a now lost Simonidean poem, when he describes the Cean *aoidos* "singing varied song to a many-stringed *barbitos*" (αἰόλα φωνέων | βάρβιτον ἐς πολύχορδον, *Idyll* 16.44–45) as he praises his royal Thessalian patrons.[78] Simonides' *vita* certainly indicates that he was interested in novel intellectual and verbal *tekhnai*, but, unlike his contemporary rival Lasus of Hermione, he does not seem to have been at the forefront of technical innovation in *mousikê*.[79]

In Aristophanes' *Clouds*, produced in 423 BCE, Simonides is in fact singled out as a leading light of *arkhaia mousikê*, his compositions preserved as *skolia* to be reperformed by amateurs at old-fashioned symposia (1355–1356).[80] The idea of Simonidean *polukhordia*, however, might not be derived from Simonides' actual music and poetry, but from a strain of the biographical tradition, now largely occluded, that arose from certain discursive fashionings of the Simonidean persona by figures connected to the New Music. Richard Hunter essentially makes this argument in a discussion of the "archaeology" of musico-poetic anecdotal tradition that he sees at work in Theocritus *Idyll* 16:

---

[76] Cf. Hägg 1989, especially 62–63; Wilamowitz 1903:76–77. Svenbro 1992 is a penetrating structuralist analysis of various myths surrounding the lyre's invention.

[77] Variations between eight and eleven are attested: Hordern 2002:244.

[78] Verse initial αἰόλον φων[belongs to an anonymous melic poem (SLG S286 col. iii.5). In an epigram (doubtfully) attributed to Simonides (PMG 947b) the *aulos* is called *polukhordos*, but that is a metaphor not peculiar to it (cf. Pindar *Olympian* 7.12, *Isthmian* 5.27; Plato *Republic* 399c–d, with Barker 1984:57n10).

[79] Cf. West 1992:344. Rivalry of Lasus and Simonides: Aristophanes *Wasps* 1410–1411.

[80] Cf. Eupolis fr. 148.1–2 K-A, τὰ Στησιχόρου τε καὶ Ἀλκμᾶνος Σιμωνίδου τε ἀρχαῖον ἀείδειν ("It is old-fashioned to sing the songs of Stesichorus, Alcman, and Simonides").

Out of context αἰόλα φωνέων and πολύχορδον would most naturally suggest a virtuoso instrumentalist like the famous Timotheus whose *Persai* nome survives (PMG 791): both αἰόλα and πολυ- suggest the *poikilia* of 'the new music', whose novelty largely lay in its emphasis upon rapid changes and instrumental 'runs', and πολυχορδία frequently appears in descriptions of this flamboyant style.[81]

What likely appealed to New Musicians about Simonides was not anything particularly forward-looking in his musical style, but rather key ethical components of the Cean's persona (at least as imagined in his *vita*): his unapologetically professionalized and profit-driven approach to *mousikê*, backed by his bold, proto-sophistic self-promotional rhetoric.[82]

Hunter suggests that the individual responsible for a polychord Simonides was Stratonicus of Athens, a virtuoso citharist of the fourth century BCE distinguished as much for his proudly professional ethos and witty flair for self-promotion as for his musical innovations—it was Stratonicus who supposedly introduced *polukhordia* into solo *kithara* playing and was the first to construct a "diagram" to explain complex harmonic relationships (Phaenias fr. 32 Wehrli = Athenaeus 8.352c). Hunter cites Ephorus of Cyme (FGrH 70 F 2 = Athenaeus 8.352c, from the treatise *On Inventions*), who labels Stratonicus an "emulator" (ζηλωτής) of Simonides in the matter of the aphoristic witticisms for which Stratonicus became famous.[83] It would not be difficult to imagine that the citharist contributed details to Simonides' résumé, bringing his model in rhetorical performance in line with his own musical

---

[81] Hunter 1996:101–102, who notes that the αἰολ- root describes music making in a "new dithyramb" by Telestes (PMG 806.3; the text is uncertain). The word αἰόλισμα 'varied tones' describes the sound of Hermes' lyre in Sophocles *Ikhneutai* 327, which could suggest that *aiol*- terms had a place in the aesthetic vocabulary of more traditional lyre playing. Yet it is worth considering whether Sophocles in his satyr play is characterizing the mischievous god as a "new citharode" *avant la lettre*; the humorous anachronism would not be out of place in the quasi-comic satyr play. Hermes' lyric music is certainly novel in the most literal sense; he has just invented the instrument. The terms used by the satyrs to describe it, however—the lyre "scatters fantasies of sound (*tonou phasmata*) like flowers" (330–331)—evoke descriptions of the airiness and insubstantiality of the New Music, on which see Csapo 2004:228; cf. Wilson 1999/2000:441, on the possible depiction of Amphion as a "new citharode" in Euripides' *Antiope*.

[82] On these aspects of the Simonidean *vita*, see Bell 1978; Gentili 1988:161–162; Hunter 1996:97–98.

[83] Stratonicus' witticisms are collated in Gilula 2000. See Wilson 2004:291–292 on the "serious" rhetoric of professionalism underlying them.

interests as well. But Ephorus says too that the "new dithyrambist" Philoxenus of Cythera, a slightly older contemporary of Stratonicus, greatly admired (ἐσπουδακέναι) Simonides; the adoption of the Cean might then have been a more widespread phenomenon across the New Music.[84]

Simonides worked in a number of genres—this *polueideia* doubtless appealed to some among the New Musicians—but he neither performed as festival citharode nor composed *nomoi*. Nevertheless, Timotheus, who is placed immediately after Simonides in Pliny's catalogue, could have played a significant role in the "modernization" of Simonides. In addition to his *kitharôidia*, Timotheus was, like Simonides and Philoxenus, also a dithyrambist, and it was perhaps in this capacity that he engaged Simonides as model. But Simonidean poetry is an unmistakable intertext for the citharodic *Persians*, and it is after all *polukhordia* on the *kithara* with which Simonides is associated in Pliny.[85] All must remain speculation here, but could Timotheus have figured Simonides as a citharode or a citharode analogue? Conceivably the Milesian, self-conscious of his Ionian heritage, was interested in fashioning, alongside Terpander, a distinctly Ionian forerunner to his innovative practice of this traditionally Aeolian-dominated *tekhnê*.[86] Certainly Timotheus recognized that enlisting an old-school "classic" to his side, especially one at home in the elite bastions of schoolroom and symposium, the lyric redoubts of his most conservative critics, went some way toward establishing the legitimacy of his controversial music. It is worth noting too what may be a significant coincidence: Timotheus, while not a praise singer per se, did, like Simonides, enjoy the patronage of a northern royal court, that of Archaelaus of Macedon. Simonides was not linked to Macedonian patrons, but his nephew Bacchylides did compose encomiastic song for the grandfather of Archelaus, Alexander of Macedon (20B S-M).

The image of the *polukhordos barbitos* indeed resonates significantly with that of the *poikilomousos khelus* of Timotheus' Orpheus; both are tendentious portmanteaux of the innovative and the traditional. A polychord *barbitos* is indeed a deliberate paradox, for the *barbitos*, like

---

[84] Cf. Wilson 2004:290n53.

[85] See Part IV.11.ii–iii.

[86] *Persians* 234–236. Cf. PMG 802.3, however, where "Ionian-bender" is used as a slur against a rival citharode, Phrynis—evidence of some anxiety about ethnic identity? Timotheus' dialect is essentially the Doric-Aeolic *Kunstsprache* of Simonides. At *Persians* 150–161 East Ionic dialect is placed, probably for comic effect, in the mouth of a barbarian.

the *khelus*-lyre, was an instrument that rarely left the confines of the symposium or *kômos*, and it seems by the middle of the fifth century to have fallen out of use by all but the most rear-guard aristocrats.[87] The *barbitos* kept rarified company with Eastern polychord harps; Pindar fr. 125 S-M imagines its invention as inspired by the many-stringed *pêktis* played at Lydian symposia. Theocritus must have this association in mind. But only in Theocritus is the *barbitos* rendered *polukhordos*, a word that, as Hunter indicates, had very specific New Music connotations.[88] For Bacchylides, in his encomium to Alexander of Macedon, the *barbitos* still had a "seven-toned voice" (ἑπτάτονος γᾶρυς, fr. 20B.2 S-M). The same Pindaric fragment, also from an encomiastic song, attributes the invention of the *barbitos* to Terpander.[89] This attribution must itself constitute a stratum in the musico-poetic "archaeology" of the Theocritus passage, one that in turn opens onto, by way of Terpander, a more general stream of citharodic tradition. Below we will see how the Pindaric invention of the Terpandrean *barbitos* operates as a metonymic link between two lyric worlds, those of the elite symposium and the public citharodic *agônes*; Pindar also attributed to Terpander the invention of the sympotic song *par excellence*, the *skolion*, by which Pindar means the sympotic encomium ("Plutarch" *On Music* 28.1140f).

A reflex of this linkage may be evident in Theocritus 16 as well. Although Simonides is invoked as the paradigmatic encomiastic poet, a model for the would-be praise singer to kings, Theocritus himself, there is a citharodic "undertone" to be heard not only in πολύχορδον but in the phrase αἰόλα φωνέων as well.[90] Could we not make out a punning reference in αἰόλα to *Aeolic* songs (*Aiolia*), specifically Terpander's Aeolic-Lesbian *kitharôidia*? Ἀν Αἰόλιος νόμος was among the canonical compositions attributed to Terpander (*On Music* 4.1132d). We may compare a verse from an epigram of the *Palatine Anthology* that recounts a legendary Delphic performance of the Locrian citharode Eunomus, αἰόλον ἐν κιθάρᾳ νόμον ἔκρεκον 'he played a varied *nomos* on

---

[87] Wilson 2003b:190–193; Power 2007:195–196.

[88] The *hendekakhordos lura* praised by Ion of Chios in an elegiac poem (fr. 32 West) is surely not a *barbitos*, but probably a polychord *kithara* that enjoyed a vogue among musically progressive Athenian elites before it was popularized at the *agônes* by the likes of Timotheus. See discussion in Power 2007.

[89] Sympotic encomium imagines its own performance on the *barbitos*; cf. Section 15n266 below. Simonides probably also referred to the *barbitos* in an encomium for his Thessalian patrons; cf. West 1992:58n47.

[90] We may note that Theocritus' poem is addressed to Hieron II of Syracuse; Hieron I had been a patron of Lesbian citharodes. See discussion in Section 15 below.

the *kithara'* (9.584.3), in which νόμος reads almost as a gloss on the pun latent in αἰόλος. In an epigram describing Arion's music, Posidippus similarly uses the adverb αἰόλα to qualify the Lesbian citharode's singing (φωνῇ, AB 37, lines 5–6).[91] Theocritus presents us then with a thickly layered work of creative reception: an Ionian singer performing (Aeolian songs) in a flashy, virtuoso style (αἰόλα) on a (Terpandrean) *barbitos*, whose *polukhordia* assimilates it to the *kitharai* of the Athenian New Music, even as it hearkens back to the polychord harps with which the *barbitos* was associated. Again, this temporal, generic, and ethnic/regional impasto might bear the marks of an intermediate citharodic reception and reinvention of Simonides by Timotheus.[92]

7. Terpander's Orpheus

The place of Orpheus in the living citharodic performance tradition merits further discussion at this point. Timotheus' invocation of Orpheus in *Persians*, brief as it is, might reflect the practice alluded to by Socrates in Plato's *Ion* 533b–c whereby citharodes "perform explanations about Orpheus" (ἐξηγεῖσθαι ... περὶ Ὀρφέως). The "explanations" at issue here, as my translation indicates, are surely performative in nature, either textually embedded (be the text prepared or largely composed-in-performance), as is the case with *Persians*, or paratextual, and more probably biographical than text-exegetical.[93] That is, the citharode communicates notionally authoritative lore *about* his mythical predecessor, as Timotheus does with self-serving intent in his *sphragis*, and as he does for Terpander as well. This is suggested by the *Ion* passage: Socrates says that both auletes and citharists should be

---

[91] Theocritus' αἰόλα carries other associations, little surprise given the overdetermined allusiveness of Hellenistic poetry. The visual aspect of the shell of the *barbitos* could be described as αἰόλον 'checkered, dappled', as at *Homeric Hymn to Hermes* 33, Nicander *Alexipharmaca* 561–562. The αἰόλος/Αἰόλιος pun too recalls the monodic lyric of the Lesbian poets Sappho and Alcaeus, both famous exponents of the *barbitos*. We are reminded too of the Aeolic heritage of Simonides' Thessalian patrons, the Scopadai and Aleuadai (Theocritus *Idyll* 16.34–36).

[92] Hunter 1996:146–149 argues analogously that a brief description of Orpheus' performance at Apollonius Rhodius *Argonautica* 4.907, which seems to be, *pace* Hunter, implicitly citharodic rather than citharistic, is refracted through the prism of the New Music: "He played [on his *phorminx*] the swiftly moving melody of a quick-rolling song" (κραιπνὸν ἐυτροχάλοιο μέλος κανάχησεν ἀοιδῆς). (For the New Music aesthetic of speed, cf. Plato *Laws* 669e.) Orpheus is transformed into a "master of 'modern music'" (149) in the style of a Timotheus.

[93] Cf. Martin 2001:24, 32.

able to "perform explanations" about Olympus and Thamyris, respectively. Since no verbal texts were involved in auletic and citharistic performance, we must understand these instrumental performers to be speaking "paramusically" *about* the *protos*-figures themselves.[94]

Timotheus was probably not the first citharode to bundle together in performance Orphic and Terpandrean "bio-exegesis." This practice likely originated with the citharodes of the Lesbian *diadokhê*, eager to link their model, Terpander, and thereby themselves, with the talismanic musical potency of Orpheus, which was symbolically condensed in his magical lyre. A reflex of this practice could be detected in an account of the invention and early transmission of the seven-stringed lyre attributed to the Pythagorean theorist Nicomachus of Gerasa, who was writing around 100 CE. Since a variant heurematography is attributed to Nicomachus in Boethius *On Music* 1.20, it could, however, be the work of his anonymous excerptor.[95] The account follows the tradition of the *Homeric Hymn to Hermes* in making Hermes the inventor of the heptachord lyre (that is, the tortoise-shell lyre, τὴν λύραν τὴν ἐκ τῆς χελώνης, which, as in the *Hymn*, is imagined to be the primal lyre, predating both the *phorminx* and the *kithara*). Orpheus is named as its initial mortal recipient; with it he is said to have taught Linus, Thamyris, and Amphion. The account continues:

ἀναιρεθέντος δὲ τοῦ Ὀρφέως ὑπὸ τῶν Θρᾳκικῶν γυναικῶν τὴν λύραν αὐτοῦ βληθῆναι εἰς τὴν θάλασσαν, ἐκβληθῆναι δὲ εἰς Ἄντισσαν πόλιν τῆς Λέσβου. εὑρόντας δὲ ἁλιέας ἐνεγκεῖν τὴν λύραν πρὸς Τέρπανδρον, τὸν δὲ κομίσαι εἰς Αἴγυπτον. εὑρόντα δὲ αὐτὸν ἐκπονήσαντα ἐπιδεῖξαι τοῖς ἐν Αἰγύπτῳ ἱερεῦσιν, ὡς αὐτὸν πρωθευρετὴν γεγενημένον. Τέρπανδρος μὲν οὕτω λέγεται τὴν λύραν εὑρηκέναι, Ἀχαιοὺς δὲ ὑπὸ Κάδμου τοῦ Ἀγήνορος παραλαβεῖν τηνικαῦτά φασιν.

After Orpheus was killed by the Thracian women his lyre was hurled into the sea and washed up at Antissa, a city of Lesbos. Fisherman found the lyre and brought it to Terpander, and he brought it to Egypt. Having discovered it, he perfected it and showed it to the priests in Egypt, as if he had been the first inventor. Thus it is said that Terpander invented the lyre,

---

[94] For Thamyris as a model citharist, see Part II.3n51.
[95] See Jan 1895:211–234.

but they say that at that point the Achaeans received it from Cadmus son of Agenor.

Nicomachus *Excerpts* 1 = T 53b G

Nicomachus (or the excerptor) here integrates a range of conflicting or rival traditions about the myth history of *kitharôidia*. First, he apparently wants to reconcile what I have called "mainland" traditions, which promote Cadmus and Amphion, Linus and Thamyris as primeval mortal exponents of singing to the lyre, with a Lesbian-Eastern Aegean one, which spotlights Orpheus and Terpander. Second, he wants to account for a specific "problem" that arises within the latter tradition: if the lyre of Hermes that was inherited by Terpander already had seven strings, in what sense can Terpander be called its "inventor"? The inclusive logic of the proposed scenario is ingenious but, even by the elastic standards of mythical chronology, hopelessly contorted. Cadmus' gift of the lyre to Greece is placed not only after the time of Amphion, whose foundation of Thebes is elsewhere always seen as secondary to the Cadmeian foundation, but also after Terpander, who by any reckoning must be generations younger than Cadmus.[96] As a whole assemblage, the Nicomachean account is probably the idiosyncratic work of one individual compiler. Yet the discrete narrative details that inform it are surely drawn from other sources that in turn draw from more ancient lore, some of which likely goes back as far as the Archaic period.[97]

The odd story of Terpander's trip to Egypt may be no more than a contrivance of the Nicomachean account, a roundabout means of getting the lyre of Hermes into the hands of Cadmus, who elsewhere receives the lyre directly from Hermes when he marries Harmonia (Diodorus Siculus 5.49). The Egyptian episode also provides a convenient explanation for the antiquity of traditions maintaining that it was Terpander who invented the seven-stringed lyre. Although Terpander "perfected" (ἐκπονήσαντα) the instrument—a deliberately vague acknowledgement of the commonly held belief that Terpander did, in fact, add three strings to the tetrachord lyre that he inherited from Orpheus (e.g. Nicomachus *ap.* Boethius 1.20 = T 53a G)—he convinces the Egyptian priests, with what appears to be an uncharacteristic duplicity, that it was he who was its original inventor (*prôtheuretês*). Nevertheless, there might have been previous accounts about a trip taken to Egypt by Terpander, more positive in tone, which were adapted by Nicomachus

---

[96] See discussion in Gostoli 1990:119–120.
[97] See Franklin 2003:302n12 on Nicomachus' sources; cf. Franklin 2006a:54–55.

or his source and altered to undermine Terpander's claims to originality. The theme of the wise man visiting Egypt to learn arcane wisdom is attested already in Plato, who has Solon discoursing with Egyptian priests (*Timaeus* 21c; *Critias* 113a), but the theme is surely older. The Spartan lawgiver, Lycurgus, also visited Egypt and studied its native *nomima* 'customs' (Strabo 10.4.19).[98] That both of these figures are lawgivers (*nomothetai*) is notable in light of Terpander's own image as a singer of order-bringing *nomoi*. But Terpander's Egyptian sojourn may reflect more specifically the horizons of Lesbian culture. Alcaeus had supposedly visited Egypt and spoken of it in his poetry (Strabo 1.2.30); Sappho's brother, Charaxus, imported wine to Egyptian Naucratis, which had a significant presence of Lesbian traders.[99] The mercantile connections between Archaic Lesbos and Egypt surely indicate the existence of a Lesbian intrigue with Egyptian culture. We might speculate, then, that romantic tales of Terpander's Egyptian sojourn, either to play his own music or, more likely, to acquire prestigious ancient and esoteric musical knowledge, were from an early point circulated by the Lesbian Singers, who themselves may have performed in Naucratis in the course of their travels.[100] Similar tales about Terpander's journey to Lydia may lie behind Pindar fr. 125 S-M, in which the citharode is imagined as a privileged guest at Lydian banquets, where he is first exposed to the exotic harps that he will emulate in his design of the *barbitos*.

The story of Terpander and the fishermen, attested only here, could also be a distinct piece of Lesbian lore. The fifth-century BCE historian Hellanicus of Lesbos is a good candidate for its written transmitter, but behind him could stand the island's citharodes themselves, who were eager to promote a direct link between their ancestor's *kitharôidia* and the supernatural power of the Orphic lyre.[101] The story is obviously a variation on an undoubtedly very old theme, the migration of Orpheus' head and lyre to the northern shores of Lesbos, typically to Antissa, the native city of Terpander.[102] In some accounts of the legend it is said that upon arriving at Antissa the head was buried in a cave yet continued

---

[98] Cf. Szegedy-Maszak 1978:202.

[99] Herodotus 2.135; Strabo 17.1.33; Athenaeus 13.596b–c. The story of Charaxus may be a fifth-century fabrication, as Lidov 2002 argues, but Lesbian presence in Egypt during Sappho's time was nevertheless a reality. Mytileneans helped to found the "Hellenion" shrine in Naucratis in the sixth century BCE: Herodotus 2.178. Cf. Shields 1917:xii; Spencer 2001:75–76.

[100] Cf. Part I.8.iiin173 for speculation on the reception of such tales in Hellenistic Alexandria.

[101] Franklin 2003:302n12 posits Hellanicus as an early source for *Excerpt 1*.

[102] Cf. Burkert 1983:202, with a list of the sources in n30; Graf 1987:92–94.

to sing oracles. The fate of the lyre, however, is less clear. Lucian *The Uncultured Book Collector* 11 says that the Lesbians "hung up the lyre in the temple of Apollo, where it was preserved for a long time" (he does not say whether the temple was in Antissa); Phanocles fr. 1.19 Powell locates the still-resounding lyre "in the tomb" of Orpheus, along with the singing head. In both Lucian and Phanocles the Orphic lyre represents the musical patrimony of the entire island of Lesbos ("the most musical of them all," as Phanocles fr. 1.22 puts it), and belongs to no one individual. But it is entirely possible that there were distinct citharodic oral traditions, perhaps originally elaborated within the context of a local Antissan cult of Orpheus, relating how the Orphic lyre came at some point into the sole possession of Terpander; these narratives may well have involved the intercession of fishermen.

The Nicomachean story indeed bears an unmistakable resemblance to another *logos Lesbios* 'Lesbian story', no doubt of considerable antiquity, that is recorded by Pausanias 10.19.3 in connection with the cult of Dionysus *Phallên* in the city of Methymna. Fishermen from Methymna, the city nearest to Antissa on the northern coast of the island, had once recovered from the sea an uncanny wooden image that had a divine quality (*to theion*) to it; the Delphic oracle later confirmed that the image was of Dionysus and ordered the cult to be established around it.[103]

Of course, it could be the case that the role of the fishermen in the Terpander story represents a later accretion, derived perhaps from the Methymnian legend, to an older account that by some other means brought the numinous Orphic lyre into personal contact with Terpander.[104] In any case, we can only guess at the precise details involved in citharodic versions of Terpander's reception of the lyre. It is unlikely that there was one orthodox telling. Conceivably, in one account the Orphic lyre was imagined to have seven strings, as Nicomachus has it; Terpander simply inherited it (and its powers) as

---

[103] Cf. Burkert 1983:202–203 and Graf 1987:93, both of whom connect this aetiological legend with the story related by Nicomachus.

[104] Indeed, it does require a considerable suspension of temporal logic (although not necessarily an impossible one) to have Terpander acquiring the lyre so soon after the death of Orpheus, unless we are to imagine that the lyre had been moving at a glacial pace between the mouth of the Hebrus and the shores of Antissa. We may note that the people of Antissa were resettled in Methymna after the destruction of their city in 167 BCE (Livy 43.31.14, Pliny *Natural History* 5.139); cf. Mason 1995. The mention of Terpander as *Methumnaios* in Diodorus Siculus 8.28 *ap.* Tzetzes *Chiliades* 1.385–392 = T 15 G could reflect some attempt at a wholesale appropriation of Terpander and Orpheus by Methymna after the fall of Antissa. Ovid *Metamorphoses* 11.50 has the Orphic lyre washing up at Methymna.

is and so "discovered" rather than "invented" the heptachord lyre. (This account would coexist peaceably with Hermes' invention of the lyre in the *Hymn to Hermes*, which was well known by the fifth century BCE, though we should not expect that citharodes felt compelled to "square" divergent heurematographical legends as if they were rationalizing mythographers.) In another account, which promulgated the strong tradition of Terpander as technical innovator, Terpander refined the Orphic lyre, adding three strings to its four (cf. ἐκπονήσαντα 'perfected' in Nicomachus); this narrative would complement the programmatic rhetoric of Gostoli fr. 4 ("new songs to the heptatonic *phorminx*"). Terpander was also attributed the original design of the concert *kithara*; perhaps that invention too was presented in terms of a modification of the Orphic lyre, be it seven- or four-stringed.[105]

But, not surprisingly, Orpheus was himself called by some the inventor of the *kithara* (Pliny *Natural History* 7.204). On the Sicyonian metope at Delphi, Orpheus and Philammon both hold square-bottomed *kitharai*, presumably with seven strings. Again, we should not expect logical and temporal consistency in the myth history of the lyre and *kithara*, even within the oral traditions of *kitharôidia* itself.

8. Orpheus in Citharodic Performance?

The performative engagement of citharodes with Orpheus and Orphic myth was likely more extensive, however, than the sort of brief treatment that we see in *Persians*, and surely exceeded the specific concerns of the Terpandrean *diadokhê*. Indeed, we might ask whether citharodes sang Orphic poetry, that is, either texts attributed to Orpheus or texts devoted to the experiences of Orpheus that circulated under separate authorship. If so, what sort of texts were they, and in what contexts were they performed: in public, festal, and competitive ones, or strictly within the confines of private cultic ritual? Richard Martin has recently advocated the former view, warning against being "misled by the ancient evidence into thinking that private gatherings, *thiasoi*, or initiate groups were the only or even the major locus to feature

---

[105] Timotheus *Persians* 221–231 represents a creative variation on all of these traditions. Such variation and combination was probably not uncommon from one citharode to another, and one occasion to another. I discuss a curious variant in which the Orphic lyre passes, via (Lesbian) Lyrnessos, to Achilles (Philostratus *On Heroes* 11.10) in Part II.9.i.

Orphic poetic performances."[106] Orphic poetry, he argues, in particular an Orphic *Descent to Hades*, was routinely performed by professional rhapsodes at public festivals such as the Panathenaia, before mass audiences.[107] Direct evidence for this is wanting, but it seems reasonable that if, as West has it, an Orphic *Descent* and texts expounding inchoate "Orphic" cosmo-theogonic ideas were already in circulation in the sixth century BCE, then at least some of these poems would have been realized in public performances during the late Archaic and Classical periods outside of the restricted spheres of telestic ritual and religio-philosophic circles.[108] Martin points out that the humor of the Aristophanic parody of an Orphic theogony in *Birds* 693–702, with its absurdist take on the principle of the cosmic egg, would have been lost to the mass audience had such material not been "public, performed, and popular," although it could be argued in response that Aristophanes elsewhere parodies esoteric discourse only vaguely familiar to his audience, as in the burlesque of Ionian scientific theory in *Clouds*.[109]

While I remain skeptical that hardcore "doctrinal" Orphica—the stuff later packaged and sold in the "hubbub of books by Orpheus and Musaeus" criticized by Plato (*Republic* 364e)—ever made significant inroads at the *mousikoi agônes* of big festivals such as the Panathenaia, narrative poetry such as the *Descent*, both entertaining and edifying, very likely did. That is, professional performers offered exciting poetic accounts *about* Orphic exploits rather than "Orphic" poetry qua sacred, revelatory discourse. I assume that "secular" Panathenaic audiences eager for sound, story, and spectacle would have had little patience for the extended and abstruse cosmological and mystic-eschatological speculations of the latter, even if they otherwise enjoyed the "didactic" theogonic and catalogue poetry of Hesiod, which might seem boring performance material to us, but which nonetheless had an engaging combination of canonical familiarity, Panhellenic glamour alongside

---

[106] Martin 2001:23; cf. West 1983:79–80, who believes that Orphic poems "had a very limited circulation. They were not a matter of general public interest. They were not ... recited for public or social entertainment."

[107] Nagy 2005:80 also thinks that rhapsodes performed Orphic poetry at the Panathenaia, at least in the sixth century BCE, reckoning that it was eclipsed by rhapsodic performances of Homer by the fifth century.

[108] West 1983:9–12, who thinks, however, that such poems existed during the sixth century only as written texts circulating within elite Pythagorean circles. Cf. Graf and Johnston 2007:174. Bowra 1952:124, however, thinks that an Orphic *Descent* "may possibly have taken shape" in the public contexts of Peisistratean Athens, which saw the circulation of other descent narratives (Heracles, Odysseus, Theseus).

[109] Martin 2001:32.

passages of local genealogical and geographical interest, and flashes of narrative verve.[110]

Of course, it is probable that some "Orphic" theogonic material made it into publicly performed texts, particularly, I suspect, the hymnic *prooimia* that prefaced epic entertainments. The case of Onomacritus is worth considering in this regard. Onomacritus, called a *khrêsmologos* 'speaker of oracular utterances' in Herodotus 7.6, was employed by the Peisistratids for his expert manipulations of not only oracular but also Homeric poetry; the scholia claim that he interpolated three lines into the *Nekuia* section of the *Odyssey* (11.602–604). His intimacy with the tyrants and with Homer place him in the milieu of the Panathenaia, not as a behind-the-scenes "redactor" of Homeric texts—a rather anachronistic notion—but as a rhapsodic performer on the public agonistic stage.[111] In addition, a number of testimonia suggest that Onomacritus promulgated in poetic form certain themes that would come to be associated with Orphism, in particular the myth of Dionysus' *sparagmos* at the hands of the Titans. Pausanias 8.37.5 says that Onomacritus "taking over the name of the Titans from Homer composed rites for Dionysus and made the Titans the agents of the sufferings of Dionysus."[112] This "Orphic" work was thus significantly related to his Homeric endeavors. Martin argues reasonably that Onomacritus, in addition to presenting Homeric epic, indeed performed in Athens as a "rhapsode of Orphic material."[113] It is tempting to connect, however tenuously, the "Orphic" *rhapsôidia* of Onomacritus that is suggested by Pausanias' testimony to the implications of the following passage from the early Byzantine antiquarian Joannes Lydus:

---

[110] Cf. the pertinent remarks on the Panathenaia as a festival that was "always dignified but never intense, never emotionally strong," its emphasis falling rather on ceremony and spectacle, in Parker 2005:378.

[111] The report that Onomacritus was one of four authorized compilers of Homeric poetry (*Anecdota Graeca* 1.6 Cramer) suggests as well "live" rhapsodic activity. On Onomacritus, see now D'Agostino 1987, who argues that the Odyssean interpolation, an encomium of deified Heracles that is rather abruptly placed in the *Nekuia*, was meant to complement Peisistratean promotion of the cult of Heracles (95–113). Heracles played a crucial role in the tyrants' management of the Panathenaia, and it is in the performative context of that festival that the interpolation should be understood. Martin 2001:31 considers the interpolation in light of Onomacritus' interest in Orphism and the Orphic *Descent*.

[112] See Rohde 1925: "The myth of the dismemberment of Zagreus [Dionysus] by the Titans was already put into verse by Onomakritos" (341); Guthrie 1952:13, 107–108. Linforth 1941:353 and Edmonds 1999:43–44, however, make reasonable objections to the early role of Onomacritus in expounding Orphic doctrine. Cf. West 1983:249–251.

[113] Martin 2001:31.

Τέρπανδρός γε μὴν ὁ Λέσβιος Νύσσαν λέγει τετιθηνηκέναι τὸν
Διόνυσον τὸν ὑπό τινων Σαβάζιον ὀνομαζόμενον, ἐκ Διὸς καὶ
Περσεφόνης γενόμενον, εἶτα ὑπὸ τῶν Τιτάνων σπαραχθέντα.

Terpander the Lesbian says that Nyssa nursed Dionysus, the
one called by some Sabazius, born of Zeus and Persephone and
then torn apart by the Titans.

Joannes Lydus *On the Months* 4.51

It is possible that only the first part of this sentence refers to the text
attributed to Terpander. If so, the poem in question could be a proemial
citharodic hymn to Dionysus or even a dithyrambic text that went
under the name of Terpander.[114] In support of the former possibility we
may consider a volute krater of the Altamura Painter from around 470
BCE, on whose neck is depicted a victorious citharode and on whose
body Zeus is shown presenting a newborn Dionysus to the nymphs of
Nysa. The mythical scene could represent the theme of the citharode's
song, presented on some festival occasion in Athens.[115]

Yet the syntax of the Joannes Lydus passage—the participial phrases
that follow τὸν Διόνυσον τόν are all attributive and so subordinate to
the clause in which Terpander is explicitly cited—in fact encourages
us to take the whole sentence as a description of the contents of a
"Terpandrean" text that treated the Orphic myth of Dionysus' first birth
from Zeus and Persephone and his death at the hands of the Titans, and
presumably the second birth of the god as well, to which the story of
Nysa/Nyssa would be more properly attached. If so, we might conjecture
the existence of a citharodic tradition of singing "Orphic" theogonic
material that went under the name of the first citharode, and the one
closest to Orpheus, Terpander. Dating such a tradition with precision
would be impossible; it could conceivably be quite late. But the implicit
links suggested by the testimonia concerning Onomacritus between the

---

[114] Gostoli 1990:145 thinks that the citation of Terpander ends with τὸν Διόνυσον; what
comes after is a "general definition of Dionysus-Sabazius that we find already enun-
ciated in identical terms in Diodorus (4.4)." Yet the fact that Diodorus Siculus uses
much the same phraseology to describe Dionysus-Sabazius does not necessarily rule
out a "Terpandrean" source for the general content that Joannes Lydus is reporting.
Diodorus is himself citing the "mythologizing" of unnamed sources (μυθολογοῦσι
δέ τινες), which could themselves have drawn on "Terpander." In addition, Diodorus
says nothing in his passage about the Titans, although he does mention their murder
of Dionysus-Zagreus at 5.75.4.

[115] Ferrara, Museo Archeologico Nazionale T 381 (Alfieri 1979:33–34, figs. 77 and 78); cf.
Webster 1972:161. On the other side of the vessel, however, an aulete surrounded by
athletic youths is depicted. The Dionysiac theme could be his.

rhapsodic performance of Orphica, including the myth of the Titans, and the Archaic Panathenaia might prompt us to trace it back as well to the setting of the sixth-century Panathenaia, where it emerged in concert (or in competition) with Onomacritus' rhapsodic poetry.[116] Again, we might recall the Altamura Painter's image, with its potentially meaningful collocation of citharode, Dionysus, and (nymphs of) Nysa, although there are of course no explicitly "Orphic" signifiers present in it.

Other Terpandrean fragments and testimonia yield subtle hints of Orphism, yet all are highly ambiguous. It could be argued that the proemial invocation of Zeus as the "beginning of everything, leader of everything" (Ζεῦ πάντων ἀρχά, πάντων ἀγήτωρ, fr. 3 G) recalls the language and conceit of certain Orphic hymns to Zeus, but obviously the similarities may be no more than coincidental.[117] Nor does Terpander seem to have been implicated as a propounder of eschatological wisdom in mystery cult as were Orpheus and his fellow singers Eumolpus, Musaeus, and Linus. In the *Ecphrasis* of the fifth-century CE poet Christodorus of Coptos, Terpander is said to have resolved the civic strife of Sparta with his "mystic song ... on his *phorminx* that solemnizes mystic rites" (μύστιδα μολπήν ... μυστιπόλῳ φόρμιγγι, *Palatine Anthology* 2.111–116 = T 59 G). But it is probably this late poet's own conceit to cast Terpander as a mystagogue, and his famous musico-political intervention in Sparta as a mystico-religious initiation. Of course, this metaphorical turn was not without basis in either the Orphic mysteries or the Terpandrean lore. In both traditions, the music of the lyre—and recall that Terpander had inherited the lyre of Orpheus—was endowed with supernatural powers. The two traditions must have enjoyed to some extent a dialogic relationship. The myths and rituals of Orphism and Orphic-related mysteries, including those at Eleusis, clearly integrated elements of *kitharôidia*, its practice (more on which below) and its ideology. Conceivably, it was the lore transmitted above all by citharodes about Orpheus' musical dominion over nature and death, the "cosmic force" of his lyre, that inspired and shaped the early stages of his invention as a mystagogue. At the same time, while we certainly should not imagine that professional citharodes sidelined

---

[116] The syncretism of Sabazius and Dionysus is a later-fifth-century development, at least in Athens. See Gostoli 1990:145–146. But Sabazius-Dionysus could represent a secondary accretion in an older "Terpandrean" tradition.

[117] Orphic hymns: "Zeus is head, Zeus is middle, from Zeus all things have been born" (Derveni Papyrus col. 17.12); the incantatory repetition of Zeus' name also recalls Terpander fr. 3 G. Cf. Betegh 2004:173–174 for further parallels among the Orphic hymns.

as telestic initiators, or that they sang full-blown "Orphic hymns" at the *agônes*, it is entirely possible that they in turn absorbed some Orphic ideas and imagery into their songmaking, as did other "secular" poets, such as Aristophanes.[118]

A more confident case could be made for *kitharôidia* as a medium for the popular diffusion of narrative entertainments *about* Orpheus. Citharodes are, in fact, more likely to have taken an interest in the exploits of the prototypical lyre singer than are rhapsodes.[119] It seems significant that a major mythological figure such as Orpheus is entirely absent from both the *Iliad* and *Odyssey* as we have them. Indeed, as the Sicyonian metope indicates, in the Archaic period Orpheus was imagined not as a generic "singer" or "poet," but as an idealized concert citharode projected into the mythic past. That image was no doubt fashioned and promoted in the first place by the citharodes, who sang of Orpheus' superhuman musical feats as a member of the Argonautic expedition in what amounted to a rhetoric of professional self-aggrandizement—citharodes' vaunting their own heroic legacy, and the promise of their own musical superpowers, in the very songs they sang (cf. Part II.10).[120] But was there Archaic or Classical citharodic narrative solely dedicated (and perhaps also attributed) to Orpheus, in particular a *Descent to Hades*? It is generally agreed that early poetic renderings of Orpheus' *katabasis* would have been first-person accounts of the musician's underworld journey and search for his wife.[121] Martin thus

---

[118] It is notable that in local Delphian tradition Orpheus' telestic activity was cited as the reason for his absence from the early record of the Pythian citharodic *agôn*, as if mysteries and *agônes* were incompatible: "But they say that Orpheus, because he cultivated an air of solemn detachment in his mysteries and was haughty in general, and Musaeus, because he imitated Orpheus in all things, refused to be put to the test in a contest of music" (Ὀρφέα δὲ σεμνολογίᾳ τῇ ἐπὶ τελεταῖς καὶ ὑπὸ φρονήματος τοῦ ἄλλου καὶ Μουσαῖον τῇ ἐς πάντα μιμήσει τοῦ Ὀρφέως οὐκ ἐθελῆσαί φασιν αὐτοὺς ἐπὶ ἀγῶνι μουσικῆς ἐξετάζεσθαι, Pausanias 10.7.2).

[119] Cf. Wilamowitz 1903:84n1.

[120] Although Martin 2001 argues for an Orphic *rhapsôidia*, he acknowledges that "[s]tories that attest to the power of [Orpheus'] *kithara* playing ... are probably connected to the lore and ideology of actual *kithara*-players" (32).

[121] Bowra 1952:124; West 1983:12; Graf and Johnston 2007:173–174. On the first-person narration of the *Orphic Argonautica*, see below. Bowra points out that the attribution of a *Descent* in *Suda* s.v. Ὀρφεύς (658 Adler) to one Orpheus of Camarina could also reflect the first-person nature of the tradition. I note here the possibility that Orpheus of Croton, who was supposedly employed by the Peisistratids to edit the text of Homer alongside Onomacritus (Tzetzes *On Comedy* p20 Kaibel), may, if he was real (West 1983:249–250 assumes he was a scholarly invention), have been a citharode rather than a rhapsode, as we might first think. It is interesting that Asclepiades of Bithynian Myrlea *ap. Suda* s.v. Ὀρφεύς (657 Adler; Asclepiades may also be Tzetzes' source) attributes an *Argonautica* to him.

makes the appealing argument that when rhapsodes recited an Orphic *Descent*, they were performing a *mimêsis* of Orpheus, reenacting the persona of the legendary singer in the moment of performing a text that was notionally composed by him. To support this idea of mythical reenactment by rhapsodes, Martin cites a claim, made by Alexander Polyhistor, that Terpander "emulated (*ezêlôkenai*) the epic verse (*epê*) of Homer and the melodies (*melê*) of Orpheus" (FGrH 273 F 77 *ap.* "Plutarch" *On Music* 5.1132f). Yet "Terpander is not a rhapsode."[122]

What Alexander's formulation actually captures is a mimetic logic that belongs to *kitharôidia*, not *rhapsôidia*, which had nothing to do with *melê*. Terpander's emulation of Orphic melodies provides a model for such mimetic reenactment in performance; citharodes identify with Terpander's identification with Orpheus. We have, in fact, a neat iconographical reflex of the conceptual fusion between the identities of living citharode and Orpheus on a late-sixth-century black-figured oinochoe from Athens: an agonistic citharode mounting a platform is accompanied by the inscription *khaire Orpheus* 'Hail, Orpheus'.[123] Of course, Alexander Polyhistor says nothing of Orphic poetry; it is Homeric epic with which he associates Classical *kitharôidia*, and this was no doubt largely the case in the fifth century BCE.

Faint echoes of a citharodic *Descent* might nonetheless be audible in late- and post-Classical texts and images. In Plato *Symposium* 179d Phaedrus claims that the gods refused to restore to life Orpheus' dead wife because, being a *kitharôidos*, he "seemed cowardly and soft," relying on the power of his music rather than "daring to die for his love (ἔνεκα τοῦ ἔρωτος)" as Alcestis did for her husband.[124] Phaedrus' (and Plato's)

---

[122] Martin 2001:32.

[123] Villa Giulia M 354; Seebass 1991:19, with fig. 6. Cf. Part I.4.

[124] Plato has Orpheus receiving a phantom (*phasma*) of his wife, who goes unnamed, rather than the real thing. This version of the story may be Plato's own invention, an attempt to undermine versions in which Orpheus succeeds in reviving his wife with his music (cf. Heath 1994:180n25; Sansone 1985, who thinks that Plato is borrowing from an *Orpheus* of Aristias, a tragedian of the early fifth century). As Bowra 1952:119–120 shows, Euripides *Alcestis* 357–362 (in conjunction with a variety of later texts) indicates that the fifth century knew such versions; the tragic story of Orpheus' failure seems in fact to be a Hellenistic innovation. (Not all believe that there were ever "happy-ending" accounts of the *katabasis*; see Heath 1994, who provides a comprehensive review of scholarship at 163–164.) Naturally, one would imagine that if Archaic and Classical cithardes did sing a *Descent*, they would have celebrated the transcendent efficacy of the Orphic lyre, at least in the short term. Bowra suggests that in early versions of the myth Orpheus' wife is "brought successfully to the upper world, [but then] has to return to Hades under the guidance of Hermes" (121). For Bowra, the later-fifth-century BCE relief from the Athenian Altar of the Twelve Gods, of which several Roman copies survive, may illustrate this "second death": Eurydice is

aristocratic disdain for professional citharodes is apparent, but it is improbable that Plato has independently and casually cast Orpheus in Hades as a *kitharôidos*, a word that is used only twice in Plato, and whose professional implications are surely marked; this Orpheus is no generic "singer." Rather, the quip may allude to a well-established association between the Orphic *katabasis* and *kitharôidia* in the Athenian performance culture. Again, there is no obvious written trace of an early Orphic *Descent*, citharodic or otherwise. But it is worth reading a passage from the *Orphic Argonautica* against the Platonic one. The *Orphic Argonautica*, a hexametrical account of the journey of the Argo related in the first person by Orpheus, is a work of the late Imperial period, yet scholars have argued that it draws not only on Roman and Hellenistic poetry, but Classical and even Archaic epics concerning Orpheus as well, including the Orphic *katabasis*.[125] In its opening section, a reckoning of the traditional themes of Orphic poetry, we read:

> ἄλλα δέ σοι κατέλεξ' ἅπερ εἴσιδον ἠδ' ἐνόησα,
> Ταίναρον ἡνίκ' ἔβην σκοτίην ὁδὸν Ἄϊδος εἴσω,
> ἡμετέρῃ πίσυνος κιθάρῃ, δι' ἔρωτ' ἀλόχοιο·

> And I told you everything I saw and learned
> when I went to Taenarum by the dark path into Hades,
> relying on my *kithara*, for love of my wife.

Orphic Argonautica 40–42

The phrase πίσυνος κιθάρῃ 'relying on my *kithara*' corresponds precisely to the phrase *fretus cithara* in Vergil's telling of the *katabasis* in *Aeneid* 6, even falling in the same metrical position in the hexameter line (*Threicia fretus cithara fidibusque canoris* 'relying on his Thracian *cithara* and its resounding strings', 6.120). Both the *Argonautica* and the Vergilian passages would seem to be dependent on a shared source, a passage from an Orphic *katabasis*, perhaps of some antiquity.[126] Although the instrument of Orpheus is variously described as a tortoise-shell lyre or *kithara* in the *Argonautica* and in Vergil, the use of *kithara* in the two passages seems deliberate and marked, and may have been so in the original source. Could that source text have been citharodic, or at least have referred to

---

called back to Hades by Hermes while Orpheus stands by, lyre in hand. For Touchette 1990, however, the image represents the successful restoration of Eurydice to life.

[125] See Bowra 1952:121; Nelis 2005, for whom the *Argonautica* is a "repository of traces of lost [Orphic] texts" (172).

[126] Cf. Ziegler 1942:1391; Nelis 2005:171–172: "The *katabasis* may have been a privileged model of the *Argonautica*."

a cithardic performance tradition of the Orphic *Descent*? And did Plato know this text as well? We might, after all, hear a faint echo between Phaedrus' criticism of Orpheus, that the cowardly *kitharôidos* would not consent physically to die, i.e. to commit suicide, ἕνεκα τοῦ ἔρωτος 'for love', and Orpheus' proud claim in the *Argonautica* that he went to Hades alive, confident in his musical powers, δι' ἔρωτ' 'for love' of his wife.

Fifth-century Athenian iconography yields only one representation related to the *katabasis* myth, a sculptural relief originally attached to the parapet surrounding the Altar of the Twelve Gods.[127] On it Orpheus wears the *alôpekis*, the fox-skin Thracian cap, and high Thracian boots and holds a simple *khelus*-lyre in his left hand. This "realistic" portrayal of Orpheus is in line with the majority of surviving representations of the singer in fifth-century Athens, most of which place him in scenes set immediately before his death, as he plays the lyre for enchanted Thracian men, or in scenes of his murder at the hands of the Thracian women. In these images, Orpheus, typically wearing Greek rather than Thracian attire, plays the basic *lura*; he is distinctly non-professional.[128] This representational tendency, which is markedly different from the distinctly citharodic visions of Orpheus in the sixth century, may reflect an "aristocratic" casting of Orpheus in the Athenian sympotic imaginary, with which the imagery on wine vessels intimately engages— Orpheus is made to look like one of the lyric symposiasts who consume his image.[129] The change in iconography does not mean, however, that citharodes were no longer singing Orphic narrative in Athens. In fact, *kitharôidia* is as likely a medium as any for the diffusion of not only the *katabasis* narrative, but also stories about the Thracian experiences of Orpheus, including his murder.[130] It is perhaps significant that Aeschylus, whose *Bassarids* treated the myth of Orpheus' death from a novel Dionysian myth-ritual perspective, was known to adapt musical and thematic ideas from *kitharôidia* (Aristophanes *Frogs* 1282–1300).[131] Other dramatic and dithyrambic treatments of Orphic myth, now unknown, may of course stand behind the vase paintings (the narrative details of which notably do not match those that we can reconstruct for

---

[127] Cf. n124 above.

[128] The ethnologically "correct" characterization of Orpheus on the altar relief reflects increased Athenian interest in Thracian culture in the later fifth century. Cf. Parker 1996:174. Vase paintings from the period show other Thracian singers, Thamyris and Musaeus, also attired in "authentic" garb.

[129] Discussion in Part I.5.

[130] West 1983:12 speculates that a "poem about Orpheus' descent to Hades" narrated too his death at the hands of the Thracian women.

[131] See West 1990b:38 on Aeschylus' innovations in the *Bassarids*.

Aeschylus' play), but it is possible that citharodic accounts provided the basic source for material that was creatively adapted by both the vase painters and the dramatists and choral poets.

On a series of southern Italian vases produced in the fourth century BCE, however, the "catabatic" Orpheus is fit with the glamorous garb and accoutrements of the citharode, the agonist's *skeuê*: he plays a full-scale concert *kithara* and wears an ankle-length, decorated chiton and, in some images, a fancy Phrygian headdress.[132] These vases are to be connected with local Orphic-Bacchic cults, and it is clear that on them Orpheus is imagined as "the author of the 'Orphic' texts attributed to him; he appears in these underworld scenes as a guarantor that the prescribed purification rites have been performed."[133] In a scene by the Ganymede Painter, for instance, Orpheus plays his *kithara* in a quasi-orchestic pose before a deceased initiate who holds a scroll; the citharodic performance visibly manifests, "brings to life," the written text, which surely contains sacred poetry of Orpheus about the afterlife.[134] Yet we should beware of completely abstracting the Orphic-eschatological symbolism of these images from the popular performance culture of *kitharôidia* that must have influenced the portrayal of Orpheus in them. Southern Italy, in particular Tarentum, had long been a center of Orphism (and its close relative, Pythagoreanism) as well as *kitharôidia*, and it is possible that there these two spheres of activity and expression enjoyed especially close musical and poetic contact.[135]

Orphic poetry was also the subject of "live" musical performance within the ritual practice of mystery cult. Pausanias says that the priestly clan of the Lycomidai performed as part of their cultic rites at Phyla in Attica *humnoi* of Orpheus alongside *humnoi* composed by Musaeus (1.22.7; 4.1.5) and Pamphus (9.27.2; 9.30.12).[136] Another Attic *genos*, the Eumolpidai, possessed, at least by the latter part of the fourth century BCE, a corpus of Orphic verse suited to the Eleusinian rites that they managed.[137] We cannot be sure, however, in what form these mystical Orphic poems were delivered to or by initiands and cult

---

[132] See e.g. an Apulian amphora by the Ganymede Painter, c. 340 BCE (Antikenmuseum Basel und Sammlung Ludwig S40; reproduced in West 1983, plate 2); Apulian volute krater (Munich, Antikensammlungen 3297; Maas and Snyder 1989:191, fig. 3).

[133] Maas and Snyder 1989:172.

[134] For the vase, see n132 above. Cf. discussion in Detienne 2003:135; West 1983:25–26.

[135] Cf. Bremmer 1999:78–80 on Orphism and Pythagoreanism in southern Italy. On Tarentum as a center of both Orphic-Bacchic cult and *kitharôidia*: West 1983:24–25; Part II.10n232 above.

[136] Pamphus: Duran 1996; Cassio 2000:101–102.

[137] West 1983:23–24; cf. Graf 1974:28–30.

members. Rhapsodic recital was probably common. Choral performance, in some cases certainly aulodic, in others perhaps accompanied by strings, is attested for Eleusis.[138] The name of Eumolpus, the eponymous ancestor of the Eumolpidai (and usually known as the son of Musaeus), itself bespeaks performance that combines song and dance, typically in choral formation (*molpê*).[139] But monodic lyric or even citharodic performance of certain Orphic and Orphic-related *humnoi* within the context of mystery cult ought not be ruled out.[140]

We may consider the relevant case of the Athenian Euneidai, whose members, we learn from Harpocration s.v. Εὐνεῖδαι, "were citharodes who provided service for ritual occasions" (ἦσαν δὲ κιθαρῳδοὶ πρὸς τὰς ἱερουργίας παρέχοντες τὴν χρείαν). Euripides in his *Hypsipyle* told how Euneus, the clan's mythical ancestor, was instructed in the art of playing the "Asiatic" *kithara* by Orpheus himself (μοῦσάν με κιθάρας Ἀσιάδος διδάσκεται, fr. 64, II.98 Bond).[141] The testimony of Harpocration is frustratingly vague. For what rituals exactly did these aristocratic *kitharôidoi* provide music? Public ones? A hint is provided in Pollux *Onomasticon* 8.103, which says that the Euneidai were called upon to serve as *kêrukes* 'heralds' in *pompai* 'festival processions' (cf. scholia *ad* Aeschines 1.20). Did they sing then citharodic hymns at civic festivals, accompanying sacrificial processionals? If so, there is no trace of any such activity in the literary record. It was hired, often foreign

---

[138] Sources and bibliography compiled in Hardie 2004:17–21; cf. Hardie 2005 for music in mystery cult in general. In respect to music at Eleusis, I mention the curious case of Themistius of Aphidna, who was executed for committing an act of *hubris* against a female *kithara* player (*kitharistria*) from Rhodes during the Eleusinia festival (Dinarchus 1.23, mid fourth century BCE). It is difficult to imagine that an Athenian citizen would normally be put to death for assaulting a foreign, hired "music girl." Perhaps this Rhodian was accorded sacred status because she played her stringed instrument in the Eleusinian Mysteries themselves. Cf. Omitowoju 2002:132.

[139] As suggested in Part II.12, it may have been citharodes performing in Athens who first elevated Eumolpus to the status of agonistic citharode and teacher of Heracles *kitharôidos*.

[140] Hardie 2004:28–29 suggests that the eschatological symbolism of the Orphic lyre was a feature of the "poetry ascribed to the telestic initiator Orpheus himself." It is a logical assumption that such cultic poetry was itself performed to the lyre or *kithara*. These instruments may have been directly involved in initiatory rites, played for or even by initiates. The story of Heracles' "lyric initiation" by Eumolpus might point to the latter possibility, as might an image such as that on an Apulian calyx krater, which has a young initiate taking the lyre from the hand of Orpheus (West 1983, plate 3). On the cathartic role of the lyre in Pythagorean rites, see Iamblichus *Life of Pythagoras* 110–111, 113. Pythagoras, who likely emulated Orpheus and composed "Orphic" verse (see Riedweg 2002:90–92), could himself be imagined in the guise of a citharode: Apuleius *Florida* 15.11–12.

[141] The fullest discussion of the Euneidai remains Toepffer 1889:181–206.

musicians who typically supplied the *Gebrauchsmusik* for public and private sacrifices in classical Athens, not well-born citizens; most such music was instrumental, and auletic, although the combination of *auloi* and *kitharai* is iconographically attested for sacrificial *pompai*.[142] Certain occasions, however, might have called for more dignified personnel.

It is worth considering whether the processional citharodes (or citharists, or both), probably eight in all, and matched by an equal number of *aulos* players, depicted on the (probably) idealized Panathenaic procession on the Parthenon frieze are meant to be members of the Euneid clan rather than contestants slated for appearances at the Panathenaic *mousikoi agônes*, as they have usually been taken.[143] A Roman-era inscription from the Theater of Dionysus, however, places the activity of the clan in a distinctly Dionysian milieu. It indicates that the priest of Dionysus Melpomenos, who received a seat of honor at the theater, was drawn from the ranks of the Euneidai (IG II² 5056). But even if the family played a traditional musical role in Dionysian cult predating this late period, which is indeed probable, it is impossible to say in what contexts they performed, or where.[144] Prominent Dionysian cultic and festival occasions in Classical Athens on which the music of the *kithara*, choral or monodic, had a leading role are unknown. It is possible that the Euneidai regularly performed in private, even domestic contexts, removed from the fora of large-scale civic agonistic spectacle, at events akin to the private aristocratic revels, *pannukhides*, that one scholar has argued were held in conjunction with the public rites of the Anthesteria.[145] Perhaps too their sacerdotal music was largely choral in nature. This is suggested by Hesychius s.v. Εὐνεῖδαι, who diverges from Harpocration in recording that the family was made up of "citharists and dancers." That members of the Euneidai and the Eumolpidai accompanied and danced in lyric paeanic choruses for Apollo at Delphi is well attested for the post-Classical period.[146]

---

[142] Nordquist 1992 lays out the evidence; cf. Kemp 1966. For the hiring of auletes for sacrifices, see especially Plutarch *Sympotic Questions* 632c–d; cf. Dinarchus 1.23, a hired *kitharistria* at Eleusis (n138 above).

[143] Contestants: Hurwitt 1999:223. Bundrick 2005:150–152 suggests that the musicians are citizen amateurs; cf. Part I.3.iin43.

[144] Cf. Parker 1996:297–298. Burkert 1994:46 thinks that the connection between Euneidai and Dionysus Melpomenos goes back at least as far as the fifth century. Wilson 2004:278n21 implicates the family in Apolline worship as well.

[145] Bravo 1997. Cf. Kerényi 1976:161n88 on the "rather private character" of the cult of Dionysus Melpomenos. On the Anthesteria, cf. Part IV.6n148.

[146] See references in Wilson 2004:278. It is worth keeping in mind too the epithet of Dionysus Melpomenos: *molpê* suggests song and dance. See Pausanias 1.2.5 on Dionysus Melpomenos as a *khorêgos* figure analogous to Apollo Musagetes, probably imagined as

But Harpocration's κιθαρῳδοί could be understood in its primary sense to describe solo performers of citharodic song (which does not necessarily exclude associated citharistic duties of accompanying choruses). This is the understanding of Walter Burkert, who argues that the Euneidai possessed and performed a collection of citharodic *humnoi* that they attributed to Orpheus, the *kithara* teacher of their progenitor Euneus.[147] He sees in one isolated verse preserved in the Derveni Papyrus, a heavily spondaic hexameter (or quasi-hexameter) in Attic dialect, a survival of an old tradition of Orphic *humnôidia* cultivated by the Euneidai.[148] Burkert's argument is compelling, but it leaves open the question of performance context. The singing of Orphic *humnoi* to the *kithara* by the Euneidai was, like the performance of Orphic hymns by the Eumolpidai or Lycomidai, perhaps restricted for the most part to non-agonistic religious occasions, presumably connected with the familial cult of Dionysus Melpomenos. There is no indication that they were connected to the Eleusinian Mysteries. But it is possible that members of the Euneidai competed in festival citharodic *agônes*, and perhaps brought their Orphic *humnoi* with them into this more public realm. It seems significant that in the fragmentarily preserved comedy by Cratinus called *Euneidai*—the very existence of such a play suggests that at least some members of the clan were publicly recognized for their musical activities—the verb ἀμφιανακτίζειν appears (fr. 72 K-A), which must allude to the incipit of the famous Terpandrean *prooimion* (fr. 2 Gostoli = PMG 697). If the Euneidai were cast by Cratinus as performers of Terpandrean citharodic texts, then the case is quite strong that they were known to participate in festival *agônes* alongside professionals. But we could as well imagine that the comedy involved some sort of antagonism between professional *agônistai* of the sort who sang Terpander, and the aristocratic, sacerdotal Euneidai. Polemon says that the play was especially rich in parodies (fr. 45 Preller), and Terpander's songs were presumably subject to parody as well, but this testimony does not help to determine the characterization of the Euneidai in it.

---

playing a *kithara*. Dionysus appears as such in third-century BCE choregic monumental sculpture; see Stewart 1982:212. A *kithara*-playing Dionysus was portrayed on the west pediment of the late-fourth-century BCE temple of Apollo at Delphi leading a chorus of women, an image that precisely complemented that of Apollo leading the Muses on the east pediment. Discussion in Stewart 1982, Clay 1996a:93–100.

[147] Burkert 1994:46–48, followed by Cassio 2000.

[148] Δημήτηρ Ῥέα Γῆ Μήτηρ Ἑστία Δηιώ. On the peculiar scansion, see Burkert 1994:47.

9. The Singer's Name

It is fitting that the first identifiable citharode bears a name that means 'he who gives musico-poetic pleasure, *terpsis*, to men', for the inducement of *terpsis* in his auditors is inarguably the definitive aim of the citharode's practice—even if that aesthetic, affective, sensory pleasure could serve the further goal of inducing certain orderly sociopolitical behaviors and conditions, as we see in the stories about Terpander's musico-political intervention in Sparta.[149] That Terpander has a metamusical and metageneric speaking name of this sort neatly emblematizes his ambiguous standing between history and legend. On the one hand, the name reads as a self-referential, programmatic generic fiction, just as "Homer" and "Hesiod" are names that, albeit in less obvious fashion, symbolically condense definitive aesthetic, functional, and compositional-performative aspects of the poetic genres to which they are attached.[150] In this sense, every performer of *kitharôidia* is, or has the potential to be, a "Terpander."

On the other hand, the name reflects the "show business" mentality with which even the earliest citharodes were operating. It seems to have been not uncommon for musicians of the Archaic and Classical periods to adopt or, in some cases, we may presume, if they were born into a family of entertainers, to have received at birth, names that advertised the musico-poetic skill of their bearers—*nomina omina*, as it were, assuring audiences that the talent of the composer and/or performer to whom they were listening, or were about to listen, was a foregone conclusion. We may think of Stesichorus, 'establisher of choruses', the choral composer and impresario, or Terpsicles, 'famed for giving *terpsis*', a fifth-century rhapsode who dedicated a tripod at Dodona (GDI 5786), or, in what must be a case of either blatant vanity naming or one very prescient father, the Sicyonian aulete Pythocritus,

---

[149] For *terpsis* as a "passive aesthetic reaction" that the performer may deploy to manipulate an audience into a state of action, see the analysis of Gorgianic psycho-rhetorical theory in Segal 1962:106–117. This two-step Gorgianic model is applicable to the (idealized) citharodic experience as well, as is indicated in accounts of the Spartans' being seduced by musical pleasure into putting aside their civil differences. Perceau 2007 is an insightful discussion of the psychology of musical *terpsis* in Homer.

[150] See Nagy 1979:296–300 on the semantics of Homeros 'he who fits [the Song] together' and Hesiodos 'he who emits the Voice.' Cf. the variant discussions of Homer's name in Durante 1976:194–197 and West 1999b. Nagy 1990b:86n23 interprets the name Terpander as "generic, in line with the programmatic use of the verb *terpô* 'give pleasure' *in poetry* to describe the effects *of poetry*."

who was six times victorious at Delphi (Pausanias 6.14.9).[151] A striking instance of this custom is the name of Nero's musical trainer, Terpnus, a famed agonistic citharode in his own right. This name both advertises the man's talent and unavoidably invokes the memory of the founder of his art. It should be noted, however, that Terpnus was late. Indeed, while expressive names for citharodes became more common in the Hellenistic and Imperial periods, in the Archaic and Classical periods generically referential names are less well attested than we might expect.[152] There are citharodes whose names connote, with a markedly "aristocratic" tone, agonistic success and fame, such as Pericleitus and Aristocleitus (or Aristocleides), both Lesbian successors of Terpander.

But in most cases the names of citharodes are less eloquent (e.g. Arion, Phrynis, Timotheus). One prominent exception is the Locrian citharode Eunomus, whose name broadcasts his skill both in performing *nomoi* and in musically promoting good social order (*eunomia*). A well-known story recounted how he defeated one Ariston of Rhegium at the Pythian citharodic *agôn* even after one of his strings had broken, thanks to a helpful cicada that lighted on his *kithara* and sang the missing note. Eunomus, however, may well be entirely legendary; the events of this story are obviously fictive, and no ancient author ever attempts to pin down a date for them. The Pythian contest at issue is probably not to be imagined as the historical penteteric one, but that attached to the enneateric festival, which, as we will see below, provides the convenient setting for other citharodic legends. Perhaps we should view Eunomus as a sort of western counterpart to Terpander and Arion, a culture hero within an Italian, or distinctly Locrian, citharodic tradition.[153]

Another exceptional citharodic speaking name appears in the *vita* of Timotheus of Miletus. Timotheus, who was probably born into a family of Milesian musical professionals, was according to *Suda* s.v.

---

[151] Gostoli 1990:XII, who takes "Terpander" as just such a stage name, and provides further parallels. For Terpsicles, see Graziosi 2002:25, who argues that this speaking name is intended to put the historical rhapsode "on a par" with the Homeric *aoidoi* Demodocus and Phemius Terpiades, "whose names speak of fame and enjoyment."

[152] This becomes evident from a perusal of the chronological indices in Stephanis 1988.

[153] Cf. Flach 1883:321n1. The earliest recorded version of the Eunomus story we know is that of the Hellenistic historian Timaeus of Tauromenion (FGrH 566 F 43 a–b), but it must have had life long before. Cf. Brown 2002:79; Berlinzani 2002, who sees in the legend a reflex of musically determined political rivalries in southern Italy, which enjoyed a vital citharodic culture. Strabo 6.1.9 records that a statue of Eunomus holding a cicada-graced *kithara* used to be shown in Locri, which could be some indication of a local hero cult devoted to him. The Locrian athlete Euthycles was honored with both a statue, which had supernatural powers, and hero cult in his home city (Callimachus frs. 84–85 Pfeiffer, with *diêgêsis*; cf. Fontenrose 1968:74.)

Τιμόθεος the son of Thersander, Neomusus, or Philopolis. Neomusus must be a comic moniker, a play on Timotheus' own notorious musical innovations. Thersander, the most mundane of the three, is usually taken to be the true name of the father. Its citation by the Hellenistic poet Alexander of Aetolia also supports its authenticity (fr. 4 Powell *ap.* Macrobius *Saturnalia* 5.22.4–5 = PMG 778). But Philopolis has some historical merit as well. Philopolis ('lover of/beloved by the *polis*'), an otherwise historically attested name, would well suit an itinerant celebrity citharode of the fifth century BCE. It reads as a variation on the expressively named Homeric bard Demodocus ('received by the community'; cf. the implicit gloss on the name in *Odyssey* 8.472, λαοῖσι τετιμένον 'honored by the people') made relevant to the larger-scale business of *polis* (and inter-*polis*) performance culture.[154] A more traditionally Homeric variant on the name Demodocus, Laodocus ('received by the people'), is borne by a citharode mentioned in an anecdote told by Aelian that is set in the fourth century BCE (*Historical Miscellanies* 4.2). Laodocus may be fictional, but, real or not, the name reflects what seems to have been an interest on the part of some professional citharodes to promote a sense of their continuity with the Homeric bards. We should keep in mind the central role of Homeric epic in the repertoire of the Classical citharode. Names such as Philopolis and Laodocus also indicate a politically relevant role for the citharode, which recalls the deep involvement of the Homeric *aoidos* within his local community.

In the occupational pursuit of communally pleasing *terpsis* the citharode indeed stood in a direct line from the Homeric *aoidoi*. The swineherd Eumaeus, describing itinerant craftsmen and service providers in the *Odyssey*, those he calls *dêmioergoi* 'men that work for the community', includes among them the "divine singer," the *thespis aoidos*, whom he succinctly characterizes as one "who by singing gives *terpsis*" (ὅ κεν τέρπῃσιν ἀείδων, 18.385).[155] There is indeed a direct onomastic link between the world of the epic bards and Terpander. The Ithacan *aoidos* Phemius has the expressive patronymic Terpiades

---

[154] Cf. Hordern 2002:6–7, who suggests that the name Philopolis may have "had overtones in the context of Miletus' revolt in 412 BCE; the sobriquet may ... have indicated that Timotheus remained loyal to Athens." This is an appealing suggestion, but it need not be exclusive of the possibility that Timotheus' father really was named Philopolis—or at least could have been.

[155] Cf. e.g. *Odyssey* 1.347 (of Phemius), 8.45 (of Demodocus). On the *terpsis* induced by Homeric bards, see Ford 1992:52–54; Perceau 2007. On Homeric *dêmioergoi*—seers, doctors, shipbuilders, heralds, and singers—see Tandy 1997:166–169 and Dougherty 2001:50–60.

'son of Pleasurer' (*Odyssey* 22.230).[156] The same name carried by Phemius' father, Terpes 'Pleasurer', seems also to have been given to Terpander.[157] An epigram from the *Palatine Anthology* (9.488 = *Planudean Anthology* 1a.36.14) describes a citharode named Terpes, which must be a nickname for Terpander, the figure most famously associated with *kitharôidia* at the Carneia, where Terpes performs. The epigram is post-Classical, but there is no reason to think that its author was not familiar with traditional citharodic lore surrounding Terpander in Sparta. The name Terpes is attested much earlier, on an Attic drinking cup of around 520 BCE painted by Oltos, where it identifies a satyr playing a large concert *kithara* in the *thiasos* of Dionysus.[158]

Images like that on Oltos' cup are not uncommon in the Archaic period. They offer up figures of playful inversion set within the make-believe realm of "Dionysian happiness"—the unruly satyr is imagined to be acting in burlesque the part of the orderly, Apollo-affiliated citharode.[159] Such funhouse images, we must keep in mind, were by and large consumed by elite symposiasts, who, outside of the symposium, were themselves connoisseurs, even performers of the *kitharôidia* cultivated within the civic sphere. It is of course possible that Terpes was considered a generic name for musicians, and that Oltos chose it for no other reason than to make explicit the musical *terpsis* inherent in the Dionysian *thiasos* (and by extension the mortal *kômos* and symposium); indeed, he labels an auletic satyr in the same scene Terpnon. But by giving this citharodic satyr a nickname that was linked to the most famous citharode of all, Terpander, Oltos could well have been making a deliberate allusion to real-world citharodic culture, one intended to humor sympotic *mousikoi* who would view the cup at close quarters. If so, this would be our earliest preserved reference to Terpander.

10. Terpander in and out of Delphi

"Plutarch" *On Music* 4.1132e, perhaps drawing from the *Collection of [Famous] Musicians* by Heraclides of Pontus, reports that Terpander's

---

[156] Cf. Nagy 1990b:86n23.

[157] Cf. Wilamowitz 1927:78.

[158] Tarquinia, Museo Nazionale RC 6848; LIMC VII 2, p613.

[159] Bundrick 2005:108 interprets *kithara*-playing satyrs in similar fashion. See a representative collection of images in Castaldo 2000:234, 240–242; cf. Wegner 1949:210. "Dionysian happiness" in Archaic iconography: Isler-Kerényi 2007:206–207, 222–223. Cf. Restani 1991 on strings in Dionysian scenes in Attic vase painting.

outstanding citharodic *tekhnê* won him four successive victories at Delphi, while the Pythian festival was presumably still enneateric.[160] This historical accuracy of this testimony, as Flach and Wilamowitz long ago argued, is surely dubious, regardless of whether we take Terpander to be a historical personage or a personification of the Lesbian citharodic *diadokhê*.[161] But the connections that were drawn between the Pythian games and Terpander nevertheless merit more detailed discussion. First of all, the very existence of a high-visibility citharodic contest at a pre-Amphictyonic, enneateric Pythia is highly doubtful.[162] Our most detailed account of it is recorded in Pausanias 10.7.2–3, which is cited in translation below. Also included is section 10.7.4, in which the periegete lists the (real, historical) victors in the first Pythian games offered after the reorganization of the festival following the Sacred War:

> They [the Delphian locals] relate a traditional account [*mnêmoneuousi*] that the most ancient contest and the one in which they first offered prizes was the singing of a hymn [*humnos*] to the god. Chrysothemis of Crete both sang and won the prize in singing; his father Carmanor is said to have purified Apollo [after the slaying of the dragon]. After Chrysothemis, their tradition has it [*mnêmoneuousi*], Philammon was victorious in song, and after him Thamyris, son of Philammon. But they say [*phasi*] Orpheus, because he cultivated an air of solemn detachment in his mysteries and was haughty in general, and Musaeus, because he imitated Orpheus in all things, refused to be put to the test in a contest of music. [3] They say [*phasi*] that Eleuther too won a Pythian victory for singing with a loud and sweet voice, since he sang a song that was not his own. It is related [*legetai*] that Hesiod was disqualified from the contest because he had not learned to accompany his song on the lyre. Homer came to Delphi to inquire about his needs, but, even though he had learned how to play the lyre, his learning was

---

[160] ἔοικε δὲ κατὰ τὴν τέχνην τὴν κιθαρῳδικὴν ὁ Τέρπανδρος διενηνοχέναι· τὰ Πύθια γὰρ τετράκις ἐξῆς νενικηκὼς ἀναγέγραπται ("Terpander seems to have been supreme in the cithardic *tekhnê*, for it has been recorded that he was victorious at the Pythia four times in a row").

[161] Flach 1883:192; Wilamowitz 1903:88n1. Gostoli 1990:98–99 is surely right to discount the arguments of Jacoby (FGrH II B Kommentar, p443) that Heraclides is actually referring to victories at the Sicyonian Pythia, which he would know from his consultation of the Sicyonian *anagraphê* (cf. *On Music* 3.1132a), an inscription that included information about cithardic history. Gostoli, however, accepts the historicity of Terpander's Pythian victories at Delphi, which I do not.

[162] Mosshammer 1977:27n2 thinks the enneateric festival is entirely "mythical."

of no use to him thanks to the accident that befell his eyes. [4] In the third year of the forty-eighth Olympiad [586 BCE] ... the Amphictyons offered prizes in *kitharôidia*, just as from the beginning, but they added a contest of singing to the *aulos* [*aulôidia*] and one of solo *aulos* playing.[163] Proclaimed [*anêgoreuthêsan*] as victors were Melampus, a Cephallenian, for *kitharôidia* and Echembrotus the Arcadian aulode and Sacadas of Argos in the contest of *auloi*.

Pausanias 10.7.2–4

Certainly the fancifully aggrandizing local lore recorded by Pausanias about who did—the legendary Delphic celebrities Chrysothemis of Crete and Philammon, Thamyris, and Eleuther—and who did not—Hesiod and Homer (both negatively associated with *rhapsôidia*, which was never among the *mousikoi agônes* at the Pythia), Orpheus and Musaeus (both supposedly distracted by their Mysteries from the serious pursuit of agonistic music)—participate in the proto-cithárodic *agôn* in "hymn-singing to Apollo" would by analogy put the supposed involvement of Terpander with it in the category of legend as well.[164] In reality, early Archaic Pythian musical culture must have been quite humble, and probably exclusively local, as the local color in Pausanias' legendary victor list suggests, with emphasis placed on the solid execution of paeanic cult hymns rather than creative virtuosity of any sort. Only in the early sixth century BCE, well after Terpander's notional *floruit*, would the contest grow in stature as a glamorous international

---

[163] 586/5 is Pausanias' date for the first penteteric Pythian *agôn*. For the likelihood of a 582/1 date, however, see Mosshammer 1982.

[164] The Eleuther mentioned by Pausanias is likely to be the eponymous founder of the *polis* of Eleutherna in northwest Crete. His presence in the catalogue of victors at the early Pythia speaks, as does that of the Cretan Chrysothemis son of Carmanor, to what was likely the historical role of Cretan lyre singers in structuring Delphian musical culture. In the *Homeric Hymn to Apollo* the Cretan sailors are thus Apollo's first priests at Delphi and the first mortal paean singers there as well (516–519; cf. Franklin 2006a:59–60). Eleutherna seems to have been a conspicuous center of *kitharôidia* on Crete; it was the home of the (probably legendary) citharode Ametor, whose "descendants," the Ametores or Ametoridai, were a historical fixture of the local musical culture on Crete, known for their "erotic songs" (Athenaeus 14.638b; Hesychius s.v. Ἀμητορίδας). Linus too may have been claimed by the city (Stephanus of Byzantium s.v. Ἀπολλώνια κγ΄). An inscription from fifth-century BCE Eleutherna (I.Cret. II xii 16Ab, line 2) records a law concerning the service of a *kitharistas* to the *polis*, but the inscription is too badly preserved to make sense of what that service entailed or how it was managed. See discussion in Perlman 2004:108, 112.

event, more "secular" in nature, attracting skilled soloists from all parts.[165]

But if the story about Terpander's Pythian victories is an invention, whose invention was it? Some obvious candidates present themselves. First, it could have arisen from the desire of his Lesbian *apogonoi* to magnify his (and by reflection their) fame by inserting him into the prehistory of an event that was taking on major international prestige within citharodic culture in the sixth and fifth centuries, and one in which they seem to have made relatively little impact, especially in comparison to their dominance at the Archaic Spartan Carneia. It is significant that outside of Terpander we hear of not one Lesbian victor at Delphi until the later third century BCE, and only then at the Aetolian Soteria festival, not the Pythia.[166] Alternately, but certainly not exclusively, the Spartans themselves may have promoted the story about the prestigious Pythian victories of the citharode who was "theirs" by adoption. Indeed, the Lesbian citharodic and the local Spartan traditions may have conspired to promote the figure of a Pythian Terpander. We may note that other legendary citharodes were tendentiously inserted into the fluid ranks of enneateric Pythian competitors. Demetrius of Phalerum has Demodocus and Phemius performing there, a fiction designed to explain how Agamemnon, while visiting the oracle, recruited Demodocus to serve as court singer in Mycenae.[167] Eumolpus too, the musician-priest of Eleusis, was made a Pythian victor (*Suda* s.v. Εὔμολπος), perhaps through the locally encomiastic song and myth making of citharodes performing at the Panathenaia or Eleusinia.

---

[165] Cf. the remarks of Brelich 1969:497n225. Davies 2007 assesses the evidence for the establishment of the penteteric Pythian *agônes*.

[166] Archeanax of Mytilene (FID III 4, 125.7).

[167] Fr. 144 Fortenbaugh and Schütrumpf = scholia *ad Odyssey* 3.267. Discussion in Gostoli 1986. We might speculate that a similar scenario stands obscured behind the story that the Delphic oracle bid the Spartans to send for the "Lesbian Singer" (relevant sources collected in T 12–15, 60f, i Gostoli). That is, Spartan emissaries took a victorious Terpander home with them from Delphi, as Agamemnon did Demodocus (similarly for the purpose of maintaining order in his community; cf. Scully 1981). But Delphi may have conjured up its own role in Terpander's Spartan intervention as a retroactive attempt to claim influence over the cultural politics of early *kitharôidia*. Compare the implications of Herodotus 1.65.4: the Spartan constitution of Lycurgus, with whom some synchronized Terpander (Hieronymus of Rhodes *On Citharodes* fr. 33 Wehrli *ap.* Athenaeus 14.635f = T 6 G), was said to have been outright granted to Lycurgus by the Pythia. But Herodotus records that the Lacedaemonians themselves did not hold this tradition (they thought Lycurgus brought his laws from Crete). It was, then, presumably promoted by Delphi, although the Spartans surely believed that the oracle had ratified and so legitimated the constitution (cf. e.g. Xenophon *Constitution of the Spartans* 8.5). See discussion in Crane 1998:79–80.

One assumes that the Eumolpid clan as well would have been disposed to vaunt the Panhellenic musical prestige of its mythical ancestor.[168]

The Delphians may have themselves appropriated Terpander at some point. Gostoli has argued that the verb ἀναγέγραπται 'it has been recorded', which is used in *On Music* 4.1132e to introduce the claim about Terpander's victories, suggests the victories were commemorated on an inscription (*anagraphê*) at Delphi, one perhaps based on the list of Pythian victors compiled by Aristotle and his nephew Callisthenes (frs. 615–617 Rose).[169] This argument is attractive, although not decisive. After all, one must wonder why Pausanias, who has clearly absorbed the local lore about the early history of the Pythian musical *agôn*, does not include the famous Terpander among its victors. (And even if we do accept the argument, we need not assume the historicity of the inscribed victories, as Gostoli seems to do.) However, the Terpandrean *vita* does reveal at least one other possible trace of Delphic appropriation, the information in *Suda* s.v. Τέρπανδρος that some claimed Terpander was descended from Homer through one "Boios the Phocian": οἱ δὲ καὶ ἀπόγονον Ἡσιόδου ἀνέγραψαν, ἄλλοι δὲ Ὁμήρου, Βοίου λέγοντες τοῦ Φωκέως, τοῦ Εὐρυφῶντος, τοῦ Ὁμήρου ("Some have registered that he was a descendant of Hesiod, others of Homer, claiming that he was the son of Boios the Phocian, son of Euryphon, son of Homer"). Terpander's Homeric lineage, posited alongside a Hesiodic one, may reflect some broader attempt on the part of citharodes themselves to lay historical claim to the rhapsodic repertoire with which theirs had long overlapped and which theirs was increasingly absorbing in an effort to remain competitive with the rhapsodic medium.[170]

---

[168] One Eumolpid, Agenor, actually offered a (non-agonistic) display of *kithara* playing to Apollo at Delphi: Stephanis 1988, no. 36.

[169] Gostoli 1990:99–100. Gostoli does not exclude the separate possibility that the *anagraphê* at issue is the Sicyonian *anagraphê*, from which Heraclides, a likely source for *On Music* 4.1132e, took details about early citharodic history. If so, the Classical antiquity of the Sicyonian document would indicate that Terpander's Pythian success had long been part of citharodic lore. Gostoli 1990:98-99 sensibly rejects, however, the view held by Jacoby (FGrH II B Kommentar, p44), that Terpander won his victories at the Sicyonian Pythia, which Heraclides would have known from the Sicyonian *anagraphê* (cf. *On Music* 3.1132a), although it is entirely conceivable that Archaic Sicyon would have wanted to absorb Terpander into its own citharodic history.

[170] The *Suda*'s mention of Boeotian Arne and Aeolic Cyme as alternate birthplaces, alongside Lesbian Antissa, for Terpander would also seem to fit the pattern whereby Terpander was actively assimilated to Hesiod and Homer. For another view, see Gostoli 1990:88, who believes that these alternate birthplaces were mooted to explain the attribution of the Boeotian and Aeolic *nomoi* to Terpander. But there are deeper generic and regional agendas in play: see Part II.12 above.

But could the insertion of Boios as an intermediary in Terpander's Homeric lineage represent a specifically Delphic localization? Pausanias 10.5.7–8 mentions a legendary *epikhôria gunê* 'native woman' by the name of Boio, who composed a *humnos* on the origins of the oracle, in which she ascribed to Olen, the legendary Hyperborean singer and poet, the invention of the hexametrical prophecies of Apollo. It is with her we should probably identify this Boios: Boios/Boio is a local poetic celebrity, whose most famous song had a strongly localized metapoeticality, and who was yet an *apogonos* of Homer.[171] This creative genealogizing of Terpander through Boios/Boio could reflect the desire of the Delphians to "possess" the Lesbian citharode, to credit him directly to their own local music cultural capital, while still emphasizing his Panhellenic importance, and aggrandizing their own, through the connection to Homer. That rhapsodic competitions of Homeric poetry did not take place at Delphi is significant in this respect. Homer's presence was felt rather in the citharodic *agôn*, to which he was directly linked "by blood," as it were, through his "Phocian" descendant Terpander. Of course, the link between Terpander and Boios need not have been Delphic propaganda alone; it could have been offered up by Lesbian citharodes eager to ingratiate themselves with Pythian authorities by singing their own lineage into the myth history of Delphic musical culture. The first citharode to sing Homer at the Pythia was supposedly Stesander, from the Ionian island of Samos (Athenaeus 14.638a = Timomachus FGrH 754 F 1). This testimony could suggest that Lesbian and Ionian citharodes struggled over the authorized performance of Homeric *kitharôidia* at Delphi, and in such a context the Homer-Boios-Terpander lineage would carry obvious rhetorical force.

Both *On Music* and the *Suda*, which also presents the testimony about Boios, record what seems to be another facet of the confrontation between the Terpandrean tradition and Delphi, this one particularly ambivalent, even agonistic:

---

[171] For the identification of Boios with the female poet Boio, see Knaack 1899; Platthy 1985:61–62. I wonder whether the *humnos* attributed to Boio was not itself performed by citharodes in Delphi. Its lyric hexameters in Doric dialect (Pausanias quotes four lines) would neatly fit the morphological profile of early citharodic song. Given the metapoetic focus of the piece, the invention of hexameter song, its performance in Delphi would celebrate the privileged, ancient nexus there between epic, oracular poetry, and *kitharôidia*, all hexametrically based forms.

νόμους λυρικοὺς πρῶτος ἔγραψεν· εἰ καί τινες Φιλάμμωνα
θέλουσι γεγραφέναι.

Terpander first wrote lyric *nomoi*, even if some would have it
that Philammon wrote them.

Suda s.v. Τέρπανδρος

τινὰς δὲ τῶν νόμων τῶν κιθαρῳδικῶν τῶν ὑπὸ Τερπάνδρου
πεποιημένων Φιλάμμωνά φασι τὸν ἀρχαῖον τὸν Δελφὸν
συστήσασθαι.

They say that Philammon, the Delphian of old, actually
constructed some of the citharodic *nomoi* composed by
Terpander.

"Plutarch" *On Music* 5.1133b

Both sources seem eager to put these reports in a dubious light. That
Philammon composed the *nomoi* later canonized under the name of
Terpander was clearly a partisan view—wishful thinking, as the *Suda*
has it—at odds with the mainstream consensus that has Terpander as
undisputed *prôtos heuretês* of agonistic citharodic music. But still, the
outside opinion was sufficiently well known to have been reported;
the unidentified party (*tines*) who made the claim must have had some
degree of influence. I would suggest that the *tines* were Delphians
wanting to contest the Panhellenically mainstream Lesbian claim to the
invention of agonistic *kitharôidia* and to position it instead as their own
legacy by rooting the history of its competition pieces in the legendary
past of the Pythian contests. The account preserved in Proclus
Chrestomathia ap. Photius *Bibliotheca* 320b.1–4 that has Chrysothemis
first performing *nomoi* at Delphi could represent an alternative local
tradition, but one motivated by the same impulse to locate the origins
of competitive *kitharôidia* deep in the institutional history of the
Pythia.[172] One need not go so far as to say that the prioritization of

---

[172] The history of the aulodic *nomos* as recorded in "Plutarch" *On Music* 5.1133a offers
a parallel case of contested origins. According to the mainstream tradition, the
aulodic *nomos* was devised by Clonas, whose ethnicity was disputed between two
musically preeminent regions competing for the prestige attached to this seminal
figure, Arcadia (the Arcadians made him a Tegean) and Boeotia (the Boeotians made
him a Theban). But another, more locally restricted Troezenian tradition made the
counterclaim that the *prôtos heuretês* of aulodic music and indeed the *aulos* itself was
the epichoric music hero Ardalus, son of Hephaestus and the founder of a line of
Troezenian aulodes, the Ardalids (Pausanias 2.31.3; Pliny *Natural History* 7.204). The

Philammon or Chrysothemis represents a revision of citharodic tradition that is hostile to Terpander.[173] It is one rather that shades over his contributions, and the preeminence of the Lesbian line of citharodes, in favor of an epichoric Cretan-Delphic tradition. Terpander's prestige as a *prôtos heuretês* was thus diminished at Delphi, but, if his Pythian victories and Phocian paternity were tenets of local propaganda, it is possible that at the same time his fame was co-opted for the greater glory of an invented Pythian legacy.

11. *Kitharôidia* on Lesbos

The social and cultural context in which the Terpandrean *diadokhê* emerged and operated on Archaic Lesbos is highly obscure. When we glimpse a Lesbian Singer, he is always abroad: Terpander in Sparta or Delphi or Lydia; Arion in Corinth or plying the seas like a long-distance trader, earning large sums of money performing in Italy and Sicily, as Herodotus 1.23–24 portrays him. Sappho acknowledges the superlative agonistic talent of the Lesbian Singer, but for her, he is already a definitively Panhellenic phenomenon, circulating through foreign lands like a precious commodity exported from her island (πέρροχος ὡς ὅτ' ἄοιδος ὁ Λέσβιος ἀλλοδάποισιν 'Outstanding, like the Lesbian Singer against foreign rivals', fr. 106). Her own poetry may show the influence of local citharodic epic, but she says nothing explicit about the situation, practical or socioeconomic, of the Lesbian citharodes at home, although fr. 106 certainly indicates her esteem for them.[174]

---

musical clan of the Ardalids was presumably responsible for inventing its illustrious ancestor and transmitting his *nomoi* as well as aggrandizing lore about him, which it did with some success, enough to have the tradition recorded as a footnote to the mainstream history of *aulôidia*. Plutarch *Banquet of the Seven Sages* 150a posits the existence of two Ardaluses, the aulode and a more ancient figure, the first "priest of the Troezenian Muses." But this is a rationalization akin to what we see in the reception of the *vita* of the aulete Olympus (cf. n20 above); the two figures were likely identical, and the Ardalid aulodes were surely attached to the cult of the Troezenian Muses (cf. Nagy 1990b:29n66).

[173] We might read Delphi's agonistic challenge to Terpandrean primacy as an expression of a broader tension between a "mainland" citharodic tradition and an Eastern Aegean one. For the ambivalent relationship between Philammon and Orpheus—now rivalrous, now cooperative—as another such expression, see Part II.10n225.

[174] Demetrius *On Style* 146, who quotes the line, indicates that Sappho compared the triumphant citharode ἐπὶ τοῦ ἐξέχοντος ἀνδρός 'to the man who is preeminent.' This *anêr* 'man' may well be the enviable groom to a girl for whom Sappho sings a wedding song. In other wedding songs, Sappho compares grooms to gods and heroes (cf. frs. 31.1, 105b, 111.5). The comparison of groom to citharode indicates the considerable

Perhaps Sappho even viewed the Panhellenic renown of the Lesbian Singer as a model for the diffusion beyond Lesbos of her own song and name, which she expected would eventually win "fame everywhere" (πάντᾳ κλέος, fr. 65).

Alcaeus makes no reference at all to Terpander or the Lesbian Singers. As with Sappho's, hymnic and epic elements in his poetry may bear the mark of *kitharôidia* as well as *rhapsôidia*, but his attitude toward the citharodic tradition of his island is a complete mystery, which prompts radically different hypotheses. We might speculate that his silence reflects certain ideological differences that were in place between Alcaean lyric monody, which was an aristocratic, primarily sympotic affair, and the more demotic tenor of *kitharôidia*, which perhaps had the support of Alcaeus' populist rivals (i.e. the tyrants Myrsilus and Pittacus). Indeed, the "stasiotic" nature of much of Alcaean song would seem to put it at odds with Terpandrean *kitharôidia*, whose reputation was for resolving factional disputes and establishing communal consensus—qualities that made it appealing to tyrants. But that scenario must remain pure speculation. The reality, obscured by the vagaries of textual preservation, may have been quite the opposite. Perhaps Alcaeus sought to link the local and Panhellenic prestige of Terpandrean *kitharôidia* and its Orphic patrimony to his own poetry and music, as Sappho seems to have done, if her praise of the Lesbian Singer in fr. 106 is any guide. (Alcaeus' hymn to the river Hebrus, fr. 45, may have mentioned Orpheus, and in turn alluded to historical Lesbian *kitharôidia*; cf. Part I.22.iv.) Or perhaps he assumed a more ambivalent position toward *kitharôidia*, some mixture of socio-ideological estrangement combined with musical admiration and emulation.

Despite the lack of explicit literary testimony for citharodic activity on Archaic Lesbos, I would argue that at least three fundamental assumptions can be made to explain its early emergence on the island and the Panhellenic prominence it soon acquired. First, that there was a native Lesbian tradition of paean singing that was of considerable antiquity (i.e. predating the seventh century BCE) and repute is shown by a fragment of Archilochus: αὐτὸς ἐξάρχων πρὸς αὐλὸν Λέσβιον παιήονα 'myself leading off the Lesbian paean to the *aulos*' (fr. 121W). While it is possible to read the fragment as indicating that the Lesbian paean was originally sung to the *aulos*, an instrument that was in fact

---

esteem in which Sappho and her audience held the latter, and might suggest already his recognized status as "sex symbol." Green 1998:58 qualifies fr. 106 as "fierce, and justified, insular pride."

a part of Archaic Lesbian musical culture (cf. Sappho fr. 44.24; Alcaeus fr. 307b), the phrase πρὸς αὐλόν nevertheless seems marked. That is, Archilochus announces emphatically that what is being sung is an aulodic (and perhaps distinctly Ionian) adaptation of the traditionally *lyric* Lesbian paean.[175] Archilochus (or perhaps the speaker in a narrative poem) takes on the role of *exarkhôn*, the one who "leads off" the choral performance with a solo song (cf. fr. 120W, in which Archilochus acts as *exarkhôn* for a dithyrambic chorus). This role would correspond to that played in the Lesbian practice by the *kitharistês*, who introduced the choral song with a solo *prooimion* sung to the lyre.

As we saw in Part II.3, such choral lyric performance was the ground from which solo *kitharôidia* likely emerged; the *kitharistês* evolved into the citharode. There is a reflex of this process implicit in the lore about early *kitharôidia* at Delphi, where the Cretan Chrysothemis stepped forth from the paeanic chorus to sing the first citharodic *nomos*. We might easily imagine that a similar scenario played out on Lesbos. Its early-established paeanic culture would have provided a seedbed for the flowering of *kitharôidia*; the first Lesbian Singers would have been *kitharistai* turned citharodes. Further, the paeanic origins of Lesbian *kitharôidia* likely marked its later practice and reception. A primary function of the Lesbian paean may have been to bring about communal purification, both physical and spiritual, as was the case with the Cretan paean.[176] It is significant that the healing paean sung by the Achaean youths to lift a plague in *Iliad* 1.472–474 is offered to appease Sminthian Apollo (39), whose cult was firmly established throughout the Aeolis, including Lesbos, from a very early point.[177] An Imperial-era inscription from Methymna calls a local prophet of Apollo Smintheus a "maker of songs" (τὸν τῶν μελῶν ποιητήν, IG XII 2.519). Although the inscription is late, it points to what was likely the long-observed role of music—and paeanic music is a reasonable assumption—in the Lesbian cult of the god. The Achaeans' performance may thus reflect Lesbian song culture in particular, including its beliefs about the cathartic power of paean singing, beliefs that may have left their traces in notions about the extramusical powers of the Lesbian citharodes.[178]

---

[175] Sappho fr. 44.33 might suggest too that the Lesbian paean was generally lyric: the Trojan men call upon Paean "skilled in the lyre" (*euluras*; for the epithet, see Part II.9.i).

[176] Cf. Rutherford 2001:15, with discussion below.

[177] Cf. Farnell 1907(IV):164–166; Shields 1917:1–2.

[178] For the impact of Lesbian song traditions on the *Iliad* in general, see Dué 2002. We may wonder too whether Achilles' visit to Lesbos in the *Aethiopis* to sacrifice to Apollo prior to his purification for the murder of Thersites did not involve cathartic music making (summary of Proclus p106 Allen). We may compare the implications

A second assumption: from at least the early seventh century BCE, the Lesbian citharodes must have benefitted from their cultural contacts with Mermnad Lydia, and through Lydia with the Near East, in terms of constructing and refining the seven-stringed concert *kithara*, also known as the "Asiatic" *kithara*, which would become the standard instrument of the virtuoso solo *agônistês*, replacing the *phorminx* or lyre that had been in use by previous generations of musicians, including the choral *kitharistês*.[179] The image of Terpander as an elite reveler at a Lydian banquet that is presented in Pindar fr. 125 S-M is a romanticized, even, as we will see below, tendentious expression of what was nevertheless a real, historical initiative on the part of enterprising Lesbian musicians to import "Asiatic" musical technology from Lydia to Lesbos and from there to points abroad during the Orientalizing period.[180] Along with the new technology of the lyre, notions about the magical properties of the instrument, particularly in its seven-stringed form, were also imported to Lesbos. Or rather, such ideas, once lost, were rediscovered, since Bronze Age Greece seems to have already been familiar with them, as is indicated by their persistence in what are surely the very ancient myths of Orpheus and Amphion, whose lyric music could suborn wild nature and bring an entire city into being.[181] We might imagine that a unique ideological fusion of inherited mythos about the transcendental powers of the Orphic lyre, which Terpander legendarily possessed, a native tradition of "cathartic" Apollonian paeanic song, and more recently absorbed Near Eastern musical cosmology took shape on Lesbos in the early Archaic period, which would find expression in the belief promoted by the Lesbian *diadokhê* that Terpander could sway men's minds and bring communities to good order with the charm of his song.

Third, the accounts of both Terpander's and Arion's building an agonistic musical culture from the ground up in Sparta and Corinth (and perhaps in the cities of Italy and Sicily) suggest the historical

---

of Apollo's visit to Crete after his slaying of the Pythian serpent to be purified by Carmanor, the father of Chrysothemis the lyre singer (Pausanias 2.7.7; 10.16.5).

[179] Cf. n8 above. The heptachord *kithara* begins to appear in the archaeological record in the seventh century BCE: Maas and Snyder 1989:31–32, 41.

[180] See Franklin 2002 and 2008 for details; cf. Campbell 1988:265. Spencer 1995 discusses Lesbian trade with Anatolia.

[181] See Franklin 2006b on the reinfusion throughout Archaic Greece of a lost Bronze Age "wisdom of the lyre" recovered from and elaborated in the Near East. The Minoan-Mycenaean ideal of the lyre singer as a guarantee of peace and stability persists, if in diluted form, also in the picture of the Homeric *aoidos*, who has the ability to maintain social order with musical *terpsis*. See Scully 1981.

development of a vibrant, sophisticated culture of *mousikoi agônes* on Lesbos, which its citharodes, acting as much in the capacity of agonistic impresarios as performers, were able to export and reproduce abroad. One probable setting for the competitive performance of *kitharôidia* was the Pan-Lesbian festival, celebrated at the shrine of Zeus, Hera, and Dionysus, located in the federal district of Messon. In this "middle space" near the center of the island, *mousikoi agônes* of different sorts, both choral and monodic, appear to have been established at an early point.[182] Lesbian cities presumably hosted their own civic *agônes* featuring *kitharôidia*. In Mytilene, Pompey attended the local ἀγὼν πάτριος τῶν ποιητῶν 'ancestral contest of the poets', whose name advertises an antiquity that it no doubt possessed, even if in Pompey's time its archaism was probably rather touristically put on (Plutarch *Life of Pompey* 42.4). The festival may be the same as the one devoted to Apollo Maloeis that is described in Thucydides 3.3.3. There is evidence that this festival featured choral performances: Callimachus fr. 485 Pfeiffer mentions the *Maloeis khoros*, which, given the poet's antiquarian interests, must have been an institution of long standing; a first-century CE inscription from Hiera, across the bay from Mytilene, names an *arkhikhoros* 'chorus leader' of Artemis and Apollo Maloeis (IG XII 2.484). A Lesbian festival of Apollo with a conspicuous musical component almost certainly would have included *kitharôidia*.

The archaeological record provides one extraordinarily suggestive, if indirect, witness to the existence of an advanced citharodic contest culture on early Lesbos. We have visual evidence from the early Archaic period for what would appear to be a citharodic contest on Lemnos, a northern Aegean island that would have been in close cultural contact with nearby Lesbos. Depicted on the shoulder of a late eighth- or early seventh-century BCE stamnos from Hephaestia, one of the two main cities of Lemnos, is a man holding what is distinctly a *kithara*, although it is prototypically small and has only six strings (which may, however, be merely an inaccurate rendering of a heptachord instrument by the artist).[183] He has in his right hand a plectrum, which is connected to the *kithara* by a cord; around his left wrist is looped the support strap for the *kithara*. He has shoulder-length hair and wears a truncated yet brightly

---

[182] Nagy 1993 and 2007b:24–25, expanding on the epigraphical studies of Robert 1960, who dates the Lesbian federation at Messon to the seventh century BCE. See too Calame 1997:122–123 on the Archaic choral-cum-beauty contests of Lesbian women (the Kallisteia), attested in Alcaeus fr. 129, that were held at Messon.

[183] Athens, National Museum 19272; Della Seta 1937:644, fig. 4; Maas and Snyder 1989:46, fig. 9b.

decorated chiton. In short, present are all the elements that make up the refined *skeuê* of an agonistic citharode as seen in later Archaic iconography. He is shown in the moment of kneeling down before a seated, elaborately attired goddess, who is probably to be identified as the Great Goddess of Lemnos and presumably a patron divinity of the festival to which this scene refers.[184] The goddess holds out a wreath, which the musician reaches out to take with his right hand. There can be little doubt that what the scene portrays is an idealized vision of a citharode—perhaps a Lesbian Singer—who has won victory at a Lemnian *agôn* and is receiving his crown directly from the hand of the presiding divinity.[185] We could compare fifth-century BCE Attic vases that symbolically idealize citharodic victory by showing Nikai delivering crowns and other token prizes directly to the musician (see e.g. Plate 13).

Political conditions on Archaic Lesbos may have worked to accelerate the organization of citharodic *agônes* there. That is, we might be inclined to consider the emergence of the citharodic culture on Lesbos as a symptom of and response to the island's notorious propensity for violent political disunity, both within and among its cities. As Peter Green puts it, "The pattern of internal politics on Lesbos—violent feuding between cities, and, in cities, between aristocratic-oligarchic and democratic, or, earlier, 'tyrannical' (i.e. anti-oligarchic) factions—was established early, and proved to be perennial."[186] Aelius Aristides 24.55 comments, as others before him surely had, on the seeming irony created by the persistence of *stasis* on Lesbos, that the island famous for its musicality, whose superlative citharodes put an end to *stasis* in other cities and which possessed the very head of Orpheus, was nevertheless

---

[184] The festival may be the festival of Hephaestus during which "new fire" was brought to Lemnos. Burkert 2001:66 argues that the Great Goddess, herself called Lemnos, was honored at it along with Hephaestus. The festival probably concluded with *agônes* meant to commemorate the mythical contests once held to celebrate the arrival of the Argonauts on Lemnos (71). A citharodic *agôn* on this occasion would be a fitting context for the performance of Argonautic epic.

[185] My interpretation differs from that of Della Seta 1937:645–646, who believes that the musician is a citharist leading a processional dance for the goddess. There is no indication, however, that the musician or the young boy who is shown walking behind him is dancing or making music; the former is clearly moving to kneel down in honor of the goddess. Cf. Maas and Snyder 1989:33. Beschi 1992 discusses other material remains of the Archaic musical worship of the Great Goddess on Lemnos.

[186] Green 1998:56. On the history of Lesbian fractiousness, cf. Mason 1993 and 1995:400, who marks the destruction of Arisba by Methymna in 700 BCE as the beginning of a "long history of distrust"; Spencer 2001 on the "continual" *stasis* in Mytilene from the late seventh century BCE onwards (81).

"so unmusically disposed" (οὕτως ἀμούσως διακείμενοι).[187] Of course, there really was no irony to this. It goes without saying that a vigorous musical life is in and of itself no guarantee of a community's sociopolitical stability. The factionalism of Mytilene was perpetuated not despite but largely because of the brilliant yet socially destabilizing musico-poetic counterculture exemplified by Alcaeus.[188] But in terms of the long-held ideological beliefs about music in ancient Greece, Aristides makes a reasonable point: the right sort of music should carry a beneficial sociopolitical surplus value that transcends aesthetic enjoyment; it should foster actual communal harmony.

As was suggested above, Archaic Lesbos was perfectly positioned to be the crucible for the formulation and articulation of this ideology in its specifically citharodic aspect, an Apollonian, Orphic, and Near Eastern-inflected ideal of the wonder-working, cosmically ordering properties of solo lyric song. What is more, the political instability of the island could have provided a strong impetus for the practical implementation of that ideal through the establishment of citharodic

---

[187] His speech is delivered to an audience of Rhodians, who are themselves on the verge of *stasis*, but here Aristides pretends that he is addressing the Lesbians: φατὲ μὲν τὴν νῆσον ἄπασαν ὑμῖν εἶναι μουσικὴν καὶ τούτου τὴν Ὀρφέως κεφαλὴν αἰτιᾶσθε, αὐτοὶ δ' οὐκ αἰσχύνεσθε οὕτως ἀμούσως διακείμενοι; καὶ κιθαρῳδοῖς μέν ποτε τοὺς Ἕλληνας ἐνικᾶτε, τῷ δ' ὑπὲρ ὑμῶν αὐτῶν μὴ δύνασθαι βουλεύσασθαι κινδυνεύετε ἡττᾶσθαι καὶ πάντων ἀνθρώπων; καὶ πρότερον μὲν παρ' ὑμῶν ἑτέρωσε βαδίζοντες ἔπαυον τὰς στάσεις, νῦν δὲ οὐδὲ παρ' ὑμῖν αὐτοῖς ὑμᾶς αὐτοὺς γνῶναι δύνασθε ("You say that your whole island is musical and you give as the cause of this the head of Orpheus. But are you not ashamed to be so unmusically disposed? And at one time you surpassed the Greeks with your citharodes, but because of your inability to take counsel with yourselves, you risk being defeated by everyone. And in the past men came from you to other places to put an end to factional crises (*staseis*), but now you are not even able to know yourselves on your home soil"). Aristides is referring to the current (second-century CE) state of conflict on Lesbos, but the *topos* he invokes is an old one; cf. Mason 1993:225.

[188] Indeed, Classical Mytilene was known to exert its hegemony over neighboring states through a form of musical repression. Aelian *Historical Miscellanies* 7.15 says that the children of those who rebelled against the Mytileneans were forbidden an education in literature (*grammata*) and *mousikê*. Aelian explains this punishment by saying that it reflects the great respect the Mytileneans had for musical culture—nothing could be worse than *amousia*. But a more pragmatic reason presents itself: Mytilene was intent on suppressing the dissident political voices that could be raised in musical practice. Isocrates in *Letter* 8 also suggests that Mytilene, which he calls "the *polis* agreed by all to be the most musical" (8.4), had been taking measures to purge its own famed musical culture of dissident influences. Isocrates writes to the rulers of the city asking them to restore citizenship to Agenor, a prominent music teacher (8.1, 8.4) who had been exiled to Athens some years before. Isocrates tactfully makes no reference to the reason for Agenor's exile except to mention that the Mytileneans were "afraid for the welfare of their city" (8.3).

agônes both in the *poleis* and at federal gatherings at Messon. Perhaps already at these *agônes* the paralegal force of the very form of citharodic song, the *eunomia* notionally effected by *nomos*, was taking shape as an item of faith. And if, ultimately, the intractable political realities of Lesbos could neither accommodate nor sustain the salutary ideological fiction of cosmic *kitharôidia*, this would not prevent the Lesbian Singers from successfully marketing that ideology and its institutional apparatus abroad, perhaps with the backing of the authority of the Delphic oracle, to *poleis* with the proper political and cultural configuration to benefit from it.[189]

12. Megaclo's *Moisai*

The third-century BCE historian Myrsilus of Methymna recorded a local myth set during the time of the primordial Lesbian colonizer-king, Macar, that expresses, in allegorical form, the defining cultural themes of early *kitharôidia* on the island. The myth as Myrsilus knew and told it likely took its shape at a relatively late date, certainly after the Archaic period. It seems to have been concocted specifically to provide an aetiology for a group of bronze statues of the Muses located somewhere on Lesbos. Yet it almost certainly musters elements of citharodic lore that go back considerably further in time, and it might contain some latent information about the historical organization of the earliest Lesbian citharodes.[190] It is worth quoting in full the passage

---

[189] Franklin 2006a:59–60 argues for the historical role of Delphi in arranging musical foundations and catharses of cities in Archaic Greece, but I am less certain of the historicity of its involvement in brokering the "real" relationship between the Lesbian citharodes and Sparta. (For what it is worth, Fontenrose 1978:285 deems the oracle concerning the Lesbian Singer "not genuine.") Needless to say, the mediation of Delphi early on became a crucial axiom of Terpandrean lore, whether at the instigation of the Lesbians, the Spartans, or the Delphians (cf. n167 above). Clearly, all parties would have had something to gain from their mutual implication. The mediating role of the oracle features in accounts of other musicians and poets brought in to "heal" Spartan social ills, most prominently Thales/Thaletas of Gortyn, Tyrtaeus, and Alcman (Aelian *Historical Miscellanies* 12.50). Yet here too the authenticity of that mediation is difficult to assess. Perhaps these accounts were secondary to the Terpandrean legend, and even stood in a relationship of agonistic emulation with it—if Terpander was summoned by the Pythia, then these other exemplars of musical media (choral melic, aulodic elegy) could have been as well.

[190] On Myrsilus, see Jackson 1995. Although his interpretation of this myth (36–40) differs radically from mine (see following note), I would agree with his contention that elements of it date back to the Archaic period. For Jacoby, it represents a "rationalization of a local Lesbian legend" (1955:380).

from the *Protrepticus* of Clement of Alexandria in which the myth is related:

> As for the Muses, whom Alcman makes children of Zeus and Mnemosyne and the rest of the poets and prose writers deify and revere, entire cities have dedicated temples of the Muses (*mouseia*) in their honor. But they were Mysian servant girls (Μύσας θεραπαινίδας), whom Megaclo, the daughter of Macar, had purchased. Macar, who ruled as king over the Lesbians, was forever quarreling with his wife, and Megaclo was upset on behalf of her mother. How could she not have been? So she brought these Mysian servant girls, as many as was their number, and called them, in her Aeolic dialect, *Moisai*. She had them taught to play the *kithara* and to sing melodiously of ancient deeds (ᾄδειν καὶ κιθαρίζειν τὰς πράξεις τὰς παλαιὰς ἐμμελῶς), and they, by continually playing the *kithara* and enchanting with their beautiful song (κιθαρίζουσαι καὶ καλῶς κατεπᾴδουσαι), charmed (ἔθελγον) Macar and checked his anger. In return for this service Megaclo dedicated as a thank-offering, on her mother's behalf, bronze statues of them, and commanded that they be honored in all the temples. Such are the Muses. The story is found in Myrsilus of Lesbos.

> Myrsilus of Methymna FGrH 477 F 7a
> *ap.* Clement *Protrepticus* 2.31

There can be no doubt that Myrsilus figures the Muses as a kind of chorus of citharodes; ᾄδειν καὶ κιθαρίζειν τὰς πράξεις τὰς παλαιὰς ἐμμελῶς 'to play the *kithara* and to sing melodiously of ancient deeds' is as clear a definition of Archaic and Classical *kitharôidia* as could be formulated. The "ancient deeds" they sing recall the epic narratives that were the subject of the Terpandrean *nomos*. Terpander himself was an ἐπαινέτης ἡρωικῶν πράξεων 'praiser of heroic deeds' (Plutarch *Laconian Institutions* 17.238c). Further, the music of the Muses has an enchanting and charming effect (κατεπᾴδειν, θέλγειν) on its listeners, soothing their mutual hostilities, a quality that is central to the image of Lesbian *kitharôidia*. Indeed, in the myth, *kitharôidia* is introduced expressly for the purpose of pacification, of restoring proper order. It is tempting to read Macar's constant quarreling with his wife as a metaphor for Lesbian civil strife—the troubled marriage of the first couple of Lesbos forecasting the island's stormy political future—and the intercession of the citharodic Muses as an *aition* for the sociomusical interventions of Terpander and the Lesbian Singers, at home and abroad.[191] The phrase, "they checked his anger" (κατέπαυον τῆς ὀργῆς), for instance, echoes the language that is used in later texts to describe Terpander's calming of the Spartans.[192]

We may note two other characteristics of these Muses that evoke Terpander and the early history of Lesbian *kitharôidia*. First, although Clement alludes to their having a set "number," he does not mention how many they are. Fortunately, other sources inform us that Myrsilus said there were seven Lesbian Muses rather than the nine of the Panhellenic tradition.[193] The theme of seven θεραπαινίδαι 'servant girls' recalls another myth connected to Lesbos and the Troad, Agamemnon's offer of seven Lesbian women to Achilles, which appears in *Iliad* 9.128–129 (cf. 19.245–246).[194] But the similarity may be merely superficial. The seven Muses may rather symbolically correspond to the seven strings of the *kithara*, the invention of the Lesbian Terpander. Second, the Muses are non-Greek Easterners, Mysians. There is obviously etymological play involved in making them Mysians (*Musai-Moisai-Mousai*).[195] This may be a late accretion to the myth, but it could express a much earlier theme, the confrontation of Lesbian and Anatolian musical culture. Mysia is just north of Lydia, which looms large, legendarily as well as historically, in early Lesbian musical culture—a Lydian inventor of the *kithara*, Tyrrhenus, was in fact put forward alongside Terpander (Duris FGrH 76 F 81).[196] The "Asiatic" origins of the citharodic Muses

---

[191] Our myth finds an echo in another local account told of Macareus, a corrupt priest of Dionysus in Mytilene who killed his wife in anger (Aelian *Historical Miscellanies* 13.2); some mythopoetic DNA must be shared here, but the resemblances are more superficial than thematic. The story of Macareus seems to reflect the belief that early Lesbian Dionysian cult involved human sacrifice (see Shields 1917:59; Macar in one tradition was himself a priest of Dionysus, *Etymologicum Magnum* s.v. Βρισαῖος). Jackson 1995:38–40 thus argues that Myrsilus' myth allegorizes the introduction to Lesbos of the cults of Hera and Zeus, which had a tempering effect on the wild excess of pre-Aeolic Dionysian worship. In light of the probable institution of cithardic contests at the federated shrine of these three gods at Messon, Jackson's reading holds some interest. But it does not sufficiently account for the myth's clear emphasis on Muses, Mysia, music, and the number seven, nor for the lack of explicit Dionysian content.

[192] Philodemus *On Music* 1 fr. 30, 31–35 = p18 Kemke, τῆς τα]ραχῆς ἔπαυσε τοὺς [Λακεδαι]-μον[ίο]υς 'he checked the Spartans from their disorder'; Aristides 24.55, ἑτέρωσε βαδίζοντες ἔπαυον τὰς στάσεις '[Lesbian citharodes] went to other places and checked factional crises'.

[193] Arnobius 3.37; *Epimerismi Homerici* Cramer A.O. I 285, 15 (= FGrH 477 F 7b, c).

[194] Cf. Jackson 1995:39–40; Shields 1917:70–71.

[195] Cf. Jacoby 1955:380.

[196] For Mysia as a metonym for other regional musical traditions in Anatolia, see Barker 1984:66n29.

of Lesbos chime with the "Asiatic" origins of the *kithara* itself, whose epithet was indeed *Asias*, "because the Lesbian citharodes who lived directly opposite Asia made use of it."[197] The importation of these seven "servant girls" to Lesbos, I suggest, mythicizes the actual flow of heptatonic musical technology from east to west during the Orientalizing period.[198] The name change, although fanciful, is thus neatly emblematic: what was foreign (*Musai*) takes on a distinctly Aeolic and Lesbian identity (*Moisai*).[199]

Macar is here called the king of Lesbos, and in one tradition Lesbos is the name of his wife (scholia *ad Iliad* 24.544). But according to another tradition, recorded by a separate scholiast to the same line of the *Iliad*, Macar had a special relationship to Antissa: after he left his home on Rhodes, he went to Lesbos, where he "founded a city [on Lesbos] and named it Antissa, after his wife" (πόλιν οἰκίσας ἀπὸ τῆς γυναικὸς Ἄντισσαν ὠνόμασεν).[200] Although other cities of Lesbos were said to be named for members of Macar's family, only Antissa was identified as his wife, who, again, is otherwise named for the entire island, Lesbos. Might the unnamed mother of Megaclo, then, be Antissa, and the setting of the myth be the city named for her? It was Antissa that could make the strongest bid to being the cradle of *kitharôidia* on Lesbos. Although Terpander would become a Pan-Lesbian axiom of *kitharôidia*, Antissa laid the most compelling claim to his origin, which must reflect the antiquity of its own citharodic tradition. Antissa could claim as well the oracular head and lyre of Orpheus, the latter of which Terpander legendarily inherited. Myrsilus recorded lore about the burial of Orpheus' head at Antissa, and how it made the nightingales there sing more sweetly than elsewhere on Lesbos (FGrH 477 F 2). Orpheus was almost certainly honored with cult in Antissa.

If the mythical setting of the Megaclo story is Antissa, then the seven bronze citharodic Muses were in all probability located in the historical city. There is a complication, however. We read in Athenaeus

---

[197] "Plutarch" *On Music* 6.1133c; cf. Duris FGrH 76 F 81.

[198] Cf. nn179–181 above. We may note, however, that Megaclo has the servant girls *taught* to play the *kithara* and to sing, presumably after she has brought them to Lesbos. It is as if there were already citharodes on the island in Macar's time. The myth thus accounts for the infusion of Eastern musical knowledge and yet maintains the "indigenous" integrity of a native Aeolic-Lesbian tradition.

[199] For the Panhellenic diffusion of Aeolic-Lesbian *Moisa*, see Cassio 2005.

[200] On the likelihood of a close alliance between Rhodes and Antissa in the second century BCE, see Mason 1995:402. Could Macar son of Rhodos and Helios (cf. Diodorus Siculus 5.56) have been a specifically Antissan creation from this period? In other, probably older traditions, Macar is a son of Zeus or of Crinacus, the son of Zeus (scholia *ad Iliad* 24.544; Diodorus Siculus 5.81).

that Euphorion of Chalcis, a third-century BCE poet, mentioned a group of Muses in Mytilene that was made by the sculptor Lesbothemis, one of whom held a *sambukê*, a polychord instrument derived from the harp named the *magadis*. We do not know when Lesbothemis lived, although Athenaeus calls him *arkhaios* (4.182e; 14.635a).[201] The *sambukê*, Euphorion says, was especially popular in Mytilene. Like other harps, it was strongly identified with its Eastern origins, and, although it surely enjoyed a vogue among Archaic and Classical elites in Mytilene, as did harps such as the *trigônos*, *magadis*, and the *pêktis*, by the Hellenistic period it was commonly played by hired women.[202] We might be tempted to see these associations registered in Myrsilus' myth, and thus to localize it and the bronzes in Mytilene; the myth would offer then a semi-comic *aition* for why one of the Mytilenean Muses plays the exotic *sambukê*. But we need not. First, it should be recalled that in Clement's telling, at least, the seven Muses emphatically *kitharizein*, a verb that is not used to denote harp playing. And second, the cult of the Muses, as the myth indicates, was Pan-Lesbian. All the cities, Megaclo had commanded, were to honor them, and we may presume that, historically, cities besides Mytilene, including Antissa, had Muse cult and locally appropriate cult statues of the Muses.[203]

If the citharodic *Moisai* of the myth do belong to Antissa, a connection to Terpander and his *genos* naturally suggests itself. That is, the early Lesbian citharodes of Antissa may have organized themselves around a local cult of the Muses, who took on the traits of the citharodes and were implicated in myths relevant to the culture of *kitharôidia*, of which Myrsilus' story is a late, composite reflex. Alex Hardie has made a good case for the "role of Muse cult in establishing group identity among practicing musicians" on early Lesbos. He cites Sappho fr. 150, in which Sappho refers to herself and her companions as μουσοπόλοι 'those who busy themselves with the Muses', as Hardie understands the term, which he speculates is an "East Greek coinage applied to professional musicians."[204] It is likely, however, that Sappho applies the term to her circle in a primarily metaphorical rather than strict sense;

---

[201] Cf. Bie 1887:19–21.

[202] On the *sambukê*, see West 1992:75–77. Sophocles *Mysians* fr. 412 Radt mentions the Phrygian triangle harp (*trigônos*) and the Lydian *pêktis*, but not the *sambukê*, although, as West notes (p77), the *sambukê* may have been conflated by some with the triangle harp.

[203] Cf. Shields 1917:70.

[204] Hardie 2005:14–15; cf. Lanata 1996:14. Hardie notes that the term was adopted by the professional musicians of the guilds of the Artists of Dionysus in the Hellenistic period (IG VII 2484, a synod of Theban *tekhnitai* and *mousopoloi*).

she and her aristocratic companions are not professional performers per se, but nevertheless devotees of the Muses and associates of their cult in Mytilene.[205] Perhaps she has appropriated the title from the wholly professionalized guild of Lesbian Singers, by her day probably a Pan-Lesbian network tied into Muse cults in cities beyond Antissa, whom she names with admiration and perhaps in a spirit of emulation (fr. 106). It is significant that Euripides refers to the citharodes who sing of Alcestis at the Carneia as μουσοπόλοι (*Alcestis* 444–447); the tragedian surely has in mind the most famous Carneian competitors, the Lesbian Singers.[206]

It is worth considering too the implications of a curious image on an Attic hydria attributed to the Group of Polygnotus that was made around 440–430 BCE.[207] On the shoulder of the vessel, a bearded man appears to have lowered himself down on a rope into a cave, where he props his foot upon a rock, below which the animate head of Orpheus rests on the ground, as he stretches his arm down toward it. Next to the head stands a Muse, perhaps Calliope, Orpheus' mother; she holds a tortoise-shell lyre, which may be meant to be that of Orpheus. (It has only six strings, but that is likely an oversight of the artist.) Flanking this Muse and the man are other Muses, six in all, who variously hold lyres or *auloi*. The scene is surely set on Lesbos, most likely at Antissa, given the preeminence of that city's claim to Orpheus. That the Muses are seven in number seems more than a coincidence in light of the tradition of the seven Lesbian Muses. It has been suggested that the man with the rope is Terpander, who will consult the oracular head and perhaps receive the Orphic lyre from the Muse.[208] What would thus be imagined is the birth of the citharode, a passing of the torch from Orpheus to Terpander. If this interpretation is correct, we might then take the association of Terpander, Orpheus, and the Muses in the

---

[205] Aelius Aristides 28.51 = Sappho fr. 193 says that Sappho claimed "the Muses had made her truly prosperous (ὀλβίαν) and enviable." Sappho might be referring to the professional aspect of Muse cult, in which the Muses grant material prosperity (*olbos*) to the musicians who observe their worship (for the idea cf. e.g. *Homeric Hymns* 15.9, 20.8). Again, however, musical professionalism is probably deployed metaphorically. For Sappho, the prosperity she receives is not material, as it would be for a professional performer, but rather a question of spiritual fulfillment and social prestige. For the semantic contestation that could take place over the meaning of *olbos* (spiritual happiness vs. financial prosperity), see Crane 1996.

[206] Cf. Hardie 2005:15, who sees in the passage a "link of sorts to the citharoedic school of Terpander."

[207] Antikenmuseum Basel und Sammlung Ludwig BS 481; Bundrick 2005:125, fig. 77.

[208] Schmidt 1972:132; cf. Lissarrague 1995:23, Bundrick 2005:126, who discusses alternative interpretations.

image as a reflection, from the temporal and geographical distance of Classical Athens, of the institutional interrelationship between *kitharôidia*, Muse cult, and the cult of Orpheus in Archaic Antissa.

Terpander's own *vita* contains another clue to the implication of *kitharôidia* in an Antissan cult of the Muses. A scholiast to Homer *Iliad* 22.391 records that "Terpander of Antissa was an *apogonos*" (ἀπόγονος Τέρπανδρος ὁ Ἀντισσαῖος) of Crinoeis, one of the Idaean Dactyls, divinely talented metalworkers, musicians—the scholiast calls them μουσικώτατοι 'terribly musical'—and magicians, whose ancestral home was Mt. Ida in the Phrygian Troad.[209] This Crinoeis was the "first to sacrifice to the Muses" (πρῶτος Μούσαις ἔθυσεν); in other words, he established the original Muse cult, of which Terpander and his *genos* were the presumed inheritors. By way of comparison, we may note that a guild of aulodes in the city of Troezen, the Ardalids, claimed that its mythical ancestor, Ardalus, was the first priest of the Troezenian Muses. That is, Ardalus established the local cult of the Muses around which the Ardalid guild organized its membership.[210] We hear nothing else of Crinoeis. It has been argued that the name is a deformation of Crinacus, who was known as both the father and the son of Macar (scholia *ad Iliad* 24.544; Diodorus Siculus 5.81.4).[211] If so, this would bring us back to Myrsilus' story, in which the household of Macar is responsible for the foundation of Muse cult on Lesbos. It could be the case that Crinoeis/Crinacus belongs to an older, Lesbian Terpandrean genealogy, and that the name has been transferred to a later, Dactylic one. The Dactyls are nowhere else connected to the Muses.

But what can we make of Terpander's descent from an Idaean Dactyl? He may simply have been linked by some late scholar to the Dactyls through a sheer coincidence of musical associations. The Dactyls were attributed the invention of the rhythm that bears their name (Clement *Stromateis* 1.15.73), and dactylic rhythms were a hallmark of the Terpandrean *nomoi*.[212] But the genealogy is probably rooted in an older stratum of the tradition. Here it is appropriate to bring the biographical testimony of the third-century BCE Parian Marble into the discussion. On the Marble, Terpander is called the son of Derdeneus

---

[209] On the Idaean Dactyls' reputation as magicians, see Johnston 1999:105–106.

[210] Cf. n172 above.

[211] Welcker 1865:142–143.

[212] Cf. Barker 1984:210n31. Alexander Polyhistor (first century BCE) says that the Phrygian Dactyls, along with the Phrygian aulete Olympus, were the first to introduce instrumental music (*kroumata*) to Greece ("Plutarch" *On Music* 5.1132f). The claim likely derives from the smithing of the Dactyls; *kroumata* literally means 'strokes' or 'blows'.

(Ep. 34). The name may be understood as a variant of Dardaneus, that is, a Dardanian, an inhabitant of the region of Dardania in the Troad.[213] Dardania and the city of Dardanos, located on the coast of the Hellespont, were settled by the native Samothracian hero Dardanus, to whom the Trojan royal line would trace its lineage. Derdeneus/ Dardaneus and Dactyls are readily linked in the geographical imaginary of the Troad. As Strabo 7, fr. 49 puts it, Dardanus established "the *polis* of Dardania"—Strabo conflates the city of Dardanos with the district of Dardania—"at the foot of Mt. Ida," which was the ancestral home of the Dactyls (cf. 13.1.25). Accordingly, we might be inclined to posit an original identity between Derdeneus and Crinoeis the Dactyl, i.e. the Dactyl from Dardania was Terpander's father or more distant ancestor.[214]

Yet the Dactylic lineage may belong to a tradition based upon yet ultimately separate from that of Derdeneus and the Dardanian connection.[215] Derdeneus looks to be an example (not necessarily historical)

---

[213] Bechtel 1917:116–117 posits the nominative Δερδενεύς 'Derdeneus' (rather than Derdenis) for the genitive Δερδένεος on the Marble and sees in Derdeneus a reminiscence of (*Anklang an*) Dardaneus; cf. already Welcker 1865:142. *Suda* s.v. Δαρδανεύς says that Δαρδανεύς is the "name of a people; also, the Dardanians" (ὄνομα ἔθνους· καὶ Δαρδάνιοι). The *ethnos* 'people' must be the Illyrico-Thracian Dardanians; these Dardanians are, interestingly, said by Strabo to have cultivated music, including that of stringed instruments, despite their primitiveness (7.5.7). The second group of Dardanians mentioned in the *Suda* must be the Dardanians of the Troad, and it is to these that Terpander must be linked.

[214] As Welcker 1865:142 suggests.

[215] A primary motive for its creation may have been to posit a genetic precedent for the wonder-working effects of Terpander's *kitharôidia*—the Dactyls were uncanny musicians and magicians. But it is tempting to consider specific local factors in its development as well. As early as the fourth century BCE, Orpheus had been made a disciple of the Dactyls, who taught him initiations and mysteries on the northern Aegean island of Samothrace (Ephorus FGrH 70 F 104), home to the Panhellenically renowned mystery cult of the Great Gods, also known as the Cabeiroi, with whom the Dactyls of Phrygian Ida were sometimes identified (Strabo 7, fr. 50). Although Terpander seems never to have been elevated to the status of an Orphic mystagogue (cf. Section 7), it is possible that he was at some point drawn into the orbit of the Samothracian musical culture—if not the mysteries themselves—through a putative Dactylic lineage. It seems likely that music played an important practical and symbolic role in the rites and their attendant festivals; cf. Kowalzig 2005:61–63; Rutherford 2007a. (In his discussion of Samothrace and its rites, Diodorus Siculus 5.49.1 tells the story of the wedding of Cadmus and Harmonia, a myth that was probably central to the mystery cult. The myth includes *aitia* for a wide range of musical practices: Hermes gives the couple his lyre, Athena her *auloi*, Electra her drums and cymbals, and Apollo plays his *kithara*. It is as if Samothrace were folding into its own myth and ritual complex the entire panoply of Hellenic musical culture.) There is every probability that Samothracian festivals hosted citharodic *agônes*; we saw above that cithathodic *agônes* were held on nearby Lemnos from the seventh century BCE. Given the relative proximity of Samothrace to Lesbos, it stands to reason that the Lesbian Singers would have been prominent

of a historical naming practice on Archaic Lesbos. Lesbians had occupied the Troad, including the city of Dardanos, since the end of the eighth century BCE. One such Lesbian settler, "Scamander, son of Macaris," was buried in Dardanos, according to the Aeolic inscription on his tumulus.[216] Scamander, the famed river that runs by Troy, is in fact one of the names given to Sappho's father (P.Oxy. 1800 fr. 1). Such evocative Anatolian names reflect the cultural and political investment of Lesbian elites in and notional possession of the Troad and its epic history.[217] Again, although the name Derdeneus evokes an actual onomastic habit and cultural pattern of Archaic Lesbos, that does not mean that Derdeneus was a real person. Terpander's Dardanian affiliation should be understood as a rhetorical fiction that suits the practices and interests of the early Lesbian Singers. On the one hand, it reflects their close engagement with Anatolian musical culture; on the other, it advertises the privileged "familial" access enjoyed by Terpander's *apogonoi* to the Aeolic epic traditions of the Troad.

---

competitors, and Terpander may have acquired his distant Dactylic ancestor in the context of such contests. Terpander's Dardanian connections offered a natural link both to the Dactyls as well as to Samothracian myth. Dardanus was a Samothracian by birth; Strabo 7, fr. 49 says that he brought his native mysteries with him to the Troad.

[216] Aksik 1971. Spencer 1995:304 observes that the name Macaris is "one which has more than a passing significance in the myths [about the founder of Lesbos, Macar] current in archaic Lesbos." The name evokes Trojan-epic glory, while the patronymic recalls the heroic foundation of Lesbos.

[217] Cf. Spencer 1995:304–305; West 2002b:208. Phrynis the Mytilenean citharode is called the "son of Kamon" in Timotheus PMG 802 (cf. Pollux *Onomasticon* 4.66). Wilamowitz 1903:65 argues that the name "ist identisch mit Σκάμων, dem Kurznamen von Σκαμανδρώνυμος," a variant of "Scamander" that is also attested for Sappho's father (cf. Herodotus 2.135.1). Timotheus may have deliberately shortened Skamon to Kamon for comedic effect; see Part IV.3n98. Phrynis presumably came from a family of musical professionals rather than old-line elites, so the name is best taken as a stage name, contrived, like Derdeneus, to advertise the citharode's privileged access to epic lore. (It is interesting to note that the Mytilenean historian Hellanicus named his son, also a historian, Skamon: *Suda* s.v. Ἑλλάνικος.) We may compare the third-century BCE citharode Archeanax of Mytilene (FD III 4, 125.7), who shares a name with one of the leading aristocrats of Archaic Mytilene, the Archeanax who supposedly built the city of Sigeion with stones from Troy (Strabo 13.1.38). The fifth-century citharode Alcaeus mentioned in Eupolis fr. 303 K-A may have been from Mytilene as well. Cf. Aloni 1986 on the role of the Mytilenean colony of Sigeion in legitimating Lesbian claims to Trojan epic. After the Athenians seized Sigeion in the sixth century BCE, the Mytileneans took refuge at the nearby settlement of Achilleion, where Achilles' tumulus was located (Herodotus 5.94.2).

13. Terpander in Sparta

It was above all at Sparta, where Terpander undertook the first *katastasis* 'establishment' of civic musical culture, that Lesbian *kitharôidia* acquired the definitive reputation of being able to guarantee political *kosmos* and social harmony, to deter *stasis*. Sparta, like Lesbos, was notoriously racked with civil disorder before the establishment of its famed *eunomia* (Herodotus 1.65; Thucydides 1.18.1).[218] There is no reason to doubt that, beginning from at least the later seventh century BCE, Terpander's *nomoi* were considered to be the paralegal musical complement of the political *nomoi* of the Spartan state.[219] Terpander was in fact synchronized with the legendary lawgiver Lycurgus by the Peripatetic scholar Hieronymus of Rhodes in his *On Citharodes* (fr. 33 Wehrli *ap.* Athenaeus 14.635f), a view that chimes with the belief expressed in starkly literal terms by Clement *Stromateis* 1.16.78 that Terpander "set to music the *nomoi* of the Lacedaemonians."[220] As was argued in Part II.4, claims such as these should not be dismissed as late, naïve confusions of the legal and musical senses of *nomos*. They are rather rationalizing expressions of a deeply traditional belief in the fundamental imbrication of music and social order. The pairing of poet-musician and lawgiver is a differentiated variation on the genuinely Archaic figure of the musical *nomothetês* 'lawgiver', such as Solon (cf. Solon fr. 31W) or Terpander's choral counterpart in Sparta, Thaletas, who was said to use song as a cover for lawgiving (Plutarch *Life of Lycurgus* 4).[221]

Demetrius of Phalerum provides the earliest surviving explicit reference to the beneficial political intervention of the Lesbian citharodes. Arguing that Homeric *aoidoi*, whom he imagines to be forerunners of the Archaic and Classical citharodes, were employed by kings to maintain the social order in their absence, he cites the historical example of Sparta to prove his point:

τοσοῦτον δὲ καὶ πρὸς τὰ πολιτικὰ διέτεινεν ἡ τῶν κιθαρῳδῶν
μουσικὴ ὡς τῶν Σπαρτιατῶν τὴν πόλιν ὠφελεῖσθαι λέγουσιν
ὑπὸ τούτων τῶν ἀνδρῶν τὰ μέγιστα καὶ πρὸς ὁμόνοιαν καὶ
πρὸς τὴν τῶν νόμων φυλακήν. ὡς καὶ τὴν Πυθώ, αὐτόθι

---

[218] On the historical circumstances of *stasis* in early Sparta, see now van Wees 1999; Meier 1998.

[219] Cf. Gostoli 1988.

[220] Cf. Plutarch *Agis* 10.6; van Wees 1999:6–7. Hieronymus may be following Aristotle; cf. n4 above.

[221] Solon: cf. van Wees 1999:25–26.

φυομένης ταραχῆς, εἰπεῖν, τὸν Λέσβιον ᾠδὸν ἀκούειν καὶ
παύσασθαι τῆς φιλονεικίας. ὃ καὶ γέγονεν.

And so much did the music of the citharodes pertain to the
affairs of state (*ta politika*) that they say (*legousin*) that the
polis of the Spartans was above all assisted by these men in
regard to both civic concord and the continued preservation
of the *nomoi*, and that the Pythian oracle, when disorder was
brewing in Sparta, told them to listen to the Lesbian Singer
and cease from their love of strife, which indeed happened.

Demetrius of Phalerum *ap.* Scholia E, Q
ad Odyssey 3.267[222]

Fourth-century BCE Athenian cultural conservatives such as Demetrius
were clearly fascinated by the Terpander in Sparta narrative for its
ideologically sympathetic elements. It represented for them the purest
fantasy of the hegemony of an "aristocratic" lyric culture, its power
to enforce an elitist vision of societal rectitude, power that was felt to
be lost in the wake of the populist New Music of late Athenian democracy.[223] Terpander's legendary harmonization of the Spartan populace
also fitted neatly with (and probably helped to inspire) theories, first
propounded by Damon of Oa, then elaborated by culturally and politically elitist Academic, Peripatetic, and, later, Stoic thinkers, about the
socio-psychagogic force of musical ethos, the power of melody and
rhythm to regulate individual and collective social behavior.[224] It has

---

[222] On the attribution of this passage to Demetrius, who is cited earlier in the scholion,
and a discussion of its connection to Peripatetic research on Homer and musical
history, see Gostoli 1986 and 1988:236n21; cf. Wilson 2004:269–272.

[223] On early Spartan culture as an idealized model for embittered Athenian musical
elites, see Csapo 2004:240–244.

[224] On Damon in his political context, see Wallace 2004; ethos theory: Wallace 1995;
Anderson 1955, 1966. For a critic of musical ethos theory such as the Epicurean
Philodemus of Gadara, Terpander's Spartan intervention was a central point of refu-
tation, since "very many of those who are mad for music (*mousoleptoi*) agree" upon
its veracity (*On Music* 4, P.Herc. 1497, col. 9, 4–19 = T 14b G); *mousoleptoi* is a swipe at
adherents of the theory—those who allow themselves to be "possessed" by the Muse.
Philodemus directly takes on Diogenes of Babylon (fl. c. 200 BCE), a Stoic proponent
of the politicized ethos theory. Diogenes had claimed that Terpander "made the
Lacedaemonians desist from their disorder by singing in their *philitia*" (Philodemus
On Music 1 fr. 30.31–35, p18 Kemke = Diogenes SVF III, p232 fr. 84 von Arnim = T 14a G).
We should note the possibly aristocratic-oligarchic implications of the setting in the
philitia, which Diogenes perhaps envisaged as the Spartan equivalent of Attic-Ionic
symposia rather than the militaristic, post-Lycurgan "public messes" of the sixth
century and after. On the anachronistic application of the terms *philitia* (a variant of
the more common *phiditia*) and *sussitia* 'public messes' (cf. Photius *Lexicon* s.v. μετὰ

395

even been suggested that Damon invented the story wholesale.[225] But although Classical Athenian intellectuals and those influenced by them might have romanticized, appropriated, and rhetorically enhanced the Terpandrean narrative—see the discussion of Choricius' tendentiously "elitist" Terpander in Section 2—it was not their invention. Demetrius' *legousi* 'they say' points to an oral tradition that we can trace back past Aristotle (fr. 545 Rose; cf. Heraclides Lembus *Excerpts from Aristotle's Politeiai* fr. 11 Dilts) to the *Cheirons* of Cratinus, a comedy of the 430s.[226] But it does not begin there. For Cratinus, who referred to the saying, "After the Lesbian Singer" (fr. 263 K-A), the respect accorded to the Lesbian citharodes at the Carneia already enjoyed proverbial status, and although we have no earlier direct allusions to it—Sappho fr. 106 celebrates the agonistic success of the Lesbian Singers, but says nothing about their political charms—the tradition must surely go back much further, to early Sparta and the Lesbian Singers themselves.[227]

We do have two pertinent Archaic references to the political power of music in Sparta. The music in question, however, is not that of Terpander, but of Thaletas (or Thales) of Gortyn in Crete, one of the composers of the post-Terpandrean "second *katastasis*." Unlike the first *katastasis*, which was centered on *kitharôidia* at the Carneia festival, this second establishment of musical culture was connected first and foremost to another Spartan festival of Apollo, the Gymnopaidiai. It was centered on choral song and dance, which

---

Λέσβιον ᾠδόν) to early Spartan private sympotic culture, see Quattrocelli 2002:17. The sympotic reimagining of Terpander goes back to the fifth and fourth centuries (cf. Pindar fr. 125 S-M, discussed below; Section 2 above, on Choricius); its presentation within the rhetorical framework of ethos theory may be Classical as well. In his critique of Diogenes, Philodemus argues by contrast that Terpander "delighted the Spartans at the *agônes*" (αὐτ]οὺς ἐπ[ὶ τῶν] ἀγώνων ἔτερπεν) but did not actually sway them to put away their *stasis* with his music (they did so because they listened to reason and obeyed the Delphic oracle). Philodemus thus simultaneously demystifies and demoticizes Terpander—he is no more than a talented agonistic citharode.

[225] Forrest 1963:164–165.

[226] This play is discussed in the following section. Neither Herodotus nor Thucydides mentions the role of Terpander or the Lesbian Singer in early Sparta. But I would note the implications of Herodotus 1.65.2, in which the historian says that, before the time of Lycurgus, the Spartans were both "the worst governed" (*kakonomôtatoi*) and "unsociable to foreigners" (*xeinoisi aprosmeiktoi*). As Crane 1998:79 observes, "Herodotus implies that the Spartans improved not simply because they adopted a new internal order but because they became better able to associate with members of other Greek states." Herodotus may be referring primarily to Lycurgus' supposed consultation of the Panhellenic Pythian oracle (described in 1.65.3), but he likely alludes as well to the traditional connection drawn between the importation of foreign musicians and poets (perhaps including Terpander) and the ordering of the Spartan state.

[227] Cf. Kiechle 1963:200–201.

was as much *aulos*-accompanied as lyric, and it also involved the introduction of agonistic singing to the *aulos, aulôidia* ("Plutarch" *On Music* 9.1134b–c).[228] The names associated with choruses at the second *katastasis*, Thaletas of Gortyn, Xenodamus of Cythera, and Xenocritus of Locri, were composers primarily of paeans, the choral genre most fitting the divine honorand of the Gymnopaidiai, Apollo.[229] In addition, two aulodes are named as exponents of the second *katastasis*, Polymnestus of Colophon and Sacadas of Argos. The most notable of these musicians was the legendary or semi-legendary Thaletas/Thales, who seems to have emerged at an early point in Spartan musical lore as a sort of choral doublet of Terpander; by the fourth century BCE he was, like Terpander, touted as an exemplary architect of musico-political order in Sparta. According to Pausanias, "in verses (*epê*) composed for the Lacedaemonians" Polymnestus of Colophon, one of the aulodic composers implicated in the second *katastasis*, says that Thales lifted plague (*nosos*) from Sparta (1.14.4).[230] And the choral poet Pratinas of Phlius, composing in the late sixth to early fifth century BCE, says in

---

[228] Two other, non-Spartan festivals are included in this passage as part of the second *katastasis*, the Arcadian Apodeixeis and the Argive Endymatia. Presumably the *mousikoi agônes* at these festivals were founded around the time those of the Gymnopaidiai were (probably later seventh century BCE, as opposed to the early-seventh-century date given to the Carneian citharodic contest; cf. Barker 1984:214n65), and some of the same musicians (e.g. Sacadas of Argos) connected to the Gymnopaidiai were also connected to the Arcadian and Argive festivals.

[229] Cf. Barker 1984:214n66; Rutherford 2001:31. The choral performance of Thaletas' songs at the Gymnopaidiai is attested by Sosibius *On Sacrifices* FGrH 595 F 5 *ap.* Athenaeus 15.678c–d. Porphyrus *Life of Pythagoras* 32 says that Pythagoras sang the paeans of Thaletas to the lyre; such solo reperformance of choral melic was common (cf. Aristophanes *Clouds* 1354–1356). It is likely that at least some of Thaletas' songs were sung to the *aulos* ("Plutarch" *On Music* 10.1134d–e, derived from Glaucus of Rhegium, who seems to have had, however, an auletic bias of sorts, as we saw in Part II.6). Cf. Rutherford 2001:79–80 on auletic accompaniment to paeans; he notes that paeans at the Spartan Hyacinthia were accompanied by *aulos* and *kithara* together (Polycrates FGrH 588 F 1). The paeanic character of the second *katastasis* was probably not total: Glaucus claims that there were disputes as to whether the songs of Thaletas were actually paeans; similar disputes arose about the genre of Xenodamus' songs, with some arguing that they were *huporkhêmata* (*On Music* 9.1134c; Athenaeus 1.15d; cf. Barker 1984:214n71). Glaucus claims too that Xenocritus' choral pieces came to be classified as dithyrambs because they included heroic narration. These were probably not unlike what Arion's Corinthian dithyrambs looked like. Cf. Ieranò 1997:191.

[230] Pausanias takes pains to distinguish Thales from the "shamanic" wise man and seer Epimenides of Knossos, who legendarily purified Athens and other cities. Indeed, while both were imagined to be administers of analogous rites of communal *katharsis*, Epimenides is not figured as a musician per se (although poetic verses were ascribed to him). On Epimenides and the tradition of Cretan purifiers, see Burkert 1992:60–63. Carmanor of Crete, however, the father of Chrysothemis, the first mortal paean-composer and citharode at Delphi, was an explicitly musical purifier in the vein of

one of his songs that Thaletas came to Sparta, like Terpander, at the prompting of the Delphic Oracle, and "through his *mousikê* healed Sparta and released it from the plague that oppressed it" (διὰ μουσικῆς ἰάσασθαι ἀπαλλάξαι τε τοῦ κατασχόντος λιμοῦ τὴν Σπάρτην, Pratinas PMG 713 iii *ap*. "Plutarch" *On Music* 42.1146c). Terpander is mentioned immediately before Thaletas in this passage of *On Music* as "having resolved *stasis* among the Lacedaemonians." (The compiler's immediate source for this testimony is unfortunately unnamed, although the Peripatetic music theorist and historian Aristoxenus of Tarentum, who is the source for much of *On Music*, is a reasonable candidate.)

Although the Apolline paean was long believed to cure epidemic (cf. *Iliad* 1.472–474), the plague described by Pratinas and Polymnestus must be intended as a metaphor for Spartan *stasis*.[231] This is made clear by Philodemus of Gadara, who, as an Epicurean critic of musical ethos theory, refutes the account held by certain *philosophoi* (i.e. proponents of ethos theory) that Thaletas, like Terpander, put an end to factionalism (not sickness) at Sparta, and by Plutarch, who provides a detailed version of that account.[232] In his *Life of Lycurgus*, Plutarch says that Lycurgus brought Thales to Sparta directly from Crete, for reasons more political than cultural, since Thales "passed as a poet of lyric *melê* and used this *tekhnê* as a screen, but in fact accomplished the work of the best of the lawgivers (*nomothetai*)."[233] Plutarch, likely following a source steeped in ethos theory, perhaps Aristotle, describes how Thales' melodies and rhythms, "having a considerable ordering and calming effect" (πολὺ τὸ κόσμιον ἐχόντων καὶ καταστατικόν), were conducive to "obedience and civic concord" (πρὸς εὐπείθειαν καὶ ὁμόνοιαν) among the Spartans, who were "insensibly softened in their dispositions as they listened" (ἀκρώμενοι κατεπραΰνοντο λεληθότως τὰ ἤθη) and so put aside their violent differences under the influence of

---

Thales; he was said to have purified Apollo after the god had killed the serpent at Delphi.

[231] On the curative powers of the paean, see Rutherford 2001:15, 37.

[232] Philodemus *On Music* 1 fr. 30.31–35, p18 Kemke = Diogenes SVF III fr. 84 von Arnim; *On Music* 4, P.Herc. 1497, col. 9, 4–19.

[233] *Life of Lycurgus* 4.1: ποιητὴν μὲν δοκοῦντα λυρικῶν μελῶν καὶ πρόσχημα τὴν τέχνην ταύτην πεποιημένον, ἔργῳ δὲ ἅπερ οἱ κράτιστοι τῶν νομοθετῶν διαπραττόμενον. Plutarch's description of Thales' music as a πρόσχημα 'screen' for his political work recalls his characterization of another *mousikos* active at the intersection of music and politics, Pericles' advisor Damon of Oa, who "attempted to use the *lura* as cover" (τῇ λύρᾳ παρακαλύμματι χρώμενος) for his political influence (*Life of Pericles* 4.2–3).

this tempering music.[234] Thales thus acted as a "forerunner" of Lycurgus (προοδοποιεῖν, 4.2).[235]

Similarly, Terpander was intimately tied to Lycurgus, and the social and affective force of his music was described in terms similar to those applied to Thales' paeans. As we saw, Demetrius of Phalerum claims that Lesbian *kitharôidia* assisted Sparta πρὸς ὁμόνοιαν καὶ πρὸς τὴν τῶν νόμων φυλακήν 'in regard to both civic concord and the continued preservation of the *nomoi*'. Diodorus Siculus describes the socio-affective power of Terpander's *tekhnê*: his "skillful performance of a *melos* on the *kithara* re-harmonized" the Spartans (τι μέλος Τέρπανδρος ἐντέχνως κιθαρίσας | αὐτοὺς πάλιν συνήρμοσε); hearing his "song of harmony" (τῆς ἁρμονίας τῇ ᾠδῇ), the fractious citizens broke into tears of joy and embraced one another.[236] Additionally, Terpander's musical establishment of political orderliness, and that of his successor Arion, were likewise metaphorized as the curing of plague, a tradition that should be considered in light of the roots of the Lesbian citharodes in their native paean culture, which, we saw, had its own reputation for *katharsis*. Boethius has it that "Terpander and Arion of Methymna rescued the Lesbians and the Ionians from the gravest diseases with the help of their song" (*On Music* 1.1). Curiously, Boethius mentions neither Sparta nor Corinth, the *poleis* with which these citharodes are most closely associated. His mention of Ionians, however, the only such mention in the Terpandrean testimonia, may point to some otherwise unattested tradition in which a Lesbian Singer "healed" an Ionian community.

Given that we have references to Thaletas' Spartan intervention made by two Archaic poets, Pratinas and Polymnestus, but none to

---

[234] Aristotle *Politics* 2.1274a29 makes Lycurgus an ἀκροατής 'listener' or 'disciple' of Thales; cf. Forrest 1963:163. On Aristotelian influence in Plutarch's *Life of Lycurgus*, see Morrow 1960:33. Another possible source may be Ephorus of Cyme, who reported on Thales' musico-political activity on Crete in connection to a discussion of the Lycurgan constitution (Strabo 10.4.16), and who, it has been argued (Kiechle 1963:200), is the source behind Diodorus Siculus' account of Terpander's harmonization of Sparta (8.28 *ap*. Tzetzes *Chiliades* 1.385–392), although this latter contention is far from certain. Ephorus' own view of music's ethical force seems to have been rather pessimistic, however: he argued that music was originally devised for deception (*apatê*) and beguilement (*goêteia*) (FGrH 70 F 8 *ap*. Polybius 4.20.5; cf. Wallace 1995:25).

[235] Cf. the discussion of this passage in Nagy 1990b:367–368, who notes that the "calming" quality (καταστατικόν) of Thaletas' music recalls his role in the second *katastasis* of music at Sparta.

[236] 8.28 *ap*. Tzetzes *Chiliades* 1.385–392. The citharodic *nomos* and the paean were thought to share the same orderly, temperate aesthetic and "Apollonian" character (Proclus *Chrestomathia ap*. Photius *Bibliotheca* 320a33–b26; cf. Rutherford 1995).

Terpander's, we might be tempted to conjecture that the legend of Terpander's pacification of the Spartans is secondary to and based upon a tradition originally attached to Thaletas. But the primacy of Terpander and the Carneian *kitharôidia* that constitutes the first *katastasis* seems to have been an axiom of the historical narrative of early Spartan musical culture, and this in itself suggests the independence of the Terpandrean musico-political tradition. Further, recall that Thaletas was ranked as an exponent of the second *katastasis*, which was focused upon choral music. His activity as a choral composer may explain why his wonder-working music is singled out for praise by Pratinas, who was himself a choral poet. That is, the praise might have had a self-interested rhetorical purpose. For Pratinas, Thaletas is a model, and the saving purification that the Cretan effected in Sparta once upon a time is an advertisement for the potential social benefits that his own choral song might confer in the here-and-now. Besides his mention of Thaletas, other fragments of Pratinas' poetry indicate that he took a keen interest in the musical culture of Sparta, and indeed they suggest that he composed songs for performance there.[237] It was Pratinas who characterized the Spartan citizen as "that cicada ready built for a chorus" (ὁ τέττιξ εὔτυχος ἐς χορόν, PMG 709). The cicada metaphor probably alludes to the summertime choral performances at the Gymnopaidiai, which is the best candidate for the occasion on which Pratinas' song was sung; this verse would thus be an instance of choral self-reference, a common enough device in Archaic and Classical choral poetry.[238] The Gymnopaidiai, we saw, was the main site of the second *katastasis*, and works attributed to Thaletas continued to be performed by choruses at that festival through the sixth and fifth centuries BCE (Sosibius *On Sacrifices* FGrH 595 F 5 *ap.* Athenaeus 15.678c–d). We hear too that Pratinas referred to another choral composer connected to the Gymnopaidiai and the second *katastasis*, Xenodamus of Cythera (PMG 713 ii *ap.* "Plutarch" *On Music* 9.1134c). Could Pratinas have commemorated Thaletas and Xenodamus, culture heroes of the Gymnopaidiai, in a song of his own composed for the festival, perhaps in the same song in which he compared the Spartan singer-dancer to the cicada?[239]

---

[237] Cf. Calame 1997:141n149; Constantinidou 1998:26–28. I leave out of the discussion Pratinas PMG 708, with its intriguing reference to the superiority of "Dorian *khoreia*" (line 17), due to its disputed authorship. Cf. Zimmermann 1986.

[238] Cf. Henrichs 1994/1995; Power 2000.

[239] Pratinas claimed that Xenodamus composed songs in the hyporchematic performance mode (cf. n229 above; Part II.3n58). Pratinas himself composed songs called

We can be more confident that the verses on Thales attributed to Polymnestus, himself a hero of the second *katastasis* and the Gymnopaidiai, belonged to an aulodic poem traditionally performed at the festival. I have argued that biographical lore about Terpander was transmitted within the very texts performed by citharodes at the Carneia. Perhaps an analogous practice reigned at the *agônes* of the Gymnopaidiai: not only were the songs of their founders reperformed, but newer poetry was introduced that celebrated the life and work of those founders.

This is not to say that the story of Thaletas' musical purification is secondary to that of Terpander's in the sense of being derived from it.[240] It is obvious that the second, primarily choral establishment of music at Sparta functioned as the ideologically inseparable supplement to the first, citharodic establishment. That is, for the good order of the Spartan state to be secured, both *kitharôidia* and paeanic choral music had first to be established—at festivals of the god of music and good order, Apollo—by musicians equally adept in their respective media at "sounding" the city's enviable constitution into being.[241] Citharode and chorus were complementary, an arrangement whose cultural logic was grounded in the ancient continuity between the media of the former and the latter. The two modes, choral and citharodic performance, produced analogous effects in different ways. The chorus was the musical expression of social collectivity *par excellence*, a metonomy of

---

huporkhêmata (Athenaeus 14.617b, although the poem cited there as a *hyporkhêma*, PMG 708, may be a dithyramb by a later fifth-century poet; cf. Zimmermann 1986). By making Xenodamus a composer of *huporkhêmata*, he may have been attempting to create a legitimating precedent for his own, perhaps innovative style of song performance at Sparta.

[240] However, none of the sources that have Thaletas working musical miracles describe him as a choral poet; he is implicitly imagined as a solo musician, presumably a citharode. Similarly, when Stesichorus is portrayed as resolving *stasis* in a city (perhaps Sparta) with his *melos*, he sings solo (Philodemus *On Music* 1, p18 Kemke = PMG 281c; cf. Part II.6n115). One reason for these monodic characterizations is anecdotal economy. But they also speak to the paradigmatic, iconic force of the image of the lone citharodic wonder-worker: Orpheus, Amphion, and (very likely) Terpander. Nagy 1990b:428 discusses the anecdotal "parallelism between Stesichorus and Terpander." On the role of the Delphic oracle in accounts of poets' visits to Sparta as perhaps originally a feature of the Terpandrean tradition, see n189 above.

[241] The Carneia and the Gymnopaidiai may have abutted one another on the Spartan religious calendar, the latter celebrated between the middle of July and the middle of August, the former between mid-August and mid-September. See arguments in Richer 2005:256–259. It is worth noting that, while the "historical" sequence of the *katastaseis* inverts the evolutionary development of citharode from chorus, within the temporal logic of the festival year, the choral performances of the Gymnopaidiai precede the solo turns of the Carneia.

the *polis*, performing before the *polis* a gracefully idealized version of its communal solidarity and cooperation—ideology in perfectly synchronized motion and sound.[242] The practice and pleasure of ritual song and dance, through the very fact of the active communal participation and physical entrainment built into it, readily promoted civic consolidation and effected self-regulating social control.

Citharodic performance entailed a more passive and top-down, yet no less effective mode of group manipulation. The charismatic virtuoso ideally produced a kind of collective *katharsis* through the *terpsis* he created; he could mobilize and align the divergent moods and temperaments of his listeners under the spell of an expert combination of music, text, and visual spectacle, stimulating a common affect among the civic audience that would become in turn conducive to amity. This cathartic consolidation of the citizenry is vividly rendered in the passage of Diodorus Siculus that was cited above (8.28 *ap.* Tzetzes *Chiliades* 1.385–392). The mutually hostile Spartans were so moved by Terpander's masterfully skillful (ἐντέχνως) performance of his "song of harmony," that, "completely changed in mood, they embraced one another, joyfully saluting one another through their tears" (μετατραπέντες ἀλλήλους περιέβαλλον, ἠσπάζοντο δακρύοις). In this reconstruction of events, the musical transformation of the individual dispositions of the listeners precipitates an emotional, even physical—note the mutual embraces, which evoke the synchronized movement of a chorus—homogenization of the entire Spartan body politic. It is purified of its *stasis*; the joyful tears that are shed by all express this communal purgation. The specific imagery deployed by Diodorus, in particular the mingling of pleasure and tears, may show the influence of Aristotelian theories of tragic *katharsis*, but the description may nonetheless reflect tenets of the social ideology of *kitharôidia* in old Sparta.

Indeed, the Spartan structure of the twin *katastaseis* is one that other cities in Archaic Greece adopted, in particular those ruled by tyrants, who were likely eager to recreate among their own divided and hostile populaces the socially stabilizing musical politics of the Spartan festivals. In contracting Arion to come to Corinth in the later seventh century BCE, the tyrant Periander was thus getting "two *katastaseis*

---

[242] Cf. Nagy 1990b:142; Rutherford 2001:85–86 notes the imbrication of ideals of aesthetic, somatic, and social order in the paean. Plato in the *Laws* emphasizes the importance of choral culture to his supremely ordered utopia, for which Sparta is an obvious model. His citizens are all chorus members (*Laws* 665c), made to enact somatically the hegemonic state ideology, to internalize and propagate it again and again through their own rhythmic dance and music making. Cf. Kowalzig 2004.

in one," as it were, a citharodic Lesbian Singer as well as a poet and organizer of choral performances that were directed not to Apollo, as at Sparta, but to the god more suitable to tyrannical policies of social engineering, the more populist Dionysus. With this Spartan-adapted dual institution of *kitharôidia* and Dionysian choruses in Corinth, Periander seems to have set the model for tyrannical musical politics to come. Cleisthenes adopted a version of it in Sicyon, where he established "tragic choruses" (Herodotus 5.67.5) and promoted *kitharôidia*.[243] The Peisistratids would follow it as well, with their establishment of the City Dionysia in 534 BCE, which perhaps at some point during their reign included dithyrambic contests (although the dating of Lasus' introduction of these is questionable) and their heavy investment in the Panathenaia, which prominently featured *kitharôidia*.[244]

14. Music, Blood, and Cult

One curious detail preserved among the Terpandrean testimonia would appear to speak to the gap thought to exist between the political inefficacy of *kitharôidia* on Lesbos and its celebrated efficacy abroad. Photius *Lexicon* s.v. μετὰ Λέσβιον ᾠδόν records that the Spartans called upon Terpander to resolve their civic strife while he "was in exile for the crime of murder" (ἐφ' αἵματι φεύγοντα).[245] Photius begins his entry by writing that the "After the Lesbian Singer" proverb appeared in a play by the comic poet Cratinus, where it was used of "those who come in second"; Zenobius 5.9 (= fr. 263 K-A) confirms that that play was Cratinus' *Cheirons*, which was probably produced around 440–430 BCE.[246] Perhaps *Cheirons*, which took *mousikê*, including that of the lyre, as one of its themes, treated Terpander at some length.[247] Photius may know, then, the story about Terpander's exile from this play.[248] And while Photius leaves the nature of Terpander's blood guilt unspecified, we may speculate that someone in the play characterized Terpander as

---

[243] Cf. Power 2004.

[244] Cf. Zimmermann 1992:32–33.

[245] *Suda* s.v. μετὰ Λέσβιον ᾠδόν repeats the same information.

[246] Geissler 1969:20–21.

[247] Music in *Cheirons*: frs. 247, 248, 254, 263, 267 K-A. Cheiron himself was renowned in myth for his lyre playing, so we might presume that the chorus of Cheirons in the play took some proprietary interest in it. Cratinus probably mentioned or at least alluded to Terpander in his *Euneidai* (fr. 72 K-A).

[248] Flach 1883:201n2 suspected that a comic poet was behind the story.

a typical representative of the violent factionalism of his island, whose music was out of tune with his murderous politics. Alcaeus, whose poetry takes *stasis* and exile as its main themes, could have been an inspiration; Sappho too was supposedly exiled from Lesbos to Sicily (Parian Marble Ep. 36). There is some indication from the fragments of *Cheirons* that the play, like many other Old Comedies, explored notions of cultural "decline," prominently including concerns about changes in musical practice and taste.[249] Perhaps a debate was staged between advocates of old and new music, and the latter put forward the story of Terpander's exile for murder as a way of discrediting traditional beliefs in the social stability brought about by Terpandrean *kitharôidia*. A secondary swipe at Sparta may have been implied as well—its famed Lesbian Singer, who supposedly brought amity to their state, was nothing more than a murderer. Or, on any number of other possible reconstructions of the context of the story in the play, this dig into the vaunted marriage between Spartan musical culture and political *eunomia* may have been its entire point.

We may compare the tale, circulated in fifth- and fourth-century BCE Athens, that when the Delphic oracle advised the Spartans, who were troubled by social ills during the Second Messenian War, to send to Athens for an advisor, the Athenians cleverly sent the worst man they could find, Tyrtaeus, a lame, mentally challenged schoolteacher.[250] It is important to note that the slanderous tale involves a parody of the traditional account of Terpander's summons to Sparta by the oracle, as is evident in its telling in Pausanias 4.15.6. The Spartans are told to "bring in the Athenian Advisor" (τὸν Ἀθηναῖον ἐπάγεσθαι σύμβουλον), an expression that unmistakably recalls the oracle's iconic advice to "call for the Lesbian Singer" (e.g. τὸν Λέσβιον ᾠδὸν μεταπέμπεσθαι, Photius s.v. μετὰ Λέσβιον ᾠδόν). It is possible, however, that the tale had deeper roots, that Tyrtaeus' Athenian origin and perhaps even his physical deformity were considerably older elements of his *vita*, well known in Archaic Sparta, which had in fact made a policy of importing poets from abroad (Aelian *Historical Miscellanies* 12.50; Plutarch *Agis* 10.5–6). These elements could have been transmitted as authorized

---

[249] As suggested by frs. 247, 248, and perhaps 254 K-A. Cf. Ruffell 2000:486–487; on political nostalgia in the play, see Farioli 2000.

[250] See the summary of the lengthy scholarly debate over the origins of the tale and its variants in Compton 2006:119–125. On its contextualization within the intricate push and pull of anti- and pro-Spartan propaganda, see Figueira 1999:230–231. Laconizing Athenians put their own positive spin on Tyrtaeus' putative Athenian origins (e.g. Plato *Laws* 629a).

biographical lore there along with his verse. Only later, in the fifth and fourth centuries BCE, were these details politicized in Athens, presented in such a way as to discredit him, and Sparta.[251] Similarly, the story of Terpander's exile, even if it was tendentiously recounted in Attic comedy, might nevertheless belong to a more profound layer of the tradition, one known to both the Lesbian *diadokhê* and the Spartans.

The Indo-European theme of the polluted, scapegoated, or marginalized hero, expelled by his own community and welcomed into another, to which he in turn brings needed assistance, is one that is variously refracted throughout the *vitae* of the Greek poets, in particular that of Tyrtaeus (despite its deliberately satiric mediation in the case of his Athenian reception).[252] The narrative of transgression, expulsion, and redemption implicit in Photius' testimony indicates its relevance to the Terpandrean tradition as well. But the presence of such generically archetypal elements in the tradition should be viewed as more than a subconscious, transhistorical expression of a generic mythical pattern. We should acknowledge too its historically determined mediation by those agents with a stake in Terpander, in particular the Lesbian citharodes, for whom it may have functioned as an aetiology, reflective of the actual sociopolitical situation of Lesbos, for their characteristic itinerary. Specifically, the story might have served to redeem the musico-political irony of Lesbian *kitharôidia*, reframing it as a sublime *conditio sine qua non*: the very social disorder that plagued *stasis*-prone Lesbos necessitated the circumstances under which Terpander/the Lesbian Singer leaves home to cure *stasis* in points abroad.

The murder and exile theme reflects especially the intimate tie between Terpander and Sparta, where, we may imagine, the story went that he was purified of his blood guilt before he in turn "purified" Sparta with his music. Nagy makes the appealing suggestion that the theme "may imply hero cult in the making" for Terpander in Sparta.[253] Indeed,

---

[251] Compton 2006:119–129 makes a good case for the Spartan antiquity of seemingly "negative" elements in the Athenian biography of Tyrtaeus.

[252] Cf. Compton 2006. Parker 1983:375–392 reviews myths involving the exile and purification of killers. Especially relevant is the case of Macar, who left home to colonize Lesbos after killing his brother (scholia *ad Iliad* 24.544; cf. Diodorus Siculus 5.56–57, 61, with McGlew 1993:159). It may be significant that the Homeric scholion mentioning Macar's crime identifies him specifically as the founder of Antissa, Terpander's city.

[253] Nagy 1990b:434n104, who compares "the myth about Oedipus at Colonus, where the hero is exiled from Thebes on account of his blood guilt and is thereafter purified at Athens, in response to which the hero donates to the Athenians his own corpse as the talisman of his represented hero cult at Colonus." Sparta likely claimed Terpander's corpse; see discussion below. Nagy 1990a:52 discusses the hero cult of the Archaic poet as a locus for the collection and elaboration of his biographical lore.

given that the right of first performance serially granted to his *apogonoi* at the Carneia was established "in honor (*timê*) and commemoration of ancient Terpander" (ἐπὶ τιμῇ καὶ μνήμῃ Τερπάνδρου τοῦ παλαιοῦ, Plutarch *On the Delay of Divine Justice* 13.558a), we might expect a hero cult for Terpander to be attached to the Carneia.[254] There his ritualized reenactment by "the Lesbian Singer" constituted a sort of immortality, as well as epiphany. In response to the annually repeated call for the Lesbian Singer, Terpander "appeared" each year, without fail, in the form of his descendants—recall that there was an "unbroken continuity" in the performance and victory of the Lesbian *diadokhê* in Sparta through the sixth century BCE ("Plutarch" *On Music* 6.1133c).[255] In this way it seems that both the Lesbians and the Spartans were complicit in the perpetuation of the cult, commemorating through ritual reenactment Terpander's original performance at the Carneia as well as the sociopolitical salvation that it brought about—his "re-harmonization" (πάλιν συνήρμοσε) of the fractured populace of Laconia with his "song of harmony," as Diodorus Siculus puts it (8.28 *ap.* Tzetzes *Chiliades* 1.385–392). Such observance would have amounted to a seasonal reconfirmation of the cosmic ideology of *kitharôidia* and a reminder of its necessity for the health of the state.

According to another bit of lore that may point to hero cult, the Carneia was also exactly, appropriately where Terpander ended his mortal life and thus, importantly, left his corpse behind. Possession of the hero's corpse was a precondition for hero cult; Terpander's death during the very celebration of the festival would locate his body not only in Sparta, but specifically in the ambience of the Carneia, to which the cult was probably annexed. A short epigram from the Hellenistic or early Imperial period describes the death of the citharode Terpes:

---

[254] Cf. Nagy 1979:118, section 1n2 for the semantics of *timê* in the context of hero cult. As Muellner 1996:28n48 puts it, "The local hero's everlasting *timê* is his cult." While there is no explicit evidence for Terpander's Spartan hero cult, it is significant that the Spartans did set up cult for other semi-legendary founding figures, the lawgiver Lycurgus (Herodotus 1.66; Plutarch *Life of Lycurgus* 31) and the ephor-poet Chilon (Pausanias 3.16.4). We should note too that Terpander's bloody past (and Spartan redemption) seems thematically well suited to the myth history of the Carneia. In one commonly held aetiological account, the festival was founded to atone for the murder of the seer Carnus and to purify the blood guilt of the offending Heracleidai. Sources collected in Burkert 1985:441n25.

[255] With the end of the continual supremacy of the Lesbian Singers in Sparta, we might presume the decline of the cult of Terpander in the sixth century. But that need not have been entirely the case. At the least, non-Lesbian cithaodes would likely have continued to perform Terpandrean *nomoi* at the Carneia.

Τέρπης εὐφόρμιγγα κρέκων Σκιάδεσσιν ἀοιδὰν
   κάτθανε νοστήσας ἐν Λακεδαιμονίοις,
οὐκ ἄορι πληγείς, οὐδ' αὖ βέλει, ἀλλ' ἐνὶ σύκῳ
   χείλεα. φεῦ, προφάσεων οὐκ ἀπορεῖ θάνατος.

Terpes, while playing to the *Skiades* a song on his lovely *phorminx*, died after having made his homecoming (*nostos*) among the Lacedaemonians. He was struck neither by a sword nor an arrow, but by one single fig, right through his lips. Ah, death does not lack for occasions!

Tryphon *Palatine Anthology* 9.488[256]

As we saw above, this "Terpes" must be Terpander (cf. *Suda* s.v. γλυκὺ μέλι καὶ πνιξάτω); the setting must be the Carneia, where celebrants traditionally gathered in nine special sun-blocking tents called *Skiades* (Athenaeus 4.141e–f).[257] In her collection of the Terpandrean testimonia Gostoli prints in line 2 κάτθανεν ἐξαπίνης 'he died suddenly'. This is the reading of the line as it appears in a later collection of Greek epigrams compiled by Maximus Planudes (1a.36.14). The manuscript containing the *Palatine Anthology* has the garbled κατθαν' εν ο στησας, which editors have reasonably corrected to κάτθανε νοστήσας 'he died after having made his homecoming'. This reading deserves serious consideration as an older variant of Planudes' rather bland κάτθανεν ἐξαπίνης, which Gostoli defends by pointing out that nowhere else do we hear of Terpander's *nostos* 'homecoming' in Sparta.[258] The singularity of the reference is no reason to do away with it. Rather, I would contend that Terpander's homecoming, not to Lesbos, but to his second home, Sparta, is a theme of the Terpandrean tradition that goes all the way back to the Archaic period, as is his perfectly iconic death at the very *agôn* he inaugurated—the sweet fruit chokes the sweet singer in the midst of his

---

[256] For dating, see Page 1981:99.

[257] Cf. Gostoli 1990:83. Pausanias 3.12.10 describes one *Skias*, a large, main pavilion located near the agora (cf. *Etymologicum Magnum* s.v. Σκιάς). This structure was used by the Spartans as an assembly hall, but it may have housed the Carneian cithatodic *agôn* as well; the confiscated *kithara* of Timotheus "still" hung on its wall in Pausanias' time. Pausanias reports that the *Skias* was built by Theodorus of Samos, which would date it to the middle or late sixth century BCE, as Theodorus was a contemporary of Croesus and Polycrates (Herodotus 1.51.3, 3.41.1). Our epigrammatist may be showing his antiquarian learning by having Terpes/Terpander play among the *Skiades* rather than in the *Skias*, which would notionally have been built after Terpander's time.

[258] Gostoli 1990:83.

song.[259] The Spartan *nostos* and the exile from Antissa have a structural harmony: Terpander cannot return "home" to die in the city from which he has been exiled, but must return to his adopted home in Sparta, which will possess his postmortem fame in the form of hero cult at the Carneia. Where had Terpander been that he had to return to Sparta? The answer is suggested by the account that has him winning multiple victories at the Pythian citharodic contest at Delphi ("Plutarch" *On Music* 4.1132e), which could have been circulated from the early sixth century BCE by both the Spartans and the Lesbian citharodes (cf. Section 10 above).[260] Sparta was Terpander's center of gravity, but he was imagined to move in an orbit around it, as did his early *apogonoi*, winning Panhellenic glory as he moved from contest to contest.[261]

15. Pindar's Terpander

Pindar attributes two inventions to Terpander; both are attested only in Pindar. The first is the longer-armed, deeper-pitched version of the tortoise-shell lyre, the *barbitos*:

> τόν ῥα Τέρπανδρός ποθ' ὁ Λέσβιος εὗρεν
> πρῶτος, ἐν δείπνοισι Λυδῶν
> ψαλμὸν ἀντίφθογγον ὑψηλᾶς ἀκούων πακτίδος

> Which once upon a time Terpander the Lesbian
> first invented, as he heard at the banquets of the Lydians

---

[259] Livrea 1993:3n4 makes the tentative suggestion that the author of the epigram, Tryphon, knew early citharodic scholarship on Terpander by Hellanicus of Lesbos or Hieronymus of Rhodes, who wrote a treatise called *On Citharodes* (fr. 33 Wehrli). The killer fig finds an analogue in an anecdote about Anacreon's choking on a grape-pip (cf. Page 1981:99; Livrea 1993:4). The theme is similar, yet tailored for the sympotic context of Anacreontic song (Valerius Maximus *Memorable Deeds and Sayings* 9.12.8; Pliny *Natural History* 7.7). Cf. Rosenmeyer 1992: "Such convenient anecdotes symbolically unite the manner of a poet's life and death" (14n12). On the iconic pose struck by Terpander at the moment of his death, see *Suda* s.v. γλυκὺ μέλι καὶ πνιξάτω, with comments in Part I.18.

[260] Cf. Livrea 1993:4.

[261] There are similarities between Terpander's *nostos* and the story of Arion as related in Herodotus 1.23–24, which draws on Lesbian and Corinthian accounts. Both were preeminent Lesbian citharodes—Arion was a "citharode second to none in his day"— who made their fame as guests in a foreign city in which they had an honored, semi-permanent status. Like Terpander, Arion left his adopted city of Corinth to display his art (in the West), and then returned with his wealth and glory not to his native city of Methymna, but to his second home of Corinth.

the plucking that sounds in answer from the tall harp.

Pindar fr. 125 S-M[262]

These lines are cited by Aristoxenus in a discussion of the plucking technique involved in the playing of the polychord Anatolian harps called the *pêktis* (Doric and Aeolic *pâktis*) and *magadis* (fr. 99 Wehrli *ap.* Athenaeus 14.635b, 635d). Aristoxenus says that they appear in what he calls Pindar's *skolion* to Hieron, the tyrant of Syracuse (ἐν τῷ πρὸς Ἱέρωνα σκολίῳ). *Skolia* were songs intended for performance in the convivial environment of the symposium. They were usually sung monodically to the singer's own lyre or *barbitos*, but they could occasionally be sung to the accompaniment of the *aulos* or simply recited as the symposiast held a sprig of myrtle; a type of "choral" *skolion* was also known.[263] In general, *skolia* were short pieces that symposiasts across the spectrum of musical talent and ability could execute, often, it seems, in a spirit of good-natured competition.[264] Yet the *skolion* was ideally an amateur genre, its performance practice reflective of the aristocratic-egalitarian and spontaneous spirit of the symposium: everyone in the drinking group could have an unpracticed go at one *skolion* or another. Content seems to have varied. Some were brief, anonymous "folk songs," such as we see collected in the corpus of the Attic *skolia*. Others were reperformed (and occasionally recomposed) classics of the Lesbian and Eastern Ionian sympotic lyric repertoire, typically requiring a bit more skill.[265] As one character, presumably a symposiast, says to another in

---

[262] On the technical issues involved in Pindar's description, see Barker 1984:295–296; West 1997:48. The harp's "plucking that sounds in answer" seems to refer to the fact that its high-pitched strings were used to "reply" to another instrument or voice sounding at an octave lower (Barker 1984:295n175).

[263] On *skolia*, see Fabbro 1995, especially the testimonia collected in 3–15. Cf. Harvey 1955:161–163; Herington 1985:49–50; Nagy 1990b:107; Maehler 2004:238.

[264] Cf. the implications of Dicaearchus *On Musical Contests* fr. 88 Wehrli = scholia *ad* Plato *Gorgias* 451e. On the ludic nature of *skolion* singing, see Collins 2004:84–98.

[265] For the recomposition of lyric classics as *skolia*, compare Alcaeus fr. 249 and its notably altered "skoliastic" version, PMG 891. Cf. Fabbro 1992. One etymology of the term *skolion*, which means "crooked," derives it from the "crooked" course the lyre would have followed as it was passed among the select symposiasts who had the skill to execute the more difficult lyric songs, which for this reason are *skolia* strictly speaking (Dicaearchus fr. 88 Wehrli). But this etymology most likely reflects assumptions based in the musical culture of the late Classical period, when fewer laypeople had the proper *paideia* to sing to the lyre a Sappho or Alcaeus composition. A variety of contrasting etymologies were known; see Barker 1984:103n16; Collins 2004:87, with further bibliography. The scholia to *Gorgias* 451e record one tradition according to which the *skolion* was so called by antiphrasis: *skolia* were actually simple songs, not at all tricky or "crooked."

Aristophanes' *Banqueters*, "Sing, please, taking a *skolion* from Alcaeus or Anacreon" (fr. 235 K-A). (We should note that both of these poets were major exponents of the music of the *barbitos*.) Pindaric and Bacchylidean *skolia* were polished, professionalized, lengthier takes on this amateur form, with extended mythical narration approximating what we have in the *epinikia*. Functionally, they were encomiastic songs commissioned by and directed toward powerful and wealthy patrons, at whose symposia they would be performed, typically, it seems, to the *barbitos*, if the several references to the instrument in the fragments of the *skolia* are a reliable indication.[266] Their performance was probably monodic, although the possibility of choral execution, presumably on a smaller scale than that of the *epinikia*, should not be entirely ruled out.[267] So when Pindar attributes the invention of the *barbitos* to Terpander, he is attributing to him the invention of the very instrument to which the *skolion* is being sung.

Indeed, probably in this same *skolion*, Pindar attributes to Terpander the invention of the genre of the *skolion* itself:

ἔτι δέ, καθάπερ Πίνδαρός φησι, καὶ τῶν σκολιῶν μελῶν Τέρπανδρος εὑρετὴς ἦν.

Furthermore, just as Pindar says, Terpander was also the inventor of songs (*melê*) called *skolia*.

Pindar *ap.* "Plutarch" *On Music* 28.1140f[268]

The scholarly response to these texts has been to read them as objective testimony either to Terpander's actual, historical invention of

---

[266] For the overlap of the Pindaric and Bacchylidean *skolion* and *enkomion*, see Maehler 2004:239 ("both terms evidently refer to the same kind of sympotic song"); cf. Harvey 1955:162–163; Cingano 2003; Fearn 2007:27n2, with further bibliography. *Barbitos*: Bacchylides frs. 20B.1, 20C.2 (an *enkomion* also to Hieron of Syracuse); Pindar frs. 125, 124d (probably from the same song as 125). On the Bacchylidean references, see Fearn 2007:41–42. It is possible, of course, that *skolia/enkomia* only *imagine* their performance to the *barbitos* and that *auloi* or even a *kithara* were actually used. But perhaps in this case we are better off taking literally the performative self-references.

[267] See Fabbro 1995:XVI–XVII; Cingano 1990:223, 2003 on possible choral execution.

[268] A majority of scholars now agree that this testimony refers to the same song from which fr. 125 is excerpted. See Gostoli 1990:89–90; cf. van Groningen 1960:118. It could be that the attribution of the invention of the Mixolydian scale (*tonos*) to Terpander, which is reported in the same section of *On Music* as the testimony about his invention of *skolia* (28.1140f = T 37 G), also derives directly or indirectly from the *skolion* of Pindar. The Mixolydian mode was intimately associated with Archaic Lesbian sympotic lyric. Aristoxenus reports the claim that Sappho was its original inventor (fr. 81 Wehrli *ap. On Music* 16.1136c–d). Yet Aristoxenus may also have reported the variant tradition that Terpander invented it, which he could have drawn from Pindar's *skolion*, with which he was familiar (fr. 99 Wehrli).

the *barbitos* and *skolia*, or at least to a Panhellenically held tradition to that effect. Terpander is clearly intended by Pindar to serve as model for his own song-making practice. What has been missing is the basic recognition that Pindar's vision of musico-poetic history is inevitably self-interested, that his representation of Terpander is shaped by a rhetorical agenda determined by the generic and occasional circumstances of his own song. This is not to say that Pindar's claims are not grounded in some mixture of historical practice and traditional belief.[269] Musical traffic between Lydia and Lesbos was very real, as we have already discussed. Harps such as the *pêktis*, redolent of Eastern refinement and *habrosunê* 'delicacy, luxury', were in vogue among Archaic Lesbian elites who prided themselves on their privileged access to the East.[270] The instrument is mentioned by both Alcaeus (fr. 36.5) and Sappho (frs. 22.11, 156.1); Sappho is even said to have been its inventor (Menaechmus FGrH 131 F 4 *ap.* Athenaeus 14.635d). The *pêktis* found a place too in the opulent symposia of Polycrates' Samian court, as Anacreon's erotic lyric attests: νῦν δ' ἁβρῶς ἐρόεσσαν ψάλλω πηκτίδα 'now I pluck delicately (*habrôs*) the lovely *pêktis*' (PMG 373; cf. 386; 374 mentions the *magadis*). The *barbitos* was played in the same class-restricted contexts as the harp (see below), and it is probable that long before Pindar's time it was viewed as a Greco-Lydian hybrid of harp and lyre, a chic, slightly decadent musical accessory to the "lifestyle

---

[269] Pindar's attribution of the *barbitos* to Terpander has no known antecedent. In the eleventh-century CE Persian verse romance *Vāmiq and 'Adhrā* by the poet 'Unṣurī, which adapts significant portions of the Greek novel *Metiochus and Parthenope*, there is a scene set at the court of the Samian tyrant Polycrates. In the scene, Ibycus (Persian: Īfuqūs) sings erotic lyric on the *barbaṭ*, which is likely the *barbitos*. Vāmiq then tells the story of Hermes' (Persian: Hurmuz) creation of the *barbaṭ* with the help of an old man, Hažrah-man, whose name would appear to be a rendering of "Terpander." See discussion in Hägg 1989, with translation of the relevant Persian text on 45–46. It is almost certainly the case that the author of the Greek novel has cobbled together in rationalizing fashion various literary traditions of lyric lore, combining Hermes' invention of the lyre as known from the *Homeric Hymn to Hermes* with the Pindaric tradition of Terpander's invention of the *barbitos* (cf. Hägg 1989:71). The presence of Ibycus, who himself sings to a *barbaṭ*, is intriguing, however. Could Ibycus have already treated Terpander's invention in a lyric song composed for the Polycratean court, where both Lesbian *kitharôidia* and sympotica were in fashion? The chances are slim, and we should note that Ibycus himself does not tell the tale in 'Unṣurī's narrative. Yet, if the tale did have pre-Pindaric currency on Polycratean Samos, much of the argumentation made below for Pindar's "sympoticization" of Terpander at Hieron's Syracusan court would hold true. I plan to return to the late chapter in the "invention of Terpander" represented by this novelistic episode in a future publication.

[270] For the identification of Archaic elites with things Eastern, see Morris 1990:171–185; Kurke 1992.

of *habrosunê*" pursued by its players.[271] Aristotle, writing long after an
elitist backlash against musical *habrosunê* had set in, groups together
with distaste *barbitos* and *pêktis* as instruments a proper gentleman
should not play, despite their former popularity with Archaic aristocrats (*Politics* 8.1341a39–41). The kinship imagined between the two
instruments was based more on cultural semiotics and overlapping
performance contexts than on objective technical and structural similarities—the *barbitos*, like the lyre, had only seven strings that were
struck with a plectrum rather than plucked—yet Pindar, probably not
uniquely, envisages the direct influence of the harp on the construction and technique of the *barbitos*.[272]

We have seen too that the Lesbian Singers advertised their particular engagement with Anatolian culture; recall the implications of
Terpander's manufactured descent from Derdeneus. Archaic Sparta
had its own romance with things Lydian, as Alcman's poetry as well as
his putative Sardian origin indicates.[273] It is conceivable that Lesbian
citharodes self-consciously "Lydianized" their *tekhnê* and personae
for a Spartan audience fascinated by Eastern exotica, playing up the
Asiatic character of the heptachord *kithara* and the "Oriental pomp"
of their *skeuê*; perhaps tales of Terpander's involvement in Lydian
high society and its harp culture were already being put into circulation.[274] References to the "Asiatic" *kithara* appear only after the
middle of the fifth century BCE—perhaps reflective of the New Music's
renewed interest in exotic glamour—but this does not mean that the
Lydian provenance of the *kithara* was not highlighted long before then.
Conceivably, this could have led to the notion that the *kithara* itself
shared certain affinities with both the harp and the *barbitos*, which

---

[271] "Lifestyle": Kurke 1999:185.

[272] There is perhaps another reflex of such assimilation of *barbitos* to harp in Theocritus, who calls the *barbitos polukhordos* (*Idyll* 16.45).

[273] Sources for Alcman's origins, Lydian or Spartan, assembled in Bowra 1961:17–18. Lydian fashion: Alcman PMGF 1.68, a "Lydian head-band"; cf. Sappho frs. 39.3–2, 98a. For a possible reference to the *magadis* in Alcman PMG 101, see West 1992:72–73.

[274] "Oriental pomp": West 1992:55. We may note the attribution of the invention of the *kithara* to the Lydian king Tyrrhenus, who was also known as the inventor of the triangle harp, which visually resembles the *kithara* (Duris FGrH 76 F 81). Another Lydian, Torebus, is credited with the invention of the Lydian *harmonia* ("Plutarch" *On Music* 15.1136c) and with adding a fifth string to the lyre (Boethius *On Music* 1.20). These traditions may be quite early; some version of them may have played a part in the citharodes' own accounts of their art. So too the tradition that Amphion, as inventor of the seven-stringed *kithara*, knew the Lydian mode through his kinship with Tantalus (Pausanias 9.5.4), may have been an early construct of "mainland" citharodes looking to compete with the Lydian prestige of the Lesbian line.

Pindar expanded by making Terpander a *barbitos* player and harp fancier.[275] As to Pindar's envisaging of Terpander as a sympotic singer, it is possible that he extrapolated from a tradition according to which Terpander and the Lesbian Singers performed in Sparta at private, aristocratic symposia of the seventh century BCE or had entertained at the quasi-sympotic, militaristic "public messes" called *sussitia, phiditia,* or *philitia* that were later instituted, probably in the sixth century BCE.[276]

---

[275] See previous note on Tyrrhenus of Lydia, inventor of both harp and *kithara*. The *barbitos* was normally played by a standing, often dance-stepping musician—the Lydianizing comasts on the late Archaic "Anacreontic" vases abundantly illustrate this posture (cf. Price 1990:143n30)—and the practice could have contributed to its conceptual interchangeability with the *kithara*, which was also played by standing, "dancing" musicians (cf. Part I.17). We might even imagine that Archaic *barbitos* players could imagine themselves "playing the citharode" in the Dionysian space of the symposium; the long chitons such players wear on Archaic vases indeed resemble those worn by citharodes. Cf. Nagy 2007a, who suggests that chiton-wearing, *barbitos*-playing Sappho and Alcaeus are implicitly cast as agonistic Panathenaic citharodes in a sympotic scene on an Attic krater of the Brygos Painter (Munich, Antikensammlungen no. 2416; 480–470 BCE). Such casting of the amateur monodists *par excellence* as professional agonists would represent the complementary inverse of Pindar's sympotic makeover of professional Terpander. Bell 1995:25–30 argues that this Attic vessel, discovered in Sicily near the ancient site of Acragas, was commissioned by the Emmenid tyrant Xenocrates of Acragas, for whose son, Thrasyboulus, Pindar composed *Isthmian 2*. That song significantly compares the erotic lyric of Alcaeus and (probably) Sappho (see scholia to line 3) with the professional poetry of Pindar (cf. Nagy 2007a:235). It could be that both vase and ode reflect a professionalization of sympotic musical culture at the Acragantine tyrannical court akin to what we see at Hieron's Syracusan court. See discussion below. An Acragantine citharode, Moschus, competed at the Panathenaia in the later fifth century BCE (scholia *ad* Aristophanes *Acharnians* 13).

[276] On the transition in Sparta from an aristocratic sympotic culture to the egalitarian "messes," see Bowie 1990b:225n16; Powell 1998:129; Hodkinson 2000:217–218; Quattrocelli 2002:16–17. Laconian vase painting of the sixth century BCE does yield several examples of lyre players entertaining at convivial gatherings, but we cannot ascertain the identity of these musicians; some may be divinities rather than mortals. See Pipili 1987:51–52; Stibbe 1992. Diogenes of Babylon and Photius both offer testimony to the effect that Terpander sang for the Spartans in their *philitia* or *sussitia*. But these reports may themselves represent the remainder of an elitist, post-Pindaric recasting of Terpander as a sympotic rather than agonistic singer, as the insistence of Philodemus, correcting Diogenes, that Terpander "sang in the *agônes*" suggests. See n224 above. Quattrocelli 2002, following Vetta 1983:XXIV–XXV, makes the argument for Terpander as a largely convivial composer, but this necessitates taking the Pindaric testimony too literally and misunderstanding the predominantly public nature of *kitharôidia*. Nor do the Terpandrean fragments support this view; the spondaic fr. 3 G is hardly "sicuramente" from a *skolion melos* (Quattrocelli 2002:18–19), and fr. 8 G, an anonymous libation song, was only attributed to Terpander, and dubiously so, by Bergk in the nineteenth century. This is not to say, however, that historical citharodes never performed on occasion in private (or semi-private) sympotic contexts; some obviously did. See discussion below.

Yet, for all this, Pindar's *barbitos*-playing, sympotic Terpander nevertheless remains a tendentious construct. It is as if one were to commemorate Paganini as the first to compose parlor songs for the guitar (which he did in fact play), when all the world knows him as the iconic violin virtuoso of the grand concert hall. In the mainstream tradition, which in all probability captures the historical situation of the Lesbian Singers in Sparta and elsewhere, Terpander was the paradigmatic professional citharode, at home in the public spectacle of the *mousikoi agônes* rather than the inscrutable confines of the symposium. Hellanicus of Lesbos knew Terpander above all as the victor at the inaugural citharodic contest at the Carneia, where the Lesbian *diadokhê* won its fame ("Plutarch" *On Music* 6.1133c). Heraclides of Pontus says emphatically in his assessment of Terpander's work that he performed his *nomoi* "in the *agônes*" (*On Music* 3.1132c). Indeed, the monumental *nomos* and its accompanying *prooimion* are the genres for which Terpander and the citharodes were best known. As for the *barbitos*, its use, on Lesbos, Samos, and in Athens, was largely confined to the Orientalizing aristocratic symposium and its attendant comastic celebrations; it was, as far as we can tell, not played in open, civic contexts, and certainly not at *mousikoi agônes*. So deeply implicated in the musical culture of the social elite was the *barbitos* that for Alcaeus it was as if the instrument were a living peer of his sympotic circle: it "makes merry as it participates in the symposium" (ἀθύρει πεδέχων συμποσίω, Alcaeus fr. 70.3–4).[277] As such, the *barbitos* was strongly marked with an elitist and amateur ethos, from which its aristocratically prized connotations of Eastern luxury were inseparable. The "Asiatic" concert *kithara* was similarly an elite instrument, but its elitism was of a radically different order: professionalized, virtuosic, technically daunting, and very much implicated in the demotic festival culture of the *polis*, not the *musica occulta* (as Nero called it) of the symposium.

The Archaic poetic and visual record makes it abundantly clear that the primary exponents of Aeolic and Ionic erotic and sympotic lyric, Sappho, Alcaeus, and Anacreon, were also the primary exponents of the *barbitos*.[278] Anacreon, who likely brought its culture to the

---

[277] Cf. discussion of this fragment in Part I.22.iv. As Sappho's poetry suggests and Classical Athenian vase painting indicates, the *barbitos* also makes its way into the hands of women in restricted contexts of domestic music making. On the instrument and its sociology, see Maas and Snyder 1989:39–40, 113–138; West 1992:58–59; Wilson 2003b:190–193; Nagy 2007a; Power 2007.

[278] See Nagy 2007a:237–243 for concise commentary and bibliography on Athenian vase paintings of Sappho, Alcaeus, and Anacreon with the *barbitos*.

aristocratic and tyrannical symposia of Athens when he relocated to the city from Samos, was so closely identified with it that he was made its inventor (Neanthes FGrH 84 F 5 *ap.* Athenaeus 4.175e). It was these poets too whose works provided the material for the *skolia* sung by later symposiasts, and this must explain the retention of the *barbitos* in the stylized *skolia* of Pindar and Bacchylides—it was the generically and occasionally appropriate instrument to use.[279]

But again, outside of Pindar, no visual or literary evidence connects Terpander to the *barbitos* or *skolia* as it does Alcaeus, Sappho, and Anacreon. Why then did Pindar choose to adopt Terpander as a model for his own composition and performance of *skolia* instead of one of these other poets? One answer could be found in the very fact that the prevalent image of Terpander was essentially that of a professional musician. Pindar too was a professional. Yet the sympotic *skolion*, as we saw, was traditionally considered an amateur genre, and the *barbitos* an amateur's instrument. By fashioning Terpander as the inventor of the genre and its hallmark accompanying instrument, Pindar creates a validating precedent for his own professional (and commercial) intervention in this decidedly amateur medium. The contributions of an Alcaeus or an Anacreon are trumped, as it were, by the foundational activity of Terpander, who is not only the iconic lyric professional but also, as Pindar envisages him, the super-elite East Greek monodist *par excellence*, drawing his music straight from the source of haute-aristocratic Lydian *habrosunê*. It is that hyper-authentic musico-sympotic practice to which Pindar's *skolion* hearkens, and whose impossible glamour its performance notionally reenacts in Syracuse.[280] Terpander's prestige is thus made to authenticate and legitimate Pindar's role in the professionalization of sympotic musical culture at the tyrannical court of Hieron, to bridge, or rather to obscure, the ideological gap between the deliberate, commercial ethos of the professional and the resolutely non-professional, egalitarian, and spontaneous ethos of the symposium and its traditional *skolia*.[281] Again, although the Pindaric scenario

---

[279] Simonides too had probably mentioned the *barbitos* in an encomium for the Thessalian Scopadai, to which Theocritus *Idyll* 16.45 probably alludes. Cf. West 1992:58n47. Proclus in Photius *Bibliotheca* 321a12 makes the *barbitos* the essential instrument for accompaniment of *skolia*.

[280] Or possibly Aetna, the city founded in 475 BCE by Hieron. Bacchylides "sends" his *enkomion* for the tyrant to the "men of the symposium at well-built Aetna" (20C.6–7).

[281] Cf. *Olympian* 1.14–18, where the professional performance of the epinician ode is assimilated into the exclusive ambience of Hieron's symposium, yet is also positively contrasted to the amateur *mousikê* that is normally made there. Discussion in Morgan 1993:3. We may compare too the rhetorico-ideological work done in Pindar *Isthmian*

may build upon preexisting themes in the cultures of *kitharôidia* and sympotic lyric, the Terpander he creates is tailored to the specific purposes of his generic and performative rhetoric.

To understand still better what was at stake in Pindar's invocation of the Lesbian citharode, however, we should consider more closely the local context of Pindar's encomiastic song and the cultural interests of its addressee. It seems that Hieron had, like tyrants before him, engaged not only choral and encomiastic poets such as Simonides, Pindar, and Bacchylides, but star citharodes as well.[282] Consider the implications of the following scholion to Aristophanes' *Clouds*, which cites the research of Ister of Cyrene, a third-century BCE historian and author of a work called *On Melic Poets*:

ὁ Φρῦνις κιθαρῳδὸς Μιτυληναῖος. οὗτος δὲ δοκεῖ πρῶτος παρ' Ἀθηναίοις κιθαρῳδικῇ νικῆσαι Παναθήναια ἐπὶ Καλλιμάχου (Meier: Καλλίου codd.) ἄρχοντος. ἦν δὲ Ἀριστοκλείτου μαθητής. ὁ δὲ Ἀριστόκλειτος τὸ γένος ἦν ἀπὸ Τερπάνδρου, ἤκμασε δὲ ἐν τῇ Ἑλλάδι κατὰ τὰ Μηδικά. παραλαβὼν δὲ τὸν Φρῦνιν αὐλῳδοῦντα κιθαρίζειν ἐδίδαξεν. ὁ δὲ Ἴστρος Ἱέρωνος αὐτόν φησι μάγειρον ὄντα σὺν ἄλλοις δοθῆναι τῷ Ἀριστοκλείτῳ. ταῦτα δὲ σχεδιάσαι ἔοικεν· εἰ γὰρ ἦν γεγονὼς δοῦλος καὶ μάγειρος Ἱέρωνος, οὐκ ἂν ἀπέκρυψαν οἱ κωμικοὶ πολλάκις αὐτοῦ μεμνημένοι ἐφ' οἷς ἐκαινούργησε κλάσας τὴν ᾠδὴν παρὰ τὸ ἀρχαῖον ἔθος, ὡς Ἀριστοφάνης φησὶ καὶ Φερεκράτης (Burges: Ἀριστοκράτης codd.).

Phrynis was a citharode from Mytilene. He seems to have been the first to win in *kitharôidia* at the Athenian Panathenaia, while Callimachus was archon (446/5 BCE).[283] He was a student of Aristocleitus. Aristocleitus was of the line (*genos*)

2.1-13—an epinician ode for a member of the tyrannical family of Sicilian Acragas—to reconcile the realities of musico-poetic professionalism (Pindar's "mercenary Muse") with the romanticized amateurism of old-time, aristocratic sympotic love lyric. See Nagy 1989, 1990:340–342; Kurke 1991:240–256.

[282] Aeschylus was also lured to Syracuse and Aetna by the tyrant. Cf. Herington 1967; Podlecki 1980:387–395.

[283] Callias, the name transmitted in the manuscripts of the scholia, was archon in 456/5, which was not a Panathenaic year. The name has thus been changed to Callimachus, in whose archon year the *agônes* of the Great Panathenaia would have been held. It is likely too that that year, 446/5, was the first in which Pericles' reformed version of the festival was instituted; thus the otherwise absurd claim that Phrynis was "the first to win in *kitharôidia* at the Athenian Panathenaia." Definitive discussion in Davison 1958:40–41.

descended from Terpander, and he was at the peak of his career throughout Greece at the time of the Persian Wars. Taking on Phrynis when the latter was still an aulode, he taught him to play the *kithara*. But Ister (FGrH 334 F 50) says Phrynis was Hieron's cook and was given along with some others to Aristocleitus. But he likely invented this story, for if Phrynis had been Hieron's slave and cook, the comic poets would not have concealed it, since they often mention him for the musical innovations he introduced, with which he made his style of song feeble and effeminate (*klaô*), in contrast to its ancient character. So say Aristophanes and Pherecrates.[284]

Scholia *ad* Aristophanes *Clouds* 971a[285]

As the scholiast indicates, Phrynis was repeatedly attacked in Old Comedy. It is possible, then, that a comic source lies behind the testimony that he began his musical career practicing *aulôidia*, a *tekhnê* of considerably lesser prestige than *kitharôidia*—this sounds like a deprecation of the citharode's skill, or perhaps some joking *aition* for the *aulos*-like complexity of Phrynis' innovative *kitharôidia*.[286] Ister's claim that Phrynis had been a cook and slave probably also derives, at least in part, from comic abuse, despite the fact that it is rejected by the scholiast on the grounds that "the comic poets would not have concealed it" had they known it. Another practitioner of the New Music, the dithyrambist Philoxenus of Cythera, was also assigned servile origins, again, probably first by a comedian.[287] The truth of the matter, however, must

---

[284] Cf. Aristophanes *Clouds* 969–971. The manuscripts have Aristocrates, but Pherecrates seems better. Phrynis is subject to attack for his New Musical innovation in Pherecrates *Cheiron* fr. 155.14–18 K-A.

[285] *Suda* s.v. Φρῦνις repeats much the same information, with some interesting variations. Instead of Aristocleitus, it has Aristocleides, who is called a *kitharistês*. It adds the information that Ister's testimony comes from his *On Melic Poets*, that Phrynis was the son of Kamon (the manuscripts have καρβωνος, but Kamon, elsewhere attested, seems better than the "Kanops" adopted in Adler's *Suda* edition; cf. Hordern 2002:259), and that "many others" besides Phrynis were given to Aristocleitus by Hieron. On the verb *klaô* as a gendered term of musical criticism, cf. LSJ s.v. κλάω 3. The *Suda* has the compound form *kataklaô*. The reference is presumably to the exharmonic "bends" (*kampai*) for which Phrynis is criticized in *Clouds* 969–971.

[286] Cf. Part I.15n273. A third possibility is that the story alludes to his compositions for dithyrambic choruses, although there is no evidence for these.

[287] Philoxenus was called Doulon because he had been a *doulos* 'slave': Hesychius s.v. Δούλωνα = fr. adesp. 74 Kock. Cf. *Suda* s.v. Φιλόξενος, which records that Philoxenus was sold to the Athenian dithyrambist Melanippides, who, we may infer, taught him the art of dithyrambic song. Similarly, Phrynis is said by Ister to have been given to Aristocleitus, who taught him *kitharôidia*. The Spartan general Lysander cuttingly

be that Phrynis was a protégé, or at least a closely affiliated successor, of the Terpandrean *apogonos* Aristocleitus; the two likely came into contact first on Lesbos.[288]

Phrynis' chronology is impossible to establish with certainty, but some general outlines can be made out.[289] He was victorious in Athens in 446 BCE, but was still performing at least into the late 420s, when he was mocked in Aristophanes' *Clouds* (originally produced in 423) and (probably) defeated by his young rival, Timotheus of Miletus (PMG 802).[290] If Phrynis appeared as a living character in Eupolis' *Demes*, which was produced sometime between 417 and 410, then his performance career presumably extended past 420.[291] Assuming Phrynis was in his early 20s when he won at the Panathenaia of 446, then he would have been born in the early to mid 460s, early enough to have been trained as a young man by an aging Aristocleitus, whose Panhellenic fame had been at its height (ἤκμασε) around 480. (Or, from a more skeptical point of view, Phrynis was born early enough at least to have made the plausible claim that he was the student of Aristocleitus, and thus a direct inheritor of the Terpandrean legacy.) By comparison, Diodorus Siculus 14.46.6 says that Timotheus was at his career peak (ἤκμασε) in 398, when he was almost 50 or slightly older, yet he lived four decades more, and presumably remained musically active throughout those years.

What is unlikely is that Phrynis would have had direct contact, as cook or citharode, with Hieron, who died in 466, although he may well have enjoyed successes in any number of *agônes* across post-tyrannical Sicily and Italy during his own life.[292] The story of Phrynis' service to the tyrant must derive rather from his relationship to Aristocleitus, who very likely did interact with Hieron. The two are chronologically

---

asked a citharode seeking his patronage if the citharode in fact wanted to be his slave: Plutarch *Life of Lysander* 18.5.

[288] Cf. Davison 1958:40–41.

[289] Cf. Telò 2007:28–33.

[290] Timotheus must have begun performing in the 420s. Parian Marble Ep. 76 dates Timotheus' death, at age 90, somewhere between 366/5 and 357/6 BCE. *Suda* s.v. Τιμόθεος records that he died at age 96. We can thus put his birthdate in the mid to late 450s or early 440s; this dating would accord with the statement of Diodorus Siculus 14.46.6 that Timotheus was in his prime in 398. Cf. Wilamowitz 1903:67n4.

[291] Cf. Taplin 1993:42–43; Storey 2003a:169–170; 112–114 for the date of the play (he proposes 417–416 BCE). Telò 2007 proposes the later date of 410, after Phrynis was long dead; he argues that the citharode appeared as a character in the Underworld.

[292] In Eupolis *Golden Race* fr. 303 K-A, a citharode named Alcaeus is addressed ὦ Σικελιῶτα Πελοποννήσιε '[Alcaeus] of Sicily and from the Peloponnese'. Could this Alcaeus be a Lesbian Singer who made his name, like his Lesbian predecessors Arion and Phrynis, at both the Spartan Carneia and in Sicily? *Golden Race* was probably produced in the mid 420s BCE; cf. Storey 2003a:267, 275.

matched. Hieron assumed power in Syracuse in 478, while Aristocleitus was still enjoying the glory of his Panhellenic fame. Ister's anecdote suggests that their connection may have amounted to a fairly intimate patronal relationship, as Arion's seems to have been with Periander of Corinth. This is not to say that Hieron did not actively support a public culture of *kitharôidia* at festivals in Syracuse and other Sicilian cities under his rule. Southern Italy and Sicily had been, after all, an enthusiastic market for *kitharôidia*, perhaps Lesbian *kitharôidia* in particular, since the late seventh century, as the story of Arion's tour of the region indicates.[293] Hieron would logically have taken an interest in attracting to Sicily the most Panhellenically renowned of all citharodes, the Lesbian Singers of the Terpandrean *genos*, to advertise the cultural prestige of his regime both on Sicily and across all Greece.

But we may speculate that the tyrant was intent too on making Aristocleitus and his musico-poetic prestige a more personal possession. That is, the Lesbian citharode might have been more closely integrated into Hieron's inner circle, as a retainer to the tyrannical house. In this capacity, he might have "represented" Hieron at Panhellenic and prominent local *agônes* abroad, including the Panathenaia, where stories such as we have in Ister about his relationship with the tyrant, stories which would later include his student/successor, Phrynis, began to circulate.[294]

---

[293] Relevant is the civic reorganization in 461 BCE of the citizenry of the Sicilian city of Camarina on the model of the strings of the lyre (or *kithara*). Cf. Cordano 1994. On the one hand, the lyrico-political ordering of the city hearkens back to ancient *doxa* that a "lyre-founded city would gain metaphysical protection and enjoy social unity" (Franklin 2006a:59); on the other, it could reflect more popular enthusiasms for contemporary *kitharôidia*, which had been stimulated throughout Sicily by the culturally ambitious and competitive tyrants of Syracuse, Gela, and Acragas. It is perhaps significant that we find two of the earliest appearances of the word *kithara* in Epicharmus (frs. 68.1; 108.2), who worked in Syracuse during the reign of Hieron. Citharodic performance per se is not at issue in either fragment, however.

[294] For a citharode's advertising the prestige of a patron at foreign festivals, cf. Part I.21n376 (Arion and Periander of Corinth); Part IV.3 (Lysander and Aristonous). At least one Olympic athlete had Hieron's name announced alongside his own in his victory proclamation: Pausanias 6.13.1. For the Sicilian tyrants' interest in Panathenaic musical prestige, see Nagy 2007a:234–235. It is tempting to compare the case of the aulete Midas of Acragas, who was a Panathenaic victor (scholia *ad Pythian* 12 inscr.). Pindar wrote an epinician ode to commemorate another of Midas' victories, this one at the Pythian auletic *agôn* (*Pythian* 12, 490 BCE). Midas is surely a professional name; cf. Clay 1992: "Midas was a Phrygian name, and the *aulos* was thought to have been of Phrygian origin" (519). The fact that Pindar mentions neither Midas' father nor family suggests too that he was a foreigner, quite possibly from Phrygia, who had adopted Acragas as his home. There is a good chance that he served as a retainer to the dynastic family of Acragas, the Emmenidai, one of whom, Xenocrates, brother of

At the Syracusan court, he might, like the professional poet Pindar, have provided citharodic music for the tyrant's symposia. We may compare the case of another royal collector of poets and musicians, Archelaus of Macedon, who hosted Timotheus, the most renowned citharode of the later fifth century BCE, at his court in Pella. One telling anecdote has the two haggling over compensation in what is clearly the context of a symposium at which Timotheus is entertaining:

> Ἀρχελάῳ δὲ δοκοῦντι γλισχροτέρῳ περὶ τὰς δωρεὰς εἶναι Τιμόθεος ᾄδων ἐνεσήμαινε πολλάκις τουτὶ τὸ κομμάτιον· 'σὺ δὲ τὸν γηγενέταν ἄργυρον αἰνεῖς.' ὁ δ' Ἀρχέλαος οὐκ ἀμούσως ἀντεφώνησε 'σὺ δέ γ' αἰτεῖς'.

> When Archelaus seemed rather grudging when it came to gifts Timotheus would often sing this phrase to remind him: 'But you praise earth-born silver'. And Archelaus would reply not unmusically (οὐκ ἀμούσως), 'But you demand it'.

> Plutarch *On the Fortune of Alexander*
334b = PMG 801[295]

Although citharodic performance was normally at home in the public festival, tyrannical symposia, larger-scale and more lavish events than the symposia of private citizens, could accommodate, and conspicuously so, command performances by musical stars such as Aristocleitus and Timotheus, who would normally be singing before crowds of thousands.[296] Such command performances, far more the exception than the rule, would obviously serve to showcase the means and distinction of the tyrant; they might even have included

---

the Emmenid tyrant Theron, won a Pythian chariot victory in 490 BCE, the subject of Pindar *Pythian* 6, the same year Midas won his musical victory. Perhaps the two traveled together to Delphi; perhaps too their victories and victory odes were celebrated in conjunction with one another in Acragas. Midas presumably had sufficient money to afford Pindar's services—and *Pythian* 12 is quite short—but there is the possibility that the Emmenidai themselves commissioned the ode for Midas—a self-promoting gift, as Pindar's song ultimately speaks to the discrimination and influence of the aulete's patrons. On tyrannical interest in *aulêtikê*, see Barker 1990:55.

[295] Cf. Plutarch *Sayings of Kings* 177b. We should understand Archelaus as actually *singing* his "antiphonal" rejoinder. Such direct participation is typical of music making in the symposium, although here its normatively amateur ethos is perverted by the commercial implications of the sung exchange. For relevant discussions of the sympotic practice of "criticizing" existing songs through recomposition—alteration or augmentation—see West 1974:17–18; Ford 1999:120; Collins 2004:63–98.

[296] For the distinction between private and tyrannical symposia, see Cingano 1990:220–223; Vetta 1992: "il simposio tirannico è il luogo della professionalità" (209).

explicitly encomiastic elements. However, the inclusion of fee-earning professional musicians—we think first of all of the χρήματα μεγάλα 'big money' amassed by Arion (Herodotus 1.24.1)—into the ethically non-professional, notionally egalitarian Archaic symposium could be ideologically problematic. We see a reflection of this in the anecdote about Timotheus at the court of Archelaus. The crass haggling of musician and king, in song no less, is a sympotic *faux pas*. Despite the fact that their relationship is mystified as one of reciprocal gift exchange, as if between companions or friends, *hetairoi* and *philoi*—we should recall how Aristocleitus is said by Ister to have received gifts from Hieron—it is in fact based on wages and services, and this fact inevitably alters the tone and integrity of sympotic musical culture.[297]

The openly commercial ideology of fifth-century professional *kitharôidia* is at odds with the professed economic disinterest of the aristocratic symposium, where *kharis*, the graceful exchange of favors and gestures of goodwill between friends is the rule. Commerce and *kharis* are a difficult fit; their suture can require the rhetorical virtuosity of a Pindar.[298] Thus, to return to Pindar's sympotic praise song for Hieron, we can be confident that the invocation of Terpander alludes to and flatters the tyrant's overall investment in citharodic culture; it highlights in particular his privileged "possession" of one of the very *apogonoi* of Terpander.[299] Yet perhaps Pindar also intends for his sympotic Terpander not only to serve as a model for his own professional contribution to the symposium, but to naturalize Aristocleitus' presence there as well. If the paradigmatic professional citharode Terpander could be invited to Lydian banquets and could invent the definitive style of sympotic drinking song, then it is only right for

---

[297] On the ideology of the wage, *misthos*, cf. Will 1975.

[298] On gift exchange as a means of mystifying the real economic relationship between aristocratic citizen and professional female "companions," *hetairai*, at the symposium, see Davidson 1997:109–111; cf. Kurke 1999:185–186. Significantly, the anecdotal tradition frames the relationship between the lyrico-aristocratic exemplar Anacreon and his tyrannical patron Polycrates as one of *kharis* and "equal" gift exchange between friends: Aelian *Historical Miscellanies* 9.4; Stobaeus *Florilegium* 4.31. See Nicholson 2005 for Pindar's rhetorical shading over of the unseemly professional realities of athletic culture in his *epinikia*. Cf. too the insights of Neer 2002:87–131, who speculates that sympotic elites in Athens encouraged the ideological fiction that the potters and painters of the drinking vessels they used were gift-giving friends and social equals, so as to "erase" the disruptive reality that these essential objects of sympotic culture were objects merely bought from commercial artisans. For Nero's idiosyncratic use of sympotic rhetoric to negotiate private and professional musical identities, see Part I.9.

[299] For a possible allusion to another Terpandrean *apogonos*, Euainetidas, at *Pythian* 4.177, see Part II.10.

one of his descendants to join in the tyrannical symposium as one of Hieron's friends and companions. That Aristocleitus was bought and paid for by the tyrant, as was Pindar, is accordingly obscured, if not entirely forgotten.

Finally, we may not want to rule out the possibility, tentative as it must be, that Pindar's *skolion* was performed for Hieron not by Pindar himself, but by a qualified intermediary, namely Aristocleitus. The openings of the two preserved Bacchylidean sympotic *enkomia*, including 20C, for Hieron, make it clear that while the poet elaborates the fiction that he is physically present at the performance and actually singing to the *barbitos*, he is in fact not present but only "sending" (*pempein*) his song to the symposium, where it will be performed by others (20B.3, 20C.6).[300] The technical demands of performing professional *skolia* were surely greater than those needed to sing a traditional *skolion*, but presumably not so great that an especially talented member of Hieron's family or circle of friends could not have mastered them. We think of *Nemean* 4.13–16, in which the father of the *laudandus* is imagined to reperform the victory ode to the lyre at a symposium, or the lyric performance of the aristocratic Damophilus at the symposium of the Cyrenean king Arcesilas described in *Pythian* 4.294–297. But the Terpandrean "signature" that distinguishes the *skolion* for Hieron would make it especially suitable for performance by a Terpandrean *apogonos*. Certainly, the evocation of the bygone Lydian glamour of Terpander's sympotic music making would take on added resonance if it were Aristocleitus, playing the part of an aristocratic symposiast, who sang the *skolion* to the *barbitos* and thus palpably reenacted his ancestor's inventions.[301]

---

[300] Carey 1989:564n49; cf. Fearn 2007:41.

[301] Of course, in this scenario it is conceivable that Aristocleitus would have sung the *skolion* to his concert *kithara*, and that the *barbitos* was only intended as an archaizing, stylized conceit; cf. n266 above. But that need not have been the case; for one, the link with the sympotic Terpander described by Pindar would have been more obvious if the *skolion* were actually sung to the *barbitos*. Vetta 1983:LII-LIII has argued for the existence of a tradition of encomiastic *kitharôidia* at tyrannical courts, yet this seems to overstate the case. It is one thing for a star citharode to entertain at a private gathering, and perhaps to compliment the patron with some choice remarks or by singing flattering mythical narratives in his *nomoi*; it is another thing to for him to serve as a dedicated praise singer in the manner of a Pindar. Nevertheless, Hieron, with his outsized narcissism and cultural ambitiousness, may have encouraged this unique combination of encomiastic poetry and *kitharôidia*, scaled to the practical and ideological horizons of the symposium: a sympotic encomium composed by Pindar and performed to the *barbitos* by a Lesbian citharode. For some suggestive associations between Timotheus, Simonides, Bacchylides, and the *barbitos* at the Macedonian court of Alexander, see Section III.6 above.

Part IV
Panathenaic *Kitharôida*

1. *Kitharôidia* Comes to Athens

B Y THE BEGINNING of the fifth century BCE, and probably still earlier, Athens had become a premier market for *kitharôidia*, its Panathenaic *mousikoi agônes* overshadowing the long-established regional contests at the Spartan Carneia and rivaling the international allure of the Pythian games at Delphi. The city's emergence as a citharodic center had everything to do with the regime of the Peisistratids, who played a key role in instituting and promoting the art at the Panathenaia from at least the middle of the sixth century BCE, when Peisistratus finally consolidated his rule in Athens (the "third tyranny").[1] It cannot be a coincidence that beginning in the period 550–540 BCE we see the first black-figured images in the Attic ceramic record of what appear to be mortal citharodes, who are very likely, if not certainly, meant to represent competitors at the Panathenaia.[2] By 530–520 BCE, citharodes (and citharists) standing on the festival *bêma* 'platform' and performing for judges and spectators are routinely represented on red-figured vases.

---

[1] I follow Shapiro 1989:2, who dates Peisistratus' third seizure of power in Athens to 546 BCE, after the Battle of Pallene.

[2] Cf. Davison 1958:37; Shapiro 1992:65–66, who notes the ambiguities inherent in interpreting these early images, which are, however, not entirely obstructive. First, we cannot be sure how many of the citharodes are meant to represent Apollo. A reasonable view might be that some are Apollo, but others very probably are not. We will return to this problem below. Second, are they citharodes or citharists? Musicians who are not depicted singing pose particular difficulty. My assumption, however, is that the great majority of figures playing *kitharai* on Attic vases, Archaic and Classical, are citharodes, given the unarguably greater popularity and prestige of *kitharôidia*. Also, there is the sheer fact that more citharodes than citharists performed: in the fourth century, five prizes were awarded to citharodes, only three to citharists (and, notably, to rhapsodes; IG II² 2311.1–11, 15–19). Cf. similar reasoning in Kotsidu 1991:106. Third, because the citharodes are not depicted on the official Panathenaic amphorae that were distributed to victors, and because neither judges nor spectators nor a *bêma* 'platform' are shown in the scenes, a Panathenaic performance setting cannot be certain. But in most images there is fortunately "an unmistakable allusion to the Panathenaia in the columns that flank the scene on both sides" (Shapiro 1992:65). A citharode appears on a Panathenaic-shaped amphora from 550–540 BCE (British Museum, London B 139; Shapiro, p. 66 with fig. 43). Images of aulodes and auletes from the same period are more distinctly shown in agonistic settings suggestive of the Panathenaia; see Shapiro 1992:61.

The setting for the majority of these images must be the Panathenaic *agônes*.[3] Furthermore, such images far outnumber those of competitors in other *mousikoi agônes* during this period, the aulodes, auletes, and rhapsodes.[4] Around 530 BCE we also begin to see images of Heracles *kitharôidos*, a figure that is unmistakably linked to Peisistratid investment in Heraclean myth and cult as well as the Panathenaia festival, and that strongly suggests the tyrants' interest in associating themselves specifically with the prestige of *kitharôidia* at the Panathenaia.

Since Peisistratus died in 528 BCE, the civic focus on *kitharôidia* that is illustrated by the later-sixth-century iconography must actually have been fostered by his sons Hippias and Hipparchus, who succeeded their father as co-rulers and governed until the murder of Hipparchus in 514 BCE—significantly, at the Panathenaia festival (Herodotus 5.55–56; Thucydides 6.56)—and then the deposition and exile of Hippias in 511/10 BCE. Hipparchus seems to have been especially involved in stimulating musical and poetic culture in the city. Aristotle refers to him as a music-lover, φιλόμουσος (*Constitution of Athens* 18.1); one modern scholar has appropriately dubbed him a "Minister for Cultural Affairs."[5] His name was linked with the composer of choral melic Simonides of Ceos and the lyric monodist Anacreon of Teos, both of whom he induced to make Athens and his tyrannical court a creative home base.[6] To Hipparchus was also attributed the regulation of the rhapsodic recitation of Homeric *epos* at the Panathenaia.[7] In the "Platonic" dialogue *Hipparchus* 228c we read that with his cultural initiatives Hipparchus was intent on "educating (*paideuein*) the citizens, so that those subject to his rule might be as good as possible." Beneath the anachronistic "Socratic" rhetoric of this statement—the ethical emphasis on securing the "goodness" of the citizens—we can detect a more practical policy of sociopolitical organization and ideological manipulation through the

---

3   Cf. Shapiro 1992:66–67; Bundrick 2005:161–163.
4   A trend that will continue through the fifth century as well. Cf. Kotsidu 1991:105. Aulodes and auletes, however, outnumber citharodes in the period 550–540 BCE; cf. Shapiro 1992:61, with discussion below.
5   Herington 1985:250n61. Cf. Aloni 1984.
6   "Plato" *Hipparchus* 228b and Aelian *Historical Miscellanies* 8.2; Aristotle *Athenian Constitution* 18.1–2 says that Hipparchus sent too for "other poets," and we should probably include the dithyrambic composer Lasus of Hermione in that group. See Herington 1985:92–93. Lasus, as Herington argues, likely produced choral dithyrambs in the time of Hipparchus. The institution of dramatic contests at the City Dionysia dates from the 530s, when Peisistratus was still in power (Herington 1985:87–91, who notes the continuities between the tragic contests and the Panathenaic musical contests).
7   "Plato" *Hipparchus* 228b–c.

spectacle of civic cultural events, a policy his father Peisistratus very likely had early on explored.[8] As we will see, *kitharôidia* was an important component of that policy; it also had a significant role to play in the tyrants' shaping of the image of Athens abroad.

But first, let us step back in time. Although some confusing testimony from Plutarch (*Life of Pericles* 13) would date the introduction of the *mousikoi agônes*, including the *agôn* in *kitharôidia*, to the middle of the fifth century BCE, scholars are now in agreement that it should not be taken literally. This testimony, which claims that Pericles was the first to pass a decree (*psêphisma*) instituting *mousikoi agônes* at the Panathenaia, cannot be taken to mean that contests were held for the first time at the festival under Pericles. The visual evidence makes this unmistakably clear.[9] It is more likely the case that Pericles undertook a reorganization of the *agônes*, no doubt seeking to recoup for himself the popular favor that the tyrants had enjoyed in the previous century with their sponsorship of festival musical culture—as Plutarch says, he acted from motives of φιλοτιμία 'desire for public recognition'.

Yet we cannot be sure exactly when or at whose initiative the *mousikoi agônes* were officially instituted at the sixth-century Panathenaia. We can be fairly certain that in 566 BCE an older civic festival of Athena was drastically reorganized and a penteteric Great Panathenaia was established, with a Lesser Panathenaia being celebrated every year. One source points to Peisistratus as the reorganizer, but the fact that he assumed power for the first time only five years after 566 makes this testimony problematic. Another, more credible source would indicate that it was the Philaid aristocrat Hippocleides who led the effort to reorganize the festival in 566, the year he was (likely) archon.[10] Although it would be about 20 years until the appearance of the first vase paintings of what appear to be Panathenaic musical performances, with *kithara* or *aulos*, there is no reason to think that musical events were not included in the reorganization of the festival from the

---

[8] On the "Socratic" biases of the *Hipparchus*, see Herington 1985:250n64.

[9] As recognized by Davison 1958:36–41 (who believes, however, that musical contests were suspended after the Persian Wars and restarted by Pericles); cf. Shapiro 1989:41, 1992:57–58; Kotsidu 1991:32; Herington 1985:86; Bundrick 2005:171, all of whom argue for the unbroken continuity of the contests from the time of the Peisistratids.

[10] A scholion to Aelius Aristides 13.189.4–5 has Peisistratus establishing the Great Panathenaia; Marcellinus *Life of Thucydides* 2–4, perhaps citing Pherecydes of Athens, says that the new festival was established in the year Hippocleides was archon (Eusebius *Chronicle* Olympiad 53.3–4 supplies the 566/5 date for the reorganization). Hippocleides likely led a "coalition of leading elites," including Peisistratus: Forsdyke 2005:117.

start. It is significant that Hippocleides—assuming it was he who led the reorganization—had conspicuous links by marriage to the tyrant Periander (Herodotus 6.128.2) and by guest-friendship to the tyrant Cleisthenes of Sicyon (6.129), both of whom were practiced manipulators of festival performance politics.[11] As to the time gap between the 566 date and the appearance of contest scenes in the iconography, conceivably it took about two decades or so for the *mousikoi agônes* to "catch on," attracting the interest of talented performers from Athens and abroad as well as the enthusiasm of Athenian audiences, in particular, Athenian elites, on whose sympotic vessels the contest scenes mostly appear.[12] We will see that this may have been particularly true of *kitharôidia*. Again, these scenes began to appear with frequency only when Peisistratus assumed his third tyranny in the mid 540s, and this synchronicity would suggest that, if Peisistratus had only inherited the musical contests, he certainly took it upon himself to promote them more vigorously than they had been before. He may also have succeeded specifically in stimulating the interest of the Athenian aristocracy in the musical culture of the Panathenaia, both as appreciative spectators and as performers.

What sort of exposure to concert *kitharôidia* did Athenians have before its official installation at the Panathenaia? Late Geometric

---

[11] Thus Herington 1985:84; cf. Kotsidu 1991:187n46. The friendship with Cleisthenes notoriously went sour when Hippocleides, spurred on by the music of the *aulos*, performed a shamelessly exhibitionist dance (*orkhêsis kai anaideia*) at the very symposium that was meant to celebrate his engagement to Cleisthenes' daughter. Hippocleides thus "danced away" his prestigious marriage in Sicyon, although he proverbially responded to the tyrant's dismissal of him by claiming, "Hippocleides doesn't care" (Herodotus 6.129). Could this tale represent a critical reflex of Hippocleides' Panathenaic politics, a piece of propaganda circulated by his rivals, the Alcmaeonids? It has been thought that Herodotus is channeling a pro-Alcmaeonid, anti-Philaid version of the events at Sicyon: McGregor 1941:269, with further bibliography. It is significant that Hippocleides' vulgar breach of aristocratic decorum is precipitated by a "contest of *mousikê*" held among the symposiasts (ἔριν εἶχον ἀμφί τε μουσικῇ), a key detail that might reflect an Alcmaeonid dig at Hippocleides' ambitious, perhaps incipiently tyrannical involvement in staging *mousikoi agônes*. However, Thomas 1989:266–270 has challenged the theory that Herodotus derived his account from Alcmaeonid tradition, arguing rather that the story has a "popular provenance" (cf. Kurke 1999:144). If the story is focalized through a popular, anti-elite perspective, then the valency of Hippocleides' performance changes; no longer a disgraceful *faux pas*, it is now rather a pointed renunciation, expressed through the socially loaded practice of *mousikê*, of aristocratic cultural pretension, elegantly capped by the proverbial counter-rejection of Cleisthenes, "Hippocleides doesn't care!" Cf. Luria 1929 on Aesopic elements in the story, which may also point to a "popular provenance." Even on the "popular" reading, the Philaid's role in the history of the Panathenaia could be at issue, in this case celebrated rather than undermined.

[12] Cf. Kotsidu 1991:105.

iconography indicates that the tetrachord *phorminx* and the *khelus*-lyre were known in Athens as early as the eighth century; the images illustrate their use in ritualized collective settings, where they provide accompaniment for choral song and dance and for sacrificial processionals.[13] The local hero Theseus is shown holding a *khelus*-lyre on the Attic François Vase (c. 570–560 BCE) as he leads a mixed chorus of Athenian youths; the instrument will remain a hallmark of his iconography throughout the Archaic period.[14] With only a few uncertain exceptions, however, there is no representation of anything like an agonistic solo performance before the apparently Panathenaic scenes of the middle of the sixth century BCE. The first certain appearance of Apollo *kitharôidos* in Attic art is on a black-figured wine bowl by Sophilus produced between 580 and 570 BCE. The scene is set at the wedding of Peleus and Thetis. Apollo, attired in the rich garb of a concert citharode and playing a full-sized concert *kithara* (albeit with only six strings), rides in a quadriga driven by Hermes; three Muses walk alongside.[15] The outfitting of Apollo in full citharodic *skeuê* could suggest that Sophilus had witnessed performances by professional citharodes who were similarly equipped.[16] Yet the fact that Apollo's *kithara* has only six strings might reflect his personal inexperience of the medium, and perhaps his dependence on older visual models.

This is not to say that traveling citharodes would never have included Athens on their itineraries; the Lesbian citharodes had, after all, been a well-established presence on the Peloponnesus since the early seventh century. Musical events were likely presented at public or semi-public gatherings in Athens before 566, perhaps even at the proto-Panathenaic festival. We know that musical contests were held at privately organized funeral games outside of Attica in the early Archaic period. The Hesiodic narrator of *Works and Days* claims that he won a tripod at a song contest, probably lyric in nature, attached to funeral games for the wealthy Amphidamas of Chalcis (654–657).[17] Such games were probably put on in seventh-century BCE Attica as well; these would have provided a venue for foreign and perhaps

---

[13]   Maas and Snyder 1989:11–23.

[14]   Cf. Shapiro 1991:126, who suggests that the lyre assimilates Theseus to Apollo.

[15]   London, British Museum 1971.11–11; Maas and Snyder 1989:46, fig. 9a.

[16]   A *kithara* player in fancy dress is included, alongside an *aulos* player, in a scene of women's festivity, probably wedding-related, on a black-figured fragment from the later first half of the sixth century BCE (Athens, National Museum, Acropolis 2203; Maas and Snyder 1989:47, fig. 10).

[17]   Cf. Koller 1956:166.

some local cithirodes to compete.[18] A few scenes of what may be solo cithirodic performance may be set at such pre-Panathenaic events. The painter of a black-figured lekythos from c. 580 BCE, for instance, has depicted what might be one such scene. While there are no explicit visual markers of an agonistic or festival context, a solo contest or concert seems implied. The sirens by which the cithirode is flanked may suggest an Odyssean or Argonautic theme for his song (Heidelberg University 68/1).[19]

But the musical culture of Athens, both in its aristocratic and demotic aspects, may in general have been dominated more by the *aulos* than by the lyre or *kithara* before the reorganization of the Panathenaia; even after the reorganization, the *aulos* and aulodic music may have remained the dominant attraction at the festival for almost three decades, overshadowing *kitharôidia*. It is telling that the images of aulodes and auletes that begin to appear around the middle of the sixth century are distinctly set in a Panathenaic agonistic context: singers and auletes stand on platforms, performing for spectators and seated judges; in some cases, the vessels are Panathenaic-shaped amphorae, and show a striding Athena on the obverse, a clear allusion to the goddess' festival.[20] By contrast, images of cithirodes from this same

[18]   Cf. Roller 1981:3–5; Kyle 1987:19.

[19]   Cf. Part II.10. Two other possible representations of solo cithirodic performance in pre-Peisistratean Athens. (1) A late seventh-century BCE fragment of a large terracotta plaque from the North Slope of the Acropolis shows a bearded man in a short-sleeved chiton holding up a seven-stringed *phorminx*, whose ornamented arms, however, anticipate those of the concert *kithara*; a pair of hands—the attached body has broken off—reaches out to touch, perhaps even take hold of (or hand over), the instrument (Athens, Agora AP 1085; Maas and Snyder 1989:43, fig. 3a; cf. Glowacki 1998:82–83, with fig. 8.1, who argues that the plaque comes from a metope or wall panel of a temple). The image recalls a slightly earlier depiction on a Delian amphora of Apollo playing a *kithara*-like *phorminx* before his sister, Artemis, who similarly extends her hands toward her brother's instrument (Delos, Archaeological Museum B 4260; Maas and Snyder 1989:45, fig. 7). (The bearded musician notably resembles too an Apollo *kitharôidos*, also wearing a short-sleeved garment, depicted on a slightly older amphora from Melos; Athens 911; Maas and Snyder 1989:42, fig. 2.) But the setting of the scene on the plaque is a mystery. The man could be a soloist, but whose hands are those? A choral dancer's? A member of a ritual procession that the musician accompanies? (2) A *phorminx* player appears on another plaque fragment from c. 580 BCE (Athens, National Museum 2523; Maas and Snyder 1989:44, fig. 5b). The musician wears a long chiton and a decorated mantle akin to the elaborate outfit of Apollo *kitharôidos*. He stands next to a flaming altar, as we see in some later "Panathenaic" scenes (e.g. Staatliche Museen zu Berlin, Preussischer Kulturbesitz F 2161 [Plate 11]). But the presence of a woman playing a rattle suggests that the context is cultic-ritual rather than agonistic.

[20]   Probably the earliest depiction of an aulodic contest has all of these features (London, British Museum, B 141, c. 550–540 BCE). Cf. Shapiro 1992:61–65; Vos 1986.

period are both fewer and far less markedly Panathenaic, agonistic, or public; there is a tentativeness about their representational status.[21] This need not indicate, however, that the citharodic *agôn* was introduced by Peisistratus only after auletic and aulodic *agônes* had already been established, but it does suggest two things. First, if Peisistratus did not himself institute agonistic *kitharôidia*, he (and his sons) were responsible for encouraging its popularity, and successfully so, for citharodic scenes would eclipse auletic and aulodic ones by the 530s. Second, despite the fact that the archaeological record shows Athenians had long known and used string music in certain ritual contexts, *aulêtikê* and *aulôidia* were nonetheless likely more familiar than *kitharôidia* to Athenian audiences of the first part of the sixth century—and not merely as spectators. It is reasonable to assume that the Athenian elites who commissioned the images of the Panathenaic contests were more comfortable singing to the *aulos* than to the lyre; some might even have competed in the contests themselves as aulodes, a performance that required far less skill than *kitharôidia* (or *aulêtikê*, for that matter). This is not to say that the lyre had no part in the *paideia* of cultured elites of the day. Theseus' possession of the tortoise-shell lyre on the François Vase suggests that the instrument already played a significant role in the formation of aristocratic identity in the earlier sixth century.

Yet it is important to keep in mind that not one prominent lyric poet is linked to Athens in the seventh and early-sixth centuries BCE. Hipparchus himself was to a significant extent responsible for the widespread adoption of East Greek lyric monody and its attendant Lydianizing style among Athenian symposiasts. His importation of Anacreon, the leading exponent of the music of the *barbitos* and its chic ethos of Eastern luxury (*habrosunê*), to Athens in the late 520s following the death of Anacreon's former patron, Polycrates of Samos, was a conspicuous expression of his fascination with the tradition of Aeolic and Ionian aristocratic lyric, and his desire to make it the possession

---

Papaspyridi-Karouzou 1938 argues that an early sixth-century amphora with a depiction of an aulete, whom she identifies as the legendary aulete Olympus, playing to an audience of two men and one very intent goose on the obverse and a horse and rider on the reverse (Athens, National Museum 559), is a "proto-Panathenaic" amphora from around 570. She accordingly submits the vessel as evidence for the possibility of equestrian events and *mousikoi agônes* at a pre-566 Panathenaia. But the amphora may be later than 566 and reflect rather auletic contests at the reorganized festival; cf. Davison 1958:27–28, Shapiro 1992:64.

[21] Cf. Shapiro 1992:61 on the "sizable corpus of both aulodes and auletes in a Panathenaic setting in the period ca. 550–530, before our earliest certain picture of a Panathenaic kitharode or kitharist."

of his city and his own court. Before the Peisistratids the only distinguished Athenian poet was Solon, who composed elegiac and iambic
poetry, two genres that relied primarily on the *aulos* for musical accompaniment. The aulodic genre of elegy was initially at home in the aristocratic symposium, but it likely made its way into the Panathenaic *agônes*
from the very beginning.[22] Indeed, we have evidence that the performance of elegy was the rule at the Panathenaic aulodic contest ἐν ἀρχῇ
'in the beginning' ("Plutarch" *On Music* 8.1134a, citing the authority of
a Panathenaic inscription, *graphê*). Even if the inscription "is the one
recording Pericles' re-establishment of the musical contests" in the
middle of the fifth century BCE (cf. Plutarch *Life of Pericles* 13.11), this
does not mean that such performance was not the custom too at the
sixth-century Panathenaia.[23] The aulodic performances at the Delphic
Pythia, instituted in 582 BCE, also featured elegiac poetry.[24]

Solon has in fact been implicated in the reorganization of the
Panathenaia festival, or has at least been seen as an influence on it.[25]

---

[22] Cf. Brown 1947:130–131 on the predominance of the *aulos* at early Athenian symposia.
But Brown overstates the case when he argues that Hipparchus and his circle
actively favored the lyre over the *aulos*. The Peisistratids after all patronized Lasus of
Hermione, a prominent aulodic composer. There may, however, be something to the
contention that Critias' later-fifth-century assessment of Anacreon as "the opponent
of the *auloi*, the lover of the *barbitos*" (αὐλῶν ἀντίπαλον, φιλοβάρβιτον, fr. 1.4 D-K *ap.*
Athenaeus 13.600e) alludes to the historical role Anacreon played under Hipparchus
in the "lyricization" of reed-centric Athenian music. For Critias' own rhetorical
appropriation of an "anti-*aulos*" Anacreon, see Wilson 2003b:190–191. By the same
token, Athenian symposiasts would of course have been somewhat familiar with East
Greek lyric songs before the time of Hipparchus. One anecdote has Solon learning a
melos of Sappho from his nephew (Stobaeus *Florilegium* 3.29.58). Perhaps Solon had
mentioned Sappho in his elegy, as he may have Arion (John the Deacon *Commentary on
Hermogenes* = Solon fr. 30aW, with Pickard-Cambridge 1962:99). It may be significant,
however, that in the anecdote it is Solon's nephew who teaches him the novel song,
suggestive perhaps of a generation gap between aulodic elegy and lyric. For pre-
Peisistratean images of the *aulos* in comastic/convivial contexts, see Shapiro 1992:64.
Stringed instruments begin to appear in comastic iconography in the third quarter of
the sixth century, well after their appearance in Laconian and Corinthian art. See e.g.
an Attic psykter with comasts dancing to a *phorminx* (Rhodes 12.200; Maas and Snyder
1989:44, fig. 6); the *phorminx* in this image anticipates the comastic role of the *barbitos*
in images that appear a decade or so later.

[23] Barker 1984:213n58; cf. Davison 1958:40.

[24] Pausanias 10.7.4–6; 586 BCE is Pausanias' date. For the likelihood of the 582 date, see
Mosshammer 1982. The story related by Pausanias, that the aulodic contests were
dropped immediately after their debut because sung elegy sounded too gloomy,
seems a clever but groundless attempt to explain a gap in the Pythian victor lists. Cf.
West 1974:5.

[25] Kyle 1987:21–22 offers convincing arguments that would link Solon's attempts to
"democratize" aristocratic athletic culture to the "civic athletics" promoted at the
Panathenaia.

Perhaps Solonian initiatives stand behind its musical contests as well, in particular its auletic and aulodic events.[26] As a recent study of the poet has shown, Solon was intent on transforming the medium of elegy from a largely aristocratic, elitist poetic tradition into an "open" civic discourse, touching on political and social concerns shared by the entire citizenry.[27] Athens' main civic festival would be a natural site for Solon to publicize this transformation. The account of his legendary performance of his *Salamis* elegy in the Athenian Agora, where he sings to a mass audience that has gathered (ὄχλου δὲ πολλοῦ συνδραμόντος) while he stands atop the *bêma*-like "herald's stone" (Plutarch *Life of Solon* 8.1–3), is perhaps an anecdotal "aetiological" reflex of aulodic elegiac performance at the festival. The contests may in fact have been held in the Agora in the sixth and earlier fifth century BCE, before they were moved to the Periclean Odeion.[28] Significantly, Solon's kinsman Peisistratus figures prominently in this story, "urging and inciting the citizens to obey the words" of the elegy (τοῦ Πεισιστράτου τοῖς πολίταις ἐγκελευομένου καὶ παρορμῶντος πεισθῆναι τῷ λέγοντι).

The late popularity of lyric culture comparative to aulodic culture in Athenian society, both in the symposium and in the public realm, may explain a curious claim made by Apollo in the *Homeric Hymn to Hermes*:

καὶ γὰρ ἐγὼ Μούσῃσιν Ὀλυμπιάδεσσιν ὀπηδός,
τῇσι χοροί τε μέλουσι καὶ ἀγλαὸς οἶμος ἀοιδῆς
καὶ μολπὴ τεθαλυῖα καὶ ἱμερόεις βρόμος αὐλῶν.

For I too am a follower of the Olympian Muses,
    for whom choruses are a concern, and the splendid path of
        song,
    and the vitality of song and dance (*molpê*) and the lovely
        roar of *auloi*.

Homeric Hymn to Hermes 450–452

---

[26]   Cf. Davison 1958:38.

[27]   Irwin 2005b. See Bowie 1986 for the complementary private/sympotic and public/ festival contexts for Archaic elegiac performance. Short-form and "personal" elegy was at home in the former; in the latter, aulodes performed "substantial narratives of their city's history, narratives that in some respects resembled hexameter epic, but that may also have had features symptomatic of their form's relationship to 'personal' poetry" (34).

[28]   Cf. Shapiro 1996:218; Bundrick 2005:160.

Hermes has just revealed the newly invented lyre to Apollo, whose enthusiasm for its novelty is initially tempered by a certain defensiveness. The god of music asserts that he is, appropriately, just as dedicated a follower of the Muses as Hermes is. Nonetheless, the *Hymn* imagines that Apollo has had absolutely no exposure to the music of strings before this point. This is meant to be startling, and a bit comic. βρόμος αὐλῶν 'roar of the *auloi*' is saved as a sort of punch line until the end of Apollo's description of the Muses' concerns, which form a résumé of his own (limited) musical experience. (And it is difficult not to hear an allusion to Dionysus in that description, and his epithet Bromios 'Roarer'.) As we will discuss in greater detail below, there is reason to believe that the *Hymn* was performed in later-sixth-century Athens, perhaps while Hipparchus was still in power.[29] If so, Apollo's surprisingly late lyric conversion would present a playful allegory for Athenians' own enthusiastic integration of the music of the lyre and *kithara* into their civic and sympotic musical lives, which had previously been centered around the *aulos*.

2. Citharodic Geopolitics

i. Athenian alternatives to Delphi

The Peisistratid promotion of *kitharôidia* figured significantly in both an international and domestic agenda of cultural politics. In terms of domestic policy, Panathenaic *kitharôidia* served as a site where Panathenaic interests, the interests of "all the Athenians," the tyrants, aristocrats, and the masses, productively converged, where potentially conflicting social energies found resolution in the mutually satisfying displays of prestige and pleasures of consumption involved in civic musical performance. The reputation for conflict resolution that *kitharôidia* had already acquired in early Sparta may have made it an especially appealing medium to Peisistratus and sons as they sought to consolidate and maintain their power over a highly fractious citizenry. But *kitharôidia* played a major role as well in the tyrants' bid for Panhellenic recognition and distinction.[30] For the Peisistratids, as for other Archaic tyrants, namely Periander, Cleisthenes, and Hieron, the possession of citharodic prestige was a conspicuous means of

---

[29] Brown 1947:102–132.
[30] Cf. Kotsidu 1991:28–29.

enhancing both their city's and their own profile and influence abroad. The effort to make Athens into a citharodic center was closely linked to the Peisistratids' proprietary interest in authoritative performances of Homeric *epos*, their desire to make it into an Athenian property, as it were, to link fundamentally its Panhellenic prestige with that of the city's premier civic festival as a sign of Athens' and their cultural mastery.[31]

Scholars have tended to focus exclusively on the rhapsodic contests and Hipparchus' "Panathenaic rule" when discussing the tyrannical drive to control epic. But that is to neglect the fact that citharodes too performed epics of the Trojan Cycle, including Iliadic and Odyssean material. It is true that by the time Hipparchus was managing the Panathenaia in the 520s the Ionian rhapsodes could make the most authoritative claims to Homer and in turn to Trojan epic. But, as was argued in Part II, in the middle of the sixth century, when Peisistratus was in charge of the Panathenaic program, a related yet rival Aeolic tradition of citharodic epic on the Trojan War had a distinct identity and prestige.[32] Significant in this regard was the Athenian occupation of the Aeolian Troad, going back to the later seventh century BCE, which included the seizure of the Mytilenean settlement of Sigeion (Herodotus 5.94–95). As Herodotus makes clear, the ongoing conflict with the Mytileneans that resulted, which flared up in the early tyranny of Peisistratus, who regained control of Sigeion after it had reverted to Mytilene (cf. Strabo 13.2.38), was as much a struggle over possession of the epic tradition of the Troad as of the territory itself.[33] In the neighborhood of Lesbian Sigeion, that tradition was predominantly Aeolic, and, in the first part of the sixth century, very likely predominantly citharodic. It would stand to reason that Peisistratus, concomitant with his making Trojan epic an Athenian possession, would want to make its authoritative Aeolic medium, *kitharôidia*, an Athenian possession as well. At the same time, citharodes may have been attractive to the tyrants for the very fact that their repertoire was more flexible than

---

[31]   See especially Nagy 1996:65–66, with bibliography; cf. Skafte Jensen 1980; Aloni 1984; Shapiro 1992:72–75, 1993; Irwin 2005b:277–280.

[32]   Citharodic epic would, however, continue to rival rhapsodic epic through the fifth century BCE. It is worth noting the fact that we have not one representation of an agonistic rhapsode from the years of the tyranny, while we have numerous depictions of citharodes (not to mention aulodes and auletes). The numbers surely reflect popular enthusiasm for the more colorful and engaging spectacle of citharodic performance. But this popularity in turn gives us some indication of the importance of *kitharôidia* in Peisistratean *Kulturpolitik*.

[33]   Cf. Part III.12n217.

the rhapsodes', open to a range of texts and traditions beyond Homer. The Terpandrean citharodic *nomoi* could be fit out with all sorts of locally and occasionally appropriate narratives, including those favorable to the tyrannical regime. Competitors at the Panathenaic citharodic *agôn* appear to have drawn material from the saga of Heracles, a hero with whom Peisistratus closely identified (cf. Part II.11). The visual evidence suggests that one showpiece was a citharodic Gigantomachy, whose starring character, Heracles *kitharôidos*, served as a heroic exemplar for the citharodes of the Panathenaic *agôn* as well as its tyrannical patrons.

The growth of Delphi as a major international center of agonistic musical culture after the establishment of citharodic, aulodic, and auletic contests there in 582 BCE (Pausanias 10.7.3–4) could be seen as a particularly strong incentive for Peisistratus to patronize the Panathenaic *mousikoi agônes*. The hostilities between the Peisistratid regime and Delphi were surely exaggerated—witness the rumor that the Peisistratids were responsible for burning down the Archaic temple of Apollo at Delphi (Philochorus FGrH 328 F 115)—but relations between Athens and Delphi under the tyrants were certainly not warm; our lack of any firm evidence that either Peisistratus or his sons consulted the oracle during a period when most other cities and tyrants did so is telling.[34] The contrastingly close relations that existed between the exiled political nemeses of the tyrants, the Alcmaeonids, and the Pythian shrine since the involvement of Alcmaeon with the First Sacred War in the 590s must have been a critical factor in the estrangement. As a consequence of these apparent tensions, Peisistratus may well have singled out the *mousikoi agônes* of the Delphic Pythia, in particular its prestigious citharodic contest, as a model to emulate and surpass at his Panathenaia.[35] The policy pursued by Hipparchus of dispensing his own wisdom (*sophia*) in the form of epigrams inscribed on herm statues strategically placed throughout the Attic countryside seems an analogous manifestation of a poetic politics aimed at appropriating for Athens authority traditionally possessed by Delphi. This policy is described in "Plato" *Hipparchus* 228d, in a passage that goes on to say that with his poetic *sophia* Hipparchus was intent on rivaling the wisdom dispensed in poetic form by the oracle of Apollo at Delphi (228e).[36]

---

[34] Shapiro 1989:50.

[35] Cf. Anderson 2003:163. On the Sicyonian Pythian games established by Cleisthenes as an analogously competitive response to the reorganized Delphic Pythia, see Power 2004.

[36] Discussion in Nagy 1990b:160–162; cf. Aloni 1984.

Further, Herodotus indicates that the tyrants had long been storing up written oracles on the Acropolis for their own use (5.90, 5.93); Peisistratus was in fact given the epithet "Bakis," the name of a legendary soothsayer (scholia *ad* Aristophanes *Peace* 1071; cf. *Suda* s.v. Βάκις). Onomacritus, a professional *khrêsmologos* 'speaker of oracular utterances', and the poet Lasus of Hermione were both employed by the tyrants in collecting, organizing, and interpreting these oracles (Herodotus 7.6).[37] Significantly, Onomacritus seems to have been a specialist in the oracles attributed to Musaeus, a distinctly Athenian mythical singer. The implication to be drawn from these testimonia is that the tyrants wanted to make their Athens into a sort of counter-Delphi, a rival site of oracular wisdom poetry. The Peisistratean Panathenaic *agônes* might thus represent a related musico-poetic "alternative" to Delphi, one with aspirations to achieve a level of Panhellenic recognition equal to the Pythian contests.[38]

We may want to consider that polysemous mascot of the Panathenaic cithharodic *agôn*, Heracles *kitharôidos*, as an emblem of the tyrants' "geomusical" competitiveness with the Pythian *agônes*. As we will see, the cultural and political symbolism of Apollo *kitharôidos* was by no means neglected by the tyrants; rather, it was vigorously appropriated. Nevertheless, the promotion of the Peisistratid-identified Heracles as a proto-Panathenaic agonistic citharode easily reads as a challenge to the musical, and specifically citharodic supremacy of Apollo and the Pythian *agônes*. It is as if Heracles has appropriated for Athens and its festival the instrument most iconically played by the god of Delphi.[39] Indeed, it is tempting to see in Heracles *kitharôidos* a variation on the theme of Heracles' appropriation of Apollo's Delphic tripod. It has been argued that the myth of the Struggle for the Tripod was allegorically deployed in both pro- and anti-Peisistratean propaganda. According to this argument, the depiction of the scene on the east pediment of the Siphnian treasury at Delphi (completed c. 525 BCE) reflected anti-Peisistratean propaganda circulated by the Alcmaeonids and the Delphians: Heracles is Peisistratus, eager to usurp Delphi's

---

[37] Cf. Nagy 1990b:159–160; Watrous 1982:167. Onomacritus was also involved in "editing" Homeric poetry; he may have performed as a rhapsode. See Part III.8; cf. Martin 2001.

[38] Relevant is the patronage of the Athenian cult of Apollo Pythios by Peisistratus, which involved some significant conflation with the (Delian-oriented) cult of Apollo Patroos (see Hedrick 1988). Peisistratus established the sanctuary of Pythian Apollo (*Suda*, Photius s.v. Πύθιον). See Shapiro 1989:50–52.

[39] The figure of Heracles *kitharôidos*, who often has a quiver slung across his back, visually and conceptually evokes Apollo: see Plate 6, with Part II.11; cf. Bundrick 2005:161 for a related line of argument.

oracular prestige; his attempted removal of the tripod represents his hubristic stance toward Delphi and Apollo, which will be checked by Zeus, who intervenes between Heracles and Apollo on the pediment.[40]

In roughly contemporary Athenian depictions of the scene, the valency is markedly different, and may reflect a pro-Peisistratid view. In these, Heracles appears to receive the support, tacit or active, of Athena against Apollo. This totalizing political-allegorical reading of the imagery has attracted severe criticism, much of it convincing.[41] Yet it is worth taking note of a black-figured Attic neck amphora now in Paris (Louvre F 58). The vase shows Heracles hefting the tripod in front of Apollo, who holds his concert *kithara* in one hand, unplayed and pointed toward the ground, while he raises the other hand above his head. Athena, holding spear and shield, stands firm behind Heracles. Some have interpreted this as a "reconciliation" scene: Heracles returns the tripod to its rightful owner.[42] However, it need not be; Apollo's raised hand may be an attempt to check rather than hail the hero. It is difficult not to read the vase against the contemporary images of the Panathenaic Heracles *kitharôidos*. Athena is positioned and attired as she often is in those images.[43] Apollo holds the *kithara*, but he has nevertheless been "upstaged" by Heracles, who, set in the center of the scene, still has possession of the tripod. We should recognize the polysemy of this latter object. It is of course meant to be *the* oracular tripod of Delphi. But in Archaic art tripods could also symbolize victory in contests, athletic as well as musical, including those of the Panathenaia.[44] A black-figured amphora by the Princeton Painter from the time of Peisistratus shows Athena facing a citharode, who wears full concert attire. As in many images of this period, it is unclear whether this citharode is Apollo or a mortal. A large tripod stands between them, which, if the citharode is meant to be a mortal musician, must represent his victory, surely at the Panathenaia, as the

---

[40] Watrous 1982:167–168, following Boardman 1978b:231; cf. Böhr 1982:50. If this interpretation is correct, the Athenian Heracles *kitharôidos* might then represent the tyrants' "re-appropriation" of this Alcmaeonid characterization of them as Heraclean anti-Apollos. But Shapiro 1989:62–64 has lodged significant objections. As Watrous points out, the (late) literary sources for the Struggle over the Tripod reflect the anti-Peisistratus/Heracles and pro-Alcmaeonid/Apollo/Delphi tradition.

[41] Cf. Shapiro 1989:62–64; more vigorously, Neer 2001:292–294.

[42] Shapiro 1989:63–64, with bibliography. The image is reproduced as Shapiro's plate 30e. The vase has been heavily restored, and this hinders confident interpretation.

[43] E.g. an amphora attributed to the Leagros Group, Worcester Art Museum, Austin C. Garver Fund (1966.63); Bundrick 2005:161, fig. 95.

[44] See Scheibler 1988; Shapiro 1992:201n82.

presence of the goddess indicates.[45] At some contests tripods were in fact distributed as prizes. Significantly, Pausanias 10.7.5–6 records that tripods were offered at the first Pythian *mousikoi agônes*.[46] Thus, although Heracles himself does not hold a *kithara*, might the Louvre neck amphora nonetheless demand that we mentally supplement the familiar, contemporary image of Heracles *kitharôidos* as we view it, and so understand the tripod to allude, if not to an actual *mousikos agôn*, then to a more notional cithardic antagonism between the hero and the god, and, further perhaps, between Athens and Delphi.[47]

Tripods appear in another iconographic context that could be linked to Heracles *kitharôidos*, the Panathenaia, and to Athens-Delphi friction:

> During the Peisistratid era, the giants in Attic gigantomachies have the tripod as their most popular shield device ... [T]he tripod ... is the emblem of Delphi. That Herakles should fight giants who are shown with a Delphic shield device, at a time when Peisistratos' opponents had gone into exile (probably to Delphi [...]), is not likely to be a coincidence.[48]

As we have seen, Heracles *kitharôidos* must not have been an independent creation of the vase painters. The figure is likely to have been inspired by a cithardic Gigantomachy performed at the Panathenaia, in which Heracles performed a lyric song to celebrate the defeat of the Giants, a performance that in turn offered an *aition* for the Panathenaic musical contests. Similarly, the tripod devices on the Giants' shields may be picking up on a latent anti-Delphic/Alcmaeonid strain in the Panathenaic Gigantomachy. However, it is important to emphasize how mistaken it would be to reduce Heracles *kitharôidos* or the Gigantomachy from which he likely emerged to mere anti-Delphic (or worse, anti-Apolline) propaganda. The rhetoric involved in both is more positive than negative; both serve to celebrate and to legitimate mythically the cultural and political achievements within Athens of the tyrants.

---

[45] Geneva, Musée d'Art et d'Histoire HR 84; Chamay and von Bothmer 1987, plate 7. Cf. discussion in Shapiro 1992:65.

[46] Cf. Neer 2001:296, who notes the interesting fact that Pausianias 10.7.6 says the first Pythian victor in *aulôidia*, Echembrotus, dedicated his winning tripod to Heracles in Thebes.

[47] Neer 2001:296 sees in the Struggle for the Tripod on the pediment of the Siphnian treasury an allusion to athletic *agônes*: "As much as it relates to the oracle, therefore, the pediment also depicts an 'athletic' contest: like the games for Patroklos, the Struggle for the Tripod is an *agôn*."

[48] Watrous 1982:165.

Yet still, the iconography does suggest an undercurrent of antagonism within the ideology of the Peisistratean Panathenaia directed outwards to Delphi and its Pythia.

ii. Delian overtures

Alongside Peisistratus' support of Panathenaic music, we might consider aspects of his religious and cultural intervention on Delos as a competitive response to Delphic musical prestige.[49] Panathenaic and Delian politics were in fact closely intertwined. Thucydides 3.104.1 relates that the tyrant purified the part of Delos that was visible from the temple of Apollo (cf. Herodotus 1.64.2), an action that seems to have been part of a larger effort to assert Athenian influence on the island, the major center of Ionian ethnic and cultural identity.[50] The Delian intervention can be dated to around 545–540 BCE, when Peisistratus was firmly in power. This was clearly a proto-imperial maneuver, and one in which the Athenian tyrant's management of musical culture, in particular *kitharôidia*, may have played a considerable practical and symbolic role.[51]

Delos had even before the tyranny of Peisistratus hosted a Panionian *panêguris* 'festival gathering'. Thucydides 3.104.3–5, adducing the Delian section of the *Homeric Hymn to Apollo* in which this *panêguris* is described (he quotes lines 146–150 and 165–172), says that this "ancient mass gathering on Delos of the Ionians and the dwellers of the surrounding islands" (τὸ πάλαι μεγάλη ξύνοδος ἐς τὴν Δῆλον τῶν Ἰώνων τε καὶ περικτιόνων νησιωτῶν, 3.104.3) included choral performances for Apollo as well as gymnastic and musical *agônes*. Thucydides 3.104.6 says that "in later times" (ὕστερον) the Delian musical and athletic *agônes* fell into neglect "thanks to misfortunes" (ὑπὸ ξυμφορῶν), and that only choral performances sponsored by Athens and the islanders were maintained, until the Athenians re-purified the island in 426 BCE and subsequently established a quinquennial festival called the Delia, restoring and elaborating the dormant contests

---

[49] See Parker 1996: "The foreign religious centre with which the Peisistratids were associated was not Delphi but Delos" (87).

[50] Cf. Shapiro 1989:49. Athenian claims to being "the eldest land of the Ionians" (πρεσβυτάτη γαῖα Ἰαονίας, Solon fr. 28a) had a long history. See Hedrick 1988:204 for the historical facts behind the claims.

[51] Cf. Shapiro 1989:48–49. Shapiro notes that Peisistratus "anticipated a political strategy used later by the Athenians, in the 470s, with the founding of the Delian League, and yet again in 426, with the second purification of Delos."

(cf. 3.104.2).[52] Thucydides' ὕστερον 'in later times' is chronologically ambiguous, but it most probably does not indicate the time before or during the activities of Peisistratus on the island. The "misfortunes" experienced by Delos are far more likely to have occurred in the earlier part of the fifth century, probably as a result of the Persian Wars and the subsequent rise of the Delian League, when Athens was usurping the place of Delos as the center of Panionian culture, than in the sixth century, when wealthy Naxos, the Peisistratids, and the Samian tyrant Polycrates, in a "competitive sport among those who sought to control the waters in which [Apollo's] birthplace lay," were pumping money and resources into the tiny island.[53] Frustratingly, the historian omits any mention of Peisistratean involvement in the *mousikoi agônes* on Delos. Thucydides 3.104.2–3 has been taken to mean that the quadrennial Delia was instituted by Peisistratus, not the fifth-century democracy. The text simply does not support this argument.[54] But it is an entirely reasonable assumption that Peisistratus and his sons continued to patronize and perhaps even reorganized the ancient festival described by the historian and the *Hymn to Apollo*, and that the festival under the tyrants' oversight offered not only choral performances but also a roster of *mousikoi agônes* including *kitharôidia*, as did the Peisistratid Panathenaia.

The existence of a rhapsodic contest on Delos at the combined Delian and Pythian festival staged by the Samian tyrant Polycrates, probably in the late 520s, suggests that solo musical contests were also held at earlier Peisistratean iterations of Delian festivals.[55] Furthermore, the

---

[52] Herington 1985:161 and 187 dates the restoration of the contests to 417 BCE, when Nicias likely sponsored a very polished theoric choral performance on Delos (Plutarch *Life of Nicias* 3.4–5). But note that this was a choral production, and Thucydides 3.104.6 makes clear that choruses had always been a part of the Delian festivities, even when the contests were not held. The restoration of the contests likely took place at a time closer to 426; cf. Parker 1996:150.

[53] Parker 1996:88. On the fifth-century dating of the neglect of the Delian *agônes*, see Barron 1983:11. Janko 1982:112 argues for the late sixth century.

[54] Shapiro 1989:48–49, who believes too that that festival would only have included choral performance. Again, this is not supported by the text.

[55] *Suda* s.v. Πύθια καὶ Δήλια and ταὐτά σοι καὶ Πύθια καὶ Δήλια; Hesiod fr. 357 M-W. Cf. Janko 1982:112–115; Burkert 1979; Aloni 1989; West 1999b:368–372. We should note the possibility that Polycrates took a special interest in promoting "Homeric" *kitharôidia* alongside *rhapsôidia*. Stesander of Samos first performed Homer, beginning with the *Odyssey*, at the Delphic cithrodic *agôn* (Timomachus FGrH 754 F 1). Stesander's primacy in performing the Homeric *Odyssey* at Delphi suggests an early date; perhaps he was a contemporary of Polycrates. Cf. Part II.7n139. Could Polycrates then also have had an interest in promoting *kitharôidia* on Delos, at the combined Delian and Pythian *agônes*? And might we suspect some competition between the Athenian and

composite Delian-Pythian *Homeric Hymn to Apollo*, which may have been first performed by the Chian rhapsode Cynaethus at the Polycratean festival, shows that Apollo *kitharôidos* was a familiar icon of the Delian cultic imaginary and performance culture. The archaeological record confirms this. A colossal marble Apollo *kitharôidos*, parts of whose chiton-bedecked upper body and *kithara* have been preserved, was erected on the island probably at some point in the later sixth century BCE, that is, during roughly the same period in which Cynaethus would have performed the *Hymn* on Delos.[56] The *Hymn* seems in fact concerned to establish the island as a bona fide center of Apollonian *kitharôidia*, with a tradition as illustrious as that of Delphi. At the transition from the Delian to the Pythian section of the *Hymn* we read the following invocation of Apollo, in which he is imagined without his chorus of Muses, as the perfect avatar of the concert citharode:

ὦ ἄνα, καὶ Λυκίην καὶ Μηονίην ἐρατεινὴν
καὶ Μίλητον ἔχεις, ἔναλον πόλιν ἱμερόεσσαν,
αὐτὸς δ' αὖ Δήλοιο περικλύστοιο μέγ' ἀνάσσεις.
εἶσι δὲ φορμίζων Λητοῦς ἐρικυδέος υἱὸς
φόρμιγγι γλαφυρῇ πρὸς Πυθὼ πετρήεσσαν,
ἄμβροτα εἵματ' ἔχων τεθυωμένα· τοῖο δὲ φόρμιγξ
χρυσέου ὑπὸ πλήκτρου καναχὴν ἔχει ἱμερόεσσαν.

Lord, Lycia too and lovely Maeonia [Lydia] and Miletus are yours, that charming city by the sea, but you yourself again are the great ruler over sea-girt Delos. And from there the son of glorious Leto goes, playing on his hollow *phorminx*, to rocky Pytho, wearing divine, perfumed garments; and his *phorminx* beneath the golden plectrum makes a charming sound.

Homeric Hymn to Apollo 179–185

Although lines 177–178 of the *Hymn* ("And I will not cease from singing far-shooter Apollo of the silver bow, whom lovely-haired Leto bore") would seem to mark the end of the Delian section, most scholars have realized that this passage nevertheless cannot be taken to mark the beginning of the Pythian section proper. We need not, however, assume, as some have, that it is a late "interpolation" or that the "authentic"

Samian tyrants for possession of cithardic prestige? By comparison, Hipparchus' recruitment of Anacreon could be read as a deliberate attempt to appropriate the sympotic-lyric prestige of Polycrates.

[56] Cf. n64 below.

opening of the Pythian section has been lost.[57] Rather, it is clear that, rhetorically and structurally, the passage serves to mediate a transition from the Delian to the Delphic realm—Apollo is literally in transit between the two—and that the perspective of the *Hymn* is at this point still Delian and Ionian. Indeed, the identity of this citharodic Apollo, "Leto's son," is distinctly Delian, and, importantly, has been so formed even *before* he leaves the island for Delphi, where, by implication, there is not yet lyric culture. The lyric tradition of Delos, by contrast, is notionally timeless, cognate with the god himself; Apollo's first demand after his birth on the island is for the *kitharis* (*Hymn to Apollo* 131). Further, the image of Apollo *kitharôidos* as he leaves Delos cannot but recall the vivid and lengthy description of the Panionian *panêguris* there (146–166). Athletic and musical contests had been established at this festival to bring *terpsis* to the god (149–150), who with his *phorminx* and his festive finery is himself a model agonist.[58]

Might we detect in the Delian characterization of Apollo *kitharôidos* the reflex of a "meta-agonistic" rhetoric, an assertion of the priority (and so greater importance) of the Delian citharodic *agôn* to that at the Pythia? Certainly, the marked subordination of Pythian to Delian *kitharôidia* makes sense in the context of a "Delian and Pythian" festival celebrated on Delos. In support of this reading, we may note that Apollo's initial trip to "rocky Pytho" from Delos is markedly otiose and premature. His real goal for the time being is Mount Olympus, where he arrives after the unexplained detour to Delphi. On Olympus he leads a chorus of Muses and gods in his role as *kitharistês*, a performance that symbolizes his definitive integration into and leading position among the Olympian pantheon (186–206).[59] But again, instead of writing off the Delphic detour as a random textual "problem," we might do better to take it as the rhapsode's deliberate attempt to express, in spatial and temporal terms, on the one hand the interconnectedness of Pythian and Delian lyric culture, and on the other hand the notional secondariness

---

[57] Cf. Allen, Halliday, and Sikes 1904 *ad* 179–182; Càssola 1975:498.

[58] Shapiro 1989:58 notes the correlation between the long "Ionian" chiton Apollo *kitharôidos* wears on later-sixth-century Attic vases and the "Ionian Greeks, who are characterized in the *Hymn* as ἑλκεχίτωνες ['with trailing chitons'] (147)."

[59] The scene of choral lyric performance on Olympus may also belong to a specifically Delian hymnic perspective, as it provides a fitting exemplar for the quasi-divine proceedings of the Delian festival, the choral performance of the Delian Maidens, "a great wonder, whose fame will never perish" (156), before an audience of notionally "immortal and unaging" Ionians (151). Cf. Lonsdale 1994/1995 for the Olympian chorus as a "prototype and paradigm" for the Delian festivity.

of the former to the latter.[60] The *Hymn* was performed under the aegis of Polycrates, and at his festival; nonetheless, the agonistic stance assumed toward the Pythia, muted as it is, might represent a legacy of Peisistratus' Delian musical politics.

Iconographic evidence from Attica could also point to the tyrant's investment of Athenian attention and resources in Delian musical culture, and his attendant interest in linking the musical events in Athens to those on Delos. From around 540 BCE depictions on Attic vessels of Apollo as *kitharôidos*—attired in the long chiton and elaborate mantle that form the *skeuê* of the festival citharode, playing the square-bottomed concert *kithara* from which is draped the characteristic intricately decorated cloth—become increasingly common. Not infrequently this Apollo *kitharôidos* appears alongside Artemis and Leto, in the configuration known as the Delian Triad, in scenes set on Delos.[61] One excellent example on a black-figured neck amphora from around 510 shows Apollo in full citharodic performance mode between Artemis and Leto, striking the strings of his large *kithara* with the plectrum before an altar that stands in front of a palm tree, a detail that explicitly localizes the scene on Delos.[62]

Alan Shapiro has made the intriguing argument that the image of Delian Apollo *kitharôidos* on these black-figured Attic vases was derived from a cult statue of Apollo as citharode in the first Athenian temple of

---

[60] In the Pythian section, when Apollo arrives at Delphi, it is as if for the first time (279–286); the initial visit after Delos has been forgotten. Indeed, the deeper into the Pythian section we go, the more the rhapsode draws exclusively upon Delphian narrative traditions (cf. West 1999b:369). In these traditions, Cretan lyric culture is recognized as the signal influence on that of Delphi; accordingly, near the end of the *Hymn*, Apollo is evoked in his specifically Pythian musical aspect as leader of the Cretan paean. The Delian Apollo *kitharôidos* has also been forgotten.

[61] Shapiro 1989:54–58, with the relevant vase paintings assembled in his plate 27.

[62] Hannover 753; Shapiro 1989, plate 28a. Note that here Leto holds a flowery frond in her hand, which may allude to the recurring motif of flower-sniffing listeners at *mousikoi agônes*, probably the Panathenaic, depicted on contemporary vases. See too a fragmentary neck amphora in Orvieto (Duomo 333, Shapiro 1989, plate 27c), on which Leto also holds a palm frond before a performing Apollo *kitharôidos*. An intriguing variation on this theme is to be seen on a black-figured neck amphora also from around 510 (Brooklyn Museum 62.147.2; Pinney and Ridgway 1979:50–51, no. 22). On the reverse side is a scene of a Dionysian revel, a maenad dancing and playing clappers, flanked by two satyrs. On the obverse Apollo plays the *kithara* in between two women, presumably Leto and Artemis; the latter holds clappers to her nose, as if she were sniffing a flower. The Dionysian coloring of the Delian scene is in line with a general tendency in later-sixth-century Athenian musical culture (and the art that reflects it) to elide the spheres of public *kitharôidia* and the Dionysian symposium. See discussion below.

Apollo Patroos in the Agora, which was dedicated by Peisistratus.[63] The Peisistratean cult of Apollo Patroos was specifically Ionian in orientation; Patroos "refers to Apollo as patron god of the Ionians, whose principal festival was the Delia."[64] As father of Ion, whose mother was the Athenian Creusa, Apollo Patroos was the ancestor of the Ionians by way of Athens (Euripides *Ion* 8–81; Plato *Euthydemus* 302c); he provided the divine legitimation for the city's claims to Delian and Ionian hegemony. The Delian identity of the Athenian Apollo Patroos may have been a matter of some contention, but that it could be asserted, even with some degree of tendentiousness, is made clear by the fourth-century BCE orator Hyperides in a markedly antiquarian passage that links fundamentally Attica, Delos, and Apollo Patroos (fr. 67, from the *Delian Oration*).[65] If Shapiro is right about the cult statue, it is remarkable that Peisistratus advertised in Athens the imperialistic, paternalistic aspirations of his Ionian foreign policy under the iconic sign of Apollo *kitharôidos*, whose Delian associations would have been unmistakable. This is not just a case of Peisistratus' nodding to Apollo's traditional possession of the *phorminx* or lyre, as attested, for instance, in the Delian portion of the *Homeric Hymn to Apollo* (131–132).[66] Nor

---

[63] Shapiro 1989:58. The second temple of Apollo Patroos in the Agora was constructed in the fourth century BCE. See Hedrick 1988.

[64] Shapiro 1989:52; cf. Hedrick 1988: Peisistratus was responsible for the civic institution of the cult (206). It is significant that the only (fragmentarily) preserved statue of Apollo *kitharôidos* from the Archaic period comes from Delos (Delos, Archaeological Museum 4092). This was not the primary Delian cult statue of the god (on which see Fehr 1979), but likely a member of a sculptural group of the Twelve Gods, the Dodekatheon (see Long 1989:11, with previous bibliography). Dating is uncertain; Long puts it c. 500 BCE, but an earlier date is entirely possible; cf. Flashar 1992:14. We cannot say whether the dedication of the statue could be connected in any way to a Peisistratean intervention on Delos, but, given its probable contemporaneity with a similar cult statue in Athens, it is tempting to conjecture a significant pairing of Ionian citharodic Apollos, meant to amplify essential political and musical resonances between Athens and the site of the Panionian festivities. On Peisistratus' construction of a stone temple and possible statuary dedications on Delos, see Courby 1931: 193–194, 207–215.

[65] Fourth-century identifications of Apollo Pythios and Patroos are also known (Demosthenes 18.141, with further evidence assembled in Hedrick 1988:200–201), but the Delian associations of Apollo Patroos, which Hyperides' oration suggests had an ancient cast, are undeniable. See Parker 1996:224; Aloni 2000:88.

[66] Cf. Shapiro 1989:58–59. Scenes of Delian Apollo with the tortoise-shell lyre are rare in sixth-century vase painting. See Bundrick 2005:226n28. Such scenes become more frequent in the fifth century, as Apollo is increasingly "deprofessionalized" in the Classical iconography, his *kithara* replaced by the lyre, his elaborate costume replaced by a simple, unadorned chiton and/or himation. The god who was before assimilated to the glamorous citharode is now cast more commonly as the amateur gentleman musician, a transition that reflects, to some extent, at least, elite divestiture from

should we be content to settle for a purely symbolic interpretation: Apollo the citharode as ordering communal archegete, the embodiment of cosmic harmony political and aesthetic. Of course, such lyrico-political symbolism must have been intended by the tyrant, and the fact that it seems to have been more at home in Aeolic regions and Dorian cities of the Peloponnese and the West—Sparta is a standout—than in Ionian ones could suggest that he was deliberately appropriating and redirecting its force for an (imagined) Athenian-led Ionian community.[67] What should not be ignored, however, is that the image of a distinctly citharodic Apollo promoted by Peisistratus, as depicted on the vases and, again, if Shapiro is correct, displayed prominently in statuary in the new temple of Apollo Patroos in the Agora, would resonate with the contemporary citharodic performance culture. That is, the Peisistratean Apollo, a strategically charged elision of Apollo Delios and Patroos, absorbed and reflected the glamorous aura projected by the modern-day citharodes the tyrant was intent on having sing in Athens, some of whom may have sung as well at the Delian *agônes*. Citharodic cultural capital generated in Athens and on Delos would here have been visibly converted into political capital supporting the Panionian aspirations of the Peisistratids.

The feedback loop between mortal and divine citharodic glamour is well illustrated by a black-figured neck amphora, now in London, produced around 550–540 BCE, the same decade in which Peisistratus likely performed his Delian intervention and dedicated the temple of Apollo Patroos.[68] On the obverse, Apollo, dressed in a patterned mantle over a long, white chiton, plays for his sister, who holds her bow; on the reverse, a bearded mortal citharode, wearing similar garb, playing

---

the public culture of *kitharôidia*. Cf. Sarti 1992. See e.g. a red-figured amphora from around 460 BCE (London, British Museum E 274; Bundrick 2005:147, fig. 86), showing Apollo holding the lyre and pouring a libation before his sister and a Delian palm tree.

[67] Wilson 2004:280 notes the markedly non-Athenian character of such lyrico-political symbolism: myths of the musical formation of city walls attach to Megara and Thebes; Sparta's good constitution was linked to the citharodic *nomoi* performed at the Carneia; the Dorian city of Camarina reorganized its citizenry on the model of a lyric *harmonia* (see Cordano 1994). On the Ionian aesthetic in tyrannical Athens as a response to Peloponnesian style, see Boardman 1995:12–13. In his *Persians*, Timotheus of Miletus perhaps imagines a political dimension to his own "Ionian" appropriation of the "Aeolic" lyre of Orpheus and Terpander. After vaunting his eleven-stringed *kitharis* (229–231), he refers to the Ionian confederacy as the "twelve-walled people" (δυωδεκατειχέος λαοῦ, 235–236). The subtext of the passage would appear to be Amphion's building of the walls of Thebes. It is as if the cosmic power of the lyre were now an Ionian property. See discussion in Section 11.iii below.

[68] On the coincidence of these events, see Shapiro 1989:51. Vase: London, British Museum B 260; Shapiro 1992:66, fig. 42a, b.

an identical *kithara* and striking almost the same pose as Apollo, stands alone between two sphinx-topped columns, an iconographic motif that refers to the Panathenaia.[69] The assimilation of the citharodes is surely deliberate; the two are effectively made to "impersonate" one another.[70] The motivation for this must be in large part to flatter the mortal citharode. But musical geopolitics also enter the picture. While Leto is absent from the scene of Apollo and Artemis, a Delian setting could nonetheless still be intended. If so, the metonymical links between the two scenes on the vase might reflect a broader ideological continuity between the music of two festivals promoted by the Peisistratids, the Panathenaic and the Delian, and a further connection of both to the Athenian cult of Apollo Patroos.[71]

3. Late Classical Interlude

The strategic links between Athenian and Delian musical cultures would be renewed a century after the death of Peisistratus, when the later-fifth-century democracy restored the *mousikoi agônes* on Delos, a move that recalled, and perhaps served as political balance to, Pericles' reestablishment of *mousikoi agônes* at the Panathenaia in the 440s.[72] These renewals of musical prestige in Athens and then on Delos, we will see, had a meaningful part to play in the Athenian imperial agenda of the second half of the fifth century. But here let us flash forward to the later fourth century BCE and to what may yet be another echo of Peisistratean citharodic culture: the new colossal statue of Apollo *kitharôidos* produced by the sculptor Euphranor that was installed in the new temple of Apollo Patroos in the Agora. The statue has been excavated, minus head, arms, and *kithara* (Plate 3), but later copies allow us to fill in our picture of the original with these missing components.[73] Shapiro, noting the general conservatism of Greek cults and

---

[69] Shapiro 1992:65. Cocks are more common on top of Panathenaic columns, but sphinxes and other forms can stand in. See the pairing of sphinx and cock columns on reverse and obverse of a black-figured amphora attributed to Group E in San Antonio (Picon and Shapiro 1996, no. 40).

[70] See comments in Bundrick 2005:162. As Shapiro 1992:65–66 notes, the only detail that really distinguished the two figures is the beard of the mortal citharode.

[71] Cf. Bundrick 2005:144.

[72] Parker 1996:149–151 notes the "curious echoes" between the Delian interventions of Periclean Athens and those of Peisistratus. Cf. Smarczyk 1990:504–525.

[73] On the statue, see Palagia 1980:13–20, with figs. 6–17; Flashar 1992:50–60. See too Roccos 1989, who argues convincingly that the Apollo of the Palatine temple

cult statues, argues that this statue was modeled on an earlier one commissioned by Peisistratus.[74] Euphranor portrays Apollo *kithar-ôidos* in the usual himation and chiton, which we presume the Archaic statue wore, but added a peplos reminiscent of that worn by Athena Parthenos. The peplos was almost certainly not a feature of an Archaic cult statue—no sixth-century vase painting depicts Apollo wearing one.[75] The innovation is surely significant; it brings to the image a politically and culturally meaningful semiotic polyvalency. On the one hand, the peplos transforms Apollo into a more socially abstracted symbol; as far as we know, real-life citharodes, even in the fourth century, did not wear this garment as a part of their *skeuê*. The visual and conceptual looping between mortal and divine citharode that we see illustrated on the London amphora is short-circuited. The peplos vividly assimilates Apollo to Athena, the transvestism reinforcing his position as authoritative *Stadtgott* alongside the city's patron goddess. But this symbolization also divorces him from the real-life cultural practice of *kitharôidia*.[76] On the other hand, we could read the peplos as symbolically reinforcing the Athenian identity of Apollo Patroos qua citharode and thus reflecting a civic recommitment to an Athenian patronage of actual citharodic culture. It could telegraph specifically a reference to the Panathenaic festival, which even into the late fourth century (and well after) remained an important center of agonistic *kitharôidia*.[77]

---

dedicated by Augustus in 28 BCE, which also wore the peplos (Roccos, p580), was not the Rhamnusian Apollo of Scopas, as is usually thought, but a "neo-Attic" Roman work modeled on Euphranor's Apollo. Other Imperial statues of Apollo *citharoedus* feature the peplos (see Plate 4).

[74] Shapiro 1989:58.

[75] Roccos 1989: "Apollo Patroos is the first citharodic type to wear the Attic peplos" (580n45).

[76] Palagia 1980:18 notes that "the affinity of the Patroos with the Athena Parthenos may indicate an affiliation of the patron deities of Athens." Arguably, this reimagining of Apollo *kitharôidos* as practically transcendent ideal is a "civic" reflex of the fifth-century process, motivated by the sociocultural elite of Athens, whereby the god was gradually transformed from professional *agônistês* to amateur lyre player. The study of statuary of citharodic Apollo by Flashar (1992) confirms a general trending away from "professional" toward idealized—the nude, seated Apollo with *kithara* or lyre is a striking instance—portrayals in the Hellenistic and Roman periods.

[77] An early third-century BCE inscription found at the Athenian Theater of Dionysus that records the multiple victories of the Tarentine citharode Nicocles graphically attests to the preeminence of the Hellenistic Panathenaia. In the center of the inscription, in outsized letters, Nicocles' citharodic victory at the Great Panathenaia is commemorated, flanked by mentions of victories at presumably lesser contests such as the Pythian and Isthmian games (IG II² 3779). Cf. Reisch 1885:23n5 and especially Bélis 1995:1052–1053 (with photograph of the inscription on p1053). Bélis notes that the graphic arrangement of the victories represents a hierarchy of "dignity"

Such conflation of the two deities under the sign of *kitharôidia* and the Panathenaic festival that frames it would present a bold variation on an iconographic theme attested over 150 years earlier. A red-figured Panathenaic-shaped amphora by the Nikoxenos Painter from c. 500 BCE shows Athena, in her guise as helmeted, striding Promachos, assuming the customary place of Apollo, vigorously sweeping a plectrum across the strings of the large concert *kithara* she holds (Plate 11).[78] On the reverse an ephebic-looking citharode wearing a long, puffy-sleeved robe is shown striking the strings of his instrument in a nearly identical gesture (Plate 12). This citharode is most likely a mortal, but his countenance evokes Apollo's; his posture too, unlike that of Athena's dynamic gait, is stiff and statuesque, like that of Apollo *kitharôidos* in earlier sixth-century depictions. Both figures play before an altar; both are framed by the distinctive cock-topped columns that evoke the Panathenaic contests. As on the earlier amphora in London discussed above, mortal and divine citharodes are assimilated, but here the city's patroness gets in on the game, "playing the citharode" and thereby vividly enacting the city's possession of the medium.[79] Indeed, the citharodic Athena might be viewed as a post-tyrannical, democratic response to the Peisistratid-identified images of Heracles *kitharôidos*, in which Athena had been consigned to the role of spectator.[80] Although

---

and "prestige." Yet her comments on the inscription seem to me mistaken in two respects. First, she claims that Nicocles won at the Great Panathenaia in the dithyrambic contest. This is unlikely. For although, like Timotheus, Nicocles was a dithyrambic composer as well as a citharode, he was first and foremost a citharode—a sculpture on the Sacred Way in Athens represented him as such (Pausanias 1.37.2; cf. Stephanis 1988:328); and while a dithyrambic victory at the Lenaia is mentioned (explicitly marked *dithuramboi*), we have no reason to think that the other victories, unmarked as to contest, were not citharodic. Although dithyrambs were performed at the Panathenaia (cf. Wilson 2000:36), *kitharôidia* was still the better-known event at that festival. Second, Bélis implies that since the inscription was set up in Athens, Nicocles showed favoritism to the city by centering his Panathenaic victory. This may be true in part, but it is still not a strong argument against the Hellenistic prominence of the Panathenaia. The monument, after all, was meant primarily to celebrate the comprehensive prestige of Nicocles' own career. We have the remains of what appears to be a white-ground Panathenaic prize amphora from the early second century BCE, with Athena in peplos on the obverse and a chiton-wearing citharode in performance on the reverse: Edwards 1957:346, with plate 84. The amphora was presumably only a supplement to the cash prizes won by citharodes at the highly remunerative Panathenaic *agôn*, as the fourth-century BCE prize inscription IG II² 2311 attests.

[78] Staatliche Museen zu Berlin, Preussischer Kulturbesitz F 2161; Schauenburg 1979:72, Abb. 21 and 22.

[79] On earlier vases Athena is depicted as a citharodic spectator: Shapiro 1992:65–66.

[80] Bundrick 2005:164 also reads the image as heralding the newly democratic tenor of the Panathenaic contests.

the Euphranor Apollo inverts the terms of the Nikoxenos Painter's image—Apollo is "playing Athena"—it communicates a similar message. But beneath the Attic imposition of the peplos the Ionian-Delian traces of Apollo Patroos, dating back to the Archaic period, must have remained. This emerges in an expert analysis of the statue and its historical context, which concludes that "[C]ostume, haircut, and kithara were intended to recall a traditional Ionian costume, and the musical contests held on the island of Delos."[81]

The Panathenaic, Delian, and citharodic themes that inform Euphranor's Apollo Patroos hearken back to the sixth century BCE, but very much reflect the tenor of the religious and cultural aspirations of later-fourth-century Athens. The new temple and cult statue were dedicated during Lycurgus' tenure as state treasurer, probably around 330 BCE, and the reactivation of Athenian citharodic capital signaled by the colossal statue is indeed in line with his costly investments in civic culture, which were aimed at raising the lowered profile of Athens to its "Classical" eminence.[82] Lycurgus took a keen interest in recouping the glory of the premier Athenian musico-poetic medium of the fifth century, tragedy. He financed the reconstruction of the Theater of Dionysus, where he had erected statues of Aeschylus, Sophocles, and Euripides, and he commissioned authorized state texts of the plays of these canonical tragedians.[83] His interventions in the Panathenaic festival mainly concerned its ceremonial and religious aspects, but in his speech *Against Leocrates* (102) he makes much of the city's "ancestral" legacy of Homeric recitation at the Panathenaic rhapsodic *agôn*.[84]

Outside of the implications of the Apollo Patroos statue, we hear nothing specific about Lycurgan interest in citharodic culture. Star citharodes were, however, playing increasingly prominent roles in the interstate politics of the later fourth century. It is hard to imagine that

---

[81] Hedrick 1988:200. However, he overlooks the distinctly Attic ethos brought to the traditional Ionian elements by the peplos. Fehr 1979 makes the relevant argument that the fifth-century Athena Parthenos of Pheidias, a work whose influence is detectable in the Euphranor Apollo (cf. Palagia 1980:18–19), was modeled on the Archaic cult statue of Apollo on Delos. There was thus a significant circulation of Delian and Athenian imagery around the figure of Apollo Patroos.

[82] Lycurgus and the statue of Apollo Patroos: Mitchel 1970:34–35, 44; Hedrick 1988:209; Flashar 1992:58–59.

[83] Plutarch *Lives of the Ten Orators* 841d–842a.

[84] Lycurgus and the Panathenaia: Shear 2001:569–575. Lycurgus financed the building of a new Panathenaic stadium: Plutarch *Ten Orators* 841d. Plutarch also attests to Lycurgus' interest in musical contests outside the Panathenaia and Dionysia. He added comic competitions to the Anthesteria (841f) and instituted the performance of cyclic choruses at a festival of Poseidon in the Piraeus (842a).

Athens would want to be left out of the action, especially since its dominant rival Macedon was clearly intent on emerging as a major center of *kitharôidia*.[85] Lycurgus evinces a pious interest in ancient Delian culture in his speech "Against Menesaechmus, Concerning the Sacrifice on Delos" (fr. XIV Conomis), roughly contemporary to the *Delian Oration* of Hyperides, which also seeks to reclaim ancient Delian prestige for Athens.[86] The *mousikoi agônes* on the island, including *kitharôidia*, were still being celebrated in style, but other states, including the Delians themselves, had been challenging the hegemony of Athens on Delos since the end of the Peloponnesian War.[87] Inscriptions recording victors at the Delian citharodic *agônes* are preserved only from the third century BCE, but we should note that the earliest victor we know from this period is an Athenian, Memnon, in 284 BCE (IG XI 105).[88]

At another (non-Panathenaic) festival in which the Athenians took great interest in the fourth century BCE, the Amphiaraia at Oropus, on the border of Attica and Boeotia, we have inscriptional evidence of the victory of another Athenian citharode in the *agônes*, one Cleonicus (IG VII 414).[89] In what may not be a coincidence, Cleonicus' victory took place in 329, the first year the Athenians hosted the Amphiaraia after Oropus was returned to Athens from Thebes and the festival's penteteric reorganization was proposed in 331.[90] Given that the cult of Amphiaraus, with its attached festival, was something of a political football passed back and forth between between Thebes and Athens, it also may not be a coincidence that the winner in the less prestigious contest of boys' solo *kithara* playing—an event that was also offered at the fourth-century Panathenaia—was a Theban named Lysander.[91] Perhaps we might see in the record of the agonistic string culture the traces of some political negotiation between the two cities?

After the Athenian defeat at Aegospotami, which marked the end of the Peloponnesian War, Sparta made its own Delian overtures. The Spartan general Lysander, in what was surely a provocative gesture

---

[85] Macedonian cithradic ambitions go back to the later fifth century, when Timotheus of Miletus was a guest of Archelaus: Plutarch *On the Fortune of Alexander* 334b. On the political intrigues of fourth- and third-century BCE cithrodes, see Part I.21.

[86] Epigraphic evidence shows that *kithara*-accompanied theoric choruses from Lycurgan Athens were well represented in the musical culture of Delphi. See Wilson 2004:278; Parker 1996:250.

[87] Parker 1996:222–223.

[88] Cf. Stephanis 1988, no. 1638.

[89] Cf. Stephanis 1988, no. 1448.

[90] On the dating, see now Knoepfler 1993.

[91] See Parker 1996:146–149 on the politics of the Amphiaraia.

intended to counter traditional Athenian prerogatives, made dedications at the temple of Apollo on Delos.[92] There is no evidence that Lysander intervened in the musical contests on the island, but it is clear that the Spartan general understood how to manipulate musical culture in the game of international power politics. His methods merit a brief digression. There is the fascinating testimony in Plutarch's *Life of Lysander* that Lysander destroyed the walls and burned the triremes of Athens to the sound of *auloi* played by the *aulêtrides* 'female auletes' he had summoned from the city. This appropriation of distinctly Athenian musical resources—the *aulos* was the instrument most prominently associated with the civic music of Athens, the *aulêtrides* were the hired entertainers at its symposia—to provide the festive soundtrack for the humiliation of the physical manifestations of Athenian civic and imperial power was a cannily orchestrated performance indeed, fraught with deep symbolic irony.[93] For, if democratic Athens was a predominantly "auletic" city, oligarchic Sparta was a city whose musical identity was traditionally bound up with the music of the lyre. We could perhaps connect to Lysander's auletic gloating over the fall of Athens the erection in Amyclae—the site of the Apolline Hyacinthia festival and, as such, a resonant locus of Spartan musical culture—of a statue meant to be the personification of Sparta, a woman holding a lyre. Pausanias, who was an eyewitness of this statue of lyric Sparta, says that it was dedicated with funds from the spoils of Aegospotami (3.18.8). The timing of the dedication and the source of its funding conspire to suggest that this monument was a deliberate reassertion of Spartan cultural values, a memorial to triumphant Spartan musical

---

[92] I.Délos 104.82, 120; cf. Parker 1996:222.

[93] Plutarch *Lysander* 15.4 (an elaborated version of a shorter account in Xenophon *Hellenica* 2.2.23): ὁ δ' οὖν Λύσανδρος ... πολλὰς μὲν ἐξ ἄστεος μεταπεμψάμενος αὐλητρίδας, πάσας δὲ τὰς ἐν τῷ στρατοπέδῳ συναγαγών, τὰ τείχη κατέσκαπτε καὶ τὰς τριήρεις κατέφλεγε πρὸς τὸν αὐλόν, ἐστεφανωμένων καὶ παιζόντων ἅμα τῶν συμμάχων, ὡς ἐκείνην τὴν ἡμέραν ἄρχουσαν τῆς ἐλευθερίας ("After Lysander sent for many *aulêtrides* from the city and gathered together all of those in the camp, he tore down the walls and burned the triremes to the music of the *aulos*, while the allies [of the Spartans] donned crowns and danced, since they believed this was the first day of their *eleutheria* 'freedom'"). Two other *détournements* of Athenian musical and political culture are enacted here. First, the crowns (*stephanoi*) donned by the allies as they revel to the music of the *aulêtrides* evoke the comastic/convivial ambience of the Attic-Ionic symposium. Second, the Athenian catchword of *eleutheria* is turned against the defeated "tyrant city."

and political order (*kosmos*), built from the imperial capital of Athens itself.[94]

Lysander ambitiously enlisted rhapsodic poets in the service of promoting his own fame. He kept Choerilus of Samos on retainer "to adorn his deeds in verse" (ὡς κοσμήσαντα τὰς πράξεις διὰ ποιητικῆς), and supposedly paid Antilochus a capful of silver for an encomiastic poem. The Samian Heraia festival was renamed in his honor as the Lysandreia; performers at the attached musical contests lost no time in competing to glorify the new honorand. No surprise, as Lysander himself served as judge at the initial offering of the rededicated *agônes*. Antimachus of Colophon was supposedly defeated by Niceratus of Heracleia in the rhapsodic contest; both were reciting poems about the Spartan admiral in his presence (Plutarch *Lysander* 18.4–5).[95]

A final anecdote related by Plutarch links Lysander directly to citharodic culture. He was approached (perhaps at the Lysandreia) by Aristonous, one of the most successful citharodes of the later fifth and early fourth centuries, a six-time Pythian victor and winner of the Panathenaic *agôn* in 398.[96] Aristonous told the Spartan in what was perhaps an overly direct show of goodwill (φιλοφρονούμενος) that if he were victorious once more at Delphi, he would have the *kêrux* 'herald' "proclaim him as Lysander's" (Λυσάνδρου κηρύξειν ἑαυτόν). The reply: "As my *doulos* 'slave', you mean?"[97] This anecdote refers to what was probably a historical practice, the citharode's advertisement of a powerful patron's name alongside his own in the official victory announcement delivered during the crowning ritual, which would allow the patron to share in the glory of the victory at its most intense and concentrated moment. More typically, the name of a victor in a *mousikos agôn* would be proclaimed alongside his home *polis* and the

---

[94] Cf. comments of Wilson 2004:280. The identification of musically conservative Sparta with the seven-stringed lyre long persisted: Plutarch *On Monarchy, Democracy, and Oligarchy* 827b.

[95] On the festival, see Habicht 1970:243–244. *Lysander* 8.4 explicitly cites the tyrant Polycrates of Samos as a model for Lysander. Plutarch here and elsewhere in the biography likely draws on traditions hostile to Lysander's imperialist ambitions after the Peloponnesian War; cf. Bearzot 2004.

[96] Aristonous' Panathenaic victory is recorded in Parian Marble Ep. 67; cf. Stephanis 1988, no. 369. We do not know from what *polis* Aristonous came. Could he have been an Athenian? His probably slightly older Athenian contemporary, Execestides, was also a Pythian and Panathenaic citharodic victor (Polemon fr. 47 Preller *ap.* scholia *ad* Aristophanes *Birds* 11).

[97] Plutarch *Lysander* 18.5: ἐπεὶ μέντοι ὁ κιθαρῳδὸς Ἀριστόνους ἑξάκις Πύθια νενικηκὼς ἐπηγγέλλετο τῷ Λυσάνδρῳ φιλοφρονούμενος, ἂν νικήσῃ πάλιν, Λυσάνδρου κηρύξειν ἑαυτόν, 'ἦ δοῦλον;' εἶπεν.

name of his father.[98] But as international "free agents" citharodes were presumably open to publicizing at this marquee moment the name of a high-bidding patron. Such selling (or rather leasing) of high profile "advertising space" at the Panhellenic and major regional festivals might have constituted a lucrative revenue stream for the professional agonistic musician. Analogous to the proposition made by Aristonous is the case of the professional athlete Astylus of Croton, who on two occasions had himself "announced as a Syracusan in order to please Hieron" (ἐς χάριν τὴν Ἱέρωνος ... ἀνηγόρευσεν αὐτὸν Συρακούσιον, Pausanias 6.13.1).[99]

What seems fabricated about the story is Lysander's cutting response to Aristonous, which notably, however, does not amount to a flat-out rejection. Lysander's desire for widespread recognition and power was historical fact, even if his detractors exaggerated his aspirations into tyrannical proportions.[100] Lysander does not seem to have objected to being deified and honored by rhapsodes on Samos. He undertook his own Panhellenic self-promotion at Delphi by dedicating a bronze statue of himself there (Plutarch *Lysander* 18.1). It is difficult to believe that Lysander would resist the opportunity to have his name publicized at the Pythia by a citharode as renowned as Aristonous. It could be the case that Aristonous did have himself announced under the name of Lysander, presumably with the blessing of the latter (and his financial incentivizing—compare the story about the rich compensation of Choerilus and Antilochus), and that the anecdotal reply of the Spartan is a secondary reflex. As such, it could be read from two points of view. First, it could have emerged from a hostile tradition that emphasized the haughty peevishness and overweening behavior supposedly exhibited by Lysander (*Lysander* 18.2, 19.1), who is made to humiliate,

---

[98] Both ethnic and patronymic are indicated in a fragment of Timotheus, PMG 802, in which the citharode "quotes" the *kêrux* who once announced his victory over his older rival, Phrynis of Mytilene: μακάριος ἦσθα, Τιμόθε᾽, ὅτε κᾶρυξ | εἶπε· νικᾷ Τιμόθεος | Μιλήσιος τὸν Κάμωνος τὸν ἰωνοκάμπταν ("Blessed you were, Timotheus, when the herald said, 'Timotheus, a Milesian, defeats the son of Kamon, that bender of Ionian melody'"). Cf. Kurke 1993:142–144 on the wording of athletic victory announcements. Phrynis' father may have actually been named Skamon; cf. Part III.12n217. The shortened version (also recorded in Pollux *Onomasticon* 4.66) could be Timotheus' own punning allusion to the melodic *kampai* 'bends' for which the comedians (Aristophanes *Clouds* 970–972, with scholia *ad loc.*) as well as Timotheus himself (ἰωνοκάμπταν) criticize Phrynis.

[99] See Kurke 1993:158n39. The *kharis* 'favor' that Astylus repaid the tyrant was surely a return for monetary payment. Cf. Nicholson 2005:9 for further discussion and related examples.

[100] See Bearzot 2004.

454

"enslave" the world-famous citharode, while not, however, rejecting his attractive offer. Indeed, in Plutarch's account this anecdote caps a series of examples of behavior that illustrate Lysander's increasingly hubristic enjoyment of power. But perhaps the story reflects Lysander's own disingenuous self-fashioning: the noble Spartan, the champion of *eleutheria*, styles himself as shocked by the citharode's offer; he is seemingly made uncomfortable by the tyrannical implications of the patronage arrangement proposed by Aristonous.[101] *Kitharôidia* was, after all, a medium central to the establishment of the communal peace at Sparta going back to the time of Terpander. Perhaps the thought of one powerful individual's undue influence over its performers was too far out of tune with the traditional Spartan ideal of the citharode as resolver of civil strife.

4. Apollo Patroos: Ideological Resonances in Athens

I have argued that the citharodic envisioning of Apollo Patroos in his ancestral aspect chimed with the imperialistic assumptions by Athens of its own "foundational" status in the Panionian community and iconicized its leading role within that international context, exemplified most strongly in the city's recurrent exertions of influence on Delos. Such influence, we saw, may have included the patronage of citharodic *agônes* on the island. But might Apollo Patroos also have played some symbolic role in the ordering of the musical culture *within* the city? In Plutarch's telling of an anecdote that has a young Alcibiades vehemently refusing to learn the *aulos*, Alcibiades refers to Apollo Patroos as an exemplar of Athenian musico-political identity, saying, "We Athenians, as our fathers say, have Athena as foundress (*arkhêgetis*) and Apollo as our ancestral god (*patrôios*); the former threw away the *aulos*, while the latter flayed the very *aulos* player [Marsyas]" (*Life of Alcibiades* 2.6). It has been argued that, despite Alcibiades' seemingly collective evocation of "we Athenians," his appeal to ancestral Apollo actually reflects a tendentiously elitist, exclusionary vision of both citizenship and musical practice: "We can certainly point to no known role of Apollo Patroos in the musical 'formation' of 'the Athenians' at large."[102] Indeed, the old-line clans, the *genê*, which not uncommonly provided

---

[101] For Hieron as tyrannical patron of citharodes, see Part III.15.
[102] Wilson 2004:301.

a social frame for aristocratic identity and activity, from an early point took a proprietary interest in the cult of Apollo Patroos.[103] We might imagine that the lyric character of this "family" Apollo validated aristocratic notions of an elite-only "lyric birthright," the privileged, restricted access to lyric music in the schoolroom and the symposium. Alcibiades' rejection of the demotic *aulos* in favor of the lyre also has a *hauteur* that could reflect the elitist ideology inherent in the Patroos cult. His self-justifying allusion to the Apollo and Marsyas myth, which portrays the god as an implacable defender of aristocratic social and aesthetic supremacy, is notable in this respect as well.[104]

But it is just as likely that by the time of Alcibiades' youth Apollo Patroos was a divinity with a broader civic identity, his *kithara* a source not only of aristocratic identification but also of citywide (democratic) cultural pride—which Alcibiades would of course have exploited for his own self-interested rhetorical purposes.[105] For it is entirely possible

---

[103] Parker 1996:64; cf. Hedrick 1988:203. See Wilson 2004:278 on the aristocratic affiliations of the *genê* in respect to musical activity.

[104] Rejection of *aulos*: Wilson 1999, with the important qualifications in Martin 2003. (Palagia 1980:16 argues that the Lycurgan cithardic Apollo Patroos referred to the Marsyas myth, but there is nothing to indicate why this would be the case.) I would note the deliberately mixed signals sent by aristocrats such as Alcibiades and Critias in regard to auletic culture, which suggest that their rejection is a disingenuous sociocultural performance aimed at maintaining their own distinction. Critias significantly marks the *aulos* as a distinctly unsympotic instrument in comparison to the stringed *barbitos*, which he associates with his aristocratic sympotic exemplar Anacreon (1.4 D-K; cf. Wilson 2003b:190–191). But Critias also composed 'public' aulodic music (for tragedy) and, like another famous rejecter of the *aulos*, Alcibiades, enjoyed playing it himself (Chamaeleon of Heraclea *ap.* Athenaeus 4.184d, where we learn too that Alcibiades supposedly studied the *aulos* under the star virtuoso Pronomus). There clearly developed in the fifth century a double standard about what was appropriate musical practice where and for whom: elites could both denigrate and play the *aulos*, but always on their own terms; it was a sign of their own cultural mastery that they could make the rules under which such behaviors were not contradictory. I would take this as a strategic response to the challenge to elite musical hegemony presented by the rising musical professionalism of later-fifth-century Athens.

[105] A later-fifth-century BCE allusion, darkly ironic in tone, to the citharodic Apollo Patroos may be heard in Euripides *Ion* 897–906: Creusa criticizes Apollo for neglecting her and their son, Ion, while he "makes a racket on the *kithara* (κιθάρᾳ κλάζεις), singing paeans." Paternal Apollo is anything but; he is antisocially absorbed in his *kitharôidia*. Further, the god's apathy and hypocrisy are ironically underscored by the fact that he sings solo paeans; paeans were normally a choral form that celebrated healthy social integration. Creusa thus imagines a "perversely autistic performance," as Wilson 2004:279 well puts it; cf. Rutherford 1994/1995. (We might also suspect that some deliberate antiquarianism is in play here, an allusion to the belief that the citharodic *nomos* had in time past evolved from the paean.) I would argue, however, that Euripides is drawing on the contemporary superstar status of the professional

that the Peisistratid dedication of a temple and statue in the Agora was aimed specifically at opening up the restricted ambit of this upper-class cult to a broader demotic constituency, a move that would be in line with broader tyrannical policies that aimed at exposing and diffusing, while not completely diminishing, concentrations of gentilician influence over the cultural and religious life of the *polis*.[106] The cult would remain in a sense an aristocratic possession, and provide opportunity for elite display, but possession and display would then be framed and monitored by civic space and *polis* ideology. Felix Jacoby makes a similar argument, but assigns the public promotion—indeed, the invention—of the cult of Apollo Patroos to Solon. There are valid chronological objections to Jacoby's argument.[107] Nevertheless, the motivation he ascribes to Solon's promotion of the cult, to unite the *dêmos* while "absorb[ing] the aristocracy without destroying it," surely suits the approach of the tyrants to their own management of civic cult and ritual, which, as another scholar describes it, "had a dual purpose: it served to articulate and strengthen collective identity, and to grant the elites a prominent place in the social order."[108] It is in light of these negotiations between private and public and aristocratic and demotic that we may view the adornment of the public cult statue of Apollo Patroos with the trappings of the citharode, which, on Shapiro's reasonable argument, originated with the Peisistratids. Alcibiades' claim gives us a glimpse of the ideological middle ground occupied by the musical Apollo Patroos—an aristocratic icon with popular appeal, not unlike Alcibiades himself. A scholiast to Aristophanes *Clouds* 984 gives us another glimpse. Glossing the word τέττιγες 'cicadas', which the personified Worse Argument, a proponent of all that is novel, uses to mock old-school Athenian musical culture, the scholiast reports that "the ancient Athenians wore golden cicadas in their hair, because, [cicadas] being musical (*mousikoi*), they were sacred to Apollo, who was Patroos to the *polis*."

Thucydides mentions these golden cicada hairpins in his description of the sumptuous Ionian dress that was integral to the "lifestyle of luxury" (τὸ ἀβροδίαιτον) practiced by Archaic Athenian elites

---

citharode in his depiction of this aloof Apollo Patroos rather than the god's aristocratic, "lyric" narcissism.

[106] Kolb 1977:107 views the tyrants' interest in Apollo Patroos (an "*Aristokratengott*") as being at odds with their *Volksinteresse*. Yet the dedication of the shrine in the Agora is rather a characteristically strategic negotiation of the claims of *Adel* and *Volk*.

[107] Jacoby 1944:72–73; cf. Hedrick 1988:203; Parker 1996:49n26.

[108] Jacoby 1944:74; Forsdyke 2005:116, with further bibliography. On similarities in the style of social and cultural management of Solon and Peisistratus, see now Irwin 2005b:263–280.

(1.6.3).[109] That lifestyle, it should be noted, was one surely promoted by the *philomousos* Hipparchus, as his importation to Athens of Ionian Anacreon, that exponent of East Greek lyric *habrosunê*, makes clear. We will see its imprint too on sixth-century images of Panathenaic citharodic performance. The Aristophanic scholiast describes a meaningful nexus, likely shaped by Peisistratean cultural politics, between elite display, the cultivation of music, and Apollo Patroos, who is, despite the special claims made upon him by the aristocracy, markedly identified as an inclusionary civic entity: he is "Patroos to the *polis*" (Πατρῷος τῇ πόλει). The god's citharodic aspect would accordingly, I suggest, have been subject to such a "double vision" in terms of its social significance.

We should recall too the way that the sixth-century ceramic evidence suggests a connection between a Delian citharodic Apollo, a figure that was probably identified with Athenian Apollo Patroos, and the Panathenaic citharodic *agônes*. Indeed, the public display of the ostensibly "aristocratic" Apollo Patroos as festival citharode could well emblematize the strategic thrust of the domestic politics of Panathenaic *kitharôidia* practiced by the Peisistratids. There can be no doubt that the *mousikoi agônes* of the Panathenaia, a free dispensation of musical mass entertainment, were exploited by the tyrants to secure their popularity with the *dêmos*.[110] At the same time, however, the tyrants likely recognized the value of musical contests as a site where the social and cultural ambitiousness of the aristocracy could be productively channeled into the demotic sphere, and thus better contained and controlled. Elites would themselves have seen the contests, perhaps at first mainly the aulodic ones, but increasingly the citharodic ones as well, as opportunities for high-visibility public display of their sociocultural distinction, as discerning, top-tier spectators and judges, and, at least in some cases, as performing competitors. Similar arguments have been made for the Peisistratids' management of the Panathenaic athletic *agônes*, which were, of course, a more traditional area of aristocratic recognition seeking.[111] Indeed, a surplus function of Heracles *kitharôidos* might have been to forge a symbolic link between the familiar world of the athletic contests and the less

---

[109] Cf. Hedrick 1988:200.

[110] Cf. Kotsidu 1991:28. And perhaps by Hippocleides the Philaid as well, if he was the festival's primary reorganizer. Further, if musical contests had been put on by wealthy families at privately funded festal events prior to their rule, the tyrants obviously would have been eager to trump these shows of aristocratic largesse on a grand civic scale.

[111] See Stahl 1987:246–255. Cf. Zimmermann 1992:32–33 on the tyrants' use of Dionysian choral culture to integrate the various social strata of Athens.

familiar one of the musical contests, modeling and inviting elite interest and participation in the latter.[112] The citharodic Apollo Patroos (as well as the other citharodic refractions of Apollo under the tyrants) could have fulfilled an analogous symbolic function, exerting an ennobling influence on agonistic *kitharôidia*, and in a sense legitimating its consumption and practice for the aristocratic elite.

5. Brilliant Spectators

The experience of Panathenaic *kitharôidia* in the sixth century BCE and, as we will see, through a good part of the fifth century thus belonged to "all the Athenians"—it was popular music broadly speaking—but it was still one in which aristocratic citizens cultivated a proprietary interest as privileged connoisseurs and occasionally as quasi-professional agonists. Sixth-century Attic vase painting provides vivid evidence for the elite investment in the spectatorship of festival *mousikê*. Unlike those of aulodes and auletes, the earliest images of citharodic (and citharistic) performance, from the middle of the century, do not include an audience, or at least a mortal audience. But by around 530 BCE black- and red-figured vases do begin to depict citharodes standing atop the *bêma* and performing before spectators. Among the earliest such vases is a red-figured amphora attributed to the Andokides Painter (Louvre G 1), which well exemplifies themes in the later-sixth- and early-fifth-century iconography of citharodic spectatorship. On the reverse of the amphora a beardless young man in full citharodic *skeuê*, including a wreath of victory on his head, stands on a two-tiered *bêma*; he has just run the plectrum across the strings of his large *kithara*, whose arms jut up impressively into the decorative frame running above the scene (Plate 9).[113] The player is depicted in a static, almost statuesque pose, which is typical of citharodic scenes at this time, but we need not think that the real-life musician this figure portrays did not display the kind of orchestic dynamism we see in many representations from later in the century.[114] The image on the obverse of the amphora may in fact suggest the excitement of the performance: two heroic warriors fight

---

[112] See Kotsidu 1991:114 for Heracles as an agonistic "Vorbild und Schutzpatron." On the inherent athleticism of citharodic performance, see Part I.18.

[113] Cf. Bundrick 2005:162, with 230n104 on the frame-breaking *kithara*. We may note how the sides of the decorative frame approximate the appearance of the columns that in other images connote Panathenaic performance.

[114] Cf. Shapiro 1992:66–67.

a duel, the top-pieces of their helmets breaking into the upper decorative frame like the arms of the *kithara* on the reverse. Is the duel the subject of the citharode's epic song? Or is the heroic contest meant to reflect and glorify the agonistic struggle of the musician? Perhaps we should not rule out either possibility. The dueling warriors are flanked by divine spectators, Hermes and Athena, whose presence may allude to the Panathenaic setting of the musical *agôn* on the reverse.

There, similarly disposed around the citharode, stands a pair of mortal spectators. These spectators, both beardless young men, represent the *kaloi k'agathoi* of the cultured elite of tyrannical Athens. Their elegant and costly Ionian costumes, no less impressive than that of the citharode, long hair, and staffs clearly distinguish them as such.[115] The two in fact appear to be consummate exponents of the Ionian "art of luxurious living," τὸ ἁβροδίαιτον, that Thucydides ascribed to Archaic Athenian elites (1.6.3). The citharodic *agônes*, it seems, were an attractive site for the conspicuous display, we might even say the "performance" of such elite splendor.[116] To complete the dandyish effect, both spectators hold flowers; the one on the right daintily sniffs the petals of his flower as he listens, to produce, one imagines, a sort of synaesthetic rush, the sweet smell enhancing the sweetness of the musical and visual *terpsis* unfolding before him.[117] The gesture finds a significant echo on the obverse, where Athena sniffs a flower as she watches the dueling warriors. Just as the citharode may be implicitly assimilated to the battling hero, so his fabulous spectators are gently likened to the gods. The parallelism may suggest that there is at least something

---

[115] On the staff as a marker of social privilege, see Stansbury-O'Donnell 2006:186; cf. Shapiro 1989:43.

[116] As were, and indeed from an earlier point (see discussion above), aulodic and auletic contests. Spectators of *aulêtikê* and *aulôidia* are similarly attired: examples and discussion in Shapiro 1992:62–64. Some spectators in early scenes of such contests also sit on stools. These are probably judges, but cf. Bundrick 2005:163. Seated spectators/judges would appear in citharodic scenes in the later sixth century, e.g. a black-figured pelike attributed to the Leagros Group (Staatliche Kunstsammlungen Kassel, Antikensammlung T.675; Shapiro 1992:69, fig. 47).

[117] On the flower sniffing, cf. Shapiro 1989:42. Cf. Bundrick 2005:163, who sees in the gesture an attempt to put on an "air of studied nonchalance." I would detect a greater focus and intensity in the listening postures of these spectators, although they are far less focused than the elite youth shown listening in deep concentration to citharodic performance on the early-fifth-century amphora by the Brygos Painter (Plate 2). The spectators on the amphora of the Andokides Painter are self-consciously "performing" their appreciation of the music; the youth on the Brygos Painter's seems, at least, rather genuinely "lost in the music"; cf. Bundrick 2005:165. (But is his "rapture" merely another pose? Cf. Part I.14). The Andokides Painter repeats the flower motif in a scene of an aulodic performance (Basel BS 491; Shapiro 1992:67, fig. 45)

notionally divine about such privileged spectatorship of the citharodic *agôn*.[118] Indeed, in scenes such as this, the glamour and charisma of the spectators attract the viewer's eye as much as does the star power of the citharode; the spectators are integral to the spectacle.

Given that they are likely stand-ins for the wealthy vase owners themselves, this is not surprising. These images flatter the privilege and distinction of the aristocratic festival audience, whose members consume the images at their own symposia, almost as much as they celebrate the achievement of the citharodic agonist. Relevant to these points is the marked visual identity between the spectators and citharode on the Louvre amphora, in their elegant dress as well as their physiognomy.[119] Indeed, the bodies of all three figures are similarly eroticized, and so make equal claims on the desire of the viewer; we watch the spectators watch the citharode. Our gaze is drawn especially to their protruding buttocks. As the old-school lover of boys and lyres, Better Argument, indicates in Aristophanes' *Clouds*, a πυγὴ μεγάλη 'big rump' ranked high on the list of features considered sexually attractive in the elite pederastic culture of Archaic and early Classical Athens (1014); it was indicative of good athletic and musical *paideia*. Citharodes would continue to be depicted with prominent buttocks into the fifth century BCE, a sign of the elite focalization of their sexual desirability.[120] See, for example, the Brygos Painter's citharode, alongside whom runs the inscription, "The boy is beautiful" (*ho pais kalos*); the elite listener on the reverse is similarly labeled a "beautiful boy" (Plates 1 and 2).

The Louvre amphora reveals too the way in which the civic music of the Panathenaic *mousikoi agônes* was imagined by Athenian elites to be something an exclusive encounter, a private possession. There is no direct indication of the mass audience that also attended and enjoyed the contests. Its appraising gaze, directed at the display of both musician and elite spectator, is of course implicit in the background—and very much needed for such displays to have any real validity—but the musical experience, despite its demotic frame, is envisioned as if

---

[118] Compare the slightly later eye-cup by Psiax (Plates 7a and b): a citharode and his two stylish spectators depicted on one side are on the other side "transformed" into heroic figures.

[119] We see this assimilation on other late Archaic scenes as well, e.g. a pelike in Kassel (n116 above) where citharode and seated spectator/judges are, however, all bearded, and all less flamboyantly attired than the figures on the Louvre amphora.

[120] Anderson 1994:193 notes that the prominent buttocks of the well-known citharode by the Berlin Painter (New York 56.171.38) have "an almost feminine gracefulness of line." But his contention that "this young performer deviates markedly from the physical ideals set forth for the youth of Athens by Aristophanes" is puzzling.

it were intended exclusively for the few connoisseurs who can truly appreciate it. The public is, as it were, obscured and the idealized aristocratic engagement with *kitharôidia* isolated and foregrounded. It is almost as if the *mousikos agôn* were portrayed as an intimate gathering, observed at a respectful distance by thousands of unseen yet fascinated viewers.

This effect is made especially vivid on a calyx krater by Euphronios from c. 510–500 BCE, also in the Louvre (G 103).[121] An aulete, labeled Polykles, mounts a *bêma* as he daintily lifts the back hem of his chiton with his right hand, a gesture we see *bêma*-mounting citharodes perform as well; Polykles in fact appears with a *kithara* on a contemporary black-figured oinochoe (Villa Giulia 20839-40). The audience is made up of three seated, young elites, each, like Polykles, labeled by inscriptions. Among them is Leagros, who makes numerous appearances on vase paintings of the time; his name is accompanied by a "tag *kalos*," which marks him as an eroticized cynosure of Athenian high society.[122] Again, the spectators are as much on display as the musician is. The intimacy of the scene would appear to suggest that "this is a private occasion, not a public festival."[123] Despite appearances, however, the setting is very likely meant to be a civic festival, probably the Panathenaia. The focus is merely restricted to the aristocratic members of the audience; the festal contest is rendered as a simulacrum of an informal domestic concert, offered for these privileged few.[124]

In the fourth century BCE, Aristotle advises his elite readership to avoid the demotic culture of *mousikoi agônes*, lest they be morally corrupted by its vulgarity (*Politics* 8.1341a9–13, 1341b10–32, 1342a16–27), and to resist as well the charms of the concert *kithara*, a thoroughly

---

[121] Bundrick 2005:163, fig. 97.

[122] On the "tag," see Shapiro 1989:43; cf. Shapiro 2004. Another aristocratic name with *kalos* inscription, [Me]las, is inscribed on the *bêma*, probably a reminder of another member of this fashionable coterie who is not pictured; cf. Bundrick 2005:164, with further scholarship. From the early fifth century, citharodes (and citharists), both young and older, are occasionally designated *kalos* (see Plates 1 and 13).

[123] Thus Shapiro 1989:43.

[124] Cf. Bundrick 2005:164, with relevant observations on the scene as occasion for display of aristocratic social status. However, there is no need to speculate that actual physical attendance at the Panathenaic *mousikoi agônes* was "a privilege of the elite." That would go very much against the socially integrative agenda of the Peisistratean *Kulturpolitik* in which they took root. Again, the vase paintings only idealize the exclusivity of the Archaic *agônes*. Of course, it is entirely conceivable that elite spectators took in the contests from privileged viewing positions, "front row seats," as it were. Judges, who were presumably drawn from the upper ranks of society, would certainly have taken positions close to the performer.

"banausic" *tekhnikon organon*, ideologically toxic to elite amateurs (*Politics* 8.1341a18–19). As we saw in Part I.9, these proscriptions reflect the tenor of a more general practical and sentimental turn taken by some, although certainly not all, Athenian elites, beginning as early as the middle of the fifth century and intensifying in response to the growing popularity of the New Music toward its end, away from civic *mousikê* and toward a "gentlemanly ideal" of *mousikê* restricted to the use of the amateur's lyre in the private confines of the schoolroom and symposium. Yet, as the Archaic iconography indicates, the socio-musical landscape of Peisistratean and Cleisthenic Athens was much less ideologically "uptight," much more hedonistically experimental; the politicized distinctions between *khelus*-lyre and *kithara*, lyre or *kithara* and *aulos*, sympotic/paideutic and agonistic, Apollonian and Dionysian, Greek and other were not nearly the sensitive issues they would become in the discursive elaborations surrounding the New Music in the late democracy.[125] Archaic elites apparently felt entitled to assume any number of musical identities, both as listeners and as performers.

In the *Politics*, Aristotle refers disapprovingly to this freedom of musical behavior, as if it were an embarrassing offense against proper decorum, out of character with the normally exemplary ethics and politics of the ancients. Both before (*proteron*) and in the aftermath of the Persian Wars, he says, the Athenians, flush with wealth and the leisure it afforded, eager to display their excellence (*aretê*), and proud of their accomplishments, "pursued every kind of learning, experimenting without discrimination" (πάσης ἥπτοντο μαθήσεως, οὐδὲν διακρίνοντες ἀλλ' ἐπιζητοῦντες, *Politics* 8.1341a28–32). This indiscriminate enthusiasm included *aulos* playing, which a few Archaic elites, Spartan and Athenian, went so far as to practice not only in private but in public, showing off their skills at *agônes* before festival audiences.[126] Later, however, they would reject the *aulos*, as they would too the "hedonistic," exotic stringed instruments of the Anacreontic sympotic culture originally promoted by Hipparchus, the *barbitos* and the harp (8.1341a32–42). That is, by around the middle of the fifth century, some Athenian elites, at least, were beginning to move away from the patterns of musical production and consumption that had

---

[125] See Martin 2003 for a sympathetic approach to the representations of the *aulos* in Archaic Athens. The diversity of musical references in Pindaric poetry also suggests the catholicity of elite Archaic attitudes to *mousikê*; see Barker 1984:54–61.

[126] Aristotle *Politics* 8.1341a33–36 names one Thrasippus, a *khorêgos* who supplied auletic accompaniment for his own chorus. Cf. Wilson 2000:131.

been established under the Peisistratids and had continued through the Persian Wars, choosing instead to display their leisured wealth and excellence in other fora. As we will see, however, the qualifier in "some elites" should be emphasized; the evidence does not support an absolute sundering of mass and elite musical cultures at any point. Other Athenian elites remained active and visible in the public culture of *kitharôidia* through the second half of the fifth century.

Although Aristotle focuses on the old-time aristocratic romance with the *aulos*, which, we saw, did in fact have considerable antiquity, the sheer number of Archaic and early Classical sympotic vessels featuring images of *kithara* players, many of them including elite spectators, indicates the extent to which the culture of *kitharôidia* was embraced and appropriated by the Athenian aristocracy, no doubt with the encouragement of the tyrants.[127] Elites not only participated publicly in that culture, they also incorporated it into the collective imaginary of their exclusive sympotic culture. Indeed, the sympotic validation of *kitharôidia* should be viewed as the ideologically necessary complement of its public consumption by elites in the Agora, or in whatever civic space the *agônes* were held at the time. Although concert *kitharai* themselves seem not to have been regularly played at Archaic symposia—the tortoise-shell lyre, the *barbitos*, and the *aulos* were the primary musical resources—valorized images of competitive *kitharôidia* pervaded it. The line between the agonistic world and the sympotic one was conceptually, if not necessarily in practice, fluid and permeable; there was not the rigid ideological barrier imagined by Aristotle. Archaic Athenian elites were clearly drawn, as fans, to the charismatic citharodes of the Panathenaia. They wanted to celebrate the agonistic fame (*kleos*) of their musical favorites by possessing commemorative images of their victorious performances, performances at which they themselves had been present as spectators and which now could be re-lived in the symposium.[128] Self-congratulation was mixed with admiration in the commissioning of such images. As we see on the Louvre amphora, elite fans glamorized their personal proximity to the action, promi-

---

[127] For the significantly greater number of citharode/citharist images relative to those of other agonistic musicians in the sixth and indeed throughout the whole of the fifth century, see Vos 1986:123 (who counts c. 90 citharodes/citharists from 550–540 to the end of the fifth century, out of around 140–150 scenes of agonistic music); cf. Kotsidu 1991:105.

[128] Cf. the remarks on the circulation of images of cherished athletic victors through Athenian symposia in Neer 2002:93–95.

nently inscribing, as it were, their own Panathenaic *kleos*, their artful performance of spectatorship, alongside that of the citharodic victor.

The sympotic imagery of citharodic performance could even prompt the merger of the bicameral roles of spectator and performer, inviting the symposiast to assume, in his imagination, the identity of the citharode. A remarkable example of an image that would inspire such fantasy is to be seen on the obverse of a red-figured pelike by the Argos Painter from c. 480 BCE (Plate 10). A citharode is posed on the *bêma* in an unusual fashion, facing left, with his back to the viewer of the vase as he sings and plays for his audience, which includes two spectators leaning on staffs and one seated spectator or judge. Citharodes are on other vases always posed facing right, so we have a clear view of their profiles, their garb, and their instruments; these elements are all strangely obscured on this pelike.[129] The Argos Painter's defiance of convention must have been intentional, however. The reversed pose in fact seems to have given him some trouble, as the awkward representation of the citharode's hands shows: it is unclear which hand is doing what, and where. Perhaps the confusion is comically deliberate, however; the artist may have wanted to illustrate the fact that this citharode is a rank amateur who has not the slightest bit of form or technique. We will return to that interpretation below. For now, let us consider the *in situ* visual effect created for the sympotic viewer of the pelike. As he reclines and looks at the image, perhaps while holding his own lyre or *barbitos*, the symposiast assumes the point of view of the performing citharode as he looks out from the *bêma* at the festival gathering, represented by the elite staff-leaners, one old and bearded, one beardless and young, as well as the seated spectator or judge, who stares straight ahead, seemingly at the performer, but actually at the viewer, whose gaze he almost disarmingly returns. Which one is being appraised, citharode or symposiast? What the image does, then, is offer a simulation of festival citharodic performance. From the comfort of his couch, the symposiast projects himself onto the *bêma*; he mimetically "plays the citharode," briefly experiencing the vertiginous thrill of singing before thousands.[130] This ludic fusion of sympotic and agonistic musical personae would of course be greatly enriched if we were to imagine the symposiast engaging the image while singing a lyric song, or even simply singing a *skolion* to *aulos* accompaniment.

---

[129] Cf. Kotsidu 1991:109–110.

[130] For a vivid evocation of the thrill of performing before a mass Panathenaic audience, see Plato *Ion* 535e.

Such mimetic role-playing would be entirely at home in the Dionysian ambience of the Archaic symposium, where the quasi-theatrical assumption of new identities was part of the ritual experience (and the fun). Music making played a crucial role in mediating this sympotic transformation of identity.[131] The so-called "Anacreontic" vases, which show Athenian elites trying on effeminate, Lydian personae in a sympotic-comastic environment while they play and dance to *barbitoi* and *auloi*, vividly illustrate this process.[132] It is appropriate, then, that on the Argos Painter's pelike the citharode may well be a satyr, the Dionysian play-actor *par excellence*, who here functions as whimsical alter ego for the elite symposiast.[133] Because his face is hidden by the *kithara* and his body by his flowing robes, we cannot be sure, but the shape of his head and what appears to be his deeply receding hairline hint at his satyric identity. Perhaps this very ambiguity is a deliberately playful, "surprise" effect. The reverse of the vase, however, shows a young satyr leading a camel, which strengthens the viewer's hunch that the citharode on the other side is a satyr.[134] (Is this exotic yet sentimental image perhaps meant to represent the subject of the satyr-citharode's song?)

---

[131] On the Archaic symposium as a theatrical, mimetic experience, see now Nagy 2007a; cf. Lissarrague 1990.

[132] See Frontisi-Ducroux and Lissarrague 1990. On the relationship of sympotic to comastic performance in the "Anacreontic" vases, see Nagy 2007a:240–241. On the mimesis of concert citharodic performance permitted by comastic performance on the barbitos, see Part III.15n275. In respect to this last point, it is worth noting that, on two vases from the last quarter of the sixth century BCE, a woman who is very likely meant to be Sappho is depicted with a *kithara* instead of a lyre or *barbitos*: a fragment from a belly amphora of c. 525 BCE, perhaps by the Andokides Painter (Stuttgart, Landesmuseum, 4.692; Schefold 1997:74–75, fig. 11); a black-figured lekythos of c. 500 BCE attributed to the Diosphos Painter (Hamburg, Museum für Kunst und Gewerbe 1984.497). See discussion in Yatromanolakis 2001:161n16. The casting of this icon of aristocratic lyric-sympotic song as a citharode reflects, I suggest, not so much the reality that her songs were sung to the *kithara* at symposia (or at *agônes*), but rather the citharodic fantasy in which Athenian symposiasts themselves could engage as they performed the Lesbian poet's songs. On the flirtation with *kitharôidia* inherent in Sapphic poetry, see Part II.9.i.

[133] Cf. Shapiro 2004:9–10 (with bibliography in his n34) on the "trend of the Late Archaic, to show satyrs mimicking the mores and manners of the Athenian élite. The humor seems to reside in the utter incongruity of the bestial satyrs masquerading as good Athenian citizens, sometimes even in citizen dress."

[134] Cf. Padgett 2000:57. The frontal view of the bald spectator/judge's face might also add to the intimations of satyric humor in the scene. Sympotic auditors of music sometimes face the viewer, e.g. a calyx krater of Euphronius (Munich, Antikensammlung 8935; c. 520–505 BCE), on which a frontal-faced symposiast listens to an *aulêtris*; cf. Bundrick 2005:113, with fig. 69.

The implicit satyric identity of the citharode could thus explain what may be his "bad technique"—this minion of Dionysus has surreptitiously gotten his bestial hands on the virtuoso instrument of Apollo. But satyrs in fact have a long history with the *kithara* in the Athenian sympotic imaginary, going back to the time of the Peisistratids. Satyric enthusiasm for the *kithara* seems in fact to have become a humorous commonplace by the fifth century: the chorus of Euripides' satyr play *Cyclops* claims that no sound is sweeter than that of the "Asiatic" *kithara* (443–444).[135] The *kithara* had a prominent place in late Archaic imagery of the make-believe Dionysian *thiasos*, where it was played, expertly it seems, by reveling satyrs, as well as the occasional maenad. Again, these images reflect the exuberant embrace of citharodic culture by elite symposiasts, its essential integration into the convivial realm of Dionysus.[136] We saw in Part III.9 that one such image, on a drinking cup from c. 520 BCE, may have included an allusion to Terpander in the form of a citharodic satyr labeled Terpes (Tarquinia, Museo Nazionale RC 6848). But the Argos Painter's citharodic satyr finds its closest parallel on a red-figured column-krater produced roughly 20 years later: a satyr, decked out in full citharodic regalia, the very model of the Panathenaic citharode, performs for two seated spectators or judges, Hermes and Dionysus, the latter of whom holds a thyrsos and a wine cup.[137] The image is, like that on the pelike, clearly humorous. Indeed, it would appear to allude to an older scene type, with Apollo *kitharôidos* similarly playing for a seated Hermes and Dionysus, such as we see depicted on a black-figured amphora in the manner of the Lysippides Painter from c. 530–520 BCE.[138] This latter scene splendidly emblematizes the virtual continuity between *agôn* and symposium that had taken shape under the tyrants. The model citharode entertains at once Dionysus, the god of the symposium and revel, and Hermes, who invented not only the sympotic tortoise-shell lyre, but also, as the *Homeric Hymn to Hermes* has it, the very

---

[135] On the satyric propensity for *kithara* playing, cf. Hedreen 2007:166–167.

[136] See Wegner 1949:210; representative images in Castaldo 2000:234–237, 240–241. Hedreen 2007:168 notes that, before around 520 BCE, reveling satyrs were portrayed exclusively with *auloi*; their novel adoption of *kitharai* thus reflects the increased interest in *kitharôidia* among the sympotic aristocracy at this time. As a variant of these scenes we may note vases that depict a citharodic contest on one side and a scene of Dionysian revelry on the other, e.g. a black-figured kylix, Group of London B 460 (London, British Museum B 460); a black-figured pelike attributed to the Leagros Group (Staatliche Kunstsammlungen Kassel, Antikensammlung T.675). Cf. Webster 1972:160.

[137] Ferrara, Museo Archeologico Nazionale 4110; Castaldo 2000:241, fig. 125.

[138] Norfolk, VA, Chrysler Museum of Art 2003.18. Apollo does not, however, stand on a *bêma*. For other examples of the schema, see Castaldo 2000:120.

art of citharodic performance. In addition, as god of the Agora, the presence of Hermes could allude to the Panathenaic *agônes*, which may have been held in the Agora before they were transferred to the Odeion.[139]

It is tempting to read the satyric variation on the earlier scene as a negative parody, a critical comment on the increasingly Dionysian and theatrical elements creeping into a traditionally conceived Apollonian *kitharôidia*, a subject we will take up later. Indeed, it may be significant that images of Apollo as a concert citharode begin to fall out of the iconographic record around the time this column krater was produced, a sign perhaps of elite disenchantment with trends in the popular culture of *kitharôidia*.[140] But the column krater likely looks backward, rather than forward to changes in the sociology of *kitharôidia* to come. Its citharodic satyr is not a figure of derision or anxiety, but an emblem of the continued elite interest in public *kitharôidia*, his performance reflective of the cultural continuum still felt to exist between the festival *bêma* and the symposium.[141]

6. Lyric Politics in the *Hymn to Hermes*

The continuum between the festival *bêma* and the symposium may find its mythical foundation in the *Homeric Hymn to Hermes*, which was probably composed in the form we have it in the later sixth century BCE.[142] Norman O. Brown, noting certain resonances between the themes

---

[139] I follow an interpretation of Hermes' presence as spectator of Heracles *kitharôidos* offered by Bundrick 2005:160.

[140] Cf. Sarti 1992; cf. Wilson 2004:283–286. Sarti (p101) notes the sociomusical implications of the appearance in late-fifth-century vase painting of the *kithara* in the hands of Marsyas, the one-time auletic opponent of Apollo *kitharôidos*. On her reading, the images signal that *kitharôidia* has been fully integrated into the demotic sphere of Dionysian aulodic, civic *mousikê* and is no longer the "possession" of the lyric elite. Boardman 1956 thinks these images were inspired by a dithyramb of Melanippides, which might suggest a deliberate attempt on the part of aulodic composers to appropriate the music of the *kithara*; cf. Csapo 2004:213.

[141] Wilson 2004:287n45 reads the scene attractively as a "positive, if playful, proclamation of the increased assumption—from 'below'—of a proud place in the *technê*, and one in which the influence of Dionysos was increasingly felt." But the cultural transformation in *kitharôidia* that Wilson would see reflected might be premature c. 460 BCE, and I am somewhat less inclined to accept it than I was in Power 2007:191. The satyric *kitharôidos* seems rather a reconfirmation of elite mastery of citharodic culture "from above."

[142] See Janko 1982:141–143; Görgemanns 1976 would date the *Hymn* to the early fifth century. His interpretation, however, strongly favors an Athenian context for its composition (see below).

of the *Hymn* and in the cultural politics of the tyrants, not least the emphasis on lyric *mousikê*, offers a compelling argument for the *Hymn's* creation in Athens under Hippias and Hipparchus. He proposes a date for its performance there in the years immediately following 522/1 BCE, when the Altar of the Twelve Gods was dedicated in the Agora. The *Hymn*, Brown argues, alludes to this monument when Hermes portions out 12 sacrifices to the gods (126–129). This model sacrifice takes place on the banks of the river Alpheios, and so presumably near Olympia (although Olympia goes unnamed), where there was a cult of the Twelve Gods (cf. Pindar *Olympian* 10.48). It seems clear that, by the topographical logic of the narrative itself, Hermes' sacrifice is meant to provide an *aition* for the Olympic cult. But this need not mean that the *Hymn* was performed at Olympia, as a number of scholars have argued. An Athenian audience would naturally take the *Hymn* to refer secondarily to their cult of the Twelve Gods, localized in the Agora, a site closely associated with Hermes in the Peisistratid era, and where in fact the first performance of the *Hymn* may have taken place, conceivably at the Panathenaia.[143] A Peisistratid context would certainly suit the "lyric politics" implicit in the *Hymn*, the way in which it presupposes the ideologically unproblematic overlap between symposium and *kitharôidia*, amateur and professional, that, I have argued, characterized the musical scene of late Archaic Athens. Further, while our *Hymn* is a rhapsodic production, its preoccupation with lyric and citharodic themes may suggest the existence of a separate citharodic Hermes *humnos*, also responsive to an Athenian cultural context, from which the rhapsodes derived their own *prooimion*. Citharodes obviously would

---

[143] Brown 1947:102–110. Brown's arguments are too complex and in some ways problematic to deal with in detail here. The salient points are expressed above (although Brown seems to believe too that the *Hymn* was performed before a private audience at the court of Hipparchus, which seems to me unlikely). Brown's scenario for the *Hymn's* Athenian performance finds a notable adherent in Webster 1975:92; on Atticisms in the text, see Càssola 1975:174. Among proponents of an Olympic performance are Càssola 1975:174, Janko 1982:142, Burkert 1984, and West 2003:14. The fact that Athens is not mentioned in the text is no indication that it was not first performed there; Olympia, after all, is not named either. The *Hymn* was a Panhellenically oriented composition that would have been carried by rhapsodes from place to place. An overt reference to Athens would be out of place in its mythical topography, and would thus compromise the supra-local potential of its performance. Against the Olympic scenario, we may also recall that *mousikoi agônes* were not held at the Olympic Games. More recently, Johnston 2002 has proposed a number of alternatives to performance at Olympia, including Delos and Delphi, but she leaves Athens out of consideration.

have had more of a vested interest in elaborating the divine origins of the lyre and their own *tekhnê*.[144]

In the *Hymn*, Hermes invents the tortoise-shell lyre, which is repeatedly envisioned as being ultimately destined for use in the symposium, where the instrument was in fact most at home. Hermes addresses the tortoise as χοροιτύπε δαιτὸς ἑταίρη 'companion of the feast who strikes up the dance' (31), thus evoking the sympotic-comastic ambience of courtesans (*hetairai*) and string-accompanied, quasi-orchestic revels such as we see on the "Anacreontic" vases.[145] Later, Hermes will hand his lyre over to Apollo, again figuring it as a *hetaira*, and telling his brother to bring it to the "rich feast and the lovely dance (*khoros*) and to the glorious revel (*kômos*)" (480–481; cf. 436–437).[146] On the other hand, however, it is important to note that

---

[144] It is worth noting that Alcaeus composed a hymn to Hermes, perhaps a lyric response to a citharodic hymn already in the repertoire of the Lesbian Singers (fr. 308). It is unclear, however, whether Alcaeus' hymn dealt with the god's invention of the lyre; cf. Hägg 1989:51–52. Perhaps Hermes' invention of the lyre was a "mainland" rather than Eastern Aegean/Lesbian citharodic tradition; cf. Part II.9.i. Hermes is notably left out of the Aeolic-Ionic lyric genealogy described in Timotheus *Persians* 221–231, which includes only Orpheus, Terpander, and Timotheus; Apollo is the only lyric god acknowledged in the text.

[145] On the lyre as *hetaira*, see now Richardson 2007:88–89.

[146] The *khoros* here likely refers to dance in the sympotic environment, bookended as it is by feast and revel. For the "Dionysian chorus" of the symposium, see Part I.6.i. But another possible identity for the "lovely *khoros*" should be considered. On a black-figured Attic amphora from c. 550 BCE, four men playing lyres move in choral proces-sion, two of them taking giant steps as they go, a movement that recalls the "fine and high step" of Apollo the paeanic *kitharistês* in *Homeric Hymn to Apollo* 516 (Paris, Louvre G 861; Maas and Snyder 1989:51, fig. 15c). Could these musicians themselves be engaged in a paeanic choral performance of some kind? At the Spartan Hyacinthia *kithara*-playing boys marched in a paeanic procession, strumming to the tune piped by an accompanying aulete (Polycrates FGrH 588 F 1). There is, however, no *aulos* in the Attic procession. That is not a problem, but the lack of any known festival occasions for paeanic performance in Athens is (cf. Wilson 2007:165–166). Perhaps the procession is part of some other civic festival, even the Panathenaia (although these lyre players are presumably not cithardic agonists). Alternatively, some sort of private festivity is possible. The aristocratic clan of the Euneidai (see Part III.8) were known to provide lyric music for festival processions (Pollux *Onomasticon* 8.103), although Pollux does not specify occasion. Indeed, the ceremonially attired lyre players on the Louvre amphora may as well be Athenian elites rather than professional musicians; perhaps the image even captures the Euneidai in action. Interpretation is complicated, however, by a series of images on late-sixth- and early-fifth-century black-figured vases that visually resemble the lyric procession depicted on the amphora. These images feature marching satyrs playing *kitharai* (and in one case lyres) in processional groups, sometimes high stepping as well (Szilágyi 1977:361; Hedreen 2007:164–168; images collected in Castaldo 2000:242–244). These images have been read as representations of real-life proto-satyr-play choral performances (e.g. Hedreen 1992:113–114) or pre-aulodic, "Arionic" satyric-citharodic dithyrambs,

both of Hermes' performances involve what are distinctly citharodic forms, the *anabolê* 'prelude' and hymnic *prooimion* (52–61; 425–433; cf. Part II.1–2). Recall that in the world of the *Hymn*, the *kithara* has not yet been invented; Apollo has only had experience of the *auloi* (450–452). But Hermes wields the lyre, which is called *kitharis* (499, 509, 515) and *phorminx* (64, 506)—the wooden "box lyres" that are actually the ancestors of the *kithara*—as well as *lura* (418, 423) *and khelus* (153, 242), as if it were both the prototype of the concert *kithara* and the future musical resource of the symposium; the instrument is performatively and functionally overdetermined.[147] Extended hymnic *prooimia* are not at home in the symposium; they are the province of the skilled festival

---

for which there is, however, no good evidence outside of the images themselves and an arbitrary synthesis of some disparate nuggets of testimony in the *Suda* entry on Arion. (*Pace* Koller 1962, there is no reason to believe that Arion composed his Corinthian dithyrambs for *kitharai* rather than *auloi*; also, Pratinas PMG 708 is almost certainly a late-fifth-century aulodic dithyramb rather than an Archaic "citharodic dithyramb," as Zimmermann 1986 shows.) Another scenario: men—including the Euneidai, perhaps, who had connections with Dionysian cult (IG II² 5056)—dressed as satyrs could have marched with *kitharai* at the Anthesteria, where "satyr play" and behavioral inversion were at home (cf. Seaford 1984:7), and where there may have been string contests as well (Friis-Johansen 1967:192; Smith 2007:162). It seems preferable, however, to read the marching satyrs, who are notably not depicted as men in costume but as purely mythical beings, as creatures of fantasy (cf. Hedreen 2007:167), akin to the *kithara*-playing satyrs in the make-believe hyperspace of the Dionysian *thiasos* depicted on contemporary Attic vases. Like those satyrs, these processional satyrs represent the culture of citharodic music in Dionysian, sympotic drag; they are ultimately figures of fun and the sympotic imagination rather than cultic reality (cf. Castaldo 2000:122; Part III.9n159). The sort of lyric processional we see on the Louvre amphora may well be their primary point of reference. But the satyrs may offer up too a funhouse reflection of competitive citharodes at the Panathenaia. On an early fifth-century lekythos (Taranto 6250; Castaldo 2000:244, fig. 129, with comments on p121), three satyrs proceed through "an urban religious sanctuary defined by herm, bema, and altar. The architectural elements suggest the kind of place where competitive song and dance was performed, such as the Agora at Athens" (Hedreen 2007:166). But the central place of the *bêma* suggests above all a citharodic *agôn*; one of the satyrs is in fact shown mounting it, as citharodic agonists commonly do. The "Singers at the Panathenaia" krater by Polion from c. 425 BCE represents a late variation on the motif of the citharodic satyr procession (New York, The Metropolitan Museum of Art, Fletcher Fund 1925 [25.78.66]; Hedreen 2007:165, fig. 54). Here the costumed satyrs are clearly intended to parody Panathenaic citharodes, rather more critically, it seems, than those in the Archaic images; the scene, which includes an aulete, is likely based on a dramatic model, either a satyr play (Froning 1971:25–26) or perhaps a comedy (Roos 1951:227; cf. Storey 2003b on satyric comic choruses). For the *kithara* in Dionysian ritual and comastic contexts in Laconian art, see Stibbe 1992.

[147] Cf. Richardson 2007:86. On the alternation of the names for the lyre in the *Hymn*, see Càssola 1975:166–170. See Hägg 1989 on various traditions of Hermes' invention of the lyre. On the lyre as the notionally "primitive" antecedent to the sophisticated concert *kithara*: Part III.5n60.

citharode, and when Hermes sings them to his lyre, he takes on the identity of the citharode.

The *Hymn* nevertheless suggests that both proto-citharodic performances are also paradigmatic performances of sympotic lyric. Before Hermes sings his first *prooimion*, the song of his own birth, and so a model "Hymn to Hermes," his "beautiful singing" (καλὸν ἀείδειν) to the lyre, "improvisatory and experimental" (ἐξ αὐτοσχεδίης πειρώμενος)— this is after all the first time such a citharodic *humnos* has been sung— is compared to "young men at feasts, who boldly trade jibes with one another" (κοῦροι | ἡβηταὶ θαλίῃσι παραιβόλα κερτομέουσιν, 54–56). The spontaneous spirit of Hermes' performance, despite its clearly polished, virtuosic execution, is markedly figured as the sort of confidently unpracticed, improvisatory, yet nonetheless graceful expression that is characteristic of sympotic speech and music making. Similarly, Hermes' performance of his second *prooimion* is imagined at once as paradigmatically citharodic and sympotic. Before striking up the *anabolê*, he takes his stand "to the left" of Apollo (ἐπ' ἀριστερά, 424). The significance of this positioning is made clear when Apollo, who has interrupted Hermes to express his amazement at the music, claims that while he knew the music of the *aulos*, "Yet I have never thought of anything else like this—like the passing to the right (ἐνδέξια ἔργα) at young men's feasts (ἀλλ' οὔ πώ τί μοι ὧδε μετὰ φρεσὶν ἄλλο μέλησεν, | οἷα νέων θαλίης ἐνδέξια ἔργα πέλονται, 453–454). What Apollo is referring to is the well-known sympotic tradition of singing convivial songs (*skolia*). Martin West comments,

> At the symposium a myrtle branch and/or a lyre was passed round the guests from left to right, and each in turn was expected to sing or improvise a few verses. Our poet represents the practice as already existing in outline and as just waiting for the lyre to be invented for its perfection.[148]

We realize now that Apollo and Hermes have been arranged in a distinctly sympotic configuration. Having finished his song, Hermes will hand the lyre over to Apollo, who stands to his right; it is as if the two gods are laterally positioned, as they would be at a reclining symposium, rather than facing one another, as performer and spectator at a citharodic performance. The handover will thus be a model

---

[148] West 2003:149; the translation of these lines is also West's. On lyric ἐνδέξια cf. Storey 2003a:322.

for the ἐνδέξια ἔργα of the historical symposium.[149] Appropriately, Apollo, immediately upon receiving the lyre, launches expertly into his own song, emulating precisely the technique of Hermes (499–502; cf. 418–420), and implicitly even bettering it, for it was the custom of *skolion* singing that the "receiver" of the the lyre would have to "cap," that is, show up, the previous singer's song.[150] It is likely that this game of "capping" is already alluded to in the comparison of Hermes' first lyric performance to the mutual jibes of young symposiasts (55–56).[151] By implication, then, Hermes' virtuosic citharodic *humnos* is imagined as a *skolion*; his citharodic performance is a prelude, as it were, to the symposium. At the same time, we may be invited to see the implicitly competitive exchange between Hermes and Apollo as a mythical prefiguration of the competition between citharodes at the Panathenaic citharodic *agôn*.

Just as the *Hymn* collapses distinctions between citharodic and sympotic performance, so it provides a divine model for the cultural symbiosis of professional and amateur musicians. One would not want to adopt uncritically the class-based reading of the *Hymn* offered by Brown, according to which Hermes is the projection of the "aspirations and achievements" of an emerging merchant class and so the antipode of the old guard paragon of aristocratic values, Apollo.[152] But it

---

[149] A few sources claim that lyric *skolia* were so called because of the "crooked" course the lyre took as it was passed, out of order, among the most skilled singers (*sunetôtatoi*) in the room, i.e. *skolia* did not simply go "to the right." The earliest proponent of this theory is the late-fourth-century BCE Peripatetic Dicaearchus (fr. 88 Wehrli). But there is no compelling reason to think that his etymology reflects sixth-century practice (cf. Part III.15n265); his scholarly predecessor Aristoxenus (fr. 125 Wehrli) by contrast proposed that the songs were called *skolia* because of the crooked (yet sequential) path they traveled due to the arrangement of couches at the symposium. However, if Dicaearchus' claim is somehow reflective of Archaic practice, then we might assume that Hermes and Apollo are facing each other, and that the lyre will go "out of order," i.e. to the left, as it is passed from god to god, both *sunetôtatoi*. The *Hymn* would thus imagine the gods' citharodic-sympotic encounter as a "breaking of the rules" of *endexia* before the fact. Such cleverness would not be out of keeping with the sophisticated wit of the *Hymn*, but the "lateral" reading proposed above seems more probable.

[150] On sympotic "capping," see Aristophanes *Wasps* 1219–1227 (where the singing of *skolia* to the *aulos* rather than the lyre is described), with Collins 2004:84–146, who notes intriguing formal parallels between sympotic song performance and Panathenaic *rhapsôidia*, despite the ideological differences between the two institutions.

[151] Cf. Barker 1984:103n16.

[152] Brown 1947:97. See Kurke 2003:97n29 for a perhaps too harsh critique of Brown's "crude sociologizing." It is true that Brown's Marxist-influenced reading of the *Hymn* verges on naïve allegorizing, but his attention to its socioeconomic subtext and context does in fact anticipate more sophisticated New Historicist-inflected approaches to literary production taken by Kurke and others.

would not be too reductive to see Hermes in part as an exemplar of the professional citharode, one who proudly views his music as a source of economic livelihood—his lyre is a "priceless treasure" (μυρίον ὄλβον, 24) and a source of profit and means of social advancement (34–35)—yet who also knows as an entertainer and teacher how to appeal to the sensibilities of the aristocracy. He presents his music as a desirable combination of gentlemanly, "sympotic" spontaneity—lyre playing should be "devoid of grievous effort" (ἐργασίην φεύγουσα δυήπαθον, 486)—and the performer's "knowledgeable application of skill and expertise" (τέχνῃ καὶ σοφίῃ δεδαημένος, 483), which requires, of course, the oversight of the professional instructor—Hermes fashions himself now as the model *kitharistês*, the schoolmaster in charge of lyric *paideia*.[153] Apollo, representing the aristocratic audience, is first awed by the novelty of Hermes' *kitharôidia*, then he recognizes the value of the lyre for the elite symposium; he is willing to exchange for it and the didactic service of Hermes his precious cattle (436–437). Hermes himself is welcomed into the Olympian ranks—that is, Athenian high society—where Apollo guarantees him "prestige and fortune among the gods" (κῦδρον ἐν ἀθανάτοισιν καὶ ὄλβιον, 461) thanks to his invention of the lyre; Apollo will, however, from now on personally assume mastery of it. Far from being the allegory about the conflict between Hermes and the professional class and Apollo and the aristocracy envisioned by Brown, the *Hymn* imagines instead the negotiation and integration of the two, at least in their musical capacities, with the latter, of course, assuming a leading role.[154]

There is no doubt that we need to make room for a certain degree of wish fulfillment on the part of the agonistic professionals who created

---

[153] On the rarified socioeconomics of lyric *paideia*, see Plato *Protagoras* 326b–c: only the richest and most powerful citizens have access to it. Winnington-Ingram 1988 discusses the identity and status of professional teachers of *mousikê* in fifth-century Athens. Socrates' *kitharistês*, Konnos, may have had a career as a citharode (scholia *ad* Aristophanes *Wasps* 675).

[154] On the theme of Hermes' integration into the Olympian order, see Clay 1989:100–103, 149–151. It is important to note that in other accounts of the myth Apollo and Hermes did come into direct conflict over possession of the lyre. Pausanias 9.30.1 describes a bronze sculpture on Helicon that portrayed Apollo and Hermes "fighting over the lyre" (καὶ Ἀπόλλων χαλκοῦς ἐστιν ἐν Ἑλικῶνι καὶ Ἑρμῆς μαχόμενοι περὶ τῆς λύρας). The theme seems to be illustrated on two red-figured Attic vase paintings of the fifth century BCE as well: see Overbeck 1889:419–420. At Argos, however, Hermes' role as inventor seems to have been acknowledged by and integrated into Apollonian cult: Pausanias 2.19.7 reports that in the sanctuary of Apollo Lycius there was a statue of Hermes taking hold of the tortoise to make the lyre. Unfortunately, there is no indication in the text of the monument's date.

this scenario. The exaltation and ennobling of Hermes the citharode is heavily idealized. Non-elite citharodes, despite being admired and feted by politically powerful birth elites and interacting with them as entertainers and teachers, would for the most part not have been recognized as their social equals (*hetairoi*). In reality, the profoundly amateur mentality of the aristocratic symposium would not easily have accommodated the socioeconomic values of the career citharode.[155] But the *Hymn* is accurate in capturing, and valorizing, the ideological openness of late-sixth- and early-fifth-century Athenian musical culture, in which the elite symposiast was potentially a citharode and the citharode potentially an aristocratic lyre singer, even if those potentials were in real life only occasionally realized.[156] We may thus detect in the *Hymn* the outlines of an originally Peisistratean musico-political agenda, one aimed at opening up a self-entrenched aristocratic culture to the influence of the civic *mousikê* patronized most conspicuously by the tyrants themselves.

7. Aristocratic Agonists

Ideology and practice did occasionally align, however; some aristocrats became musical agonists. In Section 1, I suggested that some of the earliest agonistic aulodes at the Panathenaia may have been members of the aristocracy, who had acquired experience singing elegy at symposia. By the later sixth century, some Athenian elites may have felt sufficiently confident in their lyric *paideia* to train for competition

---

[155] In his study of Attic vases featuring musical contest scenes, T. B. L. Webster presumes that the vases were commissioned by friends, family, and admirers of musical victors for sympotic celebrations, at which the victors would have been guests of honor (Webster 1972:158–171). That may be true in some cases, in particular those vases with name-labeled musicians, at least some of whom represent "aristocratic agonists" (Webster, p49, with discussion in Section 7 below), but there is no reason to think that professional citharodes would regularly have been invited to participate at symposia as "equals," even if their charismatic images were welcome there.

[156] For such "egalitarian fictions" operative in the production and consumption of Athenian painted pottery at this time, see Neer 2002:131–132. It is notable that some of the "Pioneer" vase painters who portrayed themselves (or their colleagues) as if they were the aristocratic "equals" of their clients depict themselves (or their colleagues) making music in elite milieux, e.g. a hydria by Phintias (Munich 2421): on the body of the vase the painter Euthymides is shown receiving instruction in the lyre; on the shoulder above, a *hetaira* reclining at a symposium toasts him, "This one's for you, Euthymides!" Discussion in Neer 2002:102. Cf. Hedreen 2003, however, for the view that the scene is parodic.

at the Panathenaic citharodic and citharistic *agônes*.[157] This does not mean that the late Archaic *agônes* were by any means dominated by the enthusiastic local gentry. We should assume that itinerant professionals incorporated the Panathenaia into their schedule of festival appearances from a relatively early point, and that the Peisistratids actively encouraged the participation of eminent foreign musicians, offering high-value prizes to that end.[158] The testimony of "Plato" *Hipparchus* 228b–c, that Hipparchus sent nothing less than a penteconter to escort Anacreon to Athens and retained Simonides there μεγάλοις μισθοῖς καὶ δώροις 'with large fees and gifts', speaks to the

---

[157] The early-fifth-century BCE "schoolroom" cup by Douris (Antikensammlung, Staatliche Museen zu Berlin, Preussischer Kulturbesitz F 2285) suggests that Archaic elite youths would learn some bits of the citharodic repertoire as part of their training with the *kitharistês*. A boy studies a scroll containing a hexametric verse that appears to represent the *prooimion* to a citharodic song (PMG 938e). See West 1971:308; Part II.9.ii.

[158] We have no idea what sorts of prizes were given to musical victors at the Peisistratean Panathenaia, or in the fifth century for that matter, but there is every reason to believe that lucrative cash-and-valuables awards were granted, as they were in the fourth century (IG II² 2311). As Aristotle *Constitution of Athens* 60.3 puts it, "The prizes for winners in the *mousikoi agônes* are of silver and gold." Most agonists were, after all, itinerants, who would appreciate cash-and-carry prizes (cf. Herington 1985:246n28). The lack of true Panathenaic amphoras showing musical contests strongly indicates that musicians were not awarded olive oil as were athletic victors. There is one example of what would seem to be a fifth-century Panathenaic oil amphora representing a citharodic performance (St. Petersburg 17295; c. 430–425 BCE), but its size is irregular—54 cm compared to the 59.9 to 69 cm that are standard in the sixth and fifth centuries—and its status as an official prize amphora thus in doubt; cf. Davison 1958:38; Kotsidu 1991:90. At most it represents an *ad hoc* exception to the cash rule. There are not strong grounds for the claim, made by Kotsidu 1991:100, that after 403/2 BCE cash-and-valuables prizes suddenly replaced less explicitly "chrematitic" crown-and-oil awards (cf. Davison 1958:37–38, who anticipates Kotsidu, though far less vigorously). Kotsidu (p91) points to an inscription from 402/1 (IG II² 1388.36–37) that records the dedication of a citharode's golden crown to Athena, but there is no reason to take this as evidence of a change in prize policy during that year. Her appeal to the thesis elaborated in Valavanis 1987 (cf. Davison, p37), that after the fall of the Thirty the Panathenaia was reformed, is unpersuasive: changes to the Panathenaia may well have been made under the restored democracy, but there is no reason to believe that the prize policy was affected. Further, two pieces of literary testimony point to cash-and-valuables prizes before the fourth century. At Plato *Ion* 530d (set in the late fifth century) the rhapsode Ion says he deserves to win the "golden wreath" at a contest that is almost certainly the Panathenaia; cf. also his mercenary observation (535e) that if he makes his audience cry, he will in turn laugh when he gets his cash prize (αὐτὸς γελάσομαι ἀργύριον λαμβάνων). At Athenaeus 15.698d–699a we learn that the parodic singer Hegemon of Thasos won a second prize of 50 drachmas cash at Athens. Kotsidu makes the argument that this victory took place at the Panathenaia between 420 and 412 BCE, when *parôidia* seems to have been introduced into the *agônes* (p89, with sources collected there). See Shapiro 1992:58–59 for visual indices of cash prizes in the iconography.

tyrants' lavish expenditures on recruitment of musical talent from abroad.[159] Indeed, the earliest Panathenaic musical victor whose name we know, the aulete Midas, was a citizen of Sicilian Acragas (probably a Phrygian by birth) and an international competitor; his victory at the Pythia in 490 BCE was celebrated by no less than Pindar (*Pythian* 12, with scholia *ad* inscr.). The earliest known victor in *kitharôidia* is Phrynis of Mytilene (scholia *ad* Aristophanes *Clouds* 971c), whose victory leads us to suspect that other members of the famed Lesbian *diadokhê* had made appearances at Panathenaic *agônes* before his victory, which probably took place in 446 BCE. Yet there is some circumstantial evidence that suggests at least a few socially distinguished Athenians did try their hand at agonistic *kitharôidia* and *kitharistikê*, competing against the professionals, sometimes, it seems, with success, in the later sixth and well into the fifth century BCE. It is worth reviewing the main pieces of evidence, such as they are.

First, in the decade leading up to and that following 500 BCE, two victorious citharodes made dedications on the Athenian Acropolis. These dedications probably took the form of costly bronze statues of the citharodes in their moment of victory, for which we have the inscribed bases. These bases also would have represented the *bêmata* on which the sculpted musicians stood. It seems a reasonable assumption that the victories these dedications commemorated were at the Panathenaia.[160] The earlier inscription, dated by Raubitschek to 510–500, reads, "Alkibios | the *kitharôidos* | dedicated [this] | Nesiotes" (IG I[3] 666).[161] "Nesiotes" might indicate Alkibios' provenance; the island of Nesos is close to Lesbos, so it would be a suitable homeland for an Archaic citharode. But it far more likely belongs to the artist who crafted the dedication, despite the fact that the expected *m'epoiêse* 'made me' is missing. Nesiotes was a prominent figure in post-Peisistratean Athens, most famous for creating, in collaboration with Kritios, the Tyrannicides group as well as a number of other prominent pieces of monumental sculpture on the Acropolis.[162] To engage a Nesiotes, Alkibios must have been a person of considerable means and

---

[159] The "large fees and gifts" for Simonides mentioned in the *Hipparchus* refer to the maintenance of the poet in his public and private capacities, respectively. As a composer of civic choral melic, Simonides worked openly for *misthos* 'fee'; as a private, sympotic companion of the tyrant, he received instead "gifts," in accord with the non-professional ideology of the symposium; cf. Part III.15n298 for Anacreon's monetary disinterest at Polycrates' court.

[160] Cf. Davison 1958:40; Kotsidu 1991:76.

[161] Raubitschek 1949, no. 84.

[162] Cf. Kotsidu 1991:79.

connections in the *polis*. The later inscription, dated c. 500–480, reads, "Ophsi[os the *kith*]*arôidos* ded[icated me] in Ath[ens]" (IG I³ 754).[163] Another fragment of an Acropolis base inscription, IG I³ 753, "Kalon the Aeginetan made [this]," has been thought to belong to Ophsios' dedication. Like Nesiotes, Kalon was a "name" craftsman of his time.[164] Again, we must presume Ophsios was a man of wealth and standing, who could afford the services of a Kalon. It is entirely possible that both Alkibios and Ophsios were foreign-born professionals who had grown rich playing at festival *agônes* and could afford to be commemorated in style at Athens, an emerging center of *kitharôidia*. Recall that the aulete Midas of Acragas, whose income would presumably have been less than a top-rank citharode's, was apparently able to afford the epainetic services of Pindar.[165] But both citharodes "bear good Attic names."[166] And although the absence of patronymics in both inscriptions might give us some pause—could these men have been Athenians of humble birth who "made it big" with their *kitharôidia*?—the most likely scenario is that Alkibios and Ophsios were both "aristocratic agonists," who marked their achievements with a reflexively elitist flair for conspicuous self-promotion.[167] We might even want to view the later dedication of Ophsios as an agonistic response to the earlier one of Alkibios. The two would likely have been close enough in age to compete against one another. Perhaps their competitiveness spilled over into the high-status game of monumental prestige, with Ophsios matching, even trumping Alkibios' ostentatious Acropolis dedication with one of his own, commissioned from an equally famous artist.

Attic vases provide another set of evidence, perhaps more definitive. Beginning at the end of the sixth century BCE, a number of vases were produced featuring musical agonists identified by name. These

---

[163] Raubitschek 1949, no. 86.

[164] Raubitschek 1949, no. 85; cf. Kotsidu 1991:77–78.

[165] Although his tyrannical patrons, the Emmenidai, may have brokered (and perhaps paid for) the commission; cf. Part III.15n294.

[166] Davison 1958:40.

[167] Cf. the prudent assessment of Wilson 2004: "Fine and costly states need not entail *kaloikagathoi* dedicators, but at this period, they certainly point in that direction" (284). We may note that the only other bronze statue of a mortal musician erected on the Acropolis of which we know was that of the ultimate exemplar of aristocratic lyric *mousikê*, Anacreon (Pausanias 1.25.1); the dedicator was surely a wealthy elite. See Part II.13n333. Also relevant is the fact that the patronymics of assuredly professional citharodes such as Phrynis and Nicocles seem to have been included in their victory announcements and inscriptions (PMG 802; IG II² 3779, Nicocles son of Aristocles); perhaps we should consider another factor besides class behind the absence of patronymic on the Acropolis monuments.

named agonists, all but one of them string players, appear on other vases in contexts that suggest they were of an aristocratic background. It has been plausibly argued that the vases commemorating their agonistic victories were commissioned specifically for symposia at which they were lauded by their elite friends and family.[168] The earliest of these are two contemporary vessels featuring a musician named Polykles. In Section 5, we looked at the scene on the calyx krater of Euphronius (Louvre G 103), in which a musician labeled Polykles mounts the *bêma* with *auloi* in hand, presumably to compete in an auletic *agôn*. A musician labeled Polykles similarly mounts a *bêma* with his *kithara* on a black-figured oinochoe (Villa Giulia 20839–40).[169] Presumably these two Polykles are the same person. Shapiro speculates that he may have been a professional musician, perhaps a "Panathenaic victor, much in demand as an entertainer in 'high society'."[170] That scenario is certainly possible. But could Polykles rather have been himself an ambitious member of high society turned "professional" competitor, one of the voraciously experimental late Archaic elites discussed by Aristotle, turning his hand to *aulêtikê* as well as *kitharôidia* (or *kitharistikê*) at the *agônes* of the Panathenaia or some other festival?[171]

---

[168] Webster 1972:49; but see cavils about Webster's reading of *all* contest scenes as commissions for epinician symposia in n155 above.

[169] The vase (ABV 673) is unpublished. Shapiro 1989:43n210 describes it.

[170] Shapiro 1989:43; Bundrick 2005:164, less specifically, calls him a "proficient musician."

[171] Shapiro 1989:43 compares Kydias of Hermione, a musician and poet—one of his erotic songs is cited in Plato *Charmides* 155d—who is depicted making music among aristocrats in comastic contexts on two Attic vases from c. 515–510 BCE. On a psykter by the Dikaios Painter in London he is shown as a satyrically balding, bearded *bon vivant* playing the *barbitos* (London E 767; Shapiro 1982, plate 26c); on a cup in Munich, a youthful reveler labeled Kydias plays the *aulos*, although the label might apply rather to the bearded *barbitos* player who stands nearby (Munich 2614; Shapiro 1982:73, fig. 1). Kydias must, like his fellow Hermionean, Lasus, have come to Athens under the tyrants. As Plato's reference and the vase paintings suggest, he was mainly known, like Anacreon, as a habitué of the aristocratic symposium and *kômos*, treating erotic themes to the *barbitos* and *aulos*, rather than a citharode or aulete on the festival *bêma*; cf. Webster 1972:53–54; Shapiro 1982:72. Of course, it is not impossible that he moved between the two worlds. The scholia to Aristophanes *Clouds* 967 provide further testimony to the activity of Kydias, who is called in them, however, Kydides (cf. PMG 948; Kydias/Kydides presumably is not to be confused with Kedeides or Kekeides, an old-fashioned dithyrambic composer mentioned at *Clouds* 985, for whom see Stephanis 1988, no. 1391). From the scholia we glean that elite schoolboys of old learned pieces by Kydias and Lamprocles of Athens. At *Clouds* 967, Better Argument quotes with approval the dactylic opening of an old song by the former, τηλέπορόν τι βόαμα 'A far-sounding cry', a reference to the sound of the *lura* itself (according to the scholia). The song's genre is impossible to determine; a short lyric piece is likely. One scholiast, however, says that the verse comes from Κυδίδου τοῦ Ἑρμιονέως κιθαρῳδοῦ 'Kydides (Kydias) the citharode'. The cithrode identification is intriguing; the dactylic meter

Other examples of named cithAROdes appear further into the fifth century. On a red-figured bell krater by Polygnotus from around the middle of the fifth century, a young *kithARA* player—it is not clear whether he is a cithAROde—labeled "Nikomas *kalos*" performs before an admiring group of elite spectators, two bearded men, one seated, one standing, and a youth leaning on a stick.[172] Beazley takes the name Nikomas to be an abbreviated form of Nikomakhos, which appears written alongside a young symposiast on a contemporary stamnos, also by Polygnotus (Villa Giulia 3584). Nikomas the agonist and Nikomakhos the symposiast are presumably the same person.[173] It is possible that Nikoma[kho]s was a professional musician who won access to the symposia of the elite, but, as with Polykles, the situation may have been the opposite: he may have been an elite who won fame in the *agônes*.

The same would seem to hold true for the victorious young *kithARA* player depicted on a red-figured pelike by the Epimedes Painter in Plovdiv, Bulgaria from c. 430 BCE (Plate 13). This musician—again, it is unclear whether he is a cithAROde or citharist—stands on the *bêma*, which has a *kalos* inscription, attired in long chiton and mantle and holding his *kithARA*. The make of the instrument is somewhat peculiar; we will return to it below. His name, Alkimakhos, is inscribed above his wreath-crowned head. Four winged Nikai flutter about him. Since their appearance on vases by the Berlin Painter and his peers in the first quarter of the fifth century, such Nikai, bearing *kithARAi* or prizes such as crowns and libation bowls (*phialai*) for the victor, had become a commonplace in cithARODic contest scenes. In fact, soon after their introduction, *kithARA*-bearing and even *kithARA*-playing Nikai were so popular a motif on vases produced in the second quarter of the fifth century that they became virtual stand-ins for the victorious cithArodes whom they were meant to honor.[174] The Nikai on the Plovdiv

---

would be in keeping with early *kithARôidia*, and schoolboys may in fact have learned excerpts of cithAROdic song, as the Douris school cup suggests. But the scholiast may simply be making an inference from the putative reference to the *lura* in the quoted fragment. On Lamprocles, known primarily as a dithyrambic composer and aulete, as well as a music teacher with ties to the aristocratic intelligentsia of Athens, see Wallace 2003. The song of his that Aristophanes has the boys learning, possibly a hymn to Athena, was presumably an aulodic composition. Its initial verse, partially quoted by Better Argument (Παλλάδα περσέπολιν δεινάν) was also dactylic, and some ancient scholars attributed it to Stesichorus.

[172] New York, The Metropolitan Museum of Art 21.88.73; Richter and Hall 1936, no. 126.
[173] Cf. Webster 1972:50.
[174] On the Nikai motif in Periclean Athens, see Shapiro 1996: "Fluttering Nikai are now an almost indispensable accompaniment of musical victors. The victor himself is seldom seen actually performing, but instead stands quietly receiving his accolades ... These

pelike, however, are unique in that they are all tagged with inscriptions marking them as personifications of the festivals at which Alkimakhos has won victories. These inscriptions are very faintly visible on the vase; the line drawing included in this book shows only the inscription above the head of the upper-left Nike, "at Marathon." She represents a victory at the Herakleia, a local Attic festival held at Marathon.[175] The three others symbolize victories at the Panathenaia and the games at Isthmia and Nemea. Alkimakhos appears to be a local and Panhellenic success story.

Before we consider further the significance of these victories, let us first consider what else we can say about Alkimakhos. More so than Polykles or Nikoma[kho]s, his noble pedigree is almost certain. Young men labeled with his name (or, in one case, the name alone) appear on several other roughly contemporary vases, in scenes that would indicate his background of aristocratic privilege and distinction, if, as seems very likely, they do represent the same Alkimakhos as the one on the pelike. Alkimakhos appears on a bell krater by the Lykaon Painter in London as a reclining symposiast in elite company; another bell krater by the same painter in Warsaw, featuring a scene of Dionysus,

---

vases not only reflect the allegorizing tendency of High Classical art, but also seem for the first time to elevate the victorious musician to a heroic stature equal to that of athletic victors" (218). (I would, however, qualify the latter observation. As we have seen, citharodes had in fact been implicitly assimilated to the image of the athlete and hero in Archaic art; the figure of Heracles *kitharôidos* emblematizes such assimilation.) Cf. Kotsidu 1991:117–122; Bundrick 2005:167–168 (with further bibliography at 231n30), who sees in the Nikai motif an increased appreciation of the "professionalism and personal achievement" of the citharode, which is also reflected in the increased isolation of the "spotlit" citharode from his audience, although I am not as sure as she is that these developments reflect an increasingly "democratic" re-envisioning of the contests. As we see on the Brygos Painter's amphora, the elite spectator continues to play a "starring role," isolated in equal splendor on his own side of the vase. It was previously thought that the absence of musical contest scenes in the iconographical record indicated a suspension of the contests after the Persian Wars, until Pericles revived them at mid-century (so Davison 1958). But Schafter 1991 argues compellingly that the *kitharai*-bearing Nikai represent the ongoing *agônes*. The temporary turn away from depicting musical contestants with their *kitharai* was more likely motivated by an artistic fashion set by the Berlin Painter than sociological or ideological factors. Cf. too Vos 1986:128. An early Classical neck amphora by the Providence Painter depicting a Nike with *kithara* includes the inscribed *kalos* name Timonides, perhaps an aristocratic victor (Vienna 698; cf. Webster 1972:164). Webster 1972:67–68 discusses two earlier neck amphoras by the Dutuit Painter that also involve Nikai and a named victor: on one an isolated citharode is labeled "Arkhinos *kalos*" (Naples 3155); on the other two Nikai are depicted on the neck; "Arkhinos *kalos*" is written along both sides (Louvre G 137). Webster thinks that the two vases were "a pair made to celebrate Archinos' victory in a contest for citharodes."

[175] Wilson 2000:43, 327n177; Parker 2005:473.

satyrs, and meanads, is inscribed with the *kalos* names Alkimakhos and Axiopeithes, who was probably Alkimakhos' first cousin.[176] The father of Axiopeithes was also named Alkimakhos. Like his namesake nephew, he seems to have cut an impressive figure in Athenian society as a young man; he is singled out as *kalos* on several vases from c. 470–460 BCE. One of these is particularly notable in light of his nephew's interest in the *kithara*. "Alkimakhos *kalos*, son of Epikhares" is inscribed on the body of an unattributed lekythos in Boston showing a scene of the murder of Orpheus, lyre in hand, by a Thracian woman. Perhaps a dedication to lyric music that went beyond the routine *paideia* accrued by elite Athenians ran in this family.[177] The younger Alkimakhos appears as well in another distinctly aristocratic context, as a competitive athlete, on a cup by the Eretria Painter of c. 430, an image to which we will return.[178] "Alkimakhos *kalos*" appears on the exterior of a contemporary cup by the Kalliope Painter, where the inscription might tag a youth with a lyre who stands in a mixed group of youths and women; in the tondo of the cup Apollo sits with his lyre by a Muse.[179] The cup evokes the exclusive glamour of Classical lyric *paideia*, for which the lyric (rather than cithariodic) Apollo is the aristocratic icon. That glamour is evoked as well on the reverse of the Plovdiv pelike. An elegant youth plays his lyre surrounded by two admiring women. Indeed, the pelike invites us to see a natural progression between its two scenes. The lyre-playing youth is Alkimakhos as elite schoolboy, who will bloom into the star of the *kithara* we see on the other side.[180]

It has been plausibly argued that the two women flanking the young lyre player are Nikai, and that the scene alludes to the contests in lyre playing and singing to the lyre that Alkimakhos had won as

---

[176] London E 495; Warsaw 142355. On the latter vase, which may commemorate a dramatic or dithyrambic production in which the two kinsmen were involved, see discussion in Beazley 1928:54–56, Webster 1972:71–72; on the former, see Matheson 1995:285, with plate 177.

[177] Boston, Museum of Fine Arts, 13.202; cf. Caskey and Beazley 1954:43–44, who discuss this distinguished family and provide an inventory of the vases on which the name Alkimakhos, referring to both uncle and nephew, appears.

[178] Louvre G 457. Webster 1972:57 thinks that this is "probably a younger Alkimakhos than the successful citharode," but the chronology certainly allows the identification. The tondo of the cup shows a mythical schoolroom scene featuring two famous lyre singers: Linus holds a book scroll before Musaeus.

[179] Ferrara, Museo Archeologico Nazionale T 617; cf. Webster 1972:58.

[180] A contemporary stamnos in Florence invites a similar reading (Museo Archeologico 4066; CVA Florence 13, plate 640, 3 and 4). On the obverse, an unnamed young man stands atop a *bêma* with his *kithara* (distinctly a Thamyris *kithara* like that of Alkimakhos—see below), attended by two Nikai. On the reverse, a youth with a *khelus*-lyre stands between two young male admirers.

a schoolboy.[181] Such school contests, some of which include winged Nikai, others, like the Plovdiv pelike, wingless women who may represent either Nikai, mothers, or generic female admirers (suggesting the burgeoning sexual appeal of the boy), are depicted beginning around 480 BCE on red-figured vases that were presumably commissioned by the families of the victors.[182] School musical contests were in all likelihood private events, restricted primarily to family and friends of the elite student body, but the iconography indicates that the contestants and their families looked to the Panathenaic *agônes* as a model, even if few students would have been able or would even have aspired to compete at the civic level. In the case of an Alkimakhos, however, experience at these "play" contests may well have been a prelude to success in the serious world of professional *mousikê*.[183] Nevertheless, it may have been fairly common for schoolboys, even those less talented and ambitious than Alkimakhos, to emulate with their lyres the technique and flair of the citharodic stars they saw at the Panathenaia.

There is some indication of this in the critique of contemporary *paideia* delivered in Aristophanes' *Clouds* by Better Argument, who notes with distaste the "clowning around" (*bômolokheuesthai*) of today's boys in imitation of the virtuoso citharode Phrynis of Mytilene, whose signature *kampai* 'bends', harmonically bold melodic figures, scandalized conservatives (967–972). For this decidedly amateur enthusiast of lyric *paideia*, at least, it is as if the "show business" of *kitharôidia* threatens to corrupt and deform the cultural innocence of the lyre—a sentiment apparently not shared by the family of Alkimakhos. Such "clowning around" may have taken place at private lessons, but perhaps

---

[181] Cf. Vergara 2003:65.

[182] See inventory in Webster 1972:166–170; representative images in Beck 1975, plates 44–46. There are considerably earlier black-figured genre scenes of school contests without Nikai, e.g. a Nikosthenic pyxis from c. 520 BCE (Vienna, Antikensammlung, Kunsthistorisches Museum IV 1870; Shapiro 1992:54, fig. 32a, b, c).

[183] The boys' contest in *kitharistikê* at the Panathenaia may have been dominated largely by elite Athenian youths (and perhaps sons of the gentry from neighboring *poleis*) eager to display their excellent lyric *paideia* to the city. If so, it would have served as a bridge between the schoolroom and the adult festival *bêma*. We are uninformed about the demographics of the Panathenaic contest, however. Conceivably, the sons of musically professional Athenian families could have prevailed in the contests. The most famous citharist of the fourth century, the probably non-elite Stratonicus of Athens, presumably competed in (and won at) the boys' contest at the later-fifth-century Panathenaia. We can be more certain that it was aristocratic youths who displayed their musico-poetic learning in the boys' rhapsodic *agôn* at the Apatouria festival, which is described in Plato *Timaeus* 21b–c (with Proclus *Commentary on Plato's Timaeus* 1.88–89). The prizes in the contest were provided by the boys' fathers; schoolroom prizes similarly were provided by parents (Theophrastus *Characters* 22).

we should imagine a setting at school *agônes* that would be open to the likes of aristocratic voyeurs such as Better Argument (cf. his ogling of boys at the Panathenaic armed dances, 987–989). In fact, his claim that schoolboys of yore would have been beaten for "effacing the Muses" (τὰς Μούσας ἀφανίζων) as they do now with their fancy "bends," may contain an allusion to what Aeschines *Against Timarchus* 10 calls *Mouseia en didaskaleiois*, which seem to be "something like a schoolroom contest in matters musical under the auspices of the Muses."[184]

Let us now return to Alkimakhos' victories. The references to the Panhellenic festivals of Isthmia and Nemea are intriguing yet highly problematic, so we will have to leave them aside for the moment and focus on the Panathenaia. It is probable, but not certain, that the Plovdiv pelike was commissioned to commemorate a recent victory at the Panathenaia rather than at one of the other festivals mentioned. Was he victorious in *kitharôidia* or *kitharistikê*? The iconography is unhelpful here; the fact that Alkimakhos is not shown singing tells us nothing. As to his age, he is young and beardless, but it would be going too far to call him a boy (*pais*). He appears rather to be a *neaniskos*, and adolescent male in his very late teens or early 20s.[185] We know from the early-fourth-century BCE Panathenaic prize inscription (IG II^2 2311) that there were two separate contests for citharists, one for *paides* 'boys', presumably those under 18, and one for *andres* 'men', which included all those who were older.[186] There was, however, only one contest for citharodes, which would have been open exclusively to those who were at least 18 years or older.[187] We cannot be certain whether these age classes were in effect before the fourth century, or, still less so, before the Periclean reinstitution of the Panathenaic *mousikoi agônes*. But these divisions are logical and fair: *kitharôidia* is entirely too difficult for the young, while the less demanding art of solo *kithara* playing is manageable for older adolescents and teens; men, older and younger, nevertheless practice it at a much higher skill level, so there is a need for two separate contests. Thus there is little reason to think

---

[184] Wilson 2000:338n97. On the schoolroom Mouseia, cf. Fisher 2001:136 and Murray 2004:379, with references to further testimonia.

[185] On *neaniskos* vs. *pais*, see Dover 1989:85–86; cf. Austin and Olson 2004:99.

[186] See lines 15 and 22d in the restored text in Shear 2003:103–104.

[187] See discussion in Part I.7. One suspects, however, that, unlike the athletic *agônes*, where age divisions were very strictly patrolled, if rather hazy (to us, at least: see Golden 1998:104–112), more leeway was allowed at the *mousikoi agônes*, at least for slightly younger competitors who wanted to compete against older ones.

that these sensible categories would not have been the rule going as far back as the Peisistratids.[188]

What this means for the interpretation of the iconography of musical contests is that beards and "youthful" looks are not clear indices of agonistic category.[189] Both bearded and unbearded competitors would have performed against one another in the citharodic *agôn* as well as the men's contest in *kitharistikê*. There was no intermediary *neaniskos* class between boys and men in either. Talented citharodes and citharists, whether from professional backgrounds or elite ones, would have begun their mature agonistic careers as soon as possible, in their late teens and early 20s, when they would have gone up against considerably older (and bearded) opponents. Thus the Brygos Painter's beardless and beatific young citharode, labeled only figuratively a "beautiful boy (*pais*)," would have competed against more experienced (and bearded) citharodes such as those depicted on contemporary vases by the Pan and Berlin Painters.[190] The beardless Alkimakhos likewise could have competed against the bearded citharode on a slightly later calyx krater by the Peleus Painter.[191] The idealizing style of High Classical art additionally complicates attempts to identify citharodes and citharists by age.[192] Indeed, Alkimakhos, when he won his Panathenaic victory,

---

[188] Cf. Kotsidu 1991:58. A Panathenaic-type amphora of c. 530 BCE (Reggio 4224; Kotsidu 1991, Tafel 8) illustrates what appears to be the performance of a boy citharist. On boy aulodes, a class also attested in IG II² 2311 (line 22a in the text of Shear 2003), on sixth- and fifth-century vases, cf. Shapiro 1992:60–62, who notes that "all the extant representations [of *aulôidia*] from the time of Perikles and later show a boy aulode." Images of agonistic solo auletes, for whom there was only one Panathenaic contest, are correspondingly rare in the fifth century. The relatively low prize amounts for both men's aulodic and auletic Panathenaic victors attested in IG II² 2311.12–14, 20–22 are relevant. Athenians seem to have been far more invested in *rhapsôidia* and *kitharôidia* than in the agonistic music of the *aulos*. Perhaps the boys' contest in *aulôidia* continued to be the subject of vase painting in the later fifth century because elite Athenian boys continued to enter the contest; mature professional aulodes and auletes attracted far less attention. We may note that the inscription attests that only two prizes, first and second, were issued to the men's aulodes and to the (men's) auletes; perhaps only two were granted to winning boy aulodes as well. Because of the fragmentary nature of IG II² 2311, we do not know the value of the boys' prizes in *aulôidia* or *kitharistikê*. At the festival of Artemis in Eretria, boy aulodes received 50 and 30 drachmas (IG XII ix 189). At this festival there does not seem to have been a contest for adult aulodes.

[189] *Pace* Vos 1986:128.

[190] Berlin Painter: Panathenaic-shaped amphora (formerly in the Hunt Collection; Shapiro 1992:58, fig. 37); pelike by the Pan Painter, whose bearded citharode mounts a *bêma* labeled *kalos* (New York, Solow Art and Architecture Foundation; Bundrick 2005:167, fig. 98).

[191] London, British Museum E 460; Bundrick 2005:169, fig. 99.

[192] Shapiro 1992:58; cf. Part I.7n123.

might conceivably have had a beard, or at least the beginnings of one, which the artist may have "shaved off."

Alkimakhos could thus have won his Panathenaic victory as a citharode or as a citharist. Two factors might point to the latter possibility, however. The first is that, by the second half of the fifth century, competition at the Panathenaic citharodic *agônes* must have become incredibly stiff, making it difficult for even the most talented "aristocratic agonist" to compete with success. While the Periclean reinstitution of the *mousikoi agônes* may have recharged elite as well as demotic interest in the music of the festival, it was very likely marked by a recommitment to making the Panathenaia into an international center of *mousikê*, which meant attracting the best itinerant professionals.[193] That Phrynis appears to have been the victor at the first Periclean Panathenaia could, as was proposed above, be in line with the pre-Periclean festival's ability to attract top talent from abroad; nevertheless, it seems significant that the inaugural victory was won by this citharode in particular, who would make a name for himself later in the century as a virtuoso exponent of the New Music.[194] The victory reads as a harbinger of the hyperprofessionalization that

---

[193] And we should not overlook the small but notable pool of apparently non-elite Athenian citharodic professionals. We have the names of two such musicians from the fifth century BCE. (1) Meles son of Peisias, father of Cinesias the new dithyrambist (Pherecrates fr. 6 K-A; Plato *Gorgias* 501e; cf. Stephanis 1988, no. 1630). (2) Arignotus son of Aristomenes; like Meles, a member of a family of music and dramatic professionals (Aristophanes *Wasps* 1275–1283, *Knights* 1278; cf. Stephanis 1988, nos. 301 and 399). (3) A debatable case: Polemon fr. 47 Preller *ap.* scholia *ad* Aristophanes *Birds* 11 records that Execestides, who is mocked in Aristophanes *Birds* 11, 764, and 1527 for being a phony Athenian citizen, was a victor at the Pythia, the Carneia, and twice at the Panathenaia, perhaps one of those times in 414 BCE, the year *Birds* was produced, which would explain why Aristophanes mentions him three times. Davison 1958:40 takes literally the comedian's abuse: "In spite of his fine old Athenian name [Execestides] was apparently an interloper." Perhaps he was a resident alien (*metoikos*) who pretended to citizen status. In a fragment from Eupolis' *Prospaltians* an Exekestos is mentioned in proximity to the words *kitharôidos* and *metoikos* (fr. 259). Could this Exekestos be our citharode? Cf. Storey 2003a:233. The name Execestides (the name of Solon's father) might then be a comic sobriquet playing on his aspirations to Athenian citizenship. Yet Aristophanes' invective excess—the citharode is called a slave and a barbarian from Caria—might be taken to suggest that the opposite is in fact the case, that he was in fact an Athenian. Cf. Stephanis 1988, no. 842; MacDowell 1993:364–365. Could Execestides' itinerancy have prompted the joke that he was a foreigner? At *Birds* 11 he is invoked as a paradigmatically "homeless" wanderer. Further, could the "Eastern" associations of *kitharôidia* have prompted his characterization as a barbarian?

[194] The date of Phrynis' victory/the first Periclean Panathenaia was probably 446 BCE: Davison 1958:41. The claim made in the scholia to Aristophanes *Clouds* 969 that Phrynis was the "first" (*prôtos*) to play the *kithara* for the Athenians must express the

would define musical culture in Athens by the end of the fifth century and into the fourth, and was probably already in the making in the first half of the fifth, a transformation of the field of musical practice that would exclude all but the most able career musicians from the major *agônes*. Additionally, citharodes were increasingly expected to be composers and poets of their own show-stopping *nomoi* as well as reperformers of the traditional Terpandrean repertoire of epic *nomoi* (more on this below). And then there were the ideological barriers. As we have discussed, a certain degree of reactionary anti-professionalism set in among certain factions of the elite as a result of their exclusion, making it still less likely that well-born Athenians would attempt even to qualify for these displays of "banausic" skill.

Since the early sixth century BCE solo *kithara* playing had been practiced by professional virtuosos, such as Epicles of Hermione, an associate of Themistocles and probably a Panathenaic victor (Plutarch *Themistocles* 5.3; more on this musician below). In the fourth century its greatest exponent, Stratonicus of Athens, was the consummate professional *agônistês* of the New Music.[195] Yet *kitharistikê* was acknowledged to be an easier *tekhnê* to master than *kitharôidia*; the existence of the boys' contest shows as much. Perhaps enthusiastic amateurs continued to find that they could make a showing at this relatively less technically challenging and creatively demanding, if less distinguished contest. (Prize amounts in *kitharistikê* were considerably less than in *kitharôidia*, but this may not have bothered non-professionals seeking glory and exposure rather than money; for those troubled by the commercial implications of cash prizes, it may even have been a welcome point of distinction.) This brings us to a second factor. The ribbed arm of the *kithara* that Alkimakhos holds suggests that the instrument is the so-called Thamyris or Thracian *kithara*, which appears primarily in the hands of younger agonists attended by Nikai on Attic vases after around 450 BCE, some of whom may even be *paides*.[196] This type of *kithara* may have been favored not only by youths, but specifically by those in the contests of *kitharistikê*. (In the case of Panathenaic *paides*, the two

---

fact that he was the first winner at the reformed Periclean *agôn* (cf. Davison, p40). Cf. Part III.15n283.

[195] On early *kitharistikê*, see Barker 1984; Power 2004:432–434.

[196] Cf. Vergara 2003:65. The long hair of the victorious player of a Thamyris *kithara* on a pelike by the Painter of Athens 1183, contemporary with the Plovdiv pelike, suggests that he is pre-ephebic, although such details are not always to be taken literally (Athens, National Archaeological Museum 1183; Bundrick 2005:29, fig. 16). See, however, the following note.

groups would overlap.) Thamyris himself may have been imagined in the later fifth century as the mythical exemplar of the citharist.[197]

Yet the iconographical record shows that the Thamyris *kithara* was not completely restricted to *kitharistikê*, so we should remain open to the chance that Alkimakhos was a citharode. One possibility to consider is that Alkimakhos did not win first prize in the Panathenaic citharodic *agôn*, but took a second-, third-, or even fifth-place "victory." The fourth-century Panathenaic inscription indicates that five citharodes were in fact awarded prizes at the *agôn* (IG II² 2311.4–11), more so than in any other musical contest at the festival, including that in *rhapsôidia*, which, like *kitharistikê*, awarded only three prizes—a clear indication of the medium's enormous popularity with Athenian audiences, but no doubt also of the larger pool of would-be contestants. Although only the first-place citharode received a crown, the other four competitors received hefty cash awards. Assuming that the citharodic field at the Panathenaia was as wide in the fifth century as it was in the fourth, a talented and determined elite such as Alkimakhos would conceivably have had decent odds at qualifying for the competition. Perhaps other citharodic (or citharistic) "victors" we see commemorated on Attic vases are also such qualifying prizewinners.

The Panathenaic *agôn* was not, however, the only game in town for *kitharôidia*, although it was the most important. Throughout the fifth century a number of Attic festivals offered musical *agônes*, less prestigious and remunerative than those of the Panathenaia, but just for that reason probably more welcoming to non-professional enthusiasts. One such festival was the penteteric Herakleia at Marathon, where Alkimakhos apparently triumphed (whether in *kitharôidia* or *kitharistikê*, however, we can again not say). A fragment from a red-figured vase of c. 430 BCE depicts an elegant young man in a short-sleeved chiton holding a large concert *kithara* (not a Thamyris *kithara*) and mounting a *bêma* before a shrine of Heracles.[198] The setting of this

---

[197] Cf. Part II.8n172. A late-fifth-century fragmentary *khous* has a group of what are clearly *paides*, two with tortoise-shell lyres and one with a Thamyris *kithara*, engaged in a musical contest, presumably at the Anthesteria, and presumably, in light of their age, a citharistic one (Basel, Collection of Herbert A. Cahn 649; Smith 2007:163, fig. 8.8, with comments on 162–164). Boy lyre players are commonly portrayed on *khoes* (references in Smith, p162n27; cf. Friis-Johansen 1967:192 on musical contests at the Anthesteria). Wilson 2004:281n30 makes the appealing proposition that the Anthesteria "may have remained a home for the 'amateur ideal' of public string performance." There is, however, no clear evidence for a men's cithradic contest, but cf. n146 above.

[198] Bucharest 03207; CVA Bucharest 1, plate 32, 1.

contest is presumably the Herakleia. Aristophanes' *Frogs* may contain an allusion to the citharodic contest at the festival. Dionysus asks Aeschylus whether he took the old-fashioned citharodic tunes that supposedly influenced his choral odes, tunes that to Dionysus' modern ears sound as dully repetitive as work songs, "from Marathon" (1296–1297). Perhaps the joke here is that the Marathonian Herakleia had a reputation for preserving older citharodic traditions, unlike the urban Panathenaia, where the flashy New Music of Timotheus and his like were in vogue. If so, we might surmise that the conservative Herakleia attracted a less professional and perhaps more distinctly aristocratic pool of competitors.[199]

It has been suggested that the Anthesteria remained a redoubt throughout the fifth century for the musical display of aristocratic amateurs. Depictions on the small wine pitchers called *khoes* that are associated with the Anthesteria indicate that boys' contests in *kitharistikê* were held at this Dionysian festival, but we can be less sure that citharodic *agônes* were held for older musicians.[200] We hear of musical contests, surely including *kitharôidia*, being offered at the Eleusinia, the Epitaphia, and perhaps the Hephaistia as well.[201] These contests themselves likely attracted big names from abroad as well as local professionals, but it is a reasonable assumption that *kitharôidia* was performed at a variety of other, lesser festivals of the city and demes at which willing elites could mount the *bêma* and win a prize. We should also remain open to the possibility that citharodic and citharistic *agônes* were held at the yearly Lesser Panathenaia. If so, such contests might have attracted a less star-studded roster of competitors.[202] At least some of the contest scenes on Attic vases must be set at such festivals rather than the Great Panathenaia. Indeed, for all we know, a few might commemorate second- or third-place finishes at one of these smaller-scale festivals.

---

[199] Cf. Part II.6n119.

[200] Cf. n197 above.

[201] Testimony in Wilson 2004:281. On the problematic inscriptional evidence (IG I³ 82.14, 31–33) for music at the Hephaistia, see Kotsidu 1991:154–158; Miller 1997:233n94; Wilson 2000:35 and 2009:74. On music at the Eleusinia, cf. Part II.12n280.

[202] Our ancient sources for the festival are unhelpful in this important question. *Ex silentio* we may infer that citharodes did not formally compete at the Lesser Panathenaia. The penteteric model of *agônes* at the Panhellenic festivals on which the Panathenaia was based supports this inference. But Reisch 1885:18 reasons that since dithyrambic choruses were presented yearly at the Panathenaia, at least by the later fifth century (cf. Lysias 21.1), we may do well not to disregard completely the possibility of yearly *mousikoi agônes* as well; cf. Hose 1993:9n37.

Finally, there are Alkimakhos' Isthmian and Nemean victories. The presumption has been that Alkimakhos was victorious at *mousikoi agônes* attached to these prestigious Panhellenic festivals, and that he must therefore have been an itinerant professional.[203] We have seen, however, that Alkimakhos was a member of the Athenian aristocracy. Of course, his elite status would not have prevented him from competing in music at these biennial games, just as his peers competed at them in athletics. A decree passed in the later 430s BCE—that is, in the same decade Alkimakhos was winning his victories—granted permanent *sitesis* 'board' in the Athenian Prytaneion to gymnastic and hippic victors at Olympia, Delphi, Isthmia, and Nemea. It has been argued that in a lost section of the inscription recording the decree (IG I³ 131) it was indicated that musical victors at these games were also to be granted this honor.[204] Yet, while we know that the Pythia had featured *mousikoi agônes* since its inception, there is no evidence, outside of what is suggested by the Nikai on the Plovdiv pelike, that they were on the program of the Nemean or Isthmian games during the Classical period. It is certain, however, that musical contests were not held at the resolutely athletic Classical Olympics. The evidence we do have suggests that musicians in general and citharodes in particular only began to compete at Nemea and the Isthmus in the Hellenistic period, which saw an exponential increase in *mousikoi agônes* throughout all of Greece.[205] On the inscribed monument erected in Athens by the third-century BCE citharode Nicocles to celebrate his multiple victories, we read that Nicocles was the first (*prôtos*) to win at the Isthmia, presumably in *kitharôidia* (IG II² 3779).[206] While we could allow for some exaggeration on the part of this self-aggrandizing star or perhaps conjecture some reorganization of preexisting Isthmian *mousikoi agônes* that would allow Nicocles to claim he was the "first" winner (of a reformed contest), the best course is to take the inscription at its word.[207]

The complete lack of literary references to music at the Classical Isthmian games is notable as well. As for Nemea, the earliest attestation

---

[203] Cf. Bundrick 2005: "[C]learly he must have been one of the star performers who traveled from contest to contest" (173).

[204] Morrissey 1978:122, who bases his argument largely on the probability that the decree was proposed by Pericles, whose interest in musical *agônes* is otherwise attested by his reform of the Panathenaia and his building of the Odeion (Plutarch *Pericles* 13.10–11); cf. Wilson 2004:302n76.

[205] Cf. Kotsidu 1991:26, with bibliography in 186n41.

[206] Cf. West 1992:373; 2002:131.

[207] Phrynis was said to be the "first" (*prôtos*) citharodic victor at the Panathenaia, i.e. at the reformed *agônes*; cf. n194 above.

of musical contests is Plutarch *Philopoemen* 11, which describes the performance in the (Hellenistic) theater of Nemea by the citharode Pylades of Timotheus' *Persians*. The date was 207 BCE.[208] Of course, there is no indication that this was the first Nemean citharodic contest, but again, the silence of the literary and epigraphical sources on music at the Archaic and Classical festival is striking. Attestations of musical competition at the Roman-era games abound.[209]

The Plovdiv pelike thus remains our only potential piece of evidence for *agônes*, citharodic or citharistic, at the fifth-century Isthmian and Nemean festivals. Keeping in mind Alkimakhos' aristocratic background, however, we might venture another interpretation of the vase. Could the victories at the Panhellenic games have been in athletics rather than music? Recall that Alkimakhos is pictured as an idealized athlete on a cup by the Eretria Painter (Louvre G 457). Conceivably, he could have excelled as both an athletic and musical agonist, perhaps winning his Panhellenic athletic victories as a boy and his musical victory at the Panathenaia as a young adult. (The Herakleia had athletic and musical contests, so perhaps there too Alkimakhos competed as an athlete.)[210] The pelike would thus represent Alkimakhos as the perfect product of gymnastic and musical *paideia*, the rare individual who has successfully proved his aristocratic excellence at the highest levels of competition in both fields.[211]

8. Tyrannical Leitmotifs in Democratic Athens

Although it was conspicuously promoted by the Peisistratids, *kitharôidia* did not suffer from the taint of tyranny after the expulsion of Hippias in 510 BCE and the subsequent establishment of the democracy. That emblem of Peisistratean citharodic politics, Heracles *kitharôidos*, in fact would continue to appear on Attic vases until the very end of the sixth century. The appearance around 500 BCE of the Nikoxenos

---

[208] The performance is also recorded in Pausanias 8.50.3. Cf. Miller 2001:8n13.

[209] Miller 2001:13.

[210] Pindar *Olympian* 9.88–89 commemorates the victory his client Epharmostos of Opous won as a *pais* at the Marathonian Herakleia; cf. *Pythian* 8.79.

[211] Alkimakhos' crossover success would find a parallel in the fascinating agonistic career of Hedea of Tralles in Asia Minor, who won the children's contest of *kitharôidia* at the first-century CE Athenian Sebasteia, as well as athletic victories at the Nemean and Isthmian games (SIG³ 802). But the familial and cultural circumstances surrounding Hedea's achievements are radically different from those of Alkimakhos'. Cf. Part I.7n118.

Painter's Athena *kitharôidos* (Plate 11) probably signaled a wider reaction to tyrannical musical and festal policy, yet one that involved not the rejection but the redefinition of Panathenaic *kitharôidia* within the new political order; its prestige would now truly belong to "all the Athenians."[212] As we have seen in the preceding sections, members of the aristocracy remained invested in citharodic culture both during and after the Cleisthenic period, both as fans and occasionally as agonists. And there is every reason to believe that *kitharôidia* continued to claim the attention of the *dêmos*. As an Aristophanic scholiast concisely reports, Athenians of the Classical period were "fanatical about *kitharôidia*."[213] The enormous prize amounts given by the city to the five contestants at the citharodic *agôn* of the fourth-century Panathenaia clearly support this claim.

It is not surprising that two of the most prominent figures of the fifth-century democracy, Themistocles and Pericles, both emulated the tyrants in their promotion of agonistic music. Plutarch tells how Themistocles, still a "young unknown" (νέος καὶ ἀφανής), but driven by an outsized desire for public recognition (φιλοτιμία) "entreated upon Epicles of Hermione, a citharist very popular (σπουδαζόμενον) among the Athenians, to practice at his home, since he was eager for the recognition (φιλοτιμούμενος) that would come from many people (πολλούς) seeking out his house and visiting him."[214] Themistocles was born c. 524 BCE, so we can presume these events to have taken place in the last years of the sixth century or the beginning of the fifth. As a populist leader on the make, Themistocles takes his cue from the recently departed Peisistratids and looks first to civic musical and festival culture—we may assume that Epicles is in town for the Panathenaia—to realize his social and political ambitions. That Epicles comes from Hermione, the home of Lasus and Kydias, two "name" musicians from earlier in the sixth century, would appear to make his emulation of the Peisistratids

---

[212] A more aggressive strain of anti-tyrannical sentiment might, however, manifest itself in early-fifth-century musical iconography: scenes of young Heracles beating to death his *kitharistês*, Linus. Might we see in these images the reflection of some politicized mythical revisionism, the tendentious transformation of the tyrants' citharodic hero into a paradigmatic figure of *amousia*? On the theme, which appears only in the late Archaic and early Classical periods, see Bundrick 2005:71–74.

[213] Scholia *ad* Aristophanes *Clouds* 965c: ἐσπούδαζον δὲ οἱ Ἀθηναῖοι περὶ κιθαρῳδίαν.

[214] Plutarch *Themistocles* 5.3: τῇ δὲ φιλοτιμίᾳ πάντας ὑπερέβαλεν, ὥστ' ἔτι μὲν ὢν νέος καὶ ἀφανὴς Ἐπικλέα τὸν ἐξ Ἑρμιόνος κιθαριστὴν σπουδαζόμενον ὑπὸ τῶν Ἀθηναίων ἐκλιπαρῆσαι μελετᾶν παρ' αὐτῷ, φιλοτιμούμενος πολλοὺς τὴν οἰκίαν ζητεῖν καὶ φοιτᾶν πρὸς αὐτόν.

only more obvious.[215] Themistocles makes popular music his private possession, as it were, a (temporary) property of his household, but he generously shares its pleasures with the masses. This "democratic" dispensation of lyric *terpsis* is in line with Peisistratean policy; it reads as well as a challenge to the proprietary claims made by the Athenian aristocracy on the prestige of string music, both sympotic and, to a lesser but still significant extent, agonistic. That Themistocles was himself notoriously, and, if the anecdotal tradition is accurate, proudly *amousos*—he supposedly boasted that, while he had not enjoyed the lyric *paideia* his elite rivals had, he nevertheless "knew how to make a *polis* great and wealthy" (Ion of Chios FGrH 326 F 13)—only complicates and enriches his gambit.[216] He exploits the fame of Epicles to make his own name, but at the same time the ostentatious display of his direct access to musical celebrity advertises his own already considerable distinction, which is indeed a match for that of his rivals.[217] We see an earlier generation of elites, such as the *kaloi k'agathoi* on the Louvre amphora of the Andokides Painter, similarly showing off their privileged proximity to the stars of the Panathenaia.

That Themistocles housed a citharist and not a citharode, however, is likely a significant point. As we have seen, professional citharists ranked considerably lower on the socioeconomic scale than did

---

[215] Plutarch *Themistocles* 5.6 suggests the intimacy between Themistocles and another fixture of late Peisistratid musico-poetic culture, Simonides.

[216] For Themistocles' *amousia*, see Harmon 2003; Wilson 2004:299–300. The context in which Ion of Chios cites his boast is significant. Ion is relating, in his quasi-travelogue *Epidemiai*, how as a young man he witnessed Cimon, the primary aristocratic rival of Themistocles, performing a song at an Athenian symposium. The other symposiasts laud him as being "more sophisticated" (*dexiôteros*) than Themistocles, who cannot *kitharizein* (FGrH 326 F 13 by way of Plutarch *Cimon* 9.1–2). Lyric *mousikê* apparently played a part in the two men's political self-positioning vis-à-vis one another. We might view Themistocles' association with Epicles as a specific attempt to trump the elitist musical capital of Cimon, although the chronology—Cimon is over ten years younger—makes this somewhat difficult. Themistocles' musical "open house," however, possibly finds an echo in Cimon's populist policy of opening up his fields and his house to Athenian citizens in need of free fruit or dinner (Plutarch *Cimon* 10.1; cf. Aristotle *Constitution of Athens* 27.3–4). (Stesimbrotus of Thasos, a contemporary of Ion, records a contradictory biography of Cimon, according to which he had, like Themistocles, acquired no musical education at all, but rather had a genuinely noble, "Peloponnesian" character unaffected by Attic sophistication [FGrH 107 F 5 by way of Plutarch *Cimon* 4.5]. Stesimbrotus' account is more likely than Ion's to be tendentious, however. It may derive from sources hostile to Cimon, as Jacoby thought, or it may represent an attempt to distinguish Cimon from his later rival, the musically accomplished Pericles.)

[217] Cf. Duplouy 2006:30 on this type of strategy of social recognition, which "makes evident the rank of the individual at the same time as it contributes to the acquisition of the prestige necessary for [the realization of his social] ambitions."

citharodes. As a "young unkown," Themistocles may not yet have had the resources, financial or social, to attract a famous citharode to his side, and so perhaps settled for the next best thing, a popular citharist of Hermionean provenance. His later forays into musical politics would be more impressive. He undertook the *khorêgia* of a tragedy by Phrynichus, probably *Phoenician Women*, in 476 BCE (Plutarch *Themistocles* 5.5). Later, while in exile, he assumed the "tyrannical" role of agonothete, establishing Anthesteria and Panathenaia festivals in Magnesia in Asia Minor (Athenaeus 12.533d), the latter of which, at least, presumably included *mousikoi agônes*. And one tradition had it that Themistocles constructed an early version of the "Periclean" Odeion, the Athenian public music hall, with the masts and spars of captured Persian ships (Vitruvius 5.9.1). If true, the project would have recapitulated on a far grander scale his earlier, more humble offer of a musical "open house." Whatever function this "proto-Odeion" may have actually served, however, its status as precursor, whether real or imagined, to the Periclean public music hall surely reflects in part a broader commitment on Themistocles' part to the democratization of Athenian musical culture.[218]

According to Plutarch, it was the desire for public recognition (φιλοτιμία) that drove Pericles to enter the field of musical politics, just as it had Themistocles. Pericles' musico-political activity took on a much more dramatic form than Themistocles' had, however, given the extent of his power in mid-century Athens:

> φιλοτιμούμενος δ' ὁ Περικλῆς τότε πρῶτον ἐψηφίσατο μουσικῆς ἀγῶνα τοῖς Παναθηναίοις ἄγεσθαι, καὶ διέταξεν αὐτὸς ἀθλοθέτης αἱρεθείς, καθότι χρὴ τοὺς ἀγωνιζομένους αὐλεῖν ἢ ᾄδειν ἢ κιθαρίζειν ἐθεῶντο δὲ καὶ τότε καὶ τὸν ἄλλον χρόνον ἐν Ὠιδείῳ τοὺς μουσικοὺς ἀγῶνας.

> Then first did Pericles, out of his desire for public recognition, pass a decree (*psêphisma*) that a musical *agôn* be held at the Panathenaia. And having himself been elected manager of the contests (*athlothetês*), he prescribed how the contestants must play the *aulos*, or sing, or play the *kithara*. And at that time and thereafter they watched the *mousikoi agônes* in the Odeion.

> Plutarch *Pericles* 13.11

---

[218] Cf. Wilson 2004:300; Mosconi 2000:250–270. See further discussion of the Themistoclean structure below.

The first "Periclean" *agônes* have been persuasively dated to 446/5 BCE.[219] In that year, as Plutarch says, the contests were moved to the Odeion, a large, roofed concert hall near the Theater of Dionysus on the southeastern slope of the Acropolis. Its construction—or massive renovation, if Themistocles had already erected a smaller prototype on the site—was overseen by Pericles himself amidst considerable political controversy.[220] Pericles' opponents apparently seized upon this large and innovative building, and presumably his grand plan to house the Panathenaic musical contests within it, as an indication of his tyrannical ambitions and tried to have him ostracized for it.[221] It has recently been argued that the Odeion was not built to be a concert hall and was not used in the fifth century to house the *agônes*, despite its name (the "place of song") and the fact that Plutarch, along with several other, admittedly late sources, indicates that it was.[222] It is true that the Odeion served in the fourth and fifth centuries as a gathering place for a variety of political and cultural activities, including the vetting of dramas for the City Dionysia, the *proagôn*.[223] That is logical, since the Odeion would probably only have been used for *mousikoi agônes* at the penteteric Great Panathenaia, leaving it empty for much of the time.[224] One scholar has expressed legitimate concerns about reconciling the enormous size of the Odeion with "the few days a year it would provide the 'vital' function of housing the hitherto open-air *proagônes* and music contests."[225] But we must not overlook the fact that musical

---

[219] Davison 1958:41.

[220] The Odeion's construction has been variously dated, from the 450s to the 430s; see Bundrick 2005:233n160.

[221] Plutarch *Pericles* 13.9–10 (= Cratinus fr. 73 K-A). Cf. Mosconi 2000:276–280; Hose 1993. On the shadowy role of Damon, a sophist and *mousikos* who served as a close advisor to Pericles, see Wallace 2004, who speculates that Damon's own ostracism may have been prompted by his musico-political activities in connection to Pericles' Panathenaic interventions, including the construction of the Odeion. Cf. Wilson 2004:292–293.

[222] Kotsidu 1991:141–149; Miller 1997:218–242, who believes the Odeion was not constructed for the purpose of housing the *agônes*, but that they were held there "possibly quite soon after construction" (234). Cf. Robkin 1976:92–94. Odeion and music: *Suda* s.v. ᾠδεῖον; *Anecdota Graeca* 317.33; Hesychius s.v. ᾠδεῖον says that the contests of rhapsodes and citharodes are held in the theater, but before were held in the Odeion. The move to the theater may have taken place as early as the fourth century BCE (see Kotsidu 1991:154).

[223] Kotsidu 1991:145 assembles the relevant sources; cf. Miller 1997:220, a "wild heterogeneity" of functions.

[224] Cf. Hose 1993:6.

[225] Miller 1997:234, who observes that the Odeion "was almost twice as long as the Parthenon and twice the width." It was the largest roofed structure in the Greek world: Meinel 1980:155.

contests, centered as they were in the programs of major civic festivals, did play a vital role in the cultural experience of the Greeks, and that a large venue specially appointed for their display could very well be appreciated by a majority of the Athenians as performing a vital function. By comparison, no one would question the vital function of the Theater of Dionysus as a place to watch dramas.

We might go further, however, and argue that it was precisely the seeming disparity between the Odeion's grand ostentatiousness and its limited functionality as a concert hall that contributed to its cultural significance. The "excess" of the structure—the great expenditure of money and labor it represented, the immense amount of prime civic space it consumed—would have sent a clear message. It was a physical monument to the unstinting spiritual investment of Athens in the promotion of musical culture (and to the economic and political resources that support such an investment), one conspicuous to all Greeks who came to witness the Panathenaic *mousikoi agônes*. In other words, the Odeion was a classic status symbol, asserting the cultural prestige and distinction of the Athenian *polis*. That it had no real equivalent in the Greek world only adds to its symbolic efficacy in this regard. We will return to the Odeion below.

As we saw in Section 1, the iconographic record makes it certain that Plutarch's testimony cannot be taken literally to mean that musical contests were not held at the Panathenaia before Pericles' decree (*psêphisma*). It must be the case that the decree marked a second reorganization of the *agônes*, a reinstitution, fundamentally connected to the construction of the Odeion. But besides the novel staging of the contests in the Odeion, it is unclear what changes Pericles brought to their management and practice. Plutarch says that, as manager of the *agônes* (*athlothetês*), Pericles "prescribed how the competitors should αὐλεῖν ἢ ἄδειν ἢ κιθαρίζειν." The three infinitives surely constitute a condensed reference to contests in *kitharôidia, aulôidia, kitharistikê, aulêtikê,* and *rhapsôidia*, all of which appear in the fourth-century Panathenaic prize inscription (IG II^2 2311) and are attested in the pre-Periclean iconographical record. So it does not seem as if Pericles added or took away any *agônes* from the festival program.[226] Plutarch's testimony does indicate that Pericles regulated *how* the contestants were to perform, however. But what exactly does that mean?

---

[226] Vos 1986:129 thinks that Pericles may have introduced the boys' aulodic contest, but the iconography does not support this; cf. Bundrick 2005:232n155.

It could be that he formalized new rules and requirements, or relaxed preexisting ones; perhaps he made the contests more accommodating of the innovative and experimental tendencies of virtuoso professionals—recall the possible implications of Phrynis' victory at the first Periclean citharodic *agôn*. But Pericles might simply have insured that the musicians followed the rules—with the exception of the rhapsodic Panathenaic Rule, probably more general rules about comportment and competitive fairness than specific prescriptions about song content—that had existed long before the reinstitution.[227] Indeed, it may well be the case that, both as proposer of the new *psêphisma* and as *athlothetês*, Pericles effected nothing practically substantial besides the Odeion, only a ceremonial and symbolic repitching of the festival's ideological tenor. That is, the reinstitution was intended to authorize the democratic transfiguration of the *agônes*, which may still have borne the mark of the tyranny, under the rhetorical and procedural sign of the *psêphisma*, a political action that required the ratification of the democratic assembly.[228] We note too the emphasis on democratic rhetoric and process in the fact that Pericles takes care to be "elected" (αἱρεθείς) *athlothetês*.[229] There can be no doubt that Pericles was following in the footsteps of the tyrants and their Panathenaic populism; the claim in Plutarch that he acted out of φιλοτιμία has the tone of a hostile tradition—recall the threat of ostracism that attended Pericles' reforms—but it nonetheless has a grain of truth.[230] There was all the more reason, then, for Pericles to take care to preserve democratic proprieties as he "democratized" the *agônes*.

Pericles may have even sought to recuperate the musical, and specifically citharodic, politics of the Peisistratids in their international aspect. A red-figured Panathenaic-shaped amphora by the Nausicaa Painter contemporary to the Periclean reinstitution evinces a conflation of Delian and Panathenaic musical imagery that recalls the significant overlaps we see in Archaic black figure, but in a notably more assertive mode. Sheramy Bundrick offers the following reading:

---

[227] "Plutarch" *On Music* 8.1134a cites an "inscription (*graphê*) on the Panathenaic *mousikos agôn*" that attests to the performance of aulodic elegy at the Panathenaia. If this *graphê* is connected to the Periclean reforms, it would probably indicate that Pericles' regulations for performers were not innovative, since aulodic elegy had long been practiced at *mousikoi agônês*.

[228] On *psêphismata* in the fifth-century Athenian democracy, see Hansen 1978:316.

[229] Cf. Davison 1958:36.

[230] Cf. Shapiro 1992:57 for the tyrannical precedent for the Periclean reforms; Wilson 2000:36–37.

Here the performing kitharode is Apollo himself, mounting the two-stepped *bema* (inscribed *kalos*) in the presence of his half-sister, Athena. The presence of Athena, along with the distinctive shape of the vase, places Apollo's performance in the realm of the Panathenaic festival. Indeed, the pairing of Apollo and Athena may reflect the political importance of the Delian League. The figures on the reverse—Hermes with his kerykeion and Poseidon with his trident—further suggest Periklean interests. The cults of both gods were extremely important in Classical Athens; with Poseidon as god of the sea and Hermes as a god associated with agricultural practices and the land, together they metaphorically indicate the extent of Athenian power.[231]

The vase thus presents us with an expansive vision of "citharodic imperialism" as conceived under the Periclean democracy, one that both echoes and surpasses the ambitious Panionian agenda of the tyrants. Apollo *kitharôidos*, triumphant in the premier *mousikos agôn*, and Athena, armed with spear, together orchestrate the harmonious convergence of Panathenaic and Delian prestige and Attic-Ionic power, extending far and wide. We should note an important divergence from the sixth-century iconography, and the Peisistratid ideology that informs it. There Delian Apollo *kitharôidos* is typically portrayed in the guise of a mortal *agônistês*, sometimes in proximity to a Panathenaic festival setting, but he is never explicitly depicted as a Panathenaic competitor. On the fifth-century amphora, he is explicitly depicted as such. This explicit Panathenaic framing of Apollo is an innovation, and may speak to a more concerted attempt under the Athenian democracy, undertaken in conjunction with the reestablishment of the Panathenaic *agônes*, to appropriate Delian musical tradition. This would accord with the more aggressively controlling tenor in contemporary Athenian policy toward Delos. In the years during which the amphora was produced, the Panathenaia was taking on an increasingly central role in Athen's imperial agenda as leading city of the Delian League, arrogating to itself the traditional Panionian investment in Delos. In 454 BCE the Delian treasury was removed to the Athenian Acropolis (Plutarch *Pericles* 12.1).[232] Probably at or near this time, the Athenians

---

[231] Bundrick 2005:172. Amphora: Boston, Museum of Fine Arts 96.719. Cf. Shapiro 2001 for a broader discussion of red-figured Panathenaic amphoras against the background of Delian politics.

[232] Cf. Barron 1983:11.

compelled members of the League to send tribute to the city during the celebration of the Great Panathenaia.[233] The premier event of the newly organized festival, the citharodic *agôn*, is appropriately imagined as the focal point of this centralization of geopolitical power and cultural prestige.

It has been observed that there is a "sudden surge in depictions of musical contests and victors about 440, suggesting that whatever Pericles did made these contests more visible and more popular with the Athenian audience than they had been at any time since before the Persian wars."[234] Pericles was, we saw, intent on bringing the Panathenaic *agônes* into ideological alignment with the democratic *polis*, and, to a reasonable extent, it is possible to speak of a democratization of the experience of music at the Panathenaia. The notional possession of Panathenaic music by the aristocracy, as privileged consumers and critics and occasionally as agonists, was likely challenged, deliberately so, by the Periclean reforms. Indeed, it is tempting to see in the Nausicaa Painter's scene a marked reclamation of the "aristocratic" Apollo *kitharôidos* for the new democratic *agônes*, one that would resonate with the tyrants' earlier citharodic rendering of Apollo Patroos. The image could play specifically against the burgeoning iconographical trend (and the elitist ideology behind it) whereby Apollo was being divested of his citharodic *skeuê* and "professional" aspect in images intended for consumption by aristocrats, who preferred to see the god content with an amateur's lyre.[235] The Panathenaic contests were now held in a publicly funded structure expressly intended for musical performance, an arrangement that would have reminded the

---

[233] For the inscriptional evidence, see Smarczyk 1990:525–592. For the mid-fifth-century date, see Shapiro 2001:122. Cf. Parker 1996:149–151 on Periclean Athens' Delian appropriations.

[234] Shapiro 1992:58.

[235] Cf. Sarti 1992:100–101. We should not, however, be misled by this partially indicative yet nonetheless isolated trend or by the pessimistic absolutism of fourth-century elites such as Plato into imagining a complete rupture between mass and elite at the fifth-century Panathenaic *agônes*. After all, aristocratic agonists such as Alkimakhos continued to make a showing at the contests, and elites must have continued to patronize the contests as spectators, although there may have been a new sense that such individual displays must now be safely integrated into the democratic structure of the festival. For the Classical Panathenaic procession as a site of democratically contained aristocratic display, see Shapiro 1996:221; Maurizio 1998. The *kithara* players on the idealized procession of the Parthenon frieze may represent elite Athenians rather than professional agonists; cf. Part I.3.iiin43.

audience that the *mousikos agôn* was fundamentally a demotic property, supported and framed by the civic apparatus of Athens.[236]

Non-elite Athenians accordingly grew more self-confident and expressive in their appreciation and critique of the musicians who performed for them. The connoisseurship (of sorts) displayed by Dicaeopolis, the "average" citizen hero of Aristophanes' *Acharnians* (produced in 425 BCE), in his withering assessment of the citharodes who competed at the Panathenaic contests of 430 and 426 BCE may represent a relatively recent sociocultural development (13–16), although one that would soon become more common. Indeed, in Dicaeopolis' aesthetic assertiveness we may detect the seeds of what Plato would call in the fourth century *theatrokratia*, the putative control of civic *mousikê* by the masses to the exclusion of the elite. Plato's Manichean vision of music as class struggle is no doubt exaggerated, but it does reflect the historically real assertion of the demotic voice in the city's citharodic culture, which could be traced back to the changes of the 440s (cf. Part I.14). On the side of the performers, the marked flirtation between the citharodic *nomos* of the later fifth century and drama and dithyramb suggest that citharodes were trying to appeal to the preferences of the Athenian demotic audience, albeit with mixed success. We will see that this audience could be quite traditional in its tastes in *kitharôidia*, rejecting the same *poikilia*, stylistic variety and heterogeneity, in citharodic *nomoi* that for Plato supposedly defined the multifarious political character of the late democratic Athenian citizenry (Plato *Republic* 561d).

9. Dionysian Deformations: The New *Nomos*

As late as 425 BCE, Athenians could still expect to hear the Classical Terpandrean *nomoi* performed at the Panathenaia. In the passage from *Acharnians* just cited, Dicaeopolis praises the Boeotian *nomos* performed by Dexitheus and condemns the *Orthios nomos* of Chaeris. Aristophanes *Knights* 1278–1279 suggests that the rendition of the *Orthios* by the Athenian citharode Arignotus was well known to everyone in Athens. The fact that Execestides, probably an Athenian citharode as well, won victories at both the Panathenaia and the Spartan Carneia, whose conservative regulations notoriously discouraged citharodic

---

[236] On the democratization of Athenian musical ideology signaled by the Odeion, see the exhaustive study of Mosconi 2000; cf. Musti 2000.

innovation, suggests that he too maintained the classics in his repertoire.[237] But alongside the retention of this older tradition, a new style
was emerging. Certain citharodes were beginning to break from the
rigid presets and protocols of the Terpandrean *nomoi* by composing
melodies and texts for their own *nomoi*. They diversified the rhythms,
introduced adventurous harmonic modulations made possible by *polukhordia*, the increase of the *kithara*'s strings beyond seven, and imported
into their conventionally Apollonian lyric art the language, narrative
content, and histrionic mimeticism of the Dionysian genres of dithyramb and tragedy. The traditional heroic narratives set to inherited
melodic frameworks that defined the older practice were replaced by
freshly created treatments of events from myth and history set to original music—new *nomoi*. On the one hand, these changes can be viewed
as a pragmatic response the growing predominance of the "democratic"
Panathenaic *agônes* as a center of citharodic culture and the influence of
the sophisticated tastes of the drama- and dithyramb-savvy Athenian
audience. On the other hand, however, the Dionysian turn was not pure
market calculation; it offered a viable creative strategy for innovating
the centuries-old form and practice of the *nomos*.

The most prominent of these innovators, Phrynis, and, still more
notably, his younger rival Timotheus, who also composed dithyrambs (*Suda* s.v. Τιμόθεος), were at the vanguard of the Athenian New
Music, that loosely affiliated, mutually influential group of citharodic, dithyrambic, and dramatic composers and performers intent
on various forms of musical and poetic experimentation (*kainotomia*)
and complexity (*poikilia*).[238] The preserved titles of works by Timotheus
that we are certain or at least quite confident are *nomoi*, *Persians* (PMG
788–791), *Nauplios* (PMG 785), *Cyclops* (PMG 780–782), and *Niobe* (PMG

---

[237] On Execestides, see n193 above. He seems to have been an influential citharode, as is
suggested not only by his multiple victories but also by Hesychius s.v. Ἐξηκεστιδαλκίδαι·
παρὰ τὸν Ἐξηκεστίδην καὶ Ἀλκίδην τοὺς κιθαρῳδούς ("Exekestidalkidai: from the
citharodes Execestides and Alcides"). We hear nothing else of Alcides, although he
may be the same as the Alcaeus, perhaps a Lesbian citharode, who is mentioned
in Eupolis *Golden Race* fr. 303 K-A; cf. Storey 2003a:275. In any case, Execestides and
Alcides were stylistically linked. Together they were figured (probably in Old Comedy)
as new Terpanders, the co-founders of a line of citharodes, the "Exekestidalkidai."

[238] We do not know the titles of *nomoi* composed by Phrynis, as we do for those by
Timotheus. Phaenias fr. 10 Wehrli *ap.* Athenaeus 14.638c remarks on the classic status
of the *nomoi* of Phrynis as well as Terpander, which could suggest that the former
were still being performed as late as the end of the fourth century BCE. See Aristotle
Metaphysics 1.993b15 for the profound influence of Phrynis on Timotheus: εἰ δὲ μὴ
Φρῦνις, Τιμόθεος οὐκ ἂν ἐγένετο ("If there had been no Phrynis, there would have
been no Timotheus").

786–787)—titles which are derived significantly from the narrative content exclusive to each *nomos*, rather than from some character- istic of the text-transcendent musical setting, as was the case with the Terpandrean *nomoi*—could easily belong to tragedies or dithyrambs.[239] Like tragedies or dithyrambs, they are autonomous, solely authored works. Indeed, the generic status of *Niobe*, *Nauplios*, and *Cyclops* has long been debated: are they *nomoi* or dithyrambs? The debate is symp- tomatic of the extent to which Timotheus' *kitharôidia* resembled his dithyrambs, which in turn had a distinctly tragic cast, e.g. *Birth Pangs of Semele* (PMG 792) or *Madness of Ajax* (PMG 777).[240]

The diction of the Timothean dithyrambs and *nomoi* is virtually indistinguishable.[241] Early on in his career, Heraclides of Pontus tells us ("Plutarch" *On Music* 4.1132e), Timotheus had experimented with "mixing dithyrambic diction" (διαμιγνύων διθυραμβικὴν λέξιν) into the *epê* of his citharodic *nomoi*—probably lyric hexameters or quasi- hexameters—and thus, it is implied, displacing the traditionally epic diction those *epê* would otherwise have contained. Timotheus was anticipated in this by Phrynis, who "innovated the *nomos* and attached hexameter to 'free verse'" (ἐκαινοτόμησεν αὐτόν [the *nomos*]· τό τε γὰρ ἑξάμετρον τῷ λελυμένῳ συνῆψε, Proclus *Chrestomathia ap.* Photius *Bibliotheca* 320b8–10). This testimony resembles that of Heraclides about the early *nomoi* of Timotheus, that they were *epê* with an admix-

---

[239] I leave out of account the *Artemis* (PMG 778), which seems to have been a *humnos* for Artemis of Ephesus rather than a *nomos*, although the latter genre is not to be entirely excluded (cf. Hordern 2002:11). No fragments of or testimonia about Timotheus' *Laertes* (PMG 784) and *Phineïdai* (PMG 795) survive, so both must remain generically indeterminate. As for the latter, the violent and grotesque aspects of the myth— Phineus' blinding of his sons, the attacks of the Harpies—would suggest a highly dramatic, volatile musical score. Argonautic-related myth was probably a common subject of early *kitharôidia*, which might be a point in favor of supposing the *Phineïdai* was a *nomos*.

[240] Wilamowitz 1903:81 argues cogently that Timotheus' *Niobe* was a *nomos* rather than a dithyramb. *Cyclops* was very likely a *nomos*: Wilamowitz 1903:81, 107; cf. Power 2011 (forthcoming). Timotheus did, however, deal with Odyssean themes in two dithy- rambs, the *Scylla* (PMG 793–794) and *Elpenor* (PMG 779). It has been argued that he composed an Odyssean dithyrambic "cycle," including the *Elpenor*, *Cyclops*, *Scylla*, and *Laertes*; cf. discussion in Hordern 2002:12–13, who is skeptical. Odyssean scenes had likely been a definitive resource for earlier Classical *kitharôidia*, and the *Scylla* and *Elpenor* (and perhaps the *Laertes*, if it is not a *nomos*) could rather represent a dithy- rambic appropriation of traditionally citharodic material. Cross-generic influence went both ways; cf. Philoxenus' dithyrambic *Cyclops*, discussed below.

[241] For the dithyrambic language of the new *nomos*, see Csapo 2004:215 ("the language [of the *nomos* was] altered to give it the pathos and volubility of the dithyramb"); Hordern 2002:47–50 on the compounds that were characteristic of new dithyrambic and nomic texts.

ture of dithyrambic diction. From the later viewpoints of Heraclides and Proclus, both citharodes negotiate a dialectic of convention and innovation: with a traditional constraint, hexameter, Phrynis contrasts an innovative feature, "free verse"; Timotheus contrasts the language of regular epic verse with the innovation of dithyrambic diction. The latter is a lexical innovation, but the nature of the dialectic is nevertheless similar. It is reasonable to speculate that the use of dithyrambic diction would have itself necessitated the use of lyric meters to some extent as well, resulting in a polymetric composition. Conversely, we can safely assume that Phrynis' "free verse" implies some degree of lexical experimentation as well—probably, as in Timothean *nomoi*, borrowings from dithyramb.[242]

What was happening in the new *nomoi* was the breakdown of textual and musical categories and proprieties that would later be decried as no less than a sociocultural catastrophe by Plato in *Laws* 700e: citharodes such as Timotheus "imitate (*mimoumenoi*)"—this very mimetic tendency is for Plato already a symptom of the corruption of *kitharôidia*— "aulodic song genres (*aulôidiai*) in their citharodic songs (*kitharôidiai*)." At the sonic level, we must imagine that Timotheus with his eleven-stringed *kithara* was intent on emulating the mimetic and tonal sophistication of the dithyrambic *aulos*, the instrument that was considered by Plato to be "the most polychord of all" (*Republic* 399d).[243] The titles and fragments of the *nomoi* indicate the complementary relationship between such musical *kainotomia* and the textual subject matter. Timotheus gravitated specifically toward sensationalistic mythical and historical material, involving markedly "othered," exotic, violently irrational, emotionally extreme subjects

---

[242] Cf. Hephaestion *On Poems* 3.3 for the "free verse" of Timotheus.

[243] In the same passage, "polychord and panharmonic" stringed instruments are called *mimêmata* 'imitations' of the *aulos*. The *polukhordia* 'many-notedness' of the *aulos* was due to the "aulete's capacity for generating a wide variety of notes from only a few finger-holes, by means of techniques for breath- and lip-controls" (Barker 1984:132n29). Cf. "Plutarch" *On Music* 29.1141c; Pindar *Isthmian* 5.27, *Olympian* 7.12; Simonides fr. 46 = PMG 947b. Pindar *Pythian* 12 is a vivid testament to the inherent mimetic capability of the *aulos*. The "polychord" mimeticism of the *aulos* was itself increasingly elaborated throughout the fifth century; see, e.g. "Plutarch" *On Music* 21.1137f–1138b; Athenaeus 14.631e; cf. Barker 1984:97. The emulation of the *aulos* by the Apollonian *kithara* finds a comic reflection on a bell krater by Polion (New York 25.78.66, c. 425 BCE). Three men costumed as aged satyrs play *kitharai* in a confrontational manner before an aulete, who holds his *auloi* at his sides unplayed, as if he has been upstaged by the satyrs. An inscription running above the heads of the satyrs bills them as "Singers at the Panathenaia"—that is, they are citharodes. The image may be based on a comedy or a satyr play that was critical of "modern" trends in *kitharôidia*. The middle satyr has a polychord *kithara* with eight strings.

and characters—storms, gruesome monsters, distraught and dying barbarians and women—whose musical depiction demanded the tonal *poikilia*, sonic and affective intensities, and mimetic pyrotechnics, both audible and visual, that were the hallmarks of the New Music. The old "rules" of the *nomos* had to be broken to capture these intensities.

A parallel could be drawn with a recurrent phenomenon of modern European narrative and dramatic music: the deliberate conjunction of representations of madness, especially feminine hysteria, with the exploitation of extraordinary musical figures and devices—highly elaborate ornamentation, rhythmic and metrical irregularity, chromaticism, virtuosic display, formal discontinuity and fragmentation.[244] That is, madness and other irrational subjects have traditionally offered composers a liberating mimetic scope for working out sonic and formal fantasy and experimentation. The representations of psychologically disordered and emotionally excessive characters—what are called in opera mad scenes, e.g. the Queen of the Night's "Der Hölle Rache" aria in Mozart's *Die Zauberflöte,* or the hysterical woman awaiting her errant lover in Arnold Schoenberg's experiment in form and tonality, *Erwartung*—call for, in some cases one might say excuse or justify, deviant and excessive compositional (and performative) procedures. As one music historian argues:

> Even as late as Mozart's time the forms of music were so rigid that the only way the average composer could wriggle out of the restraints even momentarily was to seize upon certain genre pieces such as the storm. A storm is not expected to follow strict logic, so the composer could break away for a moment and upset the furniture. The Mad Scene offered similar freedom, both formally and expressively."[245]

Not surprisingly, Timotheus did compose at least one musical storm. In his *Memoirs,* the second-century BCE collector of anecdotes Hegesander told of how a famous aulete, Dorion, dismissed the storm conjured up in Timotheus' *Nauplios,* saying he had seen a bigger one in a boiling pot (FHG IV 416 *ap.* Athenaeus 8.338a). On the basis of this anecdote, Wilamowitz argues that the *Nauplios* must have been an aulodic dithyramb.[246] But there is no reason to believe that cross-generic rivalries

---

[244] Cf. McClary 1991:80–111.

[245] Henehan 1980:24, quoted in McClary 1991:101–102.

[246] Wilamowitz 1903:80n2.

were any less intense than intra-generic ones.[247] Dorion's criticism might better be read as an expression of the territorial rhetoric of musical professionalism. For the new *kitharôidia*, with its *polukhordia* and harmonic expansiveness, its focus on mimeticism and treatment of Dionysian themes, could be perceived, from the point of view of a working aulete, as an unwelcome encroachment on *aulos*-based music. The storm in the *Nauplios* was in all likelihood a sensational, arresting piece of musical mimesis, but its very effectiveness was what provoked Dorion to disparage it publicly as a failure.[248] At least one dithyrambic composer, Philoxenus of Cythera, responded to the citharodes' appropriation of dithyrambic music in kind. In Philoxenus' quasi-dramatic dithyramb of the early fourth century BCE, *Cyclops* or *Galateia*, Polyphemus was "played" by a solo singer holding a *kithara*, a *coup de théâtre* that was probably intended as a semi-parodic allusion to Timotheus' nomic *Cyclops*.[249] It has been argued that Melanippides composed a dithyrambic *Marsyas*, in which was described, or rather acted out, the satyr's startling transformation from aulete to citharode.[250]

The imbrication of *nomoi* and dithyrambs elaborated in the Athenian New Music would be taken still further, by at least one citharode, in the Hellenistic period. Inscriptions from late third- and second-century BCE Teos record that on several occasions Demetrius of Phocaea "citharodized" (ἐκιθαρῴδει) dithyrambs, that is, he apparently performed dithyrambs in virtuoso solo renditions rather than with choral accompaniment.[251] The performance of citharodic dithyramb may have become fairly widespread, but there is no unambiguous testimony for it outside of the Tean inscriptions.[252] Perhaps it was Demetrius' specialty.

---

[247] Cf. Hordern 2002:11.

[248] The story about the dithyrambist Cinesias' critique of the Timothean *Artemis* (n260 below) may be a reflex of the same sort of territorial rhetoric.

[249] Philoxenus PMG 819, 822; cf. Power 2011 (forthcoming).

[250] Boardman 1956; cf. n140 above.

[251] The dithyrambs performed by Demetrius were a *Persephone* (by another composer, Nicarchus of Pergamon), an *Andromeda* (his own composition), and a *Horse* (Kallippos of Maronea). The inscriptional evidence is now assembled and convincingly restored in Ma 2007:221, 234, who argues for the solo performance of these pieces. On Demetrius cf. Stephanis 1988, no. 636.

[252] Cf. Ma 2007:232n28. An earlier record of a victory in dithyramb at the Athenian Lenaia, which is inscribed alongside numerous citharodic victories on a monument that was erected for the early-third-century citharode Nicocles of Tarentum (IG II² 3779), has been taken to mean that Nicocles accompanied the winning dithyramb with his *kithara* (e.g. Pickard-Cambridge 1927:76, Bélis 1995:1052–1053). But this conclusion is far from certain. Like citharodes such as Arion and Timotheus before him, the talented Nicocles more likely composed dithyramb qua poet for regular choral, aulodic performance (cf. Sutton 1989:100). Another possible Hellenistic

Attic tragedy too was integral in the remaking of *kitharôidia*. The relationship between tragedy and *kitharôidia* dated back to the early fifth century BCE: Aeschylus himself had looked to the citharodic *nomos* for inspiration (Aristophanes *Frogs* 1281–1300). The later fifth century, however, witnessed a heavy increase in the traffic of music and themes between the two genres. Timotheus' *Persians*, suffused with tragic and oriental color, finds an obvious antecedent in Aeschylus' *Persians*. The stories of Niobe and Nauplios (the younger) provided the plot for plays by both Aeschylus and Sophocles. *Cyclops*, while drawing, like older citharodic *nomoi*, from Homeric epic, nevertheless shares its title with a satyr play of Euripides, whom the biographical tradition makes an admirer of Timotheus and a collaborator on the composition of his *Persians* (Satyrus *Life of Euripides* T 4.24 Kovacs). That collaboration, however, is probably less historical fact than narrative condensation of the notable continuities between the works of the two composers. The verbal and scenic parallels are indisputable; they speak to mutual influence. The linguistic, metrical, and conceptual similarity between the barbarian laments in *Persians*, in particular the pidgin Greek imprecations of the captured Phrygian (146–161), and the polymetric "messenger aria" of the Phrygian eunuch in Euripides *Orestes* 1400–1502 is the most striking example.[253] Wilamowitz argues convinc-

---

cithodic hybrid, however, is attested in Polybius 4.20.8–9: the third-century Arcadians chorally reperformed the *nomoi* of Timotheus and Philoxenus to the music of the *aulos*. But perhaps Polybius means to say dithyrambs rather than *nomoi*, or he is using *nomoi* in a generic sense ("melodies"), as Philoxenus did not compose citharodic *nomoi* and Timotheus did compose choral dithyramb. Cf. Pickard-Cambridge 1927:78; West 1992:381–382. The report in Clement of Alexandria *Stromateis* 1.133 that Timotheus was the first to perform citharodic *nomoi* with a chorus is highly improbable; it is perhaps based on a misunderstanding of Polybius' testimony, or the simple fact that Timotheus also composed choral dithyramb. Cf. Hordern 2002:27.

[253] See Porter 1994:199–207; cf. Basset 1931:159–161, with further parallels. Herington 1985:276n37 sums up Bassett's key points: "[Bassett] names Euripides' *Antiope*, *Hypsipyle*, and *Phoenissae*, besides *Orestes* [as showing the influence of Timotheus]. Perhaps the most remarkable parallel to which he points is the verbal and metrical correspondence between *Orestes* 1397 Ἀσιάδι φωνᾷ βασιλέων and line 147 of Timotheus' poem, Ἀσιάδι φωνᾷ διάτορον." Cf. Csapo 2004:240, who notes what could be the allusive mention of *nomoi* in the Eunuch's song (1426, 1430). To the echoes adduced by Bassett and others I would add a phrase from an earlier play, *Trojan Women*, καινοὶ ὕμνοι (511), which may echo καινά in Timotheus PMG 796 (cf. Schönewolf 1938:37). This is the only example of *kainos* describing music in Euripides. It is conceivable that not only Timotheus' music but also his programmatic vocabulary influenced Euripides. The plots of *Antiope* and *Hypsipyle* deal with mythical lyre players and thus draw upon currents in the contemporary Athenian culture of *kitharôidia*: see Wilson 1999/2000. For Euripides and the New Music in general, see Csapo 1999/2000.

ingly that the heroine's death scene in *Niobe*, which featured a lament involving a hallucination of the voice of Charon calling from beyond (PMG 786, 787), is based upon the death of the Euripidean Alcestis (cf. *Alcestis* 252–263).[254] The new *nomos* must also have involved a new style of physical performance, the citharode's histrionic deployment of his body to complement visually the mimetic extremities of text and music.[255]

10. Comic Critique and Popular Ambivalence

The cross-fertilization of new *kitharôidia* and tragedy finds a fittingly boundary-crossing emblem in Aristophanes' evocation in *Women at the Thesmophoria* 101–129 of the tragedian Agathon, who, probably to an even greater extent than Euripides, was an enthusiastic adopter of trends in the New Music.[256] Agathon, in all the splendor of his "soft," luxurious, Asiatic-Ionic visual style (130–167), appears on stage to sing, by himself, a duet between a solo singer and a women's chorus. We do not know if this song is meant as a parody of an actual song from a tragedy by Agathon, but it points in a general sense toward Agathon's interest in the music of East Greek citharodes such as Timotheus.

This is signaled even before Agathon begins his song proper. Mnesilochus, the protagonist of *Women at the Thesmophoria*, asks Euripides, who has brought him to Agathon's house, "Ant tracks (μύρμηκος ἀτραπούς), or what is it he is about to sing through?" (100). The image of "ant tracks," which refers to the melodic and modal intricacies of the New Music, is used specifically of the polychord *kitharôidia* of Timotheus in the attack on the New Music composers in Pherecrates *Cheiron* fr. 155 K-A (ἐκτραπέλους μυρμηκιάς 'perverse ant tracks', 23).[257] Since the singing has not yet begun, Mnesilochus is presumably responding to an instrumental prelude, sounded on the *aulos* or perhaps on a lyre or *barbitos* played by Agathon himself, that

---

[254] Wilamowitz 1903:81n1.

[255] See discussion in Part I.17.

[256] Agathon supposedly introduced the "effeminate" chromatic genus into tragic music (Plutarch *Sympotic Questions* 645e), an innovation that was alternately ascribed to Euripides (Michael Psellus [?] *On Tragedy* 5). Cf. Austin and Olson 2004:87. It may be significant in this regard that Aristoxenus *ap.* "Plutarch" *On Music* 20.1137e claims *kitharôidia* employed the chromatic genus "from the start." Cf. Hordern 2002:34n97; Part II.5n98.

[257] Cf. Muecke 1982:46. The metaphor was also applied to dithyramb, however; Philoxenus earned the nickname Myrmex 'Ant' (*Suda* s.v. Φιλόξενος).

parodies the many-noted complexity of the New Music.[258] Agathon's song proper, in an astrophic, polymetric sequence not unlike what we see in Timotheus' *Persians*, takes the form of a hymn to Apollo, Artemis, and Leto, a subject that is not out of keeping with the "Apollonian" character of *kitharôidia*, but one that is distinguished by a consistently orientalizing, Dionysian flavor that resonates with the markedly Dionysian (and yet still Apolline) image of the singer.[259] We think of Timotheus' *Artemis*, which apparently hymned the goddess in an exotic, "Bacchic" fashion that was perhaps at home in Ephesus, where it was first performed, but was shockingly inappropriate to secondary Athenian audiences. So shocking was it that, according to one anecdote, even Cinesias, supposedly the most outrageous dithyrambic composer of the New Music, stood up in the audience to voice his disapproval at the verse describing Artemis as θυιάδα φοιβάδα μαινάδα λυσσάδα 'thyiadic, frantic, maenadic, fanatic'.[260]

In Agathon's hymn, Apollo is praised as an Easterner, the founder of Phrygian Troy, perhaps with a subtle allusion to the god's lyric foundation of that city (cf. Ovid *Heroides* 16.179–180; Martial 8.6.6).[261] Indeed, the hymn includes two explicit references to the *kithara*; the curiously emphatic attention to this instrument again suggests that Aristophanes is alluding to a marked sympathy between Agathon's tragic *melos* and the *kitharôidia* of the day. First, Agathon sings of the "notes of the Asiatic *kithara*" (κρούματα ... Ἀσιάδος, 120) that accompany the dance of the Phrygian Graces. Later, Agathon, taking the part of the female chorus, sings, "I revere mistress Leto and the *kitharis*, the mother of songs (*humnoi*) esteemed on account of its masculine cry" (σέβομαι Λατώ τ' ἄνασσαν | κίθαρίν τε ματέρ' ὕμνων | ἄρσενι βοᾷ δοκίμων, 123–125).[262] Like Agathon's Apollo, it is as Asiatic that the *kithara* is first invoked. The exotic cast of the instrument is further underscored by its fanciful association with the Graces of Phrygia, known to be the ancestral home of the *aulos*—a deliberate mixing of Dionysian

---

[258] Cf. Muecke 1982:46.

[259] For Agathon as Dionysus, see Bierl 2001:164–168, 173, 321n60; as Apollo, Muecke 1982:44.

[260] PMG 778 = Plutarch *On Superstition* 10; cf. Plutarch *How the Young Man Should Listen to Poetry* 4.

[261] Bothe 1845:111 thinks that the chorus represented by Agathon consists of Trojan girls, and that the hymn parodies a choral song from a play of his on the fall of Troy. That must remain pure speculation, but it is interesting to note the apparent prominence of the theme in *kitharôidia* (cf. Part II.9.ii); Euripides' choral song on the fall of Troy in his *Trojan Women* alludes to the conventions of the citharodic hymn (511–515).

[262] See Austin and Olson 2004:96 for the preferability of δοκίμων (Schöne) to the transmitted δόκιμον; cf. Muecke 1982:48.

and Apollonian musical identities is strongly implied. Euripides too was fascinated by the notionally Asiatic character of the *kithara*; it is in his plays that we first see the term *Asias (kithara)* used.[263] Webster argues that Euripides coined it in "homage" to Timotheus, who was an "Asian" Ionian of Miletus.[264] While it is true that Euripides may have been the first poet to employ the actual term *Asias (kithara)*, doubtless drawn to its exoticizing and vaguely Dionysiac connotations, the idea behind it surely predates him, having its roots in the Archaic lore of Lesbian *kitharôidia*.[265] Nevertheless, it seems probable that Euripides was responding to an actual exoticizing trend in the contemporary culture of *kitharôidia*. That is, Timotheus and citharodes like him, themselves inspired by tragedy's romance with barbarian, Eastern cultures, likely emphasized the "archaic exoticism" of their *tekhnê* and their own performative personae.[266] The reception of *kitharôidia* by tragedy thus involved its theatricalizing, its "othering." But there was a sort of feedback loop at work. Citharodes were already, under the influence of Dionysian forms, "othering" themselves and their art.

One expression of the exoticizing trend in *kitharôidia* may be detected in the appearance of the foreign-looking Thracian or Thamyris *kithara* in the hands of agonists in later-fifth-century BCE contest scenes. The use of these instruments may have been inspired by a tragedy, Sophocles' *Thamyras*, which in its turn may have represented a dramatic engagement with the emergence of innovatory trends in Athenian citharodic culture.[267] Agathon's "look" and bearing in *Women at the Thesmophoria* are surely meant to evoke the persona of the modern-day citharode, at least in part. Agathon claims that he emulates poets associated with sympotic and erotic lyric, Ibycus, Anacreon, and Alcaeus, "who gave new flavor to *harmonia*; they wore headbands and they adopted a lifestyle of Ionian luxury" (160–163). His

---

[263] A scholiast to *Women at the Thesmophoria* 120 in fact claims that Ἀσιάδος κρούματα is a parody of a passage from the *Erechtheus* of Euripides (= Euripides fr. 64 Austin = 370 N). Other mentions of the Asiatic *kithara*: *Cyclops* 443–444; *Hypsipyle* fr. 64 II.98 Bond. Strabo 10.3.17 cites a line from an unnamed poet of uncertain date that mentions the *kithara Asiatis*; cf. Cassio 2000:106.

[264] Webster 1967:18.

[265] The glosses of *Asias kithara* by Duris of Samos (FGrH 76 F 81) and in "Plutarch" *On Music* 6.1133c (perhaps drawn from Heraclides of Pontus) both explain the term in connection with the Lesbian citharodes and their proximity to Asia, by which Lydia above all is meant. See Cassio 2000:107; for Pindar's reception of this tradition in fr. 125 S-M, see Part III.15.

[266] Cf. Wilson 2004:305n82; Cassio 2000:109–110.

[267] See Wilson 2009. The satyric Panathenaic citharodes on Polion's bell krater play Thracian *kitharai* (cf. n243 above).

style must then recall primarily the glamorous, Lydianizing comasts we see on the late Archaic "Anacreontic" vases; that a *barbitos* and a tortoise-shell lyre are among the various "props" scattered about him (137–138)—perhaps held or even played by him—only reinforces that impression.[268] Yet the hypermimetic Agathon, wearing a long, saffron-dyed chiton (the *krokôtos*, 138) and singing a "citharodic" hymn, inevitably "plays the citharode" as well.[269]

It is worth noting the implications of the scholion on line 162, which says that "the older copies" (τὰ παλαιότερα ἀντίγραφα) of the play had "Achaios," the name of a tragedian of Euripides' generation, instead of "Alcaeus."[270] The Alexandrian scholar Aristophanes of Byzantium supposedly recognized that "Alcaeus" the lyric poet of Mytilene was the correct reading. A later Alexandrian scholar, Didymus, disagreed with Aristophanes, arguing that Alcaeus was not sufficiently familiar to the Athenians "on account of his [Aeolic] dialect." That objection, as the scholiast notes, is wholly ungrounded. But what Didymus proposed instead is interesting: "Alcaeus" could be accepted as the correct reading, but only if it were taken to refer to a citharode by that name rather than the lyric poet. Alcaeus appears to have been a famous citharode of the later fifth century, a contemporary of Phrynis and Timotheus. He was sufficiently well known in Athens to appear

---

[268] Cf. Austin and Olson 2004:111–112. For Agathon as Anacreon, see Snyder 1974; Muecke 1982:50. It is unclear whether one or both of the stringed instruments are held or played by Agathon. They are mentioned by Mnesilochus in an inventory of seemingly random objects, including an oil-flask, a mirror, and a sword, that have apparently come out with Agathon on the *ekkuklêma* (137–140). Most of them must be on the ground around Agathon, but he is presumably wearing the chiton and the headband that are mentioned as well. It is worth noting that the lyre could act as the default sign for poet-composer or trainer in any genre, even aulodic ones, and this probably reflects real compositional and rehearsal methods. On the Pronomus vase, Pronomus is shown with his *auloi*, while the poet Demetrius sits near a lyre (cf. Wilson 2000:352–353). Another figure, standing next to Pronomus and holding a lyre, named Charinus, is probably the chorus trainer (cf. Waywell 1973:268, Trendall and Webster 1971:29). So it would be appropriate to show Agathon with a stringed instrument as he composes. Of course, if he does hold the lyre or *barbitos*, he may be only pretending to play it. That is, the comic aulete may be supplying the actual musical accompaniment. The visual-aural effect would nicely iconicize the Dionysian "aulization" of the Apollonian *kithara* that is thematized in the song itself.

[269] Such "playing the citharode" may already have been a part of the Dionysian boundary-blurring of the Anacreontic symposium/*kômos*; see Part III.15n275. The *krokôtos* was typically worn by women (Austin and Olson 2004:102)—Agathon is explicitly cross-dressing—but agonistic musicians also wore costly dyed garments. The famous aulete Antigeneidas wore a *krokôtos* when he accompanied a dithyramb called *The Comast*, perhaps a work of Philoxenus (*Suda* s.v. Ἀντιγενίδης = PMG 825).

[270] Cf. Austin and Olson 2004:110–111.

as a character in Eupolis' *Golden Race*, which was probably produced in the mid 420s.[271] The Aristophanic scholiast cites a line from that play in which someone addresses Alcaeus ὦ Σικελιῶτα Πελοποννήσιε '[Alcaeus] of Sicily and from the Peloponnese' (fr. 303 K-A). Alcaeus may have been a Lesbian citharode, named propitiously after his island's famous *melopoios*, who won fame at the Spartan Carneia and, like Arion before him, in the lucrative citharodic markets of Western Greece, but also competed, as did the Lesbian Phrynis, at the Panathenaia. Didymus may have been (and very probably was) merely speculating on this point, drawing his own connection between the text of Eupolis and that of Aristophanes without any external support. Nevertheless, his reasoning invites a more worthwhile interpretation. Could we read "Alcaeus" as an example of the allusive density that Aristophanes so commonly displays? That is, Alcaeus the Lesbian lyric poet would be the primary referent of "Alcaeus," but, secondarily, the audience would hear an allusion to the well-known Lesbian citharode. That "Alcaeus" comes last in Agathon's list of influences, after the unambiguous Ibycus and Anacreon, and so perhaps timed as a punch line, would underscore the cleverness and humor of the referential ambiguity. Both identities, that of the glamorous, aristocratic, Ionic symposiast and that of the charismatic, exotic-seeming festival citharode in his splendid *skeuê* are fused in the mimetic *poikilia* of the Aristophanic Agathon's fabulous "self-staging."[272]

Although Alcaeus the citharode was not explicitly linked to the New Music, it is worth noting that in another fragment of the *Golden Race* of Eupolis, someone is addressed as ὦ καλαβρὲ κιθαροιδότατε 'O most citharodic barbarian' (fr. 311 K-A; for καλαβρός as βάρβαρος, see Hesychius s.v.). The addressee of this paradoxical designation— the master of Hellenic musical culture figured as the very opposite of the cultured Hellene—may well be our Alcaeus. If so, his putative "barbarian" status would likely have more to do with his choice of material for his *nomoi* and his performative self-presentation than with his actual ethnicity. Similarly, Aristophanes' abuse of the star citharode Execestides, who was probably an Athenian citizen and certainly a free Greek, as a slave from barbarian Caria (*Birds* 11, 764, 1527) may represent an analogous comic response to the increasingly "exotic" persona of the citharode. The supposed barbarity of the citharode remained a comic topos in the fourth century. Aristotle *Rhetoric*

---

[271] Cf. n237 above.

[272] "Self-staging": Nagy 2007a:245–246; cf. Bierl 2001:158–165.

3.11.1412a33–1412b3 records an insult to a citharode named Nicon, surely delivered first in a Middle or New comedy: "You are a Thracian slave girl."[273]

The comic conflation of gender and ethnicity—the citharode as female barbarian—made explicit in the insult directed at Nicon is implicit in Agathon's hymn as well. Agathon's "chorus" claims to revere, along with Leto, "the *kitharis*, the mother of songs (*humnoi*) esteemed on account of its masculine cry" (123–125). First, we should note that *kitharis* is an archaizing designation for the concert *kithara* that is used by Timotheus in his *Persians* to describe both the *kithara* of Apollo (202) and his own eleven-stringed instrument (231). On the one hand, Agathon's maternal characterization of the *kitharis/kithara* marks its hymnic assimilation to Leto, mother of Apollo and Artemis. On the other, however, "the more significant point is that the instrument—grammatically feminine—is confused about its gender, like Agathon and a number of other characters in the play."[274] The *kitharis* is, like Agathon, androgynous, a mother of songs that yet has a "masculine cry" (ἄρσενι βοᾷ).[275] But the feminizing of the instrument, which was by tradition "patriarchal," almost entirely confined to use by male musicians—Pindar *Pythian* 4.176 appropriately calls the ur-citharodic Orpheus ἀοιδᾶν πατήρ 'father of songs'—likely refers beyond the characterization of Agathon and the "gender-bending" thematics of the play to the role of the *kithara* in the Dionysiac experimentation of the new *nomos*, which included the melodramatic mimesis of women (e.g. Niobe, a maternal figure indeed) and a preference for pathetic, sensual melodies that many heard as effeminate and potentially effeminizing. As Mnesilochus exclaims upon the completion of Agathon's hymn, ὡς ἡδὺ τὸ μέλος ... καὶ θηλυδριῶδες 'how sweet the song ... and smelling so of women!' (130–131).[276]

The gendered critique of New Music was a common theme in Old Comedy, which was at least ostensibly culturally and aesthetically conservative, and in the reactionary elite intellectual discourse of

---

[273] See Cooper 1920.

[274] Austin and Olson 2004:96.

[275] On the "travesties of gender" in the representation of Agathon, see Zeitlin 1996:383–384; cf. Muecke 1982, who sees the hymned *kitharis* as "the deified personification of Agathon's μελοποιία" (48).

[276] For θηλυδριῶδες, see Austin and Olson 2004:98, with bibliography. Mnesilochus' exclamation of wonder at the New Music of Agathon may allude to the eroticized awe shown by Apollo at Hermes' proto-citharodic performance in *Homeric Hymn to Hermes* 436–462. Like Agathon, Hermes has sung a lyric hymn; like Mnesilochus, a somewhat confounded Apollo interrupts to ask a series of questions about the identity of the performer and his "new" *tekhnê*. Of course, Mnesilochus' reaction is far less politely expressed and far more qualified than Apollo's.

the fourth century that to a large extent inherited and elaborated the musical critical tropes of comedy. And it is not only the music that was so criticized; the musicians themselves came under fire for their supposed effeminacy. Such *ad hominem* critique was deployed with force against the dramatic and dithyrambic exponents of the New Music, above all Agathon.[277] The question Mnesilochus asks of the bewildering Agathon is emblematic: "Am I to seek out who you are then based on your song (*melos*)?" (144–145). But, as the case of Nicon the "Thracian slave girl" shows, citharodes were not exempt from the politics of musical identity. Phrynis' musical and personal masculinity appears to have been especially vulnerable to abuse. He was called, as Agathon is by Mnesilochus (136), a *gunnis* 'sissy', and was said to have "enfeebled" the harmony of the *kithara*, making it "softer" (*malthakôteron*) (scholia *ad* Aristophanes *Clouds* 971a, b). Aristophanes makes punning reference to the supposed pathic and promiscuous homosexuality of the Athenian Arignotus, "a man beloved by all men and greatly skilled, a citharode in the fullest sense, whom charm attends" (ἅπασι φίλον ἄνδρα τε σοφώτατον, | τὸν κιθαραοιδότατον, ᾧ χάρις ἐφέσπετο, *Wasps* 1277–1278).[278] Arignotus was doubtless a talented citharode, although his *kharis* 'charm' may have had as much to do with the feminine whiteness of his skin as the excellence of his rendition of the *Orthios nomos*, something Aristophanes insinuates in a separate reference at *Knights* 1278–1280, in which he also figures the citharode as a promiscuous *erômenos*, sexually gratifying his many fans.[279] The uncontracted superlative κιθαραοιδότατος 'most citharodic, a citharode in the fullest sense', however, generalizes the insinuations against Arignotus, elevating his putative effeminacy into a constitutive feature of the citharodic character. Similarly, Eupolis' use of the same superlative to describe a "barbarian" citharode, perhaps Alcaeus, in his *Golden Race*, suggests that alterity and exoticism were also becoming essential to the perception of the citharode, at least in the comic imagination. Effeminacy and barbarism (or at least uncultured, banausic vulgarity—ethnic difference displaced onto class distinction) were for Plato and his musically elitist congeners of the fourth century definitive traits of the citharode and other agonistic

---

[277] See Csapo 2004:230–232.

[278] Cf. Totaro 1991:153–154 for the erotic double entendres in the passage.

[279] "For now everyone knows Arignotus who knows the color white (*to leukon*) and the *Orthios nomos*." See Totaro 1991:155–157 for the sexual punning. At *Women at the Thesmophoria* 191–192, we learn that Agathon is good looking, white skinned (*leukos*), clean shaven, and has the voice of a woman (*gunaikophônos*). Arignotus, we might surmise, is similarly a citharodic exponent of this glamorously androgynous New Music "look."

musicians. Phaedrus, in Plato *Symposium* 179d, is made to assume that all citharodes, even Orpheus, are unmanly; he claims that Orpheus could not save Eurydice from Hades because μαλθακίζεσθαι ἐδόκει, ἅτε ὢν κιθαρῳδός 'he was likely to have been soft and effeminate, since he was a citharode'.[280] Aristoxenus laments the "utter barbarization" of the theaters in his day (fr. 124 Wehrli), as well as the profound "feminization" of the music that was performed in them (fr. 70).

It would be misguided to read these marginalizing characterizations of citharodes as unmediated reflections of their perception in the popular culture. Certainly the extreme views of Plato or Aristoxenus were far from the mainstream. But what about Old Comedy's critique? First, it is worth keeping in mind that the transformations of citharodic culture may have been viewed by the comic poets as a professional challenge. Although citharodes were not in direct competition with comic poets, as their "acts" grew more theatrical, they must have entered into indirect rivalry with comic spectacle for the attentions of the Athenian public.[281] The rough treatment of citharodes in comedy could be seen in part then as a self-interested strategy. Comic poets undercut their prestige—they are nothing but barbarians and effeminates—while at the same time importing some of their undeniable allure from the Panathenaia to the comic stages of the Dionysia and Lenaia.[282] We have one instance of this double-edged engagement in Agathon's quasi-cithardic turn in *Women at the Thesmophoria*. There is good reason to believe that Phrynis appeared on stage as a character in Eupolis' *Demes*, in which he had a hostile confrontation with Pyronides, the play's hero and likely no fan of the melodic "bends" (*kampai*) for which Phrynis was mocked by Aristophanes in his *Clouds* (969–972).[283] It

---

[280] Cf. Dover 1989:74.

[281] In light of such an implicit rivalry, it is worth considering Timotheus' own conspicuous attempts at humor. In the *sphragis* of *Persians*, he borrows the tropes and verbal style of the comic invective that was leveled at the New Music composers (himself included) to attack his own New Music rivals: μουσοπαλαιολύμαι 'defilers of the Old Muse', λωβητῆρες ἀοιδᾶν 'debauchers of songs' (215–218; for the imagery, cf. Pherecrates fr. 155 K-A). Similarly, at PMG 802, from the *sphragis* of another *nomos*, he uses the comic compound ἰωνοκάμπτας 'bender of Ionian melody' to undercut his rival Phrynis (cf. n98 above for other comic elements in this fragment). Probably also comedic is the speech of the Phrygian captive in *Persians* 146–161, with its solecistic Ionic Greek. The speech may well have been played for laughs; it has clear affinities with comic imitations of barbarians trying to speak Greek. Cf. Herington 1985:156; Hall 2006:279; Colvin 1999:56; van Minnen 1997:255.

[282] For the rivalry and even appropriation inherent in comedy's critique of New Music in general, see Zimmermann 1993; Dobrov and Urios-Apirisi 1995.

[283] The evidence is the fourth-century BCE Paestan bell krater by Asteas (Salerno Pc 1812), which appears to illustrate a scene from *Demes*. See Taplin 1993:42, with ill.

is conceivable that the play featured a "para-citharodic" performance by Phrynis that put his musical and sexual deviance on full display. Eupolis' *Golden Race* apparently included a cameo by the citharode Alcaeus, who may have performed a song expressive of his "barbarian" character.[284]

Beneath the representational agendas and invective excesses of comedy, however, we may well detect a shift in the popular perception of the professional citharode—a shift helped along, of course, by comedy itself, but also by the citharodes' own Dionysian deformations of their *tekhnê*. To some extent, the outraged reactions to innovations in the music and performance of *kitharôidia* staged by the comic poets must have reflected attitudes shared by members of their audience as well, who were, if not outright scandalized, then at least made uneasy by the "softening" of the traditional proprieties of *kitharôidia*. "New" citharodic performance style had become objectively more flamboyant than the old-school variety; conceivably, not only comedians and conservative elites but average citizens as well imputed a gendered difference to the professional citharodes who entertained them, which in turn rendered their music morally suspect (if not less enjoyable).

Mnesilochus' response to Agathon's strange music and stranger image is at once sensually pleasurable—an erotic "tickle" (*gargalos*) comes over him as he listens (132–133)—and perplexed, and even borderline hostile (cf. the rude interrogation at 137–144, which is compared to Lycurgus' contemptuous interrogation of Dionysus). Scripted and exaggerated though it is by Aristophanes, this response may well capture something of the ambivalence felt by the Panathenaic mass audience when confronted by a Phrynis or Timotheus. It is significant that we catch a glimpse of the effeminate citharode in tragedy as well as comedy. In Euripides' *Antiope*, produced around the time of the *Women at the Thesmophoria*, Zethus, a paradigm of manly virtue, accuses his bother, the proto-citharode Amphion, of softness and effeminacy. Zethus tells Amphion, "You are conspicuous by your womanly appearance" (γυναικομίμῳ διαπρέπεις μορφώματι, fr. IX Kambitsis), by which an anachronistic allusion to the glamorous *skeuê* of the fifth-century

---

16.16; cf. Storey 2003a:169–170, 332. On Phrynis' clean-shaven appearance, perhaps a reflection of his androgynous New Music persona, see Part I.7n123.

[284] Cf. Storey 2003a:275, 333. Two other possible "para-citharodic" scenes: (1) In Plato *Women Returning from Sacrifice* fr. 10 K-A someone (a citharode?) asks to be brought a *kithara* and costume; perhaps a citharodic performance followed. (2) If the satyric "Singers at the Panathenaia" on Polion's krater were inspired by a comedy or satyr play (cf. n146 above), we might assume some parodic *agôn* was enacted in the original drama.

citharode is probably intended.[285] Indeed, we might read the epithet γυναικόμιμον (literally 'woman-imitating') as expressly evoking the mimetic and theatrical aspect of new citharodic performance and persona. The word makes a significant appearance in Euripides *Bacchae* 980, where it describes the costume worn by Pentheus as he makes his paradigmatically dramatic and Dionysiac transformation from man to woman.

11. Legitimating the *Nomos*: Timotheus' Persians in Athens

i. The wages of *paranomia*

Timotheus' *Persians* is a work fundamentally shaped by and responsive to the specific conditions of the democratic culture of *kitharôidia* in post-Periclean Athens. The subject of the *nomos*, the defeat of the Persian forces at Salamis, is quintessentially Athenian in its market appeal; it is also inherently theatrical, thanks to its consecrated treatment by Aeschylus. The style of *Persians* has all the hallmarks of the new *nomos*, musical, textual, and performative, that bear the stamp of Athenian drama and dithyramb. The central narrative section (1–201), what Pollux *Onomasticon* 4.66 calls the *omphalos*, is studded with dithyrambic diction and surely elicited a full range of innovative vocal and instrumental effects to capture the intensities of the text and the representations they entail. There are frenzied battle scenes, evoked no doubt with all manner of melodic, instrumental, and rhythmic *poikilia*. The polymetrical irregularity of the text implies a quick-changing, even spasmodic rhythmic articulation that would emphasize the chaos and upheaval of the conflict. The narrative flow is routinely disrupted by sudden "jump-cuts" from one scene to another, abrupt changes in focus and mood that were likely underscored by a musical

---

[285] Kambitsis 1972:38 compares the portrait of a cross-dressing Agathon in *Women at the Thesmophoria*. Bothe 1825–1826 *ad loc.* already noted the allusion to the citharodic *skeuê* in γυναικόμιμον μόρφωμα. For the commentary on contemporary *kitharôidia* built into *Antiope*, see Wilson 1999/2000, who shows Euripides' Amphion to be a socio-musically overdetermined figure, not entirely dissimilar to Agathon: part new-style citharode wowing the masses with his musical flights of fancy (fr. 911 N, with Wilson, p441), part anti-demotic aristocrat entrenched in the "lyric counterculture" of the symposium.

lambency; we should imagine harmonic modulations, changes of tempo and volume, extreme timbral contrasts, and other such devices. Descriptions of physical violence inflicted on objects and bodies suggest highly imitative, often high-decibel sound effects: the crashing and capsizing of ships (11–20; 86–93); the confused screams and shouts of the combatants (κρ]αυγᾶι βοὰ δὲ [πα]μμι[γ]ὴς κατεῖχεν, 34); the gruesome drowning death of a barbarian (40–85). The action is periodically interrupted by four aria-like "mad scenes," in each of which the citharode casts himself in the role of a lamenting barbarian *in extremis*, impersonating with his *kitharôidia* the "mad, sad, and foreign voices" that audiences would normally hear impersonated by an actor-singer or chorus on the tragic (or occasionally comic) stage.[286]

Further, we may assume that these scenes were "realistically" infused with orientalizing musical modes and stylemes, as well as any number of experimental instrumental and vocal techniques. The various ethnicities and dispositions of the suffering barbarians suggest a range of harmonic colors and special effects. There is a mentally deranged, drowning commander (*anax*, 42), probably a Persian.[287] As he goes under, he curses the sea and invokes his lord Xerxes (72–81) "in a piercing and babbling voice" (ὀξυπαραυδήτῳ φωνᾷ) while saltwater fills his mouth (64–71).[288] At 105–138 Timotheus presents a composite voice belonging to "a group consisting of barbarians including Mysians and Lydians, who sing to us jointly like a tragic chorus."[289] The third "aria" is the confused and desperate supplication of a Greek warrior by a Phrygian from Kelainai (150–161). We might expect at this point a modulation into the Phrygian *harmonia*. The last barbarian voice we

---

[286] "Mad, sad, and foreign voices": Hall 1999:101n27.

[287] Cf. Gambetti 2001:49–50, who identifies the drowning *anax* as Xerxes' brother Ariamenes. The man is apparently called an "islander" at line 47, however. If the epithet is to be taken literally—and not as a metaphorical description of his shipwrecked state—Hordern's suggestion that he is from the islands of the Red Sea appeals (2002:156).

[288] A recurring theme/image in *Persians* is the barbarians' loss of control over their mouths (*stoma*, cf. 85, 91, 148), grotesquely marking their divorce from reason and articulate *logos*, their animalistic reduction to pathetic bodies emanating unrestrained sound. The teeth gnashing (γόμφους ἐμπρίων, 69) of the drowning man recalls a feature of the auletic *Puthikos nomos*, an instrumental representation of Apollo's slaying of the Pythian serpent. Pollux *Onomasticon* 4.84 says that one section of the *nomos* includes "gnashings (ὀδοντισμόν) like those of the serpent as it grinds its teeth (συμπρίοντος τοὺς ὀδόντας) after being pierced with arrows" (trans. Barker 1984:51). Timotheus may have taken this bit of auletic mimesis as a model for his aria. The gaping mouth of the lamenting Gorgon was the source of the "music" Athena first adapted for the *aulos*: Pindar *Pythian* 12.20–21.

[289] Hall 2006:278.

hear is that of the Persian King himself, Xerxes (178–195). His song
erupts out of an implicit antiphonal *kommos*, as around him his entou-
rage (*panêguris*, 171) engages in the typically overwrought gestures
of staged barbarian lament, scratching their faces and rending their
garments (166–169).

The description of this lament suggests a shrill, intense, and chaotic
music that likely carried over into the King's aria: "A high pitched
Asiatic wailing was attuned to their polyglot lamentation" (σύντονος δ'
ἁρμόζετ' Ἀσιὰς | οἰμωγὰ πολυ<γλώσσῳ> στόνῳ, 169–170).[290] σύντονος
'high pitched' perhaps indicates a musical setting in the Syntonolydian
harmonia, which Plato *Republic* 397e associates with lament and effeminacy (cf. "Plutarch" *On Music* 15.1136b).[291] Might we also hear an allusion
in Ἀσιὰς to the "Asiatic" *kithara* of Timotheus, which is itself "attuned"
to the stylized representation of this wild lament? All this, battles and
and barbarians, we might imagine would have been brought to visual
life with a good deal of histrionic physical mimesis.[292]

Yet for all its apparent typicality as a product of the New Music, I
would argue that *Persians* is also a work that reflects Timotheus' awareness of the potentially ambivalent reception of his innovative *kitharôidia*.
The anecdotal tradition records that Timotheus had fallen out of favor
thanks to his innovations. Satyrus, the third-century BCE biographer of
Euripides, records that Timotheus, unpopular "among the Greeks" on
account of his *kainotomia*, was on the verge of suicide, until "Euripides
alone laughed back at the audiences" (μόνος Εὐριπίδης ἀνάπαλιν
τῶν μὲν θεατῶν καταγελάσαι). The tragedian gave the citharode
encouraging words and even composed the *prooimion* to *Persians*. As
a result, Satyrus says, Timotheus "was victorious and immediately
ceased to be despised."[293] Plutarch closely follows: "Timotheus was
hissed because he seemed to transgress against the laws of music
(παρανομεῖν εἰς τὴν μουσικήν) due to his *kainotomia*" (*Whether an Old
Man Should Engage in Public Affairs* 23.795d = Euripides T 57 Kovacs). The
verb *paranomein* must refer specifically to innovations in the citharodic
nomos (cf. "Plutarch" *On Music* 4.1132e; Plato *Laws* 700d). Euripides again
comes to the rescue, assuring Timotheus that he will "soon have the

---

[290] On the text and translation, see Hordern 2002:219. On the debt of the King's lament to
the choral *kommos* of Aeschylus' *Persians*, see Rosenbloom 2006:153.

[291] Cf. "Plutarch" *On Music* 15.1136b; Janssen 1984:115.

[292] The performance of *Persians* has been masterfully reconstructed along similar lines in
Herington 1985:151–160; cf. Hall 2006:275–280; West 1992:363.

[293] τ‹ῷ› τε νικῆ[σ]αι παύσασθ[αι] καταφ[ρ]ο[νού]μενον [αὐτίκα τὸ]ν Τ‹ι›[μόθεον], Satyrus
Life of Euripides (P.Oxy 1176 fr. 39 XXII, with supplements of Wilamowitz = T 4.24 Kovacs).

theaters in his power." Neither Satyrus nor Plutarch is a reliable biographer.[294] We may well be skeptical of the historicity of a personal and collaborative relationship between the tragedian and the citharode, which could derive specifically from their depiction in Old Comedy as fellow travelers in the Athenian New Music or could be some more broadly literalizing reflex of the (real) mutual influence between the two poets, which is apparent in their texts.[295] Stories of collaboration may have derived too from the fact that the poets were known to have been contemporaneous (or nearly so) "artists in residence" at the Macedonian court of Archelaus.[296] Timotheus was said by some to have composed the epigram on Euripides' cenotaph in Athens, which records the tragedian's death in Macedon (Thucydides *vel* Timotheus FGE 1 = *Life of Euripides* 14), where Timotheus was also said to have ended his life (Stephanus of Byzantium s.v. Τιμόθεος).

We may be less skeptical, however, about the veracity of the backstory to the collaboration, Timotheus' difficulty securing popular success. The anecdotal tradition no doubt exaggerates the suicide-inducing intensity of his failure, as well as the "overnight" success he achieved with *Persians*. Timotheus had clearly enjoyed some measure of success before the positive reception of that *nomos*. PMG 802 attests to a victory over Phrynis, which likely took place relatively early in Timotheus' career, perhaps in Athens. Phrynis, who was himself a controversial citharode, won the Panathenaic *agôn* in 446 BCE, relatively early in his own career. But the *nomos*, as we have seen, was a conservative form and *kitharôidia* a highly traditional *tekhnê*. Not only might the culturally retrograde Spartans, whom Timotheus singles out as his most vociferous critics in the *sphragis* of *Persians*, and their elitist ilk in Athens have opposed Timotheus, but the broader Athenian audience may have felt alienated from his experimentations as well. We may note that, although Satyrus says that Timotheus was unpopular "with

---

[294] On Satyrus as biographer, see now Schorn 2004.

[295] Cf. Schorn 2004:344–345 for the latter possibility. Maas 1938:1336 is inclined to accept the collaboration with Euripides, arguing that "das συμποιεῖν ist in jener Zeit nicht selten." He compares Aristophanes *Frogs* 944, where Aristophanes has Euripides acknowledge his collaboration in the writing of his monodies with a man named Cephisophon; cf. *Frogs* 1408, 1452–1453; 596 K-A, where Cephisophon's help in writing music (*melôidia*) is emphasized. See further references and discussion in Sommerstein 2003/2004. But that collaboration may have had more basis in the comic imagination than in reality; Cephisophon was said to have been Euripides' slave and the seducer of his wife. At *Women at the Thesmophoria* 157–158, dramatic collaboration (on a satyr play) is figured as a sex act. Cf. Hordern 2002:16.

[296] Cf. Hordern 2002:5. Scullion 2003 argues that Euripides' Macedonian sojourn was a posthumous biographical fiction.

the Greeks" (παρὰ τ[οῖ]ς Ἑλλη[σι]ν), the tradition clearly concerns foremost his Athenian reception, as the involvement of Euripides (historical or not) indicates.[297] Furthermore, there is no mention of the Spartans, as we might expect if the tradition were simply extrapolating from Timotheus' description of his struggles in *Persians*, nor is there any sense that it is specifically the Athenian elite or the comic poets who attack Timotheus. Rather, the hostile laughter and hissing that the anecdotes report strongly suggest the displeasure of mainstream Athenian audiences; in fact, Timotheus' *kitharôidia* is imagined to have a distinctly elitist appeal—only Euripides, whose own disregard of popular acclaim was legendary (and surely exaggerated), can understand its value.[298]

The screeds of culturally reactionary and anti-democratic elites of the fourth century BCE tend to create the impression that the radical innovations of the New Music composers of the fifth century, citharodes, tragedians, and dithyrambists alike, were met with unanimous acclaim by the "theatrocratic" *dêmos*. Plato imagines that the dissolution of the boundaries between Classical song genres was spurred on by the frenzy for novelty among the Athenian democratic masses (*Laws* 700a–701b); the source behind "Plutarch" *On Music* 12.1135d, probably Aristoxenus, directly equates Timotheus' "love of novelty" (he is *philokainos*) with "what is nowadays called the popular and money-making style" (τὸν φιλάνθρωπον καὶ θεματικὸν νῦν ὀνομαζόμενον τρόπον). While there is some validity to these claims, they nevertheless gloss over the nuanced complexity of popular reception, as does Old Comedy with its cartoonish polarities of old and new (even if the extremist visions of comedy to some extent did reflect and inevitably inform popular perceptions of musicians). To win demotic favor at the Panathenaia, and the prestigious and highly lucrative victory prizes that went with it, Timotheus and Phrynis before him had to create consensus among as broad a swath of the audience as possible. This likely meant that they had to negotiate a delicate balance between innovation and tradition, on the one hand borrowing from the Dionysian musical and poetic forms that were so well established in the democratic city, on the other

---

[297] A point made by Schorn 2004:345n853.

[298] For Euripides' controversial reception, see Stevens 1956; Roselli 2005. From the perspective of fourth-century conservative elites, the fifth-century New Music was an entirely populist phenomenon. But there are indications that in reality certain fifth-century elites were the earliest appreciators of modern musical techniques; cf. the praise of the eleven-stringed lyre in the sympotic elegy of Ion of Chios (fr. 32 West, with discussion in Power 2007).

maintaining the traditional decorum associated with Apollonian *kithar-ôidia* and the Terpandrean *nomoi*, which some citharodes were still performing successfully at the Panathenaia through at least the 420s BCE.[299] If this balance was skewed too far toward *kainotomia*, charges of *paranomia*, citharodic "illegitimacy," could ensue, jeopardizing chances of agonistic success. In a revealing passage of "Plutarch" *On Music* that was discussed in the previous section, we read that Timotheus "sang his first *nomoi*, at least, in *epê*, while mixing in dithyrambic diction, so that he would not appear to be directly transgressing against the laws of classical music" (ὅπως μὴ εὐθὺς φανῇ παρανομῶν εἰς τὴν ἀρχαίαν μουσικήν, 4.1132e). This sociological interpretation of the formal character of the early Timothean *nomoi*, which is probably derived from Heraclides of Pontus (or some other Peripatetic music historian), presupposes the same sensitive fifth-century reception conditions for *kitharôidia* that inform the anecdotes of Satyrus and Plutarch. Timotheus was initially, at least, careful to avoid the impression of *paranomia*. Accordingly, he played by the generic rules of the Terpandrean style, maintaining the cultural legitimacy and familiarity of his *nomoi* while at the same time introducing change into this legitimate, familiar context.[300]

As Timotheus' career progressed into the later fifth century, however, he may have become less adept at maintaining this balance; his *kainotomia* increasingly sounded to audiences like *paranomia*. Contests were probably lost. *Persians*, however, may represent an attempt to redress this imbalance and to win back a mass audience. Again, we need not imagine that anything like the dramatic reversal of fortune described in the anecdotes attended the performance and reception of the *nomos*. But Satyrus' testimony, that with *Persians* Timotheus was victorious, seems perfectly reasonable. And it is difficult not to connect the triumphant reception of the work to its emphatic traditionalism, which is apparent in the choice of narrative subject, Salamis, as well as the startlingly conservative positions taken by the citharode himself in the concluding section of the work, the *sphragis*. With *Persians*, Timotheus was clearly

---

[299] Cf. Power 2011 (forthcoming) on the lower tolerance for innovation in the *nomos* versus dithyramb and drama. It is notable that in the litany of the New Music transgressors against *Mousikê* in Pherecrates fr. 155 K-A, Phrynis and Timotheus (qua citharode) top the list, trumping the dithyrambists Melanippides and Cinesis with their outrages.

[300] Proclus *Chrestomathia ap.* Photius *Bibliotheca* 320b8-10 preserves testimony that suggests Phrynis similarly attempted to avoid excessive *kainotomia*, perhaps more carefully at an earlier point in his career, when he won at the Panathenaia. We should recall that Timotheus may have produced "adaptations" of Terpandrean *nomoi*. See Part III.5.

intent on crafting a rhetoric of legitimation for the new *nomos*. The work is an ideologically unassailable vehicle for the expression of citharodic *kainotomia*, perfectly designed to neutralize any perception of *paranomia*. In it we see the self-conscious making of a classic.

ii. Salamis in Athens, without Athens

The victory referred to by Satyrus, as the Athenian setting of the anecdote suggests, is very likely to have been at the Panathenaia. The majority of recent scholarly treatments of *Persians* have accepted or only slightly modified arguments made by Samuel Bassett to the effect that the *nomos* was first performed in Athens between 412/11 and 408/7 BCE.[301] 412/11 was the year that Sparta entered into a treaty with Persia against Athens (Thucydides 8.18; cf. 8.37, 8.58). A fragmentary line from the *nomos*, Ἄρης τύραννος· χρυσὸν Ἑλλὰς οὐ δέδοικε 'Ares is a tyrant; Greece does not fear gold' (PMG 790), may allude to the treaty, which stipulated Persia's contribution of gold to the Spartan war effort. Zenobius 2.47, who quotes the line, claims that it became proverbial thanks to the success (εὐημερία) of *Persians* in Athens. The song's Salamis theme and its description of Timotheus' unfair victimization by the aggressive Spartans (206–212) suggest that it was composed in response to the events of 412. Further, in that year a number of Ionian cities, including Miletus, defected to the side of the Spartans; Timotheus appears to allude to these troubles in lines 235–236 of the *sphragis*. We will return to them below. The *terminus ante quem* of 408/7 is perhaps less sound. Bassett and others settle on 408/7 because it was supposedly in that year that Euripides left Athens for the Macedonian court of Archelaus. But we have seen that there is little reason to insist on the veracity of Satyrus' claim that Euripides composed the *prooimion* of *Persians*. However, the linguistic and conceptual similarities between *Persians* and the song of the Phrygian eunuch in *Orestes*, produced in 408 BC, are so suggestive that 408/7 may serve in any case as an approximate *terminus ante*. The Great Panathenaia of 410/9 BCE falls within this window, and Bassett's tentative proposal that Timotheus success-

---

[301] Basset 1931; cf. Hansen 1984 (which includes a review of earlier conjectures); Janssen 1984 (who opts for the lower end of the 412–408 window); Herington 1985:151–152; van Minnen 1997; Phillips 2003:211–213; Wilson 2004:305–306. Hordern 2002:15–17 is critical of the arguments for an Athenian first performance, but offers no conjectures of his own.

fully presented the work at the festival in that year remains a most compelling scenario.[302]

In the study of *Persians* that accompanied his *editio princeps*, Wilamowitz argued that the *nomos* could not have been performed in Athens because the text as preserved on the papyrus found at Abusir makes no mention of Athens. It is a "Salamis without Athens." That is, the fragment of the *nomos* as we have it describes a sea battle that is certainly meant to be Salamis, yet contains no explicit references to Athens or to the Athenians who played crucial roles in the victory. Indeed, the battle itself is not even identified as Salamis.[303] Wilamowitz believed that by "ignoring" Athens Timotheus was in fact insulting the city. By this logic, Athens is to be entirely ruled out as the site of the premiere, and, we might add, as the site of any subsequent reperformance of the piece. Wilamowitz concluded that *Persians* was premiered in the Spartan-dominated Greek East in the early fourth century.[304] Several scholars have arrived at similar conclusions based upon similar reasoning.[305]

---

[302] Bassett 1931:163n1; Herington 1985:151–152 and Phillips 2003:212–213 are more confident in assigning the premier to the Panathenaia of 410/9. Hansen 1984 dates the Athenian premier to 410/9, but thinks *Persians* was performed at the festival of Artemis Munichia, which involved the annual commemoration of the battle of Salamis. The idea is appealing, but there is no evidence for *mousikoi agônes* at this festival, which had considerably lower wattage than the Panathenaia. The Panathenaia had its own historical Salamis connections. Bowra 1961:344 has suggested that Simonides' choral melic *Sea-battle of Salamis* (PMG 536) was sung as a *prosodion* in the Panathenaic procession, accompanying the ship-cart whose "sail" was the peplos of Athena. Cf. Rutherford 1990:200–201, who speculates that the *Sea-battle* (and/or its companion, piece, the *Sea-battle at Artemision*) was a paean; cf. Rutherford 1996:169–173. (Heliodorus *Aethiopica* 1.10.1 says that a paean for Athena was sung by ephebes during the procession of the ship-cart at the Great Panathenaia.) The date of the introduction of the ship-cart is uncertain. One scholar has recently offered convincing arguments for a date "shortly after the Persian Wars," which would suit the chronology of the Simonides poem. She argues for the use of "one of the boats from the battle of Salamis to celebrate and recall the saving of the city," a symbolic gesture that would be in line with the overall focus of the festival on the "common theme of salvation" (Barber 1992:114, 209n27; cf. Mansfield 1985:54, 68, 101). The emphasis on political salvation in the epilogue of *Persians* (237–240) is notable in this respect.

[303] Wilamowitz 1903: "Kein Themistocles, kein Aristeides, weder Salamis noch Psyttaleia genannt, überhaupt kein Eigenname" (61).

[304] Wilamowitz 1903:63 proposed a specific occasion, the Panionion at Mycale in 398–396 BCE. However, in a follow-up to his study of *Persians* published three years later (1906:49–50) Wilamowitz changed his mind about the location, deciding now in favor of Miletus, on the grounds that there is no evidence for *mousikoi agônes* at the Panionion; cf. Janssen 1984:13.

[305] Aron 1920:37, 40 and Ebeling 1925:318 argue for a performance at the Ephesia festival in Ephesus between 399 and 396 BCE. Rosenbloom 2006:149 has recently advocated this line as well: "The song's first performance fits better between 396 and 394 [at

Proponents of an Athenian *Persians* have already offered sufficient rebuttal to the arguments of Wilamowitz.[306] But two interrelated points in defense of an Athenian premiere for the *nomos* bear emphasis. First, to argue that Timotheus would be willing to ignore or insult Athens is to misunderstand the professional and economic pragmatics of the agonistic *kitharôidia* practiced by the likes of Timotheus. As Nashville has been to contemporary American country music or Broadway to the musical, so was the later-fifth- and fourth-century Panathenaia to agonistic *mousikê* in Greece. The Athenian scene was where stars were made and musical reputations confirmed and contested, where styles of performance and composition were elaborated and exchanged—witness the vitalizing interplay between *kitharôidia*, dithyramb, and tragedy—and where fortunes were to be made. For a citharode of Timotheus' stature and ambition to ignore, much less slight Athens in the late fifth or early fourth centuries would be utterly illogical, an act tantamount to artistic and commercial suicide.[307] Satyrus' claim that Timotheus was in fact contemplating suicide in response to his failure in Athens is overdramatic, but nonetheless apposite.

This brings us to the second point. If success in Athens would have been so crucial to Timotheus, whose previous reception there had apparently been fraught with difficulty, why then do we have in *Persians* a "Salamis without Athens?" Salamis was no doubt a subject matter supremely amenable to an Athenian audience. But why then does the *nomos* lack any specific reference to Athenian participation? Why does even Salamis go unnamed? It has been argued that had we more of the *nomos* (in its present condition we have less than half of the work), then explicit Athenian references would be more evident.[308] Yet the utter lack of such references in the major sections of the *nomos* that we do have, the long description of the naval rout and its aftermath, as well as the whole of the *sphragis*, understandably raised the suspicions of Wilamowitz. We might look, then, to alternative explanations for "Salamis without Athens." One is aesthetic. Timotheus may have

---

Ephesus] when the Spartan king Agesilaus led an invasion of the Persian empire." Gambetti 2001:63 proposes a first performance in Miletus in 404–403 BCE "davanti un pubblico spartano o filo-spartano."

[306] See especially Janssen 1984:13–22.

[307] Cf. the remarks of Wilamowitz 1903:39 on the continuing Athenian cultural hegemony in the fourth century. In the *Harmonides* of Lucian a dialogue is imagined between the fourth-century BCE Theban aulete Timotheus and his ambitious student Harmonides, in which the status of Athens as the musical "big time" is taken for granted. Cf. Wilson 2000:336n82.

[308] Basset 1931:153–154; Janssen 1984:15.

been trying to lend Salamis a historically transcendent, mythic quality. Another explanation, not necessarily exclusive from the aesthetic, is one that takes into account the "double bind" effect that must have been an important aspect of itinerant citharodic practice in the later fifth century, that is, the two competing market demands put upon the production of the citharodic *nomos*: on the one hand, the special interests of the important Athenian market, which would have been especially acute for Timotheus, a maverick who was struggling to establish a secure place in it; on the other, the inevitable reality that the *nomos* could not be too obviously an Athenocentric production, but had to be a mobile, supra-national commodity, a traveling, reperformable entertainment whose content would appeal to, or at least not alienate, audiences at a wide circuit of Panhellenic and regional *agônes* beyond the Panathenaia. We may thus expect that a certain degree of Athenian "localization" had to be balanced with the pragmatics of Panhellenic diffusion in order to ensure maximum economic and professional success for the *nomos* and its performer.[309]

A "Salamis without Athens" is a savvy textual strategy for negotiating this "double bind" inherent in the marketing of the citharodic *nomos*. It is a celebration of a classic Panhellenic moment in which the preeminent position of Athens is left implicit or unmarked.[310] As such, *Persians* is a work that is "automatically" localized when performed in Athens—we will examine some of these local effects below—but it is also one whose value would not suffer when taken on the road and performed elsewhere, at other times, in the Greek world, conceivably even in cities that were inimical to Athens and friendly to Sparta. The generic character of Timotheus' Salamis narrative allows nearly all Greeks, not only the Athenians, to identify with the timeless, politically transcendent, near-mythic victory over the Persians. The fact that the text of *Persians* has invited such radically divergent views concerning its performance history is a testament to the sophistication of its

---

[309] Cf. Hordern 2002:129. On similar attempts to maintain a balance between Athenian "localization" and interpolitical appeal in the genre of tragedy, see Taplin 1999.

[310] On the potential of Salamis to express at once both Panhellenic and Athenian pride, see Hall 1996:1–12, with specific reference to Aeschylus' *Persians*, which is also notably reticent to name (Greek) names. Goldhill 1988:192 sees this reticence as reflective of democratic ideology: "[T]he subsumption of the individual into the collectivity of the *polis* is a basic factor in fifth-century Athenian democratic ideology. This may provide an interesting light in which to view the anonymity of the Greek soldiers in [Aeschylus'] *Persae*. It is as if they are being portrayed as a unified, collective body (which can be contrasted with the lists of Persian contingents, Persian dead, and Persian kings)." Perhaps a similarly democratic subtext lies beneath the anonymous collectivity of Timotheus' Greeks.

discursive ambiguities. Timotheus' characterization of his Spartan critics in the *sphragis* is emblematic of the extent of the strategic diglossia of the text. To one audience (or scholar), the lines "Sparta's great leader, well-born and age-old, a people teeming with the flowers of youthful manhood" (206–208), might sound like an honorific compliment. (One could even imagine Timotheus singing them with a straight face at the Carneia.) Other audiences (or scholars) might hear coded in the lines a caricature of Sparta's aggressive, overweening aristocracy.[311]

Let us consider Timotheus' choice of Salamis to be the theme of his self-legitimating *nomos* in light of its likely first performance in Athens in 410 BCE. The valorization of Salamis as a touchstone of Athenian patriotism and imperial pride by the broad spectrum of the Athenian *dêmos* cannot be underestimated, and we may assume that the collective memory of the battle took on added emotional and ideological resonance immediately following Persia's entry into the Peloponnesian War in 412. In addition, in the aftermath of the failed Sicilian Expedition and during the dispirit that followed, Timotheus' recollection of the glory of Salamis would have served as a highly effective utopian entertainment, nostalgic and escapist, but also inspiring and hopeful.[312] However, after the victory of the Athenian fleet at Cyzicus in the spring of 410 over combined Peloponnesian and Persian forces, which was followed shortly by the collapse of the oligarchic government in Athens, it would have been heard too as an epinician celebration of Athenian naval success: Salamis would stand as a kind of heroic exemplar for current victories, echoing them on a grand mythic-historic scale. We may imagine that *Persians*, in its timely response to current events and moods, was received by the Athenians in the same enthusiastic spirit in which Plutarch tells us the audience at the Nemean Games met its third-century BCE reperformance by the citharode Pylades of Megalopolis: "The Greeks broke into joyful applause, since in their hopes they were recovering their ancient prestige (*to palaion axiôma*) and in their confidence coming close to the spirit of those earlier days."[313] We will return to the historical context of this reperformance below.

To be sure, there were some Athenian elites, especially those with strong oligarchic sympathies, who felt an ideological, even aesthetic distaste for the democratic cast of this naval victory. Some scholars

---

[311] Cf. n347 below. Compliment: Wilamowitz 1903:61.

[312] Cf. Phillips 2003:212–213 on the morale-building effect of *Persians* in this context of geopolitical anxiety.

[313] Plutarch *Philopoemen* 11; trans. Campbell 1993a:92. Cf. Pausanias 8.50.3.

have argued that an ideological rift existed in the fifth and fourth centuries between the "mass" naval victory at Salamis and the "elite" hoplitic victories at Marathon and Plataea.[314] For the staunchly anti-democratic Athenian Stranger of Plato's *Laws* and his Spartan inter-locutor Megillus, Marathon and Plataea, not Salamis—as the *polloi* 'masses' have it—brought salvation (*sôtêria*) to the Greeks; the former battles made the Greeks better (*beltious*, an aristocratic descriptor), the latter worse (707b–c; cf. 707a–b). It has been argued that the *Persians* of Aeschylus stands on the other side of the ideological divide, revealing a markedly democratic bias in its neglect of Marathon and the relatively short shrift it gives to Plataea. But there is a risk of placing too much weight on Plato's tendentious extremism or Aeschylus' omissions. Christopher Pelling reviews the sources for a conflict between Salamis and Marathon/Plataea and sees little compelling evidence for all-or-nothing ideological "battle of the battles" in the fifth century.[315]

We should accordingly be wary of taking Timotheus' celebration of Salamis as an outright gesture of anti-elitism, as opposed to a straight-forward attempt to consolidate large-scale, pandemic support among the "average" Athenians who formed the bulk of the Panathenaic audi-ence. While we should not be surprised that Aristophanes' aristocratic Better Argument draws a direct line between old-time *paideia* in lyric *mousikê* and the "elite" Athenian victory at Marathon (*Clouds* 985–986), it is probably too much to assume an anti-elite cultural/political agenda behind the linking of the New Music and the victory at Salamis in *Persians*.[316] This linkage would not necessarily by default alienate the majority of elite audience members. Indeed, it is possible that specific elite/hoplitic interests were addressed in *Persians*. It has been observed that the battle of Salamis was split into "two simultaneous episodes—the well-known naval battle and the hoplitic battle at Psyttaleia."[317] The land battle on Psyttaleia is described in Herodotus 8.95, where the noble Athenian Aristides, who, significantly, had been ostracized from

---

[314] Podlecki 1966:8–26; cf. Loraux 1986:161–163; Euben 1986, 1997:66, 89–90.

[315] Pelling 1997:9–12, who concludes, "We can believe that from the outset both Marathon and Salamis became Panathenian themes, themes which all Athenians would thrill to, not the stuff of partisan ideology" (12).

[316] Cf. n353 below. It is fair to note, however, that one later-fifth-century oligarchic elite, "Xenophon" (the Old Oligarch), who criticizes the bullying political hegemony of the oarsmen in democratic Athens (*Constitution of the Athenians* 1.2), claims that the *dêmos* has done away with elites who practice traditional *mousikê*, which it ironically does not consider *kalon* 'noble', while it "sings ... and dances and mans the fleet" (1.13). See Wilson 1997:93–94 on this passage.

[317] Loraux 1986:161.

Athens and was an enemy of Themistocles (8.85), has his *aristeia* with a handpicked troop of hoplites. Aeschylus *Persians* 447–465 describes the battle as well, although in a perhaps less aggrandizing light.[318] Psyttaleia is probably meant to be the scene of Timotheus *Persians* 140–161, which is clearly set on land: a "steel-bladed Greek" (σιδαρόκωπος Ἕλλαν, 143) carries off a Phrygian by the hair. The Greek is presumably a hoplite rather than a sailor. The avoidance of place and (Greek) personal names in the scene is, as we have seen, characteristic of the Panhellenizing tenor of the *omphalos* as a whole. But could it in this case also reflect a disinclination to align the *nomos* with one specific, politicized intra-Athenian version of Salamis?

It is significant, however, that Sparta had a conspicuously small share in the Panhellenic and Panathenaic glory of Salamis.[319] Indeed, according to Herodotus, Sparta's participation in the battle was a matter of great contention; the Lacedaemonian fleet under Eurybiades would have pulled out in the eleventh hour if not for the active intervention of Themistocles (8.42–63). Herodotus singles out not one Spartan for distinguished service in the battle. The contemporary reality of the post-412 Sparta-Persia alliance would only have deepened the perception of Sparta's estrangement from the legacy of Salamis, which Timotheus must have implicitly exploited to win Athenian favor. It is perhaps no coincidence that over 200 years later Pylades chose to reperform *Persians* on the occasion he did, and that it was such a spectacular hit with the Panhellenic audience at the Nemean festival. For Philopoemen, the general of the Achaean League, was in attendance at the theater of Nemea, having just defeated the Spartans at Mantinea (207 BCE).[320] That is, the ability of *Persians* to galvanize Panhellenic sentiment at the expense not only of Persia but of Sparta may have been an effect traditional to the reception of the *nomos*, going back to its first Athenian performance. Timotheus' self-dramatizing defiance of Spartan cultural persecution, scripted into the text of *Persians*, would clearly have enriched the effect. As a native of Megalopolis, the perennial enemy of Sparta, Pylades must have been an especially suitable

---

[318] Thus the argument of Loraux 1986:161–162. Cf. the counter-arguments of van Wees 1997:172n16, who sees in the scene an expression of Aeschylus' pro-hoplitic sympathies.

[319] So of course did Miletus and the cities of Ionia, which fought on the losing side at Salamis (Herodotus 7.94). The lack of definite historical referents in the *Persians* serves, however, to obscure that memory.

[320] Though Plutarch *Philopoemen* 11 sets it up as a happy coincidence: Philopoemen and his troops "had just entered the theater, when by chance (*kata tukhên*) Pylades the citharode was singing the *Persians* of Timotheus."

reperformer of *Persians* and a still more sympathetic reenactor of Timotheus himself. Megalopolis was burned down by Spartan forces under Cleomenes in 223 BCE; it would be restored by Philopoemen (Pausanias 8.27.16). How evocative then would be Pylades' performance 16 years later of the lines from the *sphragis*, "The [Spartan] populace buffets me, flaming, and drives at me with fiery blame" (209–210)? Timotheus' original resistance to Sparta's musical oppression thus took on new extramusical resonance in the Peloponnesian politics of the Hellenistic period.

Beyond its broad patriotic appeal, however, it was surely the consecrated status of Salamis in the collective political and cultural identity of Athens that attracted Timotheus. The consecrated ideological space occupied by Salamis was significantly occupied too by Aeschylus, whose *Persians* was "the most important contribution to the aesthetic and ethical shaping of the story" of the victory.[321] The absolute classic of Attic tragedy thus became the de facto model for Timotheus' theatrical *kitharôidia*. His conspicuous emulation of Aeschylus perhaps had the intentional effect of diverting attention away from his more controversial affinities with the likes of Euripides and Agathon.[322] By contributing to the reproduction and elaboration of the great tradition of the victory, whose prime exponent was no less than Aeschylus, the music of *Persians* could become part of it and benefit from its hallowed aura. Salamis offered the Athenian audience a traditional and highly sympathetic political and cultural frame of reference through which to engage the novel experience of Timotheus' music. In dramatizing the

---

[321] Hall 1996:1. An earlier, influential tragic treatment of Salamis was Phrynichus' *Phoenician Women*. The music from this play endured as representative "classical music" into the later fifth century, beloved by the older generation. The chorus of "good old boys" in Aristophanes *Wasps* 219–221 calls Philocleon out of his house by singing the "old-fashioned honeyed Sidon songs of Phrynichus"; cf. *Frogs* 1299–1300.

[322] It may be significant that Aeschylus was known for borrowing from the old-time citharodic *nomoi* of his time when he composed his choral odes (Aristophanes *Frogs* 1281–1300), making him an especially appropriate model for a citharode in need of traditional credibility. On the verbal and narrative echoes of the tragic *Persians* in the *nomos*, see Croiset 1904:330–335, Reinach 1903:78n2; Brussich 1970:69–71, 78–79; Janssen 1984, index s.v. Aeschylus *Pers.*; Hordern 2002:122; Hall 2006:275–280; Rosenbloom 2006:153–154. There were revivals of Aeschylean dramas, including *Persians*, in the later fifth century (Hall 1996:2; Biles 2006/2007). We may note the apparent irony in the fact that Timotheus' own "revival" of Aeschylus likely anticipated by five years the tragedian's more fantastically imagined revival (from the dead) in the *Frogs* of Aristophanes, that great critic of the New Music. But for both poets, Aeschylus represents an effective figure of rhetoric, a means of mobilizing the nostalgia for an idealized past to authorize their respective cultural (and, more so for Aristophanes, political) positions.

battle with his *kitharôidia*, Timotheus could justify and indulge any and all experimentation and innovation; the broadest possible Athenian audience could enjoy them too, without reservation. Indeed, what is effected is a kind of manufacture of consent: Salamis not only invites but demands the legitimation and consecration of Timotheus' controversial style of *nomos*. The latter is positioned as a "politically correct" cultural expression through its identification with the former.[323] Who could object?

This identification is made in the first line of the *nomos* (PMG 788): κλεινὸν ἐλευθερίας τεύχων μέγαν Ἑλλάδι κόσμον 'Fashioning a famous and great adornment of freedom for Greece'. Both Plutarch and Pausanias (8.50.3) quote this line in their respective accounts of the performance of *Persians* by Pylades. It has often been thought to come from the *prooimion*, but the *arkha*, the opening section of the *nomos* proper, is a more appealing possibility.[324] The use of the verbs ἐνάρξασθαι by Plutarch and κατάρξασθαι by Pausanias to describe its performance might suggest the *arkha* rather than the *prooimion*, which was very likely a detached composition transmitted separately from the *nomos* itself. (The tradition ascribing the composition of the *prooimion* to Euripides may in fact reflect its semi-autonomous status.) The line is a hexameter, which could point to a *prooimion*. Yet, by beginning his *nomos* proper with a "traditional" lyric hexameter section before the build-up of rhythmic, melodic, and verbal *poikilia* in the *omphalos*, Timotheus may have wanted to avoid the immediate appearance

---

[323] Bassett 1931:159 gestures toward this interpretation. Cf. Euben 1997:64–90 on how Salamis "became bounded, memorialized, and culturally inscribed, thereby organizing and *legitimating* certain forms of Athenian thought and action" (p66). The historical epic *Persika* by the innovative rhapsode-poet Choerilus of Samos offers some interesting parallels to *Persians*. The two works were probably composed and performed in Athens at roughly the same time (cf. Huxley 1969:12–13). The *Persika* was a more expansive work than *Persians*, but the poem is cited in *Suda* s.v. Χοιρίλος as *The Victory of the Athenians over Xerxes*, which suggests that the battle of Salamis was the focus of the work or at least a central episode. The *Suda* attests to the enormous success of the epic in Athens: "Choerilus received a golden stater per line of the poem and it was decreed that it be publicly recited along with the works of Homer." If (at least partly) true, the testimony indicates that *Persika*, or rather an Athenocentric excerpt (probably devoted to Salamis), was so popular that it surmounted the long-established Panathenaic Rule of the Panathenaia, whereby only the *Iliad* and *Odyssey* were performed (cf. Kotsidu 1991:41). This speaks to the compelling power of the Salamis theme to legitimize (and reward monetarily) new works at the Panathenaic *agônes*, something Timotheus clearly also recognized.

[324] Cf. Hansen 1990:192; Korzeniewski 1974:38. On the secondary proemial function of the *arkha*, see Part II.15.

of *paranomia* (cf. "Plutarch" *On Music* 4.1132e, on Timotheus' shrewd combination of *epê* and dithyrambic lexis).[325]

Because the line is cited in isolation, it is impossible to determine with certainty the subject of the participle τεύχων 'fashioning'. We may note, however, the verbal and thematic echoes between PMG 788 and two earlier lyric poems memorializing episodes from the Persian Wars. First, in lines 8–9 of Simonides' encomium of the Spartan warriors at Thermopylae (PMG 531), King Leonidas is said to have "left behind a great *kosmos* of excellence (*areta*) and eternal fame (*kleos*)" (ἀρετᾶς μέγαν λελοιπὼς | κόσμον ἀέναόν τε κλέος). Second, Pindar's dithyramb composed for Athens mentions the naval victory at Artemision in 480 BCE, "where the sons of the Athenians laid a brilliant foundation of freedom" (ὅθι παῖδες Ἀθαναίων ἐβάλοντο φαεννὰν | κρηπῖδ' ἐλευθερίας).[326] Both of these passages may be deliberate intertexts of PMG 788. By alluding to them, Timotheus would be setting a classic tone at the very beginning of the *nomos*, making claim to the consecrated poetic capital of Simonides and Pindar and suggesting that his song is to be ranked alongside the immortal songs of these masters of musico-poetic commemoration. By analogy to these passages, we may be tempted to supply a Greek actor in the battle of Salamis as the subject for PMG 788. Bassett, who sees a distinct allusion to the Pindaric dithyramb, would supply "some Athenian" (such as Themistocles) or, less specifically, "the Athenian force."[327] Such explicit Athenian localization would, however, be out of keeping with the demands of Panhellenic diffusion put upon the citharodic *nomos*. If Timotheus' hexameter does refer to Pindar's dithyramb, it more likely involves a latent allusion whose implications would be understood by an Athenian audience.

It would thus be more appropriate to supply a subject along the lines of "the Greek force that repulsed the barbarians."[328] Yet there is another possibility: the citharode himself.[329] PMG 788 would thus

[325] Cf. Herington 1985:154 on the traditionalizing rhetoric of the hexameter.

[326] Fr. 77 S-M *ap.* Plutarch *On the Fame of the Athenians* 7.350a. The dithyramb was sufficiently well known in later fifth-century Athens to be parodied in Aristophanes *Knights* 1239 (according to scholia *ad Acharnians* 637). See Zimmermann 1992:53–54. Athens is called the Ἑλλάδος ἔρεισμα 'bulwark of Greece' in the opening lines of the dithyramb (fr. 76 S-M); the phrase may be faintly echoed by Ἑλλάδι κόσμον in PMG 788. Cf. Hordern 2002:121–122.

[327] Bassett 1931:155; cf. Hordern 2002:128, who proposes "the Athenian *dêmos*" and reviews other suggestions.

[328] Reinach 1903:67 suggests either the battle itself or Ares as subject. Cf. Bassett 1931:155n1.

[329] A reading proposed in Rosenbloom 2006:148; already developed in Power 2001: 122–124.

constitute a reference in the *nomos* to the composition/performance of the *nomos* itself. The verb τεύχειν is used elsewhere as a metaphor for songmaking. For a relevant application of the verb to making music on the *kithara*, we might consider Pindar *Pythian* 1.4, in which the chorus apostrophizes the *phorminx* of Apollo, saying, "You fashion (τεύχῃς) the beginnings of chorus-leading *prooimia*."[330] Significantly, in *Persians* itself Timotheus refers to his Apolline archetype as χρυσεοκίθαριν ἀέξων Μοῦσαν νεοτευχῆ ("you who foster a new-fashioned Muse [*neoteukhês Mousa*, i.e. 'new-fashioned music'] of the golden *kitharis*," 202–203). Further, κόσμος can refer to "the beautiful 'arrangement' or adorned 'composition' of a song."[331] Aristophanes *Frogs* 1027 offers an example of this sense of κόσμος that is directly relevant to *Persians*. Aeschylus boasts that with his *Persians* he "adorned through music and poetry a most excellent achievement" (κοσμήσας ἔργον ἄριστον).[332] Timotheus' *Persians* is similarly a κόσμος, a musico-poetic arrangement/adornment, of the *eleutheria* achieved at Salamis. The semantics of the term as used in reference to music are important to note: music is a κόσμος in its orderliness and ordering, its expression of absolute, objectively valid aesthetic values.[333] By employing the term as a programmatic description, Timotheus would be making just such essentialist claims for his new *nomos*—the same ones Aristophanes will assume for the canonical art of Aeschylus a few years later. The musical "freedom" exhibited by the new *nomoi* of Timotheus is by implication anything but chaotic; rather, it is, like the Athenian-led establishment of *eleutheria* at Salamis it celebrates, a perfectly formed imposition of proper order on the world.[334]

---

[330] Cf. the description of Pindar's own songmaking as *teukhein* at *Isthmian* 1.14. On Pindaric metaphors of "songcraft," see Ford 2002:113–130.

[331] Nagy 1990b:145n45, citing Pindar fr. 194 S-M and *Odyssey* 8.489. Cf. Walsh 1984:8–13; Stehle 2001:111; Ford 2002 *passim*. Epinician song regularly refers to itself as a *kosmos* and its effects as *kosmein*, e.g. Bacchylides 3.95, 12.7; Pindar *Nemean* 6.46.

[332] Cf. Walsh 1984:95.

[333] *Kosmos* may analogously describe political constitutions (e.g. Herodotus 1.65.4) as well as the transcendent ordering of the universe (e.g. Xenophon *Memorabilia* 1.1.11): Nagy 1990b:145; cf. Ford 2002:36–37. Nagy suggests that the expression τειχίζωμεν ... ποικίλον κόσμον 'let us construct an intricate *kosmos*' in fr. 194.2–3 S-M figures the act of choral songmaking and performance as Amphion's construction of the walls (*teikhê*) of Thebes, an idealized conflation of musical and political *kosmos*. Could there be a latent reference to the Amphionic myth in PMG 788 as well? We will return to Timotheus' claims to a "cosmic *kitharôidia*" below.

[334] One could see in the final word of the *nomos*, *eunomia* (240), a sort of ring-composition echo of *eleutheria* in the first line. It is as if Timotheus wanted to appropriate as equivalent programmatic terms for his new music the ideologically resonant catchwords of both the fifth-century Athenian democracy (see Hordern 2002:128 on the

Indeed, κόσμος describes equally well the achievement of the Salamis victors, who are themselves "artificers" of the *eleutheria* that adorns fifth-century Greece.[335] As such, its referential ambiguity has the rhetorical effect of conflating *kosmos* as the Greeks' glorious deed of freedom and as its mediation through the musical composition of Timotheus. The ambiguity will in a sense be "resolved" in the second or third line of the *prooimion* with the articulation of the subject of τεύχων, but not before the conflation effected by the emphatic position of the first line has made its impact. The singer and the heroes he celebrates are thus fused together as authors of this Panhellenic *kosmos*. Such conflation is indeed implicit in Timotheus' (probable) Simonidean model. The "great *kosmos* of *areta*" left behind by Leonidas is his own act of valor as well as the commemoration of it by Simonides.[336] Subjective and objective poetic *kosmos* might also be identified in Simonides' *Plataea* elegy, although the reading of the relevant lines relies on major restoration and is far from certain.[337] Simonides calls upon his "auxiliary" (*epikouros*) Muse to "Fit out too this pleasing *kosmos* of my song" (ἔντυνο]ν καὶ τόνδ[ε μελίφρονα κ[όσμον ἀο]ιδῆς | ἡμετέρης, fr. 11.23–24 W²). That is, the Muse is asked to assist Simonides in recalling the praise-worthy *kosmos* of Plataea as well as in arranging and adorning it in song.[338] There is a good chance that Timotheus alludes to this same Simonidean invocation of the Muse later in the *Persians*, when he calls upon Apollo to be his *epikouros* 'auxiliary' in his struggle against the Spartans (204).[339] It is possible, then, that the opening line of the *nomos* packs a twin allusion to Simonides in his capacity as an "adorner" of the two most famous Spartan-led victories in the Persian Wars, Thermopylae and Plataea. If so, this would entail the bold appropriation of poetic and historical prestige from these Simonidean and Spartan classics of *kosmos* for Timotheus' new *kosmos* of Athenian-led Salamis.

"highly emotional associations" of *eleutheria* in Athens) and the Spartan oligarchy (on *eunomia*, see Section 11.iii below).

[335] Similarly, Pindar can refer to the victor or his victory as a *kosmos* for his *polis*, e.g. *Nemean* 2.8, where Timodemus is a κόσμον Ἀθάναις 'kosmos for Athens'.

[336] Cf. Ford 2002:111. Similarly, if more obliquely, the "brilliant foundation (*krêpis*) of freedom" laid by the Athenian sailors at Artemision also describes its choral celebration through Pindar's song (fr. 77 S-M). For *krêpis* 'foundation' as a musico-poetic and performative metaphor, see Pindar fr. 194.1 S-M, with comments in Ford 2002:125.

[337] See Perysinakis 2006 for discussion of variant supplements and readings.

[338] Cf. Stehle 2001:111; Perysinakis 2006.

[339] Cf. n349 below.

iii. Eunomian Strategies

The self-presentation of the citharode in the *sphragis* (202–236) is remarkably conservative and traditionalizing.[340] It has no trace of the all-or-nothing radicalism of Timotheus' rhetoric of innovation in PMG 796, a fragment probably from another nomic *sphragis*:

οὐκ ἀείδω τὰ παλαιά,
καινὰ γὰρ ἁμὰ κρείσσω·
νέος ὁ Ζεὺς βασιλεύει,
τὸ πάλαι δ' ἦν Κρόνος ἄρχων·
ἀπίτω Μοῦσα παλαιά.

I sing not the old songs, for my new ones (*kaina*) are better. The Zeus who is young/new (*neos*) reigns; long ago Kronos ruled. Away with the old Muse!

Timotheus PMG 796

There is no wider context supplied in the Athenaeus passage in which these lines are quoted that would allow us to date them with any certainty.[341] It is a reasonable supposition, however, that they were sung in the years before the *Persians*, when Timotheus was more extreme in vaunting his *kainotomia*, and accordingly courted charges of *paranomia*.[342] If so, the far more temperate, conciliatory rhetoric of the *sphragis* of *Persians* might be intended in the spirit of a palinode. Timotheus claims that his music transcends generational differences, and implicitly the cultural and political divisiveness associated with them: ἐγὼ δ' οὔτε νέον τιν' οὔ- | τε γεραὸν οὔτ' ἰσήβαν | εἴργω τῶνδ' ἑκὰς ὕμνων ("But I keep neither young nor old man nor my peer away from these *humnoi* of mine," 213–215).[343] The definitive polarity set up

---

[340] Cf. Herington 1985:158; Nieddu 1993; Wilson 2004:305–306; Power 2007:204–205.

[341] Athenaeus 3.122c–d. The context of the citation is itself interesting, however. Timotheus is quoted by Cynulcus, who is defending his less-than-classical use of the Greek language against the (anticipated) criticism of the classicizing lexicist Ulpian. An interesting, witty choice on Cynulcus' part: Timotheus is invoked as a classical "authority" to justify the rejection of (oppressive) classical authority! The perception of Timotheus as a "classic of anti-classicism" articulated here well reflects the paradoxical nature—consecrated iconoclasm—of his *Nachleben*.

[342] Cf. Herington 1985:152; Nieddu 1993:526–527; Wilamowitz 1903:65. Alternately, they could have been sung after the success of *Persians*, when Timotheus was more confident in the reception of his *kainotomia*. On possible Terpandrean allusions, see Part III.5.

[343] For the democratic musico-political subtext of these lines, contrasted with the negative image of the closed-off "Spartan aristocracy" that criticizes Timotheus' music, see Wilson 2004:306; Power 2007:205.

between old and new citharodic styles in PMG 796, τὰ παλαιά and τὰ καινά, is here collapsed. And while the citharode of PMG 796 figures his conflict with citharodic tradition as Zeus' primal parricidal attack on the oppressive Kronos, in *Persians* 221–231 he is instead at pains to position his new Ionian *kitharôidia* within the validating "paternal" Aeolic tradition of Pierian Orpheus and Lesbian Terpander. His *kitharis*—a rhetorically marked archaism—with its eleven strings—the potentially controversial *polukhordia* euphemized as "eleven-struck meters and rhythms"—represents the natural continuation of the lyric *tekhnê* of these worthies, who are themselves, however, cast as "new citharodes" *avant la lettre*, pioneers of *poikilia*.[344] What is new is old, and vice versa.

Although Timotheus begins the *sphragis* by associating himself (and Apollo) with the "new-fashioned Muse," he goes on to style himself a defender of the very "older Muse" dismissed in PMG 796. The Spartan *laos* 'people' (209), he claims, unfairly "drives at me with fiery blame (*mômos*) because I disrespect the older Muse with new *humnoi*" (ἐλᾷ τ' αἴθοπι μώμῳ, | παλαιοτέραν νέοις | ὕμνοις Μοῦσαν ἀτιμῶ, 210–212; cf. ἀπίτω Μοῦσα παλαιά 'Away with the old Muse!' PMG 796.5). However, it is not Timotheus, but rather his New Music rivals who deserve blame:

> τοὺς δὲ μουσοπαλαιολύ-
> μας, τούτους δ' ἀπερύκω,
> λωβητῆρας ἀοιδᾶν,
> κηρύκων λιγυμακροφώ-
> νων τείνοντας ἰυγάς.

> It is the defilers of the old Muse, those who disgrace songs, whom I fend off, those stretching out the shouts of shrill, loud-voiced heralds.

Timotheus Persians 216–220

In this passage, Timotheus savvily appropriates the same conservative critical tropes involving the moral and aesthetic degradation of music that were used against him to distinguish himself from his innovative peers.[345] Compare PMG 802, in which he dismisses Phrynis as an

---

[344] See Part III.5 on Timotheus' self-promotional re-envisioning of citharodic tradition in these lines.

[345] The comic-sounding compound μουσοπαλαιολύμαι 'defilers of the old Muse' has been taken to mean "people who spoil the Muse in an old-fashioned manner" (Janssen 1984:135; similarly, Wilamowitz 1903:27, Meyer 1923:156, Nieddu 1993:525, Hordern 2002:239). Brussich 1970:73n80 notes "una forte ambiguità di significato (μουσοπαλαιολύμης = corruttore dell'antica musa o antico corruttore della musa"). But

ἰωνοκάμπτας 'bender of Ionian melody', thereby redirecting actual or potential criticism of himself—an Ionian—toward his rival.[346]

In the *sphragis*, then, Timotheus is constructing not only his own musical identity, but those of his would-be critics as well; he is writing the script of his own reception. Like Orpheus' and Terpander's, his music is classically, and, in a broad politic sense, "democratically" all-inclusive. Conservative Athenian critics of his "new *humnoi*" are implicitly aligned with the aristocratic-oligarchic Spartans; they are anti-democratic.[347] But, just as damningly, they are by default shown to be no more respectful of the old Muse than the New Music composers they claim to despise; they are anti-classical. By contrast, Timotheus, a poet of the classical mold, knows how authoritatively to assign praise

---

Campbell's "corrupters of the old muse" is more in keeping with the rhetorical sophistication of the *sphragis* (1993a:111); cf. Wilson 2004:306n83. On the invective force of *kêrukes* 'heralds', cf. Hordern 2002:240. There is likely a "meta-agonistic" level of humor. Timotheus could be saying that his foils are no more artful than the heralds or criers who announce victories to the large crowds at *agônes* (cf. κᾶρυξ, PMG 802.1). The inference would be that his opponents should not be competing at citharodic *agônes*, but rather performing the less elevated, unmusical duty of the herald. Heralds themselves did have their own contests, as Hordern notes (cf. Pollux *Onomasticon* 4.91; Demosthenes 19.338); these had, of course, none of the prestige of the citharodic contests.

[346] Cf. n98 and n281 above.

[347] The Spartan hostility described by Timotheus was surely real. He was no doubt *persona non grata* at the Carneia thanks to his *polukhordia* and related innovations (although the anecdotal tradition about the ephors cutting his strings more probably derives from the *Persians* itself than from any one historical event). But the Spartans of the *Persians* are above all a rhetorical construct designed to secure Athenian favor, on two levels. First, Timotheus pointedly conflates their essential aristocratic-oligarchic character and their excess hostility ("the great leader [*megas hagemôn*] of Sparta, well-born and age-old, a people teeming with the flowers of youthful manhood, buffets me, flaming, and drives at me with fiery blame," 206–210). The implication is that for an Athenian to resist Timotheus on the grounds that he dishonors music is to take a typically Spartan position. The Spartans are at war with Athens, and with Timothean *kitharôidia*; a de facto alliance is intimated between the latter. Thus Timotheus' new *humnoi* become a political issue: what is at stake in their reception is not merely the expression of individual taste but the affirmation of shared political identity. Cf. Janssen 1984:17–20. Further, the curious reference to Sparta's *megas hagemôn* 'great leader' may serve to assimilate Sparta to Persia and its *megas Basileus* 'great King' (cf. Hordern 2002:325). Such assimilation would be especially noticeable if *Persians* was performed in 410 BCE, soon after Sparta had formed an alliance with Persia. We may note too that the image of Sparta as "a people teeming with the flowers of youthful manhood (*hêba*)" echoes the lament of Xerxes, who refers to his lost force as the "many-manned *hêba* of young men" (ἥβαν νέων πολύανδρον, 180–181). This phrase recalls a series of lines from Aeschylus' *Persians*, in which the army of Persia is said to be its *anthos* 'flower' and *hêbê* (59, 252, 512, 922–927). Cf. Tuplin 1994: "Sparta and Persia could strike any Athenian as a natural pair, since they were states whose enmity played a crucial role in creating, defining and (conjointly) destroying the Empire" (136).

and blame. He in fact is the true bulwark against the corruption, musical and social, introduced by *kainotomia*, that is, *kainotomia* that lacks the proper respect for tradition that Timotheus' has, of which the present *nomos* is the proof. In the epilogue of the *nomos*, which takes the form of a condensed paean, Timotheus calls upon the god of the lyre in his capacity as protector of cities:

ἀλλ' ἑκαταβόλε Πύθι' ἀγνὰν
ἔλθοις τάνδε πόλιν σὺν ὄλβῳ,
πέμπων ἀπήμονι λαῷ
τῷδ' εἰρήναν θάλλουσαν εὐνομίᾳ.

Far-shooter Pythian Apollo, come to this holy city with pros-perity, sending to this people, that they may be untroubled, a peace that flourishes through good order (*eunomia*).

Timotheus *Persians* 237–240

The final word of the *nomos* is thus *eunomia*, which surely refers not only to the proper sociopolitical order overseen by Apollo, but also to the good musical order of the present *nomos*.[348] Timotheus thus answers, at the emphatic final cadence of his song, the charges of *paranomia* that had been brought against him, not only in Sparta, but, more impor-tantly, in Athens; the present *nomos* is in no way transgressive, but wholly legitimate. Timotheus is not only defending the aesthetic and generic integrity of his music, however. More profoundly, he is laying claim to the storied legacy of the cosmic power of *kitharôidia*, which is recalled by the praise of his predecessors Orpheus and Terpander, as well as Apollo, who is invoked not only in the epilogue, but also in another paeanic section at the beginning of the *sphragis*, in which the god is enlisted as the special *epikouros* 'auxiliary' of the citharode in his struggle with the oppressive Spartans: "O you who foster the new-fash-ioned Muse of the golden *kitharis* (ὦ χρυσεοκίθαριν ἀέ- | ξων μοῦσαν νεοτευχῆ), come, healer Paean, as auxiliary to my *humnoi*" (202–205).[349] Timotheus is thus suggesting that with his *nomos* he has the same

---

[348] For the hard-to-miss musico-political punning of *eunomia* in *Persians*, see Bassett 1931:163; Janssen 1984:148; Csapo 2004:239–240; Wilson 2004:306.

[349] Rutherford 1996:182 and 2007b notes the probability of an allusion in *epikouros* (202) to Simonides' Plataea elegy, in which Simonides also invokes the Muse as an *epikouros* in praising the Spartan-led victory at Plataea (fr. 11.21 W²). On the "agonistic" tenor of the allusion, see Wilson 2004:305n82, with further bibliography. On the semantics of *epikouros* in Simonides' poem, cf. Stehle 2001. For Simonides as a model of innova-tion for Timotheus, see Part III.5–6.

Apollonian mandate to effect proper sociopolitical order in Athens (or indeed in any city) that Terpander once brought to bear with his *nomoi* at the Carneia, when he sounded Sparta's famed *eunomia* into being. Ironically, the Spartans, or any of the critics implicitly aligned with them, cannot appreciate this; their hostility to Timotheus may in fact indicate that they have become alienated from the pacificatory effects of *kitharôidia*, that it is they who have lost their *eunomia*.

The image of Timotheus' *humnoi* cutting across the social divisions of age and uniting the entire populace (213–215) now takes on a still deeper resonance. It evokes at once the transcendent charms of the Orphic lyre as well as Terpander's legendary harmonization of the fractious Spartans.[350] While the invocation of Pythian Apollo (237), "the helping and hymnic god of the musical Old Guard," is on the one hand a legitimating and archaizing gesture, on the other hand it may be meant to underscore a specific link to Terpander, whose own connections to Delphi—the oracle supposedly instructed the Spartans to listen to the Lesbian Singer—and the Pythia, where he was said to have won four victories, were an integral part of his legend.[351] In addition, Apollo's epithet ἑκαταβόλος 'far-shooter' is highly traditional, almost generic, but it may not be a coincidence that we find it in a Terpandrean *prooimion* (fr. 2 Gostoli = PMG 697).

If *Persians* was performed at the Panathenaia in 410 BCE, Timotheus' self-fashioning as an Orphic/Terpandrean/Apollonian master of lyric *eunomia* would have been especially timely. The oligarchic coup of the Four Hundred had taken place the year before. In the context of this recent social turmoil, Timotheus would conceivably be offering himself to the Athenians as an Ionian Terpander, promising to guarantee with his music, under the guidance of Apollo, continued peace and order in the restored democracy.[352] Of a piece with Timotheus' (Ionian-Athenian) adaptation of the (Spartan) Terpandrean tradition is his manipulation of the term *eunomia*. While *eunomia* could be viewed as a virtue of Solonian democracy (Solon fr. 4.31–38W; cf. Demosthenes 18.255)—the democratic citizen's adherence to the egalitarian constitution—it was colored above all by its aristocratic-oligarchic associations, not only in Sparta, but in Athens as well, where it served as a catchword for the pro-Spartan, anti-democratic oligarchs, some of

---

[350] For a possible reference in these lines to the age-graded choral culture of the Spartan Gymnopaidiai, see Power 2007:205n97.

[351] "Old Guard": Wilson 2004:305.

[352] Cf. Bassett 1931:163.

whom may have been among Timotheus' most prominent critics.[353] Timotheus' appropriation of *eunomia* entails its ideological transvaluation: true musical and political *eunomia* now belongs to democratic Athens, which heeds the *nomoi* of Timotheus—*nomoi* dedicated to demotically friendly narratives such as Salamis—just as the Spartans, now neglectful of true *eunomia*, once paid heed to those of Terpander.[354] Of course, secondary audiences beyond Athens presumably picked up on none of these local political complexities, nor did they need to. For them, Timotheus (or a reperformer of *Persians*) would simply have been fulfilling the classic function of the citharode, bringing order, musical and political, to their cities and communities.[355]

[353] See e.g. "Xenophon" (the Old Oligarch) *Constitution of the Athenians* 1.8–9, who rails against Athenians' rejection of *eunomia* in place of democratic *kakonomia*. Stenger 2004:294n115 is a concise review of scholarship on *eunomia* in fifth-century Athens; cf. Bowra 1961:414–415 on the semantic evolution of the word in poetry. The Old Oligarch is also a stern critic of demotic musical culture (1.13). It would be a mistake, however, to assume that with his assertion of *eunomia* Timotheus is trying only to answer elite, anti-democratic critics. Accusations of *paranomia* were probably more widely made among the *dêmos*, as the testimony of Satyrus and Plutarch suggests.

[354] Cf. Wilson 2004:306. *Eunomia* may already at the time of the performance of *Persians* have been a politically contested concept, just as *eleutheria* was contested and claimed by the Spartans in the later fifth century; cf. Boegehold 1999:34 on the ambiguous status of personified *Eunomia* in late-fifth-century Attic vase painting. Of course, the concept had cosmic implications that transcended any one city-state. Hesiod *Theogony* 902 has *Eunomia* flourishing alongside *Eirênê* 'Peace' (Εὐνομίην ... καὶ Εἰρήνην τεθαλυῖαν) and *Dikê* 'Justice' as children of Zeus and Themis (collectively, the *Horai* 'Seasons'). *Persians* 240 (εἰρήναν θάλλουσαν εὐνομίᾳ) may well allude to this line, but the association is traditional. Cf. related references in Hordern 2002:248; Ostwald 1969:62–75, with more on the Athenian context. Hansen 1990 argues that PMG fr. adesp. 1018b, a prayer to the Fates to send *Eunomia*, *Dikê*, and *Eirênê* to "this city" (*tande polin*) is a fragment from the *prooimion* to *Persians*, because its diction and choriambic meter echo those in the epilogue of the *nomos*. But Bowra's attribution of the verses to a choral song of Simonides, tentative as it is, remains far more convincing (1961:404–415). For Simonidean poetry as an intertext for *Persians*, see n349 above and the discussion of PMG 788 on allusions to the Plataea Elegy. If Bowra is correct to suspect that the "Prayer to the Fates" was composed to support the dominance of an oligarchic faction (perhaps in post-Persian War Corinth, p415), then an allusion to it by Timotheus would represent an analogous repurposing of oligarchic poetic capital within the "democratic" *nomos*.

[355] Note the generic deictics (τάνδε πόλιν, λαῷ τῷδε) of the epilogue. As Herington 1985:158–159 observes, "The final quatrain of the song seems designed to be sung anywhere, any time, not merely at the premiere in Athens ... from now on the *Persians* will presumably become a standard item in our migrant poet's baggage." Cf. Janssen 1984:147. Wilamowitz 1903:64 understood Timotheus to be indicating his pro-Spartan leanings by ending the *nomos* with *eunomia*. While this is to overlook the sly, appropriative rhetoric that attended the announcement of the term in Athens, it is entirely possible that secondary audiences in oligarchic and pro-Spartan cities heard Timotheus' claim to *eunomia* in a straightforward, totally unironic sense.

Another timely promise of a citharodic restoration of political order might be latent in lines 235–236, which come immediately before the epilogue. Timotheus styles his home *polis* of Miletus as ἁ δυωδεκατειχέος | λαοῦ πρωτέος ἐξ Ἀχαιῶν 'the city of a twelve-walled people that is foremost of the Achaeans'.[356] The "twelve-walled people" must be the Ionian confederation of 12 cities, which dates to the Archaic period (Herodotus 1.141–146). Herodotus 8.95 refers to the members of the confederation as οἱ δυωδεκαπόλιες Ἴωνες 'the Ionians of the twelve cities'. The epithet δυωδεκατειχής 'twelve-*walled*' sounds like a marked deviation from this more straightforward formulation.[357] We may note that the valorizing invocation of Miletus and the political strength and unity of the Ionian confederation is prefaced by Timotheus' optimistic appraisal of his innovative *kitharôidia*:

---

[356] On the difficulties presented by the form πρωτέος, see Basset 1931:162n1; Janssen 1984:145; Horden 2002:246. The meaning, however, is clearly not temporal, but "first" in the sense of "foremost." The reference to "Achaeans" in line 236 has caused more strictly interpretive problems. Janssen 1984:145 argues reasonably that it should be taken as an expression of Panhellenic sentiment, in keeping with the generic tenor of the *nomos*. The synecdoche is traditional, Homeric. Wilamowitz 1903:62 cannot admit this, because it would read as an insult to Sparta. He would see instead an oblique invocation of the supposed ancestral links between Ionians and Achaeans in the Peloponnese (Herodotus 1.145), and thus a deliberate snub of Athens and compliment to Sparta (i.e. the implication that soil shared in the deep past trumps Ionian-Athenian blood ties). Cf. now Rosenbloom 2006:150. But, as Wilamowitz admits, this argument is weakened by the fact that it was the Achaeans who supposedly drove the Ionians out of the Peloponnese (according to Herodotus). Basset 1931:162 also sees a reference to the ancient Peloponnesian ties between Ionians, Achaeans, and Spartans, but one that suggests an entirely different political position-taking: Timotheus is implicitly claiming that the Ionians are the "real" Achaeans, and so represent a challenge to the Peloponnesian hegemony of the Spartans (cf. the use of *laos* here to 209, where it describes the Spartans). Herodotus 1.145 emphasizes the fundamental homology between the 12 cities of Achaea and Ionia, which is something Timotheus may be picking up on as well. Some combination of Janssen's generic interpretation and Bassett's passive-aggressive one is certainly possible.

[357] The markedness of the epithet was perhaps still more striking in light of the fact that, at least in the 420s BCE, the cities of Ionia were unwalled (Thucydides 3.33.2). Gorman 2001:237–238 suggests that the absence of walls was a deliberate consequence of Athenian imperial policy, and that after the revolt of 412 Miletus would have been free to build a wall. The temptation might then be to read Timotheus' δυωδεκατειχὴς λαός as a coded defiance of Athenian imperialism. But there is no real indication in Thucydides' narrative of the Athenian attempts to retake the city (8.24–27) that anything like a proper wall had or had not been constructed in Miletus after 412. Archaeological remains of a Milesian city wall date to the early fourth or late fifth century (Gorman, p241), but it is impossible to connect with any certainty its construction to the events in 412. (Conceivably, the wall could have been constructed before 412, when Athens and Miletus were still allies.) The metaphorical/mythical sense of "walls" in δυωδεκατειχής is uppermost.

νῦν δὲ Τιμόθεος μέτροις
ῥυθμοῖς τ' ἐνδεκακρουμάτοις
κίθαριν ἐξανατέλλει
θησαυρὸν πολύυμνον οἴ-
ξας Μουσᾶν θαλαμευτόν·

And now Timotheus makes the *kitharis* again spring up with
eleven-struck meters and rhythms, having opened the many-
songed, chambered treasure-house of the Muses.[358]

Timotheus *Persians* 229–233

The close proximity of *kithara* and city walls in lines 229–236 cannot
but evoke Amphion's construction of the walls of seven-gated Thebes
with his heptachord lyre. At *Seven Against Thebes* 284 Aeschylus refers
to the ἑπτατειχεῖς ἐξόδους 'seven-walled exits' of Thebes; Timotheus'
δυωδεκατειχής may specifically recall the Aeschylean epithet, under-
scoring the allusion to Amphion and Thebes. The numerology of the
Persians sequence is impressionistic but nevertheless suggestive. We are
meant to draw a meaningful connection between Milesian Timotheus'
eleven-stringed *kitharis*—itself an outgrowth of Aeolic Terpander's "ten
songs" (225–226)—and the notionally twelve-walled Ionian confederation: the former has, Timotheus implies, the Amphionic power to
provide the musical foundation for the unity of the latter.[359]

In the historical context of 410 BCE, such power was desperately
needed, for by this point the confederation, to the extent that it was
still recognized to exist, and the cities in it were in violent disorder.[360] In 412 Alcibiades, in exile from Athens, had used his personal
contacts with certain leading men in Miletus, presumably aristocrats,
to provoke its defection from the Delian League, along with several
other Ionian cities, to the side of the Spartans. The Milesian revolt
was immediately followed by the treaties between the Spartans and
the Persians, which essentially entailed Sparta's selling out of Miletus
to Persia (Thucydides 8.17; cf. 8.18, 8.37, 8.58 for the treaties). During
this traumatic period, Timotheus, who may have belonged to one of
the democratic factions in his native city, probably made Athens his

---

[358] For the emphasis placed upon the civic inclusiveness of Timothean *kitharôidia* by the
image of the "treasure-house of the Muses," see Power 2007:205.

[359] Indeed, Timotheus seems to use the (archaizing) word *kitharis* to mean not just the
kithara but the entire medium of *kitharôidia*. Cf. Pindar *Pythian* 5.65.

[360] As Hordern 2002:245 notes, "Although the confederation may not have been in existence in the later fifth century, it is possible that its memory was strongly preserved
and had a deep emotional content."

home base.[361] Athens was itself badly shaken by the loss of its Ionian allies, particularly Miletus, whose recovery it saw as vitally important to its chances of success against Sparta in the East (Thucydides 8.25.5). The idealized vision of Ionian unity in *Persians* thus corresponds to no current reality; it is purely idealized nostalgia and wishful fantasy, whose realization, however, notionally lies in the hands of Timotheus. Just as the citharode "makes the *kitharis* again spring up with eleven-struck meters and rhythms," so might the "twelve walls" of the Ionian confederation be re-harmonized, made to spring to new life under the exemplary influence of its music, as the walls of Thebes had once arranged themselves (for the second time) under the spell of Amphion's *kitharôidia*. The promise of an orderly, unified Miletus and Ionia would of course appeal to Athenians nostalgic for a time before Ionian fractiousness and rebellion had become the rule, when their city's Panionian dominance was still firmly in place. The post-Periclean Panathenaia was a fitting context for such an appeal, given its strong imperial and Panionian agenda. Indeed, a Panathenaic audience would likely have appreciated that Timotheus was reminding not only the Athenians, but, just as importantly, the wavering Ionian allies, those present and those now absent, of Athens' glorious service against the Persians, the "great *kosmos* of freedom" that legitimated its empire.[362]

iv. Paeanic frames

The fact that the entire *sphragis* section itself takes the form of a virtual paean, bookended as it is by the two paeanic invocations of Apollo (202–205, 237–240), further reinforces Timotheus' rhetoric of musico-political salvation (whether or not it is specifically responsive to the events of 411 BCE).[363] The paean, although never as common in Athens as in other *poleis*, including Sparta, was nevertheless acknowledged to be the classic choral expression of communal cohesion and stability, an "an icon for solidarity among male members of the community."[364] Timotheus draws upon that politico-choral ideology to enrich his claims for the social inclusiveness and ordering properties of his music—although monodic, it has the effect of orchestrating consensus and cooperation in the manner of a paeanic performance. The paeanic

---

[361] Cf. Phillips 2003:224n79; cf. Hordern 2002:6–7.
[362] Cf. Bassett 1931:159; Phillips 2003:212–213.
[363] On the verbal and metrical parallels between the two passages, see Korzeniewski 1974:23.
[364] Rutherford 2001:85.

framing of the *sphragis* also has the effect of fusing Timotheus' personal appeal to "healer Paean" to help him defend his music against the Spartans with his appeal to the god to protect the broader interests of the *polis* in which he is performing the *nomos* (τάνδε πόλιν 'this city', 238). The successful reception of Timotheus' *nomos* is made inseparable from its success in securing the favor of Apollo for all.

Further, Timotheus' assimilation of his *nomos* to a paean is a conspicuously archaizing gesture. The citharode brings the new *nomos* back to its earliest roots, as it were, in the old-time song culture, tendentiously overwriting its more contemporary Dionysian models, dithyramb and drama. The definitive influence of those genres had of course been on full audible and visual display for the previous 200 plus verses of the *omphalos*. Yet the transition from the chaos of the the narrative to the orderly stability of the *sphragis* is itself cannily mediated by a narrated paean, the choral celebration of victory performed by the Greeks:

οἱ δὲ τροπαῖα στησάμενοι Διὸς
ἁγνότατον τέμενος, Παιᾶν·
ἐκελάδησαν ἰήιον
ἄνακτα, σύμμετροι δ' ἐπε-
κτύπεον ποδῶν
ὑψικρότοις χορείαις.

But when they [the Greeks] had set up victory monuments (*tropaia*) to Zeus to be a most holy sanctuary, they called on Paean healer lord and in equal time (*summetroi*) they began stamping with high-pounding dances (*khoreiai*) of their feet.

Timotheus *Persians* 196–201

This paeanic performance, no doubt mimetically reenacted by Timotheus with his *kithara*, marks a fitting end to the narrative of the battle of Salamis, but it also marks a transition in musical and performative style and ethos.[365] The fragmented and scattered "mad, sad, and foreign voices" heard in the preceding laments are capped by the organized choral song (*keladein*, 198) of the triumphant paean.[366] Set

---

[365] Cf. Herington 1985:158.

[366] The verb *keladein* and the noun *kelados* are regularly used to describe the traditional style of singing practiced by (male, Greek) paeanic (e.g. Aeschylus *Persians* 388; Bacchylides 16.12; Euripides *Heracles* 691–694, *Ion* 93) and epinician choruses (e.g. Pindar *Nemean* 4.16, *Olympian* 1.9). The verb notably occurs in a non-choral context as

against the pathetic and unrestrained postures of the suffering barbarians is the image of the disciplined, "symmetrical" *khoreiai* of the victorious Greeks.[367] The contrast would be dramatically registered in the alteration of Timotheus' own bodily mimesis; after "playing the other," his own citharodic identity, Hellenic and Apolline, at this point would begin to reemerge in preparation for his appearance *in propria persona* in the *sphragis*. We can expect that this contrast in characterization was reflected in the musical score as well.[368] Text, score, and performance thus would have conspired to express the subordination of the exotic and the experimental "Dionysian" music of the *omphalos* to the ordered "Apollonian" music of the archaic paean, which in turn leads into the paeanically framed nomic *sphragis*.[369] The Salamis paean marks the restoration of proper order to Greece and to the *nomos*; in terms of the latter, Dionysian *paranomia* makes way for Apollonian *eunomia*.

This "bipolar" structural logic of *Persians* is, I argue, ideologically and rhetorically determined. The sonic and mimetic excess and otherness of the New Music are fully explored—and their pleasures no doubt fully enjoyed by the audience—but they are in the end safely contained, closed off from the *sphragis*, in which Timotheus speaks for himself, or rather, plays an idealized version of himself: the audience is presented with Timotheus of Miletus, the classically grounded citharodic innovator. Unlike Aristophanes' Agathon, the poet-musician whose identity is inextricably bound up with multiple mimetic fantasies, Timotheus *kitharôidos* is a distinct, stable, indisputably Greek and masculine figure.[370]

---

a self-referential "performative future" in one of the Terpandrean citharodic *prooimia* (fr 4.2 Gostoli).

[367] For the sociopolitical connotations of this term, see van Minnen 1997:253. The chorus, itself a symbol of communal solidarity, here "performs" the harmonious political equality that exists among its members.

[368] Perhaps involving a modulation to the Dorian mode. Paeans and Dorian: "Plutarch" *On Music* 17.1136f; scholia *ad* Pindar *Olympian* 1.26. Cf. Rutherford 2001:80. Rutherford makes the point that references to the Lydian and Locrian *harmoniai* in the paeans of Pindar and later composers suggest that modes besides the Dorian could be used in the genre (80–81; cf. 383–384). This was probably the case, but it seems clear that the most traditional/male/Hellenic choral song genre was generally associated with the most traditional/male/Hellenic *harmonia*. Moderate, manly ethos of Dorian: Plato *Republic* 399a–c is the *locus classicus*; cf. too Plato *Laches* 188d, Heraclides Ponticus *ap.* Athenaeus 14.624d; "Plutarch" *On Music* 16.1136d–f.

[369] The regularity of the Aeolic meter that is introduced in 196–201 is continued through much of the *sphragis*. This suggests a continuity of mood and perhaps music.

[370] Cf. McClary 1991, who examines the way that "mad scenes" in Western vocal music—representations that typically invite a range of innovatory procedures—are often tempered by cadential "frames" of traditional, familiar musical discourse. These

By juxtaposing his own invocation of "Healer Paean" with the paeanic *khoreiai* for "Paean healer lord" around the *tropaia*, Timotheus invites the identification of the performance of the *nomos* with the performance that is the paean. The latter serves as a validating model for the former, imparting its aura of classical, indeed near-mythical grandeur and sanctity to the music of the here-and-now.[371] In line with the Panhellenically genericizing tendency of *Persians*, the singers and dancers at Salamis are a unified collective without specific political identities.[372] But the *primus inter pares* status of Athens that is operative in all things Salamis may be implicit here as well. It is tempting to speculate that Timotheus is intending to evoke one particularly resonant scene from the Athenian history of the battle (or at least its lore), that of a sixteen-year-old Sophocles leading a chorus at the Salamis *tropaion* with his lyre (*Life of Sophocles* 3; cf. Athenaeus 1.20e–f).[373] If this story is authentic, or at least if it had currency in the later fifth century, Timotheus' Athenian audience may well have been inclined to call to mind the image of this iconically patriotic performance, whose lyre-playing protagonist would grow up to become a beloved star of the tragic stage—as such, a fittingly aspirational archetype for the dramatizing citharode *par excellence*.

v. Greek music in the Persian tent

It is tempting too to speculate that the exemplary performance of the Greeks at the Salamis *tropaia* was intended also to recall the political and architectural history of the very structure in which Timotheus performed *Persians* in Athens, the Periclean Odeion. The history of

---

frames instantiate "the musical voice of reason," insuring that "the ravings of the madwoman will remain securely marked as radically 'Other', so that the contagion will not spread" (86). Hall has discussed an analogous logic of excess and frame in the epirrhematic scenes of Attic tragedy, in which impassioned lyric arias, almost always sung by women and/or barbarians, are contained, or restrained, by the rational iambic trimeters spoken by Greek men (1989:131; 1999:117–118). There is an ideological dimension to this framing of song by speech. While the singing voice of women and/or non-Hellenes *in extremis* elicits fascination and pleasure, its difference and excess, if not properly framed, can also produce embarrassment, anxiety; its "contagion" can pose a threat to the masculine political order. Cf. Sultan 1993 on historical legislation against women's lament and its refraction in tragedy.

[371] The juxtaposition also invites identification between the Greeks' struggle against Persia and Timotheus' against the Spartans. See Janssen 1984:125; Nieddu 1993:521; van Minnen 1997:253, 256; Rutherford 2001:122.

[372] So the pre-battle paean described at Aeschylus *Persians* 388–394 is Panhellenic.

[373] Cf. Bassett 1931:157.

the Odeion is in fact fundamentally connected to Salamis and the second Persian War in general; indeed, it may well have been viewed by Athenians of Timotheus' day as a *tropaion* of Athenian victories over Persia. The primary sources for the Odeion attest to its constitutive appropriation of Persian materials and visual motifs. According to Plutarch *Pericles* 13.9, "They say that the Odeion was a visual replica (*mimêma*) of the tent (*skênê*) of the Persian King" (εἰκόνα λέγουσι γενέσθαι καὶ μίμημα τῆς βασιλέως σκηνῆς); Pausanias 1.20.4 describes the Odeion as a "structure that is said to have been built as a replica (*es mimêsin*) of the tent (*skênê*) of Xerxes (κατασκεύασμα, ποιηθῆναι δὲ τῆς σκηνῆς αὐτὸ ἐς μίμησιν τῆς Ξέρξου λέγεται). A different angle is presented in Vitruvius 5.9.1: "[O]n your left as you leave the theater is the Odeion, which Themistocles roofed over with the masts and spars of ships from the Persian spoils when its stone columns were arranged in order." So the Odeion of Pericles is said to have been a replica of the tent (*skênê*) of Xerxes; Vitruvius adds the information that Themistocles was involved in the construction of a "proto-Odeion" before Pericles' in the same or a nearby location, and that he used naval spoils from the Persian wars (probably Salamis, perhaps Artemision) for the roof. It would be exhausting to rehearse in full the various theories that have been put forward to make sense of these disparate reports.[374] The following syncretic account is reductive, but it may suffice.[375]

Soon after 479 BCE a structure was erected near the Theater of Dionysus, under the supervision of Themistocles, that incorporated elements of the spoils from the Persian wars—the masts and spars of barbarian ships to which Vitruvius refers, but also the tent of Xerxes captured at Plataea.[376] Accordingly, the structure would have served as

---

[374] See especially Broneer 1944; Davison 1958:33–36; Robkin 1976; Meinel 1980; Kotsidu 1991:141–149; Miller 1997: 218–242; Camp 2004:101.

[375] I primarily follow Davison 1958:33–35 and Kotsidu 1991:141–144, although Kotsidu, unlike Davison, does not think that either Themistocles' or Pericles' "Odeia" were used for musical contests. Miller 1997:221 is skeptical of Vitruvius' testimony about a Themistoclean prototype for the Odeion.

[376] The tent was in fact occupied by Mardonius at Plataea (Herodotus 9.70), but Herodotus 9.82 strongly implies that Xerxes had given Mardonius his tent on his retreat from Greece. The word Herodotus uses there is κατασκευή, which, as Kotsidu 1991:141 points out, is echoed in Pausanias' description of the Odeion as a κατασκεύασμα (1.20.4). Of course, the Themistoclean structure need not have incorporated the actual tent of Xerxes (or Mardonius), but it was perhaps, like Pericles' Odeion, a replica of it. This view is taken by Kotsidu 1991:144 (with previous scholarship); it helps to answer the legitimate objection that "it is very unlikely that of all the Greeks at Plataia the Athenians rather than the Lakedaimonians were awarded the greatest prize" (Miller 1997:236). Herodotus 9.70 does not mention to whom the tent was

a sort of massive *tropaion*, commemorating victories both at Salamis and Plataea.[377] The question remains what function, if any, this "proto-Odeion"—which may not have been called the Odeion at all—served beyond its not unimportant significance as a monument of victory. Was it used as a music hall? The testimony of Plutarch *Pericles* 13.11, which indicates that only in Pericles' time were the *agônes* held in the Odeion, would suggest not. We should keep in mind, however, that Themistocles knew how to appropriate musical culture for political ends, so the possibility remains.[378]

Whatever its original function, the "proto-Odeion" was either renovated or totally reconstructed by Pericles as the Odeion, where the Panathenaic *mousikoi agônes* were to be held. The tent-like, Persoid appearance of the Periclean Odeion was a holdover from the older building. As such, it would have constituted an "archaic" layer of architectural symbolism that projected a visual and conceptual association between the new building, the old Themistoclean "*tropaion*," and the victories at Salamis and Plataea that the former structure commemorated. The retention of this connection to the valorized Athenian past, indeed to the very events upon which the empire was based, must have had an ideological purpose, one that was closely tied to Pericles' renewed promotion of Panathenaic musical culture and to the city's broader imperial agenda. When the Athenians and their allies and visitors gathered together in the Odeion to witness the spectacle of the *mousikoi agônes*, the very structure under whose roof they assembled was an impressive testament to both the political and musical hegemony of the city.[379] The architectural and functional rhetoric of the building in fact suggests that the two were mutually complementary.

---

awarded. For Athenian dedications of captured Phoenician triremes, see Herodotus 8.121; cf. Thompson 1956.

[377] Cf. Kotsidu 1991:143.

[378] Cf. Davison 1958:35, who attempts to reconcile Vitruvius' testimony with Plutarch's. Broneer 1944 argues that Xerxes' tent was originally used by Themistocles as the scenic backdrop for his production of Phrynichus' *Phoenician Women* and later Pericles' production of Aeschylus' *Persians*. Cf. the modifications of Kotsidu 1991:143–144; counter-arguments of Miller 1997:235–236.

[379] Miller 1997 takes a different approach to the history of the Odeion, arguing against any relation between the Odeion and the tent of Xerxes and seeing it rather as influenced directly by royal Apadana palace architecture, which the Athenian *dêmos* had appropriated to glorify its own imperial status. But her assessment of the Odeion's symbolic valency is nevertheless in line with the notion that it was a replica of Xerxes' tent: "Resonating against its Persian models, [the Odeion] is a proud statement of empire" (241).

If Timotheus did sing his *Persians* in Athens, then it was in this ideologically resonant space that he sang it. The temptation is strong to view the *nomos* as a deliberately "metatheatrical" response to the Odeion, a musico-poetic echo of its potent historical and political aura. Indeed, both *Persians* and Odeion are in their respective forms stylized mimetic artifacts of the barbarian culture vanquished, or, perhaps better, "captured," in the second Persian War. The Odeion is a replica (*mimêma*) of the captured Persian tent designated to show-case the primacy of Panathenaic musical culture; *Persians* is devoted in large part to the representation of barbarian laments following the Battle of Salamis, stylized and performed for the pleasure, ideological and aesthetic, of the Athenian audience. Like the Odeion, the *nomos* is ultimately a celebration of empire. If the Odeion serves to advertise at once Athens' privileged "possession" of the sublime prestige of the Persian wars and the culture of Panhellenic *mousikê* at its Panathenaia, then *Persians* represents a *kitharôidia* expressive of and commensurate with these imperial ambitions.[380]

Timotheus' descriptive reenactment of the paean at the *tropaia* might then carry a specific, Athenian-localized reference to the Odeion's storied connections to Salamis and its spoils. The reference might come across rather obliquely on the page, but we may assume that it took on a greater immediacy when sung out in the "Persian tent," before an audience that was familiar with the layered historical meanings of the building.[381] Another allusion to the Odeion might be heard toward the end of the King's lament (178–195), when he commands his men to load his riches onto wagons and to burn the *skênai* 'tents' so that the Greeks may not profit from his wealth (191–195). The setting of the scene is probably meant to be the foot of Mt. Aegaleos, from which point Xerxes watched the battle of Salamis unfold (Herodotus 8.90; Aeschylus *Persians* 466–467). Neither Herodotus nor Aeschylus mentions the fate of the Persian tents at Salamis, however, and Herodotus makes it seem as if there was indeed no immediate danger posed to the mobile wealth of the Basileus after the rout of the Persian naval forces (8.97). The singular presence of the *skênai* in Timotheus'

---

[380] Cf. Phillips 2003:224n82.

[381] We may note that in the paeanic epilogue of *Persians* (237–240), Timotheus refers to the city in which he is performing (i.e. Athens, foremost) as ἁγνά 'holy' (237). The epithet recalls the description of the place where the Salamis victors set up their *tropaia* and performed the paean: the "most holy sanctuary of Zeus" (Διὸς ἁγνότατον τέμενος, 196–197). Cf. van Minnen 1997:253, who argues that the adjective *hagnos* should have the more politically inflected sense of 'inviolable' in both passages.

account—placed emphatically at the end of the King's lament, no less—seems purposeful, and more than a little arch, for Timotheus and his audience, assembled in the Odeion, would have had the satisfaction of knowing that Xerxes' command was not entirely carried out. The royal *skênê*, at least, was in fact conveyed to Plataea, and from there to Athens, where it had been (at least notionally) transformed into the splendid music hall where *Persians* was being performed.

What emerges from the close constellation of references to the *skênê* of Xerxes, the *tropaia* at Salamis, and the victory song of the Greeks sung at the *tropaia* is a kind of impressionistic aetiological pastiche of the Odeion, accounting for the traditions behind the architectural history of the building as well as its function as a music hall, a "place of song," and so in a sense tracing in the heroic past the continuum between its present form and function. Gorgias records in his *Epitaphios* the commonplace notion that the *tropaia* of victories over the barbarians demand songs (*humnoi*).[382] Like the archaic paean sung around the *tropaia* at Salamis that it invokes as a model, *Persians* could be heard as a modern musical response to the Odeion, still in its sophisticated Periclean incarnation a vestigial *tropaion* of the victory over Xerxes.

12. Timotheus the Classic

By the fourth century BCE, the new *nomos* had become the dominant practice in *kitharôidia*, and the once-controversial compositions of Timotheus—thanks in large part to his own extramusical self-promotional genius, well evidenced in *Persians*—had become classics in their own right, subject to reperformance on a Panhellenic scale, just as the Terpandrean *nomoi* had previously been. Pylades' reperformance of *Persians* to an enthusiastic audience at the Nemean games in the late third century BCE vividly attests to the undisputed popularity of the Timothean *nomos*.[383] The popular canonization of Timotheus' works began in the citharode's own lifetime. Before his death around 360 BCE, the citharist Stratonicus, known more for his criticisms than commendations, could vouch for the classic status of the Milesian's

---

[382] τὰ μὲν κατὰ τῶν βαρβάρων τρόπαια ὕμνους ἀπαιτεῖ (*Epitaphios* fr. 5b).

[383] For more on the post-Classical reception of Timotheus, see Hordern 2002:73–79. Despite Timotheus' canonization, however, for certain conservative elites of the Hellenistic and Imperial eras, his name—alongside those of other composers of the Athenian New Music—would remain a rhetorically convenient byword for cultural scandal and iconoclasm. See n341 and Part I.22.ii.

nomoi: they possessed the authority of "laws" (*nomoi*), while those of a younger rival, Philotas, a student of Polyeidus, were mere *psêphismata* 'decrees' (Athenaeus 8.352b).[384] Another indication that Timotheus' *nomoi* had achieved wide-scale cultural legitimacy in his own time is the testimony of Aristoxenus to the effect that Timotheus had inspired a dedicated school of citharodic parodists: "Just as some devised comic parodies of [epic] hexameter poetry, so Oenopas first devised parodies of *kitharôidia*. Polyeuctus of Achaea and Diocles of Cynaetha emulated him" (Aristoxenus fr. 135 Wehrli *ap.* Athenaeus 14.638b).[385] Athenaeus elsewhere cites Aristoxenus as saying that the earliest of these parodists, Oenopas (or, as he is also called, Oenonas), was an Italian, and that he "brought on stage the Cyclops whistling and a shipwrecked Odysseus speaking bad Greek" (Κύκλωπα εἰσήγαγε τερετίζοντα καὶ ναυαγὸν Ὀδυσσέα σολοικίζοντα, Athenaeus 1.20a). The object of the parody may well have been Timotheus' *Cyclops*, which inspired separate parodies in early-fourth-century dithyramb and comedy.[386] We can probably date Oenopas' parody to the early fourth century as well.[387]

The fourth century saw rival schools of citharodes emerge, however, and some of these must have enjoyed considerable popularity. We have already mentioned Philotas, the disciple of Polyeidus of Selymbria, who was, like Timotheus, a dithyrambic composer as well as citharode.[388] A fourth-century writer cited in "Plutarch" *On Music* 21.1138b, very likely

---

[384] Stratonicus' career overlapped with that of Timotheus, but he really belongs to the next generation of professional musicians (he was active from around 410 to 360 BCE; West 1992:367–368). It is probable that his own instrumental music was influenced by that of the older citharode, however. Phaenias fr. 32 Wehrli says that he "introduced *polukhordia*" into instrumental *kithara* playing; in so doing he was likely taking his cue from the master of the eleven-stringed *kithara*, Timotheus, who had paved the way for the legitimacy of this innovation (*Persians* 229–231). But we should be wary about taking Stratonicus' praise of the Milesian at face value (cf. Wilson 2004:290). It is more likely the case that Timotheus was praised *because he had lost*; he was no longer a (cross-generic) rival of Stratonicus. Indeed, another anecdote has Stratonicus viciously criticizing Timotheus' dithyramb *Birth Pangs of Semele* (Athenaeus 8.352a)— the citharist, whose stock in trade was musical mimeticism, may have felt especially threatened by the ambitious (auletic) mimeticism of this work. The citharodic style of Polyeidus, however, was ascendant by the mid-fourth century, temporarily eclipsing the novelty of Timothean *kitharôidia* ("Plutarch" *On Music* 21.1138b), and Stratonicus would have been eager to put it in its place. This strategy of praising the "classics" by way of denigrating contemporaries and rivals is one Timotheus himself deploys in the *Persians*.

[385] On the practice of epic parody in the fourth century, see Olson and Sens 1999:5–13.

[386] Philoxenus *Cyclops* or *Galateia* (PMG 815–827); Aristophanes *Wealth* 290, with scholia. See Power 2011 (forthcoming).

[387] Cf. West 1992:366.

[388] Parian Marble Ep. 68; Diodorus Siculus 14.46, who adds that he was also a painter.

Aristoxenus, claims that in his own time "the citharodes have virtually (*skhedon*) rejected the style (*tropos*) of Timotheus in favor of *kattumata* and the compositions (*poiêmata*) of Polyeidus."[389] First, it is important to note the adverb *skhedon* 'virtually', which is a deliberately understated qualifier of what is surely an overstated observation—it is clear in fact that a majority of later Classical citharodes had not "virtually" abandoned the style of Timotheus. Our writer, a conservative critic of the legacy of the New Music, seems somewhat too eager to consign Timotheus to oblivion.[390] But there can be no doubt that the style of Polyeidus had its moment in the sun, and then some. Inscriptional evidence suggests that his *nomoi* were ranked alongside those of Timotheus by late Hellenistic citharodes, one of whom, Menecles of Teos, performed pieces by Timotheus and Polyeidus while on a diplomatic mission-cum-concert tour in Crete in the second century BCE (I.Cret. I xxiv 1). Unfortunately, it is impossible to say how exactly his *nomoi*, and those of his protégés, differed in style and content from those of Timotheus. A late Roman source observes that the compositions of Timotheus and Polyeidus exhibit the same manner of metrical freedom, but that is not saying much.[391]

It is possible, however, that the *On Music* passage means to equate the compositions of Polyeidus with *kattumata*. These are literally leather shoe patches, but here the word probably refers to "medleys, by contrast with structurally more organized pieces."[392] We might connect these post-Timothean citharodic *kattumata* with a fourth-century style of composition described in a play of Middle Comedy, Antiphanes' *Third Actor*: "Today's poets compose ivy-twisted, fountainy, flowerflitting, wretched songs, with wretched words, into which they weave (*emplekontes*) melodies from other compositions (*allotria melê*)" (fr. 207 K-A).[393] The speaker is invidiously comparing the insipid music and poetry of his day with the now-classic "new dithyramb" of Philoxenus. The contemporary style he describes is thus primarily dithyrambic, but his comment probably applies equally to the *nomos*, given the assimilation of the two genres that had begun in the later fifth century. The speaker seems to be criticizing makers of medleys (cf. *allotria melê*

---

[389] τῶν δὲ κιθαρῳδῶν τοῦ Τιμοθείου τρόπου, σχεδὸν γὰρ ἀποπεφοιτήκασιν εἴς τε τὰ καττύματα καὶ εἰς τὰ Πολυείδου ποιήματα. Translation based on Barker 1984:227.

[390] I discuss the complex critical agenda of this passage of *On Music* in a forthcoming article, "Aristoxenus and the Neoclassicists."

[391] Censorinus 6.608 Keil.

[392] Barker 1984:227n139.

[393] οἱ νῦν δὲ κισσόπλεκτα καὶ κρηναῖα καὶ | ἀνθεσιπότατα μέλεα μελέοις ὀνόμασιν | ποιοῦσιν ἐμπλέκοντες ἀλλότρια μέλη.

'melodies from other compositions'); the metaphor of "inweaving" resembles that of patching in *kattumata*.[394] What seems to be happening in both *kitharôidia* and dithyramb is the recycling of stock melodies, presumably popular tunes of past and present, to cobble together musical pastiches or potpourris. The reduced emphasis placed upon original melodic composition surely reflects the ever-increasing popularity of virtuoso cithanodic and auletic performance. Agonistic music of the fourth century, it seems, was increasingly focused on the star singer rather than the song.[395] Other citharodes may have attempted to revive the Archaic and Classical style of the *nomos*, or stylized recreations thereof. We have no direct fourth-century evidence for this, but Aristoxenus refers to an archaizing tendency among dithyrambic composers, which would suggest a parallel affectation in *kitharôidia* (fr. 76 Wehrli *ap.* "Plutarch" *On Music* 31.1142b–c; cf. 21.1137f–1138c).[396]

Nero surely inherited, broadly speaking, the "classical" Timothean tradition, as did his teachers and contemporaries. While it is unlikely that the original musical settings of Timotheus' *nomoi* remained intact hundreds of years after their original performances, their texts were written down at an early point—the Abusir papyrus containing the poetic text, without musical notation, of *Persians* dates to the fourth century BCE—and probably maintained their integrity well into the Imperial period, although some creative customization is not unimaginable.[397] Dio Chrysostom 19.5 says that most of what citharodes and actor-singers perform in his era, the later first and early second centuries CE, are "ancient works" (*arkhaia*), by which he seems to mean only the old texts—with what degree of modification we can only guess—but not the old music. An inscription from the first half of the second century CE makes the claim that C. Aelius Themison, a Milesian

---

[394] Cf. West 1992:372.

[395] Besides Polyeidus and Philotas, we may have the names of two other composers of cithanodic *kattumata*: Argas, who is mentioned, alongside one Telenicus of Byzantium, by the fourth-century BCE scholar Phaenias as a composer of μοχθηρὰ ᾄσματα 'worthless songs' that could not compare to those of both Terpander and, more tellingly, that forerunner of Timotheus in the new *nomos*, Phrynis (Phaenias fr. 10 Wehrli *ap.* Athenaeus 14.638c). Cf. discussion in Part II.12.

[396] Demetrius of Phalerum may have encouraged the revival of "Homeric" *kitharôidia*: see Part II.8.

[397] On the papyrus containing *Persians*, see Hordern 2002:62–73 and van Minnen 1997, who compellingly reconstructs the reception the *nomos* (qua written text) among the Hellenomemphite community of Ionian Greeks in Egypt, one of whom had owned the papyrus. One wonders if that community was familiar with a living cithanodic performance tradition of *Persians* as well. For possible remains of cithanodic texts on papyri from Ptolemaic Egypt, see West 1999a; n399 below.

musician, probably a citharode, was the "first and only to set Euripides, Sophocles, and Timotheus to music (*melê*) of his own" (SEG xi 52c). The claim is difficult to take at face value.[398] Perhaps what is meant is that Themison was the "first and only" to present all three of these poets' complete texts in entirely new musical settings, which was no doubt an impressive feat. But tragic singers and citharodes, including Nero, had long been rescoring selected works of Classical tragedy, or even setting to music the iambic sections of tragedy that were originally spoken without melody, a procedure that had already become exceedingly popular by the time of Dio Chrysostom.[399] Similarly, Themison's adaptation of Timotheus was probably not unique, although we might understand the language of the inscription to suggest that some citharodes, at least, were not singing Timotheus' *nomoi* to their own *melê*, but were following a score that was, or, more likely, was thought to be, the original.

It has been suggested that the *nomos* Nero sang at his debut performance in Naples is the same piece he would perform the following year at the Neronia in Rome, a treatment of the tragic myth of Niobe (Suetonius *Nero* 21).[400] Could this *Niobe* have been the same *nomos*, or some adapted version thereof, composed by Timotheus over 400 years earlier (PMG 786–787)?[401] We know that Nero had a citharodic song called the *Nauplios* in his repertoire, which is also the name of a Timothean composition (PMG 785), very probably a *nomos*.[402] Nero

---

[398] Cf. discussion of issues involved in Part III.5.

[399] Dio says that sung iambic excerpts from tragedy were in fact more popular than original lyric parts (19.5). On the recycling of passages from Classical tragedy by virtuoso singers in the Hellenistic and Roman theater, see Gentili 1979. West 1999a speculates that some unpublished papyrus scraps in the Ashmolean Museum (inv. 89B/29–33), from third- to second-century BCE Egypt, may contain texts (with some musical notation) from a "citharodes' repertoire, either excerpts from tragedies or citharodic nomes or dithyrambs" (53). West thinks that one scrap may even preserve the traces of the *sphragis* of a *nomos* (C13; p57). We hear of an early-second-century performance at Delphi by the aulete Satyrus of Samos of a "*kitharisma* from Euripides' *Bacchae*" (FD III 3, 128 = SIG 648 B). The nature of this *kitharisma* is a mystery. Was it a purely instrumental interpretation of scenes from the tragedy played on the *kithara* by the multi-talented Satyrus? Or did it involve the singing of the chorus that is also mentioned in the inscription? In that case, was an *aulos* employed in addition to a *kithara*? See Sifakis 1967:96–97; West 1992:376; Wilson 2000:308–309. In any case, it suggests that citharodic settings of Attic tragedy may not have been uncommon as early as the Hellenistic period.

[400] Lesky 1949:400 = 1966:346 makes this assumption; cf. Champlin 2003:116.

[401] Wilamowitz 1903:81. Some manuscripts of the Suetonius *Nero* give the title in its Greek (accusative case) form, *Nioban* (instead of Latin *Niobem*). West 1992:382 also supposes that both Nero's *Niobe* and his *Nauplios* may have been Timothean *nomoi*.

[402] Nero's *Nauplios*: Suetonius *Nero* 39.3; cf. Part I.22.i.

composed his own *nomoi* as well, in which he seems to have followed the Timothean preference for tragically colored, pathos-suffused, and affectively intense mythical subject matter. Indeed, Nero's other great artistic pursuit, *tragoedia cantata*, the singing of monodic arias adapted from tragic drama to accompanying pipes, would not have been so far from Timothean *kitharôidia* in its performative techniques and modes of self-presentation, and it is likely that the same themes, if not the same texts, could have straddled both media, sung now as tragic arias, now as citharodic *nomoi*.[403] Nero is said to have set to citharodic *melê* versions of the *Oresteia* and the *Antigone* (Philostratus *Life of Apollonius of Tyana* 4.39), while, as a tragic singer, he performed in the roles of Orestes and Antigone.[404] According to Dio Cassius 61.20.2, at his performance during the Juvenalia of 59 Nero sang a song called, alternatively, *Attis* or *Bacchae*—we do not know if the composition was Nero's own—which, as one scholar argues, "under either name and sung in either voice, whether of a lamenting castrato or maenad, has plenty of room in it for falsetto histrionics, and the effeminate/feminizing nature of the song is clearly an issue for Dio in his account of its premiere performance."[405] The emperor's musico-dramatic representation of the exotic "other" is a distinct echo of the Timothean aesthetic of extremes.

[403] Cf. Part I.17. See Kelly 1979 on the overlap between *citharoedia* and *tragoedia* in Nero's time and the later Empire; cf. Lesky 1949 = 1966.

[404] As well as other associated characters. Sources and discussion in Champlin 2003:77. The tragic roles ascribed to Nero in Suetonius *Nero* 21.3 all have a touch of the Grand Guignol: Canace Giving Birth, Orestes the Matricide, Oedipus Blinded, Hercules Insane.

[405] Freudenburg 2001:169. Sullivan 1978 supports the view presented in the scholia to Persius *Satires* 1 that lines 93–106 of that poem parody several specific verses from a Neronian composition, which Sullivan presumes to be the *Attis* mentioned by Dio. It is true that Catullus 63 might have been an influence on the citharodic *Attis* (if it is Nero's work), but we should, I think, assume that Nero sang his *Attis* in Greek rather than in Latin, as contemporary citharodes, almost all Greek, would have sung their *nomoi*. Therefore, while Persius might be allusively mocking the overwrought and socially inappropriate poetry performed by Nero, direct quotation from the citharodic *Attis* is unlikely. (Pure speculation, but could the *Attis* that Nero sings, if it was not his composition, be the work of a Hellenistic citharode?) Of course, Nero could have written an independent, non-citharodic treatment of the Attis story in Latin hexameters. Similarly, although he wrote an epic poem in Latin called the *Troica*, which he *recited* at the Second Neronia (Dio Cassius 62.29; cf. Griffin 1984:151), the *Capture of Troy* (*Halôsis Iliou*), which he *sang* as a citharode in 64 CE (Dio Cassius 62.18.1; Suetonius *Nero* 38.2, who also gives the Greek title), was probably a separate citharodic *nomos*, with text in Greek.

Plates

Plate 1: Red-figured amphora by the Brygos Painter with citharode, c. 480 BCE. Boston, Museum of Fine Arts, John Michael Rodocanachi Fund, 26.61.

Plate 2: Reverse of the amphora in Plate 1, with youth listening to citharode on obverse.

Plate 3: Statue of Apollo Patroos by Euphranor, c. 330 BCE. Athens, Agora Museum S 2154.

Plate 4: Roman statue of Apollo *citharoedus* (probably early Imperial period). Staatliche Museen zu Berlin K 163.

Plate 5: Late Republican wall painting with seated woman holding a *kithara*, from Room H of the Villa of P. Fannius Synistor at Boscoreale, c. 40–30 BCE. New York, Metropolitan Museum of Art, Rogers Fund, 1903 (03.14.5).

Plate 6: Black-figured neck amphora by the Andokides Painter with Heracles *kitharôidos* mounting platform before Athena, c. 525 BCE. Munich, Staatliche Antikensammlungen und Glyptothek 1575.

Plate 7, a and b: Red-figured eye cup by Psiax, c. 520 BCE.
Cleveland Museum of Art 1976.89. *Side A:* citharode with spectators.

Side B: warriors.

Plate 8: Metope from the Sicyonian Monopteros at Delphi, with Orpheus and Philammon (?) with *kitharai* and Castor and Polydeuces on horseback, second quarter of the sixth century BCE. Delphi Archaeological Museum.

564

Plate 9: Red-figured amphora by the Andokides Painter with citharode and spectators, c. 530–525 BCE. Paris, Musée du Louvre G 1.

Plate 10: Red-figured pelike by the Argos Painter with citharode and spectators, c. 480 BCE. St. Petersburg, State Hermitage Museum Б 1570.

Plate 11: Red-figured Panathenaic-shaped amphora by the Nikoxenos Painter with Athena playing the *kithara*, c. 500 BCE. Staatliche Museen zu Berlin, Preussischer Kulturbesitz F 2161.

Plate 12: Reverse of the amphora in Plate 11, with citharode.

Plate 13: Red-figured pelike by the Epimedes Painter with
citharode and Nikai, c. 430 BCE. Plovdiv, Departmental
Archaeological Museum 1812.

Bibliography

Aksik, I. 1971. "Recent Archaeological Research in Turkey." *Anatolian Studies* 21:5–58.

Alcock, S. 1994. "Nero at Play? The Emperor's Grecian Odyssey." In Elsner and Masters 1994:98–111.

Alfieri, N. 1979. *Spina. Museo Archeologico Nazionale de Ferrara* I. Bologna.

Allen, T. W. 1907. "The Homeridae." *Classical Quarterly* 1:135–143.

———, ed. 1912. *Homeri Opera* V. Oxford.

Allen, T., W. R. Halliday, and E. E. Sikes, eds. 1904. *The Homeric Hymns*. Oxford.

Aloni, A. 1984. "L'intelligenza di Ipparco. Osservazioni sulla politica dei Pisistratidi." *Quaderni di Storia* 19:109–148.

———. 1986. *Tradizione archaiche della Troade e composizione dell' Iliade*. Milan.

———. 1989. *L'aedo e i tiranni. Ricerche sull'Inno omerico a Apollo*. Rome.

———. 2000. "Anacreonte a Atene." *Zeitschrift für Papyrologie und Epigraphik* 130:81–94.

———. 2006. *Da Pilo a Sigeo: poemi, cantori e scrivani al tempo dei tiranni*. Rome.

Ampolo, C. 1993. "La città dell'eccesso: per la storia di Sibari fino al 510 a.C." *Sibari e la Sibaritide. Atti del trentuduesinzo Convegno di studi sulla Magna Grecia, Taranto-Sibari, 7–12 Ottobre 1992* (eds. A. Stazio and S. Ceccoli) 213–254. Taranto.

Amyx, D. A. 1976. "The Orpheus Legend in Art." *Archaeological News* 5:25–41.

Anderson, Graham. 2000. "Some Uses of Storytelling in Dio." *Dio Chrysostom: Politics, Letters, and Philosophy* (ed. S. Swain) 143–160. Oxford.

Anderson, Gregory. 2003. *The Athenian Experiment: Building an Imagined Political Community in Ancient Attica, 508–490 B.C.* Ann Arbor.

Anderson, W. D. 1955. "The Importance of Damonian Theory in Plato's Thought." *Transactions of the American Philological Association* 86:88–102.

———. 1966. *Ethos and Education in Greek Music.* Cambridge, MA.

———. 1994. *Music and Musicians in Ancient Greece.* Ithaca.

Aneziri, S. 2003. *Die Vereine der Dionysischen Techniten im Kontext der hellenistischen Gesellschaft.* Historia Einzelschriften 163. Munich.

Arafat, K. W. 1997. *Pausanias' Greece: Ancient Artists and Roman Rulers.* Cambridge.

Aravantinos, V. 1996. "New Archaeological and Archival Discoveries at Mycenaean Thebes." *Bulletin of the Institute of Classical Studies* 41:135–136.

Arnold, I. R. 1960. "Agonistic Festivals in Italy and Sicily." *American Journal of Archaeology* 64:245–251.

Arnott, W. G. 1979. *Menander II.* Loeb Classical Library. Cambridge, MA.

———. 1996. *Alexis: The Fragments.* Cambridge.

Aron, K. 1920. *Beiträge zu den Persern des Timotheos.* PhD diss., University of Erlangen-Nürnberg.

Aubreton, R., ed. and trans. 1972. *Anthologie Grecque. Première Partie: Anthologie Palatine. Tome X (Livre XI).* Paris.

Auslander, P. 2006. "Musical Personae." *The Drama Review* 50:100–119.

Austin, C. and G. Bastianini, eds. 2002. *Posidippi Pellaei quae supersunt omnia.* Milan.

Austin, C. and D. Olson, eds. 2004. *Aristophanes Thesmophoriazusae.* Oxford.

Austin, J. C. 1922. *The Significant Name in Terence.* University of Illinois Studies in Language and Literature 7. Urbana, IL.

Barber, E. 1992. "The Peplos of Athena." In Neils 1992:103–117.

Barchiesi, A. 2005. "Learned Eyes: Poets, Viewers, Image Makers." *The Cambridge Companion to the Age of Augustus* (ed. K. Galinsky) 281–305. Cambridge.

Barker, A. 1982. "The Innovations of Lysander the Kitharist." *Classical Quarterly* 32:266–269.

———. 1984. *Greek Musical Writings.* Vol. 1, *The Musician and his Art.* Cambridge.

———. 1989. *Greek Musical Writings.* Vol. 2, *Harmonic and Acoustic Theory.* Cambridge.

———. 1990. "Public Music as 'Fine Art' in Archaic Greece." *Antiquity and the Middle Ages: From Ancient Greece to the Fifteenth Century* (ed. J. McKinnon) 45–67. London.

———. 1995. "*Heterophonia* and *Poikilia*: Accompaniments to Greek Melody." In Gentili and Perusino 1995:41–60.

———. 2001. "La musica di Stesicoro." *Quaderni Urbinati di Cultura Classica* 67:7–20.

Barron, J. P. 1964. "The Sixth-Century Tyranny at Samos." *Classical Quarterly* 14:210–229.

———. 1983. "The Fifth-Century *Horoi* of Aigina." *Journal of Hellenic Studies* 103:1–14.

Bartol, K. 1998. "The Importance of Appropriateness: Rethinking the Definition of *Nomos.*" *Philologus* 142:300–307.

Bartsch, S. 1994. *Actors in the Audience.* Cambridge, MA.

Basset, S. E. 1931. "The Place and Date of the First Performance of the *Persians* of Timotheus." *Classical Philology* 26:153–165.

Beacham, R. 1999. *Spectacle Entertainments of Early Imperial Rome.* New Haven.

Bearzot, C. 2004. "Lisandro tra due modelli: Pausania l'aspirante tiranno, Brasida il generale." *Contro le 'leggi immutabili'. Gli Spartani fra tradizione e innovazione.* Storia. Contributi di Storia Antica 2 (eds. C. Bearzot and F. Landucci) 127–160. Milan.

Beazley, J. D. 1922. "Citharoedus." *Journal of Hellenic Studies* 42:70–98.

———. 1928. *Greek Vases in Poland.* Oxford.

———. 1948. "Hymn to Hermes." *American Journal of Archaeology* 52:336–340.

———. 1964. *The Development of Attic Black-Figure.* Oxford.

Bechtel, F. 1917. *Die historischen Personennamen des Griechischen bis zur Kaiserzeit.* Halle.

Beck, F. A. G. 1975. *Album of Greek Education: The Greeks at School and at Play.* Sydney.

Becker, H. S. 1951. "The Professional Dance Musician and His Audience." *American Journal of Sociology* 57:136–144.

Beecroft, A. 2008. "Nine Fragments in Search of an Author: Poetic Lines Attributed to Terpander." *Classical Journal* 103:225–242.

Bélis, A. 1995. "Cithares, citharistes et citharôdes en Grèce." *Comptes rendus de l'Académie des Inscriptions et Belles-Lettres* 1995:1025–1065.

———. 1999. *Les Musiciens dans l'antiquité.* Paris.

Bell, H. I. 1925. "A Musical Competition in the Third Century B.C." *Raccolta di Scritti in Onore di Giacomo Lumbroso*, 13–22. Milan.

Bell, J. M. 1978. "Simonides in the Anecdotal Tradition." *Quaderni Urbinati di Cultura Classica* 28:29–86.

Bell, M. 1995. "The Motya Charioteer and Pindar's *Isthmian 2.*" *Memoirs of the American Academy in Rome* 40:1–42.

Bergk, T. 1872, 1883. *Griechische Literaturgeschichte* I, II. Leipzig.

———. 1882. *Poetae Lyrici Graeci.* Leipzig.

Berlinzani, F. 2002. "Leggende Musicali e Dinamiche Territoriali: Reggio e Locri nel VI Secolo." *Identità e Prassi Storica nel Mediterraneo Greco* (ed. L. M. Castelnuovo) 23–32. Milan.

Bernabé, A., ed. 1988. *Poetae Epici Graeci. Testimonia et Fragmenta.* Pars I. Leipzig.

Beschi, L. 1992. "Una Dea della Musica a Lemnos Arcaica." *Kotinos. Festschrift für Erika Simon* (eds. H. Froning, T. Hölscher, and H. Mielsch) 132–138. Mainz.

Betegh, G. 2004. *The Derveni Papyrus: Cosmology, Theology and Interpretation.* Cambridge.

Bethe, E. 1914–1927. *Homer: Dichtung und Sage.* 3 vols. Leipzig.

Bie, O. 1887. *Die Musen in der antiken Kunst.* Berlin.

Bieber, M. 1956. "Another Note on the Murals from Boscoreale." *American Journal of Archaeology* 60:283–284.

Biehl, W., ed. 1970. *Euripides: Troades.* Leipzig.

Bierl, A. 2001. *Ritual und Performativität (unter besonderer Berücksichtigung von Aristophanes' Thesmophoriazusen und der Phalloslieder fr. 851 PMG).* Munich and Leipzig.

Biers, W. R. and D. Geagan. 1970. "A New List of Victors in the Caesarea at Isthmia." *Hesperia* 39:79–93.

Biles, Z. 2006/2007. "Aeschylus' Afterlife: Reperformance by Decree in 5th C. Athens?" *Illinois Classical Studies* 31/32:206–242.

Bing, P. 2005. "The Politics and Poetics of Geography in the Milan Posidippus." *The New Posidippus: A Hellenistic Poetry Book* (ed. K. Gutzwiller) 119–140. Oxford.

Binney, E. H. 1905. "The Alcestis as a Folk-Drama." *Classical Review* 19:98–99.

Boardman, J. 1956. "Some Attic Fragments: Pot, Plaque and Dithyramb." *Journal of Hellenic Studies* 76:18–25.

———. 1972. "Herakles, Peisistratos and Sons." *Revue archéologique* 1972:57–72.

———. 1975. "Herakles, Peisistratos and Eleusis." *Journal of Hellenic Studies* 95:1–12.

———. 1978a. "Exekias." *American Journal of Archaeology* 82:11–25.

———. 1978b. "Herakles, Delphi, and Kleisthenes of Sikyon." *Revue archéologique* 1978:227–234.

———. 1980. *The Greeks Overseas.* London.

———. 1989. *Athenian Red Figure Vases: The Archaic Period.* London.

———. 1995. "Culture and the City." *Culture et Cité: L'avènement d'Athènes à l'époque archaïque* (eds. A. Verbanck-Piérard and D. Viviers) 1–14. Brussels.

Boatwright, M. T. 2002. *Hadrian and the Cities of the Roman Empire.* Princeton.

Boegehold, A. 1999. *When a Gesture Was Expected: A Selection of Examples from Archaic and Classical Greek Literature.* Princeton.

Böhme, R. 1953. *Orpheus: Das Alter des Kitharoden.* Berlin.

———. 1970. *Orpheus. Der Sänger und seine Zeit.* Bern and Munich.

———. 1991. *Der Lykomide. Tradition und Wandel zwischen Orpheus und Homer.* Bern and Stuttgart.

Böhr, E. 1982. *Der Schaukelmaler.* Mainz.

Bolton, J. D. P. 1948. "Was the *Neronia* a Freak Festival?" *Classical Quarterly* 42:82–90.

Bonnet, A. 2001. "En Parcourant le Val des Muses. Remarques sur un concours musical: les Mouseia des Thespies." *Musique et poésie dans l'antiquité: actes du colloque de Clermont-Ferrand, Université Blaise Pascal, 23 mai 1997* (ed. G.-J. Pinault) 53–70. Paris.

Borthwick, E.K. 1959. "ΚΑΤΑΛΗΨΙΣ—A Neglected Technical Term in Greek Music." *Classical Quarterly* 9:23–29.

———. 1965. "Suetonius' Nero and a Pindaric Scholium." *Classical Review* 15:252–256.

———. 1970. "The Riddle of the Tortoise and the Lyre." *Music & Letters* 51:373–387.

———. 1994. "New Interpretations of Aristophanes *Frogs* 1249–1328." *Phoenix* 48:21–41.

Bothe, F., ed. 1825–1826. *Euripidis Dramata.* 2 vols. Leipzig.

———, ed. 1845. *Aristophanis Comoediae* III. Leipzig.

Bowersock, G. W. 1965. *Augustus and the Greek World.* Oxford.

Bowie, A. 1981. *The Poetic Dialect of Sappho and Alcaeus.* Salem, NH.

Bowie, E. L. 1986. "Greek Elegy, Symposium and Public Festival." *Journal of Hellenic Studies* 106:13–35.

———. 1990a. "Greek Poetry in the Antonine Age." *Antonine Literature* (ed. D.A. Russell) 53–90. Oxford.

———. 1990b. "*Miles ludens?* The Problem of Martial Exhortation in Early Greek Elegy." *Sympotica: A Symposium on the Symposion* (ed. O. Murray) 221–229. Oxford.

———. 2007. "Ancestors of Historiography in Early Greek Elegiac and
Iambic Poetry?" *The Historian's Craft in the Age of Herodotus*
(ed. N. Luraghi) 45–66. Oxford.

Bowra, M. 1952. "Orpheus and Eurydice." *Classical Quarterly* 2:113–126.

———. 1961. *Greek Lyric Poetry: From Alcman to Simonides.* Oxford.

———. 1963. "Two Lines of Eumelus." *Classical Quarterly* 13:145–153.

Boyd, T. 1994. "Where Ion Stood, What Ion Sang." *Harvard Studies in
Classical Philology* 96:109–121.

Bradley, K. R. 1978. *Suetonius' Life of Nero: An Historical Commentary.*
Collection Latomus 157. Brussels.

Braswell, B. K. 1988. *A Commentary on the Fourth Pythian Ode of Pindar.*
Berlin and New York.

Bravo, B. 2001. "Un frammento della *Piccola Iliade* (*P.Oxy.* 2510), lo
stile narrativo tardo-arcaico, i racconti su Achille immortale."
Quaderni Urbinati di Cultura Classica 67:49–114.

Braund, S. 1992. "Juvenal—Misogynist or Misogamist?" *Journal of
Roman Studies* 82:71–86.

———. 2004. *Juvenal and Persius.* Loeb Classical Library. Cambridge, MA.

Brelich, A. 1969. *Paides e Parthenoi.* Rome.

Bremmer, J. 1999. "Rationalization and Disenchantment in Ancient
Greece: Max Weber amongst the Pythagoreans and Orphics?"
From Myth to Reason? Studies in the Development of Greek Thought
(ed. R. Buxton) 71–86. Oxford.

Brillante, C. 1991. "Le Muse di Thamyris." *Studi classici e orientali*
41:429–453.

Brize, P. 1980. *Die Geryoneis des Stesichoros und die frühe griechische Kunst.*
Beiträge zur Archäologie 12. Würzburg.

Broneer, O. 1944. "The Tent of Xerxes and the Greek Theater."
University of California Publications in Classical Archaeology
1.12:305–311.

Brown, M. K. 2002. *The Narratives of Konon: Text, Translation and
Commentary on the Diegeseis.* Beiträge zur Altertumskunde 163.
Munich and Leipzig.

Brown, N. O. 1947. *Hermes the Thief: The Evolution of a Myth.* Madison, WI.

Brussich, G. F. 1970. "La Lingua di Timoteo." *Quaderni Triestini per il
Lessico della Lirica Corale Greca* 1:51–80.

———. 1990. "L'inno ad Artemide di Timoteo." *Quaderni Urbinati di
Cultura Classica* 34:25–40.

Bundrick, S. 2005. *Music and Image in Classical Athens.* Cambridge.

Burgess, J. 2001. *The Tradition of the Trojan War in Homer and the Epic Cycle*. Baltimore and London.

———. 2004. "Performance and the Epic Cycle." *Classical Journal* 100:1–23.

Burkert, W. 1972. "Die Leistung eines Kreophylos. Kreophyleer, Homeriden und die archaische Heraklesepik." *Museum Helveticum* 29:74–85.

———. 1979. "Kynaithos, Polykrates, and the *Homeric Hymn to Apollo*." *Arktouros: Hellenic Studies Presented to B. M. W. Knox* (eds. G. W. Bowersock, W. Burkert, and M. C. J. Putnam) 53–62. Berlin.

———. 1983. *Homo Necans: The Anthropology of Ancient Greek Sacrificial Ritual and Myth*. Berkeley and Los Angeles.

———. 1984. "Sacrificio-Sacrilegio: Il 'Trickster' Fondatore." *Studi Storici* 25:835–845.

———. 1985. *Greek Religion*. Trans. J. Raffan. Cambridge, MA.

———. 1987. "The Making of Homer in the Sixth Century B.C.: Rhapsodes versus Stesichorus." *Papers on the Amasis Painter and His World* (eds. M. True et al.) 43–62. Malibu, CA.

———. 1992. *The Orientalizing Revolution: Near Eastern Influence on Greek Culture in the Early Archaic Age*. Cambridge, MA.

———. 1994. "Orpheus, Dionysos und die Euneiden in Athen: Das Zeugnis von Euripides' *Hypsipyle*." *Orchestra: Drama Mythos Bühne* (eds. A. Bierl and P. von Moellendorff) 44–49. Stuttgart.

———. 2001. *Savage Energies: Lessons of Myth and Ritual in Ancient Greece*. Cambridge, MA.

Burn, N. 1987. *The Meidias Painter*. Oxford.

Burnett, A. 1988. "Jocasta in the West: The Lille Stesichorus." *Classical Antiquity* 7:107–154.

Cairns, F. 1979. *Tibullus: A Hellenistic Poet at Rome*. Cambridge.

Calame, C. 1996. "Montagne des Muses et Mouseia: la consécration des Travaux et l'héroïsation d'Hésiode." *La Montagne des Muses* (eds. A. Hurst and A. Schachter) 43–56. Geneva.

———. 1997. *Choruses of Young Women in Ancient Greece: Their Morphology, Religious Role, and Social Functions*. Trans. D. Collins and J. Orion. Lanham, MD.

Caldelli, M. L. 1993. *L'Agon Capitolinus: Storia e Protagonisti dall'Istituzione Domizianea al IV Secolo*. Rome.

Cameron, A. 1976. *Circus Factions: Blues and Greens at Rome and Byzantium*. Oxford.

Campbell, D. A. 1988. *Greek Lyric.* Vol. 2, *Anacreon, Anacreontea, Choral Lyric from Olympus to Alcman.* Loeb Classical Library. Cambridge, MA.

———. 1993a. *Greek Lyric.* Vol. 5, *The New School of Poetry and Anonymous Songs and Hymns.* Loeb Classical Library. Cambridge, MA.

———. 1993b. Review of Gostoli 1990. *Gnomon* 65:70–71.

Camp, J. 2004. *The Archaeology of Athens.* New Haven.

Camps, W. A., ed. 1967. *Propertius, Elegies Book II.* Cambridge.

Capponi, M. 2003. "Fins d'hymnes et *sphragis* énonciatives." *Quaderni Urbinati di Cultura Classica* 75:9–35.

Carey, C. 1989. "The Performance of the Victory Ode." *American Journal of Philology* 110:545–565.

Cartledge, P. and A. Spawforth. 1989. *Hellenistic and Roman Sparta: A Tale of Two Cities.* London and New York.

Caskey, L. D. and J. D. Beazley. 1954. *Attic Vase Paintings in the Museum of Fine Arts Boston.* 2 vols. Oxford.

Cassio, A. 2000. "Esametri orfici, dialetto attico e musica dell'Asia Minore." In Cassio et al. 2000:97–110.

———. 2005. "I dialetti eolici e la lingua della lirica corale." *Dialetti e lingue letterarie nella Grecia antica. Atti della IV Giornata ghisleriana di Filologia classica* (eds. F. Bertolini and F. Gasti) 13–44. Pavia.

Cassio, A., D. Musti, and L. Rossi, eds. 2000. *Synaulía: cultura musicale in Grecia e contatti Mediterranei.* Naples.

Càssola, F. 1975. *Inni Omerici.* Milan.

Castaldo, D. 2000. *Il Pantheon musicale: Iconografia nella ceramica attica tra VI e IV secolo.* Ravenna.

Ceccarelli, P. and A. Milanezi. 2007. "Dithyramb, Tragedy—and Cyrene." *The Greek Theatre and Festivals: Documentary Studies* (ed. P. Wilson) 185–214. Oxford Studies in Ancient Documents. Oxford.

Chamay, J. and D. von Bothmer. 1987. "Ajax et Cassandre par le peintre de Princeton." *Antike Kunst* 30:58–68.

Champlin, E. 2003. *Nero.* Cambridge, MA.

Chaniotis, A. 1988. "Als die Diplomaten noch tanzten und sangen: Zu Zwei Dekreten kretischer Städte in Mylasa." *Zeitschrift für Papyrologie und Epigraphik* 71:154–156.

Chapouthier, F. 1935. *Les Dioscures au service d'une déesse. Etude d'iconographie religieuse.* Paris.

Cillo, P. 1993. "La 'cetra du Tamiri': Mito e realtà musicale." *Annali dell'Istituto Universitario Orientale di Napoli, Dipartimento di Studi del mondo classico e del Mediterraneo antico, Sezione filologico-letteraria* 15:205–243.

Cingano, E. 1990. "L'opera di Ibico e di Stesicoro nella Classificazione degli Antichi e dei Moderni." *Annali dell'Istituto Universitario Orientale di Napoli, Dipartimento di Studi del mondo classico e del Mediterraneo antico, Sezione filologico-letteraria* 12:189–224.

———. 1993. "Indizi di esecuzione corale in Stesicoro." In Pretagostini 1993:347–361. Rome.

———. 2003. "Entre Skolion et Enkomion: Réflexions sur le <<Genre>> et la Performance de la Lyrique Chorale Grecque." *La Poésie Grecque Antique* (eds. J. Jouanna and J. Leclant) 17–45. Paris.

Cizek, E. 1972. *L'Époque de Néron et ses Controverses Idéologiques.* Leiden.

Clay, J. S. 1989. *The Politics of Olympus: Form and Meaning in the Major Homeric Hymns.* Princeton.

———. 1992. "Pindar's Twelfth *Pythian*: Reed and Bronze." *American Journal of Philology* 113:519–525.

———. 1996a. "Fusing the Boundaries: Apollo and Dionysus at Delphi." *Métis* 11:83–100.

———. 1996b. "The Homeric Hymns." *A New Companion to Homer* (eds. I. Morris and B. Powell) 489–507. Leiden.

Cody, J. 2002. "Iannis Xenakis." The Ensemble Sospeso. http://www.sospeso.com/contents/composers_artists/xenakis.html.

Coleman-Norton, P. R. 1948. "Cicero Musicus." *Journal of the American Musicological Society* 1:3–22.

Collins, D. 2001. "Homer and Rhapsodic Competition in Performance." *Oral Tradition* 16:129–167.

———. 2004. *Master of the Game: Competition and Performance in Greek Poetry.* Hellenic Studies 7. Washington, DC.

Colvin, S. 1999. *Dialect in Aristophanes and the Politics of Language in Ancient Greek Literature.* Oxford.

Comotti, G. 1989. *Music in Greek and Roman Culture.* Trans. R. V. Munson. Baltimore.

Compton, T. 2006. *Victim of the Muses: Poet as Scapegoat, Warrior and Hero in Greco-Roman and Indo-European Myth and History.* Hellenic Studies 11. Washington, DC.

Constantinidou, S. 1998. "Dionysiac Elements in Spartan Cult Dances." *Phoenix* 52:15–30.

Cook, R. M. 1962. "Spartan History and Archaeology." *Classical Quarterly* 12:156–158.

Cooper, L. 1920. "A Pun in the *Rhetoric* of Aristotle." *The American Journal of Philology* 41:48–56.

Connolly, J. 2001. "Reclaiming the Theatrical in the Second Sophistic." *Helios* 28:75–98.

Conomis, N. C., ed. 1970. *Lycurgus*. Leipzig.

Cordano, F. 1994. "La città di Camarina e le corde della lira." *La Parola del passato* 49:418–426.

Courby, F. 1931. *Les temples d'Apollon*. Exploration archéologique de Délos faite par l'École française d'Athènes 12. Paris.

Courtney, E. 1980. *A Commentary on the Satires of Juvenal*. London.

———. 1993. *The Fragmentary Latin Poets*. Oxford.

Crane, G. 1996. "The Prosperity of Tyrants: Bacchylides, Herodotus, and the Contest for Legitimacy." *Arethusa* 29:57–85.

———. 1998. *Thucydides and the Ancient Simplicity: The Limits of Political Realism*. Berkeley.

Croally, N. T. 1994. *Euripidean Polemic: The Trojan Women and the Function of Tragedy*. Cambridge.

Croiset, M. 1904. "Observations sur les Perses de Timothée." *Revue des études grecques* 16:323–348.

Cropp, M., K. Lee, and D. Sansone, eds. 1999/2000. *Euripides and the Tragic Theatre in the Late Fifth Century*. Special issue, *Illinois Classical Studies* 24/25. Urbana, IL.

Crowther, N. B. and M. Frass. 1998. "Flogging as a Punishment in the Ancient Games." *Nikephorus* 11:51–82.

Csapo, E. 1999/2000. "Later Euripidean Music." In Cropp et al. 1999/2000:399–426.

———. 2002. "Kallipides on the Floor-Sweepings: The Limits of Realism in Classical Acting and Performance Styles." In Easterling and Hall 2002:127–147.

———. 2004. "The Politics of the New Music." In Murray and Wilson 2004:207–248.

Csapo, E. and W. J. Slater. 1994. *The Context of Ancient Drama*. Ann Arbor.

Currie, B. 2004. "Reperformance Scenarios for Pindar's Odes." *Oral Performance and Its Context* (ed. C. Mackie) 49–69. Menemosyne Supplement 248. Leiden.

CVA = *Corpus Vasorum Antiquorum*.

D'Agostino, H. 2007. *Onomacriti Testimonia et Fragmenta*. Pisa and Rome.

Dale, A. M., ed. 1954. *Euripides, Alcestis*. Oxford.

D'Alfonso, F. 1994. *Stesicoro e la performance: Studio sulle modalità esecutive dei carmi stesicorei.* Rome.

Danielewicz, J. 1990. "Il *nomos* nella parodia di Aristofane (*Ran.* 1264 sgg.)." *Annali dell'Istituto Universitario Orientale di Napoli, Dipartimento di Studi del mondo classico e del Mediterraneo antico, Sezione filologico-letteraria* 12:131–142.

Davidson, J. 1997. *Courtesans and Fishcakes: The Consuming Passions of Classical Athens.* London.

———. 2006. "Revolutions in Human Time: Age-class in Athens and the Greekness of Greek Revolutions." *Rethinking Greek Revolutions* (eds. S. Goldhill and R. Osbourne) 29–67. Cambridge.

Davies, J. K. 2007. "The Origins of the Festivals, Especially Delphi and the Pythia." *Pindar's Poetry, Patrons, and Festivals, from Archaic Greece to the Roman Empire* (eds. S. Hornblower and C. Morgan) 47–70. Oxford.

Davies, M. 1988. "Monody, Choral Lyric, and the Tyranny of the Handbook." *Classical Quarterly* 38:52–64.

Davison, J. A. 1955. "Peisistratus and Homer." *Transactions of the American Philological Association* 86:1–21.

———. 1958. "Notes on the Panathenaea." *Journal of Hellenic Studies* 78:23–42.

Degani, E. 1984. *Studi su Ipponatte.* Bari.

Della Seta, A. 1937. "Arte Tirrenica di Lemno." *Archaiologike Ephemeris* 1937:628–854.

Detienne, M. 2003. *The Writing of Orpheus: Greek Myth in Cultural Context.* Trans. J. Lloyd. Baltimore.

Diehl, E. 1936. *Anthologia Lyrica Graeca.* 2 vols. 2nd ed. Leipzig.

Di Marco, M. 1997. "Minima Terpandrea." *Quaderni Urbinati di Cultura Classica* 56:31–33.

D-K = Diels, H. and W. Kranz, eds. 1951–1952. *Die Fragmente der Vorsokratiker.* 3 vols. 6th ed. Berlin.

Dobrov, G. W. and E. Urios-Apirisi. 1995. "The Maculate Music: Gender, Genre and the *Chiron* of Pherecrates." *Beyond Aristophanes: Transition and Diversity in Greek Comedy* (ed. G. W. Dobrov) 139–176. Atlanta, GA.

Dougherty, C. 1993. *The Poetics of Colonization: From City to Text in Archaic Greece.* Oxford.

———. 2001. *The Raft of Odysseus: The Ethnographic Imagination of Homer's Odyssey.* Oxford.

Dougherty, C. and L. Kurke, eds. 1993. *Cultural Poetics in Archaic Greece: Cult, Performance, Politics.* Cambridge.

———, eds. 2003. *The Cultures within Ancient Greek Culture: Contact, Conflict, Collaboration.* Cambridge.

Dover, K. 1989. *Greek Homosexuality.* Cambridge, MA.

———, ed. 1993. *Aristophanes Frogs.* Oxford.

Dué, C. 2002. *Homeric Variations on a Lament by Briseis.* Lanham, MD.

Dugas, C. 1944. "Héraclès Mousicos." *Revue des études grecques* 57:61–70.

Dupont, F. 1985. *L'Acteur-Roi, ou le théâtre dans la Rome antique.* Paris.

Duplouy, A. 2006. *Le Prestige des Élites: Recherches sur les modes de reconnaissance sociale en Grèce entre les Xe et Ve siècles avant J.-C.* Paris.

Duran, M. 1996. "Pamfos." *Anuari de Filologia* 19:45–63.

Durante, M. 1976. *Sulla Preistoria della Tradizione Poetica Greca* II. Rome.

Dyer, G. 1997. *But Beautiful: A Book about Jazz.* New York.

Dyer, R. 1975. "The Blind Bard of Chios (*Hymn. Hom. AP.* 171–76)." *Classical Philology* 70:119–121.

Easterling, P. and E. Hall, eds. 2002. *Greek and Roman Actors: Aspects of an Ancient Profession.* Cambridge.

Ebeling, H. L. 1925. "The *Persians* of Timotheus." *American Journal of Philology* 46:317–331.

Eden, P. T., ed. 1984. *Seneca: Apocolocyntosis.* Cambridge.

Edmonds, R. 1999. "Tearing Apart the Zagreus Myth: A Few Disparaging Remarks on Orphism and Original Sin." *Classical Antiquity* 18:35–73.

Edwards, C. 1994. "Beware of Imitations: Theatre and the Subversion of Imperial Identity." In Elsner and Masters 1994:83–97.

———. 1997. "Unspeakable Professions: Public Performance and Prostitution in Ancient Rome." *Roman Sexualities* (eds. J. P. Hallett and M. Skinner) 66–95. Princeton.

Edwards, G. R. 1957. "Panathenaics of Hellenistic and Roman Times." *Hesperia* 26:320–349.

Eliade, M. 1964. *Shamanism: Archaic Techniques of Ecstasy.* Princeton.

Elsner, J. and J. Masters, eds. 1994. *Reflections of Nero: Culture, History, and Representation.* Chapel Hill and London.

Euben, J. P. 1986. "The Battle of Salamis and the Origins of Political Theory." *Political Theory* 14:359–390.

———. 1997. *Corrupting Youth: Political Education, Democratic Culture, and Political Theory.* Princeton.

Evans, A. J. 1928. *The Palace of Minos* II. London.

Fabbro, E. 1992. "Sul riuso di carmi d'autore nei simposi attici (*Carm. conv.* 8 P. e Alc. Fr. 249 V)." *Quaderni Urbinati di Cultura Classica* 41:29–38.

———. 1995. *Carmina Convivalia Attica. Introduzione, testimonianze, testo critico, traduzione e commento.* Rome.

Fantham, E. 1996. *Roman Literary Culture: From Cicero to Apuleius.* Baltimore and London.

Fantuzzi, M. and R. Hunter. 2004. *Tradition and Innovation in Hellenistic Poetry.* Cambridge.

Farioli, M. 2000. "Mito e Satira Politica nei *Chironi* di Cratino." *Rivista di Filologia e di Istruzione Classica* 128:406–431.

Farnell, L. R. 1907. *Cults of the Greek States* III, IV. Oxford.

FD = Ecole française d'Athènes. 1902–. *Fouilles de Delphes.* Paris.

Fearn, D. 2007. *Bacchylides: Politics, Performance, Poetic Tradition.* Cambridge.

Fehr, B. 1979. "Zur religionspolitischen Funktion der Athena Parthenos im rahmen des delisch-attischen Seebundes I." *Hephaistos* 1:71–91.

Feld, S. and C. Keil. 1994. *Music Grooves: Essays and Dialogues.* Chicago.

Ferrari, G. 1994/1995. "Heracles, Pisistratus and the Panathenaea." *Métis* 9/10:219–226.

FGE = Page 1981.

FGrH = Jacoby, F., ed. 1923–1958. *Fragmente der griechischen Historiker.* Berlin and Leiden.

Figueira, T. 1999. "The Evolution of the Messenian Identity." *Sparta: New Perspectives* (eds. S. Hodkinson and A. Powell) 211–243. London.

Fisher, N., ed. and trans. 2001. *Aeschines, Against Timarchos.* Oxford.

Flach, H. 1883. *Geschichte der Griechischen Lyrik.* Tübingen.

Flashar, M. 1992. *Apollon Kitharodos. Statuarische Typen des musischen Apollon.* Cologne.

Fleming, T. J. 1977. "The Musical Nomos in Aeschylus' *Oresteia*." *Classical Journal* 72:222–233.

Follett, S. 2004. "Philostratus' *Heroikos* and the Regions of the Northern Aegean." *Philostratus' Heroicus: Regional and Cultural Identity in the Third Century C.E.* (eds. E. Aitken and J. Maclean) 221–236. Leiden.

Fontenrose, J. 1968. "The Hero as Athlete." *California Studies in Classical Antiquity* 1:75–104.

———. 1978. *The Delphic Oracle: Its Responses and Operations, with a Catalogue of Responses.* Berkeley.

Ford, A. 1992. *Homer: The Poetry of the Past.* Ithaca.

———. 1999. "Odysseus After Dinner: *Od.* 9.2–11 and the Traditions of Sympotic Song." *Euphrosyne: Studies in Ancient Epic and its Legacy in Honor of Dimitris N. Maronitis* (eds. J. N. Kazazis and A. Rengakos) 109–123. Stuttgart.

———. 2002. *The Origins of Criticism: Literary Culture and Poetic Theory in Classical Greece.* Princeton.

———. 2003. "From Letters to Literature: Reading the 'Song Culture' of Classical Greece." *Written Texts and the Rise of Literate Culture in Ancient Greece* (ed. H. Yunis) 15–37. Cambridge.

———. 2004. "Catharsis: The Power of Music in Aristotle's *Politics.*" In Murray and Wilson 2004:309–336.

Forrest, W. G. 1963. "The Date of the Lykourgan Reform in Sparta." *Phoenix* 17:157–179.

Forsdyke, S. 2005. *Exile, Ostracism, and Democracy: The Politics of Exclusion in Ancient Greece.* Princeton.

Fortenbaugh, W. and E. Schütrumpf, eds. 1999. *Demetrius of Phalerum: Text, Translation, and Discussion.* New Brunswick, NJ.

Fraenkel, E. 1918. "Lyrische Daktylen." *Rheinisches Museum* 72:161–197, 321–352. Reprinted in *Kleine Beiträge zur klassischen Philologie* I (Fraenkel 1964) 165–233. Rome.

Frame, D. 2006. "The Homeric Poems after Ionia: A Case in Point." *The Homerizon: Conceptual Interrogations in Homeric Studies.* Center for Hellenic Studies, Washington, DC. September 2006. http://chs. harvard.edu/publications.sec/classics.ssp. Center for Hellenic Studies.

Franklin, J. 2002. "Musical Syncretism in the Greek Orientalizing Period." *Archäologie früher Klangerzeugung und Tonordnungen* (eds. E. Hickmann, R. Eichmann, and A. Kilmer) 441–451. Studien zur Musikarchäologie 3. Rahden.

———. 2003. "The Language of Musical Technique in Greek Epic Diction." *Gaia. Revue interdisciplinaire sur la Grèce archaïque* 7:295–307.

———. 2004. "Structural Sympathies in Ancient Greek and South-Slavic Heroic Song." *Musikarchäologische Quellengruppen: Bodenurkunden, mündliche Überlieferung, Aufzeichnung* (eds. E. Hickmann and R. Eichmann) 241–251. Studien zur Musikarchäologie 4. Rahden.

———. 2006a. "Lyre Gods of the Bronze Age Musical Koine."
The Journal of Ancient Near Eastern Religions 6:39–70.

———. 2006b. "The Wisdom of the Lyre: Soundings in Ancient Greece,
Cyprus and the Near East." *Studien zur Musikarchäologie. Vol. 5,
Musikarchäologie im Kontext: Archäologische Befunde, historische
Zusammenhänge, soziokulturelle Beziehungen* (eds. E. Hickmann,
R. Eichmann, and A. Both) 379–398. Rahden.

———. 2008. "'A Feast of Music': The Greco-Lydian Musical Movement
on the Assyrian Periphery." *Anatolian Interfaces: Hittites, Greeks
and Their Neighbours: Proceedings of an International Conference on
Cross-cultural Interaction, September 17-19, 2004, Emory University,
Atlanta, GA* (eds. B. J. Collins, M. Bachvarova, and I. Rutherford)
193–204. Oxford.

Freiert, W. K. 1991. "Orpheus: A Fugue on the Polis." *Myth and the Polis*
(eds. D. C. Pozzi and J. M. Wickersham) 23–48. Ithaca.

Freudenburg, K. 2001. *Satires of Rome.* Cambridge.

Friis-Johansen, K. 1967. "Am Chytrentag." *Acta Archaeologica*
38:175–198.

Froning, H. 1971. *Dithyrambos und Vasenmalerei in Athen.* Würzburg.

Frontisi-Ducroux, F. and F. Lissarrague. 1990. "From Ambiguity to
Ambivalence: A Dionysiac Excursion through the 'Anakreontic'
Vases." *Before Sexuality: The Construction of Erotic Experience in
the Ancient Greek World* (eds. D. M. Halperin, J. J. Winkler, and F.
Zeitlin) 211–256. Princeton.

Gambetti, S. 2001. "Alcuni elementi per una interpretazione storica
dei *Persiani* di Timoteo." *Simblos* 3:45–66.

GDI = Collitz, H. et al., eds. 1884–1915. *Sammlung der griechischen
Dialekt-Inschriften.* Göttingen.

Geer, R. M. 1935. "The Greek Games at Naples." *Transactions of the
American Philological Association* 66:208–221.

Geissler, P. 1969. *Chronologie der altattischen Komödie.* Zürich.

Genette, G. 1997. *Paratexts: Thresholds of Interpretation.* Cambridge.

Gentili, B. 1954. "Il Ditirambo XVII Sn. di Bacchilide e il cratere Tricase
da Ruvo." *Archeologia Classica* 6:121–125.

———. 1977. "Preistoria e formazione dell'esametro." *Quaderni
Urbinati di Cultura Classica* 26:7–37.

———. 1979. *Theatrical Performances in the Ancient World: Hellenistic and
Early Roman Theatre.* London Studies in Classical Philology 2.
Amsterdam.

———. 1988. *Poetry and Its Public in Ancient Greece.* Trans. T. Cole. Baltimore and London.

———. 1993. "Metro e ritmo nella dottrina degli antichi." In Pretagostini 1993:5–16.

———. 1995. "Preistoria e formazione dell'esametro." Revised version of Gentili 1977. *Struttura e Storia dell'Esametro Greco* II (eds. M. Fantuzzi and R. Pretagostini) 11–41. Rome.

Gentili, B. and F. Perusino, eds. 1995. *Mousiké: metrica ritmica e musica greca in memoria di Giovanni Comotti.* Pisa and Rome.

Gerber, D. E. 1997. *A Companion to the Greek Lyric Poets.* Leiden.

Gernet, L. 1981. *The Anthropology of Ancient Greece.* Trans. J. Hamilton and B. Nagy. Baltimore.

Gerson-Kiwi, G. 1980. *Migrations and Mutations of the Music in East and West.* Tel Aviv.

Gilula, D. 2000. "Stratonicus, the Witty Harpist." *Athenaeus and his World* (eds. D. Braund and J. Wilkins) 423–433. Exeter.

Glowacki, K. 1998. "The Acropolis of Athens before 566 B.C." *STEPHANOS: Papers in Honor of Brunilde Sismondo Ridgway* (eds. K. Hartswick and M. Sturgeon) 79–88. University Museum Monograph 100. Philadelphia.

Goehr, L. 2007. *The Imaginary Museum of Musical Works: An Essay in the Philosophy of Music.* 2nd ed. Oxford.

Goertzen, V. W. 1996. "By Way of Introduction: Preluding by 18th- and Early 19th-Century Pianists." *The Journal of Musicology* 14:299–337.

Golden, M. 1998. *Sport and Society in Ancient Greece.* Cambridge.

Goldhill, S. 1988. "Battle Narrative and Politics in Aeschylus' *Persae.*" *Journal of Hellenic Studies* 108:189–193.

———. 1994. "Representing Democracy: Women at the Great Dionysia." *Ritual, Finance, Politics: Athenian Democratic Accounts Presented to David Lewis* (eds. S. Hornblower and R. Osborne) 347–370. Oxford.

———. 2005. "Music, Gender, and Hellenistic Society." *The Soul of Tragedy: Essays on Athenian Drama* (eds. V. Pedrick and S. Oberhelman) 271–290. Chicago.

Gombosi, Otto. 1939. *Tonarten und Stimmungen der antiken Musik.* Copenhagen.

Görgemanns, H. 1976. "Rhetorik and Poetik im homerischen Hermes- hymnus." *Studien zum antiken Epos* (eds. H. Görgemanns and E. Schmidt) 113–128. Meisenheim.

Gorman, V. 2001. *Miletos, the Ornament of Ionia: A History of the City to 400 B.C.E.* Ann Arbor.

Gostoli, A. 1985. "L'uso metaforico del termine *aikhmê* (Terp. fr. 6 Bgk 4 = 4 D.2; Pind. fr. 199, 2 Sn.-Maehl.; Aeschyl. Ag. 483; Choeph. 630)." *Quaderni Urbinati di Cultura Classica* 19:185–188.

———. 1986. "La figura dell'aedo preomerico nella filologia peripatetica ed ellenistica: Demodoco tra mito e storia." *Scrivere e recitare* (ed. G. Cerri) 103–126. Rome.

———. 1988. "Terpandro e la funzione etico-politica della musica nella cultura spartana del VII sec. a.C." *La Musica in Grecia* (eds. B. Gentili and R. Pretagostini) 231–237. Rome and Bari.

———, ed. and trans. 1990. *Terpander: Introduzione, testimonianze, testo critico, traduzione e commento.* Rome.

———. 1993. "Il *nomos* citarodico nella cultura greca arcaica." In Pretagostini 1993:167–178.

———. 1998. "Stesicoro e la tradizione citarodica." *Quaderni Urbinati di Cultura Classica* 59:145–152.

Gouw, P. 2006. "Keizer Augustus en de Griekse atletiek." *Lampas* 39:211–225.

Gow, A. S. F., ed. and trans. 1952. *Theocritus.* 2nd ed. Cambridge.

———, ed. 1965. Machon. *The Fragments.* Cambridge.

Graf, F. 1974. *Eleusis und die Orphische Dichtung Athens in vorhellenistischer Zeit.* Berlin.

———. 1987. "Orpheus: A Poet among Men." *Interpretations of Greek Mythology* (ed. J. Bremmer) 80–106. London and Sydney.

———. 2006. "Der Kult des Eros in Thespiai." *Plutarch: Dialog über die Liebe* (ed. H. Görgemanns) 191–207. Tübingen.

Graf, F. and S. I. Johnston. 2007. *Ritual Texts for the Afterlife: Orpheus and the Bacchic Gold Tablets.* London and New York.

Gray, V. 2001. "Herodotus' Literary and Historical Method: Arion's Story." *American Journal of Philology* 122:11–28.

Graziosi, B. 2002. *Inventing Homer.* Cambridge.

Green, P. 1998. *Classical Bearings: Interpreting Ancient History and Culture.* Berkeley.

Greiser, H. 1937. *Nomos: Ein Beitrag zur griechischen Musikgeschichte.* Heidelberg.

Griffin, A. 1979. "A New Fragment of Dionysios of Halikarnassos O MOUSIKOS." *Historia* 28:241–246.

———. 1982. *Sikyon.* Oxford.

Griffin, M. 1984. *Nero: The End of a Dynasty.* London and New York.

Griffith, M. 1990. "Contest and Contradiction in Early Greek Poetry." *Cabinet of the Muses: Essays on Classical and Comparative Literature in Honor of Thomas G. Rosenmeyer* (eds. M. Griffith and D. Mastronarde) 185–207. Atlanta.

Griffiths, F. T. 1979. *Theocritus at Court*. Leiden.

Gronewald, M. and R. Daniel. 2005. "Lyrischer Text (Sappho-Papyrus)." *Zeitschrift für Papyrologie und Epigraphik* 154:7–12.

Groningen, B. A. van. 1955. "A propos de Terpandre." *Mnemosyne* 8:177–191.

———. 1960. *Pindare au Banquet*. Leiden.

Gropengiesser, H. 1977. "Sänger und Sirenen." *Archäologischer Anzeiger* 1977:582–610.

Gulick, C. B., ed. and trans. 1937. *Athenaeus*. Vol. 6, *The Deipnosophists*. Loeb Classical Library. Cambridge, MA.

Guthrie, W. K. C. 1952. *Orpheus and Greek Religion*. Princeton.

Gutzwiller, K. 2004. "Gender and Inscribed Epigram: Herennia Procula and the Thespian Eros." *Transactions of the American Philological Association* 134:383–418.

Gyles, M. F. 1947. "Nero Fiddled While Rome Burned." *Classical Journal* 42:211–217.

———. 1962. "Nero: Qualis Artifex?" *Classical Journal* 57:193–200.

Habicht, C. 1970. *Gottmenschentum und griechische Städte*. 2nd ed. Zetemata 14. Munich.

Hägg, T. 1989. "Hermes and the Invention of the Lyre: An Unorthodox Version." *Symbolae Osloenses* 64:36–73.

Hall, E. 1989. *Inventing the Barbarian: Greek Self-Definition through Tragedy*. Oxford.

———, ed. 1996. *Aeschylus Persians*. Warminster.

———. 1999. "Actor's Song in Tragedy." *Performance Culture and Athenian Democracy* (eds. S. Goldhill and R. Osborne) 96–122. Cambridge.

———. 2002. "The Singing Actors of Antiquity." In Easterling and Hall 2002:3–38.

———. 2006. *The Theatrical Cast of Athens: Interactions between Ancient Greek Drama and Society*. Oxford.

Hallet, C. 2005. *The Roman Nude: Heroic Portrait Statuary 200 BC–AD 300*. Oxford.

Hansen, M. H. 1978. "*Nomos* and *Psephisma* in Fourth-Century Athens." *Greek, Roman and Byzantine Studies* 19:315–330.

Hansen, O. 1984. "On the Date and Place of the First Performance of Timotheus' *Persae*." *Philologus* 128:135–138.

———. 1990. "The So-called Prayer to the Fates and Timotheus' *Persae*." *Rheinisches Museum* 133:190–192.

Hardie, A. 1983. *Statius and the Silvae: Poets, Patrons and Epideixis in the Graeco-Roman World*. Liverpool.

———. 2004. "Muses and Mysteries." In Murray and Wilson 2004:11–37.

———. 2005. "Sappho, the Muses, and Life after Death." *Zeitschrift für Papyrologie und Epigraphik* 154:13–32.

———. 2007. "Juno, Hercules, and the Muses at Rome." *American Journal of Philology* 128:551–592.

Harmon, R. 2003. "From Themistocles to Philomathes: *Amousos* and *amousia* in Antiquity and the Early Modern Period." *International Journal of the Classical Tradition* 9:351–390.

———. 2005. "Plato, Aristotle and Women Musicians." *Music and Letters* 86:351–356.

Harvey, A. E. 1955. "The Classification of Greek Lyric Poetry." *Classical Quarterly* 5:156–175.

Hasebroek, J. 1965. *Trade and Politics in Ancient Greece*. New York.

Heath, J. 1994. "The Failure of Orpheus." *Transactions of the American Philological Association* 124:163–196.

Hedreen, G. 1992. *Silens in Attic Black-figure Vase-painting*. Ann Arbor.

———. 2003. Review of Neer 2002. *Bryn Mawr Classical Review* 2003.03.20 (2003), http://ccat.sas.upenn.edu/bmcr/2003/2003-03-20.html.

———. 2007. "Myths of Ritual in Athenian Vase-Paintings of Silens." *The Origins of Theatre in Ancient Greece and Beyond: From Ritual to Drama* (eds. E. Csapo and M. Miller) 150–195. Cambridge.

Hedrick, C. W. 1988. "The Temple and Cult of Apollo Patroos in Athens." *American Journal of Archaeology* 92:185–210.

Heitsch, E. 1961. *Die griechischen Dichterfragmente der Romischen Kaiserzeit*. Göttingen.

Henderson, J. 1975. *The Maculate Muse: Obscene Language in New Comedy*. New Haven.

Henehan, D. 1980. "Why They Were Crazy about Mad Scenes." *New York Times*, Sept. 21, 1980, Arts and Leisure, 21 and 24.

Henrichs, A. 1994/1995. "'Why Should I Dance?' Choral Self-Referentiality in Greek Tragedy." *Arion* 3.1:56–111.

Herington, J. 1967. "Aeschylus in Sicily." *Journal of Hellenic Studies* 87:74–85.

———. 1985. *Poetry into Drama. Early Tragedy and the Greek Poetic Tradition.* Berkeley and Los Angeles.

Higgs, P. 1994. "The Cyrene Apollo." *History Today*, Nov., 50–54.

Hodkinson, S. 2000. *Property and Wealth in Classical Sparta.* London.

Holmberg, I. 1998. "The Creation of the Ancient Greek Epic Cycle." *Oral Tradition* 13:456–478.

Hordern, J. H. 2002. *The Fragments of Timotheus of Miletus.* Oxford.

Hose, B. 1993. "Kratinos und der Bau des perikleischen Odeions." *Philologus* 137:3–11.

Hunter, R. 1996. *Theocritus and the Archaeology of Greek Poetry.* Cambridge.

Hurwitt, J. 1999. *The Athenian Acropolis: History, Mythology, and Archaeology from the Neolithic Era to the Present.* Cambridge.

Hutchinson, G. O. 2001. *Greek Lyric Poetry: A Commentary on Selected Larger Pieces.* Oxford.

Huxley, G. 1969. "Choirilos of Samos." *Greek, Roman and Byzantine Studies* 10:12–29.

I.Cret. = Guarducci, M., ed. 1935–. *Inscriptiones Creticae, Opera et Consilio Friderici Halbherr Collectae.* Rome.

I.Délos = Durrbach, F. et al., eds. 1926–1950. *Inscriptions de Délos.* Paris.

I.Didyma = Rehm, A., ed. 1958. *Didyma.* Vol. 2, *Die Inschriften.* Berlin.

Ieranò, G. 1992. "Arione e Corinto." *Quaderni Urbinati di Cultura Classica* 41:39–52.

———. 1997. *Il ditirambo di Dionisio.* Rome.

IGR = Cagnat, R., ed. 1911–1927. *Inscriptiones Graecae ad res Romanas pertinentes.* Paris.

I.Iasos = Blümel, W., ed. 1985. *Die Inschriften von Iasos. Inschriften griechischer Städte aus Kleinasien* 28. 2 vols. Bonn.

Irwin, E. 1998. "Biography, Fiction and the Archilochean *AINOS*." *Journal of Hellenic Studies* 118:177–183.

———. 2005a. "Gods Among Men? The Social and Political Dynamics of the Hesiodic *Catalogue of Women.*" *The Hesiodic Catalogue of Women: Constructions and Reconstructions* (ed. R. Hunter) 35–84. Cambridge.

———. 2005b. *Solon and Early Greek Poetry: The Politics of Exhortation.* Cambridge.

IGSK = 1972–. *Inschriften griechischer Städte aus Kleinasien.* Bonn.

Isler-Kerényi, C. 2007. *Dionysos in Archaic Greece: An Understanding through Images*. Leiden.

Jackson, S. 1995. *Myrsilus of Methymna: Hellenistic Paradoxographer*. Amsterdam.

Jacoby, F. 1904. *Das Marmor Parium*. Berlin.

———. 1944. "GENESIA: A Forgotten Festival of the Dead." *Classical Quarterly* 38:65–75.

———. 1955. *Die Fragmente der Griechischen Historiker. Dritter Teil. Geschichten von Städten und Völkern. Kommentar zu Nr. 297-607 (Text)*. Leiden.

Jamot, P. 1895. "Fouilles de Thespies, les jeux en l'honneur des Muses." *Bulletin de Correspondance Hellénique* 19:311–385.

Jan, K. von. 1895. *Musici Scriptores Graeci*. Leipzig.

Janko, R. 1982. *Homer, Hesiod and the Hymns*. Cambridge.

———. 1986. "The Shield of Heracles and the Legend of Cycnus." *Classical Quarterly* 36:38–59.

Janni, P. 1965. *La Cultura di Sparta arcaica I*. Rome.

Janssen, T. H. 1984. *Timotheus Persae: A Commentary*. Amsterdam.

Jauss, H. R. 1982. *Aesthetic Experience and Literary Hermeneutics*. Trans. M. Shaw. Minneapolis, MN.

Jeanmaire, H. 1939. *Couroi et Courètes: essai sur l'éducation spartiate et sur les rites d'adolescence dans l'antiquité hellénique*. Lille. Reprint 1975. New York.

Johnson, J. 1996. *Listening in Paris: A Cultural History*. Berkeley.

Johnston, S. I. 1999. *Restless Dead: Encounters between the Living and the Dead in Ancient Greece*. Berkeley.

———. 2002. "Myth, Festival, and Poet: *The Homeric Hymn to Hermes* and its Performative Context." *Classical Philology* 97:109–132.

Jones, C. P. 1973. "The Date of Dio of Prusa's Alexandrian Oration." *Historia* 22:302–309.

Kambitsis, J. 1972. *L'Antiope d'Euripide. Édition commentée des fragments*. Athens.

Kaufman-Samara, S. 1997. "'Οὐκ ἀπόμουσον τὸ γυναικῶν' (Εὐριπ. Μήδ. 1089): Γυναῖκες μουσικοὶ στὰ ἀττικὰ ἀγγεῖα τοῦ 5ου αἰ. π.Χ." *Athenian Potters and Painters: The Conference Proceedings* (eds. J. H. Oakley, W. Coulson, and O. Palagia) 286–290. Oxford.

Kauppi, L. 2006. *Foreign But Familiar Gods: Greco-Romans Read Religion in Acts*. London and New York.

Kavoulaki, A. 1999. "Processional Performance and the Democratic
    Polis." *Performance Culture and Athenian Democracy*
    (eds. S. Goldhill and R. Osborne) 58–95. Cambridge.

Kay, N. M. 1985. *Martial Book XI: A Commentary*. London.

———, ed. and trans. 2006. *Epigrams from the Anthologia Latina: Text,
    Translation and Commentary*. London.

Kelly, H. A. 1979. "Tragedy and the Performance of Tragedy in Late
    Roman Antiquity." *Traditio* 35:21–44.

Kemp, J. A. 1966. "Professional Musicians in Ancient Greece."
    Greece & Rome 13:213–222.

Kennell, N. 1988. "ΝΕΡΩΝ ΠΕΡΙΟΔΟΝΙΚΗΣ." *American Journal of
    Philology* 109:239–251.

Kenney, E. J., ed. 1996. *Heroides XVI-XXI*. Cambridge.

Kerényi, K. 1976. *Dionysos: Archetypal Image of Indestructible Life*.
    Trans. R. Manheim. Princeton.

Kiechle, F. 1963. *Lakonien und Sparta. Untersuchungen zur ethnischen
    Struktur und zur politischen Entwicklung Lakoniens und Spartas bis
    zum Ende der archaischen Zeit*. Munich.

Kirby, M. 1965. *Happenings*. New York.

Knaack, G. 1899. *Paulys Realencyclopäde der classischen
    Altertumswissenschaft* (ed. G. Wissowa), s.v. "Boio," cols. 633–634.
    Stuttgart.

Knell, H. 1998. *Mythos und Polis: Bildprogramme griechischer Bauskulptur*.
    Darmstadt.

Knoepfler, D. 1993. "Adolf Wilhelm et la *pentétèris* des Amphiaraia
    d'Oropos. Réexamen de A.P. LIV 7 à la lumière du catalogue *IG*
    VII 414 + *SEG* I 126." *Aristote et Athènes* (ed. M. Piérart) 279–302.
    Paris.

———. 1996. "La réorganisation du concours des Mouseia à l'époque
    hellénistique: esquisse d'une solution nouvelle." *La Montagne des
    Muses* (eds. A. Hurst and A. Schachter) 141–167. Geneva.

Koch-Harnack, G. 1983. *Knabenliebe und Tiergeschenke: Ihre Bedeutung im
    päderastischen Erziehungssystem Athens*. Berlin.

Kolb, F. 1977. "Die Bau-, Religions- und Kulturpolitik der
    Peisistratiden." *Jahrbuch des Deutschen Archäologischen Instituts*
    92:99–138.

Koller, H. 1956. "Das kitharodische Prooimion: Eine formgeschich-
    tliche Untersuchung." *Philologus* 100:159–206.

———. 1962. "Dithyrambos und Tragödie." *Glotta* 40:183–195.

Korzeniewski, D. 1974. "Die Binnenresponsion in den Persern des Timotheus." *Philologus* 118:22–39.

Kotsidu, H. 1991. *Die musischen Agone der Panathenäen in archaischer und klassischer Zeit. Eine historisch-archäologische Untersuchung.* Munich.

Kovacs, D. 2004. *Euripidea.* Leiden.

Kowalzig, B. 2004. "Changing Choral Worlds: Song-Dance and Society in Athens and Beyond." In Murray and Wilson 2004:39–65.

———. 2005. "Mapping out *Communitas*: Performances of *Theoria* in Their Sacred and Political Context." *Pilgrimage in Graeco-Roman and Early Christian Antiquity: Seeing the Gods* (eds. J. Elsner and I. Rutherford) 41–72. Oxford.

Kramer, L. 2001. *Musical Meaning: Towards a Critical History.* Berkeley and Los Angeles.

Kranz, W. 1933. *Stasimon. Untersuchungen zu Form und Gehalt der griechischen Tragödie.* Berlin.

Krummen, E. 1990. *Pyrsos Hymnon: Festliche Gegenwart und mythisch-rituelle Tradition als Voraussetzung einer Pindarinterpretation.* Berlin.

Kurke, L. 1991. *The Traffic in Praise: Pindar and the Poetics of Social Economy.* Ithaca.

———. 1992. "The Politics of ἁβροσυνή in Archaic Greece." *Classical Antiquity* 11:90–121.

———. 1993. "The Economy of *Kudos*." In Dougherty and Kurke 1993:131–163.

———. 1994. "Crisis and Decorum in Sixth-Century Lesbos: Reading Alkaios Otherwise." *Quaderni Urbinati di Cultura Classica* 47:67–92.

———. 1997. "Inventing the *Hetaira*: Sex, Politics, and Discursive Conflict in Archaic Greece." *Classical Antiquity* 16:106–150.

———. 1999. *Coins, Bodies, Games, and Gold: The Politics of Meaning Archaic Greece.* Princeton.

———. 2003. "Aesop and the Contestation of Delphic Authority." In Dougherty and Kurke 2003: 77–100.

Kyle, D. G. 1987. *Athletics in Ancient Athens.* Leiden.

La Coste Messelière, P. de. 1936. *Au Musée de Delphes.* Paris.

Lachmann, R. 1929. "Die Weise vom Löwen und der pythische Nomos." *Festschrift für Johannes Wolf* (eds. W. Lott, H. Osthoff, and W. Wolffheim) 97–101. Berlin.

Lamberton, R. 1988. "Plutarch, Hesiod, and the Mouseia of Thespiai." *Illinois Classical Studies* 13:491–504.

Lanata, G. 1996. "Sappho's Amatory Language." *Reading Sappho: Contemporary Approaches* (ed. E. Greene) 11–25. Berkeley.

Landels, J. 1999. *Music in Ancient Greece and Rome.* London.

Lang, M. 1969. *The Palace of Nestor.* Princeton.

Langdon, S. 1992. *From Pasture to Polis: Art in the Age of Homer.* Columbia, MO.

Lardinois, A. 2001. "Keening Sappho: Female Speech Genres in Sappho's Poetry." *Making Silence Speak: Women's Voices in Greek Literature and Society* (eds. A. Lardinois and L. McClure) 75–92. Princeton.

Laronde, A. 1987. *Cyrène et la Libye hellénistique.* Paris.

Larsen, S. 2007. *Tales of Epic Ancestry: Boeotian Collective Identity in the Late Archaic and Early Classical Periods.* Historia Einzelschriften 197. Stuttgart.

Latte, K. and H. Erbse, eds. 1965. *Lexica Graeca Minora.* Hildesheim.

Lawler, L. 1948. "Orchesis Kallinikos." *Transactions of the American Philological Association* 79:254–267.

———. 1951. "Kretikos in the Greek Dance." *Transactions of the American Philological Association* 82:62–70.

Leaf, W. 1912. *Troy: A Study in Poetic Geography.* London.

Lefkowitz, M. 1981. *The Lives of the Greek Poets.* London.

Leppert, R. 1993. *The Sight of Sound: Music, Representation, and the History of the Body.* Berkeley and Los Angeles.

Lesky, A. 1949. "Neroniana." *Annuaire de l'Institut de Philologie et d'Histoire Orientales* 9:385–407. Reprinted in *Gesammelte Schriften* (Lesky 1966) 335–351. Bern.

Leutsch, E. von. 1856. "Metrische Fragmente, 1. Die Namen der metrischen Füsse." *Philologus* 11:328–350.

Lezzi-Hafter, A. 1976. *Der Schuwalow-Maler. Eine Kannenwerkstatt der Parthenonzeit.* Mainz.

Liberman, G., ed. and trans. 1999. *Alcée. Fragments.* Paris.

Lidov, J. 2002. "Sappho, Herodotus, and the 'Hetaira'." *Classical Philology* 97:203–237.

Lightfoot, J. 2002. "Nothing to Do with the *Technitai* of Dionysus?" In Easterling and Hall 2002:209–244.

Ligt, L. de and P. W. de Neeve. 1988. "Ancient Periodic Markets: Festivals and Fairs." *Athenaeum* 66:391–416.

Linforth, I. M. 1931. "Two Notes on the Legend of Orpheus." *Transactions of the American Philological Association* 62:5–17.

———. 1941. *The Arts of Orpheus.* Berkeley.

Lissarrague, F. 1990. *The Aesthetics of the Greek Banquet: Images of Wine and Ritual*. Trans. A. Szegedy-Maszak. Princeton.

———. 1995. "Images grecques d'Orphée. La tête oraculaire d'Orphée." *Les Métamorphoses d'Orphée* (eds. C. Camboulives and M. Lavallée) 19–23. Brussels.

Livrea, E. 1993. "Terpandrea." *Maia* 45:3–6.

Lloyd-Jones, H. 1967. "Heracles at Eleusis: *P.Oxy.* 2622 and *PSI* 1391." *Maia* 19:206–229.

Loman, P. 2004. "Travelling Female Entertainers of the Hellenistic Age." *Arctos* 38:59–73.

Long, C. 1987. *The Twelve Gods of Greece and Rome*. Leiden.

Longo, V. 1966. "Nerone o Vespasiano? (Anth. Pal. xi, 185)." *Tetraonyma. Miscellenea Graeco-Romana* (eds. L. de Regibus et al.) 175–179. Pubblicazioni dell'Istituto di Filologia Classica di Università di Genova 25. Genoa.

Lonsdale, S. 1994/1995. "*Homeric Hymn to Apollo*: Prototype and Paradigm of Choral Performance." *Arion* 3.1:25–40.

Loraux, N. 1986. *The Invention of Athens: The Funeral Oration in the Classical City*. Trans. A. Sheridan. Cambridge, MA.

Luria, S. 1929. "Der Affe des Archilochos und die Brautwerbung des Hippokleides." *Philologus* 39:1–22.

Ma, J. 2007. "A *Horse* from Teos: Epigraphical Notes on the Ionian-Hellespontine Association of Dionysiac Artists." *The Greek Theatre and Festivals: Documentary Studies* (ed. P. Wilson) 215–245. Oxford Studies in Ancient Documents. Oxford.

Maas, M. and J. Snyder. 1989. *Stringed Instruments of Ancient Greece*. New Haven.

Maas, P. 1938. *Paulys Realencyclopäde der classischen Altertumswissenschaft* VI A (ed. G. Wissowa), s.v. "Timotheos," cols. 1331–1337. Stuttgart.

MacDowell, D. M. 1993. "Foreign Birth and Athenian Citizenship in Aristophanes." *Tragedy, Comedy and the Polis: Papers from the Greek Drama Conference, Nottingham, 18-20 July 1990* (eds. A. H. Sommerstein et al.) 359–371. Bari.

Mackay, E. A. 1995. "Narrative Tradition in Early Greek Oral Poetry and Vase-Painting." *Oral Tradition* 10:282–303.

Macleod, M. D., ed. and trans. 1967. *Lucian* VIII. Loeb Classical Library. Cambridge, MA.

Maehler, H., ed. 2004. *Bacchylides. A Selection*. Cambridge.

Malkin, I. 1994. *Myth and Territory in the Spartan Mediterranean.*
      Cambridge.

Mansfield, J. M. 1985. *The Robe of Athena and the Panathenaic "Peplos."*
      PhD diss., University of California at Berkeley.

Marshall, E. 2000. "Death and Disease in Ancient Cyrene: A Case
      Study." *Death and Disease in the Ancient City* (eds. V. M. Hope and
      E. Marshall) 8–23. London and New York.

Marshall, L. 2006. "Bob Dylan: Newport Folk Festival, July 25, 1965."
      Performance and Popular Music: History, Place and Time
      (ed. I. Inglis) 16–40. London.

Martin, R. 1989. *The Language of Heroes: Speech and Performance
      in the Iliad.* Ithaca.

———. 1993. "The Seven Sages as Performers of Wisdom." In
      Dougherty and Kurke 1993:108–130.

———. 2001. "Rhapsodizing Orpheus." *Kernos* 14:23–33.

———. 2003. "The Pipes are Brawling: Conceptualizing Musical
      Performance in Classical Athens." In Dougherty and Kurke
      2003:153–180.

———. 2005. "Pulp Epic: The *Catalogue* and the *Shield.*" *The Hesiodic
      Catalogue of Women: Constructions and Reconstructions*
      (ed. R. Hunter) 153–175. Cambridge.

Mason, H. 1993. "Mytilene and Methymna: Quarrels, Borders and
      Topography." *Échos du monde classique* 37:225–250.

———. 1995. "The End of Antissa." *American Journal of Philology*
      116:399–410.

Matheson, S. B. 1995. *Polygnotos and Vase Painting in Classical Athens.*
      Madison, WI.

Maurizio, L. 1998. "The Panathenaic Procession: Athens' Participatory
      Democracy on Display?" *Democracy, Empire, and the Arts in
      Fifth-century Athens* (eds. D. Boedeker and K. Raaflaub) 297–317.
      Cambridge, MA.

McClary, S. 1991. *Feminine Endings: Music, Gender, and Sexuality.*
      Minneapolis, MN.

McClure, L. 2003. *Courtesans at Table: Gender and Greek Literary Culture in
      Athenaeus.* London and New York.

McGahey, R. 1994. *The Orphic Moment: Shaman to Poet-thinker in Plato,
      Nietzsche, and Mallarmé.* New York.

McGlew, J. F. 1993. *Tyranny and Political Culture in Ancient Greece.* Ithaca.

McGregor, M. F. 1941. "Cleisthenes of Sicyon and the Panhellenic Festivals." *Transactions of the American Philological Association* 72:266–287.

McKay, K. J. 1974. "Alkman Fr. 107 Page." *Mnemosyne* 27:413–414.

Meinel, R. 1980. *Das Odeion: Untersuchungen an überdachten antiken Theatergebaüden.* Frankfurt am Main.

Meier, M. 1998. *Aristokraten und Damoden: Untersuchungen zur inneren Entwicklung Spartas im 7. Jahrhundert v. Chr. und zur politischen Funktion der Dichtung des Tyrtaios.* Stuttgart.

Meriani, A. 2003. *Sulla Musica Greca Antica: Studi e Ricerche.* Salerno.

Merriam, A. 1964. *The Anthropology of Music.* Evanston, IL.

———. 1979. "Basongye Musicians and Institutionalized Social Deviance." *Yearbook of the International Folk Music Council* 11:1–26.

Meuli, K. 1975. *Gesammelte Schriften* II. Basel.

Meyer, G. 1923. *Die Stilistische Verwendung der Nominalkomposition im Griechischen.* Leipzig.

Miller, J. F. 2000. "Triumphus in Palatio." *American Journal of Philology* 121:409–422.

Miller, M. 1997. *Athens and Persia in the Fifth Century BC: A Study in Cultural Receptivity.* Cambridge.

Miller, S. 2001. *Excavations at Nemea.* Vol. 2, *The Early Hellenistic Stadium.* Berkeley.

———. 2004. *Ancient Greek Athletics.* New Haven.

Mills, S. 1997. *Theseus, Tragedy, and the Athenian Empire.* Oxford.

Minchin, E. 2001. *Homer and the Resources of Memory.* Oxford.

Minnen, P. van. 1997. "The Performance and Readership of the *Persai* of Timotheus." *Archiv für Papyrusforschung* 43:246–260.

Mitchel, F. 1970. *Lycourgan Athens: 338-322.* Cincinnati.

Monbrun, P. 2001. "Apollon: de l'arc à la lyre." *Chanter les dieux. Musique et religion dans l'antiquité grecque et romaine. Actes du colloque des 16, 17 et 18 décembre 1999* (eds. P. Brule and C. Vendries) 59–96. Rennes and Lorient.

Morford, M. 1985. "Nero's Patronage and Participation in Literature and the Arts." *Aufstieg und Niedergang der römischen Welt* II 32.3:2003–2031.

Morgan, K. 1993. "Pindar the Professional and the Rhetoric of the ΚΩΜΟΣ." *Classical Philology* 88:1–15.

Morris, I. 2000. *Archaeology as Cultural History: Words and Things in Iron Age Greece.* Oxford.

Morrissey, E. 1978. "Victors in the Prytaneion Decree (*IG* I² 77)." *Greek, Roman and Byzantine Studies* 19:121–125.

Morrow, G. 1960. *Plato's Cretan City: A Historical Interpretation of the Laws.* Princeton.

Mosconi, G. 2000. "La democrazia ateniese e la 'nuova' musica: l'Odeion di Pericle." In Cassio et al. 2000:217–316.

Mosshammer, A. H. 1977. "Phainias of Eresos and Chronology." *California Studies in Classical Antiquity* 10:105–132.

———. 1982. "The Date of the First Pythiad—Again." *Greek, Roman and Byzantine Studies* 23:15–30.

Muecke, F. 1982. "A Portrait of the Artist as a Young Woman." *Classical Quarterly* 32:41–55.

Muellner, L. 1996. *The Anger of Achilles: Mēnis in Greek Epic.* Ithaca.

Mullen, W. 1982. *Choreia: Pindar and Dance.* Princeton.

Müller, F. 1994. *The Wall Paintings from the Oecus of the Villa of Publius Fannius Synistor in Boscoreale.* Amsterdam.

Munn, M. L. Z. 2003. "From Beyond the Pillars of Herakles: Corinthian Trade with the Punic West in the Classical Period." *Corinth: The Centenary, 1896-1996* (eds. C. K. Williams II and N. Bookidis) 195–217. Princeton.

Murgatroyd, P., ed. 1994. *Tibullus, Elegies II.* Oxford.

Murray, O. 1993. *Early Greece.* 2nd ed. Cambridge, MA.

———. 1996. "Hellenistic Royal Symposia." *Aspects of Hellenistic Kingship* (ed. P. Bilde) 15–27. Oakville, CT.

Murray, P. 1996. *Plato on Poetry.* Cambridge.

———. 2004. "The Muses and their Arts." In Murray and Wilson 2004:365–389.

Murray, P. and P. Wilson, eds. 2004. *Music and the Muses: The Culture of Mousike in the Classical Athenian City.* Oxford.

Musti, D. 2000. "Musica greca tra aristocrazia e democrazia." In Cassio et al. 2000:7–55.

M–W = Merkelbach, R. and M.L. West, eds. 1967. *Fragmenta Hesiodea.* Oxford.

Nagy, G. 1974. *Comparative Studies in Greek and Indic Meter.* Cambridge, MA.

———. 1979. *The Best of the Achaeans: Concepts of the Hero in Archaic Greek Poetry.* Baltimore.

———. 1989. "The 'Professional Muse' and Models of Prestige in Ancient Greece." *Cultural Critique* 12:133–143.

———. 1990a. *Greek Mythology and Poetics.* Ithaca.

———. 1990b. *Pindar's Homer: The Lyric Possession of an Epic Past.* Baltimore.

———. 1993. "Alcaeus in Sacred Space." In Pretagostini 1993:221–225.

———. 1996. *Homeric Questions.* Austin.

———. 2002. *Plato's Rhapsody and Homer's Music.* Washington, DC.

———. 2003. *Homeric Responses.* Austin.

———. 2004. "Transmission of Archaic Greek Sympotic Songs: From Lesbos to Alexandria." *Critical Inquiry* 31:26–48.

———. 2005. "The Epic Hero." *A Companion to Ancient Epic* (ed. J. M. Foley) 71–89. Oxford.

———. 2007a. "Did Sappho and Alcaeus ever Meet? Symmetry of Myth and Ritual in Performing the Songs of Ancient Lesbos." *Literatur und Religion 2. Wege zu einer mythisch-rituellen Poetik bei den Griechen* (eds. A. Bierl, R. Lämmle, and K. Wesselmann) 211–270. Berlin and New York.

———. 2007b. "Myth and Greek Lyric." *The Cambridge Encyclopedia of Classical Mythology* (ed. R. D. Woodard) 52–82. Cambridge.

Neer, R. 2001. "Framing the Gift: The Politics of the Siphnian Treasury at Delphi." *Classical Antiquity* 20:272–336.

———. 2002. *Style and Politics in Athenian Vase-Painting: The Craft of Democracy, ca. 530–460 BCE.* Cambridge.

———. 2007. "Delphi, Olympia, and the Art of Politics." *The Cambridge Companion to Archaic Greece* (ed. H. A. Shapiro) 245–264. Cambridge.

Neils, J. 1987. *The Youthful Deeds of Theseus.* Rome.

———, ed. 1992. *Goddess and Polis: The Panathenaia Festival in Ancient Athens.* Hanover and Princeton.

Nelis, D. P. 2005. "The Reading of Orpheus. The *Orphic Argonautica* and the Epic Tradition." *Roman and Greek Imperial Epic* (ed. M. Paschalis) 170–192. Rhethymno.

Nettl, B. 1983. *The Study of Ethnomusicology: Twenty-nine Issues and Concepts.* Chicago and Urbana, IL.

Newby, Z. 2002. "Reading Programs in Greco-Roman Art: Reflections on the Spada Reliefs." *The Roman Gaze: Vision, Power, and the Body* (ed. D. Fredrick) 110–148. Baltimore.

Nicholson, N. 2005. *Aristocracy and Athletics in Archaic and Classical Greece.* Cambridge.

Nieddu, G. F. 1993. "Parola e metro nella *sphragis* dei *Persiani* di Timoteo." In Pretagostini 1993:521–529. Rome.

Nietzsche, F. 1968. *The Portable Nietzsche.* Trans. W. Kaufmann. London.

Nilsson, M. P. 1971. *The Minoan-Mycenaean Religion and Its Survival in Greek Religion*. London.

Nisbet, G. 2003. *Greek Epigram in the Roman Empire: Martial's Forgotten Rivals*. Oxford.

Nordquist, G. C. 1992. "Instrumental Music in Representations of Greek Cult." *The Iconography of Greek Cult in the Archaic and Classical Periods. Proceedings of the First International Seminar on Ancient Greek Cult, Delphi, 1990* (ed. R. Hägg) 143–168. Kernos Supplement 1. Athens and Liege.

Ober, J. 1989. *Mass and Elite in Democratic Athens: Rhetoric, Ideology, and the Power of the People*. Princeton.

Olson, S. D., ed. 2002. *Aristophanes Acharnians*. Oxford.

Olson, S. D. and A. Sens. 1999. *Matro Of Pitane and the Tradition of Epic Parody in the Fourth Century BCE: Text, Translation, and Commentary*. Oxford.

Omitowoju, R. 2002. *Rape and the Politics of Consent*. Cambridge.

Ostwald, M. 1969. *Nomos and the Beginnings of the Athenian Democracy*. Oxford.

Overbeck, J. A. 1889. *Griechische Kunstmythologie* IV. Leipzig.

Padgett, J. M. 1995. "A Geometric Bard." *The Ages of Homer: A Tribute to Emily Townsend Vermeule* (eds. J. Carter and S.P. Morris) 389–406. Austin.

———. 2000. "The Stable Hands of Dionysos: Satyrs and Donkeys as Symbols of Social Marginalization in Attic Vase Painting." *Not the Classical Ideal: Athens and the Construction of the Other in Greek Art* (ed. B. Cohen) 43–70. Leiden.

Page, D. L. 1955. *Sappho and Alcaeus: An Introduction to the Study of Ancient Lesbian Poetry*. Oxford.

———. 1981. *Further Greek Epigrams*. Cambridge.

Palagia, O. 1980. *Euphranor*. Leiden.

Palisca, C. V. 1989. *The Florentine Camerata: Documentary Studies and Translations*. New Haven.

Pallone, M. R. 1984. "L'epica agonale in età ellenistica." *Orpheus* 5:156–166.

Palumbo Stracca, B. M. 1994. "Sull'iscrizione della coppa de Duride (*PMG* adesp. 938e)." *Studi Micenei ed Egeo-Anatolici* 33:119–129.

———. 1997. "Il decreto degli Spartani contro Timoteo." *Annali dell'Istituto Universitario Orientale di Napoli, Dipartimento di Studi del mondo classico e del Mediterraneo antico, Sezione filologico-letteraria* 19:129–160.

Papaspyridi-Karouzou, S. 1938. "A Proto-Panathenaic Amphora at Athens." *American Journal of Archaeology* 42:492–505.

Pappano, A. E. 1937. "The False Neros." *Classical Journal* 32:385–392.

Paquette, D. 1984. *L'instrument de musique dans la céramique de la Grèce antique: Études d'organologie.* Paris.

Parker, H. 2005. "Sappho's Public World." *Women Poets in Ancient Greece and Rome: New Critical Essays* (ed. E. Greene) 3–24. Norman, OK.

Parker, R. 1983. *Miasma: Pollution and Purification in Early Greek Religion.* Oxford.

———. 1996. *Athenian Religion: A History.* Oxford.

———. 2005. *Polytheism and Society at Athens.* Oxford.

Parker, V. 1994. "Some Aspects of the Foreign and Domestic Policy of Cleisthenes of Sicyon." *Hermes* 122:404–424.

Pavese, C. O. 1972. *Tradizioni e Generi Poetici della Grecia Arcaica.* Rome.

———. 1991. "L'inno rapsodico: analisi tematica degli inni omerici." *Annali dell'Istituto Universitario Orientale di Napoli, Dipartimento di Studi del mondo classico e del Mediterraneo antico, Sezione filologico-letteraria* 13:155–178.

———. 1998. "The Rhapsodic Epic Poems as Oral and Independent Poems." *Harvard Studies in Classical Philology* 98:63–90.

Pearl, O. 1978. "Rules for Musical Contests." *Illinois Classical Studies* 3:132–138.

Péché, V. and C. Vendries. 2001. *Musique et spectacles à Rome et dans l'Occident romain sous la République et le Haut-empire.* Paris.

Pelling, C. 1997. "Aeschylus' *Persae* and History." *Greek Tragedy and the Historian* (ed. C. Pelling) 1–19. Oxford.

Perceau, S. 2007. "Héros à la cithare. La musique de l'excellence chez Homère." *Mousikè et Aretè. La mousique et l'éthique de l'antiquité à l'âge moderne. Actes du colloque international tenu en Sorbonne les 15-17 décembre 2003* (eds. F. Malhomme and A. G. Wersinger) 17–38. Paris.

Perlman, P. 2004. "Tinker, Tailor, Soldier, Sailor. The Economies of Archaic Eleutherna, Crete." *Classical Antiquity* 23:95–136.

Perysinakis, I. N. 2006. "Κόσμον or κόμπον? A Note on Simonides' Elegy on Plataea, fr. 11.23 W²." *Zeitschrift für Papyrologie und Epigraphik* 157:19–21.

Pfrommer, M. 1992. *Göttliche Fürsten in Boscoreale: Der Festsaal in der Villa des P. Fannius Synistor.* Trierer Winckelmannsprogramme 12. Mainz am Rhein.

Phillips, D. 2003. "Athenian Political History: A Panathenaic
        Perspective." *Sport and Festival in the Ancient Greek World*
        (eds. D. Phillips and D. Pritchard) 197–232. Swansea.

Pickard-Cambridge, A. 1927. *Dithyramb, Tragedy and Comedy*. Revised
        2nd ed. 1962 by T. Webster. Oxford.

Picon, C. A. and H. A. Shapiro. 1996. *Greek Vases in the San Antonio
        Museum of Art*. San Antonio.

Pinney, G. Ferrari. 1988. "Pallas and Panathenaea." *Proceedings of
        the Third Symposium on Ancient Greek and Related Pottery*
        (eds. J. Christiansen and T. Melander) 465–477. Copenhagen.

Pinney, G. and B. Ridgway. 1979. *Aspects of Ancient Greece*. Allentown,
        PA.

Pipili, M. 1987. *Laconian Iconography of the Sixth Century B.C.* Oxford.

Platter, C. 2007. *Aristophanes and the Carnival of Genres*. Baltimore and
        London.

Platthy, J. 1985. *The Mythical Poets of Greece*. Washington, DC.

Pleket, H. W. 2004. "Einige Betrachtungen zum Thema 'Geld und
        Sport'." *Nikephoros* 17:77–90.

PMG = Page, D., ed. 1962. *Poetae Melici Graeci*. Oxford.

PMGF = Davies, M., ed. 1991. *Poetarum Melicorum Graecorum Fragmenta* I.
        Oxford.

Podlecki, A. 1966. *The Political Background of Aeschylean Tragedy*.
        Ann Arbor.

———. 1980. "Festivals and Flattery: The Early Greek Tyrants as
        Patrons of Poetry." *Athenaeum* 58:371–395.

Porter, J. 1994. *Studies in Euripides' Orestes*. Leiden.

Powell, A. 1998. "Sixth Century Lakonian Vase Painting." *Archaic
        Greece: New Approaches and New Evidence* (eds. N. Fisher and
        H. van Wees) 119–146. London.

Powell, J. 1925. *Collectanea Alexandria*. Oxford.

Power, T. 2000. "The Parthenoi of Bacchylides 13." *Harvard Studies in
        Classical Philology* 100:67–81.

———. 2001. *Legitimating the Nomos: Timotheus' Persae in Athens*. PhD
        diss., Harvard University.

———. 2004. "Cleisthenes and the Politics of *Kitharôidia* at Delphi and
        in Sicyon." *Aevum Antiquum* 4:415–437.

———. 2007. "Ion of Chios and the Politics of Polychordia." *The World
        of Ion of Chios* (eds. V. Jennings and A. Katsaros) 179–205. Leiden.

———. Forthcoming. "*Kyklôps Kitharôidos*: Dithyramb and *Kitharôidia* in Play." *Dithyramb and Society: Texts and Contexts in a Changing Choral Culture* (eds. B. Kowalzig and P. Wilson). Oxford.

Prauscello, L. 2006. *Singing Alexandria: Music between Practice and Textual Transmission*. Leiden.

Pretagostini, R., ed. 1993. *Tradizione e Innovatione nella Cultura Greca da Omero all'Età Ellenistica: Scritti in Onore di Bruno Gentili*. 3 vols. Rome.

Price, S. D. 1990. "Anacreontic Vases Reconsidered." *Greek, Roman and Byzantine Studies* 31:133–175.

Privitera, G. A. 1965. *Laso di Ermione*. Rome.

Prott, H. von and L. Ziehen. 1906. *Leges Graecorum Sacrae*. Leipzig.

Puelma, M. 2006. "Arions Delphin und die Nachtigall. Kommentar zu Poseidippos ep. 37 A.-B. (= *P.Mil.Vogl.* VIII 309, Kol. VI 18–25)." *Zeitschrift für Papyrologie und Epigraphik* 156:60–74.

Quattrocelli, L. 2002. "Poesia e Convivialità a Sparta Arcaica. Nuove Prospettive di Studio." *Cahiers du Centre Gustave-Glotz* 13:7–32.

Raubitschek, A. 1949. *Dedications of the Athenian Akropolis*. Cambridge, MA.

Reinach, T. 1903. "Les Perses de Timothée." *Revue des études grecques* 16:62–83.

Reisch, E. 1885. *De musicis Graecorum certaminibus capita quattuor*. Vienna.

Restani, D. 1991. "Dionysos tra *aulos e kithara*: un percorso di iconografia musicale." *Dionysos, Mito e Misterio: Atti del convegno internazionale, Comacchio 3-5 novembre 1989* (ed. F. Berti) 379–395. Ferrara.

Richardson, L. 2000. *A Catalog of Identifiable Figure Painters of Ancient Pompeii, Herculaneum, and Stabiae*. Baltimore and London.

Richardson, N. J. 2007. "The Homeric Hymn to Hermes." *Hesperos: Studies in Ancient Greek Poetry Presented to M. L. West on his Seventieth Birthday* (eds. C. Collard and P. J. Finglass) 83–91. Oxford.

Richer, N. 2005. "Les Gymnopédies de Sparte." *Ktéma* 30:237–262.

Richter, G. 1965. *The Portraits of the Greeks* I. London.

Richter, G. and L. F. Hall. 1936. *Red-Figured Athenian Vases in The Metropolitan Museum of Art*. New Haven.

Ridgway, B. S. 1999. "An Issue of Methodology: Anakreon, Perikles, Xanthippos." *American Journal of Archaeology* 102:717–738.

Riedweg, C. 2002. *Pythagoras: Leben, Lehre, Nachwirkung. Eine Einführung.* Munich.

Ritschl, F. 1978. *Opuscula Philologica.* Hildesheim.

Robbins, E. 1992. Review of Gostoli 1990. Classical Review 42:8–9.

Robert, C. 1920. *Die griechische Heldensage.* Berlin.

Robert, F. 1939. *Thymélè: recherches sur las signification et la destination des monuments circulaires dans l'architecture religieuse de la Grèce.* Paris.

Robert, L. 1938. *Études épigraphiques et philologiques.* Paris.

———. 1960. "Recherches Épigraphiques." *Revue d'études antiques* 62:276–361.

———. 1984. "Discours d'ouverture." *Praktika of the Eighth International Congress of Greek and Latin Epigraphy* I (ed. A. G. Kalogeropoulou) 35–45. Athens.

Robertson, M. 1969. "*Geryoneis*: Stesichorus and the Vase-Painters." *Classical Quarterly* 19:207–221.

Robertson, N. 1980. "Heracles' 'Catabasis'." *Hermes* 108:274–299.

———. 2002. "The Religious Criterion in Greek Ethnicity: The Dorians and the Festival Carneia." *American Journal of Ancient History* n.s. 1:5–67.

Robkin, A. L. H. 1976. *The Odeion of Perikles: Some Observations on its History, Form, and Function.* PhD diss., University of Washington.

Rocchi, M. 1980. "La Lira di Achilleus (Hom. *Il.* IX 186)." *Studi storico-religiosi* 4:259–268.

———. 1989. *Kadmos e Harmonia. Un matrimonio problematico.* Rome.

Rocconi, E. 2003. *Le Parole delle Muse. La formazione del lessico tecnico musicale nella Grecia antica.* Rome.

Roccos, L. J. 1989. "Apollo Palatinus: The Augustan Apollo on the Sorrento Base." *American Journal of Archaeology* 93:571–588.

———. 2002. "The Citharode Apollo in Villa Contexts: A Roman Theme with Variations." *The Ancient Art of Emulation: Studies in Artistic Originality and Tradition from the Present to Classical Antiquity. Memoirs of the American Academy in Rome, Supplementary Volume I* (ed. E. K. Gazda) 273–294. Ann Arbor.

Roesch, P. 1982. *Études Béotiennes.* Paris.

Roller, L. 1981. "Funeral Games for Historical Persons." *Stadion* 7:1–18.

Rohde, E. 1925. *Psyche: The Cult of Souls and Belief in Immortality among the Greeks.* Trans. W. B. Hillis. London.

Roos, E. 1951. *Die tragische Orchestik im Zerrbild der altattischen Komödie.* Lund.

Rose, V., ed. 1967. *Aristotle. Fragmenta.* Stuttgart.

Roselli, D. K. 2005. "Vegetable-Hawking Mom and Fortunate Son: Euripides, Tragic Style, and Reception." *Phoenix* 59:1–49.

Rosenbloom, D. 2006. *Aeschylus: Persians.* London.

Rosenmeyer, P. 1992. *The Poetics of Imitation: Anacreon and the Anacreontic Tradition.* Cambridge.

Rostovtzeff, M. 1922. *A Large Estate in Egypt in the Third Century B.C.: A Study in Economic History.* Madison, WI.

RPC = Burnett, A. M., M. Amadry, and P. Ripolles. 1992. *Roman Provincial Coinage.* Vol. 1, *From the Death of Caesar to the Death of Vitellius (44 B.C.-A.D. 69).* London and Paris.

Ruffell, I. 2000. "The World Turned Upside Down: Utopia and Utopianism in the Fragments of Old Comedy." *The Rivals of Aristophanes* (eds. D. Harvey and J. Wilkins) 473–506. London.

Russell, D. A. and N. G. Wilson, eds. 1981. *Menander Rhetor.* Oxford.

Russo, J. 1999. "Stesichorus, Homer, and the Forms of Early Greek Epic." *Euphrosyne: Studies in Ancient Epic and its Legacy in Honor of Dimitris N. Maronitis* (eds. J. N. Kazazis and A. Rengakos) 339–348. Stuttgart.

Rutherford, I. 1990. "Paeans by Simonides." *Harvard Studies in Classical Philology* 93:169–209.

———. 1994/1995. "Apollo in Ivy: The Tragic Paean." *Arion* 3.1:112–135.

———. 1995. "Apollo's Other Genre: Proclus on NOMOS and his Source." *Classical Philology* 90:354–361.

———. 1996. "The New Simonides: Towards a Commentary." *Arethusa* 29:167–192.

———. 2001. *Pindar's Paeans: A Reading of the Fragments with a Survey of the Genre.* Oxford.

———. 2007a. "Theoria and Theatre at Samothrace. The *Dardanos* of Dymas." *The Greek Theatre and Festivals. Documentary Studies* (ed. P. Wilson) 279–293. Oxford Studies in Ancient Documents. Oxford.

———. 2007b. "Two Notes on Simonides' Plataea-Poem." *Akten des 23. Internationalen Papyrologenkongresses* (ed. B. Palme) 633–636. Vienna.

Sachs, C. 1940. *The History of Musical Instruments.* New York.

Sadurska, A. 1964. *Les Tables Iliaques.* Warsaw.

Salmon, J. 1984. *Wealthy Corinth.* Oxford.

Sansone, D. 1985. "Orpheus and Eurydice in the Fifth Century." *Classica et Mediaevalia* 36:53–64.

Sardis = Buckler, W. H. and D. Robinson, eds. 1932. *Sardis: Publications of the American Society for the Excavation of Sardis.* Vol. 7, *Greek and Latin Inscriptions, Part I.* Leiden.

Sarti, S. 1992. "Gli strumenti musicali di Apollo." *Annali dell'Istituto Universitario Orientale di Napoli, Dipartimento di Studi del mondo classico e del Mediterraneo antico, Sezione di archeologia e storia antica* 14:95–104.

Scanlon, T. F. 2002. *Eros and Greek Athletics.* Oxford.

Schachter, A. 1981. *Cults of Boiotia I.* London.

Schafter, D. 1991. "Musical Victories in Early Classical Vase Painting." *American Journal of Archaeology* 95:333–334.

Schaik, M. van. 2004. "Terpandros of Lesbos in Medieval and Renaissance Music Theory." *Meer dan muziek alleen: In memoriam Kees Vellekoop* (ed. R. E. V. Stuip) 313–328. Hilversum.

Schamp, J. 1976. "Sous le signe d'Arion." *L'Antiquité classique* 1976:95–120.

Schatz, T. 1996. *The Genius of the System: Hollywood Filmmaking in the Studio Era.* Minneapolis, MN.

Schauenburg, K. 1961. "Eine neue Amphora des Andokidesmalers." *Jahrbuch des Deutschen Archäologischen Instituts* 76:48–71.

———. 1979. "Herakles Musikos." *Jahrbuch des Deutschen Archäologischen Instituts* 94:49–76.

Schefold, K. 1992. *Gods and Heroes in Late Archaic Greek Art.* Trans. A. Griffiths. Cambridge.

———. 1997. *Die Bildnisse der Antiken Dichter, Redner und Denker.* Basel.

Scheibler, I. 1988. "Dreifussträger." *Kanon: Festschrift Ernst Berger* (ed. M. Schmidt) 310–316. Beiheft zur Halbjahresschrift Antike Kunst 15. Basel.

Schmidt, M. 1972. "Ein neues Zeugnis zum Mythos von Orpheushaupt." *Antike Kunst* 15:128–137.

Schönewolf, H. 1938. *Der jungattische Dithyrambos.* PhD diss., University of Giessen.

Schorn, S. 2004. *Satyros aus Kallatis: Sammlung der Fragmente mit Kommentar.* Basel.

Schubert, C. 1998. *Studien zum Nerobild in der lateinischen Dichtung der Antike.* Beiträge zur Altertumskunde 116. Stuttgart and Leipzig.

Scullion, S. 2003. "Euripides and Macedon, or the silence of the *Frogs.*" *Classical Quarterly* 53:389–400.

Scully, S. 1981. "The Bard as the Custodian of Homeric Society: *Odyssey* 3, 263–272." *Quaderni Urbinati di Cultura Classica* 37:67–83.

Seaford, R., ed. 1984. *Euripides: Cyclops.* Oxford.

Sear, F. 2006. *Roman Theatres: An Architectural Study.* Oxford.

Seebass, T. 1991. "The Power of Music in Greek Vase Painting." *Imago Musicae* 8:11–37.

Segal, C. P. 1962. "Gorgias and the Psychology of Logos." *Harvard Studies in Classical Philology* 66:99–155.

Sens, A., ed. 1997. *Theocritus: Dioscuri (Idyll 22). Introduction, Text, and Commentary.* Hypomnemata 114. Göttingen.

Severyns, A. 1938. *Recherches sur la Chrestomathie de Proclus.* Liege.

Simms, R. 1975. "The *Eleusinia* in the Sixth to Fourth Centuries B.C." *Greek, Roman and Byzantine Studies* 16:269–279.

Shapiro, H. A. 1982. "Kallias Kratiou Alopekethen." *Hesperia* 51:69–73.

———. 1984. "Herakles and Kyknos." *American Journal of Archaeology* 88:523–529.

———. 1989. *Art and Cult Under the Tyrants.* Mainz am Rhein.

———. 1991. "Theseus: Aspects of the Hero in Archaic Greece." *New Perspectives in Early Greek Art* (ed. D. Buitron-Oliver) 123–139. Washington, DC.

———. 1992. "*Mousikoi Agones*: Music and Poetry at the Panathenaia." In Neils 1992:53–76.

———. 1993. "Hipparchos and the Rhapsodes." In Dougherty and Kurke 1993:92–107.

———. 1996. "Democracy and Imperialism: The Panathenaia in the Age of Perikles." *Worshipping Athena: Panathenaia and Parthenon* (ed. J. Neils) 215–225. Madison, WI.

———. 2001. "Red-Figure Panathenaic Amphoras: Some Iconographical Problems." *Panathenaika: Symposion zu den Panathenäischen Preisamphoren, Rauischholzhausen 25.11-29.11 1998* (eds. M. Benzt and N. Eschbach) 119–124. Mainz am Rhein.

———. 2004. "Leagros the Satyr." *Greek Vases: Images, Contexts and Controversies* (ed. C. Marconi) 1–12. Columbia Studies in the Classical Tradition 25. Leiden.

Shaw, P.-J. 2003. *Discrepancies in Olympiad Dating and Chronological Problems of Archaic Peloponnesian History.* Historia Einzelschriften 166. Stuttgart.

Shear, J. L. 2001. *Polis and Panathenaia: The History and Development of Athena's Festival.* PhD diss., University of Pennsylvania.

———. 2003. "Prizes from Athens: The List of Panathenaic Prizes and the Sacred Oil." *Zeitschrift für Papyrologie und Epigraphik* 142:87–108.

Shields, E. L. 1917. *The Cults of Lesbos*. Baltimore.

Sifakis, G. M. 1967. *Studies in the History of Hellenistic Drama*. London.

Silberberg-Pierce, S. 1993. "The Muse Restored: Images of Women in Roman Painting." *Woman's Art Journal* 14:28–36.

Skafte Jensen, M. 1980. *The Homeric Question and the Oral-Formulaic Theory*. Copenhagen.

Slater, N. 1999. "The Vase as Ventriloquist: *Kalos*-Inscriptions and the Culture of Fame." *Signs of Orality: The Oral Tradition and its Influence in the Greek and Roman World* (ed. E. A. Mackay) 143–162. Leiden.

Slater, W. J. 1994. "Pantomime Riots." *Classical Antiquity* 13:120–144.

———. 2007. "Deconstructing Festivals." *The Greek Theatre and Festivals: Documentary Studies* (ed. P. Wilson) 21–47. Oxford Studies in Ancient Documents. Oxford.

SLG = Page, D., ed. 1974. *Supplementum Lyricis Graecis*. Oxford.

S–M = Snell, B. and H. Maehler, eds. *Pindari Carmina cum Fragmentis*. Pars II. Leipzig.

Smarczyk, B. 1990. *Untersuchungen zur Religionspolitik und politischen Propaganda Athens im Delisch-Attischen Seebund*. Munich.

Smart, M.-A. 2004. *Mimomania: Music and Gesture in Nineteenth-century Opera*. Berkeley and Los Angeles.

Smith, A. C. 2007. "Komos Growing Up among Satyrs and Children." *Constructions of Childhood in Ancient Greece and Italy* (eds. A. Cohen and J. Rutter) 153–172. Hesperia Supplement 41. Princeton.

Smyth, H. W. 1900. *Greek Melic Poets*. New York.

Snodgrass, A. 1998. *Homer and the Artists*. Cambridge.

Snyder, J. M. 1974. "Aristophanes' Agathon as Anacreon." *Hermes* 102:244–246.

Solomon, J. 1984. "Towards a History of Tonoi." *The Journal of Musicology* 3:242–251.

———. 1994. "The Lyrical Aspects of Apollonian Music." *Apollo: Origins and Influences* (ed. J. Solomon) 37–46. Tucson and London.

Sommerstein, A. H. 2003/2004. "Cuckoos in Tragic Nests? Kephisophon and Others." *Leeds International Classical Studies* 3:1–13.

Sourvinou-Inwood, C. 1971. "Theseus Lifting the Rock and a Cup near the Pithos Painter." *Journal of Hellenic Studies* 91:94–109.

Spencer, N. 1995. "Early Lesbos between East and West: A 'Grey Area' of Aegean Archaeology." *The Annual of the British School at Athens* 90:269–306.

———. 2001. "Exchange and Stasis in Archaic Mytilene." *Alternatives to Athens: Varieties of Political Organization and Community in Ancient Greece* (eds. R. Brock and S. Hodkinson) 68–81. Oxford.

Stahl, M. 1987. *Aristokraten und Tyrannen im archaischen Athen: Untersuchungen zur Überlieferung, zur Sozialstruktur und zur Entstehung des Staates.* Stuttgart.

Stansbury-O'Donnell, M. 2006. *Vase Painting, Gender, and Social Identity in Archaic Athens.* Cambridge.

Stehle, E. 1997. *Performance and Gender in Ancient Greece.* Princeton.

———. 2001. "A Bard of the Iron Age and His Auxiliary Muse." *The New Simonides: Contexts of Praise and Desire* (eds. D. Sider and D. Boedeker) 106–119. Oxford.

Steiner, D. 2001. *Images in Mind: Statues in Archaic and Classical Greek Literature and Thought.* Princeton.

Steinrück, M. 2005. "*Lagaroi*: Le Temps de la Re-Rythmisation de l'Hexametre." *Mnemosyne* 58:481–498.

Stenger, J. 2004. *Poetische Argumentation: Die Funktion der Gnomik in den Epinikien des Bakchylides.* Berlin and New York.

Stephanis, I. E. 1988. *ΔΙΟΝΥΣΙΑΚΟΙ ΤΕΧΝΙΤΑΙ. ΣΥΜΒΟΛΕΣ ΣΤΗΝ ΠΡΟΣΩΠΟΓΡΑΦΙΑ ΤΟΥ ΘΕΑΤΡΟΥ ΚΑΙ ΤΗΣ ΜΟΥΣΙΚΗΣ ΤΩΝ ΑΡΧΑΙΩΝ ΕΛΛΗΝΩΝ.* Herakleion.

Stephens, S. 2004. "For You, Arsinoe." *Labored in Papyrus Leaves: Perspectives on an Epigram Collection Attributed to Posidippus (P. Mil. Vogl. VIII 309)* (eds. B. Acosta-Hughes, E. Kosmetatou, and M. Baumbach) 161–176. Washington, DC.

Stern, J., ed. 1996. *Palaephatus: On Unbelievable Tales.* Wauconda, IL.

Stevens, P. T. 1956. "Euripides and the Athenians." *Journal of Hellenic Studies* 76:87–94.

Stewart, A. 1982. "Dionysos at Delphi: The Pediments of the Sixth Temple of Apollo and Religious Reform in the Age of Alexander." *Macedonia and Greece in Late Classical and Early Hellenistic Times* (eds. B. Barr-Sharrar and E. Borza) 205–228. Washington, DC.

———. 1983. "Stesichorus and the François Vase." *Ancient Greek Art and Iconography* (ed. W. Moon) 53–74. Madison, WI.

Stibbe, C. M. 1992. "Dionysos mit einer Kithara." *Kotinos: Festschrift für Erika Simon* (eds. H. Froning, T. Hölscher, and H. Mielsch) 139–145. Mainz am Rhein.

Storey, I. 2003a. *Eupolis, Poet of Old Comedy.* Oxford.

———. 2003b. "But Comedy Has Satyrs Too." *Satyr Drama: Tragedy at Play* (ed. G. Harrison) 201–218. Swansea.

Strasser, J.-Y. 2002. "Choraules et pythaules d'époque impériale. À propos d'inscriptions de Delphes." *Bulletin de Correspondance Hellénique* 126:97–142.

Studnizcka, F. 1924. "Imagines illustrium." *Jahrbuch des Deutschen Archäologischen Instituts* 39:57–128.

Sullivan, J. P. 1978. "Ass's Ears and Attises: Persius and Nero." *The American Journal of Philology* 99:159–170.

———. 1985. *Literature and Politics in the Age of Nero.* Ithaca.

Sultan, N. 1993. "Private Speech, Public Pain: The Power of Women's Laments in Ancient Greek Poetry and Tragedy." *Rediscovering the Muses: Women's Musical Traditions* (ed. K. Marshall) 92–110. Boston.

Sutton, D. F., ed. 1989. *Dithyrambographi Graeci.* Munich and Zürich.

Svenbro, J. 1976. *La parole et le marbre: aux origines de la poétique grecque.* Lund.

———. 1992. "'Ton luth, a quoi bon?' La lyre et la pierre tombale dans la pensée grecque." *Métis* 7:135–160.

Szegedy-Maszak, A. 1978. "Legends of the Greek Lawgivers." *Greek, Roman and Byzantine Studies* 19:199–209.

Szilágyi, J. 1977. "Ein Satyrchor." *Acta Antiqua* 25:359–370.

Tandy, D. W. 1997. *Warriors into Traders: The Power of the Market in Early Greece.* Berkeley.

Taplin, O. 1993. *Comic Angels.* Oxford.

———. 1999. "Spreading the Word through Performance." *Performance Culture and Athenian Democracy* (eds. S. Goldhill and R. Osborne) 33–57. Cambridge.

Telò, M. 2007. *Eupolidis Demi.* Florence.

Thomas, R. 1989. *Oral Tradition and Written Record in Classical Athens.* Cambridge.

Thompson, D. B. 1956. "The Persian Spoils in Athens." *The Aegean and the Near East: Studies Presented to Hetty Goldman on the Occasion of Her Seventy-fifth Birthday* (ed. S. S. Weinberg) 281–291. Locust Valley, NY.

Toepffer, J. 1889. *Attische Genealogie.* Berlin.

Totaro, P. 1991. "Il bianco Arignoto (Ar. *Eq.* 1279)." *Eikasmos* 2:153–157.

Touchette, L.-A. 1990. "A New Interpretation of the Orpheus Relief." *Archäologischer Anzeiger* 1:77–90.

Trendall, A. D. and T. B. L. Webster. 1971. *Illustrations of Greek Drama.* London.

Tuplin, C. 1994. "Xenophon, Sparta and the *Cyropaidia.*" *The Shadow of Sparta* (eds. S. Hodkinson and A. Powell) 127–182. London and New York.

Valakas, K. 2002. "The Use of the Body by Actors in Tragedy and Satyr-play." In Easterling and Hall 2002:69–92.

Valavanis, P. 1987. "Säulen, Hähne, Niken und Archonten auf Panathenäischen Preisamphoren." *Archäologischer Anzeiger* 102:467–480.

Varner, E. 2004. *Mutilation and Transformation: Damnatio Memoriae and Roman Imperial Portraiture.* Leiden.

Velardi, R. 1992. *Enthousiasmos: Possessione rituale e teoria della communicazione poetica in Platone.* Rome.

Veneri, A. 1995. "La cetra di Paride: l'altra faccia della musica in Omero e nei suoi interpreti antichi." In Gentili and Perusino 1995:111–132.

———. 1996. "L'Elicona nella cultura tespiese intorno al III sec. a.C.: la stele di Euthy[kl]es." *La Montagne des Muses* (eds. A. Hurst and A. Schachter) 73–86. Geneva.

Vergara, F. 2003. "As Representações dos *Agônes* Musicais na Pintura dos Vasos Áticos: os atributos iconográficos, os instrumentos musicais, as vestimentas, a idade, o gênero e o corpo dos músicos." *Olhares do Corpo* (eds. N. Theml, R. da Cunha Bustamante, and F. de Souza Lessa) 56–71. Rio de Janeiro.

Vetta, M. 1983. *Poesia e simposio nella Grecia antica: Guida storica e critica.* Rome and Bari.

———. 1992. "Il simposio: la monodia e il giambo." *Lo spazio letterario della Grecia antica* I (eds. G. Cambiano, L. Canfora, and D. Lanza) 208–215. Rome.

Vetter, W. 1934. *Paulys Realencyclopäde der classischen Altertumswissenschaft* V A (ed. G. Wissowa), s.v. "Terpandros," cols. 785–786. Stuttgart.

———. 1936. *Paulys Realencyclopäde der classischen Altertumswissenschaft* XVII (ed. G. Wissowa), s.v. "Nomos," cols. 840–843. Stuttgart.

Veyne, P. 1989. "Diaskeuai. Le théâtre grec sous l'Empire (Dion de Pruse, XXXII, 94)." *Revue des études grecques* 102:339–345.

———. 2000. "Inviter les dieux, sacrifier, banqueter: Quelques nuances de la religiosité gréco-romaine." *Annales. Histoire, Sciences Sociales* 2000:3–42.

Vian, F. 1952. *La Guerre des Géants. Le mythe avant l'époque Hellenistique.* Paris.

Visconti, A. 1999. *Aristosseno di Taranto: Biografia e Formazione Spirituale.* Naples.

Vojatzi, M. 1982. *Frühe Argonautenbilder.* Würzburg.

Vollgraff, W. 1901. "Inscriptions de Béotie." *Bulletin de Correspondance Hellénique* 25:359–361.

Vorreiter, L. 1975. "The Swan-Neck Lyres of Minoan-Mycenean Culture." *The Galpin Society Journal* 28:93–97.

Vos, M. F. 1986. "Aulodic and Auletic Contests." *Enthousiasmos: Essays on Greek and Related Pottery Presented to J. M. Hemelrijk* (ed. H. Brijder) 121–130. Amsterdam.

Voutiras, E. 1980. *Studien zu Interpretation und Stil griechischer Porträts des 5. und frühen 4. Jahrhunderts.* Bonn.

Walker, H. J. 1995. *Theseus and Athens.* Oxford.

Wallace, R. 1995. "Music Theorists in Fourth-century Athens." In Gentili and Perusino 1995:17–39.

———. 1997. "Poet, Public, and 'Theatrocracy': Audience Performance in Classical Athens." *Poet, Public, and Performance in Ancient Greece* (eds. L. Edmunds and R. W. Wallace) 97–111. Baltimore.

———. 2003. "An Early Fifth-Century Athenian Revolution in Aulos Music." *Harvard Studies in Classical Philology* 101:73–92.

———. 2004. "Damon of Oa: A Music Theorist Ostracized?" In Murray and Wilson 2004:249–267.

Wallner, C. 2001. "M. Ulpius Heliodoros und T. Flavius Archibios. Beobachtungen zu ihren Ehreninschriften (IG IV 591; I. Napoli I,51)." *Nikephoros* 14:91–108.

Walsh, G. B. 1984. *Varieties of Enchantment: Early Greek Views of the Nature and Function of Poetry.* Chapel Hill.

Warmington, B. H., ed. 1977. *Suetonius, Nero.* Bristol.

Watrous, L. V. 1982. "The Sculptural Program of the Siphnian Treasury at Delphi." *American Journal of Archaeology* 86:159–172.

Waywell, G. B. 1973. Review of E. Simon, *Das Antike Theater* (Heidelberg, 1972). *Journal of Hellenic Studies* 93:268–269.

Webb, R. 2002. "Female Performers in Late Antiquity." In Easterling and Hall 2002:282–303.

Webster, T. B. L. 1953. *Studies in Later Greek Comedy.* Manchester.

———. 1964. *From Mycenae to Homer.* New York.

———. 1967. *The Tragedies of Euripides.* London.

———. 1972. *Potter and Patron in Classical Athens.* London.

———. 1975. "Homeric Hymns and Society." *Le monde grec: Hommages à Claire Préaux* (eds. J. Bingen, G. Cambier, and G. Nachtergael) 86–93. Brussels.

Wees, H. van. 1995. "Politics and the Battlefield: Ideology in Greek Warfare." *The Greek World* (ed. A. Powell) 153–178. London.

———. 1999. "Tyrtaeus' *Eunomia*: Nothing to do with the Great Rhetra." *Sparta: New Perspectives* (eds. S. Hodkinson and A. Powell) 1–41. London.

Wegner, M. 1949. *Musikleben der Griechen*. Berlin.

Weil, H. and T. Reinach, eds. 1900. *Plutarque, De la musique*. Paris.

Welcker, F. G. 1865. *Der epische Cyclus, oder Die homerischen Dichter*. Bonn.

West, M. L. 1971. "Stesichorus." *Classical Quarterly* 21:302–314.

———. 1973. "Greek Poetry 2000–700 B.C." *Classical Quarterly* 23:179–192.

———. 1974. *Studies in Greek Elegy and Iambus*. Berlin and New York.

———. 1981. "The Singing of Homer and the Modes of Early Greek Music." *Journal of Hellenic Studies* 101:113–129.

———. 1982. *Greek Metre*. Oxford.

———. 1983. *The Orphic Poems*. Oxford.

———. 1986. "The Singing of Hexameters: Evidence from Epidaurus." *Zeitschrift für Papyrologie und Epigraphik* 63:39–46.

———. 1990a. "Notes on Sappho and Alcaeus." *Zeitschrift für Papyrologie und Epigraphik* 80:1–8.

———. 1990b. *Studies in Aeschylus*. Stuttgart.

———. 1992. *Ancient Greek Music*. Oxford.

———. 1997. "When is a Harp a Panpipe?" *Classical Quarterly* 47:48–55.

———. 1999a. "Sophocles with Music? Ptolemaic Music Fragments and Remains of Sophocles (Junior?), Achilleus." *Zeitschrift für Papyrologie und Epigraphik* 126:43–65.

———. 1999b. "The Invention of Homer." *Classical Quarterly* 49:364–382.

———. 2002a. "'Eumelos': A Corinthian Epic Cycle?" *Journal of Hellenic Studies* 122:109–133.

———. 2002b. "The View from Lesbos." *EPEA PTEROENTA: Beiträge zur Homerforschung. Festschrift für Wolfgang Kullmann zum 75. Geburtstag* (eds. M. Reichel and A. Rengakos) 207–220. Stuttgart.

———, ed. and trans. 2003. *Homeric Hymns, Homeric Apocrypha, Lives of Homer*. Loeb Classical Library. Cambridge, MA.

———. 2005. "*Odyssey* and *Argonautica*." *Classical Quarterly* 55:39–64.

Westphal, R. 1869. *Prologomena zu Aeschylus Tragödien*. Leipzig.

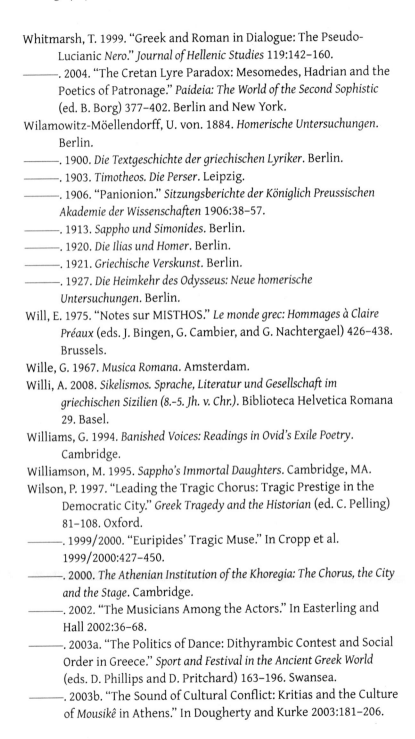

Whitmarsh, T. 1999. "Greek and Roman in Dialogue: The Pseudo-Lucianic *Nero*." *Journal of Hellenic Studies* 119:142–160.

———. 2004. "The Cretan Lyre Paradox: Mesomedes, Hadrian and the Poetics of Patronage." *Paideia: The World of the Second Sophistic* (ed. B. Borg) 377–402. Berlin and New York.

Wilamowitz-Möellendorff, U. von. 1884. *Homerische Untersuchungen.* Berlin.

———. 1900. *Die Textgeschichte der griechischen Lyriker.* Berlin.

———. 1903. *Timotheos. Die Perser.* Leipzig.

———. 1906. "Panionion." *Sitzungsberichte der Königlich Preussischen Akademie der Wissenschaften* 1906:38–57.

———. 1913. *Sappho und Simonides.* Berlin.

———. 1920. *Die Ilias und Homer.* Berlin.

———. 1921. *Griechische Verskunst.* Berlin.

———. 1927. *Die Heimkehr des Odysseus: Neue homerische Untersuchungen.* Berlin.

Will, E. 1975. "Notes sur MISTHOS." *Le monde grec: Hommages à Claire Préaux* (eds. J. Bingen, G. Cambier, and G. Nachtergael) 426–438. Brussels.

Wille, G. 1967. *Musica Romana.* Amsterdam.

Willi, A. 2008. *Sikelismos. Sprache, Literatur und Gesellschaft im griechischen Sizilien (8.-5. Jh. v. Chr.).* Biblioteca Helvetica Romana 29. Basel.

Williams, G. 1994. *Banished Voices: Readings in Ovid's Exile Poetry.* Cambridge.

Williamson, M. 1995. *Sappho's Immortal Daughters.* Cambridge, MA.

Wilson, P. 1997. "Leading the Tragic Chorus: Tragic Prestige in the Democratic City." *Greek Tragedy and the Historian* (ed. C. Pelling) 81–108. Oxford.

———. 1999/2000. "Euripides' Tragic Muse." In Cropp et al. 1999/2000:427–450.

———. 2000. *The Athenian Institution of the Khoregia: The Chorus, the City and the Stage.* Cambridge.

———. 2002. "The Musicians Among the Actors." In Easterling and Hall 2002:36–68.

———. 2003a. "The Politics of Dance: Dithyrambic Contest and Social Order in Greece." *Sport and Festival in the Ancient Greek World* (eds. D. Phillips and D. Pritchard) 163–196. Swansea.

———. 2003b. "The Sound of Cultural Conflict: Kritias and the Culture of *Mousikê* in Athens." In Dougherty and Kurke 2003:181–206.

———. 2004. "Athenian Strings." In Murray and Wilson 2004:269–306.

———. 2007. "Performance in the *Python*: The Athenian Thargelia." *The Greek Theatre and Festivals: Documentary Studies* (ed. P. Wilson) 150–184. Oxford Studies in Ancient Documents. Oxford.

———. 2009. "Thamyris the Thracian: The Archetypal Wandering Poet?" *Wandering Poets in Ancient Greek Culture* (eds. R. Hunter and I. Rutherford) 46–79. Oxford.

Winnington-Ingram, R. P. 1956. "The Pentatonic Tuning of the Greek Lyre: A Theory Examined." *Classical Quarterly* 6:169–182.

———. 1988. "Kónnos, Konnâs, Cheride e la Professione di Musico." *La Musica in Grecia* (eds. B. Gentili and R. Pretagostini) 246–263. Bari.

Woodman, A. J. 1993. "Amateur Dramatics at the Court of Nero: Annals 15.48–74." *Tacitus and the Tacitean Tradition* (eds. T. J. Luce and A. J. Woodman) 104–128. Princeton.

Yatromanolakis, D. 2001. "Visualizing Poetry: An Early Representation of Sappho." *Classical Philology* 96:159–168.

Younger, J. 1998. *Music in the Aegean Bronze Age*. Jonsered.

Zanker, P. 1995. *The Mask of Socrates: The Image of the Intellectual in Antiquity*. Trans. A. Shapiro. Berkeley.

Zeitlin, F. 1996. *Playing the Other: Gender and Society in Classical Greek Literature*. Chicago.

Zhmud, L. 2006. *The Origin of the History of Science in Classical Antiquity*. Trans. A. Chernoglazov. Berlin.

Ziegler, K. 1942. *Paulys Realencyclopäde der classischen Altertumswissenschaft* XVIII (ed. G. Wissowa), s.v. "Orphische Dichtung," cols. 1322–1417. Stuttgart.

Zimmermann, B. 1986. "Überlegungen zum sogenannten Pratinas-Fragment." *Museum Helveticum* 43:145–154.

———. 1992. *Dithyrambos: Geschichte einer Gattung*. Göttingen.

———. 1993. "Comedy's Criticism of Music." *Intertextualität in der griechisch-römischen Kömödie* (eds. N. W. Slater and B. Zimmermann) 39–50. Stuttgart.

Index Locorum

General Index

CPSIA information can be obtained at www.ICGtesting.com
Printed in the USA
270231BV00004B/2/P